Government Policies and Ethnic Relations in Asia and the Pacific

CSIA Studies in International Security

Michael E. Brown, Sean M. Lynn-Jones, and Steven E. Miller, series editors
Karen Motley, executive editor
Center for Science and International Affairs (CSIA)
John F. Kennedy School of Government, Harvard University

Published by The MIT Press:

Allison, Graham T., Owen R. Coté, Jr., Richard A. Falkenrath, and Steven E. Miller, *Avoiding Nuclear Anarchy: Containing the Threat of Loose Russian Nuclear Weapons and Fissile Material* (1996)

Allison, Graham T., and Kalypso Nicolaïdis, eds., *The Greek Paradox: Promise vs. Performance* (1996)

Blackwill, Robert D., and Michael Stürmer, *Allies Divided: Transatlantic Policies for the Greater Middle East* (1997)

Brown, Michael E., ed., *The International Dimensions of Internal Conflict* (1996)

Elman, Miriam Fendius, ed., *Paths to Peace: Is Democracy the Answer?* (1997)

Falkenrath, Richard A., *Shaping Europe's Military Order: The Origins and Consequences of the CFE Treaty* (1994)

Feldman, Shai, *Nuclear Weapons and Arms Control in the Middle East* (1996)

Forsberg, Randall, ed., *The Arms Production Dilemma: Contraction and Restraint in the World Combat Aircraft Industry* (1994)

Shields, John M., and William C. Potter, eds., *Dismanting the Cold War: U.S. and NIS Perspectives on the Nunn-Lugar Cooperative Threat Reduction Program* (1997)

Published by Brassey's, Inc:

Blackwill, Robert D., and Sergei A. Karaganov, eds., *Damage Limitation or Crisis? Russia and the Outside World* (1994)

Johnson, Teresa Pelton, and Steven E. Miller, eds., *Russian Security After the Cold War: Seven Views from Moscow* (1994)

Mussington, David, *Arms Unbound: The Globalization of Defense Production* (1994)

Published by CSIA:

Allison, Graham, Ashton B. Carter, Steven E. Miller, and Philip Zelikow, eds., *Cooperative Denuclearization: From Pledges to Deeds* (1993)

Campbell, Kurt M., Ashton B. Carter, Steven E. Miller, and Charles A. Zraket, *Soviet Nuclear Fission: Control of the Nuclear Arsenal in a Disintegrating Soviet Union* (1991)

Government Policies and Ethnic Relations in Asia and the Pacific

Editors
Michael E. Brown
Šumit Ganguly

CSIA Studies in International Security

in cooperation with the Pacific Basin Research Center

The MIT Press
Cambridge, Massachusetts
London, England

Library of Congress Cataloging-in-Publication Data

Government policies and ethnic relations in Asia and the Pacific / edited by Michael E. Brown and Sumit Ganguly.
p.   cm.—(CSIA studies in international security)
Includes bibliographical references and index.
ISBN 0-262-52245-4 (pbk.: alk. paper)
1. Asia—Ethnic relations—Government policy. 2. Pacific Area—Ethnic relations—Government policy. 3. Multiculturalism—Asia. 4. Multiculturalism—Pacific Area.
5. Asia—Politics and government—1945–   . 6. Pacific Area—Politics and government.
I. Brown, Michael E. II. Ganguly, Sumit. III. Series.
DS13.G68   1997
305.8'0095—dc21   97-25825
                                                                                              CIP

10 9 8 7 6 5 4 3 2 1
Printed in the United States of America

Contents

Preface

Most governments have to contend with ethnic problems of one kind or another. Fewer than 20 of the more than 180 states in the world are ethnically homogenous, in the sense that ethnic minorities constitute less than five percent of the country's population as a whole. Ethnic problems are tremendously important, moreover, because the evolution of a country's ethnic politics almost inevitably has significant implications for its political and economic development. In addition, as the world has seen in all too many places—from Abkhazia to Zaire—ethnic conflicts can generate horrifying levels of violence and human suffering.

This book analyzes government policies with respect to ethnic groups, ethnic problems, and ethnic conflicts—an important but under-studied issue. More specifically, it contains case studies of government policies in sixteen countries in Asia and the Pacific: India, Pakistan, Sri Lanka, Burma, Thailand, Malaysia, Singapore, Indonesia, the Philippines, China, Australia, New Zealand, Fiji, Papua New Guinea, Vanuatu, and the Federated States of Micronesia. This book traces the evolution of government policies with respect to ethnic issues in these countries, analyzes the impact these policies have had on the course of ethnic relations, develops a framework for thinking about these issues, and proposes a set of policy recommendations based on the foregoing.

Different governments, of course, have to contend with different kinds of ethnic problems, and the trajectories of ethnic problems are shaped by a wide range of factors: demographic patterns and trends, pre-colonial and colonial legacies, economic factors and developments, the political agendas and aspirations of various ethnic groups, the existence of cross-border ethnic complications, the actions of neighboring states, and the activities of international powers and organizations. Government policies are nonetheless critically important. Through neglect, by accident, and by design, they can push countries in the direction of stability, harmony, and justice, on the one hand, or instability, conflict, and inequity, on the other. In this book, we seek to analyze and advance understanding of the full range of government policies with respect to ethnic issues—the good, the bad, and the ugly.

The project that led to the production of this book was sponsored by John D. Montgomery, Director of the Pacific Basin Research Center (PBRC), Soka University of America, and Steven Miller, Director of the International Security Program at the Center for Science and International Affairs (CSIA), John F. Kennedy School of Government, Harvard University. John and Steve were present at the creation of the project, and they deserve a great deal of credit for shaping and sharpening the focus of this undertaking. John was the source of the idea to focus on government policies rather than ethnic problems, and Steve played a key role in helping us select the case studies. Their support and advice are deeply appreciated.

The fact that this rather large book was written and produced in just over one year can be traced to the prodigious efforts of many people. The eleven contributors to this volume made extraordinary efforts to focus on a common set of questions and produce first-rate studies in a very short period of time. They deserve most of the credit for whatever contributions this volume might make to scholarship on and analysis of this subject. Four leading authorities on Asian affairs—Dennis J. Encarnation, Robert Hardgrave, Sidney Jones, and Gerald Segal—took several days out of their busy schedules and helped us review first drafts of most of the chapters. The entire group is very grateful to them for their professional generosity and intellectual guidance. As the project's directors, we would also like to thank the following people for advising us at key junctures: Amitav Acharya, Zakaria Haji Ahmed, Benedict Anderson, Robyn Art, Karen Ballentine, Nayan Chanda, Jan Crawford, Patrick Cronin, Barbara Crossette, Donald Emmerson, Milton J. Esman, Trevor Findlay, Steve Hoadley, Donald Horowitz, S. Jayasankaran, Chantal de Jonge Oudraat, Stephanie Lawson, Sean Lynn-Jones, Andrew Mack, R.J. May, Traci Nagle, Vijay Nambiar, K.S. Nathan, Dwight Perkins, Lucian Pye, P. Ramasamy, Leo Rose, Stephen Stedman, Ezra Vogel, and Donald Zagoria.

Meara Keegan served as Project Coordinator and handled the complex task of orchestrating a far-flung multinational enterprise with exceptional professionalism and grace. In addition to keeping track of draft chapters that were literally flying in all directions, she produced the computer-generated maps that can be found in the pages that follow. Karen Motley, the Executive Editor of the CSIA Studies in International Security, gave us sage advice on a multitude of editorial matters and coordinated the final stages of the production process with élan. Helen

Snively copy-edited the book's twelve case studies—a truly monumental task—with skill and efficiency. Ann Callahan proofread the entire book—an equally monumental task—and helped with the production of galleys and page proofs. Deborah Kamen, Karen Motley, and Dawn Opstad went over the final set of page proofs with great care. Kristen Cashin, Lynne Meyer-Gay, Robin Regan, and Wyeth Towle provided valuable administrative and research assistance. Marie Allitto, Peggy Scannell, and Graceann Todaro of CSIA and Virginia A. Kosmo of PBRC helped to keep everything running smoothly on the administrative front. Tom D'Espinosa and his staff at Wellington Graphics handled a massive typesetting job with great skill and dexterity. We are deeply grateful to one and all.

Finally, for their generous financial support of this project, we would like to thank Soka University of America, which funds the Pacific Basin Research Center; the Carnegie Corporation of New York, which supports the Center for Science and International Affairs; and the Islamabad office of the Asia Foundation, which provided a grant that enabled experts from the region to participate in this undertaking. In particular, we would like to thank Daniel Habuki of Soka University of America; David Hamburg, David Speedie, and Astrid Tuminez of the Carnegie Corporation; and Erik Jensen of the Asia Foundation for their generosity and encouragement. This study could not have been undertaken without their help.

Although ethnic problems and conflicts are influenced by a wide range of demographic, political, and economic factors, they are shaped to a significant degree by the decisions, actions, and policies of leaders and governments. The latter must be taken into account if the scholarly community is to develop a true theory of the causes of ethnic conflict. This is critically important, and not just for academic reasons: a theory of the causes of ethnic conflict will have to emerge before a strategy for conflict prevention, conflict management, and conflict resolution can be developed. We hope that this study has made some contributions with respect to these twin goals.

Michael E. Brown
Cambridge, March 1997

Šumit Ganguly
New York, March 1997

List of Maps

List of Tables

Government Policies and Ethnic Relations in Asia and the Pacific

Introduction

Michael E. Brown and Šumit Ganguly

Ethnic problems are widespread in contemporary world affairs. They are troublesome at best; politically, economically, and socially disruptive as a general rule; and horrifyingly violent at worst. In this book, we seek to advance understanding of ethnic problems by analyzing government policies with respect to ethnic groups, ethnic issues, and ethnic conflicts in Asia and the Pacific. Our contention is that government policies almost always have a significant impact on the course and trajectory of ethnic relations in the country in question. Through neglect, by accident, and by design, they can push countries in the direction of instability, conflict, and inequity, on the one hand, or stability, harmony, and justice, on the other. However, the extent to which and the ways in which government policies can affect ethnic dynamics have not received much focused attention in research and scholarship on the subject, and government policies have not been examined from a broad comparative perspective.

We do three main things. First, we trace the evolution of government policies with respect to ethnic problems in sixteen countries in Asia and the Pacific: India, Pakistan, Sri Lanka, Burma, Thailand, Malaysia, Singapore, Indonesia, the Philippines, China, Australia, New Zealand, Papua New Guinea, Fiji, Vanuatu, and the Federated States of Micronesia. Our aim is to identify the main policy initiatives that have been undertaken, determine the ways in which policies have changed over time, and analyze the impact these policies have had on ethnic relations in the country in question. Second, we assess these policies. We try to determine how governments have fared in promoting peace, order, and stability, on the one hand, and political, economic, and social justice, on the other. We hope to identify the kinds of policies that were most effective, and the conditions under which they were effective, in promoting both peace and justice. Third, drawing on this descriptive and analytic foundation, we develop a set of general lessons and policy recommendations. The problem of managing ethnic relations will be a formidable policy challenge for most governments for the foreseeable future. We hope to develop some concrete advice for those who will have to formulate and implement government policies in this extremely sensitive and important area.

There are three reasons why this study focuses on government policies and ethnic relations in Asia and the Pacific, as opposed to some other part of the world. First, Asia is of great and growing importance in global affairs. It contains close to half of the world's population, and is home to several major powers. Asia is also the most economically dynamic part of the world, having experienced tremendous rates of economic growth in the 1970s, 1980s, and 1990s. It is important for people both inside and outside the region to understand the forces—the dynamics of ethnic relations being among the most powerful—that are shaping the region.

Second, Asia and the Pacific are extremely interesting from an analytical standpoint. The countries in the region have different kinds of ethnic settings; they have pursued different kinds of broad policies; they have launched different kinds of policy initiatives in specific policy areas; and they have experienced an array of political, economic, and social outcomes. Some governments, for example, have embraced unicultural visions, while others have favored multicultural visions. Some governments have favored policies based on coercion, while others have favored inducement. Some countries have experienced violent conflict and civil war, while others have remained comparatively peaceful. The region as a whole therefore provides rich material for a comparative analysis of government policies with respect to ethnic relations. The fact that Asia and the Pacific are undergoing rapid economic and social change and corresponding ethnic tensions—problems with which other parts of the world might well have to contend—makes this region even more valuable from an analytical standpoint.

Third, government policies with respect to ethnic relations in Asia and the Pacific have not been studied from a broad comparative perspective. Most studies of ethnic issues in the region are case studies of problems in individual countries. They are often rich in detail, but they do not focus on the same sets of issues and they do not, therefore, provide a strong foundation for comparative analysis. Most comparative studies of the region examine broader political or economic issues. The few that focus on ethnic questions do not concentrate on the roles governments have played in shaping ethnic relations in the region.[1] This book will

---

1. For studies of ethnic problems in individual countries in Asia and the Pacific, see the sources listed in the bibliography found at the end of this volume. The few studies that take a comparative perspective on ethnic issues in the region include Ralph

therefore fill an important gap in the scholarly literature on Asian studies, as well as the broader literature on ethnic studies.

The Importance of Ethnic Problems

Almost every country faces ethnic problems of one kind or another. Estimates of the number of ethnic groups in the world vary widely, depending on whether the researchers making the estimates are interested in simple ethno-linguistic distinctiveness or political salience. Those who are interested in the former estimate that there are between 3,000 and 9,000 ethnic communities in the world.[2] Those who are interested in the latter find that at least 200 groups merit attention.[3] At least 160—roughly ninety percent—of the more than 180 states in the international system are ethnically heterogeneous in the sense that minorities constitute more than five percent of the total population.[4] At least seventy-five percent of all states contain politically significant minority groups, and at least half have to contend with self-determination movements.[5]

Premdas, S.W.R. de A. Samarasinghe, and Alan B. Anderson, eds., *Secessionist Movements in Comparative Perspective* (London: Pinter, 1990); K.M. de Silva and R.J. May, eds., *The Internationalization of Ethnic Conflict* (London: Pinter, 1991); K.M. de Silva and S.W.R. de A. Samarasinghe, eds., *Peace Accords and Ethnic Conflict* (London: Pinter, 1993); David Brown, *The State and Ethnic Politics in Southeast Asia* (London: Routledge, 1994); R.H. Barnes, Andrew Gray, and Benedict Kingsbury, eds., *Indigenous Peoples of Asia* (Ann Arbor, Mich.: Association of Asian Studies, 1995); Stanley J. Tambiah, *Leveling Crowds: Ethnonationalist Conflicts and Collective Violence in South Asia* (Berkeley: University of California Press, 1996).

2. See James Minahan, *Nations Without States: A Historical Dictionary of Contemporary National Movements* (Westport, Conn.: Greenwood Press, 1996), p. xvi; Bernard Nietschmann, "The Third World War," *Cultural Survival Quarterly,* Vol. 11, No. 3 (September 1987), pp. 1–16.

3. One wide-ranging study estimates that 233 minority groups have either experienced systematic discriminatory treatment or have taken political action in support of collective interests; see Ted Robert Gurr, *Minorities at Risk: A Global View of Ethnopolitical Conflicts* (Washington, D.C.: U.S. Institute of Peace Press, 1993), pp. 5–11. Another survey identifies 210 groups that have mobilized in pursuit of political self-determination; see Minahan, *Nations Without States,* pp. xvi–xvii.

4. See David Welsh, "Domestic Politics and Ethnic Conflict," in Michael E. Brown, ed., *Ethnic Conflict and International Security* (Princeton, N.J.: Princeton University Press, 1993), p. 45.

5. For politically salient groups in the world's 127 largest states, see Gurr, *Minorities at Risk,* pp. 10–11. Gurr finds that almost seventy-five percent of these 127 states have politically salient minorities, even though he excludes groups that have fewer than 100,000 members or that constitute less than one percent of the total population of the country in question. For details on 210 self-determination movements in 91 states, see

Even in countries where ethnic minorities are minuscule in demographic terms and unassertive in pursuing political self-determination, ethnic problems have important social, economic, and political ramifications. In New Zealand, for example, Pacific Islanders constitute only five percent of the total population, but they pose difficult policy problems even though the country's citizenry is comparatively tolerant of ethnic diversity. Pacific Islanders, as well as New Zealand's larger, indigenous Maori population, tend to suffer from low income and education levels, high unemployment and incarceration levels, and more than their share of housing and health problems. The fact that these problems have persisted over time is a source of understandable concern both in policy circles in Wellington and in the general public.[6]

In countries where ethnic groups are politically active, ethnic issues are even more complicated and potentially volatile. Groups that are discriminated against socially, economically, and politically often form political organizations and make efforts to seek redress through established political channels. This almost inevitably leads to at least nonviolent conflict because political and economic gains for some usually involve losses for others. The formation of political parties along ethnic lines can be particularly divisive and polarizing. This has proven to be problematic in Canada, Czechoslovakia, India, Pakistan, South Africa, Sri Lanka, and the United Kingdom, to cite just a few examples.[7] Even when ethnic conflicts remain nonviolent, they can interfere with a country's political and economic development, and undermine civil society.

A critical threshold is reached when ethnic minorities decide that the best way to seek social, economic, and political justice is through self-government and regional autonomy arrangements. This is almost always seen by central authorities and ethnic majorities as the first step onto a slippery slope that may lead to secessionism and the disintegration of the state. Moves to acquire more autonomy are therefore almost always resisted energetically by these authorities and majorities. In Burma, for example, both civilian and military leaders have opposed regional auton-

---

Minahan, *Nations Without States*, especially pp. 651–668. Another survey that admits to being less than comprehensive finds self-determination movements in some 70 countries; see Morton H. Halperin and David J. Scheffer with Patricia L. Small, *Self-Determination in the New World Order* (Washington, D.C.: Carnegie Endowment for International Peace, 1992), pp. 123–162.

6. See Andrew Sharp's chapter on New Zealand in this volume.

7. For a fuller discussion of the complicated interrelationship between ethnicity and party politics, see Donald L. Horowitz, *Ethnic Groups in Conflict* (Berkeley: University of California Press, 1985), chaps. 7–10.

omy arrangements on the grounds that starting down this path would probably lead to the disintegration of the state. Leaders in Indonesia have held the same position ever since the country became independent. In these as in many other cases, genuine concerns about maintaining the territorial integrity of the state are reinforced by more parochial political and economic interests: central authorities in highly centralized states are generally keen to maintain their dominant political positions and to keep receiving the economic and financial benefits that flow from running the show. As noted above, conflict over self-government and regional auton-omy is a widespread problem: at least 210 groups in 91 countries seek more regional autonomy or self-determination. In Asia alone, this is an acute political problem in, for example, Burma, China, India, Indonesia, Pakistan, Papua New Guinea, the Philippines, and Sri Lanka.

In some cases, groups manage to resolve their differences without resorting to violence. In Belgium, Dutch-speaking Flemish and French-speaking Walloons have instituted regional autonomy arrangements without bloodshed. Czechoslovakia successfully implemented a "velvet divorce" in January 1993. In Asia, Thailand has experienced little sus-tained ethnic violence. In the Pacific, New Zealand has been, literally, an island of ethnic tranquility compared to what has transpired in other parts of the world.

Sadly, ethnic conflicts often become violent. In the 1990s alone, ethnic groups have engaged in open warfare in Afghanistan, Angola, Azerbaijan, Bosnia, Burma, Burundi, Croatia, Georgia, India, Liberia, Moldova, Rus-sia, Rwanda, Sierra Leone, Sri Lanka, Sudan, Tajikistan, and Zaire. Ethnic conflicts simmer in countless other locations—Bangladesh, Bhutan, China, Estonia, Fiji, Indonesia, Iran, Iraq, Israel, Kenya, Lebanon, Mace-donia, Pakistan, Papua New Guinea, the Philippines, Serbia, Slovakia, South Africa, Turkey, Ukraine, and the United Kingdom, for example. Ethnic wars often produce high levels of death and destruction because they frequently involve direct, deliberate attacks on civilian populations. The numbers of people killed, wounded, or displaced in such conflicts are often counted in ten and hundreds of thousands, and in some cases in millions.[8] In the worst cases—Bosnia and Rwanda—genocide is carried out against specific ethnic groups.

Long-term trends are worrying. The most comprehensive statistical analysis of the issue concludes that all forms of communal conflict have increased markedly since the 1950s: nonviolent protest has more than

8. For an overview of major internal conflicts as of late 1995, see Michael E. Brown, "Introduction," in Brown, ed., *The International Dimensions of Internal Conflict* (Cambridge, Mass.: MIT Press, 1996), pp. 4–7.

doubled; violent protest has increased fourfold; and open rebellion has increased almost fourfold. Since the 1950s, over one hundred minority groups have engaged in some form of rebellion.[9] One should note that, at the same time, the incidence of inter-state war has plummeted compared to previous historical eras. No great power wars have taken place since 1945. Western Europe, North America, and South America have experienced only one inter-state war, over the Falkland Islands. Only 30 of the 164 wars fought since 1945—eighteen percent of the total—were classic inter-state wars.[10] In 1990, only one of the 31 major armed conflicts then under way was an inter-state war.[11] In 1995, none of the 35 major armed conflicts then in progress was fundamentally inter-state in character. Internal conflict is the most pervasive form of armed conflict in the international system today; most of these conflicts have important ethnic dimensions; and it appears that this state of affairs will continue into the future.

Ethnic conflicts—in both their nonviolent and violent manifestations—often have important regional and international implications. Ethnic conflicts can send large numbers of refugees fleeing across international borders into neighboring states. Ethnic conflicts can also create economic and military problems for neighboring states. Trade can be disrupted, and neighboring states can be used as supply conduits and bases of operations. In the worst case, instability and conflict can spread from one state to another. This often happens when ethnic groups straddle formal borders, as they frequently do. In addition to being the passive victims of ethnic turmoil, neighboring states often take active steps to intervene in nearby conflicts—in some cases for defensive reasons, in some cases to protect ethnic brethren, and in some cases for opportunistic reasons.[12] Distant international powers and international organizations often become engaged in ethnic conflicts as well—for humanitarian reasons, to restore regional stability, to maintain principles of international law and order, or for narrower interest-based reasons.

---

9. Gurr, *Minorities at Risk*, pp. 98–100.

10. Kalevi J. Holsti, *The State, War, and the State of War* (Cambridge, U.K.: Cambridge University Press, 1996), pp. 21–25. For more discussion, see John Mueller, *Retreat From Doomsday: The Obsolescence of Major War* (New York: Basic Books, 1989).

11. A major armed conflict is one in which at least one thousand people have been killed. This is a widely used definition.

12. For more discussion of the regional dimensions and implications of ethnic and internal conflicts, see Michael E. Brown, "The Causes and Regional Dimensions of Internal Conflict," in Brown, *The International Dimensions of Internal Conflict*, pp. 590–600.

For all of these reasons, it is important to understand the dynamics of ethnic relations, the causes of ethnic conflicts, the processes by which ethnic conflicts become violent, and what well-meaning leaders and governments can do about these problems.

The Importance of Government Policy

Ethnic relations in any given country can be influenced by a wide range of factors. At the domestic level, these include demographic patterns and trends, pre-colonial and colonial legacies, economic factors and developments, the political agendas and aspirations of individual ethnic groups, governmental neglect, and governmental policy initiatives (which are not always framed with the well-being of society as a whole in mind). At the regional level, ethnic problems can be influenced by cross-border ethnic complications and the actions of neighboring states, which are often unhelpful. At the international level, developments in the economic arena and the actions of international powers and international organizations can influence the course of events.

Government policies, therefore, constitute only one part of the overall equation—although they constitute an important part of it. One way to frame this issue is, first, to distinguish between factors that are internal and external to the country in question, and second, to distinguish between elite-level and mass-level factors.[13] Therefore, four main sets of factors need to be taken into account in the analysis of ethnic relations and ethnic conflicts, and they can be depicted in a two-by-two matrix. (See Table 1.)

First, there is no doubt that ethnic relations are influenced to a very great degree by domestic, mass-level factors. These factors include the ethnic composition and geographic distribution of ethnic communities in the country in question, pre-colonial and colonial legacies that affect

---

Table 1. Influences on Ethnic Relations.

	Internal	External
Elite-level	Domestic Elites and Government Policies	Regional and International Actors
Mass-level	Domestic Factors and Developments	Regional Factors and Developments

---

13. This draws on and is adapted from ibid., pp. 572–590.

relations between and among ethnic groups, and group histories more generally. A very large body of scholarship—representing, one could argue, the dominant approach to the study of ethnic relations and attendant political problems—focuses on other factors that operate domestically and at a mass level: intra-state security concerns, economic problems, the impact of modernization on societal relations, and patterns of social and cultural discrimination.

Some scholars focus on the security concerns that develop when states become weak and individual ethnic groups within these states feel compelled to provide for their own defense.[14] The problem is that, in taking steps to defend themselves, groups often threaten the security of others. This can lead these other groups to take steps that diminish the security of the first group. This spiral of escalation is known as the security dilemma. Other scholars give great weight to the economic problems that most states experience at one time or another, and the impact these economic problems can have on intra-state and inter-group tensions.[15] Unemployment, inflation, and resource competitions, especially for land, contribute to societal tensions and frustrations, and can provide the breeding ground for conflict. Discriminatory economic systems, which often discriminate along ethnic lines, can also generate feelings of resentment and levels of frustration that can lead to violence.[16] Many scholars have pointed to economic development and modernization as sources of domestic political turmoil.[17] The process of modernization, the advent of

---

14. See Barry R. Posen, "The Security Dilemma and Ethnic Conflict," in Brown, *Ethnic Conflict and International Security*, pp. 103–124; David A. Lake and Donald Rothchild, "Containing Fear: The Origins and Management of Ethnic Conflict," *International Security*, Vol. 21, No. 2 (Fall 1996), pp. 41–75; Milton J. Esman, *Ethnic Politics* (Ithaca, N.Y.: Cornell University Press, 1994), pp. 244–245.

15. For a general discussion and several case studies, see S.W.R. de A. Samarasinghe and Reed Coughlan, eds., *Economic Dimensions of Ethnic Conflict* (London: Pinter, 1991). For a detailed discussion of the economic roots of the wars in the former Yugoslavia, see Susan L. Woodward, *Balkan Tragedy: Chaos and Dissolution After the Cold War* (Washington, D.C.: The Brookings Institution, 1995), especially chap. 3. For a discussion of the economic sources of turmoil in the developing world, see Sandy Gordon, "Resources and Instability in South Asia," *Survival*, Vol. 35, No. 2 (Summer 1993), pp. 66–87.

16. For an overview of Marx on the economic roots of domestic violence, see James B. Rule, *Theories of Civil Violence* (Berkeley: University of California Press, 1988), chap. 2; A.S. Cohan, *Theories of Revolution* (New York: Wiley, 1975), chaps. 4–5.

17. See Samuel P. Huntington, *Political Order in Changing Societies* (New Haven, Conn.: Yale University Press, 1968); Samuel P. Huntington, "Civil Violence and the Process of Development," in *Civil Violence and the International System*, Adelphi Paper No. 83 (London: International Institute for Strategic Studies [IISS], 1971), pp. 1–15; Ted

industrialization, and the introduction of new technologies, it is said, bring about a wide variety of profound social changes: migration and urbanization disrupt existing family and social systems and undermine traditional political institutions; better education, higher literacy rates, and improved access to growing mass media raise awareness of where different groups stand in society. At a minimum, this places strains on existing social systems. It also raises economic and political expectations, and can lead to mounting frustration when these expectations are not met. Entrenched patterns of social and cultural discrimination constitute another set of factors that operate to a very great degree at a mass level.

A second set of factors, supported by a large but less voluminous body of scholarship, emphasizes the importance of mass-level factors that originate beyond the borders of the country in question. Journalists and policymakers often talk about conflicts "spilling over" from one place to another or spreading "like wildfire."[18] In thinking about how conflicts spread from one place to another, they often rely on crude analogies to floods, fires, diseases, and other forces of nature. Scholars often get caught up in this kind of thinking as well. Indeed, there is a sizable scholarly literature that frames this problem as a "contagion" problem.[19] One can bring more analytical precision to this discussion by identifying specific problems and mass-level mechanisms that can lead conflicts to spread from one place to another. These include the economic, political, and security problems generated by large flows of refugees; the economic problems that develop when cross-border patterns of economic activity

---

Robert Gurr, *Why Men Rebel* (Princeton, N.J.: Princeton University Press, 1970); Walker Conner, "Nation-Building or Nation-Destroying?" *World Politics,* Vol. 24, No. 3 (April 1972), pp. 319–355; Walker Conner, *Ethnonationalism: The Quest for Understanding* (Princeton, N.J.: Princeton University Press, 1994). For an overview of this literature, see Saul Newman, "Does Modernization Breed Ethnic Conflict?" *World Politics,* Vol. 43, No. 3 (April 1991), pp. 451–478. For critiques of this approach, see Rod Aya, "Theories of Revolution Reconsidered: Contrasting Models of Collective Violence," *Theory and Society,* Vol. 8, No. 1 (July 1979), pp. 1–38; Charles Tilly, "Does Modernization Breed Revolution?" *Comparative Politics,* Vol. 5, No. 3 (April 1973), pp. 425–447.

18. For details and discussion, see Brown, "Introduction," *The International Dimensions of Internal Conflict,* pp. 23–26.

19. See, for example, John A. Vasquez, "Factors Related to the Contagion and Diffusion of International Violence," in Manus I. Midlarsky, ed., *The Internationalization of Communal Strife* (London: Routledge, 1992), pp. 149–172; Ralph R. Premdas, "The Internationalization of Ethnic Conflict: Some Theoretical Explorations," in de Silva and May, *The Internationalization of Ethnic Conflict,* p. 10; Gurr, *Minorities at Risk,* pp. 132–135. For an excellent overview of this literature, see Stuart Hill and Donald Rothchild, "The Contagion of Political Conflict in Africa and the World," *Journal of Conflict Resolution,* Vol. 30, No. 4 (December 1986), pp. 716–735.

are disrupted; the military problems that emerge when the territory of neighboring states is used for sanctuary or resupply; and the instability problems that can be transmitted from one country to another when ethnic groups straddle international borders.

A third set of factors is also regional and international in character, but operates at the elite level and features the discrete decisions and actions taken by neighboring states and other international actors. Neighboring states often involve themselves in the domestic ethnic conflicts of others, but there are only a few studies that analyze the ways in which this comes about.[20] In some cases, the motivations of neighboring states are comparatively benign, and their actions can be framed as either humanitarian or defensive interventions. In many cases, however, neighboring states launch protective interventions designed to aid ethnic brethren or opportunistic interventions designed to exploit internal turmoil elsewhere. Neighboring states often support insurgents involved in hostilities against regional rivals, hoping to keep rivals preoccupied with internal affairs and weaken them over time. Examples of this abound, including Pakistan's support of Kashmiri rebels in India and India's support of insurgents in the Pakistani province of Sindh. Russia has taken advantage of ethnic turmoil in post-Soviet Azerbaijan and Georgia to advance its position in the Caucasus. In the most extreme cases, neighboring states take advantage of momentary weaknesses caused by internal turmoil to launch invasions of rivals. Examples include the Syrian invasion of Jordan during the latter's civil war in 1970.[21]

The fourth and final set of factors that influences ethnic relations operates domestically at the elite level and includes the decisions, actions, and policies of political elites and governments. Some scholars and analysts have examined the roles played by domestic elites and inter-group

---

20. See James N. Rosenau, ed., *International Aspects of Civil Strife* (Princeton, N.J.: Princeton University Press, 1964); Karl W. Deutsch, "External Involvement in Internal War," in Harry Eckstein, ed., *Internal War: Problems and Approaches* (New York: Free Press, 1964), pp. 100–110; Hedley Bull, "Civil Violence and International Order," in *Civil Violence and the International System*, Adelphi Paper No. 83 (London: IISS, 1971), pp. 27–36; Evan Luard, *The International Regulation of Civil Wars* (London: Thames and Hudson, 1972); Alexis Heraclides, "Secessionist Minorities and External Involvement," *International Organization*, Vol. 44, No. 3 (Summer 1990), pp. 341–378; James Mayall, *Nationalism and International Society* (Cambridge, U.K.: Cambridge University Press, 1990); Midlarsky, *The Internationalization of Communal Strife*; de Silva and May, *The Internationalization of Ethnic Conflict*; Brown, *Ethnic Conflict and International Security*. An attempt to examine this issue in a systematic way can be found in Brown, "The Causes and Regional Dimensions of Internal Conflict," pp. 590–600.

21. For more discussion, see Brown, "The Causes and Regional Dimensions of Internal Conflict," pp. 590–600.

politics in the evolution of ethnic conflicts.[22] Considerable attention has been paid, in particular, to the impact of nationalist ideologies and political institutions, which are generally shaped by domestic elites, on ethnic problems.[23] However, little attention has been focused on government policies per se—the main focus of this book.

We believe that government policies merit investigation for three reasons. First, they almost always have a significant impact on the course and trajectory of ethnic relations in the country in question. A few examples will suffice for the moment. India is a country of extraordinary ethnic diversity, a country that could have fallen apart in the decades since it came out from under colonial rule in 1947. There is a good case to be made that it has stayed together because of its commitment to democratic and secular principles, and because the central government in New Delhi has undertaken a number of constructive policy initiatives. Specifically, the government's flexible language policies and its willingness to reorganize the country's state system on more than one occasion have

---

22. See Human Rights Watch, *Slaughter Among Neighbors: The Political Origins of Communal Violence* (New Haven, Conn.: Yale University Press, 1995); V.P. Gagnon, Jr., "Ethnic Nationalism and International Conflict: The Case of Serbia," *International Security*, Vol. 19, No. 3 (Winter 1994/95), pp. 130–166; Warren Zimmermann, *Origins of a Catastrophe* (New York: Times Books, 1996); Mark Thompson, *Forging War: The Media in Serbia, Croatia and Bosnia-Hercegovina* (London: Article 19; International Centre Against Censorship, 1994); Gérard Prunier, *The Rwanda Crisis: History of a Genocide* (New York: Columbia University Press, 1995); Joseph Rothschild, *Ethnopolitics: A Conceptual Framework* (New York: Columbia University Press, 1981); Horowitz, *Ethnic Groups in Conflict*.

23. On nationalistic ideologies, see Jack Snyder, "Nationalism and the Crisis of the Post-Soviet State," in Brown, *Ethnic Conflict and International Security*, pp. 79–101; Jack Snyder and Karen Ballentine, "Nationalism and the Marketplace of Ideas," *International Security*, Vol. 21, No. 2 (Fall 1996), pp. 5–40; E.J. Hobsbawm, *Nations and Nationalism since 1780: Programme, Myth, Reality* (Cambridge, U.K.: Cambridge University Press, 1990); Benedict Anderson, *Imagined Communities: Reflections on the Origin and Spread of Nationalism*, 2nd ed. (London: Verso, 1991); Paul R. Brass, *Ethnicity and Nationalism: Theory and Comparison* (Newbury Park, Calif.: Sage, 1991); Human Rights Watch, *Slaughter Among Neighbors*; Gagnon, "Ethnic Nationalism and International Conflict." On institutional problems and institutional solutions to ethnic problems, see Arend Lijphart, *Democracy in Plural Societies* (New Haven, Conn.: Yale University Press, 1977); Horowitz, *Ethnic Groups in Conflict*, chaps. 7–13; Donald L. Horowitz, "Democracy in Divided Societies," *Journal of Democracy*, Vol. 4, No. 4 (October 1993), pp. 18–38; Ted Robert Gurr and Barbara Harff, *Ethnic Conflict and World Politics* (Boulder, Colo.: Westview Press, 1994), chap. 5; James G. March and Johan P. Olsen, *Rediscovering Institutions: The Organizational Basis of Politics* (New York: Free Press, 1989); James Q. Wilson, *Political Organizations* (Princeton, N.J.: Princeton University Press, 1995); R. Kent Weaver and Bert A. Rockman, eds., *Do Institutions Matter? Government Capabilities in the United States and Abroad* (Washington, D.C.: The Brookings Institution, 1993).

served the country well.[24] Since the late 1800s, successive governments in Thailand have successfully forged a national identity while avoiding the intolerant, militant nationalism that has exacerbated ethnic relations in many countries. As a result, Thailand has experienced little sustained ethnic violence in recent decades.[25] Sri Lanka, however, is a country with a strong democratic tradition that should have been able to avoid descending into civil war. However, a series of misguided, ethnically biased policies with respect to citizenship, language, religion, education, and government employment alienated the country's Tamil minority and pushed the country's main ethnic groups into a violent confrontation. Ironically and tragically, the government's 1995 offer to give Tamils more regional autonomy probably would have prevented the war from breaking out in the first place if this offer had been made in the 1950s, 1960s, or 1970s. By the 1990s, however, parts of the Tamil community had become radicalized and unwilling to settle for anything other than complete political independence.[26]

Second, if scholars are going to develop a grand unified theory of the dynamics of ethnic relations and the causes of ethnic conflicts, they will have to take government policies into account. They constitute an important part of the broader analytical equation. However, because government policies with respect to ethnic relations have not been studied in a focused, systematic manner from a broad comparative perspective, little relevant data has been compiled and an analytical framework for thinking about these issues has not been developed. There are, in short, important gaps in the scholarly literature on this subject from both descriptive and analytical standpoints—problems that we hope to address over the course of this study.

Third, of all the factors that influence ethnic relations and ethnic conflicts, government policies are comparatively manipulable. Ethnic demography and geography, for example, usually change at a glacial pace. Ethnic histories and group attitudes also change slowly. Broad economic developments and modernization processes are difficult to control with precision. Government policies are not infinitely flexible, but they are comparatively elastic. If one hopes that scholarly study of the dynamics of ethnic relations will ultimately lead to a theory of the causes of ethnic conflict and a strategy for conflict prevention, conflict management, and conflict resolution, then it makes sense to pay particular attention to

24. See Kanti Bajpai's chapter on India in this volume.
25. See Charles Keyes's chapter on Thailand in this volume.
26. See Amita Shastri's chapter on Sri Lanka in this volume.

government policies. This is an area where academic research could generate considerable leverage over important real-world problems.

A Framework for Analysis

Since the focus of this book is on government policies with respect to ethnic relations, we should start by defining we mean by "government policies," "ethnic groups," and "policy success."

We define "government policies" broadly to include federal (national), provincial (state), and local policies. In addition to examining the formal decisions and actions of duly constituted governing bodies, we will consider informal practices as well as patterns of neglect: non-decisions and inaction can also influence ethnic problems, and therefore merit attention. However, we will limit our focus to the decisions and actions (along with the non-decisions and inactions) of governments constituted in the countries in question. The activities of corporations (local, national, or multinational), nongovernmental organizations, regional and international powers, and international organizations are also important matters, but they are beyond the scope of this book.

Since we think there will be value in looking at a wide range of inter-communal relations, we will employ a broad definition of ethnicity. For our purposes, an "ethnic group" is a human population that has a name and thinks of itself as a group; possesses a common ancestry, historical ties, and historical memories; and shares a culture, which can be based on a combination of race, language, religion, laws, customs, institutions, dress, music, crafts, and food.[27] In this book, ethnic groups will include both majority and minority communities, groups based on both linguistic and religious identifications, indigenous peoples, settlers, and, in some cases, immigrants and migrant workers. Calling indigenous peoples "ethnic groups" will be at odds with the terms of discourse in Australia and New Zealand, for example, but we think there is a good case to be made for including these peoples in our discussion. We will not examine groups defined primarily by shared ideological agendas (communist parties, for example) or economic agendas (labor unions). Obviously, ethnic markers vary from country to country, so groups will have to be categorized on a country-by-country basis.[28]

Finally, since we seek to distinguish successful policies from their less

---

27. This definition is derived from Anthony D. Smith, "The Ethnic Sources of Nationalism," in Brown, *Ethnic Conflict and International Security*, pp. 27–41.

28. There is no simple or perfect solution to the problem of defining ethnicity and categorizing specific groups and individuals. Many people have mixed ethnic backgrounds and multiple ethnic identities. New Zealand, for example, has a large number

successful counterparts, we need to have a clear sense of what we mean by "success" and "failure." For the purposes of this book, success will be defined in terms of the promotion of peaceful intra-state ethnic relations, order, and stability, *and* the promotion of political, economic, and social justice.[29] The latter will be defined in terms of fair treatment under the law and equal access to the political, economic, and social levers of power in a country. Creating equal access might involve, in the short term, affirmative action programs that create temporary inequalities designed to eliminate structural inequalities. The challenge for governments, of course, is to promote stability and justice at the same time. Authoritarian governments are often effective at maintaining political order, at least in the short term, but their methods leave much to be desired and they often do not get good grades on the "justice" dimension.

Our framework for analyzing government policies has three main elements: policy settings, policy parameters, and policy areas. (See Table 2.)

POLICY SETTINGS

The starting point for analyzing government policies has to be a consideration of policy settings—the arrays of ethnic problems and challenges with which governments have to contend. Policies, after all, are not formulated or implemented in vacuums. Different governments have to contend with different kinds of ethnic problems and challenges; these problems change over time, both in response to whatever governments do and do not do, and in response to other domestic, regional, and international developments. Drawing on our earlier discussion of the factors that can influence ethnic relations and ethnic conflicts, we will organize our discussion of policy settings by looking at five clusters of factors: demographic patterns and ethnic geography; pre-colonial and colonial legacies; group histories, fears, and goals; economic factors and trends; and regional and international influences.

Although the new governments of countries that are coming out from

---

of people with mixed Maori-Pakeha backgrounds. In India, people are identified by both religious and linguistic markers.

29. Peace, order, and stability are easy to measure. Political, economic, and social justice is not, and is highly subjective. One group might see a particular policy as fair and just, while another might see things quite differently. Which group is right? Since policies will usually favor some groups at the expense of others, this will generally be a problem for those who seek to evaluate policy initiatives. In addition, what one sees as "just" depends to a very great degree on one's political, economic, and social values. Whereas a scholar from the United States might place great value on individual rights and multi-party political processes, some Asian leaders place more value on political order and economic development and prosperity.

Table 2. A Framework for Analysis.

Policy Settings
Demographic Patterns and Ethnic Geography
Pre-colonial and Colonial Legacies
Group Histories, Fears, and Goals
Economic Factors and Trends
Regional and International Influences

Policy Parameters
Policy Goals
Policy Instruments
Policy Patterns
Policy Problems

Policy Areas
Political Structures and Institutions
Citizenship Policies
Civil and Minority Rights Policies
Policies on Religion and Religious Groups
Language Policies
Education Policies
Economic Policies

under colonial rule are in effect presented with sets of ethnic problems, these settings begin to change immediately in response to what governments do and do not do and in response to other internal and external developments. One should not think of either settings or policies as static. Indeed, one has to look at the interactions between the two over time: settings influence policies, which in turn influence group fears and political agendas, for example, and so on. Among the most important processes to analyze are the ways in which the agendas of ethnic groups become radicalized over time. In many countries, groups that once had apolitical goals have come to adopt political agendas and to favor political autonomy and self-government as the solutions to their problems. In addition, as goals have become more ambitious and contentious, groups have often become more willing to use violent means to realize their ends. Why and how do group goals change? Under what conditions do groups resort to violence? What are the critical thresholds in the process of radicalization? What can well-meaning governments and outside powers do about these problems? We hope to shed some light on these questions.

POLICY PARAMETERS

With these situational factors in mind, we turn to the broad parameters that frame government policies and we discuss some basic policy problems. Four sets of issues will be examined in this context: policy goals, policy instruments, policy patterns, and generic policy problems.

National governments generally have the overarching goal of maintaining the political unity and territorial integrity of their countries. However, different governments have different visions of how ethnic relations in their countries should be structured. Some governments are obsessed with maintaining political unity in and the territorial integrity of their states, and they engage in vigorous efforts to create single national identities, to suppress other ethnic identities, and to squash ethnic movements. These governments, one could say, have unicultural visions of their countries. Many governments have unicultural visions, but for more parochial reasons. Many governments are run by one or more ethnic groups who want to stay in power, which means keeping other groups out of power; want and need to maintain the support of their ethnic constituents; and do not care about or want to help other ethnic groups or minorities.[30] Many governments have ethnic affiliations and constituencies that strongly shape their policy agendas; these governments are not ethnically neutral "policy machines." Other governments, however, are either more tolerant of ethnic diversity or more resigned to diversity as a fact of life in their countries. Some go far to preserve cultural and ethnic diversity. Some are aware of and sensitive to ethnic problems, and are interested in making good-faith efforts to promote political, economic, and social justice. One could say that such governments have multicultural visions of their countries. In this study, we hope to develop a better understanding of the origins of ethnic visions and goals, the reasons why they change over time, and the ways governments seek to balance the need for a national identity and the realities of ethnic diversity.

This leads to the issue of governmental actions, and the instruments they utilize to translate ethnic visions into reality. What policy instruments do governments rely on most frequently and with greatest success? Drawing on the foregoing, we will try to identify notable policy patterns in the sixteen countries under investigation in this book. What combinations of goals and instruments have been most common? How have policies evolved over time? Which policies were most successful from the narrow perspective of the governments concerned and more broadly in terms of peace and justice? Under what conditions were policies most successful?

Three broad sets of policy problems also merit attention: timing problems, implementation problems, and political dilemmas. Govern-

---

30. We would like to thank Ron May for suggesting this characterization of the problem.

ments are often slow to respond to ethnic problems, acting only when they have to respond to emerging crises. This, however, is when problems are intense and comparatively intractable. To what extent are governments inclined to neglect ethnic problems? Why are governments often slow to get off the mark? Why do they miss windows of opportunity? When governments do launch policy initiatives, what kinds of implementation problems are most common and most pernicious? When and how have policies had unintended or unforeseen consequences? What implementation problems are distinctive to ethnic issues? Finally, we will analyze the kinds of political dilemmas that complicate governmental action in the ethnic arena.

POLICY AREAS

With this general framework in mind, we analyze government policies in several specific policy areas: political structures and institutions; citizenship policies; minority rights policies; policies on religion and religious groups; language policies; education policies; and economic policies. In this study, we will try to identify the policy initiatives and programs that have had the most impact—good or bad—on ethnic relations and problems, and to account for these policy successes and failures, both of which can be instructive. Because policies that work well in one place at one particular point in time do not necessarily work well under other conditions, we will endeavor to identify the conditions under which policies succeeded and failed in terms of the criteria outlined above.

Case Selection

To be comprehensive, a comparative study of ethnic issues in Asia and the Pacific would have to examine over sixty countries and territories. Such a study would be unwieldy at best and analytically muddled at worst. In order to make this enterprise both more manageable and analytically sharper, cases were selected for inclusion on the following bases.

First, we only included countries with demographically significant ethnic minorities. Our rationale is straightforward: it is unlikely that one could draw general lessons from countries with minuscule ethnic minorities that would be applicable to countries with more complex ethnographic pictures. Japan, North Korea, South Korea, Kiribati, Palau, Tonga, Tuvalu, Western Samoa, the Marshall Islands, and the Solomon Islands were excluded for this reason.

Second, we only included politically independent entities. Again, our rationale is straightforward: independent countries have control over government policies—our main concern—in ways that colonies and territories do not. American Samoa, the Cook Islands, French Polynesia, Guam, Macao, New Caledonia, Niue, the Northern Marianas, Tokelau, and Wallis and Futuna are colonies or territories of other powers, and were excluded for this reason.

Third, in the interest of making this exercise manageable, we excluded the countries of West Asia (also known as the Middle East). We excluded the six Central Asian states that emerged from the collapse of the Soviet Union in late 1991—Kazakhstan, Kyrgyzstan, Russia, Tajikistan, Turkmenistan, and Uzbekistan—because they became independent under extraordinary circumstances and because they face a wide range of unique political and economic problems. Mongolia, which came out from under the Soviet umbrella around the same time, albeit under different circumstances, was excluded for this reason as well. Afghanistan, which was occupied by the Soviet Union until 1989, has since fragmented as a political entity and was therefore left out of this investigation.

Our focus in broad regional terms, therefore, is South Asia, Southeast Asia, East Asia, and the Asia-Pacific. Significantly, the sixteen countries that are examined in this study—India, Pakistan, Sri Lanka, Burma, Thailand, Malaysia, Singapore, Indonesia, the Philippines, China, Australia, New Zealand, Fiji, Papua New Guinea, Vanuatu, and the Federated States of Micronesia—are representative of the region as a whole.[31] More importantly, they have the rich variation in ethnic settings, policies, and outcomes that we need to conduct a wide-ranging comparative analysis of these issues. The comparative advantage of this book is comparative analysis: books devoted to just one country or a single conflict will inevitably be able to provide more historical and descriptive detail than one will find in this volume. The contributors to this book, however, will focus on a common set of questions and issues, and thereby provide an empirical and analytical foundation for the development of generalizations and policy recommendations that, we trust, will cut across individual countries and regions.

Organization of the Book

This book is divided into four main parts. The first three parts contain the case studies that provide the empirical foundation for the study as a whole. They are organized along regional lines, and they examine South

---

31. In the end, difficult decisions had to be made about what countries to include, given the practical constraints that studies of this kind inevitably operate under. Good arguments could be made for including Bangladesh, Cambodia, Laos, Nepal, Taiwan, and Vietnam in this book.

Asia, Southeast and East Asia, and Australia and the Asia-Pacific in turn. They focus on developments that have taken place since 1945 or, as appropriate, the attainment of political independence. The fourth and final part of the book draws on the foregoing, looks at government policies with respect to ethnic issues from a broad comparative perspective, and develops some analytical generalizations and policy recommendations.

SOUTH ASIA

The first part of the book focuses on South Asia, analyzing government management and mismanagement of ethnic relations in India, Pakistan, and Sri Lanka.

INDIA. According to Kanti Bajpai, India's democratic political order, despite its many shortcomings, has been critical to the management of ethnic relations within its multiethnic society. India's extraordinary ethnic diversity—encompassing divisions of language, religion, caste, tribe, and region—has posed significant challenges to nation-building. To cope with these challenges, the Indian state has relied on three main instruments: first, a political order based on liberal constitutionalism and secularism; second, power-sharing arrangements based on group rights and the devolution of authority to lower levels of government; and third, the use of force and coercion when the first two instruments have failed. Policies based on power-sharing and devolution have proved to be the most successful in containing ethnic discord and violence. The use of force and coercion has had some success in wearing down militant adversaries and bringing them to the bargaining table, particularly in Punjab and the northeast. However, these strategies, along with the centralizing propensities of a number of Indian governments, have also intensified ethnic alienation, for example, in the state of Jammu and Kashmir. Increased reliance on coercive strategies has contributed to spirals of retribution and violence. Bajpai concludes that Indian governments have a mixed record in their management of the country's ethnic problems.

PAKISTAN. Pakistan was created as a homeland for Indian Muslims from the detritus of the British Indian empire. The populations of Pakistan, though predominantly Muslim, were nevertheless ethnically heterogenous in terms of language, regional affiliation, and cultural identity. As Samina Ahmed argues, a single ethnic community, the Punjabis, came to dominate the country's civil-military bureaucracies, and the new state failed to develop viable representative institutions. Most peripheral ethnic communities therefore came to perceive the state as a partisan ethnic actor. Compounding these problems, the country's leaders neglected compelling ethnic problems and adopted strategies that transformed ethnic competition into violent conflict. In 1971, Pakistan disintegrated as a consequence of these policy failures. The majority Bengali population of East Pakistan, with assistance from India, successfully seceded from Pakistan and created the new state of Bangladesh. The ruling elite in Islamabad has since continued to ignore and mismanage the country's many ethnic problems—for example, by denying regional autonomy to ethnic groups and by pursuing cultural and educational policies that have excluded various ethnic minorities. Ahmed contends that the Pakistani government's chronic inability to address these ethnic issues in a constructive and effective fashion threatens the stability and integrity of the Pakistani state.

SRI LANKA. Even though Sri Lanka obtained its independence from Great Britain without bloodshed, it ultimately plunged into a cauldron of ethnic violence. According to Amita Shastri, the roots of ethnic violence in Sri Lanka can be traced directly to the central government's failure to accommodate the legitimate demands of its Tamil minority. After independence, the country's Sinhalese leaders adopted a centralized system of government that denied minorities regional autonomy. In addition, Sinhalese politicians, despite their commitment to a democratic state, increasingly came to conceive of democracy in majoritarian terms. "Upcountry" Tamils, in particular, faced systematic political and economic discrimination, leading over half to leave for India. Subsequent policies, especially the Official Language Act of 1956, further discriminated against Tamils and other ethnic minorities. In 1972, Sri Lanka adopted a new constitution that further centralized power, subordinated the judiciary to the legislature, and granted official status to the Sinhala language and Buddhism, the religion of the Sinhalese people. The 1977 elections, which were based on the 1972 constitution, resulted in a sweeping victory for the Sinhalese-dominated United National Party. This electoral outcome further marginalized the Tamil community. Seeing little constitutional recourse to redress their grievances, segments of the Tamil community resorted to violence. The Sri Lankan state responded with increasingly repressive measures. As a consequence of these measures, the country descended into a brutal civil war in the 1980s. Although the government has tried since 1994 to resolve the conflict—even offering regional autonomy arrangements to Tamil communities—these overtures have been rejected by Tamil militants who will now settle for nothing less than an independent state. One of the tragedies of the Sri Lankan story is that, if the government had been willing to adopt accommodative policies in the 1950s, 1960s, and 1970s, war almost certainly would not have broken out.

SOUTHEAST AND EAST ASIA

The second part of the book analyzes developments in Southeast and East Asia. The track records of government policies in Burma, Thailand, Malaysia, Singapore, Indonesia, the Philippines, and China are examined.

BURMA. Ethnic policies in Burma have failed under both civilian and military rulers since the country became independent in 1948.[32] Josef Silverstein explains that the roots of these policy failures can be traced to pre-colonial and colonial times. The Burman kings did not develop many clear-cut policies toward ethnic minorities. Some groups, such as the Mon and Arakanese, were assimilated in an unplanned fashion, while others— the Karen, Shan, Kachin, and Chin, in particular—retained very distinct identities. Weak rulers at the center often faced secessionist demands. The British further complicated the situation by pursuing a "divide and rule" policy that intensified ethnic distinctions and by opening Burma to foreign immigration, especially from India. Independent Burma's first constitution did not go far enough to address the country's underlying ethnic problems; by creating a political system that was federal in theory but centralized in practice, it did not satisfy the demands of some groups— the Karen, most notably—for political autonomy. Although the country's preeminent nationalist leader, Aung San, sought to promote an inclusive vision of Burman nationalism, Burma's citizenship laws were changed in 1948, making it harder for Indians to obtain citizenship. The country's Chinese community was also discriminated against. Following a military coup in 1962, Burma's new rulers formally scrapped the federal system and aggressively promoted both political centralization and cultural assimilation. The military junta has since developed a divide-and-conquer policy of its own, negotiating cease-fires with some minorities while escalating attacks on those who will not capitulate. Although a National Convention was convened in 1993 to write a new constitution, Silverstein believes that Burma's ethnic problems will not be resolved until

---

32. In June 1989, Burma's military leaders changed the country's name to the "Union of Myanmar" in an effort to rally nationalist sentiments and to deflect domestic and international attention from their sustained attacks on the principles of democratic governance, internationally recognized human rights standards, and democratic and ethnic dissidents. We decline to endorse the junta's action. In this book, we will refer to the country they rule as "Burma."

dictatorial rule is replaced by rule of law, political rights are respected, and a federal political system is instituted.

THAILAND.   Charles Keyes shows that, for over one hundred years, Thailand's governments have pursued a policy of ethnic inclusiveness that has enabled the country to submerge ethnic differences and limit ethnic conflict. In the nineteenth century Siam included a range of indigenous peoples as well as a large immigrant population, only some of whom had been assimilated into the Tai linguistic family. Ethnic diversity, however, was not seen as a political problem by the Siamese monarchy until the late nineteenth century, when European colonial rule was extended into Burma, Cambodia, and Vietnam. Siam's rulers correctly feared that Europeans would attempt to exploit the country's cultural diversity and try to dismember it. The country's leaders consequently embarked on a concerted effort to forge a nation-state. To this end, they promulgated three principles of Thai nationalism: an emphasis on the Thai language, an adherence to Buddhism, and loyalty to the monarchy. A military coup in 1932 brought the absolute monarchy to an end, and the new leadership sought to fashion a national identity that was based more on the Thai language and history than the monarchy. Even so, Keyes demonstrates that, over the course of the twentieth century, the country's rulers have advanced a comparatively tolerant form of nationalism: one could "become" Thai if one learned the Thai language and professed loyalty to the Thai state. Significantly, King Bhumipol took steps in the 1970s to broaden the definition of Thai nationalism to accommodate citizens who were not Buddhist. This helped to reduce the alienation of Thai Muslims, many of whom live in regions that border Malaysia. In short, Thailand's experience demonstrates that cultural differences do not have to lead to violence. Governments can successfully strike a balance between the need to develop a national identity and the need to respect cultural diversity.

MALAYSIA AND SINGAPORE.   In this chapter Šumit Ganguly demonstrates that, in Malaysia and Singapore as in other parts of Asia and the Pacific, British imperial rule created some ethnic problems and compounded others. Influxes of Indian and Chinese laborers created new and more complex ethnic realities, and the latter were encouraged by the British to pursue commercial activities, which they did with considerable success. Malay commoners were deemed by the British to be unsuitable for the task of administering the country. As a result, when Malaysia obtained its independence in 1957, the ethnically dominant Malays found themselves to be economically and socially disadvantaged. Malay resentment against the country's other communities, most notably the Chinese, culminated in ethnic violence in 1969. In the wake of the 1969 riots, the Malay elite embarked on an ambitious affirmative action program designed to redress the grievances of the majority population. A political and economic strategy based on restrictions on personal freedoms, market-oriented economic policies, and redistributive measures has since enabled Malaysia to maintain ethnic peace—albeit at a cost in terms of political liberty.

Singapore, which obtained its independence from Great Britain in 1959, notionally embraces democratic standards; however, it too has relied on harsh, authoritarian methods to maintain ethnic peace and public order. Unlike Malaysia, which openly espouses the cause of ethnic Malays, Singapore professes to be a multiracial meritocracy. However, in practice, the country's Chinese community has dominated Singapore's political and economic life. Ethnic conflict in Malaysia and Singapore has been dampened by infringements placed on political liberties and by the economic booms these countries have fortuitously experienced. Whether these patterns of stability can be sustained in the future is uncertain.

INDONESIA. Indonesia (the former Dutch East Indies) was founded in 1945 by nationalists of varying ethnic backgrounds. Formal independence came in 1949 after a four-year struggle with the Dutch. Indonesia has become a country of nearly two hundred million people spread across a four-thousand-mile archipelago. As R. William Liddle explains, it is one of the most ethnically diverse countries in the world, with significant cleavages along cultural/regional, religious, and racial lines. Since President Suharto assumed power and imposed authoritarian rule in 1966, coercion has been the main instrument used by the government to cope with the country's ethnic diversity and to maintain political order, although persuasion, exchange, and cooptation have been part of the policy equation as well. Because it is worried about holding the country together as well as holding onto power, Suharto's government is deeply attached to centralized political arrangements. However, this has exacerbated tensions between the Javanese, who constitute the largest ethnic group in the country, and other groups. The government's attachment to centralization has also exacerbated relations with ethnic groups in Aceh, East Timor, and Irian Jaya, in particular; these groups seek more autonomy and have suffered under often brutal crackdowns. Indonesia is entering a difficult period, as the central leadership ages and popular demands for political liberty and regional autonomy grow. However, as Liddle observes, there are few signs that the country's leadership is willing to embrace the gradual democratization and devolution of power that is needed.

THE PHILIPPINES.   Apart from the significant problems posed by the Moro minority, R.J. May argues, ethnicity has not played a significant role in Philippine politics. The Chinese minority has been assimilated, and tribal groups have been marginalized. Under Spanish rule, ethnic Chinese were encouraged to immigrate, but they also faced widespread discrimination and periodic repression. The conditions of the Chinese improved somewhat under U.S. rule in the first part of the twentieth century. After World War II and independence, however, immigration was eliminated and attempts to integrate the Chinese community were stepped up. Assimilation of the Chinese community has since become virtually complete.

The United States also sought to improve the conditions of the tribal Filipinos though the creation of "special provinces" and the expansion of English-language education. Under President Ferdinand Marcos, the plight of tribal peoples worsened considerably in the 1960s and 1970s. Ranchers, loggers, and miners expropriated their lands and counterinsurgency operations were launched to quell any expression of discontent. Some positive changes took place under President Corazon Aquino in the late 1980s. In particular, efforts were made to draft a new constitution that promised to promote the cultural rights of indigenous communities.

However, as May relates, the Moro problem, which has its roots in the Spanish colonization of the Philippines in the sixteenth century, has persisted over time. For three centuries the Spaniards carried out military campaigns against these Muslim islanders and created an ethnic hierarchy which consigned them to the very bottom of the social and political ladder. Harsh efforts were also made to subdue the Moros during the period of U.S. colonial rule. In the post-colonial period, the Moros continued to resist efforts at assimilation and sought to fend off encroachments on their ancestral lands, particularly during the Marcos era. The Aquino administration entered into peace talks with the Moro National Liberation Front and made some effort to satisfy Moro demands for regional autonomy. However, a turning point in the relationship between Manila and the Moros was not reached until 1996, when President Fidel Ramos signed an agreement that provided for real autonomy in Muslim areas. Whether this bold step will bring the Moro rebellion to an end remains to be seen.

THE PEOPLE'S REPUBLIC OF CHINA.   In this chapter, June Teufel Dreyer holds that, under Mao Zedong, the Chinese Communist government's policies towards the country's ethnic minorities alternated between halfhearted accommodation and aggressive assimilation. According to Dreyer, in the initial aftermath of the 1949 revolution, Beijing's policies towards minority areas were largely accommodationist—the notable exceptions being government policies towards Tibet and Xinjiang. A significant policy shift took place in the late 1950s, when the anti-rightist campaign and the Great Leap Forward pushed policy in the direction of economic collectivization and cultural assimilation. The rebellions that ensued in Tibet and Xinjiang led the government to ease off and acknowledge the "special characteristics" of minorities in the early 1960s, but relations between Beijing and minority areas deteriorated dramatically as the decade unfolded. The Cultural Revolution of 1966–68 featured a brutal campaign to destroy minority cultures and customs: broadcasting and publishing in minority languages all but ceased; traditional customs and practices were virtually banned; and many religious sites were obliterated. Some accommodative steps were taken by the government in the early 1970s, but much damage to inter-ethnic relations had already been done.

Although the government's policies during the Mao era varied in some respects, one element of continuity was the government's desire to create strong ties between central institutions and areas inhabited by ethnic minorities. A profound reversal occurred under Deng Xiaoping, whose emphasis on promoting economic growth created powerful centrifugal forces: minority areas were opened up to foreign investment, trade, and tourism, and borders became more porous. These forces were especially strong in Xinjiang, Tibet, and Inner Mongolia. By the early 1990s, the government had started to adopt a harder line in response to ethnic protests. As China moves into the post-Deng era, the country's rulers face a seemingly intractable policy dilemma: accommodationist policies may lead to secessionist demands, but assimilationist crackdowns will almost certainly lead to violent backlashes and perhaps open rebellions.

AUSTRALIA AND THE ASIA-PACIFIC REGION
The third part of the book examines the evolution of government policies with respect to ethnic relations in Australia and the Asia-Pacific region. It contains case studies of policy development in Australia, New Zealand, Fiji, Papua New Guinea, Vanuatu, and the Federated States of Micronesia.

AUSTRALIA. Christine Fletcher argues that Australia is distinctive in the Asia-Pacific region by virtue of its ancient indigenous population, its large immigrant population, and its federal form of government. For over two centuries since the formal British occupation of Australia in 1788, Fletcher notes, the Aboriginal peoples of the continent have suffered in a multitude of ways. The principal policy that successive Australian governments pursued toward indigenous peoples was assimilation; with this in mind Aboriginal families were broken up, children were taken away, laws on association and movement were enacted, and Aboriginal lands were seized. Significantly, Aboriginal rights were not mentioned in any of the state constitutions or Australia's commonwealth constitution. Indeed, until the late 1960s, Aboriginal peoples were not considered citizens under the Australian constitution, and governments were prohibited by the constitution from counting Aborigines in censuses. In addition, between 1901 and 1969, governments adhered to the "White Australia" policy, designed to keep non-white immigrants from coming to Australia. Since 1969, Australia has adopted non-discriminatory immigration policies.

Starting in the late 1960s, state and commonwealth governments began to take steps to redress the conditions of the Aboriginal population. Specifically, following a national referendum, Aborigines were counted in the Australian national census, and the commonwealth government was given the authority to enter the jurisdiction of states and make laws pertaining to the Aboriginal population. Legislation passed in the 1970s expanded the rights of Aboriginal peoples. Further positive developments emerged in the 1980s with the reorganization of the Department of Aboriginal Affairs. Since 1992, in the wake of a High Court judgment, Aborigines have gained further legal rights with respect to land claims. Despite these developments, Fletcher contends that the cultural distance between the settler communities and Aboriginal peoples remains great. Consequently, even well-meaning policies have not produced the intended results. If this fundamental problem is to be addressed, real political power will have to devolve to members of indigenous communities.

NEW ZEALAND. In many and perhaps most respects, as Andrew Sharp explains, New Zealand constitutes a success story as far as government policies and ethnic relations are concerned. Significantly, the country has not experienced significant levels of ethnic violence in decades. In addition, New Zealand's record with respect to civil and political rights is exemplary. Its system of legal protections is both broad and deep, and its political system allows the full participation of all. However, there are areas of contention in the policy arena, and there is room for improvement in policy terms. The Treaty of Waitangi, which was signed in 1840 and which has since provided the legal framework for relations between European settlers and their descendants (Pakeha) and Maori, has been interpreted in different ways by the two communities. The government has offered financial settlements to many Maori communities in the 1980s and 1990s, but those who have received settlements have not always been those in the greatest need. On the whole, Maori and Pacific Islander

communities suffer from relatively high levels of unemployment, economic problems, educational problems, health problems, and housing
problems. Although this situation has improved since the 1940s, more
needs to be done. Sharp concludes that governments can and should do
more about these economic and social inequities and to provide more
reparative justice. In all probability, however, disputes about these matters
will continue to unfold in a non-violent fashion in the political, legal, and
bureaucratic arenas.

FIJI, PAPUA NEW GUINEA, VANUATU, AND THE FEDERATED STATES OF MICRO-
NESIA.   In the book's final case study, Stephen Levine examines government policies in the four largest, multiethnic, politically independent
entities in the Pacific: Fiji, Papua New Guinea, Vanuatu, and the Federated States of Micronesia. He notes that these four states face formidable
common problems: they are newly independent; they have limited political and economic infrastructures; and they face challenges—albeit challenges of different kinds—to national unity. Since these states are still very
much works in progress, their prospects are uncertain.

Fiji, which came out from under British colonial rule in 1970, has had
to contend with imperial legacies found elsewhere in Asia and the Pacific.
In Fiji as in Sri Lanka, Burma, Malaysia, Singapore, and elsewhere, British
rule led to an influx of Indian laborers, which in turn led to a changed
demographic picture and ethnic complications. Since Indians now constitute close to half of Fiji's total population, ethnic tensions have been
severe indeed in this case. In 1987, the Fijian military, which was and is
dominated by ethnic Fijians, staged a coup and seized control of the
government to prevent an Indian-led cabinet from coming to power. A
new constitution was subsequently drawn up and put into place in 1990.
It included provisions that would preserve and strengthen the position of
traditional leadership and therefore indigenous peoples; it was designed,
in short, to keep Indians from forming a government. Steps have also
been taken to prevent Indian and European encroachment on Fijian lands.
Since the Fijian and Indian populations are intermingled to a significant
degree, regional autonomy and federal solutions to the country's ethnic
problems are not an option. Violent confrontations cannot be ruled out
for the future.

Papua New Guinea, which became independent in 1975, is larger
and far more populous than any other Pacific Island state. Moreover, it
contains an astonishing amount of ethnic diversity—over one thousand
distinct ethnic groups. Not surprisingly, therefore, many of Papua New
Guinea's problems stem from efforts to forge a national identity. These
efforts have encountered considerable difficulties due to the existence of

arbitrary colonial boundaries and the country's lack of a common history. The Papua New Guinea constitution recognizes the multiethnic character of the state and grants equal rights and privileges to all of the country's ethnic groups. Nevertheless, Papua New Guinea has experienced ethnic violence. Specifically, the peoples of the island of Bougainville did not wish to be incorporated into Papua New Guinea. Misgivings over copper mining, control over land, and the fair distribution of resources led to an insurgency. Levine believes that the bloodiness of the conflict in Bougainville will probably discourage people from resorting to violence elsewhere in Papua New Guinea, but the future of the country is uncertain. The central government is weak, provincial governments have been controversial, and many economic and social issues are still on the policy agenda.

The islands of Vanuatu (formerly the New Hebrides) were jointly administered by France and Great Britain from 1906 until 1980. Significantly, the diverse communities in this multi-island state had never been grouped together politically until Europeans came along. When independence came in 1980, the peoples of Santo and several other islands sought to secede from the fledgling entity; this revolt was put down with the assistance of Papua New Guinea, which had reasons of its own for discouraging secessionism in the region. Vanuatu has not experienced any subsequent secessionist problems or significant ethnic violence, but like many new multiethnic entities it has struggled with the problem of forging a national identity. Its liberal language laws, multilingual educational system, and strong village governments ensure that cultural differences will persevere and that the tension between national unity and ethnic diversity will persist.

The political development of the Federated States of Micronesia (FSM), which became independent in 1986 and joined the United Nations only in 1990, is still very much in flux. The FSM is one of four entities that emerged from the U.S.-governed Trust Territory of the Pacific Islands in the 1970s and 1980s—the others being the Marianas, the Marshalls, and Palau, all of which are comparatively well-endowed in terms of natural resources. The FSM exists in its current form, therefore, only because three other island groups went their separate ways and because its four main remaining islands—Chuuk, Pohnpei, Yap, and Kosrae—were bracketed together by outside agencies. The peoples of these four main islands have distinct ethnic identities and are separated by vast tracts of water. Inevitably, therefore, the FSM faces tremendous challenges in its efforts to build a sense of national identity. It has sought to strike a balance between national and local aspirations by implementing federal arrangements; it is the only true federation in the Pacific. Each of the FSM's four states has considerable autonomy; the federal government is quite weak. Levine believes that this federation could fragment, as many colonial creations do, and that this would not necessarily be a tragic outcome as far as the peoples of these islands are concerned.

GENERALIZATIONS AND RECOMMENDATIONS

In the book's concluding chapter, Michael Brown draws on this empirical and analytical foundation, develops a series of generalizations about government policies and ethnic relations, and puts forward a set of policy recommendations.

Part I
South Asia

Chapter 1

Diversity, Democracy, and Devolution in India

Kanti Bajpai

India is one of the most complex countries in the world from an ethnic standpoint. The Indian government's track record in managing the country's many ethnic problems is, perhaps inevitably, mixed. The fact that India is still intact as a political entity fifty years after being formed as an independent state in 1947 is itself a major accomplishment. At the same time, India has experienced a great deal of ethnic tension and violence over the course of these fifty years.

This chapter analyzes the policies that the Indian government has used to manage ethnic relations and the conditions under which these policies have succeeded and failed. I argue that India has used a package of instruments to manage ethnic relations, where ethnicity is understood to mean social identity based on ascribed qualities such as race, religion, caste, tribe, language, and region. The Indian government's policy package has consisted of three main elements: first, a political order consisting of liberal constitutionalism, state-backed secular nationalism, and state-led social modernization and economic development; second, power-sharing in terms of group rights and the devolution of authority to ethnic-based lower levels of government; and third, coercion and force when the first two elements have failed to contain or solve ethnic problems. The government has been most successful when it has adopted carefully engineered "great policies" built around power-sharing and devolution. Force and coercion have worked in wearing down militant opponents and pushing them to accept new power-sharing arrangements, but they have also led to ethnic alienation. In places where the government has increased its reliance on coercion and force, it has become caught in unending cycles of violence and alienation.

The chapter is organized in four sections. First, it outlines the ethnic demography of India and the political context within which Indian policies are made. Second, it shows that the government has relied on a

Table 1.1. Ethnic Composition of India (By Religion).

Group	Number	Percentage
Hindu	672,600,000	82.41
Muslim	95,200,000	11.67
Christian	18,900,000	2.32
Sikh	16,300,000	1.99
Buddhist	6,300,000	0.77
Other	6,900,000	0.84
Total	**816,200,000**	**100.0**

SOURCE: 1991 Census of India.

political order consisting of constitutionalism, secular nationalism, and state-led modernization and development to preempt and contain ethnic grievances. Third, it analyzes Indian approaches to religious, caste, tribal, linguistic, and regional separatist problems and shows that a combination of group rights, devolution, coercion, and force has been used to manage ethnic relations. Group rights have been granted to various religious, caste, tribal, and linguistic groups. Devolution has been one of the keys to managing linguistic and regional dissatisfaction. Force and coercion have most often been used against regional rebels who have demanded greater autonomy, even secession. Fourth, it assesses government policies to date and suggests that carefully engineered "great policies" stand out as policy successes. This provides the basis for some recommendations with respect to government policy in this area.

India's Ethnic Demography

India has four major religious groups: Hindus, Muslims, Christians, and Sikhs. In 1991, its population was 82 percent Hindu, 12.12 percent Muslim, 2.34 percent Christian, and 1.94 percent Sikh. Together these four religions account for roughly 98 percent of the total population of India, with Hindus and Muslims constituting 94 percent of all Indians.[1] (See Table 1.1.) Muslims are dispersed all over India, but their greatest numbers are in the north. Christians are also spread widely, with large numbers in the Northeast and in Kerala. The Sikhs dominate Punjab.

The caste system in India, which is a product of Hinduism, is enormously complex, and is regionally and even locally variegated. In

1. *Census of India 1991*, Series 1, Paper 1 of 1995 (New Delhi: Registrar General and Census Commission, 1995), p. xi; and *Census of India 1981*, p. 176.

Table 1.2. Ethnic Composition of India (By Principal Language Spoken).

Language Group	Number	Percentage
Hindi	264,500,000	31.3
Bengali	51,300,000	6.1
Telugu	50,600,000	6.0
Marathi	49,500,000	5.9
Tamil	41,800,000	5.2
Urdu	34,900,000	4.1
Gujarati	33,100,000	3.9
Malayalam	25,700,000	3.0
Kannada	25,700,000	3.0
Oriya	23,000,000	2.7
Punjabi	19,600,000	2.3
Assamese	11,000,000	1.3
Sindhi	2,000,000	.23
Kashmiri	3,200,000	.37
Other	208,400,000	24.6
Total	**846,300,000**	**100.0**

SOURCE: *India 1995—A Reference Annual* (New Delhi: Ministry of Information and Broadcasting, 1995).

religious terms, it consists of four *varnas: brahmin, kshatriya, vaishya,* and *sudra.* In addition, there are the *antyaja* or "untouchables," who stand outside the *varna* system; untouchability has been legally abolished but remains a social problem. Politically and administratively, the operative caste divisions are upper and middle castes, "other backward classes," and scheduled castes and tribes. The scheduled castes and tribes are often referred to as Dalits.[2] The scheduled castes account for 16 percent of India's population, and the scheduled tribes account for another 8 percent.

Linguistically, India is far more diverse. Fifteen major languages are recognized in the constitution. The national language is Hindi in the Devanagari script. In 1981, Hindi speakers constituted 38.7 percent of the population; no other language claimed more than 8 percent.[3] (See Table 1.2.) The fourteen other languages are the official languages of various states. English remains an "associate" language that can be used for

2. See "What is 'Dalit' and 'Dalitism,'" *Dalit Voice,* Vol. 2, No. 16 (June 1–15, 1983), pp. 1, 2, 11.

3. *Census of India,* Series 1, Part IV B (i) (New Delhi: Registrar General and Census Commission, 1988), p. x.

official transactions between the central and state governments and between state governments.

Kashmir, Punjab, and the seven northeastern states are borderlands
that have repeatedly posed challenges to Indian sovereignty. In Kashmir,
the Muslims of the Kashmir Valley have formed the core of the rebellion
against New Delhi. These Muslims constitute 64 percent of the total
population of Kashmir, and, more importantly, an overwhelming 95 percent of the valley's population.[4]

The Sikhs of Punjab have gone from being the smallest community
in the state to being the largest. Prior to partition in 1947, Hindus constituted roughly 26 percent and Sikhs some 13 percent of Punjab's population. After partition, these numbers changed dramatically—Hindus
constituted 61 percent and Sikhs 35 percent. By the time Punjab was
reorganized in September 1966, Sikhs constituted 54 percent and Hindus
44 percent of the total population.[5] In 1991, the Sikh portion of Punjab's
population had grown to 63 percent, while the Hindu portion had shrunk
to 34 percent.[6]

The Northeast is a complex zone consisting of seven states. Between
1961 and 1972, Nagaland, Meghalaya, Mizoram, and Arunachal Pradesh
were carved out of Assam.[7] Most of these states have a dominant ethnic
community but also substantial minorities. Assam remains particularly
diverse, and is divided by language, religion, and tribe. Assamese speakers dominate. Assamese Hindus are the largest religious group, but Muslim numbers are substantial and by all accounts growing due to migration, particularly from Bangladesh.[8] Assam's population is also
differentiated among tribal and non-tribal groups. Arunachal Pradesh has
fifty language groups and fifty-three major tribes, and none is clearly
ascendant.[9] In Manipur, the Meiteis dominate. Meghalaya is peopled

---

4. See Ashutosh Varshney, "Three Compromised Nationalisms: Why Kashmir Has
Been a Problem," in Raju G.C. Thomas, ed., *Perspectives on Kashmir: The Roots of Conflict
in South Asia* (Boulder, Colo.: Westview Press, 1992), p. 207.

5. See Rajiv Kapur, *Sikh Separatism: The Politics of Faith* (London: Allen and Unwin,
1986), p. 203.

6. *Census of India 1991*, Series 1, Paper 1 of 1995, pp. xvi–xvii.

7. See Myron Weiner, *Sons of the Soil: Migration and Ethnic Conflict in India* (Princeton,
N.J.: Princeton University Press, 1978), pp. 86–87.

8. See Sanjoy Hazarika, *India's Northeast and the Crisis of Migration*. RGICS Paper
No. 32 (New Delhi: Rajiv Gandhi Institute for Contemporary Studies, Rajiv Gandhi
Foundation, 1996), pp. 15–17, especially.

9. See Sanjoy Hazarika, *Strangers of the Mist: Tales of War and Peace from India's
Northeast* (New Delhi: Viking, 1994), p. 129.

India.

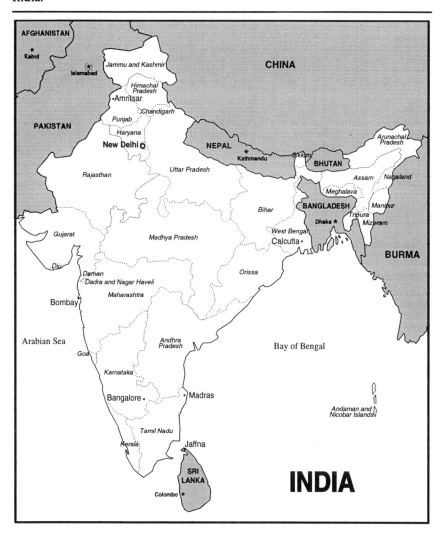

mainly by the Khasis, Garo, and Jaintia. In Mizoram, the Mizos form the largest community by far. Nagaland is dominated by the Naga tribe, but it also has Tangkhuls, Kukis, Anals, Maos, Hmars, and Haokips. Finally, Tripura has seen dramatic changes in its ethnic composition. In 1947, tribal peoples constituted 93 percent of Tripura's population; by 1981, they were only 28.5 percent due to the immigration of Bengali Hindus and Muslims.[10]

In sum, India is extremely diverse in ethnic terms, divided by religion, caste, tribe, language, and regional identity. This demographic profile does, however, point to one source of stability: the absence of a nation-wide cleavage along ethnic lines. Religious, caste, tribal, linguistic, and regional differences do not converge along a single fault line. As a result, ethnic crises tend to be localized and are therefore more easily contained by the government.

Political and Economic Context

India is a parliamentary democracy with a federal structure of government. Because India is a parliamentary democracy, government policy must be worked through a cabinet and parliament. It must also respect the basic law of the land or risk being overthrown in the courts. The press is another check on government actions. The English-language press is powerful and independent; it can either undermine or help legitimize government policy. Ultimately, government policy must pass the test of public opinion more widely, in elections. India has had eleven general elections and scores of state *panchayat* (local government) and municipal elections in its first fifty years. By and large, the electoral process has been free and fair. Although it would be difficult to prove, Indian democracy, with its checks and balances, seems to have contained the extent of ethnic restiveness in the country. An India that was not democratic would probably not have remained as united and stable as it has been since 1947.

India is also a federal union consisting of twenty-five states, six union territories, and Delhi, the national capital territory. Most of these units are demarcated ethnically. Federation itself therefore derives from an ethnic policy in the sense that ethnic groups—in this case, linguistic groups—have been given substantial power. Under the terms of the division of power, the Union List gives the federal government in New Delhi responsibility for defense, foreign affairs, currency, banking, and income taxation; the states are responsible for public order and police, welfare, health,

---

10. See ibid., pp. 123–124.

education, local government, industry, agriculture, and land revenue; and the federal and state governments are both involved in civil and criminal law and social and economic planning.[11] Here, too, it appears that the promise of federalism has limited ethnic restiveness in India, even though the practice of federalism has alienated some, particularly in Kashmir, Punjab, and various northeastern states.

The division of powers suggests that states have a considerable degree of autonomy. In practice, India has been rather centralized, often described as "quasi federal."[12] The union is responsible for national defense; it has formidable emergency powers; and it collects much revenue. Thus it runs the armed forces; it can dismiss state governments for a variety of reasons including external or internal emergencies; and it has control over key fiscal instruments as well as economic planning. The Indian government has not been shy about using this panoply of powers to manage ethnic relations. The use of these instruments has produced mixed results. While the union has successfully coerced state governments on occasion, it has also fueled resentment of the central government.

There are other centralizing elements in Indian political affairs. The all-India civil services are the "steel frame" of administration and are controlled by New Delhi. In addition, India has an army of over one million men which has been used against ethnic rebels. India also has a considerable paramilitary force. However, the most important centralizing institution in the country is the Congress Party. The Congress Party is a national party organized on regional lines. The regional or *pradesh* units, though, are subordinate to the central leadership. Particularly during Indira Gandhi's leadership of the party (1966–77, 1980–84), central control was steadily increased. The Congress Party stayed in power continuously from 1947 to 1977 and has ruled from New Delhi for forty-four of fifty years since independence.

In the nation's first years, the proclivity for a centralized structure was understandable, for at least three reasons. First, British India has been a highly centralized entity under colonial rule for two hundred years, and this legacy was difficult to overcome immediately. Second, Indian nationalists had cut their political teeth on and worked in a Delhi-centric system. Third, the partition and the ethnic complexity of the country had left an indelible mark on the political imagination of the Indian ruling elite. The

---

11. See Robert L. Hardgrave, Jr. and Stanley A. Kochanek, *India: Government and Politics in a Developing Nation*, 3d ed. (New York: Harcourt Brace Jovanovich, 1993), p. 129.

12. See ibid., p. 127.

fear that India would disintegrate was strong, and the nationalist reading of Indian history as a recurring pattern of integration and disintegration under successive empires had reinforced the view that strong central rule might periodically be necessary in order to avert chaos and collapse.

Political centralization was also necessary for the kind of economy Indian leaders wished to build. From 1947 to 1991, the government produced ambitious five-year plans and took charge of the commanding heights of the economy through a massive public sector to ensure high rates of sustained economic growth and a degree of social equity. It also regulated the workings of the private sector through a system of permits, quotas, and licenses in addition to the usual fiscal instruments.

Centralization has been under pressure since 1967. After the elections of 1967, the Congress Party continued to dominate at the center but increasingly lost control of the northern and southern state governments to various regional parties. The 1996 general elections indicated that Congress dominance at the center had also ended. Although it still won the largest share of votes nationwide (31 percent), it secured only 130 seats in Parliament. The "first past the post" electoral system gave the Bharatiya Janata Party (BJP), the rightist Hindu party, the most seats in Parliament even though it won only 25 percent of the vote. The United Front is the third most important political formation in India, but it was nonetheless asked, after some twists and turns, to form a government after the 1996 elections. The United Front government depends on the support of the so-called Federal Front, a group of regional parties. The Front's "Common Minimum Program" favors the devolution of power from the center to the states.

Economic centralization is also under pressure. First, India experienced a massive drop in foreign currency reserves in the late 1980s. Second, the central government fiscal deficit rose to 8.4 percent of the gross domestic product by 1991. Third, inflation for 1990–91 was 12.1 percent, up 3 percent from 1989–90. Fourth, annual growth in 1991–92 was a minuscule 1.2 percent, down from 5.2 percent in 1990–91 and 5.6 percent in 1989–90.[13] The economic reform program that was subsequently instituted included dismantling government planning agencies, cutting government spending, capping the public sector, reforming taxation, easing licensing procedures, loosening import and export controls, and encouraging foreign investment.

India's ethnic policies have been made and will continue to be made

---

13. Government of India, *Economic Reforms: Two Years After and the Task Ahead*, Discussion Paper (New Delhi: Ministry of Finance, n.d.), pp. 2–7.

in a political and economic context that features contrary pressures and proclivities. Indian leaders must find the golden mean between centralization and decentralization. Too much centralization can produce the ethnic restiveness it is intended to contain; too much decentralization might encourage the secessionist impulses it is intended to preempt. On balance, there is a growing feeling within the country that the pendulum has swung too far in the direction of centralization.

Political Order in a Plural Society

India's ethnic demography suggests that the ethnic management problem facing the government is not as severe as Sri Lanka's, where a single fault line divides the entire country. However, the drift towards centralization in the decades after independence has made the country increasingly prone to ethnic unrest. In response, Indian leaders have developed three elements of a political order that they hope will check the rise and radicalization of ethnic identities and demands: liberal constitutionalism, state-backed secular nationalism, and state-led social modernization and economic development. In effect, the Indian government has counted on the promise of liberal constitutional practices, a state-propagated "inclusive" nationalism, and at least some minimal level of social modernization and economic development to soften and even preempt ethnic disaffection.

The promise of Indian constitutionalism is four-fold. First, constitutionalism promises to protect fundamental rights, if necessary, through the courts. Second, it seeks to ensure that governmental and private activity in all spheres will be rule- and law-governed, not arbitrary. Third, if governmental and private actions infringe on fundamental rights, Indian constitutionalism provides ways for aggrieved parties to seek compensation. Fourth, constitutionalism attempts to protect the instruments of political participation and public accountability: elections, political parties, and legislatures. In sum, constitutionalism holds out the promise that members of any ethnic group can enjoy fundamental liberties, count on proceduralism in government, seek compensation, and organize themselves in parties to fight elections and influence the making of laws and policies. There is nothing automatic about the effectiveness of this constitutional edifice, but it is a resource for those with grievances who want justice and influence.

The second feature of the political order is a conception of nationalism that is secular and inclusivist. In this conception, being Indian does not mean belonging to any particular religious, caste, tribal, or linguistic group or inhabiting a particular region to the exclusion of others; rather, being Indian means having been born within the boundaries of India or having become a naturalized citizen and being loyal to its constitution, laws, and institutions. Thus, the official media, state-run educational institutions, and other publicity and propaganda instruments all stress pride in one's ethnic community, tolerance, even celebration of social diversity, and a commitment to a larger, national community with a common civic life. The message is simple: irrespective of one's ethnic community, one should recognize oneself as a member of the Indian nation.

The third feature of the political order that the government has brought to bear on ethnic relations is the promise of state-led modernization and development. India's legitimacy rests in part on its ability to promote social modernization and economic development. Improving access to education, electronic media, health facilities, housing, and jobs is the heart of the modernization and development effort that the government is committed to pursuing. In managing ethnic relations, the government can speed up or slow down its outreach efforts. That the government cannot be extravagant is widely understood, but at the margins some amelioration of backwardness and poverty is vital. The government reckons that in the end it is the only agency that can deliver relief to many people over a long period of time. It counts on this ability to preempt and defuse ethnic disaffection and rebellions.

In principle, these three elements should have succeeded in preempting, softening, even eliminating ethnic grievances in India. Constitutionalism, inclusive nationalism, and modernization and development promise political rationality, compensation and accountability, cultural recognition, and social justice. These would seem to be the bases of ethnic satisfaction. However, these three elements of the political order have been in decline since the 1960s. Constitutional provisions have been manipulated and extra-parliamentary regulation of the political system has increased; secular or inclusivist nationalism has developed a bad reputation as agencies of the state have behaved in a most unsecular and sectarian fashion; and entrenched social and economic interests have not allowed the benefits of modernization and development to reach most Indians. In short, while these three promises were substantially honored in the early years after independence, they have increasingly been honored in the breach since the 1960s. As a result, ethnic groups have become increasingly doubtful about their capacities to influence the central government short of violence, to be accorded respect, and to achieve a better way of life.

Religion

Managing religious relations in India is a complex endeavor. The government is involved at two levels. First, it has to manage its own relations with individual religious communities. At this first level, it is possible to distinguish between three problem areas: freedom of religion; state intervention in religious matters for the purposes of social reform; and demands made on the state by religious communities to protect their way of life and institutions. Second, the government has to manage relations between religious communities. At this level, three problem areas stand out as well: religious processions, communal violence or riots, and disputed religious sites. The government's approach at the first level has been to protect group rights, though this commitment is not absolute. At the second level, the government has been preoccupied with maintaining law and order.

RELIGIOUS FREEDOM

The government's approach to religious freedom has been a constitutional one, stressing the individual's right to freedom of conscience but most importantly the right of religious groups to preserve control of their religious institutions. Various provisions were written into the constitution; these have, by and large, been respected by the state. The constitution promises equality before the law and equal protection of all citizens. It prohibits discrimination on grounds of religion, race, caste, sex, or place of birth. It also guarantees equality of opportunity in government employment. Article 25 (1) states "Subject to public order, morality and health . . . all persons are equally entitled to freedom of conscience and the right to freely profess, practice, and propagate religion." The Indian courts have clarified that, while there can be restrictions on religious freedom under the terms of Article 25 (1), "the state can have no power over the conscience of the individual—this right is absolute."[14] In addition, according to the constitution, no one can be forced to pay taxes for religious purposes. Finally, any educational institution that receives government funds or is otherwise helped by the government cannot insist on religious instruction or attendance at worship.[15]

The constitution gives freedom of religion not only to individuals but also to religious groups. It permits incumbents of an office connected with

---

14. See Donald E. Smith, *India as a Secular State* (Princeton, N.J.: Princeton University Press, 1963), pp. 103–104.

15. *Constitution of India.*

a religious or denominational institution or governing body to be re-stricted to members of that community.[16] It also states that, subject once again to public order, morality, and health, "every religious denomination or any section thereof" has the right to establish and maintain institutions for religious and charitable purposes, manage its affairs, own and acquire immovable property, and administer such property in accordance with the law.[17]

The government has, in the main, respected the religious rights of both individuals and groups. People profess and practice their faiths with ease and do not fear government interference. The Indian government, unlike the Pakistani government, has not issued any official decrees against particular religions or sects. The Pakistani government, on the advice of Muslim religious leaders, has prohibited the Ahmediya sect from claiming to be Islamic. The religious tax imposed by the Pakistani government on Shi'ite and Sunni alike during President Zia-ul Haq's time—a decision that was later reversed—would be unthinkable in India. India has also rejected the Pakistani system of separate electorates for religious minorities.

Where the Indian government has had more serious difficulties, as we shall see, is in controlling intercommunal violence. In addition, there are areas where government actions have been questionable but not malign. It is widely believed that in the aftermath of Indira Gandhi's assassination by her Sikh bodyguards, Sikhs have been excluded from the National Security Guard, the anti-terrorist protection force. The Indian Army is said to have frozen, if not reduced, Sikh recruitment. It is also widely held that, in terms of public employment, Muslims in particular have been under-represented. Why Muslim representation is low is un-clear, but there is no evidence of systematic official discrimination. Chris-tians, from time to time, have worried about their right to proselytize. The Indian government has shown concern over religious conversion, but its focus has been on the role of foreign missionaries in the border areas of the Northeast. Even these groups have been allowed to continue their activities, by and large, and Indian Christians have been free to propagate their faith.

RELIGIOUS REFORM

The government's commitment to group rights is not absolute. In the larger social interest, the government can and has intervened in religious

---

16. *Constitution of India.*

17. *Constitution of India.*

affairs for the purpose of promoting religious reform. Hinduism has been the main target of government reform efforts. The government's record is mixed. Thus it made untouchability, essentially a problem within Hinduism, illegal. It threw open the doors of Hindu temples to all Hindus, including untouchables. It also passed legislation to stop the practice of dowry. None of these reforms, however, has been enforced stringently. On the other hand, it successfully changed and enforced Hindu personal law. While this latter intervention may seem to go against the government's commitment to group rights, it is instructive that the government worked through Hindu texts to legitimize its reforms and was therefore sensitive to group custom.

Congress Party policy in the 1930s was to retain separate personal laws as a concession primarily to Muslim opinion. With partition, the mood changed. The Muslim insistence on having separate civil codes was rejected, and the constitution directed the state to enact a uniform civil code. The government subsequently stalled. Aware that it could not enact a uniform civil code without the consent of the country's minorities, it focused instead on reform of Hindu personal law. Since Hindus constituted four-fifths of the population—the term "Hindus" here extends to Sikhs, Buddhists, and Jains—a Hindu personal law, the government argued, would at least cover the vast majority of Indians.[18]

The old personal law went back to colonial times. In general, the British were reluctant to tamper with existing practices and precepts, but under Warren Hastings they began to codify Hindu and Muslim laws and enact changes. The Act of 1781, the Special Marriage Act, and the Hindu Code Bill of 1872 were major colonial reforms. Changes in the old Hindu Code Bill were debated in 1941 and 1948 but failed to materialize. Only after independence did the Congress Party gear up to pass major legislation. Strengthened by the first general elections, Prime Minister Jawaharlal Nehru campaigned extensively for the reforms, the main parts of which were passed in separate bills in 1955 and 1956. There was substantial opposition to the bills, but it was deflected in part by reference to Hindu texts. Thus, on the Hindu Adoptions and Maintenance Bill, the government argued that Hindu texts were supportive of the proposed changes. The Nehru government had earlier used a similar approach to justify its policy with respect to the Hindu Marriage Bill.[19]

The Hindu personal law legislation of the 1950s has remained the basic code governing marriage, divorce, adoption, and succession for

---

18. See Smith, *India as a Secular State*, p. 290.

19. Ibid., p. 283.

Indian Hindus. The government's successful intervention in this area must be seen against the very long history of support for change. First of all, Hindu reformers from the eighteenth century onwards had championed the cause of change, arguing that Indians did not deserve to be free and indeed could not achieve freedom until they refurbished their own social institutions. In the twentieth century, Mahatma Gandhi and Nehru played a vital role in educating Hindu opinion on the necessity for reforms. Thus there was a long, conscious attempt to prepare community opinion for change. Second, Indian leaders guarded against the accusation that the reform was anti-Hindu. As noted, legislation was passed with appropriate references to Hindu texts, thereby indicating that the reforms had strong religious foundations.

RELIGIOUS CUSTOMS AND INSTITUTIONS

As part of its commitment to group rights, the Indian government has responded to demands that it protect religious customs and institutions. Its response has been subtle. At times, it has sloughed off direct responsibility and allowed the courts to determine what should and should not be protected. However, on key issues and at key moments, particularly with respect to Muslim personal law, it has stood behind community preferences.

Government policy in this area has hinged on whether the custom or institution in question constitutes an "essential feature" of the religion in question. The government has in general avoided the difficult if not impossible task of defining what constitutes an essential feature. However, on several occasions these judgments have been forced on the government, and it has passed on the responsibility to the courts. The courts have generally made sensible decisions, relying on a test of essentiality based on the existence of alternative but equivalent customs or institutions in the various religious traditions.

Thus, after independence, orthodox Hindus demanded that the slaughter of cows be banned. Muslims argued that on the occasion of a festival such as Bakr-i Id, it was vital to sacrifice a cow. The courts took the view that since it was permissible within Muslim custom to sacrifice a goat or camel, there were alternatives to the slaughter of cows and therefore that this practice was not an essential feature of Islam. However, the wearing of *kirpans* (daggers) by Sikhs was seen as an essential part of Sikhism because it is non-substitutable. Some Hindus argued that because sons are vital for key rituals and spiritual salvation, a man without male progeny should be entitled to have more than one wife in order to beget a son. In 1952, the Bombay High Court conceded that having a son was vital but argued that since adoption was permissible in Hinduism there was an alternative way of fulfilling this requirement.[20]

There have been other demands for religious protection, and the government has responded in defense of group rights through various legal devices. Sections of the Muslim population have insisted that the Urdu language be protected. Indeed, the constitution allows any group with a distinct language to preserve it. Muslims and Christians want to ensure that religious educational institutions and charitable trusts are allowed to function: under the constitution, they are free to establish and maintain institutions for educational and charitable purposes, and to acquire and administer property. The constitution provides that all religious and linguistic minorities have the right to "establish and administer educational institutions of their choice."[21] Christians in particular want to protect their right to proselytize; Article 25 (1) of the constitution, as noted above, allows propagation of religion.

In general, these constitutional provisions have been honored by the government. There is concern over the status of Urdu, but religious educational institutions and charitable trusts have operated freely. Christian proselytizing efforts in general have been permitted, although there has been pressure on the government to ban conversions. The government has been watchful of foreign missionaries, particularly those operating in strategically sensitive areas such as the Northeast, but the activities of Indian Christians have been largely unchecked. In addition, conversion to Islam has not been interfered with. The mass conversion of some Dalits led to protests from militant Hindus, but the government has done little to stop the practice.

The most controversial demand for protection of group rights concerns Muslim personal law. The constitution enjoins the government to enact a uniform civil code, yet since the days of Nehru it has been understood that this would not be possible without a serious national debate. Liberals of all religions, leftists, women's groups, and sections of Hindu opinion have all urged the government to enact a uniform code. However, successive Indian governments have resisted this demand—out of concern for law and order, which might be seriously jeopardized by Muslim protests, and of course out of an unwillingness to alienate Muslim voters.

The Shah Bano case illustrates how these concerns have worked, if tortuously, to protect Muslim law. In 1985, the Indian Supreme Court

---

20. See Duncan M. Derrett, *Religion, Law and the State in India* (London: Faber and Faber, 1968), pp. 446–448.

21. *Constitution of India.*

ruled that Ahmed Khan, the former husband of Shah Bano, had to provide maintenance for his former wife, who lacked other means of support. Ahmed Khan had argued that as a Muslim he had to obey Muslim law, which required him to pay support only for the so-called *iddat* period.[22] The national government initially supported the Supreme Court's decision, but Muslim protest soon gathered momentum and was turned against the Congress Party in state elections.

Reacting to the loss of a key constituency, the Congress Party government changed direction. It argued that the relevant section of the Criminal Code did not apply to Muslims. Thus in May 1986, the government passed new legislation that invalidated the court's ruling. The ensuing Muslim Women (Protection of Rights on Divorce) Bill was essentially "in accordance with the *ulema's* interpretation of the *Shariat.*"[23] There was angry reaction from liberal supporters of a uniform civil code as well as from Hindu opinion. It was widely reported that the government's opening of the Babri Masjid in February 1986 was intended to appease Hindus outraged over the government's shift of policy in the Shah Bano case.[24]

Salman Rushdie's *The Satanic Verses* was the cause of another crisis in the 1980s. The Indian government took the view that the book was hurtful to the feelings of Muslims and that its publication might lead to violent protests by the Muslim community. Once again, the Congress Party's concern about the loss of Muslim support was a factor in its thinking. The government, headed by Rajiv Gandhi, acted quickly to ban the book's entry into India, citing both the feelings of Muslims and the possibility of widespread disorder. The government's decision was criticized by the Hindu right, civil liberty groups, and leftists, but the government held firm. India was the first country to ban *The Satanic Verses*. The Rajiv Gandhi government has passed from the political scene, but the ban on *The Satanic Verses* remains in force.[25]

In both cases, group rights have been at odds with liberal tenets—a uniform civil code and freedom to publish. In both cases, the government's motives have been complex: on the one hand, it has worried about law and order, the loss of Muslim political support, and overturning a commitment (Nehru's commitment to institute a uniform civil code); on

---

22. See Kavita Khory, "The Shah Bano Case: Some Political Implications," in Robert D. Baird, ed., *Religion and Law in Independent India* (New Delhi: Manohar, 1993), p. 123.

23. Ibid., pp. 130–131.

24. Ibid., pp. 132–133.

25. Ramesh Thakur, "Ayodhya and the Politics of India's Secularism," *Asian Survey*, Vol. 33, No. 7 (July 1993), pp. 650–653.

the other, it has been concerned about the danger of widespread non-Muslim disaffection and the failure to enforce constitutional directives. In both cases, the government ultimately favored group rights over liberal policies.

MANAGING RELATIONS BETWEEN RELIGIOUS COMMUNITIES

Over time, the Indian government has become increasingly involved in efforts to manage tensions and violence between religious communities. Three major kinds of problems have confronted the government: religious processions, communal violence, and disputed religious sites. In general, the government has not tried to broker a fundamental resolution of intercommunal quarrels; rather, it has tried to stall, defuse confrontations, and maintain law and order.

RELIGIOUS PROCESSIONS.   Religious processions, celebrating various festivals, often lead to confrontations between religious communities. While there is a good deal of public tolerance of these processions, overly boisterous processions taken through localities that have large concentrations of people from other faiths do cause tensions, even violence. This is especially so between Hindus and Muslims. In response, the government has developed a standard operating procedure.

First, community groups are required to notify the authorities about large processions. Once notified, the processions are escorted by local police. If relations between religious communities in the area are already tense, the authorities may re-route the procession or refuse permission for it to be held. If violence nonetheless breaks out, the police resort to varying levels of force. Large-scale violence that cannot be controlled by the police prompts the use of paramilitaries. If the national government feels that the state government in question is not acting impartially or efficiently, it deploys its own paramilitary forces. It can even call out the army. The army has been used more and more to control communal violence arising out of these kinds of situations.

Procession control and the control of post-procession violence has generally been effective, though not without its lapses. As we will see in the following section, some of those lapses pose serious long-term problems for India.

COMMUNAL VIOLENCE.   Almost all communal riots are urban, and many begin and are sustained in areas where a large Muslim population is living among Hindus. Riots often take place in the old parts of cities, where roads and lanes are narrow and crowded. Over the past fifty years, the government has developed a routine for controlling riots and dealing with the problems of post-riot administration.

The first line of policy against communal violence is to use force to bring it under control. Law and order is a state responsibility, and the local police are the first instrument of control. As noted above, if they fail to achieve control, then the state government can turn to its own police or paramilitaries, or ask for central government assistance in the form of paramilitaries or the army.

After the violence is quelled, the government undertakes an inquiry into the incident. If the incident is serious, an inquiry commission is constituted. Almost immediately, the state or central government announces that payments will be made to the victims of violence or their families. In the case of loss of property, the government may make other forms of restitution. The police endeavor to arrest those who instigated as well as participated in the violence. To preempt further violence, the police may pick up potential troublemakers and subject them to "preventive detention" for several days. If religious organizations are suspected to have played a role in inspiring the violence, the leaders of these organizations may be arrested and charged, and their offices searched and then closed, at least temporarily.

The government has been least effective in this last regard: punishing those guilty of instigating and carrying out violence. Few rioters have been successfully charged and prosecuted. There are many reasons for this. Definitive identification is often not possible in the confusion of a riot. Witnesses fear reprisals. The police and paramilitaries in particular are often communal and sympathetic to Hindus, and the authorities find their investigations and prosecutions stalled by lower-level functionaries. The courts are almost always burdened with an enormous backlog of cases and are not enthusiastic about taking on the added burden of this forensically difficult and politically sensitive problem. Finally, politicians, moved by the prospect of political gain, interfere in the investigations. Indeed, prominent local politicians are often involved in these incidents, and they can and do use their clout to escape prosecution. The most glaring instance of the government's failure to bring guilty politicians to book has been its inability and unwillingness to punish the instigators of the 1984 anti-Sikh riots in Delhi, a lacuna that has played no small part in fueling and sustaining Sikh resentment against the central government.

In sum, the government has a mixed record in dealing with communal violence: it has developed a policing system that can control violent outbreaks; however, in failing to punish the guilty, this system often promotes resentment and sows the seeds for further rounds of communal hostilities.

DISPUTED RELIGIOUS SITES. Religious relations in India have been spoiled by several quarrels over religious sites. While the number of contested sites is not large, differences over them could explode, as they did over the Babri Masjid/Ram Janmabhoomi in Ayodhya. The Babri Masjid is a mosque that was built during the rule of the Moghul emperor Babur. It is also believed by many Hindus to be the birthplace of the god, Ram. Hindu groups want to build a commemorative temple at the site and open it for worship.

As the dispute over Ayodhya escalated, the government dithered, hoping the issue would go away. New Delhi initially ignored the controversy, choosing to postpone a thoroughgoing reckoning. Later, when public pressures increased, it attempted to manipulate opinion by what was essentially a set of tactical ploys or concessions. When this failed to divert public opinion and a confrontation threatened to develop, it used force to preserve law and order. After a massive show of force, it finally turned its attention to constructing a long-term solution to the problem. The government's policy has had mixed results. The mosque was torn down by a Hindu mob in December 1992, but subsequent government actions have succeeded in containing communal tensions. However, the government has not addressed the roots of the dispute, and has once again put this issue on the back burner.

The government's initial response to the Babri Masjid dispute was to stall. Under colonial rule, the mosque complex had been sealed off from public use. In December 1949, however, a group of Hindus smuggled some idols into the mosque and began to offer prayers at the site. Nehru ordered their eviction, but local administrative and police authorities resisted, claiming that a serious law and order problem would follow. A compromise solution was reached: once again, the site was closed to the public; a Hindu priest would be allowed to offer prayers and to care for the idols pending a final resolution of the quarrel. The government did little beyond this, hoping that with time a resolution would be found but doing nothing to fashion such a resolution.[26]

This strategy worked for over forty years, but starting in 1984–85, the government faced growing Hindu pressure. Its response was to make concessions to Hindu sensibilities. Thus, in February 1986, the lock was taken off the Masjid. At the same time, the government introduced legislation on the Shah Bano case that pacified Muslim opinion. Later, the government agreed that a foundation-laying ceremony would be performed at the Masjid complex by the Vishwa Hindu Parishad (a Hindu

26. See S.K. Tripathi, "One Hundred Years of Litigation," in Asghar Ali Engineer, ed., *Babri-Masjid Ramjanambhoomi Controversy* (Delhi: Ajanta, 1990), pp. 20–21.

organization), even as it assured Muslims that it would not allow the site to be disturbed.[27]

These ploys ultimately failed. In September 1990, the situation deteriorated and the government responded by using force. The Bharatiya Janata Party had launched a nationwide campaign with its leader, L.K. Advani, riding a van at the head of a 10,000-kilometer *ratha yatra* (chariot journey) to Ayodhya. The procession was finally stopped at the Uttar Pradesh border by the state government. Then, in October 1990, 100,000 Hindus gathered at Ayodhya and tried to march on the contested site. They were confronted by police, and approximately thirty people were killed. Hundreds more died in rioting along the *yatra* route.

The government then tried to engage the Bharatiya Janata Party, hoping to persuade it to exercise restraint.[28] It also brokered talks between Hindu and Muslim groups, hoping that the disputants would find a compromise solution. Finally, to close off Hindu demands with respect to other sites, it passed the Places of Worship Special Provision Bill of 1991. This bill maintains the status quo at all places of worship—except the Babri Masjid.[29]

The government's new policy also failed, and in December 1990, Hindu militants broke through the cordon of 10,000 police and paramilitary personnel and destroyed the Babri Masjid. The government responded, belatedly, with massive force. It temporarily banned five Hindu and Muslim communal organizations, dismissed the BJP government in Uttar Pradesh and three other states, and ordered large-scale arrests of BJP senior and middle-ranking officials. Following this use of force, the government finally initiated moves towards a long-term settlement of the problem. Its key decision was to promise that both a temple and a mosque would be built at Ayodhya. The government decided to acquire the mosque complex and surrounding lands, and to transfer this holding to two trusts—one to build a temple, the other a mosque. It also lifted the ban against worship at the site.[30]

The Babri Masjid dispute has been the most serious challenge to the Indian government's ability to manage religious relations to date. Its delaying tactics, while successful for forty years, eventually proved disastrous when it became clear that the government had no real policy for

---

27. See Asghar Ali Engineer, "Introduction," in Engineer, *Babri-Masjid,* pp. 10–11.

28. Manju Parikh, "The Debacle at Ayodhya: Why Militant Hinduism Met with a Weak Response," *Asian Survey,* Vol. 33, No. 7 (July 1993), pp. 677–678.

29. Ibid., p. 678.

30. Ibid., p. 681.

dealing with such disputed sites. The Places of Worship legislation notwithstanding, the Indian government still does not appear to have a policy in this regard. Indeed, it seems to be relying more and more on the holding actions that have been so problematic in the past.

Caste and Tribe

The Indian government has recognized that it faces considerable social problems with respect to two groups. Those known as scheduled castes and tribes still live under a stigma; those known as the other backward classes are extremely poor. The tensions between upper castes and scheduled castes and tribes, the material deprivation of the other backward classes, and the increasing political mobilization of all three groups, which between them constitute 70 percent of the population, could cause political upheavals in India.

At independence, the government had three options with respect to these problems: to change social attitudes; to generate economic development that would trickle down to the lower castes and the tribes; and to institute an affirmative action policy. It decided to emphasize a group rights policy consisting of affirmative action quotas, known in India as "reservations." The government's view was that since social attitudes would change slowly and since the benefits from economic development initiatives would be uncertain, reservations would be needed. Reservations were attractive: they could be implemented at once, would target the lower castes and tribes specifically, and would also affect social attitudes and material deprivation simultaneously.

SCHEDULED CASTES AND TRIBES

The reservations policy for scheduled castes and tribes establishes quotas in three arenas: educational institutions and universities, public employment, and political representation. Since scheduled castes and tribes make up about one fifth of India's population, they are allocated up to 22 percent of all places in educational institutions and universities and 22 percent of the posts in public employment. To ensure that these slots in education and public employment are filled, eligibility qualifications can be relaxed. Reservations in the central and state legislatures are also pegged to population levels. As a result, 119 of the 543 seats in Parliament are reserved for scheduled castes and tribes. Voters in reserved constituencies must choose from a slate consisting solely of candidates from their own groups.

While the government has remained committed to reservations and has extended the policy at ten-year intervals with no significant opposition, the achievements of the program are questionable. In higher education and public employment, quotas have seldom been filled. In public employment in 1989, for example, scheduled caste representation in high-level group A and group B positions stood at 6.51 percent and 11.65 percent, respectively. For the scheduled tribes, representation levels were 2.24 percent in group A and 2 percent in group B. Only 4.69 percent of all central government employees are from scheduled castes and tribes even though these groups now constitute nearly 25 percent of the overall population.[31]

Similarly, the effect of the reservations policy on social attitudes has not been impressive. Violence against and social stigmatization of the scheduled castes and tribes remain rampant. It is estimated that 10,000 to 15,000 acts of violence are committed every year against members of the scheduled castes. Many more incidents undoubtedly go unreported to the authorities.[32] The social stigma of caste and tribe is absent in day-to-day intercourse in urban centers, but in rural India to be from a scheduled caste or scheduled tribe is still a social burden.

Other problems have also beset government policy in this area. First, those who have benefited from reservations have tended to be a small elite within the scheduled caste and tribe communities. The spillover benefits have therefore been few. Second, this elite is self-perpetuating in that the children of those who receive benefits go on to claim benefits themselves under the reservations programs. Third, those who have won reserved seats in legislative bodies have often been manipulated by upper caste groups and politicians and have not represented the interests of their own castes and tribes as effectively as was hoped.

The government has not made a serious effort to deal with these difficulties. The first and second problems, in particular, would seem to be susceptible to administrative solutions. The most serious lacuna in government policy, though, is its unwillingness to go beyond reservations and bring about true social integration. The Indian government has been conservative in trying to shape social attitudes and practices, particularly with respect to the scheduled castes. It has abolished untouchability in a legal sense and insisted that Hindu temples be opened to all, but it has been fairly indifferent about enforcing these laws, which are largely disregarded by the populace, by temple authorities, and by local government functionaries.

---

31. S.R. Maheshwari, *Mandal Commission Revisited* (New Delhi: Jawahar Publishers, 1995), p. 5.

32. Hardgrave and Kochanek, *India: Government and Politics*, p. 191.

OTHER BACKWARD CLASSES

The Indian government has also had to deal with the economic backwardness of the other backward classes, a series of castes above the scheduled castes but below the upper castes. These groups constitute some 50–70 percent of the total population. Although it has moved more slowly with these groups, the government has pursued essentially the same policy—instituting reservations.

The government's long resistance to the idea of instituting reservations for the other backward classes was based on the assumption that any scheme modeled on the approach used for scheduled castes and tribes would be impractical. If reservations were to be based on the proportion of backward classes in the overall population, then quota levels as high as 70 percent would have to be instituted. Successive governments were therefore skeptical about instituting reservations for backward classes and postponed action for decades. In 1955, the first Backward Classes Commission recommended that 70 percent of all places in technical and professional institutes be reserved for backward classes and that reservations should be instituted in the civil services. The government rejected these recommendations, arguing that the truly needy would receive insufficient attention in such a wide-ranging program.[33] In 1980, the second Backward Classes Commission (the Mandal Commission) maintained that 52 percent of the population belonged to other backward classes. Since the Supreme Court had placed a ceiling of 50 percent on all reservations and given that 22.5 percent of educational placements and government jobs had already been set aside for scheduled castes and tribes, the Commission pegged reservations for the other backward classes at 27 percent. The government shelved the report.

In the late 1980s, the emergence of the backward classes as an increasingly cohesive electoral bloc changed the government's political calculations. In August 1990, beset by rivalries within his ruling coalition and under pressure from the Bharatiya Janata Party's mobilization of Hindus over the Babri dispute, Prime Minister V.P. Singh announced that his government would implement the recommendations of the Mandal Commission. Singh's strategy was to use caste differences to split the Hindu vote and thereby weaken the Bharatiya Janata Party.

There were strong, even violent, protests against this move, particularly in the northern states, but the government stood firm. Opposition parties, initially hostile, soon went along with the government, especially after the Supreme Court upheld the idea of reservations while reaffirming

---

33. Maheshwari, *Mandal Commission Revisited*, p. 108.

the 50 percent overall limit. Some modifications were made to the Commission's original proposal. For instance, sectors such as defense, science, technology, and space were exempted from reservations.[34] This was mere tinkering: no national party could afford to alienate 50 percent of the population.

The Mandal victory must be set in context. If half of India's population belongs to one of the other backward classes, then the number of government jobs actually reserved for these groups—at the national or state level—is a drop in the ocean. For example, of the 220,000 vacancies that materialize in the central government every year, some 60,000 will be reserved for other backward classes. This explains why, in the end, opposition to the Mandal provisions was short-lived: the new reservations did not constitute a great advance for the other backward classes or an appreciable loss for the higher castes.

Language

Language differences threatened the unity and peace of India between 1947 and 1967. First, there was an intense debate over the choice of an official language for India. Hindi, a northern language, had the largest number of speakers, but southern and eastern Indians in particular resented its enshrinement as the country's official language. The government's solution to this problem was a "three-language formula," which made Hindi the official language but allowed English and the various vernacular languages to be used within the states in government and in education.

A second problem involved the reorganization of the states. During the struggle for independence, the Congress Party had seemingly committed itself to reorganization on the basis of language. After independence, however, the government initially rejected the idea because it feared separatism and because no state was linguistically homogeneous. In the end it agreed to organize states along linguistic lines. The Indian government's handling of these two issues reflected its tendency to manage ethnic relations through group rights policies.

OFFICIAL LANGUAGE POLICY, 1947–67

One of the first ethnic issues facing the post-colonial government of India was the challenge of identifying an official language. It took the

---

34. Ibid.; and C. Rupa, *Reservation Policy: Mandal Commission and After* (New Delhi: Sterling, 1991), p. 124.

government twenty years to resolve this issue completely, but the fundamental thrust of its policy was defined between 1949 and 1956.

Government policy on language can be divided into three phases: the
1940s, 1950s, and 1960s. In the late 1940s, the basic language compact was
forged and written into the constitution. In the 1950s, a review of language policy mandated by the constitution was carried out, and some
modifications regarding implementation were made. This was followed
in the 1960s by large-scale protests, especially in the southern state of
Madras (Tamil Nadu), which led to further changes and assurances being
issued by the national government. By 1967, the official language issue
had more or less been resolved: Hindi was to be promoted as the official
language of the country as a whole, but in stages; the states were free to
choose their own official languages; and English was to be phased out.
The government, however, made an important concession to non-Hindi
speaking states: Hindi would remain the official language of the country,
but English would continue to serve as a link language between the
central and state governments and between various state governments
for as long as non-Hindi-speaking states wished.

OFFICIAL LANGUAGE POLICY: THE ORIGINAL COMPACT.   At the time of independence, the community of Hindi-Hindustani-Urdu speakers was the
single largest language group in India. Hindustani was perhaps the most
commonly spoken language in the country; it could be understood and
written by both Hindi and Urdu speakers. The Constituent Assembly
decided to use Hindustani and English as the languages of parliamentary
debate. However, proponents of Hindi began to push to have it designated as the national language; they could not tolerate Hindustani and
Urdu, with their Arabic and Persian influences. The opposition to Hindi
came from Hindustani and Urdu speakers in the north and from non-
Hindi speakers in the southern and eastern states.[35]

In 1949, after considerable debate, the Hindi bloc carried the day by
a single vote. The narrowness of the margin of victory, however, led to a
compromise. First, while Hindi would be used for the official purposes
of the country—as the language of communication between the states and
the central government, as well as between states—within states, official
business could be conducted in any one of the languages used in the state
or in Hindi.[36] Second, as a concession to non-Hindi states, Hindi would

---

35. Jyotirindra Das Gupta, *Language Conflict and National Development: Group Politics
and National Language Policy in India* (Bombay: Oxford University Press, 1970), pp. 132–
133.

36. Ibid., pp. 159–160. See also *Constitution of India*, pp. 96–97.

be introduced as the official language in two stages: in stage one, Hindi would be used in addition to English; in stage two, the use of English would be restricted and Hindi would be promoted over a fifteen-year transition period.[37] Third, the implementation of stage two would be contingent on the findings of an Official Language Commission and a Joint Committee of Parliament. Although Hindi was to be promoted in stage two of this process, the Commission was to give "due regard to the industrial, cultural and scientific advancement of India, and the just claims and the interests of persons belonging to the non-Hindi speaking areas in regard to the public services."

OFFICIAL LANGUAGE POLICY: MODIFYING THE COMPACT. In the 1950s, the mandated review of language policy was carried out and the original compact was modified. This modification further strengthened the group rights orientation of the government's language policy.

As mandated, the Official Language Commission delivered its first report in 1956. It made two recommendations: that the national government should help in developing Hindi, and, more importantly from the viewpoint of ethnic relations, that English should be replaced by Hindi after 1965 but remain as a subsidiary official language.[38] The latter recommendation was a concession to non-Hindi states because the original language compact had envisaged the complete elimination of English.

In the late 1950s, however, the government was forced to go further in the direction of retaining English and slowing down its replacement by Hindi. First, insufficient progress had been made in propagating Hindi and, second, unrest in non-Hindi areas was growing. Therefore, in September 1959, the Union Home Minister stated that as a practical matter English could not be completely phased out in the specified time frame. In addition, Prime Minister Nehru let it be known that he was skeptical of the efforts of the Hindi language associations—which he thought were aggravating relations with non-Hindi speakers. He therefore publicly urged moderation on the language issue. In the face of mounting discontent among non-Hindi speakers, he assured non-Hindi states that English would continue to be an associate language for as long as non-Hindi speakers wanted, that there would be no discrimination against non-Hindi speakers in recruitment to government services, and that Hindi would not be imposed on any state.[39]

---

37. Das Gupta, *Language Conflict*, p. 137.

38. Ibid., p. 161.

39. See ibid., pp. 226–227.

OFFICIAL LANGUAGE POLICY: THE FINAL SETTLEMENT. In the 1960s, three developments forced the Congress Party government to move towards a more flexible language formula that made further concessions to group rights: intensifying pressure from non-Hindi states and in particular from the leaders of the southern states; a rise in popular protests and violence in Tamil Nadu; and a shift of power within the Congress Party as a result of the 1962 and 1967 general elections.

First, because Nehru's pronouncement on language issues in 1959 had no legal status, it did little to reassure non-Hindi states, which therefore continued to exert pressure on the national government. In August 1961, the Chief Ministers' Conference welcomed the national government's decision to keep English as an associate language even after Hindi became the official language in 1965. It also threw its weight behind the "three-language formula" in secondary education. The idea was that students would be taught at least three languages: the regional language and their mother tongue if it was not the regional language; Hindi or, in Hindi-speaking areas, another Indian language; and English or any other modern European language. This formula was subsequently accepted by a conference of all important political parties in October 1961.[40]

The Official Languages Act of 1963 was a further response to discontent in non-Hindi states. Under the Act, English would remain as an associate language beyond 1965. However, non-Hindi groups were still not satisfied because the Act stated that "the English language may, as from the appointed day, continue to be used, in addition to Hindi." They saw the use of the word "may" as problematic.[41] Nehru's death in 1964 and the coming to power of Lal Bahadur Shastri, a Congressman from Uttar Pradesh who often expressed himself in Hindi, made them even more nervous.

A second source of pressure, more direct and coercive, therefore came to be exerted on the government in 1965. In Madras state, the opposition to Hindi turned violent. Led by students and the Dravida Munnetra Kazhagham, a regional party, a series of riots broke out. The Kazhagham leaders were arrested, leaving matters in the hands of students who bore the brunt of government repression. In February 1965, rioting and state repression intensified. This was compounded as pro-Hindi groups launched counterprotests.[42] The government was faced with the prospect of a north-south confrontation and the possibility of a secessionist

---

40. Ibid., pp. 244–245.

41. Quotation in ibid., p. 236.

42. Ibid., p. 238.

movement in Madras. The Congress Party responded with three suggestions: first, that Nehru's assurance about language policy be put into an amendment to the Official Languages Act; second, that the three-language formula in education be properly implemented; and third, that government recruitment exams be conducted in English, Hindi, and regional languages rather than in English and Hindi only. Before the government could act on these suggestions, India was at war with Pakistan, and the language problem was temporarily set aside.[43]

The third development, which caused the government to be more accommodating on language policy, was a shift in power within the ruling Congress Party between 1962 and 1967. In the 1962 general elections, the Congress Party lost seats in Hindi states and gained seats in non-Hindi states in western, eastern, and southern India. In the state elections, it lost ground to the Hindu communal parties in the north; these parties were also pro-Hindi. In short, the 1962 elections increased the influence of the Congress Party's southern, anti-Hindi constituents.[44] The general elections of 1967 brought about further changes in the Congress Party's political fortunes. First, the party won only a bare majority in Parliament. Second, it lost nearly half of the state elections, mostly to regional parties. Third, it was defeated in every Hindi state except Rajasthan. Finally, in non-Hindi states, it did better, with one critical exception—Madras—where it lost to the Dravida Munnetra Kazhagam. As a result, the Congress Party was severely weakened nationally. If it failed to deal with the language revolt, it risked further losses, especially in the south where it had a comparative electoral advantage.

The Official Languages (Amendment) Bill was passed in December 1967. The modified Act specified that English would remain an official means of communication for the nation, in Parliament, and between the central government and those states which had a non-Hindi state language. Knowledge of Hindi or English would be deemed sufficient for public servants. The new system came to have a tripartite structure: a two-language policy for official business; a three-language policy for school education; and a three-language policy for the government public service examinations.[45]

In sum, over two decades, the government developed a language policy that is sensitive to group rights and that has contained one of the country's most explosive ethnic challenges.

---

43. Ibid., pp. 245–246.

44. Ibid., p. 235.

45. Ibid., p. 259.

REORGANIZATION OF STATES: THE OTHER LANGUAGE PROBLEM

Between 1953 and 1956, the government also dealt with the language issue at a second level—in terms of the reorganization of states. Its solution to this complex problem was to demarcate states along linguistic lines, a group rights approach par excellence. Here, too, violent protest was the catalyst that brought about changes in government policy.

When India became independent, integrating the constituent units of the erstwhile British colonial empire into a coherent whole was a pressing task. These units—the former governor's provinces and the five hundred or so princely states—had existed side by side for two hundred and fifty years but were governed by different rules and administrative systems. One way of reorganizing them was to bring together areas that had a common language. This was in consonance with the Congress Party's pre-independence commitment to the creation of states organized on linguistic lines.

However, in 1948, the Linguistic Provinces Commission—the Dar Commission—concluded that a group rights approach to state formation was neither possible nor desirable. Based on its recommendations, areas were integrated or merged in different ways.[46] It was widely believed that this system was unwieldy and unfair, and that a further reorganization of India's internal map would be necessary. Subsequently, the Congress Party investigated how reorganization might be carried out, but it too rejected the formation of linguistic states. It conceded, however, that the Telegu-majority districts of Madras—a predominantly Tamil-speaking state—had a case for creating a separate state of Andhra.

The government's rejection of linguistic states increased the demand for them. Three waves of violence ultimately moved the central government to revise its policy.

The first wave of violence was triggered by an Andhra activist who fasted to death in 1953. In reaction, the government announced the formation of the state of Andhra Pradesh in October 1953. With the pressure for linguistic states mounting, the government formed a States Reorganization Commission in December to ponder the issue.[47] The Commission's 1955 report rejected the "one language, one state" formula as the fundamental basis for reorganization. Instead, it outlined four principles by which reorganization was to proceed: first, any reorganization plan must preserve and strengthen the unity and security of India; second, linguistic

---

46. M.V. Pylee, *India's Constitution* (New Delhi: Asia Publishing House, 1967), pp. 59–60.

47. Hardgrave and Kochanek, *India: Government and Politics*, pp. 136–145.

and cultural homogeneity would be taken into account in reorganization plans; third, financial, economic, and administrative efficiency should be considered in this effort; and fourth, reorganization must be compatible with economic development plans. In addition, any plan for reorganization had to be sensitive to common historical traditions, geographical contiguity, administrative considerations, and the wishes of the people insofar as these could be assessed and were not at odds with national interests. The Commission recognized that, despite these general principles, the form of reorganization would inevitably vary from region to region.[48]

Although the Commission refused to make linguistic homogeneity the guiding principle of reorganization, "the pattern that emerged from their scheme of recommendations consisted of practically unilingual States only."[49] The Commission's report did not win complete support. Given India's complex ethnic picture, any reorganization plan was bound to leave some groups insecure and unhappy. After a series of negotiations between the central government and various groups, the States Reorganization Bill was passed in November 1956.

The second wave of violence leading to the formation of linguistic states occurred in the late 1950s and early 1960s. When the States Reorganization Bill went into effect in 1956, two key states, Bombay and Punjab, were not reorganized along linguistic lines. Both eventually would be, but only after violent protests. Bombay state consisted mostly of Marathi speakers but with a substantial Gujarati-speaking minority, especially in the city of Bombay. In 1960, after widespread rioting, Bombay state was divided into Marathi-speaking Maharashtra and Gujarati-speaking Gujarat, with Bombay going to Maharashtra.

The violence in Punjab over state reorganization occurred in 1966. The government responded by creating a new Punjab state, with Punjabi in the Gurmukhi script designated as its official language. In Punjab, matters were more complex because religion and language differentiated the state's two major communities: Sikhs and Hindus. Sikhs wanted a separate state in order to protect their religion from being absorbed into Hinduism. In the 1950s, this religious concern was expressed as a linguistic issue: while both the Sikhs and Hindus of the state speak Punjabi, Sikhs write Punjabi in the Gurmukhi script. In 1955, the States Reorganization Commission rejected the demand for a Sikh-dominated state, arguing that it would not resolve communal tensions in the region. In 1966,

---

48. Pylee, *India's Constitution*, pp. 61–63.

49. Ibid., p. 64.

however, with violence brewing, the government reversed this decision. Also influenced by the Sikhs' role in the 1965 war against Pakistan and by Hindu demands for a separate Punjabi-speaking state, the government created a predominantly Sikh Punjab and a predominantly Hindu Haryana. This completed the reorganization of the major states along linguistic lines.[50]

The central government, worried about strengthening secessionist impulses, had initially been reluctant to accept linguistic states. However, deepening protests and violence threatened to undermine domestic order and stability and bring on the very demands the government feared. In the end, the government conceded that the creation of linguistic states within a federal system was most likely to bring long-term stability.

Regionalism in Kashmir, Punjab, and the Northeast States

In Kashmir, Punjab, and the Northeast states, religious, language, and other cultural differences have sustained or been used to sustain subnational identities, promote political movements for greater autonomy or secession, and mobilize groups for violent action. The Indian government has responded by devolving power through federalism, and by containing secessionism and violence when federalism has failed to accommodate regionalist demands.

When India became independent, it was understood that ethnic diversity would have to be accommodated through federal arrangements. Within this federal structure, the government has from time to time granted special degrees of autonomy to various borderland groups. When this has not sufficed or when the government has failed to honor its promises to grant more autonomy, regionalist feelings have turned into secessionist demands. The government has usually been slow to recognize and give credence to the seriousness of these demands. This, in turn, has often led to escalation and violence. The government's response to violence in the borderlands has followed a consistent pattern: first, to enter into negotiations in which it gives little away; and second, to use force in massive, sustained military operations. Along the way, the

---

50. Hardgrave and Kochanek, *India: Government and Politics*, pp. 139–140. Also rejected in 1956 were demands to form separate "Jharkhand" out of the Chhota-Nagpur area of Bihar and adjoining tribal areas of Orissa. Calls for the creation of a separate Nagaland that would have been dominated by the Naga tribes were also rejected. However, in 1963, the Indian government, as part of a settlement with militant Nagas, separated the Naga hill areas from Assam and created a new state. In neither case was the primary issue language. Rather, the divide was between tribal and non-tribal people.

government has exploited and exacerbated differences between rebel groups and between ethnic groups so as to weaken its main opponent. From the government's perspective, peace accords have usually been negotiated from a position of strength. Interestingly, however, these accords generally meet many of the demands of the rebel groups.

REGIONALISM AND FEDERALISM

Before we consider events in Kashmir, Punjab, and the Northeast in detail, we need to understand the role of federalism in the management of regional disaffection, particularly in the borderland states. India's federal system, in theory, held out the promise of a significant devolution of power. However, federalism as it has been practiced in India has involved a significant centralization of power. Virtually every Indian state has strained at the reins of central control, but in the borderland states, where regional sentiments have been strongest, the practice of federalism has pushed regional governments and peoples to agitate for much more autonomy and even political independence.

As noted earlier, India is a federal union. The constituent units for the most part are demarcated ethnically, on a linguistic basis. These linguistic states, at least on paper, have substantial power. In practice, though, India has been rather centralized. The central government very quickly asserted its primacy, taking responsibility for national security (foreign affairs, defense) and national economic policy, and controlling key institutions (the all-India bureaucracy, the army). All this was run by the Congress Party, which until 1967 dominated both national and state politics.

Indian federalism came to be marked by a dialectic. On the one hand, the central government under the Congress Party increasingly used its control of key institutions to centralize authority. On the other hand, increased control created disaffection in the states. This disaffection lowered support for the Congress Party and enhanced the support for regional parties. The more the Congress Party declined electorally, the more its leaders sought to centralize the political system. They repeatedly invoked the provision of the constitution that allows the central government to dismiss state governments in time of great danger and place states under President's Rule. President's Rule was used ten times from 1947 to 1967 and sixty-six times between 1968 and early 1989.[51]

India's federal system contains special autonomy provisions for some borderland states. Kashmir is the most extreme case. According to the

---

51. Reported in Arend Lijphart, *The Puzzle of Indian Democracy: A Reinterpretation,* RGICS Paper No. 18 (New Delhi: Rajiv Gandhi Institute for Contemporary Studies, Rajiv Gandhi Foundation, 1994), p. 19.

constitution, the central government is responsible for defense, foreign affairs, and communications, but it can make laws in other policy areas only with the concurrence of the state government. As we will see, however, the government's concerns about Kashmiri separatism led it to abridge Kashmir's autonomy in practice, fueling resentment within that state. Two other borderland states—Nagaland and Mizoram—were also given special degrees of autonomy in the constitution with respect to religious and social practices, customary procedure, civil and criminal justice, and the ownership and transfer of land. These provisions have been substantially honored but have failed to satisfy regional separatists in these states.

In response to demands for more regional autonomy, the central government has created autonomous district councils and *panchayats,* or local self-government bodies, at the village, town, and city level. These autonomous councils were specifically designed to accommodate ethnic dissidents within states and particularly in the borderland states. However, few of the autonomous councils have managed to exercise the authority formally delegated to them, at least in part because they have limited financial powers and because in the end both the state and central governments have a decisive voice in what the councils can do. The *panchayat* system has not fared much better. A new system, with significant financial and decision-making power, was introduced in 1992 and 1993 and holds out the promise of a further devolution of power. However, the state governments do not want to give real decision-making power to other bodies.

When India became independent, its leaders created a federal system that on paper seemed well balanced between the demands of a coherent, governable union, on the one hand, and states' rights, on the other. From time to time, at least on paper, the government has given more power to regional and local authorities. At the same time, the central government has resisted giving significant power to the states, and the state governments have opposed giving significant power to local bodies. Most of the efforts to devolve power in India have been undermined, partly by genuine concerns about national unity and economic planning in a looser system, and more importantly by the unwillingness of New Delhi and state capitals to share power.

KASHMIR

India's policy towards Kashmir can be divided into four phases: 1947–64, 1965–81, 1982–89, and 1990–96. The first phase was marked by government efforts to formally grant and then curtail regional autonomy in Kashmir. The second phase saw a more confident government attempt to loosen up somewhat on the reins of central control. In the third phase, the government tried to manipulate Kashmiri politics and establish tighter control over Kashmir. This degenerated into repression when Kashmiris protested. In the fourth phase, the government unleashed a massive counterinsurgency force against a full-blown rebellion. When the rebels tired, the government promised to grant more autonomy to Kashmir, and tried to bring about a return to normal political life in the state.

CURTAILING REGIONAL AUTONOMY, 1947–64. The basic thrust of Indian policy on Kashmir has been to integrate the state within the union in return for ceding it a special degree of autonomy. According to the constitution, the national government is responsible for defense, foreign affairs, and communications, but it can legislate in other areas only with the concurrence of the state governments. In addition, Kashmir was allowed to draft its own constitution. In 1952, the Kashmir government and the central government produced the "Delhi Agreement," which reaffirmed Kashmir's right to draft its own constitution and specified some of the ways in which regional autonomy would be granted to the state. According to the Delhi Agreement, Kashmiris would be Indian citizens but Kashmir would retain some special rights won prior to independence. Kashmir would be allowed to have its own flag. The *sadar-i-riyasat* (governor of the state) would be elected by the state legislature, not nominated by the central government. Finally, a state of emergency could be put into effect in Kashmir only with the agreement of the state legislature.[52]

On paper, Kashmir had been given a great deal of autonomy. However, the Indian government was skeptical about Kashmir's commitment to the union. Thus, it subsequently began to curtail Kashmiri autonomy in practice. First, the government chipped away at autonomy through a series of legal maneuvers. Between 1957 and 1966, with pliable governments in place in Kashmir, the Indian government extended various provisions of the Indian Constitution to the state.[53] In 1966, the Kashmiri Constitution was amended to convert the *sadar-i-riyasat* into a governor and the prime minister into a chief minister. Finally, the articles in the Indian Constitution relating to Presidential Rule in a state, as well as presidential and parliamentary authority to make laws during Presiden-

---

52. M.J. Akbar, *Kashmir: Behind the Vale* (New Delhi: Viking Penguin, 1991) pp. 143–144.

53. See Jagmohan, *My Frozen Turbulence in Kashmir*, 3d ed. (New Delhi: Allied, 1993), pp. 719–720.

tial Rule, were made applicable to Kashmir. For Kashmiris, these were all signs of the gradual subversion of their autonomy.

Second, the Indian government used political maneuvers to maintain control over Kashmir. Its main concern about the autonomy arrangements for Kashmir was the behavior of Kashmir's National Conference Party and its leader, Sheikh Abdullah. Increasingly, factions of the Conference and Abdullah himself were seen as obstacles to integration. The government therefore tried to remove Abdullah from the political scene and to put in his place a more pliant administration: Abdullah was arrested in August 1953, and his government was dismissed. In 1958, Abdullah was freed but almost immediately rearrested. In 1964, he was again released only to be arrested in May 1965 on his return from Mecca. It is also believed that the Indian government rigged at least the first two elections in Kashmir in order to produce state governments more palatable to New Delhi. Kashmir's first state elections were held in 1957, after the Kashmir Constitution went into effect; the second state elections were held in 1962.[54]

Third, the Indian government used economic instruments to maintain political control in Kashmir. To build a support base at both the popular and elite level, it granted general economic aid and distributed quotas, permits, licenses, and contracts. As a result, Kashmir's five-year economic development plans have been almost entirely funded by the central government, and per capita economic assistance to Kashmir has been far higher than the national average.[55]

LOOSENING UP, 1965–81. The 1965 war with Pakistan seemed to indicate that the Indian strategy of granting autonomy and then taking it away was working. When tribal invaders and Pakistani soldiers crossed into Kashmir in 1965, they found little support there; indeed, the local population cooperated with the Indian Army and civilian authorities. However little enthusiasm the Kashmiris showed about joining Pakistan, they still disliked the high degree of central government control over state affairs.

New Delhi responded cautiously: it would simply relax its hold on Sheikh Abdullah and bring him back into Kashmiri politics. He was released in 1967, and in 1968 organized the All-Kashmir States' Peoples' Convention, which was devoted to obtaining more autonomy for Kashmir. This made the Indian government nervous, and Abdullah found himself back in detention. However, by and large the government

---

54. Akbar, *Kashmir*, p. 159.
55. Jagmohan, *Frozen Turbulence*, p. 242.

continued to favor reconciliation over confrontation. In 1971, it was especially keen to ensure that Kashmir would remain loyal if India and Pakistan went to war, which in December they did.

After the war of 1971, the Indian government began autonomy talks with Abdullah. The government conceded little: virtually all of Abdullah's proposals for greater autonomy were rejected. The agreement that was ultimately reached in 1975 was intended to facilitate the Sheikh's return to state politics. According to the agreement, Kashmir would retain its own constitution. In addition, residuary powers would remain with the Kashmir assembly. The state could also review post-1953 legislation on the Concurrent List but only with the president's assent. After the accord was signed, the government arranged for the Sheikh's National Conference Party to take power, supported by the Congress Party's majority in the state.[56] Two years later, in the most free and fair elections ever held in the state, the Sheikh won handily. Abdullah was back in power, but he was tired by imprisonment and weakened by the government's manipulations of Kashmiri politics. He was therefore in no position to challenge New Delhi. For the next five years, Kashmir was stable.

MANEUVER AND REPRESSION, 1982–89.   Indian government policy towards Kashmir entered a new phase in 1982 with the death of Abdullah and the coming to power of his son, Farooq. New Delhi again turned to political maneuver as a way of limiting Kashmiri autonomy. This infuriated public opinion in Kashmir, and violence eventually broke out. The Indian government then turned to more repressive measures, which in turn radicalized segments of Kashmir's population and led to an open rebellion.

The Congress Party government in New Delhi remained suspicious of the National Conference Party under the Abdullah family, and attempted to control it by drawing it into an alliance for the 1982 elections. Farooq rejected the idea and went on to win the election. Two years later, Indira Gandhi engineered a series of defections from the party, which allowed the governor to dismiss Farooq.

After Indira Gandhi was killed in October 1984, her son Rajiv also tried to control Farooq through an electoral alliance. In 1986, fearful of being dismissed once again if he refused to join forces with the Congress Party, Farooq capitulated. The Conference-Congress coalition won the 1987 state elections, amid widespread accusations that they had been rigged. By 1988, public protests over the polls and the Conference-Congress alliance had become violent. The government responded with

---

56. Akbar, *Kashmir*, pp. 186–187.

a wave of repression: arrests and detentions without charges, police firings, the use of paramilitaries, and extraordinary law and order legislation. In 1989, Kashmiri militants organized a successful boycott of the general elections. Farooq resigned shortly afterwards.[57]

THE USE OF FORCE AND THE RETURN TO NORMAL POLITICS, 1990–96.   In 1990, the Indian government's policy towards Kashmir entered a fourth phase, one that emphasized counterinsurgency operations designed to tire the militants and to bring about a return to normal politics. On the night of January 18, 1990, Governor Malhotra Jagmohan ordered the government's paramilitary forces into action. The massive house-to-house searches that followed sparked protests that spilled into the streets. In the ensuing violence, over fifty people were killed. At this point, young Kashmiri men began to cross over into Pakistan-occupied Kashmir to be trained and to get arms.[58] Violent protests and government repression escalated thereafter. Regular Indian Army troops and Indian paramilitary forces began to carry out counterinsurgency operations reminiscent of those undertaken in the Northeast and Punjab but new for Kashmir.

By late 1995, the rebellion was starting to wane, and the government tried to return political life in Kashmir to normal. Prime Minister Narasimha Rao held out the possibility of real autonomy for Kashmir when he announced that he would be willing to discuss anything short of independence for Kashmir. Farooq Abdullah responded by demanding autonomy as envisaged in the 1952 accords. In May 1996, the National Conference and various opposition groups boycotted the general elections. Once again, there was some doubt about the fairness of the elections. The government also held state elections in Kashmir in the summer of 1996, and the National Conference participated. Farooq Abdullah was returned to power. He announced that he would negotiate more autonomy for Kashmir with the central government, devolve power within the state (to Jammu and Ladakh), set up a Kashmir human rights commission, attempt to rehabilitate militants not charged with heinous crimes, and put a local police officer—rather than the army commander—in charge of security in the region.

India's handling of problems in Kashmir exemplifies what had become a familiar pattern in its borderland regions: granting autonomy in theory but going back on it in practice; being unresponsive to normal

---

57.   Balraj Puri, *Kashmir: Towards Insurgency* (Delhi: Orient Longman, 1993), pp. 55–59.

58.   Akbar, *Kashmir*, p. 219.

agitational politics; negotiating with caution and turning to repression as agitation mounts; and finally, resorting to a massive use of force to beat down rebellions and bring about a return to political normalcy.

PUNJAB

In Punjab, Sikh demands for autonomy have been articulated in phases, and government responses have developed in commensurate phases. As noted earlier, the Sikh movement came to focus on linguistic issues in the 1950s. However, the roots of the problem in Punjab were religious differences, compounded by the Sikh community's attachment to the land and its desire to dominate the region in political terms. The fact that the Sikh community was concentrated in a single region intensified its desire for regional autonomy and political independence.

Sikh disaffection and government policies towards the Sikh movement can be divided into four phases: 1947–66, 1967–79, 1980–91, and 1992–95. In the first phase, the government sought to satisfy Sikh demands for autonomy through a reorganization of the state. The second phase involved normal agitational politics on the part of the Sikhs. When this made little impression on the government, the Sikh movement became more violent. The government then proceeded along two tracks: it countered with force but also with political responses—appeasement, elections, negotiations. By 1992, this two-track policy had failed. After a new state government was elected, the government turned to a new counterterrorism strategy based on the massive use of force. By 1995, the government had succeeded in tiring out the militants, and Punjab returned to normalcy even though none of the main demands of the Sikh rebels had been met.

AUTONOMY THROUGH REORGANIZATION, 1947–66. The Sikhs, under the leadership of the Akali Dal, had since the 1930s allied with the Congress Party with the understanding that after independence their linguistic-religious concerns would be taken into account in the new constitution. After independence, the Sikhs felt that the autonomy they had sought was being systematically denied. First, they were denied a Punjabi-speaking state by the various commissions appointed by the Congress Party government. Second, their claim to minority status in the constitution was rejected: on civil code issues, for instance, they were to be treated as Hindus. The reorganization of the state in 1956, which merged the Patiala and East Punjab States Union (PEPSU) area with Punjab, actually reduced the proportion of Sikhs in the region. In 1961, in response to violent protests, the government agreed that Punjabi was the dominant language of the state but not the official language. Only in 1966, after further Sikh protests occurred and the war with Pakistan brought home the importance of a stable Punjab, did the central government reorganize the state so that Punjabi became the official language and Sikhs came to dominate numerically.[59]

DEALING WITH NORMAL AGITATIONAL POLITICS, 1967–79. After the creation of the new Punjab, the period from 1967 to 1979 was relatively quiet. The Akalis came to power in 1967 and raised a second set of demands. Their concerns were the future of Chandigarh, territorial adjustments with neighboring states, river water allocations, and the protection and promotion of Sikhism. The Indian government's response was cautious. Thus in 1970 it agreed to award the city of Chandigarh to Punjab. In return, two Hindu-dominated sub-districts were to be given to Haryana. Neither transfer was implemented, however, nor was the division of river waters between Haryana, Punjab, and Rajasthan resolved.[60]

In reaction, the Akalis passed the Anandpur Sahib Resolution in 1973. This resolution gave expression to the idea of "Khalistan," but stopped short of advocating separatism. Most importantly, the resolution demanded that Chandigarh and other "Sikh populated Punjabi speaking areas" be merged with Punjab, that the interests of Sikhs and Sikhism be protected, and that Punjab and other Indian states be given more autonomy.[61] From 1974 to 1977, India was governed under emergency rule, and the government did not respond seriously to this resolution.

The Akali Dal returned to power in Punjab in 1977; in 1978 a revised Anandpur Resolution demanded that the central government's responsibilities be restricted to defense, foreign affairs, communications, currency, and railways. In addition, the Akalis asked for more financial powers and for the Sikhs to be listed in the constitution as a minority (as were Muslims and Christians). The Janata government in New Delhi promised to look into specific cases of financial discrimination but refused to define Sikhs as different from Hindus.[62]

NEGOTIATIONS AND REPRESSION, 1980–91. Starting in 1980, Sikh protests turned violent. Since nonviolent agitation had failed to generate an acceptable response from the government, the Sikh movement turned to

---

59. Harji Mallick, "The Historical Legacy," in Amrik Singh, ed., *Punjab in Indian Politics: Issues and Trends* (Delhi: Ajanta, 1985), pp. 35–40.

60. Hardgrave and Kochanek, *India: Government and Politics*, p. 153.

61. Kapur, *Sikh Separatism*, p. 219.

62. Kuldip Nayar and Khushwant Singh, *Tragedy of Punjab: Operation Bluestar and After* (New Delhi: Vision Books, 1984), p. 35.

terror. The government responded with repression. The two sides continued to negotiate but found it difficult to make agreements stick as pressure mounted from extremists on both sides.

From 1981 to 1984, the Akalis orchestrated a series of mass protests against the Congress Party government. The Akali agitations ran in tandem with a campaign of violence led by Sant Bhindranwale, a Sikh militant. The government's response was to play one Sikh faction against the other. This divide-and-rule policy succeeded up to a point but in the long run helped to promote Bhindranwale as an alternate force. In this sense, the government's policy backfired in the early 1980s.[63]

By October 1981, violence was spreading and the government entered into negotiations with the Akalis. These negotiations proceeded intermittently and covered the usual mix of issues, ultimately reaching no meaningful agreement.[64] Terrorist violence continued to grow, and the government responded with strong police action. It also made some concessions along the way. In October 1982, the government released 25,000 detainees and agreed to various cultural demands: relaying religious hymns through a local radio station, allowing Sikh airline passengers to carry short *kirpans*, and banning the sale of tobacco, liquor, and meat in areas around the Golden Temple at Amritsar. In March 1983, the government announced that center-state relations would be examined by an independent commission headed by a Sikh, Justice R.S. Sarkaria.[65]

This pattern of events continued. The government had no effective military strategy for dealing with heavily armed militants, but its political concessions did not satisfy Sikh demands. Even as it negotiated with its Sikh counterparts, the government relied more and more on the tools of repression. It passed an amendment to the National Security Act that allowed police to enter premises and carry out searches without warrants, to arrest and detain suspects without furnishing reasons, and to imprison suspects without trial for up to two years. In June 1984, the Indian Army seized control of the Golden Temple, killing Bhindranwale and several other senior Khalistani commanders. Although the government hoped that this would end the rebellion, the level of violence increased. Sikh troops in various parts of India mutinied and had to be put down by force. On October 31, 1984, in retaliation for the government's attack on the Golden Temple, Prime Minister Indira Gandhi was assassinated by her Sikh security guards.

63. Ibid., pp. 38, 42.

64. Ibid., pp. 44–50.

65. Kapur, *Sikh Separatism*, p. 224; and Nayar and Singh, *Tragedy of Punjab*, p. 71.

The new government under Rajiv Gandhi attempted to break the cycle of violence by signing a peace accord with the moderate Akali leader, Harcharan Longowal. To give legitimacy to the accord and hand power back to the Akalis, elections were announced. Sikh militants derailed the plan by killing Longowal. The elections nonetheless went ahead, but the new state government was unable to cope with the rising tide of violence. The central government therefore turned to more intense forms of repression. In 1987 it dismissed the Akali government in Punjab. It also went back on the accord it had signed with Longowal, fearing a Hindu backlash in Haryana. In May 1988, Indian paramilitary forces returned to the Golden Temple to flush out militants who had filtered back in.[66] This did not bring Sikh militancy to heel, however. Both Sikh terrorism and state repression escalated.

MASSIVE FORCE AND THE RETURN OF NORMAL POLITICS, 1992–95. The Sikh crisis entered a fourth phase in 1992 after state elections were held in Punjab. Even though the Akalis boycotted the elections and only 4.6 percent of the electorate voted, a new state government, under the Congress Party, was installed. With a fellow Congress government in power, the central government's strategy was to tire the militants by unleashing the state police.

Turning counterinsurgency operations over to the state police had several military advantages. The police knew the terrain intimately. They also had links with the rural population, and were not seen as instruments of New Delhi. Unlike the army, the police could respond to militant tactics in kind: kidnappings of policemen's family members were matched by police abductions of militant kin. Cash rewards were used to capture militants, and informants were given protection. Extra-judicial killings and arrests were overlooked.[67] By 1995, the government's policy had generally succeeded. Sikh militancy had been significantly weakened, the Sikh militancy had been dampened, and political life in Punjab had begun to return to normal.

Government policy in Punjab, in a broad sense, has been similar to the Kashmir policy: resistance of autonomy demands, cautious negotiations and mild repression, the use of force to tire out the military, and finally, a return to normal electoral politics.

---

66. Hardgrave and Kochanek, *India: Government and Politics*, pp. 158–159.

67. Shekhar Gupta, *India Redefines its Role*, Adelphi Paper 293 (London: Oxford University Press for the International Institute for Strategic Studies, 1995), pp. 28–29.

THE NORTHEAST

The Northeast, with its seven states, is a complex region. All of these states except Arunachal Pradesh and Meghalaya have had movements that sought political independence or greater autonomy and that have turned violent. In these five troubled states, the central government's policy has followed familiar lines: initial unresponsiveness; the initiation of negotiations when ethnic protests turn violent; the massive use of force against insurgents; and a return to negotiations and electoral politics when the rebels tire. In each case, this process has culminated in a peace accord. As a result, agitation and violence in the Northeast have subsided. However, none of the ethnic issues has been fully solved, at least in part because the terms of the accords have not been fully implemented. A closer look at one case, Assam, the most important state in the Northeast, will illustrate the broad outlines of Indian policy in this volatile border-land region.

ASSAM.   Assam presents perhaps the most complex ethnic problem in the Northeast. Some of Assam's ethnic problems were solved through reorganization of the states in the region. Arunachal Pradesh, Meghalaya, Mizoram, and Nagaland were carved out of Assam, solving many contentious issues, but present-day Assam still has ethnic difficulties. The numerically and politically dominant Hindu Assamese are arrayed against Muslim and Hindu Bengalis; the former are also resented by plains tribes such as the Bodo, Karbis, and Mishings. The Bodos, in turn, are feared by non-Bodo tribes inhabiting areas the Bodos want to control.

The Hindu Assamese revolt goes back to 1978 when, in response to massive public complaints, government tribunals were set up to investigate the numbers of foreign migrants on the electoral rolls. In June 1979, the All Assam Students Union (AASU) and other groups protested the presence of and voting rights for Bangladeshi migrants. The government, however, more or less ignored the issue. Indeed, it decided to go ahead with scheduled elections, promising to scrutinize electoral lists after the vote was in. In December, the AASU staged a protest and blocked passage of Assamese oil out of the state. After the general elections in 1980, the new prime minister, Indira Gandhi, entered into negotiations with the students.[68] The government agreed to identify and deport aliens who had come to Assam after 1971.

The situation in Assam took a turn for the worse in 1983, when Indira Gandhi called for state elections. The identification and deportation of

---

68. Hazarika, *Strangers of the Mist*, p. 143.

foreigners had not yet been carried out, and the students warned the prime minister not to proceed with the vote. The government nevertheless went ahead. In Nellie, over one thousand Bengali Muslims were massacred in retaliation. Protests against foreigners and the government's inaction on illegal migration continued. The state government cracked down. Negotiations recommenced, but little progress was made. The cycle of violence and repression continued.[69]

In late 1984, Rajiv Gandhi's new government immediately turned its attention to India's various ethnic disputes, Assam included. In 1985, it concluded an accord with the AASU, which had been fighting the central government since 1978. The accord included a pledge to deport aliens who had come to Assam after 1971, to build a third oil refinery in Assam, to reopen a nationalized paper mill that had been closed, to set up new educational institutions, to drop cases against those who had agitated against the government, and to hold elections by December 1985.[70] In return, the AASU agreed that the elections could be held on the basis of the 1971 rolls. Those who had come to Assam between 1966 and 1971 would be disenfranchised for ten years, but only after the 1985 elections. The Asom Gana Parishad, a combination of the AASU and the Asom Gana Sangram Parishad, won the subsequent elections.

However, this accord did not bring about a permanent settlement to ethnic turmoil in Assam. A second cycle of agitation, violence, and repression ensued, this time with the United Liberation Front of Asom playing the leading role. The Front's campaign took a different turn, combining kidnapping, extortion, tax collection, policing, and social and economic reform—in effect, running a parallel government.[71] The central government inevitably found this intolerable, and it went on the offensive militarily. In November 1990, it launched "Operation Bajrang," a huge counterinsurgency strike against the Front. In February 1991, the militants called for negotiations. Almost immediately, the government announced elections. In September 1991, with the elections concluded, the army was authorized to launch another counterinsurgency attack, "Operation Rhino." By December 1991, the Front was once again ready for talks. In January 1992, a Front faction was ready to surrender, and the organization split. The Assam government persuaded the central government to exploit this turn of events by funding a massive economic rehabilitation program for repentant militants. This further weakened the Front.

---

69. Ibid., pp. 143–147.

70. Ibid., pp. 148–149.

71. Ibid., pp. 175–176.

However, the split in the organization prevented the government from fully quelling the rebellion.[72] Nevertheless, a measure of stability had returned to Assam.

PEACE ACCORDS OF THE NORTHEAST.   A distinct feature of India's Northeast policies has been the conclusion of peace accords with various dissident and militant groups. These accords have not succeeded in ending insurgencies altogether, at least in part because they have not always been fully implemented. New Delhi has reached accords with the Assamese (1985), Bodos (1993), Gorkhas (1988, 1989, 1994), Mizos (1971, 1986, 1993), Nagas (1947, 1960, 1962, 1975), and Tripuris (1984, 1988, 1993).[73] A review of these accords shows that one basic model has been adapted to the needs of each state.

First, the accords all contain specific provisions relating to ending the insurgencies and rehabilitating militants and agitators. Second, all of the accords provide for the protection of ethnic identities. For instance, virtually every accord allows local religious and customary laws to govern economic activity, ownership of land and forests, civil and criminal law, and language and migration. Third, most of the accords include provisions to protect minorities within the Northeastern states. Typically, this has involved the formation of autonomous councils within states. In general, both the state and central government can modify council legislation, and the councils can review legislation on religious and social practices, customary law and proceedings, and ownership and transfers of land. Ultimately, though, the central government is supreme and can dissolve these councils. Finally, the accords specify the kinds of taxes and fees the councils can levy.[74]

The jury is still out on how well these councils function. However, a number of economic and political factors have prevented the councils from exerting real authority. State governments have impeded the flow of funds to the councils and have not taken seriously council discussions on financial matters. To compound these problems, the councils have been unable to exercise their own powers of taxation. In addition, while the councils have been given legislative, judicial, and executive authority, they have not been given a clear role with respect to economic

---

72. Ibid., pp. 192–236.

73. For the texts of the various accords on the northeast as well as those reached in Punjab and Sikkim, see P.S. Datta, *Ethnic Peace Accords in India* (New Delhi: Vikas, 1995).

74. Ibid., passim.

development—an issue of tremendous importance. Politically, council actions can be overruled by the state and central governments. Therefore, unless the same party rules both at the state and council level, friction is inevitable. Another difficulty is that councils that have been dissolved do not have to be reconstituted within a specified period of time. In sum, the councils are weak in economic and political terms, and power has devolved less than one might think.

THE INDIAN GOVERNMENT AND REGIONAL SEPARATISM

The Indian government's approach to regional autonomy and separatist movements has featured three main policy elements: the devolution of power, the control of violence, and the use of elections and peace accords to restore normal politics. Although the government has enjoyed many policy successes—more than one might expect in such a complex and difficult setting—some of its policy tendencies are less than laudatory: reneging on pledges to devolve power, using military power and violence in unrestrained ways, failing to implement peace accords fully, and generally being insufficiently sensitive to regional opinion.

Conclusions

How have the Indian government's policies with respect to ethnic issues fared? Which policies have succeeded and which have not? Under what conditions have government policies succeeded? What policy recommendations flow from this analysis?

ASSESSING GOVERNMENT POLICIES: RELIGION

With respect to religion, the Indian government, first of all, has drawn on constitutional safeguards to protect religious freedom. Numerous provisions in the constitution help to ensure that India's political order is secular. This does not mean that it is in fact at all times secular, but the government can be held to a certain standard of conduct.

Second, the Indian Constitution contains numerous provisions to protect the ways of life of all of India's many religious communities. For instance, it allows all religious groups to run their own institutions. In addition, the courts have played an adroit role in distinguishing between which customs are essential to a religion (and therefore must be protected) and which are not. The government must also be credited with holding the line against changes in Muslim personal law even though it is constitutionally bound to bring about a uniform civil code and even though public opinion supports this. The government's ban on Salman Rushdie's

The Satanic Verses must be seen as part of an effort to protect the way of life and feelings of a religious community. However much the government's motivation has been crudely political in both the civil code and Rushdie cases, it has worked to support group rights.

Third, the Indian government has moved efficiently and ambitiously to reform Hindu personal law. Although this has sparked resentment among some Hindus, it has by and large ensured that the vast majority of Indians—Hindus constitute over four-fifths of the population—lives under a uniform code.

Fourth, the government has tried to mediate disputes between religious communities, but its record in this regard has been less impressive than in the three areas mentioned above. When violence has broken out between religious groups, the government has responded with a routinized form of riot control. The government's main failing has been its inability to identify and punish those who have rioted. As a result, riots have tended to recur. The government has made infrequent efforts to mediate disputes over religious sites, but the Babri Masjid case shows that the government's tendency to avoid facing up to problems does not lead to long-term solutions.

ASSESSING GOVERNMENT POLICIES: CASTE AND TRIBE

The Indian government's policy towards the scheduled castes and tribes and other backward classes has been dominated by reservations. These three groups have benefited directly from reservations in terms of employment and education placement, but the number of beneficiaries has been small relative to the size of the overall communities. Most of the benefits have been psychological and political: there is a growing sense of personal and communitarian efficacy among these groups. Assimilation of the scheduled castes into the Hindu mainstream has not proceeded as hoped, and government policy has been weak in this regard.

ASSESSING GOVERNMENT POLICIES: LANGUAGE

The government's handling of language problems has been perhaps its biggest success. The three-language formula has worked well. The designation of Hindi as India's official language has satisfied Hindi proponents, mostly in northern India. The retention of English for official business and education, and the promotion of regional languages at the state level has assuaged the rest of India. The reorganization of states along linguistic lines has minimized conflict over language at the provincial level.

ASSESSING GOVERNMENT POLICIES: REGIONAL SEPARATISM

Government policies towards Kashmir, Punjab, and the Northeastern states have succeeded in the sense that they have kept these states within the union. A combination of violence and negotiation has pummelled and coaxed most militant groups into reaching agreements with the government. In many cases, adjustments in state relationships with the central government have helped this process along. However, these border states still lack a deep sense of being integrated into the country as a whole, Punjab being the exception. In addition, some militant groups remain unsatisfied and in a state of rebellion. Thus the government presides over a sullen and brittle peace.

IDENTIFYING THE CONDITIONS OF SUCCESS AND FAILURE

This analysis of the Indian experience suggests at least three generalizations about the conditions that lead to success and failure in the handling of ethnic relations.

First, the promise of liberal constitutionalism, secular nationalism, social modernization, economic development, group rights, and a devolution of power help to contain ethnic disaffection. The unity of India, although it has been contested, would have been under far greater pressure if this potential had not existed. Group rights and the devolution of power are crucial, and governments must be scrupulous in implementing and sustaining agreements on both counts. When governments fail to be scrupulous in this regard, trouble is likely to follow in the long run. The travails of Indian federalism and the rebellions in the borderland states are illustrative.

Second, carefully engineered "great policies" can help to generate long-term stability. Indian policies of this type included the reform of the Hindu civil code, the establishment of reservations for caste and tribal groups, the development of the official language policy, and the reorganization of states along linguistic lines. These policies were crafted with care, the final form often being achieved after a decade or more of administrative and political preparations including extensive consultation and debate within different levels and branches of government and the society at large. By contrast, the government's policies with respect to disputed religious sites and regional separatism in the borderland states have been characterized by postponement, intermittent engagement, political manipulation, and the use of force. The former have by and large been far more successful than the latter.

Third, reliance on political centralization and military force is at best a short-term option. If taken to extremes, centralization and the use of force can produce the very effects that they are intended to control. Devolution and democracy are the best long-term bases for ethnic justice and peace. When the central and state governments have made an effort to share power and when they have been sensitive to public—often group—opinion, they have done much to promote peaceful ethnic relations. The central government's motives have not always been profoundly liberal with respect to sharing power or being sensitive to public opinion; rather, it has often been moved by crude electoral calculations. That said, pluralist democracy does not require that everyone and everything at all times be imbued with liberal virtue. One of the government's greatest failings has been to signal that it can be influenced by large-scale acts of violence. This has increasingly made violence a legitimate part of the vocabulary of Indian politics.

POLICY RECOMMENDATIONS: RELIGION

In the matter of religion, three areas merit greater government effort: establishing a uniform civil code, preventing riots and punishing rioters, and reaching agreements on contested religious sites. The government, in cooperation with representatives from the country's various religions, needs to begin a serious dialogue on developing a uniform code for India. The government must also find more effective ways of preventing riots. Local politicians, administrators, police, and community activists can work together to prevent violence. In addition, the authorities must bring to justice those who are caught inciting and committing violence. Finally, governments must stop seeking political advantage with respect to controversies over contested religious sites. Good Hindu-Muslim relations are vital to India's survival. An all-party understanding on contested religious sites is therefore vital as well.

POLICY RECOMMENDATIONS: CASTE AND TRIBE

The Indian government has probably gone as far as it can in terms of instituting reservations, but it has not done enough to stop the discrimination and violence visited almost daily on members of scheduled castes and tribes and other backward classes. Civil rights abuses continue, and the Indian government must consider how economic backwardness as well as civil rights issues can be addressed more effectively. One option would be to increase the representation of these groups in the police and paramilitaries.

POLICY RECOMMENDATIONS: LANGUAGE

The development of the official language policy and the formation of linguistic states have been among the government's most successful efforts in this area. They will need further adjustment from time to time: language groups within already demarcated linguistic states will inevitably press their case for separate statehood. The creation of more autonomous councils and another reorganization of states will probably be necessary. Calls for smaller, more administratively efficient states are already being heard, and this could trigger another round of reorganization.

POLICY RECOMMENDATIONS: REGIONAL SEPARATISM

India's policies with respect to secessionism in the border states have been effective in the sense that secession has not taken place. However, none of these areas has become thoroughly integrated. A more lasting solution is required. New Delhi must turn its attention to the devolution of power through federalism. This may involve the reorganization of some states. In other cases, more autonomous councils equipped with more powers may suffice. Bringing violence to an end in Kashmir, Punjab, and the Northeast is tremendously important, and to do this the central government will have to make more than a rhetorical commitment to federalism and power-sharing.

ASSESSMENT

The Indian government has a mixed record in its handling of the country's many ethnic problems. It has done well in some areas, less well in others. Compared to some of its counterparts in Asia and Africa, however, it has performed admirably. The Indian government has managed, in the midst of enormous social diversity and economic backwardness, to maintain democracy and to contain ethnic disaffection and violence. Its reliance on constitutionalism and state-backed secular nationalism, in conjunction with policies based on group rights, devolution, and the calibrated use of force and coercion, has not been untroubled, but it has preserved India's unity and its democracy. This is no small feat.

Chapter 2

Centralization, Authoritarianism, and the Mismanagement of Ethnic Relations in Pakistan

Samina Ahmed

Ethnic relations have played a critical role in Pakistan's politics since its inception. Indeed, Pakistan came into being because of ethnic considerations: in 1947, British India was divided into two separate states to provide a separate and distinct identity for both Muslims and Hindus. In multiethnic Pakistan, with its many distinct ethno-regional communities, including the Bengalis, Punjabis, Sindhis, Pakhtuns, and the Baluchs, bargaining for access to power and resources inevitably occurred along ethnic lines.

Ethnic tensions increased over time, however, exacerbated by the absence of representative institutions and the political dominance of the civil-military bureaucracies, in which one ethnic community, the Punjabis of the west wing, were disproportionately represented. Not only was the state perceived as a partisan ethnic actor by excluded or peripheral ethnic communities, but the state's leaders either neglected pressing ethnic problems or adopted and implemented ethnic policies that transformed ethnic competition into conflict both between ethnic groups and between those groups and the state.

In 1971, this combination of neglect and consecutive policy failures led to the disintegration of the state itself: Pakistan's Bengali population seceded and formed Bangladesh. But this traumatic experience failed to alert those who have since governed Pakistan. Although Pakistan broke up as a direct result of official ineptitude, ethnic policies and official approaches have remained unresponsive to ethnic grievances, while governmental strategies have proved as ineffective as in the past. As a result, ethnic conflict is endemic in Pakistan, challenging the political stability of the state and the security of its citizens.

It is clear that the nature of Pakistan's political system and its decision-making apparatus, including the ethnic composition, interests, and goals of its decision-makers, have greatly influenced ethnic relations in

Pakistan.[1] It is equally clear that official policies have had a considerable impact on both state-group and inter-group dynamics. It is difficult, however, to determine the directions of these policies and strategies. This is because Pakistani policymakers have tried to subsume ethnicity within the rubric of larger issues such as state-building and national identity.

Under the cover of state-building, for example, Pakistan's leaders have tried to legitimize authoritarian forms of governance, to deny regional autonomy, and to create unified economic policies, which they have then used to justify the internal distribution of power. Particular cultural policies have been formulated on the grounds of nation-building, although they have been adopted to advance the ethnic and institutional interests of the decision-makers themselves.

Over time, as ethnic problems in Pakistan have increased in scope and intensity, governmental discourse and the formulation of policies to deal with issues of ethnicity have become more specific. However, policymakers have not radically changed their fundamental approaches to ethnic issues, reflecting, to a considerable extent, the continuity in internal power structures and decision-making processes.

To understand the directions of the changes in Pakistani ethnic groups and governmental responses towards ethnic problems, therefore, it is imperative to analyze ethnic relations and policies within the context of Pakistan's overall political environment. This chapter will attempt to do so by examining various turning points in Pakistan's history in order to identify the motives behind the adoption and implementation of particular policies and strategies. This historical approach will provide a framework for assessing continuity and change in Pakistani policy and for assessing the impact of particular policies on ethnic relations at critical junctures in Pakistan's political history.

While the chapter will focus on the post-colonial era, the historical legacy of colonialism will be examined insofar as it has affected the policy choices of the Pakistani political elite. After a brief overview of Pakistani ethnicity, the chapter is divided into five substantive sections, each covering a distinct phase in Pakistan's political development.

The first section examines ethnic relations during the initial years of independence, when the civil bureaucracy dominated Pakistani decision-making in conjunction with the military. The second section looks at government policies under direct military rule from the imposition of martial law in 1958 until the dismemberment of the state in 1971.

---

1. Urmila Phandis, *Ethnicity and Nation-Building in South Asia* (New Delhi: Sage Publications, 1989), pp. 100–101, 243.

Covering the period from 1971 until 1977, the third section identifies and analyzes the imperatives that shaped policy under civilian governance, while the fourth section examines policy directions following the reimposition of military rule from 1977 until 1988. The fifth and final historical section covers developments in Pakistan's political history from the military's transfer of power to civilian authorities in 1988 through March 1997. A concluding section evaluates past governmental policies to identify remedial measures Pakistani governments could institute to address the country's ethnic problems more effectively.

Historical and Ethnic Overview

When Pakistan became independent in 1947—when British India was partitioned into two sovereign states—its society was composed of several territorially, culturally, and linguistically distinct ethnic groups.

Forming a majority in the state, the Bengali population was concentrated in East Bengal,[2] separated from the second largest ethnic majority, the Punjabis of West Punjab, by 930 miles of Indian territory. Apart from refugees from the Muslim areas of India and tribal peoples from the Chittagong area, the population of the east wing was ethnically homogeneous. Even its substantial Hindu minority[3] identified itself not by the ethnic marker of religion, but by its Bengali territorial, cultural, and linguistic heritage.

The west wing, however, was home to several linguistically, territorially, and culturally distinct ethnic groups. Apart from the majority Punjabi population, the other major ethnic communities in the west wing included the Sindhis, the Pakhtuns, and the Baluchs. There was also a substantive refugee population, composed of refugees (Muhajirs) mainly from the north and the west of India, concentrated in urban areas of the province of Sindh. In the west wing, moreover, much more so than in the east, ethnicity was defined by religious and sectarian affiliation. Apart from the Hindu minority in Sindh, there were sectarian divisions within the Muslim population, including a Shi'ite minority of around 20 percent.

The ethnic picture in Pakistan was fluid, moreover, because group identities evolved over time. Pakistan's ethnic composition fluctuated as some group identities were amalgamated and new ones were created as

---

2. Bengalis constituted 54.2 percent of Pakistan's total population.

3. According to the 1951 census, Hindus composed 14.1 percent of Pakistan's population. See Y.V. Gankovsky and L. Gordon-Polonskaya, *A History of Pakistan (1947–1958)* (Lahore: People's Publishing House, n.d.), p. 97.

a result of both interethnic relations and government policy.[4] Over time, in fact, the policy choices of Pakistan's leaders completely transformed the state's ethnic composition and relations between and among its ethnic groups.

ETHNIC HISTORY

Two important factors affected the course of Pakistan's ethnic politics: its colonial legacy and the manner in which its post-independence leadership confronted the challenges of state-building and state legitimacy. The very manner in which India was divided had a major impact on Pakistani ethnicity. Communal rioting led large numbers of refugees from India to settle in urban centers of Sindh and Punjab. On Pakistan's northwestern border, the Afghan government challenged the legality of the Durand Line dividing Pakistani and Afghan Pakhtuns, and demanded that Pakistani Pakhtuns either become Afghan citizens or form their own sovereign state, Pakhtunistan.

Pakistan had been created, moreover, on the basis of the two-nations theory: that Indian Muslims had an ethnic identity separate from the Hindu majority. After independence, Pakistani policymakers found that religion alone was an insufficient foundation for nation-building for an ethnically heterogeneous but predominantly Muslim population: they therefore attempted to create an overarching Pakistani national identity, hoping to subsume preexisting ethnic loyalties and neglecting ethnic demands.

This failure to address ethnic grievances, combined with the political preeminence of an ethnically skewed civil-military bureaucracy, dominated by the Punjabi majority in the west wing, reinforced the significance of bargaining and competition along ethnic lines. The government's dependence on repression to contain ethnic dissent further accentuated ethnic divisions.

This combination of policy decisions—to neglect ethnic grievances, to maintain the ethnic composition of the bureaucracy, and to repress dissent—led to a drastic result: Pakistan disintegrated. In 1971, the majority Bengali community in the east wing opted to secede. This decision undermined the very concept on which the Pakistani state was based: the embodiment of the Muslim "nation" in South Asia.

---

4. Hamza Alavi, "Politics of Ethnicity in India and Pakistan," in Hamza Alavi and John Harriss, eds., *Sociology of "Developing Societies"* (London: Macmillan, 1989), pp. 223–224.

Pakistan.

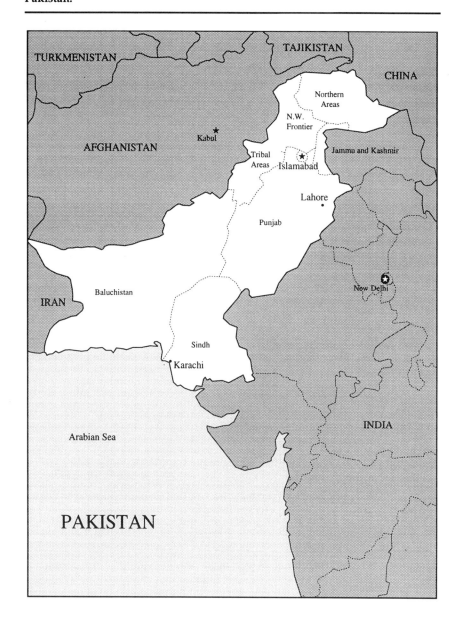

Table 2.1. Ethnic Composition of Pakistan.

Group	Number	Percentage
Punjabi	73,640,000	56.0
Sindhi	22,355,000	17.0
Pakhtun	21,040,000	16.0
Muhajir (Urdu speakers)	7,890,000	6.0
Baluch (includes Brohi speakers)	3,945,000	3.0
Other	2,630,000	2.0
Total	**131,500,000**	**100.0**

NOTE: These estimates are for 1996. No official census has been taken since 1981.

SOURCES: Gallup poll for 1996; 1981 census cited in Craig Baxter, Yogendra K. Malik, Charles H. Kennedy, and Robert C. Obert, *Government and Politics in South Asia*, 2nd ed. (Boulder, Colo: Westview Press, 1991); Charles H. Kennedy, "Ethnic Preference in Pakistan," *Asian Survey*, Vol. 24, No. 6 (June 1984); and Brian Hunter, ed., *The Statesman's Yearbook: A Statistical, Political and Economic Account of the States of the World for the Year 1996–1997*, 133rd ed. (London: Macmillan, 1996).

ETHNIC IDENTITY IN TRUNCATED PAKISTAN

Ethnicity has remained a major political force in Pakistan. The withdrawal of the majority Bengali population changed Pakistan's ethnic complexion, of course. The country's four main ethnic groups, delineated by language, territory, and a sense of historical commonality, reside within the four provinces of the federation: Punjab, Sindh, the Northwest Frontier Province (NWFP), and Baluchistan. Ethnic minorities are also present in every province.

Contemporary Pakistan's largest ethnic community, the Punjabis, constitute around 56 percent of the country's population. (See Table 2.1.) Sindhis form the second largest ethnic community, at some 18 percent of the total; Sindh province also contains a large Muhajir population. The country's Pakhtun population, approximately 15 percent of the total population, is mainly concentrated in the NWFP, although it also constitutes a minority in Baluchistan. Baluchistan covers 40 percent of Pakistan's total territory, but Baluchs comprise only 3 percent of the country's total population.[5] Due to economic migration, there are now more Baluchs outside Baluchistan than within it, particularly in Karachi, the

5. These are estimated figures since they are based on the national census of 1981, when the total population of Pakistan was 83.78 million. As of 1997, Pakistan's population is estimated at approximately 131 million. A census was to be conducted in 1991, but has been repeatedly postponed due to ethnic tensions and provincial differences over its implementation.

provincial capital of Sindh. The influx of Afghan refugees into Baluchistan has further diluted the concentration of Baluchs there.

The directions of general as well as ethnically specific governmental social, political, and economic policies have contributed to the formation of new ethnic movements and organizations. In the economically neglected regions of southern Punjab, a Seraiki movement, claiming an ethnic identity separate from the Punjabi population, is in the early stages of formation. In urban Sindh, state patronage has helped the Muhajirs to mobilize along ethnic lines.

THE POLITICS OF ETHNICITY

In post-1971 Pakistan, ethnic relations continue to be shaped by the structure of the state system itself and by the perceptions, interests, and goals of its decision-makers and their responses to ethnic demands and grievances. Ethnic competition and bargaining for access to power and resources, an expected phenomenon in a multiethnic society, have been mainly conducted through the "devices of provincial autonomy."[6] Most of Pakistan's ethnic groups have made fairly moderate demands, seeking greater regional political and economic autonomy and an official recognition of sociocultural pluralism.[7] Such bargaining, however, has often been transformed into conflict as ethnic groups have encountered authoritarian and overcentralized structures of control and unresponsive leaders. During particular periods of Pakistan's history, when ethnic groups have had no institutional, participatory mechanisms for articulating their grievances, ethnic tensions have increased.

Furthermore, the ethnic divide between Punjab and other provinces has continued to widen, since Punjab has historically controlled the decision-making processes through its predominant representation in the civil-military bureaucracies, the most powerful domestic actors in the Pakistani state. This has given Punjab a disproportionate share of political power and accompanying economic benefits.

With the state adopting policies designed to consolidate and to legitimize the social, political, and economic status quo, those ethnic communities that felt excluded or underrepresented have increasingly seen

---

6. Dietrich Reetz, "National Consolidation or Fragmentation of Pakistan: The Dilemma of General Zia-ul-Haq (1977–88)," in Diethelm Weidmann, ed., *Nationalism, Ethnicity, and Political Development: South Asian Perspectives* (New Delhi: Manohar Publications, 1991), p. 18.

7. Hamza Alavi, "Nationhood and the Nationalists in Pakistan," in Hastings Donnan and Prina Werbner, eds., *Economy and Culture in Pakistan: Migrants and Cities in a Muslim Society* (London: Macmillan, 1991), pp. 163–165.

themselves as victims of political marginalization, economic exploitation, and cultural discrimination. Successive Pakistani governments have failed to respond adequately to this ethnic alienation, and various groups have increasingly rejected state policy. This has led to outbreaks of ethnic violence, retarding economic development and undermining political stability in this weak and underdeveloped state.

Government Policies and Interethnic Relations, 1947–58

In newly independent Pakistan, the government encountered two immediate problems: acquiring legitimacy and building a new state structure, within the context of a multiethnic population. Several factors were to determine the government's approach towards ethnic relations: the country's heterogenous ethnic character, its colonial legacy, its sudden independence, and the ethnic affiliations and perspectives of the policymakers themselves.

Independence was accompanied by disputes with India over material and military resources, as well as a bloody partition in which millions of refugees, fleeing communal rioting, crossed the borders of the newly created countries.[8] Other challenges included overcoming an underdeveloped economic infrastructure and building a viable governmental system.

STATE FORMATION AND THE CREATION OF NATIONAL IDENTITY

The primary group responsible for formulating policy in independent Pakistan was the leadership of the ruling party, the Muslim League (composed mainly of Muhajirs and some representatives of the landowning Punjabi elite), which had been responsible for the creation of Pakistan and which was based in the west wing of the country. Since the newly independent state had no functioning representative institutions, the administrative apparatus inherited from the colonial era played a major role in political affairs. In its response to the issue of ethnicity, the political leadership favored an integrationist approach, attempting to create a "national" identity that could supersede existing ethnic loyalties.

This attempt to create a contrived national identity was, to some extent, a colonial heritage, reflecting the predisposition of Pakistan's leaders to the European concept of the nation-state. But it also reflected their tenuous base of support in the new state, where the formation of the state

---

8. By the 1950s, there were 7.2 million Muhajirs, mainly in the urban areas of Sindh, forming 3.3 percent of the total population of the west wing. See Gankovsky and Gordon-Polonskaya, *A History of Pakistan*, pp. 107, 152.

of Pakistan did not automatically translate into popular support for the political leadership among the country's many ethnic communities.[9] Politically vulnerable, the leadership was disinclined to work through democratic institutions. It opted instead to create a strong, centralized administrative state, to co-opt selected segments of the socioeconomic elite, and to use coercion to suppress dissent.

ETHNICITY AND THE ADMINISTRATIVE STATE

Pakistan's political leadership paid little attention to creating a constitution or representative institutions. Instead, it formed a Constituent Assembly, and the government continued to function under an amended version of a colonial act, the Government of India Act of 1935. Although the act called for the creation of a federal political structure, Pakistan's political system included no institutions for political participation nor any provision for political, economic, and cultural autonomy. Ethnic dissent was forcibly repressed through the use of the military, on which the civil leadership grew increasingly dependent.[10]

Unfamiliar with the tasks of governance and lacking a popular base, both the ruling party and the members of the Constituent Assembly—the federal legislative body elected on the basis of a very limited franchise—depended on the civil bureaucracy to run the state. This dependence on the civil service was another inheritance from colonial times; the British Indian empire had been administered and controlled by senior bureaucrats.

After independence, Pakistan's civil bureaucracy was composed mainly of personnel from the former Indian Civil Service and the Indian Provincial Service, as well as nominees from the military. They were the country's only experienced administrators, and they were more than willing to take over the tasks of policymaking and implementation from an inept and unrepresentative political leadership.

As early as 1951, after Ghulam Mohammad, a technocrat, was appointed governor-general, representatives of the civil bureaucracy, the Civil Service of Pakistan, took over key policymaking posts. Having done so, they began to manipulate the weak political leadership, with the active involvement of the military under Mohammed Ayub Khan, the first

---

9. Phandis, *Ethnicity and Nation-Building*, pp. 98–99.

10. See Wayne Ayres Wilcox, *Pakistan: The Consolidation of a Nation-State* (New York: Columbia University Press, 1963), pp. 169–170. See also H. Khuro, "Pakistan's Experiments in Democracy," in G.F. Hudson, ed., *Reform and Revolution in Asia* (London: George Allen and Unwin, 1972), p. 94.

Pakistani commander in chief. The political leadership's dependence on the civil and military bureaucracies had a considerable impact on every aspect of governmental activity, including the management of ethnic relations.

The military that Pakistan inherited from colonial India was dominated by the so-called "martial races," composed mainly of Punjabis and, to a lesser extent, Pakhtuns. Bengalis, Sindhis, and Baluchs, whom the British considered to be politically unreliable, were underrepresented or excluded.[11] This "martial races" policy was perpetuated and used to justify the continued underrepresentation of the majority Bengali population, as well as Baluchs and Sindhis, in Pakistan's armed forces. Pakistan's inherited civil bureaucracy was also predominately Muhajir and Punjabi; other ethnic groups were underrepresented.

Pakistan's civil-military bureaucracies therefore assumed broad policymaking powers, exercised through an elaborate bureaucratic structure at the central and provincial levels, headed by a powerful secretary-general and implemented with the support of a rapidly expanding military establishment. They subsequently created centralized, authoritarian political structures and denied regional autonomy in order to promote their institutional interests at the expense of rival ethnic actors.[12]

LANGUAGE AND ECONOMIC POLICIES. The bureaucracies adopted this amalgamative approach to ethnic management in order to prevent and contain potential challenges from the Bengalis, who formed a majority of the Pakistani population. In accordance with this integrationist approach, they declared Urdu the country's only official language; the mother tongue of the Muhajir population, it was commonly understood and used in urban areas of Punjab.

Officially, this language policy was aimed at creating a national identity to meet the challenges posed by regional identities and loyalties. Pakistan's founder and first governor-general, Mohammed Ali Jinnah, insisted that the official language of Pakistan had to be Urdu. "Without

---

11. See Asaf Hussain, "Ethnicity, National Identity and Praetorianism: The Case of Pakistan," *Asian Survey*, Vol. 16, No. 10 (October 1976), p. 923. See also Stephen P. Cohen, *The Indian Army: Its Contribution to Development of a Nation* (Berkeley: University of California Press, 1971), pp. 45–52.

12. Shahid J. Burki, "Twenty Years of the Civil Service of Pakistan: A Re-evaluation," *Asian Survey*, Vol. 9, No. 4 (April 1969), p. 243; and Bilal Hashmi, "Dragon Seed: Military in the State," in Hasan Gardezi and Jamil Rashid, eds., *Pakistan: The Roots of Dictatorship: The Political Economy of a Praetorian State* (Delhi: Oxford University Press, 1986), p. 156.

one State language," he declared, "no nation can remain tied up solidly together and function."[13] In practice, this language policy ensured the continued overrepresentation of the Muhajirs and Punjabis in the increasingly powerful central bureaucracy.

Ethnic alienation was further fueled by the center's economic policies, which favored the development of urban Sindh and Punjab at the expense of East Bengal, rural Sindh, the NWFP, and Baluchistan, widening existing socioeconomic disparities. The Punjabi-Muhajir central bureaucracy, responsible for formulating economic planning and for disbursing developmental expenditures to the provinces, adopted policies that favored their ethnic constituents in urban Sindh and Punjab. While one of the main sources of foreign exchange, for example, was the sale of East Bengal's jute, the proceeds were spent on developing the industry of the west wing, based in Karachi, as well as the agricultural infrastructure of central Punjab.

COERCION AND CO-OPTATION. When resentment against the central government's ethnic policies led Bengalis to demand official linguistic equality, democratic rule, and economic autonomy, the government adopted coercive policies to contain ethnic conflict. Within the west wing, too, Sindhis, Pakhtuns, and Baluchs were demanding official recognition of linguistic and regional pluralism; the center responded by forcibly suppressing ethnic dissent and co-opting segments of the ethnic leadership.

In 1948, for example, the military was used to force the Khan of Kalat, the head of the Baluch tribal confederation, to accede to Pakistan. In the NWFP, the predominantly Pakhtun and pro-Congress party, the Khudai Khidmatgar (Servants of God), under the leadership of Khan Abdul Ghaffar Khan, had opposed the division of Pakistan. After 1947, Ghaffar Khan's followers continued to oppose the Muslim League. Alienated Pakhtun nationalists called for the formation of a separate state for the Pakhtuns, Pakhtunistan, encompassing the territories of the NWFP and the Pakhtun-inhabited areas of Baluchistan. The predominantly Pakhtun National Awami Party (NAP [National Peoples' Party]), Khudai Khidmatgar's successor, merely demanded tangible provincial autonomy and democratic process. The government's response to the NAP's more moderate demand for regional autonomy consisted of enhanced centralized control over the NWFP through co-opted chief ministers, such as Abdul

---

13. Louis D. Hayes, *Politics in Pakistan: The Struggle for Legitimacy* (Boulder, Colo.: Westview Press, 1984), p. 62.

Qayyum Khan, and the use of force, particularly in the tribal areas where resentment of central intervention led to periodic outbreaks of unrest.[14]

At the same time, west-wing bureaucrats and their political allies were not in favor of representative government at the national level; they recognized that the majority Bengal population could acquire and exercise power within a democratic framework. Bengali discontent with the existing political order was manifested in the Muslim League's defeat in the first elections to the East Bengal provincial assembly in 1954. The National Front alliance won on a manifesto that called for regional autonomy, which would allow central control only over defense, currency, and foreign affairs. The center, dominated by the Punjabis and Muhajirs of West Pakistan, responded by redoubling its efforts to pursue a set of interlinked policies based on centralization, coercion, and ethnic manipulation. It proceeded to dismiss the United Front government; recognize Bengali as an official language, alongside Urdu, to divide the forces of the opposition; merge all the provinces and states of the west wing into one administrative unit, the One Unit system, to counterbalance the east wing; and dismiss the Constituent Assembly (where representatives from the east wing and the smaller West Pakistani provinces had started pressing for more provincial autonomy) and reconstitute it in a nominal form. Finally, the civil bureaucracy, in partnership with the military, consolidated its political clout by out-maneuvering the unelected and increasingly ineffective political leadership.[15]

CENTRALIZED STRUCTURES OF CONTROL

By the mid-1950s, under former bureaucrat Iskander Mirza's guidance, new mechanisms were constructed to provide legitimacy to authoritarian governance. These included Pakistan's first constitution, promulgated in 1956, which provided for a distorted parliamentary system, in which a nominated president's powers far exceeded those of the prime minister. As far as ethnic issues were concerned, the constitution acknowledged the existence of clearly demarcated territorial regions by declaring Pakistan a federal republic. Regional autonomy existed in name alone, however.

The One Unit system was given constitutional sanction, and an attempt was made to offset the numerical superiority of the Bengalis by adopting the principle of parity between the east and west wings within

---

14. Lawrence Ziring, *Pakistan: The Enigma of Political Development* (Boulder, Colo.: Westview Press, 1980), p. 77.

15. Hayes, *Politics in Pakistan*, pp. 64–65.

a unicameral legislature. The Hindu minorities of East Pakistan and Sindh were marginalized through the principle of a separate electorate, which meant that they could only vote for minority representatives, not for general seats.[16] Some distributive mechanisms were established, including regional quotas for employment and admission to educational institutions, but there was no change in ethnic socioeconomic disparities since the distribution of economic assets continued to favor the Muhajirs and the Punjabis.

The constitution's federal framework gave little autonomy to the provinces. Legislative authority, for example, was divided along the lines described by the federal, concurrent, and provincial lists, which empowered the central legislature to allocate resources. All important policy areas, including foreign policy and interprovincial trade and currency matters, were included in the federal list; other economic powers were shared between the provinces and the federation in the concurrent list; and the provinces controlled policy with respect to agriculture and education. The indirectly elected president was given the power to oversee all national expenditures; he therefore exercised great control over the provinces. In addition, not only did the president have the power to veto Provincial Assembly bills, provincial chief ministers were in no position to oppose the president's dictates.

Mirza continued to rely on the military's support and on the civil service to run the country, depriving the provinces of a role in policy-making. In fact, the terms of the 1956 constitution consolidated bureaucratic control over the provinces, since civil servants were answerable only to the central government.

In the absence of regional autonomy and representative venues for expressing grievances and demands, ethnic groups that were either underrepresented or excluded from the ruling state apparatus grew increasingly alienated. The government's response to this growing problem was to assert even more centralized control. Pakistan's first general elections were due to be held in 1959; concerned about a Bengali victory and demands for real regional autonomy, the military under Ayub Khan conducted a coup d'état in October 1958.

The Military and Ethnic Management, 1958–71

Under military rule, decision-makers were faced with the task of developing government policies that would advance their institutional

---

16. Y.V. Gankovsky and V. N. Moskalenko, *The Three Constitutions of Pakistan* (Lahore: People's Publishing House, 1978), pp. 27, 32–33.

interests, while at the same time neutralizing potential challenges from political rivals. Since the military had now assumed direct control of the state, its corporate interests, as well as its ethnic composition and preferences, determined its policy choices. This was true both of policies specifically adopted to manage ethnic relations, and of those that had more general objectives but nonetheless affected ethnic relations.

Ethnic tensions in Pakistan increased over time, since military rule precluded political participation for those ethnic groups that were underrepresented in the military. Ethnic relations were further damaged by the military's political, social, and economic policies, which discriminated against several ethnic groups, including the majority Bengali population. While the military, using coercion and co-optation, initially succeeded in countering most domestic threats, its policy directions would ultimately and irreparably divide the state.

MILITARY RULE AND ETHNIC POLITICS

Since a major goal of the new government was to legitimize and consolidate its position, it justified the coup d'état by pointing to the threat of political instability—and it subsequently further reinforced the centralized state structure. Although the military asserted complete control over all decision-making, the civil bureaucracy played a crucial role in administering the state; in return, it shared power and the attendant benefits. The military's exercise of absolute power and the implementation of centralized policies of governance had a direct effect on ethnic relations in Pakistan and were, in fact, partly motivated by ethnic factors—particularly the expectations that the Bengali-dominated opposition might win the election and take control of the central government.

The immediate pretext for the coup, however, was the outbreak of a "rebellion" in Baluchistan. Baluch resentment of the center had increased since its territory was forcibly merged into the One Unit system in 1955. Baluch alienation continued to grow as the center neglected the region's economic development while exploiting its natural resources, particularly its natural gas deposits. But without a strong political leadership or any coherent strategies, the Baluchs could not transform their feelings of resentment into concrete action. In early October 1958, however, Baluch opposition to central authority proved a useful ploy to justify the imposition of martial law; the military countered an alleged attempt by the Khan of Kalat to renounce his allegiance to Pakistan.[17]

---

17. A.B. Awan, *Baluchistan: Historical and Political Processes* (London: New Century Publishers, 1985), pp. 222–226. See also Selig S. Harrison, *In Afghanistan's Shadow:*

THE IMPERATIVES OF REGIME SURVIVAL

To manage perceived threats from rival ethnic actors, the Punjabi-Pakhtun-dominated military government retained its ethnically based and discriminatory employment policies, ensuring that the Bengalis remained underrepresented in the armed forces, while other politically suspect communities, including the Baluchs and the Sindhis, were virtually excluded from the military's higher ranks.[18] The government then promoted the institutional and ethnic interests of the military and civil bureaucrats at the expense of these excluded ethnic communities—and it used force to suppress any domestic dissent.

Since coercion failed to subdue opposition and nationalistic rhetoric failed to sustain its legitimacy, the military regime needed a political system that would provide a facade of representative rule and yet consolidate its domestic position. This was the purpose behind the Basic Democracies plan, promulgated in October 1959, which created a five-tier system of local self-government, organized along territorial lines, supposedly aimed at devolving power from the center to the periphery.

The 80,000 Basic Democrats—organized at the levels of the union (covering villages and towns), the district, the division, and the province—were to assist the local administration in such tasks as development work, maintaining law and order, and collecting taxes. But since they were elected indirectly on a non-party basis and lacked any autonomous support base, they merely served to justify authoritarian rule, acting, for example, as the electoral college, electing the army chief president, and selecting nominees to the national and provincial assemblies. Since the Basic Democrats worked under the control and guidance of bureaucrats, they also served, in tandem with the bureaucracy, to sustain the political, social, and economic status quo.[19]

The military also used other structural devices to institutionalize its control, including the 1962 constitution, which created a federal framework that actually consolidated the center's hold over the provinces,

Baluch Nationalism and Soviet Temptation (New York: Carnegie Endowment for International Peace, 1981), pp. 27–28.

18. East Pakistanis constituted less than 5 percent of the officer corps of the army. West Pakistanis held more than 75 percent of all posts above the rank of deputy secretary in the ministries of defense, foreign affairs, finance, and economic affairs. See Statement by parliamentary secretary of defense, *National Assembly of Pakistan (Debates)* (Karachi: Government of Pakistan, June 29, 1968), p. 3266. See also Rehman Sobhan, "East Pakistan's Revolt against Ayub: Old Resentments and New Needs," *Round Table*, No. 1235 (July 1969), p. 303.

19. Khalid B. Sayeed, "Pakistan's Basic Democracy," *Middle East Journal*, Vol. 15, No. 3 (Summer 1961), pp. 250–253.

disallowing any measure of provincial autonomy. Any act by the center was given constitutional protection if judged to be in the "national interest."[20]

The president was given absolute power over the central and provincial assemblies. All bills required his consent; he alone could recommend expenditure and taxation. A unicameral National Assembly, elected on the basis of parity between East and West Pakistan, could only control new expenditure in the national budget. Since the National Assembly operated as a rubber stamp for the presidency, it was, in turn, given the power to override any bill passed by the provincial legislatures and to enforce central legislation over the provinces in vital areas such as security and economic planning.

The president exercised complete authority over provincial administrations since he could appoint and dismiss provincial governors, who controlled the provincial legislatures and were answerable to the president alone. Provincial cabinets were, moreover, responsible to the governors and not to the assemblies, "making regional government . . . an extension of much resented central power."[21]

ECONOMIC POLICY

After a nominally civilian government was formed in 1962, headed by general, and then president, Ayub Khan, policymaking remained in the military's hands, while the civil bureaucracy was given the task of implementing it. Policy formation served to promote the military's corporate interests and those of its predominantly Punjabi ethnic constituency. Not only were the Bengalis, the majority ethnic community, denied participation in policymaking, but the economic policies of the center, which was dominated by the west, worked to their detriment.

Unified economic policies, envisaged through such central agencies as the Central Planning Commission and provincial planning departments and implemented by the bureaucracy, ensured that the east wing became a captive market and the supplier of raw material to the west wing. Foreign exchange earnings from its exports, such as the sale of jute, continued to finance the economic, in particular the industrial, infrastructure of the west wing, increasing the economic disparities between the Bengalis and the West Pakistanis.

In the west wing, central control over finance and developmental expenditures ensured that development efforts benefited Punjab and

20. Omar Noman, *The Political Economy of Pakistan 1947–1985* (New York: KPI, 1988), pp. 30–31.

21. Ibid., p. 31.

Sindh cities, mainly Karachi, while the underdeveloped rural Sindh, Baluchistan, and the Northwest Frontier were ignored. Constant expansion of the Punjabi-dominated military establishment, moreover, hindered socioeconomic development, while it further strengthened the military within the state.[22]

THE DISMEMBERMENT OF PAKISTAN

As ethnic grievances began to mount, the Bengali ethnic leadership, represented by the Awami League (Peoples' League) as well as Pakhtun, Sindhi, and Baluch ethnic groups and parties, issued three demands: regional autonomy, an end to the One Unit system, and the reconstitution of West Pakistan into its previous provinces. Simultaneously, students, professional groups, and opposition parties called for an overthrow of the authoritarian regime. As this opposition grew wider, the military withdrew its support from Ayub, who transferred power in March 1969 to Army Commander in Chief Yahya Khan.

Faced by increased ethnic opposition, the central government appeared to restructure its policies on state-group relations. To meet the demand for regional autonomy, it dissolved the One Unit system and reconstituted the provinces of East Pakistan, Sindh, NWFP, Punjab, and Baluchistan. In response to the demand for democracy, the government agreed to hold national elections; all adult citizens could vote, and political parties could participate without restrictions.

In East Pakistan, the Awami League fought the 1970 election on a six-point manifesto, calling for a radical reform of Pakistan's administrative and economic structures. This included the establishment of a parliamentary and federal polity in which the jurisdiction of the central government would be limited to defense and foreign affairs. Each wing would control its own financial resources, and discriminatory employment policies in the civil-military bureaucracies would be ended. Gaining an absolute majority in the national legislature and the East Pakistan assembly (160 of East Pakistan's 162 National Assembly seats and 288 out of its 300 Provincial Assembly seats), the Awami League won the right to form the central government.[23]

The Pakistan People's Party (PPP), running on a center-left platform, won an absolute majority of seats (81 out of West Pakistan's 148 National

---

22. By fiscal year 1966–67, defense expenditure was 60 percent of total governmental expenditure. See Hasan-Askari Rizvi, "Pakistan's Defense Policy," *Pakistan Horizon*, Vol. 41, No. 1 (First Quarter, 1983), p. 56.

23. Rounaq Jahan, *Pakistan: Failure in National Integration* (New York: Columbia University Press, 1972), p. 90.

Assembly seats) in the west wing as well as a majority of seats in Punjab and Sindh provinces. The NAP, basing its election manifesto on a demand for regional socioeconomic and political autonomy, won a majority in the NWFP provincial polls, and eight out of Baluchistan's fifteen provincial assembly seats.

The response of the central government to these electoral outcomes was influenced by interlinked institutional and ethnic considerations. Transfer of power to an Awami League government was unacceptable: regional autonomy would deprive the military of its claim to a disproportionate share of the state's resources. Such a transfer would also allow the Bengali majority to exercise power over the military's homeland and to alter its internal ethnic balance.

To counter these perceived ethnic threats, the government decided not to honor the electoral results. With the support of Zulfikar Ali Bhutto, whose PPP party had emerged victorious in the west wing, the military first postponed a transfer of power, leading to widespread unrest in the east wing. When disaffection in East Pakistan continued to escalate, the Yahya regime adopted coercive policies, justifying them on the grounds that the Bengali population had opted to secede. When the military tried to forcibly subdue Bengali opposition, leading to hundreds of thousands of casualties, the movement for autonomy became a struggle for secession. Despite the widespread use of force by the Pakistan military, the Bengalis gained their independence, following Pakistan's defeat in the Indo-Pakistan War of December 1971. The state of Pakistan was now cut in two.

Ethnicity in Divided Pakistan, 1971–77

In truncated Pakistan, ethnicity remained a major factor in the internal bargaining for power and resources. While the "issue of parity" was now symbolic, "the principles of autonomy, participation, and distribution were not."[24] The breakup of the state and the transformation in its ethnic composition inevitably affected the directions of ethnic politics and the policy imperatives of its central leadership.

ETHNIC REASSERTION AND POLITICAL CHANGE
The secession of the majority Bengali community meant that the Punjabis, with their preponderant representation in the politically dominant civil and military bureaucracies, became Pakistan's major ethnic group in

---

24. Phandis, *Ethnicity and Nation-Building*, p. 104.

demographic terms. At the same time, ethnic bargaining and negotiation became even more assertive since demands for regional sociocultural, political, and economic autonomy had been an essential component of the popular movement that had led to the most recent confrontation with state authorities.

The military's defeat in the 1971 war transformed the government's decision-making processes, as power was transferred to civilian leadership under President Zulfikar Ali Bhutto. For the new civilian administration, ethnic issues became an area of concern as it attempted to strengthen its base of support by reformulating government policies and priorities. Under Bhutto, himself an ethnic Sindhi, the central government adopted a comprehensive ethnic policy package, which included structural mechanisms to cope with ethnic pluralism and distributive, preferential policies specifically targeted at excluded ethnic groups.[25]

CONSTITUTIONAL REFORMS AND REGIONAL AUTONOMY. The new constitution adopted in 1973 included a federal parliamentary framework and provisions for regional autonomy. This structure was devised by candidates elected to the National Assembly from all West Pakistani provinces in 1970, thus marking a departure from past practices. The constitution, therefore, ensured a greater degree of devolution of power to the regions than in the past.

In the bicameral federal legislature, all provinces had equal representation in the upper house, the Senate. The Senate, however, actually had less authority than the National Assembly, whose bills it could not reject. The federal legislature was responsible for all areas covered by the federal legislative list, and the provinces could legislate on areas included in the concurrent list such as education, agriculture, irrigation, and police. All funding bills, however, remained the preserve of the lower house.[26]

Although provincial governors were appointed by the president, they were made subservient to their chief ministers in certain areas, including the promulgation and implementation of provincial legislation. A Council of Common Interests and a National Finance Commission were formed, each composed of representatives of the federation and the provinces, to provide policy directions on specific areas of legislation, including the allocation of resources, the provision of revenues from the center to the provinces, and the arbitration of interprovincial and center-state disputes.

25. Shahid Javed Burki, *Pakistan under Bhutto, 1971–1977* (London: Macmillan, 1980), p. 80.

26. Hayes, *Politics in Pakistan*, p. 76.

Federal revenues from locally generated resources such as gas and hydro-electric power were to be provided to their province of origin.[27]

Although the 1973 constitution enhanced provincial autonomy, it still provided considerable authority to the center. Many areas of governance remained on the federal legislative list as the responsibilities of the federal parliament. They included external finance, interprovincial trade, energy, commerce, transportation and communications, public welfare, development, foreign affairs, and defense. Provincial legislation could be declared void by the federal parliament, and the prime minister retained substantial power.[28]

LANGUAGE AND AFFIRMATIVE ACTION POLICIES.　The Bhutto government did acknowledge the existence of some long-standing ethnic, social, and economic grievances. First, it recognized linguistic pluralism, departing from earlier language policy by allowing provinces to use provincial languages for official business. Through the 1972 language bill, the PPP majority in the Sindh assembly, therefore, recognized Sindhi as an official language of the province; this was amended a year later to include Urdu, the national language of Pakistan.

The central government also promised to provide employment opportunities in the public sector and in the central and provincial bureaucracies to all ethnic groups, restoring regional quotas based on demographic distribution. In the federal quota, 50 percent of government jobs were reserved for people from Punjab, 11.5 percent for those from the NWFP, and 3.5 percent for those from Baluchistan; their respective populations in 1973 were 56 percent, 14 percent, and 3 percent of the total.[29]

Affirmative action policies were created to give underrepresented and economically backward ethnic groups better access to employment and educational facilities; quotas were set for rural areas. To reduce the sociocultural disparities and economic inequities between the privileged Muhajir-speaking urban areas and the Sindhi-populated rural regions, for example, the regional quota for state employment and for admission to state-run education institutions was based on rural-urban demarcations. The federal quota for employment was 11.4 percent for rural Sindh and

27.　Kamal Azfar, "Constitutional Dilemmas in Pakistan," in Shahid Javed Burki and Craig Baxter, eds., *Pakistan under the Military: Eleven Years of Zia ul-Haq* (Boulder, Colo.: Westview Press, 1991), pp. 66–67.

28.　Gankovsky and Moskalenko, *The Three Constitutions*, pp. 140–141.

29.　Charles H. Kennedy, "Ethnic Preference in Pakistan," *Asian Survey*, Vol. 24, No. 6 (June 1984), p. 693.

7.6 percent for urban Sindh; Sindh's population in 1973 was approximately 26 percent of the total.[30]

INSTITUTIONAL IMPEDIMENTS AND POLITICAL CONSTRAINTS

While these policies were meant to redress ethnic demands and grievances, their implementation sometimes led to increased tensions in both inter-group and state-group relations. For example, the Muhajir population, which hitherto had benefited from state political and economic patronage,[31] saw the quota policy for rural Sindh as an attempt by a Sindhi prime minister to empower his ethnic constituency at their expense. The change in language policy in Sindh also led to widespread Muhajir opposition, resulting in clashes with provincial government authorities.[32]

The quota system assumed even greater importance when the government began nationalizing assets in the private sector, enhancing the state's role as an employer. The nationalization process created anti-government sentiments among the business and industrial communities, which had benefited from preferential state policies. The central government's ethnic policies and administrative reforms also alienated the Punjabi-dominated civil bureaucracy; they were now under the control of an elected political leadership, and they watched hitherto excluded ethnic groups assume a more prominent place in policy circles.[33]

The prime minister did not attempt to challenge the ethnic-based recruitment policies of the military, aware of the considerable power the armed forces retained even after the transfer of power to civil hands. Even so, the Punjabi-dominated military was distrustful of a Sindhi prime minister, suspicious of civilian politicians in general, and disinclined towards any decentralization of power, which would threaten its institutional interests. The opposition of both the civil and military bureaucracies was to pose impediments to the proposed restructuring of state-group relations.

RESISTANCE AND REPRESSION

Facing a dual challenge—bureaucratic resistance and ethnic assertiveness—the government had only one way to strengthen its position: meet the

---

30. Ibid.

31. In 1973, Sindhis were only 2.7 percent of civil service employees, while Muhajir representation was 33.5 percent.

32. Feroz Ahmed, "Pakistan's Problems of National Integration," in Mohammad Asghar Khan, ed., *Islam, Politics and the State: The Pakistan Experience* (London: Zed Press, 1985), p. 39.

33. Noman, *Political Economy of Pakistan*, pp. 62–63.

demands of its constituents for political, social, and economic change, and defuse ethnic tensions by implementing constitutional provisions for regional autonomy. It chose not to. The PPP government confined its economic policies to rhetoric, failing to institutionalize redistributive measures at the local, regional, or national levels, thereby undermining its political legitimacy.

Moreover, mistrustful of opposition, Bhutto tended to use coercive and manipulative policies to contain perceived political threats; he increased central control over those provinces where the ruling party had little presence. In the resource-rich but economically underdeveloped provinces of the NWFP and Baluchistan, where provincial legislatures contained very few PPP representatives, predominantly Pakhtun and Baluch NAP and Jamiat-i-Ulema-Islam (JUI [Religious Scholars of Islam]) opposition coalition governments had been formed.[34] Soon after, differences emerged between the center and the NWFP and Baluchistan provincial administrations. In the NWFP, the clash took place when the centrally appointed governor attempted to intervene in the affairs of the provincial legislature.

Within multiethnic Baluchistan, state policies had led to the development of non-Baluch, predominantly Pakhtun areas, increasing interethnic socioeconomic disparities. Baluch participation in the central and provincial decision-making apparatus was minimal, while the center had exploited the province's natural resources in return for a meager royalty. When the NAP-JUI coalition in Baluchistan attempted to exercise the autonomy provided by the 1973 constitution, the center resisted.[35] The central government dismissed both the Baluchistan and NWFP provincial governments; it banned the NAP on national security grounds and created pliant provincial administrations.

The dismissal of the elected provincial governments further angered ethnic groups, particularly in Baluchistan. Opting for force rather than negotiation, the center decided to use the military to curb dissent, leading to a full-scale insurgency. Many Baluch dissidents were arrested and imprisoned; others were forced into exile in neighboring Afghanistan. As military operations continued, the Bhutto government's democratic credentials eroded. The military regained its earlier political dominance as it assumed virtual control over the political arena in Baluchistan.

In a 1974 attempt to neutralize its religious opponents, the PPP-dominated center had passed a constitutional amendment that declared

---

34. The PPP had only 3 seats in the 40-member NWFP provincial assembly and none in Baluchistan's 20-member provincial legislature.

35. Ziring, *Pakistan: The Enigma*, p. 164.

the Ahmediyas, a small Sunni religious sect, to be a non-Muslim minority. As opposition to the PPP government became more widespread and assertive by 1977, the center attempted, unsuccessfully, to retain control, on the one hand, making additional concessions to the clergy, and on the other hand, passing more constitutional amendments, which eroded such political rights and liberties as freedom of the press. The government's control slipped further after the 1977 national elections: anti-Bhutto forces disputed the result, claiming election fraud.

In the cities, this coalition of opposition forces, which included business interests and the clergy, conducted anti-government protests, forcing Bhutto to rely even more on the military to retain power. Taking advantage of mounting political unrest, the military conducted a coup d'état in July 1977, deposing the Bhutto government and once again regaining direct control of the state.

Ethnic Conflict and Authoritarian Rule, 1977–88

Once again under military rule, the government formulated and implemented a range of policies to promote its own corporate interests. The overall crisis of regime legitimacy, arising from the dissolution of an elected government and, soon after, the arrest and trial for murder of the elected prime minister, played an equally important role in determining the directions of government policy with respect to ethnic issues.

REGIME LEGITIMACY AND ETHNIC POLICY

Legitimacy problems led the government to centralize power in a variety of ways. The new regime completely transformed the existing constitutional and legal frameworks; the 1973 constitution was held in abeyance. Supreme local authority was vested in the military itself, with the promulgation of the Continuation in Force Order and the Provisional Constitutional Order of March 1981. These laws rendered redundant the entire federal framework, including all provisions for regional autonomy. All policy flowed from the center, fundamental rights were undermined by arbitrary checks on the powers of the judiciary, political parties were banned, and all avenues of political representation and discourse were closed.[36]

The military government, in alliance with the civil bureaucracy, dictated the sociopolitical, cultural, and economic policies of the provinces.

---

36.   C.G.P. Rakisits, "Center-Province Relations in Pakistan under President Zia: The Government's and the Opposition's Approaches," *Pacific Affairs*, Vol. 61, No. 1 (July 1988), p. 78.

It consolidated its control over the economy, continuing to claim a disproportionate share of the revenues from both the provinces and abroad, mainly to finance the Punjabi-dominated state apparatus.[37] The resultant uneven economic development perpetuated socioeconomic disparities between dominant and peripheral ethnic communities.

Government policy had equal relevance for ethnic dynamics in the social and cultural fields. Urgently needing legitimacy, the regime attempted to defuse domestic opposition and to justify the takeover on national security grounds. As a part of this effort, official rhetoric emphasized "national interests," depicting ethno-regional identities as inimical to the unity of the state.

The regime also tried to create a "national" identity based on the two-nations theory and the Islamic *Ummah* (universal nation) to submerge sub-state loyalties based on territorial, linguistic, and other ethnic markers. General Zia-ul-Haq claimed, for example, that Pakistan was distinct from other countries because its "basic idea was Muslim nationhood."[38]

In a related attempt to attain legitimacy, the regime embarked on a policy of "Islamizing" Pakistan, claiming that its main policy objective was to create an Islamic order. Hence, it devised new legal institutions based on the Sunni code and created institutional mechanisms such as Shari'a (Islamic law) courts to enforce Islamic legislation. The dominance of the Sunni legal code marginalized and excluded minority ethnic groups such as the 20 percent Shi'ite population, as well as Christians, Hindus, and Ahmediyas.

Structural mechanisms to consolidate military rule included the penetration of Pakistani society. While political parties were banned, Ayub Khan's Basic Democracies were revived in the form of local government institutions called "local bodies." Elected on a non-party basis, local body representatives reinforced the military regime's presence at the local level in return for political and economic patronage. Financial resources were provided to these institutions, ostensibly for local development activities, but they also created a base of support for their representatives.[39] Other new institutions included the *Majlis-i-Shura*, a federal advisory body, formed to divide the base of support of the political parties and thereby to strengthen the military's position.

---

37. The central budget, which depended on revenues generated by the provinces, increased 1.8 times more than provincial expenditures between 1950–51 and 1980–81. See Reetz, "National Consolidation," p. 137, n. 6.

38. Zia is quoted in ibid., pp. 133–134.

39. Robert LaPorte, Jr., "Administrative Restructuring during the Zia Period," in Burki and Baxter, *Pakistan under the Military*, pp. 125–126.

While the military made most policy decisions, it allowed the civil bureaucracy to play a role in policy formulation with respect to the economy. This "use of civil officers as both policy makers [and] administrators"[40] advanced the interests of Punjab, the ethnic base of the country's leaders. Other ethnic communities felt increasingly exploited and alienated, given the absence of provincial autonomy and the consolidation of authoritarian policies of governance.

THE MANAGEMENT OF ETHNIC PROBLEMS

In the provinces of Baluchistan and the NWFP, the military managed to contain ethnic dissent by adopting strategies based on co-optation and coercion. In Baluchistan, for example, military operations were ended, Baluch insurgents pardoned, and important ethnic leaders co-opted in return for state patronage, including access to substantively increased developmental funds. At the same time, the extension of communications networks across the province made it easier for the military to forcibly contain the ethnic assertion of Baluch nationalist parties and groups such as the Baluch Students Organization and the Pakistan National Party.

The use of force and the co-optation of ethnic leaders also led to a semblance of political stability in the NWFP. By the mid-1980s, however, ethnic agitation increased as Pakhtun-dominated parties, such as the Awami National Party (NAP's successor) called for regional autonomy and representative rule.

ETHNIC MANIPULATION. Government policies to manage ethnic relations proved to be least effective in Sindh. By the mid-1980s, Sindhi ethnicity had become highly politicized. Tensions between the Sindhis and Muhajirs had increased considerably over the decades, as centrally determined economic policies had consistently favored the development of Sindh's cities, dominated by the Muhajirs and Punjabis. Moreover, an influx of Punjab and Pakhtun migrant workers, as well as Muhajir refugees from the former East Pakistan, further changed the province's demographic balance to the disadvantage of the Sindhis.

Bhutto's Sindhi ethnic identity, his populist rhetoric, and his regime's affirmative action policies had helped to defuse Sindhi feelings of alienation. After the military takeover in 1977, however, representative institutions, which had provided avenues for ethnic bargaining and participation, were dismantled, and an ethnically Punjabi military had deposed and executed an elected Sindhi prime minister. The strongest opposition to military rule was, therefore, to come from rural Sindh, mainly from

40. Ibid., pp. 128–129.

PPP supporters, but also from several Sindhi nationalist parties, such as the Sindhi Awami Tehrik (Sindhi Peoples' Movement).

As Sindhi dissent spread, the military launched anti-insurgency operations in the Sindhi countryside; hundreds were killed and thousands were arrested and tried by summary military courts, run by military administrators. When force alone did not contain Sindhi dissent or weaken the PPP's base, the military adopted discriminatory policies aimed at excluding the politically suspect Sindhis from the state apparatus. Although regional quotas were formally retained, Sindhi bureaucrats were dismissed from their positions. Preferential quotas were also devised to employ military personnel in the civil bureaucracy and public sector enterprises; this benefited Punjabis and Pakhtuns.[41]

Meanwhile, the regime used divide-and-rule strategies, manipulating both inter-Sindhi differences and Muhajir-Sindhi tensions, to neutralize Sindhi and PPP opposition. Informal alliances were made with the PPP's Sindhi rivals, including some Sindhi ethno-nationalist parties, such as Jiyee Sind (Long Live Sindh). The military regime, moreover, actively supported the urban-based Muhajirs in forming their first specifically ethnic political party, the Muhajir Qaumi Movement (MQM [Muhajir National Movement]) in 1986.[42]

Central and provincial military administrators then used the MQM against the Sindhi opposition. This led to violent interethnic conflict, which first occurred between the Muhajirs and Pakhtuns competing for jobs and for the control of the lucrative arms and narcotics trade, especially in the provincial capital, Karachi. It then took the shape of widespread Muhajir-Sindhi conflict, particularly in the Muhajir-dominated urban areas of the province.

REFUGEE PROBLEMS.   The Zia regime's foreign policy initiatives undercut Pakistan's political stability in general, and ethnic relations in particular. The regime's intervention in the Afghan civil war provided it with considerable moral and material support from abroad, which helped it consolidate its domestic hold.[43] However, by letting Pakistani territory serve

---

41.   Sindhi representation in the federal government and its departments amounted to less than 4 percent of the total during the Zia years. See Shahid Kardar, *The Political Economy of Pakistan* (Lahore: Progressive Publishers, 1987), pp. 41, 43.

42.   The MQM demanded the recognition of the Muhajirs as the fifth nationality of Pakistan and called for a revision of existing quotas for employment in Sindh and the center in favor of the Muhajirs.

43.   Assistance from the United States alone was worth over $4 billion.

as a pipeline for the supply of arms to Afghan insurgents, the government undermined its domestic monopoly over the use of violence, providing easy access to sophisticated arms to sub-state, including ethnic, actors. Moreover, the narcotics trade, which helped to fund the Afghan civil war, soon penetrated Pakistan's economy and contributed to the criminalization of Pakistani politics.[44]

The influx of millions of Afghan, mainly Pashtun, refugees into the NWFP and Baluchistan had important ramifications for ethnic relations in Pakistan. Since the regime's refugee policy permitted the Afghans free movement and access to employment in Pakistan, the refugee influx in the NWFP led to tensions between locals and refugees over resources and work. In Baluchistan, the refugee presence not only depleted its scarce resources, but also changed the demographic balance of its Baluch-Pakhtun population to the detriment of the Baluchs.

DIVIDE-AND-RULE POLICIES

Although coercion and co-optation kept the military in power, it still had to attain at least some degree of domestic legitimacy to survive in the long term. Hence, it tried to create a civilian facade. Although the "civilianization" strategies of the central government were not aimed primarily at the management of ethnic relations, they had a considerable impact on state-group relations.

THE SECTARIAN CARD. As mentioned earlier, the military regime had attempted to acquire legitimacy and to counter its political opposition by claiming to "Islamize" the state, establishing close links with Sunni politico-religious parties, such as the Jamaat-i-Islami as well as Sunni *madrasses* (theological academies and schools).[45] State patronage included posts in the central cabinet for the Jamaat-i-Islami, the provision of *Zakat* funds (a religious tax) to Sunni religious trusts and schools, and the creation of a parallel legal structure, through Shari'a courts, which provided Sunni clerics with juridical powers.

These policies increased the bargaining power of Sunni religious parties with respect to their secular counterparts. State patronage fueled Sunni religious extremism, resulting in the creation of new, militant

---

44. Shahid Javed Burki, "The Management of Crises," in William E. James and Subroto Roy, eds., *Foundations of Pakistan's Political Economy: Towards an Agenda for the 1990s* (New Delhi: Sage Publications, 1992), pp. 127–128.

45. Lawrence Ziring, "Public Policy Dilemmas and Pakistan's Nationality Problem: The Legacy of Zia," *Asian Survey*, Vol. 28, No. 8 (August 1988), p. 807.

religious parties, such as the Sipah-i-Sahaba (Soldiers of the Sahara [Companions of the Prophet]). Sectarian tensions also increased as the Shi'ite minority strongly rejected state sponsorship of its religious rivals. Shi'ite alienation led to the formation of Shi'ite sectarian parties, such as the Tehrik-i-Nifaz-e-Fiqah-i-Jafaria (Movement for the Enforcement of the Shi'ite Shari'a).[46] Sectarian tensions soon escalated into violent conflict because sophisticated arms were readily available as a result of Pakistan's involvement in the Afghan war.

PARTYLESS POLITICS.   The government's policy of ostensibly devolving power to the local level through the creation of non-party local bodies had also been an effort to counter its political opposition by bypassing the political party system and co-opting some political and socioeconomic elites. But this state-directed penetration of local politics, in the absence of functioning representative institutions, only increased ethnic tensions as ethnicity gained salience in the competition for power. The predominantly Punjabi nature of the ruling regime, as well as its deliberate manipulation of ethnic tensions, including Muhajir-Sindhi differences, further exacerbated ethnic tensions. Thus state-group conflict was extended to all arenas of political interaction at the federal, regional, and local levels.

In March 1985, through the eighth amendment to the 1973 constitution and the Revival of the Constitution Order of March 1985, power was ostensibly transferred to civilian hands following non-party elections of a prime minister and national and provincial assemblies. In fact, the eighth amendment provided constitutional sanction for the military regime and distorted the constitution to enhance the powers of the president—the military dictator himself—at the expense of the prime minister and the parliament. The creation of a system of separate electorates also had direct relevance for ethnic relations: it deprived non-Muslims of the right to vote for general seats.

These attempts to create alternative structures of governance failed to legitimize military rule. In addition, the formation of even a nominal civilian government led to more demands for genuine representative institutions. The main opposition coalition, the eleven-party Movement for the Restoration of Democracy, wanted to replace the 1973 constitution's formula for center-province relations with a system that would allow more regional autonomy; this system would leave only currency,

46.   Abbas Rashid, "Pakistan: The Politics of 'Fundamentalism,'" in Kumar Rupesinghe and Khawar Mumtaz, eds., *Internal Conflicts in South Asia* (London: Sage Publications, 1996), pp. 69–70.

communications, defense, and foreign policy with the center.[47] Even as demands to restore democracy began to gain momentum across the country, President Zia-ul-Haq and several of his senior commanders were killed in a plane crash on August 11, 1988.

Continuity and Change, 1988–97

President Zia's death appeared to transform Pakistani politics. The military subsequently agreed to transfer power, and general elections were held in 1989, leading to a PPP victory under Benazir Bhutto's leadership and thereafter to her appointment as prime minister.

The military had, in fact, opted for a strategic withdrawal: it recognized that trying to prolong direct rule would generate widespread civilian resistance.[48] It therefore set a condition on the transfer of power: the new civilian government would accept the military's "guidance" in policy formation, especially in sensitive areas such as foreign policy, defense, and the economy.[49] While these general policy areas were relevant to ethnic relations, the military's dominance over policymaking also extended to specific policies regarding ethnic management.

CIVIL RULE AND MILITARY CONTROL

The Bhutto government was not inclined to restructure Pakistan's political system for fear of alienating the military. Moreover, it faced a strong opposition, under Nawaz Sharif, who headed the Islami Jamhoori Ittihad (IJI [Islamic Democratic Alliance]), a nine-party coalition that was created with the assistance of the military.[50] Hence, the PPP failed, for example, to repeal the eighth amendment, which had distorted the domestic balance of power between the prime minister and the president.

Provinces continued to have little autonomy because the center continued to control political power, economic resources, and revenues. This continued reliance on centralized decision-making was, in itself, an indicator of the directions of policymaking: defense spending and the interests of the dominant ethnic groups took precedence over the rights of the

---

47. Reetz, "National Consolidation," p. 135, n. 6.

48. Hasan-Askari Rizvi, "The Military and Politics in Pakistan," in Charles H. Kennedy and David Loucher, eds., *Civil-Military Interaction in Asia and Africa* (Leiden: E.J. Brill, 1991), p. 29.

49. William L. Richter, "Pakistan under Benazir Bhutto," *Current History*, Vol. 88, No. 542 (December 1989), p. 451.

50. Mushahid Hussain and Akmal Hussain, *Pakistan: Problems of Governance* (New Delhi: Kornak Publishers, Center for Policy Research, 1993), pp. 101, 104.

provinces to control surpluses generated within their territories.[51] Defense expenditures continued to rise, continuing to hamper socioeconomic development and redistribution and further strengthening the Punjabi-dominated military's position.[52] As the elected civilian leadership failed to implement its pledges for distributive justice, its legitimacy eroded.

The military continued to dominate the formation of Pakistan's foreign policy, and the government's interventionist policy toward Afghanistan therefore continued. This policy further damaged ethnic relations in Baluchistan: the Pakhtun population saw the Afghan refugee presence as a means of strengthening its claim to political power and access to resources; the Baluchs saw it as a threat to their ethnic interests.

The Bhutto government faced conflicting pressures: it had to meet the demands of its constituents without acquiescing completely to the military's policy preferences. The elected civilian leadership was obliged, for example, to provide at least some political and economic benefits to its Sindhi constituency, which had faced the brunt of military rule. But the PPP's slim majority in the national polls had forced it to rely on the support of other parties, including the MQM, to form the federal government; its coalition with the MQM in Sindh was an uneasy alliance in view of Muhajir-Sindhi ethnic tensions.[53] Moreover, the Punjab provincial government, which had historically decided the fate of federal governments, was under the control of the IJI, the military's political allies, and it openly defied the directives of the Bhutto administration.

Faced with multiple constraints on its exercise of power, the PPP generally tried to maintain the status quo. To placate its Sindhi constituency, the government increased Sindhi employment in the federal bureaucracy and state-owned enterprises—actions that the Muhajirs saw as discriminatory. Ethnic relations in Sindh were also damaged when the PPP could not meet several MQM demands, which had earlier been agreed upon in return for MQM support in the national parliament.[54]

---

51. Although Baluchistan, for example, receives royalties on its gas reserves, the percentage is fixed by the center and remains minimal, while its energy resources are used to promote the industrial growth of urban Sindh and Punjab.

52. Defense spending was 7.1 percent of the gross national product in 1990, up from 6.5 percent in 1989. See *World Military Expenditures and Arms Transfers 1991–1992* (Washington, D.C.: U.S. Arms Control and Disarmament Agency, 1994), pp. 7–8.

53. PPP and MQM victories in both the national and provincial assembly elections in Sindh ran along ethnic lines: the PPP won in rural Sindh and the MQM in all urban constituencies.

54. These demands included the repatriation of Muhajirs from Bangladesh and the establishment of Sindhi and Muhajir quotas for civil service employment. See Zahid Hussain, "Sindh: A Province Held to Ransom," *Newsline*, August 1989, p. 18.

Distrustful of the PPP and the Sindhis, the military high command decided in 1989 to exploit the rise in Muhajir-Sindhi tensions in order to destabilize the PPP government. With the military's active involvement, the MQM dissolved its coalition with the PPP and began to violently oppose the government's authority, especially in the urban areas of Sindh. In Karachi and Hyderabad, for example, law and order broke down completely. The military then supported the creation of an alliance between the MQM and the IJI opposition, which challenged the PPP both in the center and in the provinces of Sindh and Punjab.

Limited by a hostile military and an assertive ethnic opposition, the PPP government had little latitude to respond to these challenges. Nor was it in a position to contain Muhajir violence in Sindh without the military's support. In August 1990, the deteriorating situation in Sindh enabled the military high command to remove the PPP government, invoking the clauses of the amended 1973 constitution that empowered the president to dismiss the central legislature and executive.

ETHNIC POLICIES AND THE IJI

Elections were held once again in October 1990. Guided and supported by the military, the IJI won the rigged elections, forming not just the central government but also all four provincial governments. Ethnicity was bound to play a greater role in governmental policy since the IJI had a Punjabi leadership and the support of the Punjabi-dominated army, which had helped remove an elected government headed by a Sindhi prime minister.[55]

Since the IJI leadership, like its predecessor, depended on the military to stay in power, no radical policy changes were made to confront the country's ethnic problems. Given its Punjabi ethnic base, the IJI leadership preferred amalgamative policies; it was also disinclined to adopt any policy that could be perceived as damaging the military's institutional interests. The myth of regional economic autonomy was maintained, for example, while the resources of the provinces were again used to meet the central government's needs, including rising defense expenditures.

Faced by growing ethnic tensions, however, the central government had to appear to be responsive to ethnic problems, while in fact maintaining the status quo. In formulating its economic policy, therefore, it held negotiations, ostensibly to gain the assent of the smaller provinces

---

55. Over 65 percent of the officer corps was of Punjabi origin, rising to over 70 percent in the high command. Sindhis had virtually no representation in the military's higher ranks. See Charles H. Kennedy, "The Politics of Ethnicity in Sindh," *Asian Survey*, Vol. 31, No. 10 (October 1991), p. 946.

on the distribution of central funds and provincial revenues. But the provinces got no more control over governmental revenues than before, nor was the center's budget increased to meet local or regional demands for greater social spending.

This continuity extended to other areas of ethnic policy. Preferential devices such as the quota system for employment were retained but were distorted in their implementation. In Baluchistan, as in Sindh, the quota system was used for recruitment to the civil bureaucracy, but many posts were held by Punjabis or Muhajirs, who moved there to work.[56] In the central bureaucracy, political loyalties took precedence over preferential quotas; in the military, Sindhis and Baluchs continued to be excluded or underrepresented.

Like its military sponsors, the IJI also tended to adopt policies based on co-optation or coercion and to use religion as a legitimizing tool. These policy directions had both an indirect and a direct impact on the management of ethnic relations. The formation of political alliances with Sunni orthodox parties such as the Jamaat-i-Islami increased Sunni-Shi'ite tensions, leading to sporadic outbreaks of sectarian violence. The reinforcement of Islamic legislation, including an amended blasphemy law, severely undermined the security of the minority Christian community.

ETHNIC PROBLEMS IN SINDH

Trouble continued to brew in Sindh. Although the PPP had won a majority of seats in the Sindh provincial assembly, the IJI had formed the Sindh provincial government in alliance with the MQM, intensifying Sindhi alienation. The federal government and the IJI-MQM provincial administration decided to use the Punjabi-dominated security agencies to suppress Sindhi dissent, with the active support and involvement of the military.[57] Hence, military operations were conducted in rural Sindh with the cooperation of the provincial government, headed by co-opted Sindhi leaders such as Chief Minister Jam Sadiq Ali. These operations were justified on familiar national security grounds.[58]

Despite a common ethnic base, similar political perceptions, and a history of close relations, the IJI government was to lose the military's support. As Benazir Bhutto had learned only too well, the civil leadership could not ignore the imperatives of its own domestic constituency. Nor

---

56. Kardar, *Political Economy of Pakistan*, p. 41.

57. In Sindh, for example, the police force is predominantly Punjabi, while paramilitary forces deployed in the province, such as the Rangers, are Pakhtun or Punjabis.

58. Zahid Hussain, "Jam's Sindh," *Newsline*, March 1991, p. 21.

could it resist the temptation to adopt a more assertive role, resulting in a military backlash. The breaking point came when the IJI's coalition partner in Sindh, the MQM leader Altaf Hussain, also attempted to operate independently of his erstwhile military mentors. The military high command subsequently turned its operations against the MQM in urban Sindh.

The MQM-IJI provincial government collapsed when the MQM withdrew from the alliance in June 1992. Employing divide-and-rule tactics, the military then proceeded to create and promote a faction within the MQM, the MQM (Haqiqi), leading to unrest among the Muhajirs. When widespread civil unrest engulfed Sindh's cities, the military called on the president to dismiss the prime minister; the president complied. When the Supreme Court interceded on behalf of the federal government, the military forced both the president and the prime minister to resign in July 1993, bringing an end to the IJI government.

POLICY DIRECTIONS

After a brief interlude, during which technocrats under Prime Minister Moeen Qureshi ran a shadow military government, the PPP won a slim majority in the October 1993 elections and once again formed a government. Since its return to power depended on the military's goodwill, the new central government was even more cautious, ensuring that all of its policies suited the military's institutional interests.[59]

THE POWER-SHARING PROBLEM. The civilian government's willing acceptance of the military's dictates, combined with its own need to contain multiple domestic threats, had a considerable impact on state-group relations and ethnic dynamics in Pakistan in the 1990s. Since survival was its top priority, the government tended to tread lightly in formulating policies in areas of particular sensitivity to the military, regardless of their impact on the country's ethnic problems.

For example, in setting policy with regard to the Afghan civil war, the Bhutto administration abdicated its policymaking responsibilities to military leaders, particularly from the Inter-Services Intelligence Agency. With little government control over the military's interventionist policy, the Afghan civil war continued, retarding the repatriation of Afghan refugees from the NWFP and Baluchistan. The large numbers of Afghan Pashtuns in these provinces created problems; with the support of their Pakistani ethnic kin, they intensified Baluch-Pakhtun tensions. The

---

59. Maleeha Lodhi, *Pakistan's Encounter with Democracy* (Lahore: Vanguard, 1994), p. 298.

Baluchistan provincial government strongly opposed holding the long overdue national census until the Afghan refugees were repatriated from its territory. In the deteriorating economic climate of the NWFP, tensions between locals and refugees continued to increase.

In the domestic domain, too, the federal government pursued highly centralized administrative and economic policies favored by the powerful civil-military bureaucracies. Believing that no elected government could survive without the military's tacit support, the federal government attempted to defuse potential conflict by constantly increasing defense expenditures.[60]

The civil bureaucracy's support was also important for any elected government because it played a vital role in manipulating local and regional politics to either strengthen or undermine central governments. Although the PPP succeeded in forming provincial governments, initially in Sindh and Punjab, then in the NWFP, its position remained uncertain because of constant pressure from the opposition. Hence, it depended more and more on the central and provincial bureaucracies, enhancing the influence and power of the bureaucratic leadership.

CENTRALIZED CONTROL AND ETHNO-REGIONAL PRESSURES. To meet the needs of the civil-military bureaucracies and to assert and consolidate central control, policies were put in place that continued to erode provincial autonomy. Economic policymaking remained the preserve of the federal government, which collected most revenues. Federal agencies such as the Planning Commission and federal departments, including the Ministry of Finance, reviewed the annual development programs of provincial governments and were ultimately responsible for directing the economic policies that affected them. The provinces, therefore, remained dependent on the center for developmental funds since they had little control over the use of their domestically generated revenues.[61]

The government's failure to respond to demands for regional autonomy led to ethnic agitation, particularly in Baluchistan, the least developed of the four provinces, and in Sindh, where state-group tensions were most acute. In the Baluchistan provincial assembly, for example, both ruling and opposition members of parliament demanded more regional autonomy, particularly in the economic sphere, strongly criticizing the

60. In the federal budget for fiscal year 1996–97, the allocation for defense was 131 billion rupees, up from 110 billion rupees in 1995 and 101 billion rupees for 1994. See *The Muslim*, June 10, 1996; and *The Nation*, June 21, 1996.

61. Robert LaPorte, Jr., "Administration," in James and Roy, *Foundations of Pakistan's Political Economy*, pp. 108–109.

center's interference in Baluchistan's provincial affairs and calling on the president to intervene to ensure that the province obtained its rightful share of federally allocated funds.[62]

Baluchistan's grievances against the center were reflected, to some extent, by leaders in all the smaller provinces. Although the NWFP and Sindh had PPP-dominated provincial governments, their leaders understood the imperative of retaining the support of their domestic constituents. This impelled them, for example, to reject the federal government's proposal to build the Kalabagh Dam because it would displace many people in the NWFP, inundate valuable agricultural land, and increase Punjab's access to water at a high cost to Sindh.

The intensity of ethno-regional tensions in Pakistan was also reflected in the center's failure to obtain a consensus from all four provinces on the allocation of federal resources for the National Finance Commission award in April 1996. The three smaller provinces demanded that 90 percent of the funds from the federal tax pool should be allocated on the basis of population, and the remaining 10 percent should go to ameliorate regional backwardness and income disparities, but the Punjab provincial government disagreed.[63] Acknowledging that previous awards were based on "narrow-minded provincialism," Prime Minister Bhutto agreed to redress the grievances of the smaller provinces, but at the cost of a potentially dangerous Punjabi backlash.[64]

PARTICIPATORY PRACTICES AND COERCIVE STRATEGIES. The potential for confrontation between the federal government and the provincial governments of Baluchistan and the NWFP was blunted by the presence of representative institutions and forums for ethnic bargaining and negotiation. In Baluchistan, Baluch-Pakhtun ethnic tensions, aggravated by the presence of Afghan refugees, strengthened ethno-nationalist parties in both communities. The presence of an elected leadership and representative institutions, however, helped to contain ethnic tensions and to establish a working relationship with the center.

---

62. The Baluchistan provincial government and legislature also opposed the proposed sale of government shares in Pakistan Petroleum Limited because the sale would deprive the province of its main source of revenue, the development surcharge on natural gas. Criticizing the "colonial stance" of the federal government, the Baluchistan chief minister said that the center "considers Baluchistan its colony" and "had been plundering its resources for the past twenty four years." See *The Nation*, June 3, 1996; *The News*, June 14, 1996; and *Dawn*, June 14, 1996.

63. *Dawn*, April 20, 1996.

64. *Dawn*, June 17, 1996.

In the NWFP, the mainstream Pakhtun party, the Awami National Party, entered into an opposition alliance with the Punjabi-dominated Muslim League, showing more interest in attaining the benefits of power through the parliamentary process than in promoting its earlier ethnonationalist agenda. Any lingering sympathy for Pakhtun secessionism had dissipated in the wake of tensions between local Pakhtuns and their Afghan ethnic kin.

However, the situation was different in urban Sindh, where ethnic tensions remained high. Muhajirs in Sindh believed that the military deliberately stopped them from running in the 1993 federal elections, thereby costing them an opportunity to gain a place in the national legislature. Muhajir alienation was further fueled by the center's use of force to quell Muhajir dissent. Not only did the PPP federal and Sindh governments continue to rely on coercion rather than negotiation, but the military continued to oversee, monitor, and direct ethnic policies in the province. Having failed in its direct assault against the MQM, the military withdrew tactically, but it retained its control over anti-MQM operations through a paramilitary apparatus, the Rangers, deployed under a major general of the Pakistan army.

The centrally controlled Sindh government, with the military's support, tried to eliminate MQM hard-liners and create a more pliable Muhajir leadership. As a part of this strategy, many MQM legislators were arrested, forcing others to go underground. Meanwhile, internecine Muhajir conflict assumed serious dimensions in Sindh's urban centers. Nearly 2,000 people were injured in ethnic violence in Sindh in 1995; 15,000 have been killed since the mid-1980s.[65]

Since the MQM continued to rely on violence and civil disobedience, including frequent labor strikes, political instability hurt the country's economy, particularly in Karachi, Pakistan's major seaport. It also discouraged the foreign investment that the central government was attempting to attract for its restructured economic policies based on liberalization and privatization. The government claimed, however, to have restored peace in Sindh by eliminating the MQM's more extreme elements. At the same time, it pledged to support accommodative policies, including power-sharing arrangements, if the MQM were to denounce the use of violence.

But this official rhetoric was belied by the government's policy directions. For example, amendments in the Sindh Local Government Ordinance placed several essential branches of local administration in Karachi under bureaucratic control. New sub-districts, with a minority Muhajir and a majority Punjabi-Pakhtun migrant worker population, were also

---

65. *The Muslim,* January 29, 1996; and *Dawn,* January 1, 1996; January 21, 1996.

created in Karachi, leading to opposition charges that future elections would be rigged.[66]

While periodic outbreaks of violence continued to paralyze urban Sindh, a new potential for violence existed in the Sindhi countryside, until now an undisputed base of PPP support. In 1993, Benazir Bhutto's estranged brother, Mir Murtaza Bhutto, ran in the general elections as an opposition candidate. His party, the PPP (Shaheed Bhutto), attracted support from Sindhis who believed that Benazir Bhutto had compromised with the Punjabi-dominated establishment. It established close links with a number of Sindhi ethno-nationalist organizations, including the Sindh National Alliance. Threatened by the prospect of an internal party rift, the government arrested and prosecuted several of Mir's supporters.

On September 20, 1996, Mir was killed by police fire. Although Prime Minister Bhutto claimed that he was deliberately "targeted" and killed as "a part of a well-planned conspiracy" to destabilize her government,[67] anti-government sentiments increased among segments of the Sindhi population.

POLITICAL POLARIZATION AND ETHNIC RELATIONS. In an atmosphere of political polarization, some questioned the government's declared intention to reduce state-directed discrimination against minorities by restoring the joint electorate system; the Muslim League saw minorities as a potential PPP vote bank.[68] The proposed policy measure led the opposition to charge that it was intended to increase the PPP's chances of winning marginal seats in the 1998 elections.

Moreover, the government failed to live up to its declared aim of removing from the statute books discriminatory religious legislation, which undermined the rights of minorities, including Hindus, Christians, and Ahmediyas. There were two reasons for this. First, the Muslim League and its religious allies, such as the Jamaat-i-Islami, continued to exploit religious sentiment to undermine the government. Second, the PPP was unwilling to endanger its own alliances with some religious parties, including the Jamiat-i-Ulema-Islam (Fazlur Rehman group), which has a strong following in the NWFP and Baluchistan, and the Sunni extremist Sipah-i-Sahaba, a coalition partner in the Punjab PPP government.[69]

---

66. Unsure of its support in a climate of acute political polarization, the PPP government postponed elections to the local bodies.

67. *Dawn*, September 26, 1996.

68. Aziz Siddiqui, "One Step Forward?" *Newsline*, March 1996, p. 78.

69. Rashid, "The Politics of 'Fundamentalism,'" pp. 74–75, n. 46.

This hesitation encouraged sectarian violence among the Shi'ites: the PPP government was unwilling to address Shi'ite grievances, while the Muslim League–led opposition tacitly supported Sunni religious extremism. The government's inadequate response was often a mix of coercion and concessions, aimed at the immediate goal of reasserting state control. For example, it used force to control sectarian conflict in Kurram in September 1996, but it took no legal action against the perpetrators of violence. After the 1994 uprising in Malakand, military action was, in fact, accompanied by concessions to religious extremists, including the partial enforcement of Islamic legislation. In neither case did the government formulate a long-term policy to deal with the underlying causes of violence or to prevent future outbreaks.

The government even failed to resolve the ethno-regional differences that had prevented it from conducting the national census, which is needed to determine the distribution of state funds and the delineation of electoral constituencies. All four provinces raised objections to and placed preconditions on the census, based on conflicting perceptions of their ethno-regional interests. The fact that conducting a national census has become a controversial issue shows how salient ethnicity is as a political force in Pakistan. Unfortunately, government policies for managing the country's ethnic problems fail to reflect a sense of urgency, demonstrating a lack of direction and an inability to learn from Pakistan's troubled ethnic past.

This is amply demonstrated by the events that followed the dismissal of the PPP government in November 1996, the third consecutive military-instigated dismissal of an elected government before it completed its term of office. President Farooq Leghari cited the PPP's ethnic policies in Sindh, including the thousands of "extra-judicial" killings of MQM activists by law-enforcing agencies, as one of the causes for the dismissal.[70]

While a shadow military government headed by a PPP dissident, Meraj Khalid, declared its intention to hold a free and fair election, steps were taken to ensure the electoral victory of the military's chosen candidate, the Punjabi-dominated Pakistan Muslim League, headed by Nawaz Sharif. These measures included the appointment of anti-PPP figures and PPP dissidents to key administrative posts, such as interim Sindh and Baluchistan Prime Ministers, Mumtaz Ali Bhutto and Zafrullah Jamali, and Sindh and Punjab Governors, Kamaluddin Azfar and Kwaja Tariq Rahim respectively; the arrest and trials of a number of PPP leaders on charges of corruption; the use of the government-controlled electronic media to undermine the PPP's credibility; and the promotion of internal

---

70. Zahid Hussain, "Fall from Grace," *Newsline*, November 1996, pp. 27–28.

divisions within the party, particularly in Sindh, where the PPP's traditional Sindhi support base was already under threat due to the opposition of PPP (Shahid Bhutto) under the leadership of Mir Murtaza Bhutto's widow, Ghinwa.

At the same time, the military also ensured that any future government would be bound to publicly acknowledge its dictates through the creation of an "advisory body," the Council of Defense and National Security, composed of the President, the Prime Minister, the three service chiefs, the chairman, joint chiefs of staff committee, key cabinet ministers and senior bureaucrats. Since the purpose of the military-dominated body is to render advice to the government on a wide range of issues, including defense, foreign policy, the economy, and internal security, it will clearly undermine the authority of the Prime Minister.[71]

In the elections that followed in the wake of the Supreme Court's last-minute dismissal of a constitutional petition by Benazir Bhutto, the Muslim League won an overwhelming victory in the national assembly and in the provincial assembly of Punjab. In the NWFP, the Muslim League and its ally, the ANP, obtained a majority of seats, allowing Nawaz Sharif to form a government in the center and in Punjab, as well as a coalition Muslim League–ANP government in the NWFP.[72] Ethnic considerations played a major part in the elections in Baluchistan, where Baluch nationalist parties, the Jamhoori Watan Party (Democratic National Party) and Baluchistan National Party, managed to muster enough support to form the provincial government, although an alliance was also reached with the Pakhtun-dominated JUI (FR) and the PPP.

In Sindh, ethnic polarization, internal divisions, and the biases of the interim government all combined to dictate the electoral outcome. While the PPP managed to emerge as the largest provincial party, it lost some of its traditional seats in rural Sindh to the Muslim League and other opposition parties. The MQM, on the other hand, won in all Muhajir-majority areas of the province, demonstrating that its ethnic support base had remained intact.[73] Ethnic polarization in Sindh has since increased following the formation of an MQM–Muslim League provincial government in Sindh, since Sindhis, once again, have little voice in their own

---

71. Zahid Hussain, "Democracy on a String," *Newsline*, January 1997, p. 32; and I.A. Rahman, "A Sinister Move," pp. 33–35.

72. The Muslim League won a two-thirds majority in the National Assembly, winning 134 seats, including all but seven seats in Punjab, as opposed to the PPP total of 18 national assembly seats, all from the province of Sindh.

73. The MQM won 28 provincial assembly and 12 national assembly seats from the urban center of Sindh, while the PPP obtained 36 seats in the Sindh provincial assembly.

province and virtually none in the center, where the key posts of Chief of Army Staff, President, and Prime Minister are all in Punjabi hands. Since the military, moreover, continues to dictate the course of events in the politically sensitive province and is opposed to a key MQM demand, the withdrawal of cases registered against its supporters in Sindh, tensions are on the increase between the Muslim League and the MQM leadership.

Ethnic issues have also assumed significance in the economic sphere since the interim government's hasty passage of a National Finance Award before an elected government could take over. Since the award is perceived as inimical to the interests of Baluchistan, Sindh, and the NWFP, it has heightened the alienation and grievances of all three ethnic communities. Hence, ethnic polarization is likely to increase unless the Punjabi-dominated center and armed forces radically restructure their ethnic policies and approaches.

Conclusions

Having watched Pakistan split in 1971, those who govern it in the 1990s should be acutely aware that ethnic conflict still carries a great potential for violence and political instability. However, as we see from this historical analysis, for five decades, Pakistani governments have either neglected most ethnic problems or dealt with them in ways that transformed ethnic competition, an expected phenomenon in a heterogeneous state, into conflict between ethnic groups and between ethnic groups and the state.

ASSESSMENTS

That Pakistan's policymakers perpetuate decades-old ethnic policies, even after they clearly prove counterproductive, demonstrates the deep conservatism in the character and composition of the country's leadership. Since Pakistan's ethnically skewed civil and military bureaucracies continue to dominate all sensitive areas of state policy, their ethnic and institutional interests influence the directions of policy, and hence governmental performance in managing ethnic relations.

For example, the military's efforts to consolidate control over both national politics and the state's resources have perpetuated highly centralized structures of governance. But this very process has engendered structural imbalances in the relationship between the center and the periphery, promoting political instability and ethnic unrest. Thus, while the federal principle has been incorporated, on paper, in all three Pakistani constitutions, Pakistani governments have favored centralization in practice. The failure to allow meaningful regional autonomy has led to recurring ethnic conflict.

Moreover, centralized economic policies have deprived the provinces of control over the distribution and allocation of their internally generated surpluses—a process that has favored certain ethnic groups and regions and discriminated against others, fueling ethnic tensions. These economic policies contributed to the popular support for secession in East Pakistan in 1971, as did the center's focus on assimilation and its deliberate neglect of Pakistan's cultural diversity.

These policies of ethnic integration have, however, been selectively applied. They do not, for instance, extend to employment policies for the politically dominant state apparatus. Recruitment for the military is ostensibly based on merit, but in practice excludes the Sindhis and the Baluchs in particular. Nor are regional quotas for employment in the civil bureaucracy applied to senior policymaking posts, which are dominated by the Punjabis. Sindhi and Baluch resentment is disregarded.

Since 1971, a reliance on co-optation and coercion has managed to contain ethnic conflict in Pakistan. But it persistently recurs because the state's leaders and managers have failed to address the underlying factors responsible for such tensions. For all these reasons, the state system in Pakistan and the preferences of its leaders are directly responsible for the country's ethnic problems. Using authoritarian or semi-authoritarian structures of governance and refusing to create representative and participatory institutions, Pakistan's leaders have been able to exclude some ethnic groups and communities from the decision-making process. Knowing this, these groups consistently feel alienated.

Policies of assimilation, integration, and centralization have been most vigorously applied during periods of direct authoritarian rule. Some elected governments have tried to redress ethnic grievances and to restructure ethnic relations along more equitable lines. Representative governance has also prevented state-group tensions from assuming a secessionist shape, since even the most imperfect democracy has provided some avenues for citizens to participate and to express ethnic grievances. Elected governments have often failed, however, to implement their policy initiatives adequately, relying on coercive strategies to counter ethnic grievances rather than providing justice to all ethnic communities.

One major stumbling block prevents elected governments from bringing about structural change: the inequitable distribution of power between the political leadership and the state apparatus. Conscious of their political vulnerability compared to the powerful civil and military bureaucracies, elected leaders have been extremely reluctant to change ethnic policies favored by the state apparatus, especially in such sensitive areas as the economy and national security. The political leadership's failure to provide social and economic justice and to strengthen democratic institutions and the related ability of the state apparatus to co-opt or coerce democratically elected leaders has contributed to a growing popular disillusionment with the system of parliamentary democracy. This is particularly true for ethnic groups that see themselves as the major targets of state-directed discrimination, including Sindhi ethno-nationalists and Muhajir supporters of the MQM. Pakistan's many disgruntled ethnic actors are heavily armed and well funded, as a result of the civil war in Afghanistan and a flourishing trade in narcotics. The militarization of Pakistani society has made ethnic violence endemic, particularly in Pakistan's cities.

RECOMMENDATIONS

Ethnic relations in Pakistan must be based on political, economic, and social justice, which will require a deep evaluation of the government's ethnic policies, approaches, and strategies. Any meaningful change in ethnic policy will require, above all, structural transformation of the existing federal system to provide for tangible regional autonomy through a devolution and decentralization of power.

FEDERALISM AND REGIONAL AUTONOMY.   Of all the ethno-regional actors in Pakistan, only the Punjabi political and economic elite continue to believe that the 1973 constitution addresses the country's current political, economic, and social situation. The constitution provides the center with a level of control that should be the sole preserve of the provinces, especially over provincially generated revenues and their allocation. Meeting these growing demands for greater provincial economic autonomy will require an ethno-regional consensus on amendments to the constitutional framework. This issue will acquire even more significance in the future, as the budgetary gap widens between the state's financial resources and its expenditures.

Until regional autonomy can be enhanced and sanctioned in the constitution, other, more immediate steps can be taken. The present constitution provides for a division of power; this could at least be implemented. Ethnic tensions will ease if ethnic groups are given adequate control over their financial resources. These same factors—the impingement on provincial autonomy and the failure to redress ethno-regional grievances—played a major role in transforming moderate demands for autonomy into a movement for secession in the former East Pakistan. The same lesson remains to be learned by the central government: local and regional leaders must have enough authority and autonomy to redress the most pressing grievances of their constituents and to implement policies that address specific ethnic concerns. Otherwise, ethnic tensions will intensify.

AFFIRMATIVE ACTION POLICIES. Since past policies have perpetuated regional economic inequities, the central government must adopt more rigorous distributive policies that discriminate in favor of disadvantaged and excluded ethnic communities and groups. Their underdevelopment problems, including inadequate infrastructure in areas such as health, education, and housing, should be given priority when state funds are allocated for social development. Local and regional actors should be able to play a tangible role in identifying target areas and in formulating and implementing government policies.

Before policies based on merit can replace the quota system for education and employment in state-owned or provincially controlled institutions and bodies, the government must first reduce the gap between developed and underdeveloped ethnic communities. Preferential policies should, in fact, be extended beyond the areas they currently cover, to include, for example, quotas for the distribution of state-controlled lands and preferential access to state-provided credit. Care should also be taken to ensure that dominant ethnic communities cannot continue to exploit the system, as they can today. Monitoring of this problem could be assigned to newly created neutral institutions or to existing institutions, such as the Ombudsman.

Preferential employment policies should be adopted for ethnic communities that have been deliberately excluded from representation within the security arms of the state, including the armed forces. The military's leaders should be sensitized to the dangers of retaining ethnically skewed recruitment policies, with particular emphasis being placed on the history of the division of Pakistan. At the regional and local levels, members of underrepresented ethnic groups should be brought into law enforcement agencies and placed under the control of regional and locally elected officials, in place of the present policy of centrally directed intervention.

ETHNIC PLURALISM. The present emphasis on sustaining a "national" identity, as identified by the center's policymakers and promoted through the state-controlled education system and electronic media, should be replaced by pluralistic policies that recognize the multiethnic nature of Pakistani society. The failure of Pakistani policymakers, even after 1971, to recognize and respect pluralism has continued to exacerbate ethnic tensions. Affirmative policies, using a pluralistic approach, will help counter the ethnic grievances of groups that feel neglected or imposed upon and will help rectify the perception that cultural assimilation is the ultimate goal of the country's leadership.

INTERNAL AND EXTERNAL SECURITY. Every Pakistani citizen deserves the security that would follow an end to the cross-border traffic in arms and narcotics from Afghanistan. Shutting down this traffic would reduce ethnic conflict in Pakistan itself; this trade has financed and fueled sub-state violence, including ethnic violence, in Pakistan. But taking this step would require that Pakistan change its policy of intervening in Afghanistan, which would in turn require a reassertion of civil control over the military, the main architect of the government's Afghan policy.

There is another direct correlation between Pakistan's Afghan policy and ethnic conflict in Pakistan: the presence and activities of Afghan refugees have increased Pakhtun-Baluch tensions in Baluchistan. Steps should therefore be taken to repatriate these refugees once conditions in Afghanistan permit; in the short term, urgent measures are needed to control the political and criminal activities of Afghan refugees on Pakistani soil.

More generally, politically motivated religious violence and sectarian tension will continue in Pakistan as long as discriminatory constitutional amendments and laws continue to undermine the security of religious and sectarian minorities. These discriminatory constitutional provisions and laws must therefore be revoked by parliament, removing a major grievance among religious and sectarian minorities. Governments should also protect the security of citizens by punishing the perpetrators of religious violence, since inaction and hesitation have only strengthened the bargaining position of religious extremists.

PROSPECTS

Decentralization, the devolution of power, and the provision of justice through the institutionalization of representative decision-making processes are the keys to resolving ethnic problems in Pakistan. The country's leaders must recognize and respect the political autonomy of the various units in the national federation. Repeated efforts by central governments to override regional political preferences, for example, by dismissing or manipulating provincial governments, have played a major role in promoting political instability and increasing ethnic tensions.

There will be no tangible change in the formulation or implementation of the government's ethnic policies and no resolution of the country's ethnic problems as long as dominant state actors—and the state itself—represent, or are perceived to represent, particular ethnic interests and goals. Hence, a reduction of ethnic tension is intimately linked to the provision of a policymaking role for all ethnic groups and communities. Genuine participation will depend on an incremental strengthening of the democratic process, since these democratic institutions will oversee bargaining for access to political power and resources in the future.

The performance of elected governments and repeated interventions by the military since 1988 would seem to suggest that Pakistan will not be able to make the changes that need to be made in the political arena. The restructuring of ethnic relations proposed above could be achieved if the civil leadership on both sides of the political divide came to see the true basis of its political survival. Its political future depends not on tacit and temporary power-sharing arrangements with the state apparatus, but on an incremental consolidation and expansion of its internal bases of support. The civil leadership will acquire that support only if it provides political, economic, and social justice to the multiethnic society it governs.

Chapter 3

Government Policy and the Ethnic Crisis in Sri Lanka

Amita Shastri

Sri Lanka has been an anomaly: a vibrant democracy despite very low levels of economic development. Universal franchise was introduced as early as 1930. Within a decade of achieving independence in 1948, it experienced a peaceful transfer of power from the ruling United National Party (UNP) to the newly formed Sri Lanka Freedom Party (SLFP) and its allies. Over the next two decades, rising levels of voter turnout accompanied alternations in power between the two major parties. With its relatively generous social welfare provisions, Sri Lanka's people enjoyed high rates of literacy, longevity, and good health, more akin to those found in the developed world.

The puzzle is that, despite these positive developments, Sri Lanka slid into civil war in the 1980s, and, in the 1990s, its armed forces are faced with one of the world's most highly motivated and tightly organized insurgent movements. Ethnic hostilities in Sri Lanka have claimed over 50,000 lives, and the death toll continues to rise. The separatist insurgents of the Liberation Tigers of Tamil Eelam (LTTE) refuse to accept any political outcome except an independent Tamil state in the northern and northeastern part of the country.

In this chapter, I identify and analyze the policies of the Sri Lankan government that had a significant impact on ethnic relations in Sri Lanka. My argument is that one of the major problems in Sri Lanka has been a lack of consensus about key aspects of the political system. Moreover, the efforts by ambitious politicians to use ethnic appeals to attract, consolidate, and maintain support have exacerbated tensions between the country's major ethnic communities and played an important role in leading Sri Lanka into civil war.

The focus in this chapter is mainly on relations between the Sinhalese majority and the Sri Lanka Tamil minority, since it is the conflict between these two groups that has led the island to its tragic impasse. As a shorthand, I use the term "Tamils" to refer mainly to the Sri Lanka Tamils. However, one should note that, like any other community, both the Sinhalese and Tamil communities have individuals and sub-groups with varying interests and political orientations. The use of the blanket terms "Sinhalese" and "Tamils" allows me to focus on the initiatives and concerns of the most politically active and influential segments of each community.

The first section of the chapter will provide a historical and demographic overview of the situation on the island. The second section will focus on the policies at the time of independence in 1948 that had a long-term impact on the relationships that were developing between and among the country's various ethnic communities. The third section will examine the period after 1956, a historical and political watershed in Sri Lankan history, which brought the Sinhalese middle-class masses onto the political stage for the first time and during which relations between the Sinhalese and Tamil communities took a sharp turn for the worse. The fourth section will focus on the policies adopted by the UNP government between 1977 and 1994, when it presided over the most tumultuous and violent period in contemporary Sri Lankan history. The fifth section concentrates on the policy initiatives launched by President Chandrika Kumaratunge since 1994. The last section presents the conclusions and recommendations that may be drawn from the foregoing analysis.

The Historical and Ethnic Setting

For centuries, Sri Lanka enjoyed close relations with the South Asian mainland even while it constituted an entrepôt on the major trading routes connecting East and West Asia. This led many groups of people to play a role in constituting its plural society. Of these groups, the most important were the Sinhalese, who claim their descent from migrants who came to Sri Lanka from northern India around 500 B.C. The second largest group, the Sri Lanka Tamils, have cultural affinities to peoples living in the south of India. They claim to have settled on the island before the Sinhalese. The time of arrival and the historical contributions of each group have been the subjects of bitter controversies in the modern era. What is certain is that in pre-colonial times, Sri Lanka contained a number of kingdoms, both Sinhalese and Tamil, which rose and fell and enjoyed complex relations (including cultural exchanges, trade, marriage, and war) with peoples and kingdoms on the Indian mainland, all of which are part of the island's historical legacy today.

Sri Lanka's location was also responsible for its long exposure to

European colonial rule over a period of some 450 years. The earliest of the colonial powers, the Portuguese, came in 1505, built trading forts along the coast, drew the local population into the international trade in cinnamon, and converted some of the middle castes to Catholicism. The Dutch took over from the Portuguese around 1668, expanded their control to cover the entire coast, introduced Roman-Dutch law and Calvinism, and set up cinnamon plantations. In 1815, the British, who followed the Dutch, were the first to conquer the entire island; in 1833 they brought it under a unified system of administration. Sri Lanka developed a prosperous export sector with the growth of plantations that produced tea, rubber, and coconut in the southwest of the island after 1850. The port of Colombo became a burgeoning center of activity and the preeminent city and capital of the island. Many indigent, low-caste workers, mostly Tamil, were brought by the British from South India between 1850 and 1930 to work on the tea plantations.

The establishment and spread of colonial trade, production, administration, and education encouraged the growth of a multiethnic, Westernized, middle-class elite in Sri Lanka. Taking a cue from the movement gathering momentum in the neighboring British colony of India, leading members of this elite formed the core of a nationalist movement at the beginning of the twentieth century and demanded a greater role in the colony's administration and governance. However, unlike its Indian counterpart, the Sri Lankan movement remained elitist, moderate, and constitutionalist in nature.

The small island of Sri Lanka has a plural society with clearly defined ethnic groups.[1] (See Table 3.1.) The largest group is the Sinhalese, who constitute some 74 percent of the population. The next largest is the Sri Lanka Tamils, who form 12 percent of the population. The other group of Tamils, the Upcountry Tamils (also called the Indian, estate, or plantation Tamils), constituted 12 percent of the population at independence in 1948, but repatriation in the 1960s and 1970s has reduced their share to less than 6 percent of the total population. The other significant ethnic group is the Muslims (both Moors and Malays), who form another 7 percent of the population.

Not only are members of the different ethnic groups fairly distinct in terms of dress, diet, and customs, but they belong to different religious and linguistic groups. The Sinhalese are mostly Buddhist and speak Sinhala, while the Tamils (both Sri Lankan and Upcountry) are Hindu and

---

1. The island stretches 270 miles from north to south and 140 miles from east to west, covers an area of 25,332 square miles, and had a population of about 17 million in 1991.

Table 3.1. Ethnic Composition of Sri Lanka.

Group	Number (1946)	Percentage	Number (1981)	Percentage
Sinhalese	4,634,203	69.6	10,986,595	74.0
Sri Lanka Tamils	732,417	11.0	1,870,690	12.6
Upcountry Tamils	779,025	11.7	831,418	5.6
Muslims	426,133	6.4	1,098,659	7.4
Others (Burghers, Eurasians, and Veddahs)	86,561	1.3	59,388	0.4
Total	6,658,339	100.0	14,846,750	100.0

NOTE: The latest census was conducted in 1981. Due to disturbances, no census was taken in 1991. As of late 1996, Sri Lanka's total population was estimated at 18,270,000.
SOURCE: Sri Lanka, Department of Census and Statistics.

speak Tamil. The Muslims, depending on where they live, speak Sinhala or Tamil and are increasingly becoming familiar with Arabic. A small segment of both the Sinhalese and Tamil communities converted to Christianity during colonial rule. Elite members of all groups speak English in addition to one or more of the other languages.

These communities are demographically concentrated in different parts of the country; there has been a limited amount of intermixing. The Sinhalese live mainly in the southwest. Because of longer exposure to foreign influences, the Sinhalese in the low-lying plains tend to be less traditional than those living in the Kandyan interior, the last part of the country to be conquered by a Western colonial power. The Sri Lanka Tamils live mostly in the northeast; they constitute 86 percent of the population in the Northern Province and about 41 percent of the population in the Eastern Province. During colonial times, many Sri Lanka Tamils migrated to Colombo to work in the state services as administrators and clerks; as a result, they grew to form about 25 percent of the city's population. As their name implies, the Upcountry Tamils tend to live in the hilly center of the island on the tea plantations. A significant proportion of the Muslim community lives in the Eastern Province, mixed with Sri Lanka Tamils and the increasing numbers of Sinhalese who have settled there. Other segments of the Muslim community live in and around Colombo on the west coast.

Colonial policy was contradictory in its treatment of members of different ethnic groups. On the one hand, all individuals were considered equal under the law. On the other, faced with having to rule a large native

Sri Lanka.

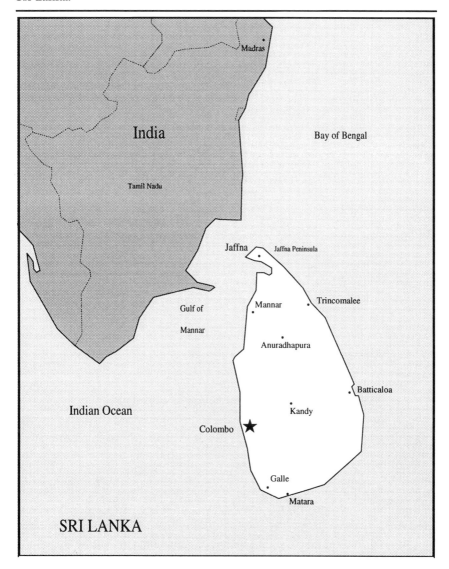

population, the colonial authorities integrated elite members of the local groups into their political and economic system. Leading members of the dominant Sinhalese caste, the Goyigama, were given positions and titles in the colonial system of government and village administration. Some of them, along with others belonging to the next highest castes (the Karavas, Salagamas, and Duravas), were integrated into the expanding circuits of wealth created by plantations, trade, and the professions. Leading members of the Sri Lanka Tamils, most often belonging to the Vellala caste, migrated south and sought jobs in the civil service in Colombo. Other Sri Lanka Tamils, along with members of the Muslim community, went into trade and finance. In traditional, rural parts of the country, leading members of each group (excluding the Upcountry Tamils) continued to exercise influence as landowners, while the large majority of each community lived as peasants. An intermediate stratum of individuals served and exercised influence in village communities as clergy, teachers, and doctors.

The Sri Lankan nationalist movement developed along two tracks. Religious revival and reform movements developed in the indigenous middle- and lower-middle class in both communities in the nineteenth century. They were followed by a growing political activity within the Westernized elite, a multiethnic group of notables, among whom members of the Sri Lanka Tamil community played a prominent role.

This changed in the 1920s when the basis for representation was shifted from a communal to a territorial one by the colonial authorities. The Sinhalese elite responded by moving to mobilize popular support along ethnic and caste lines. They used the religious and historical myths and cultural symbols that had been given prominence by the nationalist revivalist and reformist Buddhist movement. Initially used as devices for anti-colonial agitation, these later proved to be useful in delegitimating minority groups. The conservative Sinhalese elite also found them useful in their efforts to fend off the ideological challenge posed by the radical left, which became increasingly influential within the working class after the late 1920s. This ethno-nationalist channelling provided the basis for the formation of political organizations and parties in the post-independence period.

A pattern of competitive relations developed in the 1930s and 1940s between the Sinhalese and the Sri Lanka Tamil elites. As leading members of the largest minority community, which had a regional concentration and a well-developed cultural identity, and faced with an erosion in their political and economic power, Sri Lanka Tamil leaders began to take more independent stands as time went by. The Muslim elite decided to work with the Sinhalese elite. They were aggressively wooed by the Sinhalese leadership, and found it to their benefit to cooperate.[2]

In contrast, as an immigrant and largely impoverished minority group, the Upcountry Tamils faced prejudice and discrimination from the Sinhalese community. The terms on which they might gain citizenship remained disputed and ambiguous until independence. In the 1940s, they strengthened their position through massive labor strikes and developed closer ties with leftist parties and Sri Lanka Tamil associations; these moves deeply threatened the conservative Sinhalese elite.[3] Upcountry Tamils were denied citizenship after independence, and their numbers consequently declined as over half were repatriated to India. Prohibited from voting, they relied on their trade union organizations to push their economic demands and to expedite the processing of their applications for citizenship. Their conservative leadership tried to work with the major parties, especially the UNP, to achieve these goals. Citizenship was granted to the Upcountry Tamils who remained in the country by the late 1980s. Even so, for the most part, the Upcountry Tamils remain distinct as a community. They live mainly in the heart of the country, dependent on plantations for their livelihood, and do not support Sri Lanka Tamil demands for a separate state.

The Independence Arrangement and Post-Independence Changes

Sri Lanka's small size and centralized colonial administration virtually ensured that it would adopt a centralized, unitary form of government after independence. As in most other erstwhile colonies, the capital and port city of Colombo played an overwhelming role in the life of the country as its main political, administrative, business, trading, and industrial center. After independence, every important matter of government policy was defined and implemented by the national government at Colombo. Outlying regions were administered by the central government. Municipal, town, and village councils were responsible for a limited range of matters of strictly local concern, such as sanitation, roads, lighting, and traffic control.

Ethnic politics at the time of independence and in the following

---

2. For details, see Kingsley M. De Silva, *Managing Ethnic Tensions in Multi-Ethnic Societies: Sri Lanka 1880–1985* (New York: University Press of America, 1986), chaps. 8, 15.

3. Nira Wickramasinghe, *Ethnic Politics in Colonial Sri Lanka, 1927–1947* (New Delhi: Vikas Publishing House, 1995), pp. 184–246.

decade revolved around the amount of power the minorities would be able to exercise at the center. When they saw how small that amount was, they began seeking to secure greater autonomy for the regions in which they were the dominant group.

A LIMITED CONSTITUTIONAL CONSENSUS

The development of democracy is facilitated when leading members of different groups in a society can come to a consensus. This consensus forms the "bargain" on which subsequent constitutional and political interactions between the groups take place.[4]

The Sri Lankan independence constitution did not come out of a broad-based process of negotiation and bargaining between the various ethnic groups on the island. Instead, it was based on discussions between departing colonial administrators and the Sinhalese elite represented by D.S. Senanayake and the all-Sinhalese Board of Ministers. The first Sri Lanka Tamil joined the Board only in 1943, at a very late stage in the negotiating process. The negotiations with the British were dominated by Senanayake, who chaired the Board, and no other body was invited to participate in formulating constitutional proposals.

Issues of particular concern in a multiethnic state—such as citizenship, franchise, and individual and group rights—were not discussed or agreed to by representatives of the country's largest ethnic groups. The issue of citizenship was left unresolved by the British as a concession to Senanayake.[5] Tamil protests were characterized as acts that would delay or obstruct "Ceylon's march to freedom."[6] Consequently, the new constitution was not approved by five of the ten councillors elected by the two Tamil communities;[7] the five Tamil members who did vote for the proposed constitution in the State Council in 1945 lost their seats in the 1947 elections.[8]

---

4. See Guillermo O'Donnell, Philippe C. Schmitter, and Laurence Whitehead, *Transitions from Authoritarian Rule: Comparative Perspectives* (Baltimore: John Hopkins University Press, 1986); Edward Friedman, ed., *The Politics of Democratization: Generalizing East Asian Experiences* (Boulder, Colo.: Westview Press, 1994); Giuseppe Di Palma, *To Craft Democracies: An Essay on Democratic Transitions* (Berkeley: University of California Press, 1990); Adam Przeworski, *Sustainable Democracy* (Cambridge: Cambridge University Press, 1995); and Donald L. Horowitz, *Ethnic Groups in Conflict* (Berkeley: University of California Press, 1985).

5. Until independence, all inhabitants of the island were British subjects.

6. See De Silva, *Managing Ethnic Tensions*, pp. 146–147.

7. See Wickramasinghe, *Ethnic Politics*, pp. 220–221.

8. See De Silva, *Managing Ethnic Tensions*, p. 142.

A MAJORITARIAN CONSTITUTIONAL STRUCTURE

Sri Lanka adopted a constitution based on the British Westminster parliamentary model. The prime minister and his or her cabinet were to be drawn from the majority party in the lower, more powerful house of parliament. This house was to be elected through a single-member district plurality system, which tends to "manufacture majorities" in favor of the leading party or coalition. Unlike its counterpart in India, the Sri Lankan Constitution did not include an explicit bill of individual rights.

Minority rights protections that were incorporated into the constitution at independence were soon undermined. The first was an explicit provision that was put in the constitution to serve in place of a bill of rights and to alleviate minority anxieties. It prohibited the passage of any measure discriminatory to members of a particular ethnic group. The second check was implicit in the electoral system of representation, which should have given minorities as much as 40 percent of the lower house. Since any constitutional amendment had to be passed by a two-thirds majority in parliament, minorities could veto any constitutional measure that displeased them. In keeping with democratic precedent, an independent judiciary was supposed to rule on the constitutionality of all legislation. Any judicial matter that could not be satisfactorily settled on the island could be referred to the British Privy Council for its "option."[9]

POLITICAL REPRESENTATION

Political representation had been the most contentious issue in the negotiations leading up to independence. G.G. Ponnambalam, the leader of Sri Lanka's most important Tamil political organization, the Tamil Congress, had argued for a "fifty-fifty" formula for representation in the legislature. Since this would have given minority groups disproportionate influence in the parliament, this proposal was understandably rejected by Senanayake, the leader of the main nationalist organization and ruling party, the United National Party, at independence. Instead, the electoral rules devised at independence gave the more sparsely populated rural and minority areas increased weight, and provided for a number of urban multimember constituencies in multiethnic localities. This was expected to provide minority communities with 40 percent of the lower house of parliament, if people voted for candidates along ethnic lines.[10]

---

9. Much to the indignation of the parties on the left, Sri Lanka remained a "dominion" within the British Commonwealth after independence and the Queen of Britain continued to function as its monarch until 1972.

10. After the 1947 elections, the Sinhalese representation in parliament was larger than expected—67 percent. See Wickramasinghe, *Ethnic Politics*, p. 243.

In the period following independence, Senanayake, then prime minister, sought to consolidate his political strength in parliament by wooing Ponnambalam and his six Tamil Congress members of parliament. Ponnambalam consequently joined Senanayake's cabinet as minister of industries. This allowed him to channel funds and patronage to his constituency in the north until he resigned in 1953. With the disenfranchising of the Upcountry Tamils in 1949, discussed in the next section, the independence settlement relating to the representation of the minority communities was modified to the benefit of the majority community.

CITIZENSHIP AND FRANCHISE

Among the first measures passed by the parliament in newly independent Ceylon were the Ceylon Citizenship Act of 1948 and the Indian and Pakistani Residents (Citizenship) Act of 1949, which effectively deprived most Upcountry Tamils of citizenship. This was followed by the Parliamentary Elections Act of 1949, which took away the right to vote from anyone who was not a citizen of the country.

When the issue was appealed to the Privy Council, it ruled that these laws were indeed constitutional. What became clear from this ruling was that this provision in the constitution, which was supposed to protect minority communities from discriminatory action, could be rendered invalid if legislation was framed in general terms. This would be so even if legislation had a clearly discriminatory impact on a particular group.

The leadership's action was driven by economic and political calculations. Poor estate workers had begun to organize into trade unions under the leadership of the parties on the left, and thereby began to pose both a political and an economic challenge to the dominant Sinhalese elite in the interior Kandyan plantation constituencies. Following massive strike actions launched at the close of World War II, the plantation workers had succeeded in getting seven of their representatives elected and in influencing the election's outcome in favor of the left in at least fourteen other interior constituencies in the pre-independence elections in 1947. In retaliation, the ruling party, which was dominated by the conservative plantation interests, deprived the Upcountry workers of their most effective way of asserting their power and improving their lot. The ruling elite thus changed the Upcountry Tamil question from a class to a national one in one devastating stroke, leaving the most indigent, exploited, and vulnerable group on the island, many of whom were second- and third-generation residents, in a stateless limbo for the better part of the next three decades.

Just as insidiously, this measure undercut the basis of the electoral settlement that had been made at independence between the majority and minority communities. Upcountry Tamils continued to be counted in the population totals on the basis of which constituency boundaries were drawn, but their exclusion from the voting population gave additional weight to the conservative rural Sinhalese population in the Kandyan hill country. This resulted in substantial disparities in the sizes of the electorates in different constituencies across the island.[11] After redistricting in 1959, 80 percent of the country's constituencies were dominated by the Sinhalese community. This had fateful and unforeseen consequences in that it provided an additional inducement to political parties in Sri Lanka to raise issues and demands that would attract the vote of the Sinhalese electorate.[12]

Disenfranchising the Upcountry Tamils would have great implications for the position of the Tamil community as a whole. Realizing this, in 1949 a section of the moderate Tamil Congress split with Ponnambalam on the issue and formed the Federal Party (FP), which demanded a restoration of the citizenship rights of the Upcountry Tamils. Just as importantly, it sought to secure the position of the minority communities by demanding greater regional autonomy for their areas through a federal system of government.

In the following period, the tenet that "the majority is always right" was held out as the essence of democracy by the Sinhalese community, which also dismissed the idea that the will of the majority must be constrained by certain rights basic to individuals and minority groups if a political system is to merit being called democratic at all. Mobilized by the nationalist rhetoric of their elite, the Sinhalese middle and lower classes eagerly provided political support to members of their elite in return for favorable policies and patronage. In a serious failure of statesmanship, the country's founding leadership did not develop adequate constraints on the passions and appetites of legislative majorities seeking to capture partisan gains in the context of a highly competitive, developing, pluralist society.

ELECTORAL COMPETITION AND MARGINALIZATION

Initially, the distortion in ethnic representation worked to the UNP's benefit—as intended. With the Upcountry Tamils excluded from voting,

---

11. For instance, in the March 1960 election, Dehiwala-Galkissa in the Western Province had 43,172 registered voters, while the smallest constituency of Haputale in the Uva Province had 10,344 voters.

12. This electoral imbalance remained in effect until 1988, when the proportional system of elections and representation legislated by the 1978 constitution was allowed to come into play.

the UNP won easily in the numerous rural Kandyan constituencies in the 1952 general elections.

In 1956, the UNP was hoisted on its own petard when part of this voting base in rural Sinhalese and Kandyan areas was successfully wooed by S.W.R.D. Bandaranaike and his newly founded SLFP. Bandaranaike's policies relating to language, employment, and education promised to benefit the Sinhalese rural middle- and lower-middle classes in particular. For the next decade and a half, the more nationalist, Sinhalese SLFP gained an important electoral edge in rural Sinhalese constituencies. With its more regionally focused voting base, it won the elections in 1960 and 1970 by gaining more seats than the UNP even though it got a smaller proportion of the overall vote.[13]

With the emergence of a second Sinhalese party, sharp political competition became the norm. After 1956, the two major parties—the UNP and the SLFP—competed with each other to attract the vote of the Sinhalese majority, which determined 80 percent of the seats in parliament. However, each government faced serious economic problems: a chronic decline in terms of trade, slow rates of economic growth, growing budget deficits, rising rates of inflation, and increasing unemployment, especially among the youth. Responding to these problems, a small swing vote of 1–4 percent brought down one government after another. This led each major party to forge alliances with other parties and groups. The UNP found allies to its right, mainly the moderate and conservative minority ethnic parties. The SLFP found allies to its left, notably the Trotskyite and communist parties. Sharp party competition also led to escalating political rhetoric, generous promises to voters at election time, and backtracking from those promises thereafter, which in turn led to mounting political disillusionment and ethnic polarization.

The result was progressively larger parliamentary majorities for the winning party until first the SLFP (in 1970) and then the UNP (in 1977) won two-thirds and four-fifths majorities, respectively. Such majorities freed the country's ruling parties to make policy as they wished. They could even change the constitution itself—which each set about to do.

Interestingly, despite the efforts by the major parties to form broad political coalitions, the Tamil community continued to be marginalized. The promises made to the FP, the main party supported by the Sri Lanka Tamils after 1956, were broken by each new government, which feared losing the support of the majority community. Finding the two major

13. See Amita Shastri, "Electoral Competition and Minority Alienation in a Plurality System: Sri Lanka 1947–1977," *Electoral Studies*, Vol. 10, No. 4 (December 1991), pp. 334–335.

parties evenly matched in the 1960s, the FP unsuccessfully attempted to gain leverage by throwing its political support to one party or the other in return for action with respect to language issues and the decentralization of power. In the 1970s, the FP found itself completely marginalized because governments had large working majorities in parliament.

Sri Lankan politics thus entered into a pattern of competitive bidding for the support of the Sinhalese community. Once formed, this competition fed on itself and became very difficult to break.

AGRICULTURAL INVESTMENT AND COLONIZATION

A set of policies highly favored by Senanayake related to agricultural development and land colonization. Begun in the 1930s, when Senanayake was the minister of agriculture and lands, these policies continued into the 1980s and contributed to the deterioration of ethnic relations in Sri Lanka in important ways.

In a primarily agricultural country in the early stages of modern economic development, it is not surprising that the conservative Sri Lankan political elite favored greater state expenditure on irrigation projects, land development, and peasant resettlement. These policies offered major advantages. Economically, they would help lessen the country's dependence on food imports and alleviate rural overcrowding and underemployment in the Sinhalese southwest of the island. Major new irrigation projects were constructed in the north-central and eastern parts of the island, and Sinhalese peasants from villages in the densely populated southwest and central parts of the island were settled in these newly developed but sparsely populated regions.[14] Politically, these policies attracted the loyalty and support of the rural population for the Sinhalese politicians, who were seen as paternalistic benefactors.

Ideologically, this process was facilitated by the political rhetoric of the Sinhalese elite. Leading politicians compared themselves to the Sinhalese warrior kings of ancient times, who had made Sri Lanka a haven for the Sinhalese and for Buddhism and who had presided over a golden age of agricultural prosperity. Sinhalese peasants were proclaimed the children of the warrior king Duttugemunu who were helping in this grand project and reestablishing control over parts of the island that the Sinhalese had lost to Tamil invaders centuries earlier. This rhetoric shaped a popular identity in the Sinhalese population, which not only excluded members of the minority communities but carried undercurrents of hostility towards them.

---

14. The most notable of these were the Gal-Oya project in the 1950s and the Mahaveli Development Scheme in the 1970s and 1980s.

Although the settlement package became less generous as the decades went by due to increasing budgetary difficulties, the irrigation and resettlement program constituted a point of increasingly serious contention in the northeast. As far as the local Tamil population was concerned, the massive state expenditures on dam and irrigation projects benefitted the Sinhalese population disproportionately. Tamils, settled along the coastal regions of the north and east and not influential in Colombo, were neglected by development and patronage networks.

The government's agricultural investment and resettlement policies were viewed with increasing hostility by segments of the Tamil community because they also undermined the political position of Tamil communities within their own regions. The resettlement policy had a significant impact on the ethnic composition of the minority areas. With the resettlement of Sinhalese in the northeast, Tamils fell from the majority position of 51 percent that they had enjoyed in 1921 in the Eastern Province, before colonization began, to 41 percent by 1981. The Muslim proportion of the region's population fell from 41 percent to 35 percent over the same years, while the proportion of Sinhalese rose from 8 percent to 31 percent.

With their numbers diluted, members of minority groups in certain constituencies found it in their political interest to moderate their positions and cooperate with Sinhalese politicians, initially belonging to the UNP and then increasingly to the SLFP. Being a smaller minority group, which was geographically also more dispersed, the Muslims in the Eastern Province were particularly inclined to form such alliances. This was also true of the Tamils of the interior constituencies of the Eastern Province.[15] Sri Lanka Tamils, who favored autonomy and who lived mostly in the Northern Province and in the urban centers and coastal regions of the Eastern Province, viewed these changing ethnic ratios with alarm and dismay. Opposed to further deterioration of their economic and political positions, they pushed for greater regional autonomy.

The Nationalist Upsurge of 1956 and Its Aftermath

The victory in 1956 of Bandaranaike and his SLFP brought the Sinhala-speaking intelligentsia and intermediate classes of town and country to the forefront of national politics for the first time. The election had taken place in the shadow of a very different event: the 2,500th anniversary of

---

15. For details, see Amita Shastri, "The Material Basis for Separatism: The Eelam Movement in Sri Lanka," *Journal of Asian Studies*, Vol. 49, No. 1 (February 1990), pp. 65–69.

Buddha's death. Involved with celebrations of the anniversary, these groups absorbed the expectations of the Buddhist clergy and the faithful regarding the role that an independent government should play in not only protecting but also promoting the interests of the Sinhalese people, their religion, and their language on the "holy" island of Sri Lanka.

While popular expectations of the new government were high, its accomplishments would be limited by the factional tensions inherent in the governing coalition. Controlling only 51.6 percent of the seats in parliament, the SLFP-led coalition government was in a precarious position. The coalition had entered into a no-contest pact with the better organized leftist parties in the 1956 election, but faced a clear challenge from them and their trade union rank and file in the following period.

The issue of making Sri Lanka a Buddhist state and Buddhism the state religion, as the Buddhist clergy demanded, was referred to a commission to examine. The issue of making Sinhala the official state language, however, was handled differently.

LANGUAGE POLICY

Seeking to fulfill its electoral promise, the first action of the new SLFP-led government was to pass the Official Language Act of 1956, a law which declared Sinhala the country's official language. While the ostensible reason for this was to restore the national language and culture to its pride of place in the newly independent state, this measure broke with the understanding on the language issue that the different ethnic communities had reached before independence. English was spoken by less than 10 percent of the population. The question of replacing it with a language spoken by the mass of the people had arisen before independence, and had been debated in the popularly elected State Council; it had been agreed that English would be replaced with both Sinhala and Tamil as national languages. This was in harmony with another measure passed at the time, which would have allowed either of these languages to be used in government schools. In making Sinhala the country's official language, Bandaranaike and his coalition improved the position of the Sinhala-speaking middle class over both the small English-speaking elite and the Tamil-speaking middle class. The "Sinhala only" language policy was met with outrage and opposition by the Tamil-speaking middle class, who rightly saw it as exclusionary and discriminatory. It delegitimated their position as equal citizens on the island.

REGIONAL AUTONOMY

In response, the Tamils rallied to support the FP, which demanded absolute parity between the two languages as official languages, regional autonomy for Tamil areas, repeal of the unjust citizenship laws, and cessation of all state-sponsored settlement of Sinhalese in Tamil-speaking areas. An agreement was subsequently negotiated between Prime Minister Bandaranaike and S.J.V. Chelvanayagam, the leader of the FP, in July 1957. Popularly known as the Bandaranaike-Chelvanayagam Pact (or B-C Pact), it provided for popularly elected regional councils with extensive powers in the Tamil areas. The Northern Province would constitute one province, and the Eastern Province would be divided into two or more councils (in keeping with its multiethnic population); these councils would have the option of cooperating with or amalgamating with each other, so long as parliament agreed. The powers to be delegated to these regional bodies included control over agriculture, cooperatives, land and land development, colonization, education, health, industries, fisheries, housing, social services, electricity, water projects, and roads. Significantly, they would have the power to select those who would participate in colonization programs. The central government would make block grants to these regional bodies, which would also have the power to raise taxes and borrow. The FP agreed to drop its demand for "parity of status" for the Tamil language as long as Tamil was recognized as the language of the "national minority" of Sri Lanka. Tamil would be the language of government administration in the Northern and Eastern provinces, with provisions to be made for Sinhalese-speaking people in those areas. The prime minister also promised to give "early consideration" to the question of citizenship for the Upcountry Tamils.

The B-C Pact thus provided for a generous degree of regional autonomy for Tamil areas within the existing framework of the unitary state. It safeguarded the position of the Sinhalese while meeting the needs of the Tamils. Had it been implemented, much of the tragedy that followed in succeeding decades would have been avoided. However, Sinhalese extremists in the prime minister's own government and politically vociferous segments of the Buddhist clergy strongly opposed making any concessions of this type. They were joined by the UNP leader, J.R. Jayawardene, who was looking for a way out of the political wilderness. Protests and demonstrations against the B-C Pact shook Bandaranaike politically, and ultimately led him to abrogate the pact.

Particularly alarming was the mounting violence against Tamils and destruction of Tamil property. The FP's Gandhian protest against the "Sinhala only" bill in 1956 was broken up by Sinhalese hooligans, followed by the first incidence of ethnic riots in Colombo and Sinhalese settlements in the Eastern Province. Tamil protests against efforts to extend the use of Sinhala in their areas, in the aftermath of the abrogation of the B-C Pact, escalated into an even more horrific clash in which hundreds of Tamils lost their lives and over 10,000 became refugees in Colombo, and were subsequently transported to Jaffna. Only after four days of bloodshed did the government declare a state of emergency and call out the army to suppress the violence.

Following the riots, Bandaranaike made a nervous effort to solve the language issue by passing the Tamil Language (Special Provisions) Act of 1958, which sought to provide for a "reasonable use of Tamil" along lines agreed to by the B-C Pact. The enabling regulations, however, were not submitted to parliament and the act was not implemented.

The language and autonomy issues remained unresolved in the 1960s, 1970s, and 1980s. Following an electoral agreement in 1965 between the UNP leader Dudley Senanayake and Chelvanayagam, a UNP-led government developed regulations that would implement the Tamil Language Act. However, due to the opposition of the SLFP and its two leftist allies, these regulations were never put into operation. A proposal for district development councils, which would be far weaker than the regional councils proposed by Bandaranaike and which would function under the control of the central government, was abandoned in 1969. Predictably, Tamil participation in the central structures of government subsequently declined.

STATE EMPLOYMENT

The language issue became hotly contested, not only because of its emotive content, but also because it was intimately linked with employment opportunities in the government and private sector. Language policy became a particularly volatile issue in Sri Lanka because many youth had been educated in their own languages under the liberal free education policy that had been pursued since 1947. Many began entering the workforce in the late 1950s, expecting to find white-collar jobs befitting their new education and presumed status. The economy, however, grew slowly and offered few suitable employment opportunities.

The sharp competition for a limited number of employment opportunities became a zero-sum game. Members of the Sinhalese and Tamil communities attempted to expand or at least protect their positions through rhetorical rationalizations, which further strained the country's ethnic relations. Sinhalese chauvinists justified the government's actions in their favor by arguing that Sri Lanka Tamils had benefitted unduly from favorable colonial educational and employment opportunities in the past. The Tamils, in turn, attributed their disproportionate numbers in the state and civil services to their industriousness and their willingness in the past to take risks and migrate to the southwest. By implication, these qualities and pressures had not motivated the Sinhalese as a group.

The official language policy led to increased Sinhalese employment in the government and a decline in Tamil employment. The proportion of Tamils employed in state services between 1956 and 1970 fell from 60 percent to 10 percent in the professions, from 30 percent to 5 percent in the administrative service, from 50 percent to 5 percent in the clerical services, and from 40 percent to 1 percent in the armed forces.[16] This occurred despite the tremendous overall growth of the state sector and the overstaffing of state enterprises, which became the norm due to the political pressures generated by high numbers of unemployed educated youth.

IMPORT-SUBSTITUTION INDUSTRIALIZATION

The nationalist-populist SLFP-led coalition was backed by classes that favored an import-substitution model of industrial development led by the state. The expansion of the state role after 1956 led to a tremendous growth in government expenditures, subsidies, and credits to industrial and agricultural sectors, expansions in state services and employment, and a rise in minimum wages and protections guaranteed to organized labor.

While ostensibly dedicated to national economic development and to the collective good of the whole, the government did not distribute the benefits of growth apolitically. Having failed to procure a secure base within ruling party coalitions or the structure of state power, the Tamils found their economic situation deteriorating in collective terms. Very little investment flowed into the northeast after 1956.[17] As a result, to their collective dissatisfaction, they were compelled to rely increasingly on the private sector.

Although it was overturned and never implemented, the B-C Pact formed the benchmark against which all later agreements were measured. Its abandonment highlighted the difficulties and dilemmas that decentralization posed for the Sinhalese leadership in a resource-scarce developing country. Economic and political imperatives pushed government policy away from decentralization and toward greater centralization.

POLITICAL CENTRALIZATION

The political balance of power in Sri Lanka changed dramatically in 1970 when the radical populist United Front (UF)—consisting of the SLFP and the Trotskyite and the communist parties—won a two-thirds majority

---

16. Satchi Ponnambalam, *Sri Lanka: The National Question and the Tamil Liberation Struggle* (London: Zed Books, 1983), p. 174.

17. See Shastri, "Material Basis for Separatism," pp. 61–73.

in parliament. With this majority, in 1972 the UF was able to promulgate a new constitution that further centralized political power. Over the objections of the FP, Sri Lanka remained a unitary state. The positions of Buddhism and Sinhala were enhanced in that Buddhism was given a "foremost place" in the country's religious hierarchy, and Sinhala was made the country's sole official language. The new constitution obligated the state to protect and foster Buddhism, although other religious groups would be allowed to worship as they pleased. Tamil was to be used according to the provisions of the Tamil Language Act of 1958, with all regulations providing for its use to be treated as subordinate legislation. Constitutional provisions relating to citizenship and the electoral system were unchanged.

Under the new constitution, the unicameral legislature, which would disproportionately represent the Sinhalese community, became even more powerful. The judiciary was to be subordinate to the majority will as expressed by the legislature. In 1974, the legislature proclaimed that it would have the right to interpret the meaning of its own laws. The constitutional provision that had explicitly prohibited discrimination against racial or ethnic groups was done away with. Individual and minority rights were to be protected by a newly enunciated bill of rights. These rights, however, could be curtailed by the legislature in times of national emergency, in the event of a breakdown of public order, or in the public interest.

UNIVERSITY ADMISSIONS

The policy that inflamed all ranks of Tamil opinion and particularly the youth was the highly questionable university admissions policy the UF followed after 1972. The global economic recession of 1972–75 hit Sri Lanka's import-dependent economy particularly hard by quintupling food and petroleum prices, creating a severe shortage of essential goods, and creating runaway budgetary and balance-of-payments deficits. The Sri Lankan economy registered negative growth rates in 1973–74, exacerbating an already bad situation. Predictably, poverty and unemployment rates rose, the latter to an estimated 25 percent of the working population, and political agitation increased in all sectors of the population. By adopting a new university admissions policy under these conditions, the ruling elite showed how far it was willing to go to maintain its position.

The sharp competition for limited university admission slots led the UF government to adopt a policy that would standardize marks across language groups to neutralize alleged biases in grading by Tamil examiners and in the better educational facilities ostensibly enjoyed by Tamil schoolchildren. The result was higher scores and higher rates of acceptance into universities for Sinhalese students. The proportion of Tamils admitted to science-based disciplines, for example, fell from 35 percent in 1970 to 19 percent in 1975.[18]

Finding themselves increasingly excluded from higher education and training in some of the most prestigious and rewarding professional fields—such as medicine, engineering, and veterinary science—Tamil youth became alienated and cynical about the possibilities for redressing their grievances within the existing political system. Many saw only one alternative left open to them: a struggle for a separate state, by violence if need be.

The leading Tamil political organizations came together in 1976 to form the Tamil United Liberation Front (TULF), which declared it would struggle to create a separate Tamil state. Having consistently failed to get a better deal for the Tamil people through constitutional parliamentary politics, moderate Tamil politicians were pushed by the militant Tamil youth wing to, at least formally, adopt secessionism as their goal.

The Turn to the Right: The 1977 Watershed and Civil War

Ironically, just as the movement for Tamil rights committed itself to the goal of separatism, in 1977 electoral fortunes turned to make the TULF, with nineteen seats, the chief opposition party in parliament. Even so, a massive protest vote against the economic shortages and emergency rule of the UF brought the erstwhile opposition party, the UNP, into power with an overwhelming four-fifths majority of the seats in the legislature. Under these circumstances, the TULF could exert little effective pressure within the parliament.

For the next six years, the moderate TULF leadership used the possibility of violent action by militant Tamil youth as a bargaining lever in an attempt to get the government's attention and to win favorable concessions. The UNP leadership recognized the dangers inherent in the situation and tried to provide more positive responses to Tamil demands than in the past. Unfortunately, its efforts to address Tamil concerns were constrained by three factors: its blatantly partisan efforts to remain in power, the rampant ethnic chauvinism in its own ranks, and the propensity of factions within the party to resort to violence. As a result, the UNP government either agreed to measures that fell far short of Tamil demands

---

18. See Chandra R. De Silva, "The Impact of Nationalism on Education: The Schools Takeover (1961) and the University Admissions Crisis 1970–1975," in Michael Roberts, ed., *Collective Identities, Nationalisms and Protest in Modern Sri Lanka* (Colombo: Marga Institute, 1979), pp. 485–497.

or did not deliver on what it promised, repeatedly undermining the standing of the moderate TULF leadership.

A GAULLIST CONSTITUTION

Worried about recent constitutional and electoral developments, the leader of the Sri Lankan right and the new prime minister and later president, J.R. Jayawardene, argued for basic changes in the Sri Lankan political system. On assuming power, he wasted little time in adopting a presidential-parliamentary system patterned after the one that Charles de Gaulle had introduced in France in 1958. The new system revolved around an independently elected presidential executive who would nominate a prime minister and cabinet from the parliament, and preside over their workings without being personally responsible to the parliament. While the president could dissolve the parliament, the latter had only limited control over the former. The president was expected to provide political stability conducive to economic development by having a fixed term, regardless of the political majority that prevailed in parliament. With the president serving as both head of the state and head of government, the new system was more centralized than ever.

In a significant move away from the previous system, however, important changes were made to the electoral system, and this offered hope to the Tamil minority. The president would be elected on an individual preferential basis in which the winning candidate had to get 51 percent of the votes cast. Given that two well-matched parties dominated Sri Lankan politics, it was expected that the votes of minority groups would be decisive in determining the winning candidate. The unicameral legislature, in turn, would be elected on the basis of proportional representation, with individual votes cast for party lists in multimember constituencies. This was expected to make two-thirds majorities extremely difficult to get, thereby giving minority parties considerable leverage in the legislature. However, to strengthen legislative majorities, the constitution provided for a bonus seat to be awarded to the leading party list in each electoral district. The new constitution could be amended by a two-thirds majority in the legislature, but it was expected that such majorities would henceforth be more difficult to get. Some constitutional provisions, such as those relating to the unitary status of the country and the tenure of the president and the parliament, were made even harder to amend: in addition to two-thirds of the legislature's vote, they would have to attract a majority of total votes, and a minimum of one-third of the vote, in a popular referendum.

The UNP implemented several other constitutional measures to mollify the Tamils. Tamil was recognized as a "national language" along with

Sinhala, and it would be used along with Sinhala for administrative, judicial, and educational purposes in the north and east. It would also be used in court proceedings elsewhere on the island if any party in the dispute required it. "District ministers" were created to represent the interests of administrative districts to the president; these ministers were to be members of parliament, appointed from both ruling and non-ruling parties. To provide better protection to individual and minority rights, a new bill of rights was enunciated, which included unconditional guarantees against torture and arbitrary detention.

As far as the Tamil community was concerned, these measures did too little and came too late. The legal status of the Tamil language remained ill-defined but clearly subordinate to that of Sinhala, and provisions to implement these measures had not been drafted. The new district ministers were to be appointed by the president, did not have clearly defined powers, and therefore did not meet Tamil expectations for regional autonomy. Buddhism, meanwhile, continued to enjoy the "foremost place" in the Sri Lankan religious hierarchy, and the state was enjoined to foster the *sasana* (Buddhist doctrine and the Buddhist clerical order).

A belated effort was made in 1981 to provide for a very modest measure of decentralization to administrative districts (sub-units of provinces) through the newly created district development councils. However, the effort to mollify the TULF and moderate Tamils collapsed when the election to the Jaffna district development council was marred by violence and rigged by the ruling party.

ECONOMIC LIBERALIZATION

The UNP also took major steps to begin liberalizing the Sri Lankan economy in 1977. This involved several interrelated initiatives: to open up the economy to foreign trade and investment, to deregulate domestic business, and to reduce the role of the state in economic affairs more generally. Inevitably, the process of economic restructuring created winners and losers, affected different sectors, strata, and groups in different ways, and generated social tensions.

While ostensibly ethnically blind, the nature of the liberalization package adopted by the UNP favored the regions and sectors of the population from which it drew support. The efforts to increase trade, export-oriented industrial production activity, tourism, urban redevelopment, and construction activity would mainly benefit the Sinhalese-dominated southwest of the island and UNP supporters. At the same time, the UNP resisted the austerity measures advocated by the International Monetary Fund (IMF) and World Bank because they would have been politically damaging. Instead, it launched a Keynesian program that involved high levels of government spending on major construction and development projects, such as the Accelerated Mahaveli Development project; much of the funding for these projects came from foreign aid and soft loans. This pattern of spending boosted economic growth rates but generated high rates of inflation, capital-intensive investment, and sharpening income disparities.

The government's policies affected Tamils in different ways in different parts of the country. Relaxations in government controls seem to have worked to the benefit of Tamils engaged in private business and in industrial and commercial activity in the southwest of the island. In contrast, lower trade barriers led to more imports of commodities such as onions, red chilies, and other fruits and vegetables; this, coupled with declines in commodity prices, adversely affected Tamil peasants in the densely populated Jaffna peninsula who had come to depend on income from these crops. The highly centralized nature of the Sri Lankan political system and the overwhelming dominance of the UNP within it combined to keep Tamils of the north and northeast from benefitting commensurately from the government's new spending initiatives. In fact, due to the capital-intensive nature of the new economic program, unemployment remained at very high levels, especially among Tamil youth. Tamil dissatisfaction with the UNP and the government consequently intensified.

The government's economic reforms had some particularly pernicious social and psychological effects. The rapid rise in incomes of particular groups and individuals, the growth of official corruption and kickbacks, the decline in real income for many people, and the continued high rates of unemployment generated considerable resentment in the lower classes, the lower castes, and the minority groups, all of whom were marginalized by the new economic scheme. The seething discontent of lower-class urban Sinhalese and resettled rural Sinhalese was rechannelled by unscrupulous UNP politicians who claimed that mobile and prosperous Tamils in the southwest were engaging in unfair business practices and therefore coming out ahead economically. Tamils became convenient scapegoats for the shortcomings in the regime's new economic policies, and the targets of vicious rounds of ethnic violence in 1981 and 1983.[19]

---

19. See James Manor, *Sri Lanka in Change and Crisis* (London: Croom Helm, 1984); Stanley J. Tambiah, *Sri Lanka: Ethnic Fratricide and the Dismantling of Democracy* (Chicago: University of Chicago Press, 1986); and Committee for Rational Development, *Sri Lanka, The Ethnic Conflict: Myths, Realities and Perspectives* (New Delhi: Navrang, 1984).

PARTISAN CHANGES AND THE CRISIS OF LEGITIMACY

In addition to these policy changes, politically partisan measures instituted by the UNP leadership undermined its legitimacy.[20] In particular, the civil rights of the leading figure in the opposition, Sirimavo Bandaranaike, the widow of S.W.R.D. Bandaranaike and leader of the SLFP, were constrained in important ways for six years. Specifically, Bandaranaike was barred from running for president in 1982, thereby virtually assuring that Jayawardene would stay in power until 1988. This action naturally alienated Bandaranaike and kept her from working with the ruling party to solve the country's growing ethnic problem. Fearing that Bandaranaike and the SLFP would pander to Sinhalese nationalist sentiments if the UNP accommodated Tamil demands, the UNP remained wary of making any substantial concessions to the Tamils despite the escalating hostilities between the state's armed forces and militant Tamil groups.

The tenure of the UNP-dominated parliament was also extended through questionable means. The existing parliament, with four-fifths of its seats held by the UNP and elected under the single-member district system of elections, was kept in place for another term through electoral manipulation. Rather than hold general elections under the new proportional system of representation and lose their steamroller majority, the UNP held a referendum in December 1982, the results of which allowed the existing parliament to remain in power for another six years. Opposition to the government and its policies was thus undercut. Discontent could not be expressed through normal constitutional channels. This action, perhaps more than any other contributed to the growth of extremism in Sri Lanka in the years that followed.

In 1986, Sri Lanka passed another milestone in this process: a constitutional amendment requiring members of parliament to take an oath explicitly disavowing support for separatism. The moderate Tamil members of parliament, who had been elected in 1977 from the north and east on a platform that called for the establishment of a separate Tamil state, could not take such an oath and found themselves expelled from parliament. This left no legitimate representatives of the Tamil population in parliament.

When presidential elections were held again in 1988, the newly elected president, Ranasinghe Premadasa, had legitimacy problems of his

---

20. See Amita Shastri, "Constitution-Making as a Political Resource: Crisis of Legitimacy in Sri Lanka," in Subrata Mitra and Dietmar Rothermund, eds., *Legitimacy and Conflict in South Asia* (New Delhi: Manohar, 1997), pp. 173–193.

own. Although Premadasa beat Bandaranaike, the validity of his electoral victory remained under a cloud because of his close association with Jayawardene as his prime minister through the long period of UNP rule and the emergency conditions under which the elections were held.

POLITICAL VIOLENCE

As its legitimacy and popular support declined, the UNP resorted increasingly to coercion and violence in its efforts to maintain control of the country. The dangers inherent in letting unresolved ethnic differences fester acquired a particularly grim character in Sri Lanka.

The government relied heavily on its emergency powers to harass and detain Tamil insurgents. This, of course, led to even more Tamil hostility. These emergency powers were beefed up with draconian laws, such as the Prevention of Terrorism Act of 1979, which allowed the government to detain anyone suspected of any unlawful activity, without trial, for up to eighteen months. Any individual or any premises could be searched without warrant by the police or army. Property could be seized. All confessions, even oral ones that might have been made under duress, were admissible as evidence in court. In important respects, the Prevention of Terrorism Act was comparable to the Terrorism Act of 1967 in South Africa.[21] Innumerable Tamil youths were subjected to arbitrary detention and torture by the state in the 1980s and early 1990s. These acts further radicalized the Tamil community in the north in particular, which began to look on the forces from Colombo as an army of occupation. It should be noted that the government acted with even greater brutality to repress Sinhalese insurgents in the late 1980s.

Of equal concern to human rights observers were the growing activities of squads of thugs, loyal to leading Sinhalese politicians, after 1977. In addition to threatening and injuring opposition activists, these thugs systematically attacked Tamil civilians in increasingly serious rounds of ethnic violence in 1977, 1981, and 1983—conducting virtual pogroms against the Tamils. In the last of these, which Tamils refer to as their holocaust, hundreds and perhaps thousands of people were killed. As many as 100,000 persons were rendered homeless in Colombo, and another 175,000 became refugees outside Colombo.[22] The total economic loss

21. See Virginia Leary, *Ethnic Conflict and Violence in Sri Lanka: Report of a Mission to Sri Lanka in July–August 1981 on Behalf of the International Commission of Jurists* (Geneva: International Commission, 1981), pp. 46–50.

22. See Sunil Bastian, "Political Economy of Ethnic Violence in Sri Lanka: The July 1983 Riots," in Veena Das, ed., *Mirrors of Violence: Communities, Riots and Survivors in South Asia* (Delhi: Oxford University Press, 1992), p. 302.

was estimated at over $300 million.[23] In virtually all of these incidents, even when criminals were clearly identified, they were allowed to go unpunished. They were even rewarded on occasion.[24]

The collapse of the constitutional process led young, radical insurgents—Tamil and Sinhalese alike—to intensify their efforts to overthrow the government after 1983. Several Tamil groups, of whom the most notable was the Liberation Tigers of Tamil Eelam, carried out a spate of bank robberies, kidnappings, assassinations, and attacks on police stations. For the most part, these assaults occurred in the northeast. The Sinhalese youth group, the Janatha Vimukthi Peramuna (JVP), carried out a similar series of activities against the established political system in the southwest.

In retaliation, the government used the armed forces and created clandestine death squads to combat the insurgents. Arbitrary detentions, unrecorded arrests, torture, and murder—by government forces—became routine in the late 1980s.

In the ensuing cycle of violence and revenge, horrific atrocities were committed. Villagers in the northeast were hacked to death with machetes. In the southwest, maimed, charred, and mutilated bodies were found lining village roads, hung from trees, or washed up by rivers or the sea. Human rights groups estimate that some 66,000 people died in the JVP insurgency in the southwest before it was finally put down in 1990. Another 34,000 were killed in the northeast by the time UNP rule ended in 1994.

The emergence of the highly motivated, highly disciplined, militant, and ruthless LTTE is one of the main reasons why the Tamil-Sinhalese conflict has become so intractable. The leadership provided by Vellupillai Prabhakaran certainly contributes to the LTTE's success, as does its members' ideological training and total commitment to the goal of a separate state. It has become almost commonplace to mention that each LTTE fighter is willing to die for the cause and carries a cyanide capsule on a string around his or her neck, ready to be consumed in the event of capture. The LTTE has systematically attacked and killed members of other Tamil groups in order to establish and maintain its dominant position in Tamil politics. It has developed and maintains networks of Tamil supporters in India, Canada, Australia, the United Kingdom, France, the

---

23. See Tambiah, *Ethnic Fratricide*, pp. 22–23.
24. See Manor, *Sri Lanka in Change and Crisis*; and Tambiah, *Ethnic Fratricide*.

United States, and Singapore. In addition, it is said that the LTTE makes money from running arms and drugs.[25]

Another worrying aspect of the political violence on the island has been the rise of political assassinations carried out by the LTTE and to a lesser extent the JVP. The list of LTTE victims includes former Indian Prime Minister Rajiv Gandhi, Sri Lankan President Premadasa, presidential aspirants and former ministers Lalith Athulathmudali and Gamini Dissanaike, Defense Minister Ranjan Wijeratne, navy chief Clancy Fernando, army chief Denzil Kobbekaduwe and several other army generals, and moderate TULF leaders Appapillai Amirthalingam, V. Yogeswaran, and Sam Thambimuttu. The current president's popular and politically ascendant husband, Vijay Kumaratunge, was gunned down, allegedly by the JVP. Many of these assassinations were timed to inflict maximum damage to the political process, and to discourage political figures from taking actions injurious to the goals of the militants.

As if to imitate the Sinhalese Buddhist chauvinists who claimed the whole of the island as Buddha's estate, Tamil militants defined their projected separate state generously to include all territories in which Tamils were or had been in a majority position. They have consequently struck out against individuals deemed to be agents of the central government, as well as Sinhalese settlers in the northeastern region. The goal was to reduce the Sinhalese population in "Tamil areas" by killing Sinhalese and by frightening them into fleeing, thereby reestablishing the numerical dominance of the Tamil community in the "homeland" they claimed.

INTERNATIONALIZATION OF THE CONFLICT

The UNP government consistently sought to characterize the country's ethnic conflict as a domestic problem. It depicted Sri Lankan Tamil activists, even moderate ones, as troublesome, ungrateful, and unpatriotic. It accused them of being unwilling to cooperate with the majority community and the existing power structure, in return for which they could get rewards from those in power. In short, Tamils were criticized for refusing to adopt the strategy that Muslims had chosen to follow.[26]

Left with few options at home, separatist-minded Tamils decided to internationalize the issue in an effort to attract attention to their cause,

25. See "Foreign Minister at the UN," *Sri Lanka News*, Vol. 6, No. 10 (October 1996), pp. 1–3.

26. For a discussion along these lines, see De Silva, *Managing Ethnic Tensions*.

and thereby pressure the Sri Lankan government into making concessions. The Tamil diaspora and Tamil refugees became political and financial resources in this context. As the government's treatment of Tamils had become more restrictive, large numbers of educated and skilled Tamils had emigrated to developed countries in the 1960s and 1970s in search of better opportunities. Others, often of humbler backgrounds, fled to Tamil Nadu, the state in India with whose population the Sri Lankan Tamils share a substantial cultural heritage. The Sri Lankan government's harsh actions were brought to the attention of the international community by the Tamil diaspora, and used to arouse irredentist sentiments and political activity in Tamil Nadu. Moderate Sri Lankan Tamil politicians attempted to engage their counterparts in Tamil Nadu and in the central Indian government itself. Militant Tamil youth groups sought to obtain armed training and material support from the Indian government. Repeated efforts by the Indian government to mediate the conflict in Sri Lanka met with little success.

Big-power rivalry further complicated the story. President Jayawardene, faced with a mounting foreign debt problem in the early 1980s, sought to gain Western (primarily U.S.) support for the government by offering military bases to foreign powers on the island. This was opposed by India, which did not want a great-power military presence in the region. India began to back the insurgent groups in Sri Lanka with arms and training to pressure the government in Colombo on this question.[27]

Failing to get Western help against India, the Sri Lankan government signed an accord with India in 1987. Under the terms of the accord, India promised to send an Indian Peace Keeping Force (IPKF) to Sri Lanka to monitor a cease-fire in the civil war and to disarm the militants. In return, Sri Lanka agreed to stop trying to forge extra-regional ties and to resolve the Tamil problem through decentralization. The government in Colombo acknowledged that Sri Lanka was a multiethnic and multilingual society consisting of Sinhalese, Tamils, Muslims, and Burghers. While it accorded pride of place to Sinhala as the country's official language, it also recognized Tamil and English as official languages. In a significant development, the Thirteenth Amendment to the constitution and the Provincial Councils Act created a system of provincial councils and constituted a significant devolution of power. The Sixteenth Amendment made Tamil and English official languages.

Unfortunately, the accord unraveled over the next four years, and only a partial resolution of the country's ethnic problem was achieved

---

27. For a good discussion, see S.D. Muni, *Pangs of Proximity: India and Sri Lanka's Ethnic Crisis* (Newbury Park, Calif.: Sage Publications, 1993), chap. 3.

through the weakly instituted provincial councils.[28] The complex sequence of events that followed the signing of the accord created a serious crisis of credibility for its leading actors. The IPKF could not get the LTTE, the most militant of the Tamil groups, to disarm. The IPKF was consequently compelled to fight the LTTE. Due to divisions within its own ranks, the Sri Lankan government failed to devolve adequate power, and therefore failed to win over a decisive segment of Tamil opinion. Faced with Sinhalese nationalist opposition to the accord and to the IPKF, President Premadasa, who assumed power in 1989, demanded that the IPKF leave. His government even supplied arms to the LTTE to fight the IPKF. The government succeeded in getting the IPKF to withdraw and in crushing the JVP by early 1991, but the reinvigorated LTTE continued to remain beyond its control. Indeed, after a brief cease-fire, fighting was resumed by the LTTE, to Premadasa's discomfiture.

Peace Initiatives and Disappointments, 1994–97

While progress has been made on some aspects of the ethnic crisis in Sri Lanka, other aspects have proved resistant to solution.

LEGITIMACY RESTORED

The legitimacy of the political system in Sri Lanka was substantially restored when free and fair elections were held in August 1994. These elections brought a coalition of SLFP-led parties to power under the leadership of Chandrika Kumaratunge, S.W.R.D. Bandaranaike's and Sirimavo Bandaranaike's daughter. In November, Kumaratunge won the presidency with 62.3 percent of the vote. The war-weary populace was attracted to her promise to work for a peaceful resolution of the ethnic conflict through negotiations with the LTTE and a substantial devolution of power. She also promised to abolish the powerful presidency and replace it with a parliamentary cabinet system that would be more accountable.

Kumaratunge's political stock went up further, both domestically and internationally, when she offered a cessation of hostilities and unconditional talks to the LTTE. She followed this offer with a series of confidence-building measures, responding positively or at least reasonably to various demands and conditions the LTTE voiced before it would engage in talks. The Tamil population in Jaffna responded enthusiastically to the relief supplies sent from Colombo and to the visits by the

---

28. See Amita Shastri, "Sri Lanka's Provincial Council System: A Solution to the Ethnic Problem?" *Asian Survey*, Vol. 32, No. 8 (August 1992), pp. 401–421.

president's representatives. Their enthusiasm was a clear sign that the peace process was gathering momentum.[29]

SEPARATIST RECALCITRANCE

The government's promise to devolve substantial power to the provincial level was insufficient to the LTTE, which was committed to the establishment of an independent Tamil state. The LTTE stalled in the negotiations before breaking the cease-fire in April 1995 with an attack on two government frigates anchored in the port of Trincomalee in the Eastern Province.[30] A verbal attack on the government from the Sinhalese right predictably followed, accusing the government of being naive: the government had cancelled orders for arms and military equipment and cut defense spending in an effort to reassure the LTTE of its commitment to find a peaceful solution to the conflict. The government was compelled to rethink its strategy. It consequently reorganized the armed forces, giving them more offensive capabilities. A massive counteroffensive was launched over the summer. The government maintained that the offensive would last only until the LTTE came back to the negotiating table.

The peace initiative was not a wasted effort, however. It restored the government's image and international credibility. It brought the new government not only political and diplomatic sympathy, but financial and military aid, which helped to cover the escalating costs of a conflict it had clearly wanted to avoid. The support that the government received from human rights groups was also valuable. These endorsements led some foreign governments to undercut LTTE support networks in their own countries.

When fighting resumed, the Kumaratunge government showed that it was determined to control the LTTE. It made new appointments to the top positions in the armed forces, arranged for new arms and training, investigated corruption, and treated human rights violations by the armed forces more seriously. These developments boosted morale in the armed forces. Perhaps more importantly, they made the armed forces more effective militarily. This became evident when the armed forces launched an operation to reestablish control over the Jaffna peninsula, an LTTE stronghold for a decade. To the surprise of most observers, the Sri Lankan armed forces prevailed within a matter of months, taking Jaffna City in December 1995. In September 1996, the government succeeded in capturing the last major town under rebel control.

---

29. See *Tamil Times*, Vol. 14, No. 1 (January 15, 1995).

30. For details, see *Tamil Times*, Vol. 14, No. 4 (April 15, 1995).

This has forced the LTTE to rely primarily on guerrilla warfare. Rebel fighters have retreated to the jungles and rural areas of the Northern and Eastern provinces, where they can move freely and strike at will. Unless a settlement is reached, a long terrorist campaign is likely to follow.

THE PEACE PACKAGE

The other important element in the government strategy to deal with the ethnic crisis was the peace package of August 1995. The government surpassed the expectations of most observers by promising to institute a highly decentralized system of government.

Avoiding the negative image that the term "federalism" had acquired in the Sri Lankan political debate, the government's proposals called for Sri Lanka to become a "union of regions." The presidential-parliamentary structure of government at the center would be replaced by a parliamentary one. The Northern and Eastern provinces would be merged into one region (after some boundary changes), and in each of the country's eight regions (as the provinces would be called), a popularly elected regional government, consisting of chief minister, board of ministers, and assemblies, would be granted clear powers over a wide range of policy areas, including taxation, law and order, police, land, agriculture, industry, development and planning, education, culture, and communications. Both Sinhala and Tamil would be official national languages. The proposed governmental system was far more decentralized than anything that any previous government had offered. It was also more decentralized than India's quasi federal system.[31]

The government's proposals aimed at a just and balanced system in which all citizens of Sri Lanka, of whatever ethnicity, could hope to be treated equally. The proposed power-sharing arrangement would serve the needs of the Sri Lankan Tamil minority while including it in a symmetrical structure, which would enhance good governance and participation of the majority community across the island. Its bold vision gained widespread support within the Sri Lankan intelligentsia and that of friendly foreign governments.

Unfortunately, this peace initiative has stalled and could go the way of past efforts to devolve power. To become part of the constitution, the government's proposals would have to be passed by a two-thirds majority in the parliament, and then be approved by a majority of the people voting in a referendum. The government's coalition falls short of a two-thirds majority by 9 or 10 members in the 225-seat parliament. It thus

---

31. For details, see *Tamil Times*, Vol. 14, No. 8 (August 15, 1995).

needs the support of the major opposition party, the UNP, which has not been forthcoming. After a period of studied silence on the issue, the UNP proclaimed itself against the abolition of the unitary state. It remains in favor of a dominant role for the center despite the blatant biases that have characterized the center and its policies since independence and which have led the island to its tragic impasse. In taking this position, the UNP has banded with chauvinist Sinhalese opinion, including significant segments of the Buddhist clergy.[32] At the same time, all Tamil groups are opposed to continuing a unitary system. This political impasse has led moderate Tamil groups to become increasingly alienated. They have formed an alliance and threatened to withdraw their support for the government.[33]

Meanwhile, the conflict continues to prove costly in economic and political terms. Defense spending is cutting into the funds available for development.[34] Inflation, unemployment, and political unrest are rising. According to official estimates, since April 1995, the war has resulted in about 20,000 deaths and displaced some 300,000 people in the northeast.[35] There has also been a hardening of opinion within the Sinhalese community, which increasingly wonders why concessions to the Tamils are needed given that the government has seemingly won the war.

To a significant degree, Prabhakaran and the LTTE have been isolated domestically and internationally. In addition, commissions have been launched to investigate abuses of power and acts of corruption committed when the UNP was in power.[36] Meanwhile, efforts to rehabilitate war-devastated Tamil areas and to implement Tamil as an official language are being made.[37] Although these developments have not dissolved the political impasse and brought about a peaceful political settlement, they are nonetheless significant and are signs of hope to those who support the peace process.

---

32. *Tamil Times*, Vol. 14, No. 3 (March 15, 1995).

33. *Tamil Times*, Vol. 14, No. 6 (June 15, 1995), p. 13.

34. The rate of growth in the gross domestic product for 1996 is expected to be in the vicinity of 3.3 percent. Defense spending will be around U.S. $909 million, which is equal to 6.5 percent of Sri Lanka's gross domestic product. See *Tamil Times*, Vol. 15, No. 5 (May 15, 1996), p. 7; and *SLNet*, August 8, 1996, and September 14, 1996.

35. *SLNet*, August 15, 1996.

36. *SLNet*, September 21, 1996.

37. For instance, there is a plan to recruit 1,500 Tamil teachers, 500 of whom will go first to Upcountry Tamil schools.

Conclusions

Ethnic relations in Sri Lanka have been deeply influenced by state policies. Sri Lanka had free and fair elections until the 1980s, an established system of law and order, a lively and basically free press, and many political and religious freedoms. Children were educated in their own vernacular languages, Sinhala or Tamil. This relatively benign situation was undermined by the ill-conceived actions and policies discussed in this chapter. Some of these policies had a clear-cut ethnic content.

The backdrop to ethnic relations in Sri Lanka was the discourse employed by the Sinhalese political elite in the pre- and post-independence period. It was articulated in a way that generated a sense of ethnic identity. As such, it could be targeted against the colonial power, but it could also be employed against people who were perceived to be "different," "foreign," or "latecomers" to the island, such as the Christian, Muslim, and Tamil minorities. The citizenship and franchise laws passed soon after independence excluded the large Upcountry Tamil minority from participating as equal citizens in the political life of the country. Specific measures later repatriated over half the Upcountry Tamils to India. This policy undercut the earlier system, on which the imperfect independence consensus had rested, of weighing the comparative ethnic populations. The electoral bias that was created in favor of the majority community from the Kandyan areas was maintained for more than three decades. Similarly, the institutionalization of Sinhala as the country's only official language excluded large numbers of Sri Lankan Tamils from gaining employment in the burgeoning state sector. Thus, both the parliament and the government bureaucracy became increasingly dominated by the Sinhalese. Changes in university admissions policies in the 1970s also worked to the advantage of the Sinhalese community. The recognition of Buddhism's "foremost place" in Sri Lanka further exacerbated ethnic tensions in the country.

A significant development along the way was the political competition between the country's two leading Sinhalese political parties. As this competition intensified, each began to pander to the Sinhalese vote and play the ethnic card, leading to a pattern of ethnic "outbidding," which then undercut any attempts to make substantive concessions to the Tamils to resolve their grievances. With access to political power and state resources skewed in favor of the Sinhalese community, the Tamil minority remained politically and economically disadvantaged.

Most governments have not had coherent strategies to deal with the country's ethnic problems. Far-sighted leadership was particularly lacking when Sri Lanka became independent. The principles on which the new state was founded were not based on a multiethnic consensus. Similar mistakes were made when the 1972 and 1978 constitutions were developed.

Instead, most governments have acted in an ad hoc fashion in response to evolving demands and pressures. Efforts to protect short-term partisan interests inevitably led to credibility and legitimacy crises and mounting ethnic problems. The trend of events in the late 1950s under the first SLFP government and in the late 1970s and 1980s under the UNP are particularly worthy of note in this regard.

In most instances, desirable policies such as the devolution promised by the Bandaranaike-Chelvanayagam Pact of 1957 and the Senanayake-Chelvanayagam Pact of 1965 were not implemented; the leadership lacked political will. Although the UNP had an overwhelming majority in parliament in the 1980s, it failed to implement policies that might have helped to ease ethnic tensions. In fact, it manipulated the 1982 presidential election and the 1983 parliamentary election, destroying the credibility of the parliamentary process and the moderate center and polarizing ethnic relations. Political violence was subsequently justified as a mode of opposition to the government. Opportunistic power calculations, rampant factionalism, and ethnic chauvinism in the ruling party contributed in important ways to Sri Lanka's descent into civil war.

It is perhaps inevitable that ambitious politicians use partisan appeals to attract, consolidate, and maintain support. This has certainly happened in Sri Lanka. One only has to recall D.S. Senanayake's exclusion of the Upcountry Tamils to get support of the Kandyan areas, S.W.R.D. Bandaranaike's use of "Sinhala only" to attract the vote of the rising Sinhalese middle class, J.R. Jayawardene's and the UNP's opposition to the B-C Pact and competition for the Sinhalese vote, the United Front's 1972 constitution and its university admissions policy, and the UNP's 1978 constitution and its failure to deliver on various devolution schemes. The need to protect one's short-term political interests and the political and economic interests of one's constituency makes ethnic politics difficult to control unless checked by constitutional rules and strong political institutions.

There are some signs of progress, however. Proportional representation has been established in the national legislature. Tamil has been accepted as an official language at the national level. War-weariness has led to a greater willingness to accommodate diverse perspectives and demands within the political system. The clearest signs of this have been Kumaratunge's victory and her devolution package. The costs of the conflict have made leading members of both major parties wary of supporting or tolerating violence in an effort to coerce the Tamil community.

The military, for its part, is larger, better trained, and more experienced in the complexities of fighting a civil war. As its performance since 1994 has shown, it is less likely to retaliate in an undisciplined manner against civilian populations when provoked by guerrilla militants. Lastly, political elites in the country seem to appreciate the importance of free and fair elections: the irreplaceable mechanism for resolving disputes between competing political forces.

What is needed above all in Sri Lanka is comprehensive constitutional reform. Kumaratunge's proposed reforms offer a decentralized structure, individual rights, and democratic checks and balances. They would provide for a devolution of power that would allow the different peoples who make up Sri Lanka's plural society to govern themselves in important respects. Although the need for a devolution of power has gained recognition in Sri Lanka, problems relating to its operationalization are proving incredibly difficult to overcome. The most important of these is a lack of consensus on the issue between the leaderships of the country's two major parties. Perhaps the only way to solve this problem is to form a government of national reconciliation. Such a government could thrash out an agreement, present it to the people as a joint accomplishment, and share power for a specified period (perhaps five years) during which the agreement would be implemented. If no single party has the ability to impose its conception of political order on the country, then creating a government of national reconciliation is the only way to overcome ethnic divisions and build a viable political framework for the future.

Part II
Southeast and East Asia

Chapter 4

Fifty Years of Failure in Burma

Josef Silverstein

After World War II, Burma's civilian democratic leaders sincerely desired to create a state that would freely unite the majority Burmans with indigenous minorities. They envisaged a federation based on the principles of equality, mutual respect, and trust. Working in haste and under great pressure, these leaders wrote a flawed constitution. However, the problems that followed Burma's independence in January 1948 were not the result of faulty draftsmanship alone; they were rooted in the country's ethnic history, misperceptions of what various groups wanted, competing visions of how to translate principles into laws, and a lack of trust in political processes to resolve differences.

After a half-century of government failures to devise ethnic policies that would create true national unity, Burma's military leaders, who seized power in 1962 and are now organized as the State Law and Order Restoration Council (SLORC), are making another try at formulating and imposing a solution to the ethnic problem as part of a new constitution. Since 1992, the SLORC-directed National Convention has been trying to write a new basic law that would promote "non-disintegration of the Union," "non-disintegration of national solidarity," and "consolidation and perpetuation of sovereignty."[1] Although the convention has not completed its work, one can make an assessment about what it has done to date and whether the principles it has adopted will bring about peace, social unity, and economic development.

I will make five main arguments in this chapter. First, under the Burman kings, some minorities assimilated with the Burman majority, while many hill peoples did not. The Karen, in particular, retained a

---

1. "Order No. 13/92, Formation of the Convening Commission for the National Convention," *Working People's Daily* (Rangoon), October 2, 1992.

distinct culture, developing an antagonistic relationship with Burman authorities that persists today. Second, British colonial rule further complicated the picture. British "divide and rule" tactics aggravated ethnic relations in Burma in important respects. Third, although independent Burma's first constitution contained commitments to ethnic equality and federal political arrangements, these commitments were gradually undercut: citizenship laws were tightened, political power was centralized, and Burman culture was promoted. Fourth, under military rule, the centralization of power and the promotion of Burman culture were taken to new levels. The rulers saw centralization and assimilation as the keys to maintaining state unity and, not coincidentally, their own hold on power. Fifth, the military's policies have failed and will continue to fail to promote good ethnic relations and political stability in the country. It will take years to undo the damage done by fifty years of failure, but progress cannot begin until the military agrees to enter into a true dialogue with its opponents and accept the principles of political equality, ethnic diversity, and local autonomy.

Historical and Colonial Legacies

Burma has always been multiethnic, with Burmans constituting the largest, and for the most part, the dominant group in the country. (See Table 4.1.) Burmans established their political and economic center at Pagan, along the Irrawaddy River in central Burma. Various minorities have lived in coastal regions, the delta, and the plains in the south, and others have resided in the surrounding hills to the west, north, and east.

Although the Burman monarchs never articulated a discrete ethnic policy, it was implicit in the differing ways they governed and dealt with peoples on the plains and in the hill areas. As the Burmans extended their empire southward through conquest and brought the Karen, Mon, and Arakanese under their control, they moved into lower Burma and settled among the minorities. Burman kings governed these areas directly through an administrative system that was effective so long as monarchs were strong and royal succession was smooth. Burman rule, however, was marked by weak kings, rivalry, and intrigue at the palace. Since each administrator was appointed by the king and served at his pleasure, frequent upheavals at the capital led to frequent changes in local administration and periods of time when the people followed their local hereditary leaders and local traditions.

Over time, Burmans intermarried with Mon and Arakanese, who were also Buddhists, resulting in unplanned assimilation and the spread of the Burman language and culture. The same did not happen with the

Table 4.1. Ethnic Composition of Burma.

Group	Number	Percentage
Burmese (Burman)	23,532,433	69.0
Shan	2,890,437	8.5
Karen	2,122,825	6.2
Rakhine (Arakanese)	1,536,725	4.5
Mon	826,801	2.4
Chin	745,463	2.2
Kachin	465,484	1.4
Kayah (Karenni)	141,028	.4
Other indigenous	33,227	0.1
Mixed Burmese and Foreign	1,830,485	5.3
Total	**34,124,908**	**100.0**

NOTE: A complete census has not been conducted in Burma since 1931. The military rulers of Burma conducted a census in most parts of Burma in 1983. Since then, no new census has been taken. Given the continuous state of war in Burma, the exodus of alien minority refugees since 1977 and the exodus of indigenous minority refugees since 1988, there are no reliable population data for Burma. It is believed that one million people were not included in the census totals noted above. As of late 1996, Burma's population was estimated at 47,799,000.

SOURCE: This table is based on information compiled in the 1983 census conducted by the military rulers of Burma.

Karen; ethnic and religious differences, together with a long history of antagonism, kept the Burmans and Karen apart. The separation between the two widened following the arrival of Christian missionaries, who found willing converts among the Karen. The split deepened during the Anglo-Burman wars of the nineteenth century, when many Karen served as scouts for and supported the British.

Burman policy toward the hill minorities was based on indirect rule. It allowed the minorities to continue living in their traditional ways, under their own leaders, using their own languages, and practicing their own religions, while acknowledging Burman suzerainty by paying tribute and accepting the presence of Burman military representatives in the courts of their rulers. Where Burman and minority villages met, there was cultural exchange, peaceful coexistence, and some intermarriage, but little interaction beyond the thin line of contact. The largest hill groups were the Shans, Kachins, and Chins. Following the fall of Pagan in 1287, the Shans, the most numerous and best organized of the three, were the nominal successors to the Burman kings; however, they could not establish a stable kingdom because they were too divided among themselves. In the fifteenth century, the Burmans reestablished their authority and continued to rule until 1886. The Kachins in the north and the Chins in the west were smaller groups; less developed politically, they never threatened Burman rule.

The two major objectives of Burman policies toward the hill minorities were to obtain troops for their armies and to use minority villages and peoples as protective shields with respect to more distant enemies. This system was unstable, however; many of the more distant groups paid tribute in two directions in order to assure their survival. In addition, when Burman kings were weak or their dynasties in disarray, some of the more distant minorities broke away and joined foreign forces against the Burmans.

Until the nineteenth century, Burman rulers had no specific ethnic policy toward Europeans, as few settled in the country. With the Burman capital located near the country's center, Burman leaders had little contact with the Europeans who came by sea and made contact with peoples living in the coastal areas. Although Portuguese traders and soldiers established themselves among the Mon and Arakanese and fought as mercenaries in their armies, the Burmans did not see them as a threat to their rule.

Burma's relations with China were marked by war and destruction of the Pagan dynasty in the thirteenth century and several failed Chinese invasions in the nineteenth century; however, these events did not prevent Chinese peasants from migrating to Burma, moving southward from Yunnan and settling among Burma's ethnic minorities and the Burmans. Chinese settlers assimilated and intermarried easily, as religious, cultural and political barriers were few.

The British conquest of Burma brought major changes in the country's ethnic relations and ethnic policies. The British had no intention of assimilating the peoples they conquered. Rather, they justified their rule of conquered peoples as the "white man's burden." By this they meant establishing law, order, and internal peace; creating strong central authorities backed by British law, administration, military forces, and police; spreading Western culture and ideas through Christian missionaries, educators, and businessmen; and converting local economies from subsistence to exchange orientations. They established themselves at the top of all administrative, economic, and social pyramids; Burmans, along with all other ethnic groups, were treated as subordinates. While the army and police recruited from among the "martial races"—the Karen and hill peoples—missionary and state-supported schools prepared Burmans, Mon, Arakanese, and delta Karen to participate in government administration and the professions.

In what Burman nationalists later called a "divide and rule" policy,

Burma.

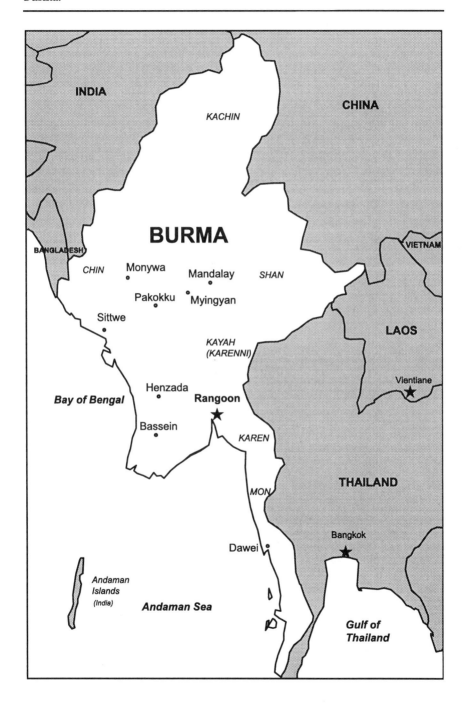

the British, like Burman rulers before them, kept the plains and hill peoples separated; they governed the former directly through centralized administrative arrangements and the latter indirectly through local leaders, according to local traditions and rules. Because Burma was made a province of India, the people in the directly ruled areas were given self-governing institutions parallel to those in India, while the hill minorities were not.[2] In 1922, the colonial government separated the Shan states from the other hill areas and formed them into the Shan States Federation under the governor of Burma.[3]

One of the most important changes in ethnic policy under British rule was the opening of Burma to foreign immigration. British recruits filled the upper ranks of the civil service, military, and police, and British firms brought in their own countrymen to fill management positions. As a province of India, Burma was opened to Indian migrants who came initially as soldiers and farmers, but then moved into the cities and large towns to become laborers and small merchants. The British also brought in Indians to fill the lower ranks of the civil service, and encouraged immigration among the money-lending castes to finance the expansion of agriculture. In general, the British favored Indians over members of the local society because the former spoke English and were familiar with the colonial system that had evolved over two centuries in India.

Toward the end of the nineteenth century, Chinese migration expanded into the cities of Burma. Chinese workers constituted a cheap source of labor, filling jobs that the indigenous population shunned. Chinese migrants also started small businesses of their own.

Changes in ethnic policy in Burma followed the introduction of popular participation in government. Initially, under the reforms of 1909, the Legislative Council included Europeans drawn from chambers of commerce and trade associations, Burmans from the Burma Chamber of Commerce, and communal representatives from the Indian and Shan communities. In 1923, a parliamentary system was introduced, comprising mainly Burman members. However, it also created special electorates and communal seats for Europeans, Anglo-Indians, Indians, and Karen. Under the 1935 Act, the governor was given "special responsibilities to protect the legitimate rights of the minorities."[4] Under this act, reserved

---

2. *Government of Burma Act, 1921.*

3. Sao Saimong Mangrai, *The Shan States and the British Occupation*, Data Paper 57 (Ithaca, N.Y.: Cornell University Southeast Asia Program, 1965), p. 304.

4. Josef Silverstein, *Burmese Politics: The Dilemma of National Unity* (New Brunswick, N.J.: Rutgers University Press, 1980), pp. 28–32.

seats and special electorates in the Parliament were expanded, with seats set aside for Anglo-Burmans and Chinese.[5] Because the hill areas remained apart from Burma proper, their residents did not benefit from any of these reforms.

Ethnic policy together with the world economic depression of the 1930s led to increased conflict between Burmans, Indians, and Chinese. Thousands of Burman farmers moved to the cities after they lost their lands to moneylenders. They could not afford new land because the price of rice had fallen so low; it did not pay to continue farming. In the cities and towns, they competed with Indians and Chinese for the few available jobs. Ethnic conflict subsequently erupted over economic and religious issues. This period also saw a rise in nationalism and political activity among the Burmans. The separation of Burma from India in 1937 and the introduction of responsible government did not end the economic competition between and among ethnic groups; nor did they silence the continuing popular demand to end Indian immigration to Burma. Cut off from administrative Burma and the world economy, the hill minorities continued to farm, hunt, and work in the forests and mines, largely unaffected by the events taking place in and around Burma's large cities.

British rule reduced the positions of Burmans with respect to indigenous minorities and opened the country to foreign immigrants who enjoyed economic and political privileges that appeared to come at Burman expense. In addition, antagonisms between Burmans and Karen intensified as each group pursued its own political agenda.

Developments during World War II

British colonial rule was interrupted in January 1942 when Japan invaded Burma and drove the British army and government out of the country. However, even before the war began, Japan had given military training to a small number of Burman nationalists, who of course opposed British rule. When war broke out in the Pacific, they were given arms and formed an army that participated in the invasion of Burma.[6] This was the first indigenous Burman army since the British overthrew the Burman monarchy in 1885; it was composed almost exclusively of Burmans.

The displacement of British rule triggered an exodus of nearly one

---

5. John L. Christian, *Burma and the Japanese Invader* (Bombay: Thacker and Co. Ltd., 1945), pp. 84–86.

6. Aung San, "Burma's Challenge," in Josef Silverstein, ed., *The Political Legacy of Aung San,* rev. ed. (Ithaca, N.Y.: Cornell University Southeast Asia Program, 1993), pp. 75–93.

million Indians who sought refuge in India, fearing Burman reprisals for their past support of the British and the various political, economic, and social benefits they had received. Immediately following the defeat of the British, elements of the new Burman army turned on the Karen, which in turn led Japanese forces to intervene and stop the bloodshed. As early as 1942, Burman leaders sent a strong signal to the Karen: they wanted to put the past behind them and build a new relationship by recruiting Karen as officers and soldiers in the army. Burmans and Karen subsequently fought together in the closing days of the war.[7]

On August 1, 1943, Japan gave Burma nominal independence. However, this did not extend to the Frontier Areas, where fighting continued or would be renewed. In response to Burman protests, Japan returned sovereignty over all but two of the Shan states, which the Japanese had transferred to Thailand, as well as the Karenni states, and the Wa territory to Burma.[8]

From the Burman point of view, the war was important in terms of ethnic issues because it restored the Burmans to primacy and put them back in direct contact with the ethnic peoples from whom they had been separated. It helped restore their sense of pride: they played a role in ending British colonial rule in 1942 and in driving out the Japanese forces in 1945. The war had less salutary effects on Burman-Karen relations. Despite the efforts of Burman leaders to forge a new relationship, traditional attitudes prevailed on both sides.

Postwar Developments

When the British civil administration returned to Burma following the defeat of Japan, it restored the Act of 1935, which reinstated the ethnic policies of the past. Burma proper again was separated from the Frontier Areas. The question of eventual unification of the two areas was left to be decided when the "inhabitants signify their desire for some suitable form of amalgamation of their territories with Burma proper."[9] In addition, Indians and Europeans were allowed to return and resume their prewar roles and exercise the rights and privileges they had previously

7. General Smith-Dun, *Memoirs of the Four-Foot Colonial*, Data Paper 113 (Ithaca, N.Y.: Cornell University Southeast Asia Program, 1980), pp. 49–50; Thakin Nu, *Burma under the Japanese: Pictures and Portraits* (London: Macmillan, 1954), pp. 99–101; and Ian Morrison, *Grandfather Longlegs* (London: Faber and Faber, 1947), pp. 197–201.

8. Government of Burma, *Burma during the Japanese Occupation* (Simla: Manager, Government of India Press, 1943), Vol. 1, p. 28.

9. *British Statement of Policy by His Majesty's Government*, 1945.

held. Because of the social and political disruptions caused by the war, the governor was authorized to rule under the emergency provisions of the Act. This meant, in practice, that he did not have to reconstitute the Burman legislature.

In a departure from the prewar state of affairs, the governor found a strong nationalist opposition, the Anti Fascist People's Freedom League (AFPFL), to British rule. The AFPFL demanded that it be given six representatives and that ethnic minorities receive five in parliament. It also called for direct access between people in Burma proper and in the Frontier Areas. The governor rejected these demands and sought to govern with the support of other Burman leaders and representatives of minority groups. He also encouraged British companies to return to Burma and help rebuild the Burman economy.

At the same time, Admiral Louis Mountbatten, the supreme allied commander for Southeast Asia, met with AFPFL leaders in Ceylon and agreed to the creation of a new army for Burma composed of an equal number of Burmans, drawn from the Burma National Army, and ethnic minority members, recruited from the British Burma Army. Modeled on the Indian Army, the new Burman army was organized along ethnic lines. Units were ethnically homogenous and led by officers from the relevant ethnic groups using vernacular languages. At command levels, English would be used.[10]

In the summer of 1946, the Karen sent a delegation to London to discuss the prospects for forming a separate Karen state. They received no official support and returned empty-handed. At the end of August, a new governor took over in Burma and introduced an important change in official policy on ethnic issues. "It will be my object," he declared, "to ensure that relations between the peoples of the hills and the plains should be as close and as intimate as possible."[11] Three weeks later, he formed a new Executive Council, with an AFPFL majority and one Karen representative; it was given authority comparable to that held by prewar ministers under the 1935 Act.

On December 20, 1946, the British prime minister invited a Burman delegation from the Executive Council to come to England and discuss Burma's transition to independence. The British failed, however, to include representatives from the Frontier Areas in their invitation. The leaders of the hill peoples saw this as an affront; the Shans, in particular, expressed their disappointment about being left out of these most important discussions.

---

10. Silverstein, *The Political Legacy*, pp. 30–38.

11. *New Times of Burma*, Sept. 3, 1946.

Even before he received the invitation to go to London, Aung San, the leader of the AFPFL and the chief councillor in the governor's cabinet, expressed his ideas on the future of ethnic relations in Burma: "we cannot confine the definition of a nationality to the narrow bounds of race, religion, etc. Nations are extending the rights of their respective communities even to others who may not belong to them except by their mere residence amongst them and their determination to live and be with them."[12]

On January 1, 1947, on the eve of the delegation's departure to London, the AFPFL called for Burma proper and the Frontier Areas to become independent simultaneously; they also demanded the immediate appointment of a representative of the Frontier Areas to the Executive Council, and the inclusion of the Frontier Areas and the Karenni state in any future constitutional assembly that would have the power to decide about the creation of a Burma federation.[13]

If the Aung San statement on nationality is read together with the AFPFL declaration, it is clear that the Burma leadership intended to pursue a liberal ethnic policy that would have embraced all the people living in the country, indigenous and alien, on a basis of equality and that it intended to create a political structure that would be erected jointly by Burmans and minorities.

The Aung San–Attlee Agreement, which was reached at the London meeting, exceeded most of the AFPFL's demands. It gave real power to the Executive Council—the same powers that had been given to the Interim Government in India—including control over the country's military forces. It extended the right to vote or to be elected to Burma nationals who were defined "as British subjects or subjects of Indian States who were born in Burma and resided there for not less than eight years or ten years immediately preceding either January 1, 1942 or January 1, 1947." The Frontier Areas and Burma proper were to be closely associated, in a manner acceptable to both, with free access to both areas by all inhabitants of both areas. Finally, the agreement created a committee to investigate the sentiments of the peoples of the Frontier Areas and to make recommendations on their future association with Burma proper.[14]

At the Panglong meeting in February 1947, the Shans, Kachins, and

---

12. Quoted in Silverstein, *The Political Legacy*, p. 150.

13. *The Times* (London), January 2, 1947.

14. *Conclusions Reached in the Conversations between His Majesty's Government and the Delegation from the Executive Council of the Government of Burma*, 1947.

Chins met with the Burman leaders, Aung San and U Tin Tut, who represented the Executive Council. The spokesmen for the hill minorities demanded that the Frontier Areas have political rights and privileges equal to those of the Burmans and that the hill peoples have political autonomy in their states and a guarantee that they would have the right to secede from the future federation; they also demanded that they receive funds from the central government as well as the right to impose local taxes.[15]

Aung San sought to allay fears of Burman domination by promising political and economic equality and by insisting that the Executive Council had no intention of interfering in local affairs. Decisions on political institutions for the state and tribal areas, he maintained, would be left for local chiefs and peoples to decide. On February 12, the two sides entered into an accord—the Panglong Agreement—which addressed all of the hill peoples' concerns but stopped short of giving them a right of secession. The appointment of a councillor and two deputy councillors for the Frontier Areas was the first step taken to implement the agreement and involve minority representatives in the administration of the country. The failure of the Karen and other minorities to participate in the discussions and sign the agreement weakened the claim that a foundation for the future of Burma had been laid that was acceptable to all. A Karen National Union spokesman declared that his organization would boycott the forthcoming election and would not participate in the new constituent assembly. The AFPFL moved to fill the breach by supporting its affiliate Karen organization, the Karen Youth League, which subsequently took the seats reserved for the Karen. This action opened a wound between the leaders of the Burmans and Karen, which widened after independence.

According to the Aung San–Attlee Agreement, the new constituent assembly would be double the size of the 1935 legislature. Noncommunal seats were increased to 182, Karen seats to 24, Anglo-Burman seats to 4, and the representatives of the Frontier Areas received 45. No seats were reserved for Indians, but they could run for noncommunal seats. Nor were any seats reserved for Europeans, Chinese, or any business organizations, contrary to the Act of 1935.[16]

The Constitution of 1947

The members of the Constituent Assembly did not formulate a discrete "ethnic policy" for independent Burma, but they formed the pillars of

---

15. *New Times of Burma*, February 11, 1947.

16. Silverstein, *Burmese Politics*, p. 116; and Burma, *Frontier Areas Committee of Inquiry*, Report, Part I (Rangoon, 1947), pp. 122–124.

such a policy in the chapters of the constitution devoted to fundamental rights and the political structure of the new federal union.

The new constitution defined citizenship in very liberal terms, opening it to indigenous and alien minorities alike. It stated that there was only one form of citizenship "throughout the Union" and that all citizens would be equal before the law, "irrespective of birth, religion, sex or race." Moreover, there would be no "arbitrary discrimination between one citizen or class of citizens and another." Anyone who had one of the following four qualifications—parents belonged to an indigenous race of Burma; born in the territory of Burma and at least one grandparent was a member of an indigenous race; born in the territory of Burma and whose parents are or were alive at the commencement of the constitution, taking into account those Indian and British residents who fled during the war and returned afterward; or born in any territories that were included in the British domain and lived in Burma for a period of not less than eight years in the ten years immediately preceding the date of the beginning of this constitution or immediately preceding January 1, 1942—and intended to elect Burma citizenship according to the laws, "shall be a citizen of the Union."[17] There was a spirit of equality and a willingness to accept aliens written into the citizenship sections of the basic law, but it was not inscribed indelibly, and could be changed by ordinary law as the new parliament saw fit.

Ethnic policy was also reflected in a unique federal system. There was to be no separate state for the Burmans. Their area, formerly called Ministerial Burma, was renamed Burma proper; it was to be administered by the prime minister, and its laws were to be made by the national parliament. Indigenous minorities who lived among the Burmans in Burma proper—the Mon, Arakanese, and smaller groups—received no special rights or privileges; this implied that assimilation would follow. For the Karen, regardless of where they lived, the constitution provided for the continuation of separate electorates and reserved seats until questions about the Karen state were resolved.

In the former Frontier Areas, the Shan states were amalgamated into a single state. It, together with the Karenni state, would continue to be led by hereditary chiefs and an elected state council. In each of these states, the chiefs were given all the seats in the upper chamber of the national assembly, while the lower house was to be elected on a noncommunal basis. In the Kachin state, representatives to the upper house of the national parliament were to be elected in equal numbers from Kachin

---

17. *The Constitution of Union of Burma*, Articles 10 and 13 (Rangoon, 1954).

and non-Kachin communities; representatives to the lower house were to be elected on a noncommunal basis. The Chins requested and received a special division rather than a state, in order to be more closely associated with Burma proper. They were to elect members to both houses of the national parliament on a noncommunal basis, and they formed a Chin Affairs Council. However, that council's authority was limited to general administration, schools, and cultural institutions. The national parliament was to be responsible for legislation on all other matters.

The heads of state in each of the three states and the Chin Special Division were to be chosen by the prime minister in consultation with the members of the appropriate state councils. These individuals would serve in the cabinet as their states' representatives, at the pleasure of the prime minister. The prime minister would also have considerable influence over the three states and the Chin Special Division in fiscal matters. He would decide how much money would be given from federal coffers to each state to supplement locally raised taxes.[18]

The constitution granted every state the right to secede from the union, except in cases where it was specifically denied. As it turned out, the Kachin and Karen states, after they were formed, were denied this right. This meant that, in practice, only the Shan and Karenni states had the right to secede. The ability to exercise this right was circumscribed, moreover, because the constitution made the Union of Burma, not states or individuals, the ultimate owner of all lands.

The Karen posed a special problem at the Constituent Assembly because they refused to accept the physical configuration of the Karen state offered to them. In order to avoid delaying independence, the assembly created a special commission to take up the Karen problem later. In 1951, the constitution was amended to create a Karen state in the eastern hill areas of Burma; the new state did not include the Karenni area. The Karen state received representation in the national parliament on a noncommunal basis. Karen living outside the Karen state lost their communal seats and special electorate; they would henceforth have to contest seats in the states in which they resided on a noncommunal basis.[19]

The authors of the constitution created a federal system that was intended to meet the needs and demands of various ethnic minorities who were working with the Burmans for the first time to build a new state. Because the minorities who received separate states were primarily

---

18. Silverstein, *Burmese Politics*, pp. 185–205.

19. *The Constitution Amendment Act, 1951* (Act No. LXII of 1951).

concerned with having control over local affairs and sufficient funds to operate their states, they agreed to a federal union that created political inequities. Although many of the delegates to the Constituent Assembly raised this issue, they were persuaded to accept these arrangements in order to finish drafting the constitution on time. Since the constitution could be amended after it came into effect, these protests were withdrawn.

Unfortunately, the Burma Constitution contained internal contradictions, which were bound to generate confusion, mistrust, and disunity between ethnic groups and between their leaders and followers, both at the center and in the states. The constitution gave considerable power to the Burman-dominated national government, power sufficient to penetrate the states and to control their leaders and peoples. Although the constitution was supposed to allow multiculturalism to flourish, it placed power in the hands of leaders at the center who wanted to spread Burman culture throughout the country. Reflecting on the authority of the parliament to modify the constitution and the center's ability to interfere in the internal affairs of the states, Burma's attorney general accurately described the country's political structure as federal in theory and unitary in practice.[20]

Ethnic Policy in Practice, 1948–97

REDEFINING THE STATUS OF ALIEN MINORITIES

Once Burma became independent in January 1948, Parliament began narrowing the definition of citizenship. In particular, it passed a Union Citizenship Act later that year that made it more difficult for Indians to gain citizenship. Under the new law, applicants were required to show that their ancestors had made Burma their home for at least two generations, and that applicants as well as their parents were born in Burma. Those who could not meet the new test could acquire citizenship through naturalization. However, until their status was resolved, they were required to register as aliens; registered aliens were given identity cards, which allowed them to live in Burma and to vote in national elections.

The government also took steps against Chinese immigrants living in the country. Because China's governments, both Nationalist and Communist, had claimed that their nationals could not relinquish Chinese citizenship even if they moved abroad and adopted citizenship in another country, the Burma Parliament amended the Citizenship Act in 1954 to outlaw dual citizenship. The new law required anyone who claimed dual

---

20. *The Nation* (Rangoon), July 2, 1952.

citizenship to renounce allegiance to the foreign government in question or lose his or her Burman citizenship.

After the military seized power in Burma in 1962, it set the 1947 constitution aside and ruled by decree. The Revolutionary Council, the military's ruling body, made an important change in the way the 1948 citizenship law was interpreted when it withdrew recognition of the Rohingyas—Indian Muslims living mainly in Arakan—as citizens of Burma. Every citizen was subsequently issued and required to carry a national registration card, but the Rohingyas were given foreign registration cards. Many Rohingyas refused to accept this new classification and held onto documents that showed they were proper citizens. The new government also discontinued the practice of registering and giving registration cards to alien children when they reached ten years of age. Without an identity document, the status of these children was in doubt.[21]

In 1974, the military adopted a new constitution, under which all non-citizens were required to apply for foreign registration certificates. To receive the new documents, applicants had to surrender their old identity cards; but, as many Rohingyas discovered later, new cards were not always issued.

In an identity check conducted in 1977 in several parts of the country but with particular intensity in Arakan, government officials "scrutinized each individual living in the state, designating citizens and foreigners in accordance with the law and taking actions against foreigners who [had] filtered into the country illegally."[22] This triggered an exodus of more than 200,000 Rohingyas, who sought refuge in Bangladesh. The Burma government declared that those who left Burma had been illegal aliens because they did not have Burma identity papers. This escalated into an international incident between Burma and Bangladesh, which partially ended only after Burma entered into an agreement to repatriate those who fled. Working with the office of the United Nations High Commissioner for Refugees, Burma agreed to accept returnees in stages, initially taking back those with identity cards, and later accepting those who could provide evidence of residency in Burma through old village records.

In 1982, the Burma Parliament passed a new citizenship law that narrowed the definition of citizenship still further and undercut the principle of ethnic equality. It created three categories of citizens: full, associate, and naturalized. Full citizenship was given to indigenous peoples

---

21. Human Rights Watch/Asia, *Burma: The Rohingya Muslims: Ending A Cycle of Exodus* (New York: Human Rights Watch, September 1996), pp. 11, 24.

22. Ibid., p. 11.

who had settled in Burma before 1823, the year preceding the first Anglo-Burman War. Associate citizenship was given to people who could
not prove that all of their ancestors had come from Burma. Applications
for associate citizenship had to be made within one year of the law's
promulgation. A person could qualify for naturalized citizenship if one
parent was a full citizen and the other a foreigner, or if one parent was
an associate citizen and the other a naturalized citizen or a foreigner. The
applicant in question had to demonstrate good character, a sound mind,
and an ability to speak one of the national languages well.[23]

The timing and framing of the new law strongly suggested that it was
directed mainly against the Rohingyas. However, it also was applied to
indigenous ethnic minorities whose citizenship should not have been
questioned; many members of minority groups did not have identity
cards, either because they lived in areas where armed insurgencies raged
or because they were victims of the government's general unwillingness
to register them. They therefore lost their equal standing with other
indigenous peoples of Burma and were treated as stateless.[24]

MODIFYING THE FEDERAL SYSTEM AND INDIGENOUS MINORITY
PROTECTIONS

If narrowing the definition of citizenship was the government's way of
dealing with its alien minorities, making incremental changes in the
structure of government and the political process was its way of modifying policy toward indigenous minorities. The motivation for these
changes was fear: would the new state survive, given the demands of the
minorities and various ethnic wars? Faced with the possibility of secession and disintegration, the ideals of local autonomy and ethnic equality
were set aside in favor of centralized political power and Burman domination throughout the country. There were three proximate causes of these
changes: demands for greater autonomy in the minority states, the border
war with China, and the military's determination to centralize power
under its control. These three considerations resulted in a steady push to
create a unitary state and a single national culture by leaders, both civilian
and military, who believed that this was the only way to hold the people
and the country together.

Almost from the day Burma became independent and the new federal
system began to operate, the new state faced a revolt by the Burma

---

23. *Burma Citizenship Law* (*Pyithu Hluttaw* Law No. 4 of 1982).

24. K.S. Venkateswaran, *Burma: Beyond the Law* (London: Article 19, 1996), p. 55.

Communist Party (BCP) and a variety of ethnic insurgent groups.[25] Whereas the war against the BCP was a civil war between two Burman-dominated forces over who should rule and what ideology should guide the state, the conflicts with ethnic minorities were seen by the leaders in Rangoon as a fight for the state's survival against forces determined to break away and withdraw their lands from the Union of Burma.

The revolt of the Karen, which started in 1949, continues to this day. Given the long history of antagonism between Burmans and Karen, the Burma army's unprovoked attacks in 1942 reinforced the Karen's belief that there could be no peace if the Burmans succeeded the British in governing Burma. Though Aung San and others had tried to heal ethnic wounds and share power, neither the majority of Karen nor Aung San's successors—he was assassinated in the midst of the Constituent Assembly—were willing to seek a solution to their problems through negotiation and accommodation.

When the authors of the constitution refused to offer the Karen a state that was economically viable and that included most of the Karen population, the Karen were convinced that they were being treated unfairly and that this state of affairs would continue under Burman rule. Divided by strong cultural and political differences, the two sides prepared for war. Fighting broke out within a year of independence. The armed forces of the Karen, the Karen National Defence Organization (KNDO), won early victories and the war spread to the southern Shan state and throughout Burma proper. Many Burman leaders and people came to believe that only the defeat of the Karen would ensure the safety of the union.

The revolt of the Karenni, which began at about the same time, had a different origin. The Karenni sought an independent state of their own, claiming that before Burma came under British rule, they had been independent and were recognized as such by Burman kings. Thus, when the British left in 1948, they wanted to recover their political independence. Although Karenni leaders accepted a state in the union in the closing hours of the Constituent Assembly, they did so reluctantly and without the full support of the Karenni people. The war that followed was largely confined to Karenni territory.

Between 1948 and 1960, several smaller minorities rebelled over the lack of political autonomy, government intrusion into their political and social affairs, and fears of being assimilated into the Burman mainstream. The ethnic groups that revolted never formed a permanent united

---

25. See Martin Smith, *Burma: Insurgency and the Problems of Ethnicity* (London: Zed Books Ltd., 1991).

opposition to the government because they could not agree on common goals: some wanted independence outside of the union, while others were willing to remain within it if they received more autonomy and better defined territories.

These internal wars ruined the government's effort to make the ethnic-based army work. Several brigades of Burma Karen Rifles defected and joined the opposition. What was left of the original army was reorganized quickly. Under the leadership of General Ne Win, the army became an integrated force led mainly by Burman officers and constituted mainly of Burman soldiers. Although existing brigades continued to use their old ethnic names, new formations were numbered instead of named and had no ethnic associations. In the new army, members of minority groups were gradually replaced by Burmans; recruitment from minority communities all but ended. The Burmanization of the army emphasized the ethnic character of most of Burma's internal wars with the Burman-dominated national army fighting several ethnic minorities. Many of these conflicts were exceptionally bitter. They hardened the beliefs of Burman civilian and military leaders about minority desires to destroy the union. At the same time, minorities grew more certain that the army of Burma was determined to destroy them.

The KNDO invasion of the southern Shan state was followed by the intrusion of Chinese Nationalist armed forces, which fled China in 1949 and took refuge in the Shan state. These Chinese forces resisted the Burman government's efforts to disarm and intern them. The joint Karen and Chinese threat led the government to proclaim martial law in 1952 in twenty-two of the thirty-three Shan state subdivisions. During the two years when martial law was in effect, the Burma army interfered in local administration in a multitude of ways. More specifically, without legal authority and without prior consultation with the Shan *Sawbwas*, who were legally responsible for deciding such questions, the military changed local administrative structures and replaced civilian administrators with members of the armed forces. During the martial law period, members of the armed forces abused the local Shan population; this contributed to the former's reputation as domineering violators of human rights. The army, in short, created fear and hostility among peoples whom they were supposed to protect.[26]

In 1953, Burma experienced a second invasion from the north. This time, the People's Liberation Army of China crossed into Burma over unresolved border issues. This, too, affected ethnic problems in Burma. A

---

26. Silverstein, *Burmese Politics*, pp. 214–217.

cease-fire halted the fighting in 1956, as the two sides agreed to resolve border problems through negotiations. The talks ended successfully in 1960, with an agreement that called for Burma to transfer three villages in the Kachin state to China in exchange for some Chinese territory and for China to recognize the remainder of the border as defined by Burma.[27]

The Burma Constitution permitted Parliament to pass legislation on border changes, provided the agreement in question had the approval of the appropriate state council.[28] In this case, the government in Rangoon pressured Kachin leaders to give their consent to the agreement and surrender the territories demanded by China, saying that it was a small price to pay for a recognized border and peace with the country's large northern neighbor. But many people in the Kachin state did not see the issue in these terms; they saw themselves being pressured to make sacrifices the rest of the country did not have to make. They saw the demand to give up part of their historic land as inconsistent with the promises made at both Panglong and the Constituent Assembly; their resentment lasted long after the agreement was executed. The government in Rangoon tried to compensate the Kachins by promising to help promote economic development in the Kachin state and, later, to name a Kachin leader as the next president of the union. The Kachins, however, never saw this as sufficient compensation for the sacrifices they were forced to make.

Ethnic relations in Burma took yet another turn for the worse when the government in Rangoon brought pressure to bear on the Shan *Sawbwas* to surrender their constitutional as well as historical rights to govern in their state. When General Ne Win formed a caretaker government in 1958 and assumed the office of prime minister, he pledged to uphold the constitution, restore internal peace, and create the conditions for a free and fair election to be held. However, using his political and administrative power and backed by the army, he imposed political and constitutional change on the Shan state. He and his government colleagues were aware that for almost a decade the chiefs had been considering the voluntary surrender of their feudal powers. The chiefs had talked with the previous government in Rangoon about what such a surrender would mean for them and their people, but no agreement was reached. In 1959, under pressure from the caretaker government, the *Sawbwas* accepted a cash payment and a promise that they could continue

---

27. Daphne Whittam, "The Sino-Burmese Border Treaty," *Pacific Affairs*, Vol. 34, No. 4 (Summer 1961), pp. 174–181.

28. *The Burma Constitution*, Article 200.

to use their hereditary titles and retain their personal property in exchange for their constitutional right to govern. Parliament later passed a constitutional amendment confirming this new arrangement.[29]

Also in 1959, the caretaker government resurrected the Frontier Areas Administration (FAA)—an instrument of British rule—in the most backward and least developed areas of the Shan and Kachin states, replacing local administration under the state councils. The state councils were pressured to surrender their authority over these areas for seven years; a provision in the agreement allowed for this period to be extended.[30] This represented a major change in government policy because the FAA extended the authority of the national government in the territories constitutionally under state rule. As a result, the states lost a great deal of control over local affairs. State leaders naturally resented this development, but they could not resist: the national government was backed by the army. Imposing this kind of agreement on the states was technically unconstitutional, but it nonetheless went into effect.

The restoration of an elected government in April 1960 provided what proved to be the last chance to reaffirm the ethnic policies of 1948 or redefine them in ways that would be satisfactory to all concerned. Faced with a possible Shan move to secede and the emergence of insurgent groups in the Shan and Kachin states and other areas during the period of the caretaker government, Prime Minister Nu sought to defuse explosive ethnic issues by holding talks with minority leaders. In 1961, he met with Shan leaders and listened to their complaints about the 1947 constitution as well as their proposals for ending the disputes between the Shans and the government in Rangoon. Nu subsequently convened a federal seminar, inviting leaders of all ethnic groups to come to Rangoon and discuss ways of ending the country's many ethnic disputes and several internal wars. Trusting the prime minister, leaders of every group attended. The seminar never concluded: on March 2, 1962, the military seized power, abrogated the constitution, and arrested many of those in attendance. General Ne Win, the leader of the coup, formed a Revolutionary Council and henceforth ruled by decree.

BURMA UNDER MILITARY RULE

One of the first acts of the Revolutionary Council was to end the federal system. On May 9, 1962, it replaced existing political and administrative

---

29. *The Constitution (Second Amendment) Act, 1959* (Act No. X of 1959).

30. Silverstein, *Burmese Politics*, pp. 216–217.

arrangements in both Burma proper and the states with a centralized system of security administrative councils composed of military, administrative, and police officers. These councils were directed by a single body, the Security and Administrative Central Council. Through this network, the military controlled the entire country, ending popular rule under constitutional guarantees. Ethnic policy, as it emerged in 1948 and was modified over the next fourteen years, ended; the promises made at Panglong and the Constituent Assembly were broken beyond repair.

Centralization did not bring peace, however. In June 1963, the Revolutionary Council invited political and ethnic groups to send representatives to a meeting and discuss ways of ending the country's civil wars and insurgencies. Representatives of the Communists, Karen, Mon, Karenni, and Chins took part, but there was no real dialogue between participants, and no agreements were reached on how to end warfare in Burma. Talks broke off in November and never resumed; warfare did.[31]

The Revolutionary Council then adopted a new ethnic policy—based not on equality, but inequality. General Ne Win used Union Day, 1964, to issue a "Declaration of the Conviction of the Revolutionary Council on the Question of Union Nationalities."[32] The new policy elevated the Burma nation above all ethnic groups and placed the common good before individual rights. It identified areas where all of the country's nationalities would share responsibility and areas where each group would act individually and independently. Economic development and social welfare were identified as common tasks for the whole country; language, literature, religion, and culture were to be responsibilities of individual groups. In either case, individual actions could not be politically or socially divisive, and they could not adversely affect the welfare of other nationalities.

To implement the new policy, the Revolutionary Council created an Academy for the Development of National Groups. The academy's purpose was to train representatives of all ethnic groups to convey the state's goals of socialism and national unity and to teach basic health, social, and education subjects. Once trained, these cadres were expected to go to the hinterland, teach, assume leadership positions, and help people improve their standards of living. The academy failed largely because of poor

---

31. Revolutionary Council, *Internal Peace Parley*, Historical Document No. 1 (unpublished, Rangoon, 1963); and Silverstein, *Burmese Politics*, pp. 232–233.

32. "A Report on Ten Years of Social Revolution in Burma," *Working People's Daily*, March 2, 1972, p. 6.

recruiting and the unwillingness of its graduates to work among rural minorities.[33]

Despite the efforts of the military leadership to use new institutions to promote national unity, disunity persisted. Year after year, Ne Win and other military leaders would complain about impediments to national unity—ethnic prejudice, narrow ethnic outlooks, a lack of cooperation from minority groups, and foreign influences. Colonel Hla Han declared in 1969 that the country's minorities were divided between those who wanted unity, peace, and security and those who wanted to keep fighting.

When the Revolutionary Council turned to writing a new constitution in 1969, Ne Win declared that it must embody two new principles: first, that people should be able to live wherever they wanted, regardless of ethnic affiliation, language, and historical origins; and second, that the Burmans and minorities should grow closer to one another. When this was achieved, he said, "we will not need to have separate governments within the Union."[34] In so saying, Ne Win implied that toleration of diversity was to be replaced by assimilation and nationalization.

The new constitution was written by the Burma Socialist Program Party (BSPP), which itself had been created by the military. The new constitution declared that all groups had the right to preserve and protect their languages, cultures, and religions, provided that they did not undermine the "unity and solidarity of the national groups, security of the State and the socialist social order."[35] For administrative purposes, the former Burma proper was divided into divisions, and the minority areas into states. To satisfy the demands of the Mon and Arakanese, their areas were removed from Burma proper and named as states; the Chin Special Division was reconstituted as a state.

Burma's new ethnic policy, as deduced from the 1974 constitution, aimed to create a single united nation in which all citizens would share a common identity and loyalty. Burmese was to be the national language, although—within limits—minority languages could be taught and used, and minority cultures could be practiced and passed on.

Unofficially, inequality was the rule. The members of the BSPP and the leaders of the military, the administration, and other institutions of

---

33. *The Guardian* [Rangoon daily], December 3, 1971.

34. *Address Delivered by Gen. Ne Win, Chairman of the Burma Socialist Program Party at the Opening Session of the Fourth Party Seminar on 6 November 1969* (Rangoon: Burma Socialist Programme Party Central Press, 1969).

35. *The Constitution of the Socialist Republic of the Union of Burma* (Rangoon, 1974), article 153(c).

authority were overwhelmingly Burman. Burmese was the official language of education and both official and unofficial communications, and it was the main language of the country's biggest cities; Burman culture spread throughout the country at the expense of local languages and cultures.

The new policy did not solve the ethnic question in Burma. The minorities in revolt continued their wars, and the country's military rulers made no effort to accommodate minority interests and sensitivities.

In 1988, peaceful summer-long demonstrations started in Rangoon and spread throughout the country. The BSPP government's failure to respond to the growing unrest and demands for political change triggered a military coup d'état. The military formed SLORC, seized power, and ruled by decree and martial law. It gave as its reasons for seizing power the fear of the breakup of the union, the disintegration of national unity, and the collapse of authority throughout the country.

The new rulers continued the ethnic policies of their predecessors. This time, however, they placed greater emphasis on ending the country's internal wars. With an enlarged army and newly purchased weapons, they turned the full might of the armed forces against the ethnic opposition. At the same time, they offered the opposition a choice: accept a cease-fire or suffer complete defeat.

SLORC had an unexpected opportunity to halt some of the fighting when the BCP broke up in early 1989, following the revolt of its cadres who were mostly drawn from local ethnic groups in the area under their control. The Burman leaders of the BCP were driven out of Burma and into China; their former cadres formed ethnic-based political groups and abandoned communist ideology in favor of ethnic nationalism and autonomy. SLORC quickly sent representatives to meet with the leaders of the new groups, offering cease-fires to prevent the eruption of new challenges to the Burman army. However, SLORC refused to discuss fundamental political issues; instead, in exchange for halting their attacks against the government and breaking off contact with elements still in revolt, it offered the groups the right to keep their weapons, administer the areas they held, and pursue their economic agendas. Other political issues, SLORC said, would be discussed only after a new constitution and government had been put into place.

The success of the new cease-fire policy led to similar offers to other insurgent groups. To prove its determination to gain control of all ethnic groups in Burma, SLORC demonstrated that it had no reservations about waging war against both the armed forces and civilian members of those groups that refused the cease-fire offer. In the past, the army had pursued a "four-cut" policy of depriving its enemies food, finance, intelligence, and recruits;[36] in the new phase, it put extra pressure on rebels by expanding its attacks upon women, children, and older men, forcing them to move away from their homes, making them dependent on the military for food and shelter, making them serve as porters in battle zones, and forcing them to walk ahead of army units in mined areas. The army carried out brutal assaults on those who did not comply with its demands quickly enough.[37]

These tactics succeeded: fifteen insurgent groups accepted cease-fires. However, this approach did nothing to repair the widening breach between SLORC and Burma's ethnic minorities. Indeed, it hardened divisions within the country.

For those ethnic minorities at peace with the BSPP government before the 1988 coup and accepting of the new regime in Rangoon, SLORC permitted the formation of political parties and participation in the 1990 election. Later, these minorities, along with ethnic groups that accepted cease-fires before the opening of the National Convention in January 1993, were permitted to participate in the convention's deliberations and the drafting of the principles for the future constitution of Burma.

As of early 1997, two ethnic minorities, the Karen and the Shans, are still at war with the government. The Karen continue to demand that political questions be discussed in conjunction with the cease-fire as the first step to removing the issues that provoked and sustain their wars. The Shan opposition is composed of former members of the Mong Tai Army, whose leader, Khun Sa, surrendered to SLORC in early 1996. Many Shans refused to follow; instead, they have formed new resistance organizations and continue to fight the Rangoon government. The long Karenni war against the government ended with the signing of a cease-fire in 1995; however, the war quickly reignited when the army broke the agreement. Thus far, despite all its efforts, SLORC has not been able to impose peace throughout the country on its own terms.

With regard to alien minorities, SLORC has continued the policy of the BSPP government. Although it appeared initially to have taken a more liberal stand by allowing the Rohingyas to form political parties in 1989 and contest for seats in the *Pyithu Hluttaw* (National Assembly) 1990 election, it changed its course after the vote. The Rohingya parties were dissolved in August 1991, and of the four Rohingyas elected, two were

---

36. Smith, *Burma: Insurgency,* p. 259.

37. K.S. Venkateswaran, *Burma: Beyond the Law,* pp. 46–53.

arrested and tortured, one died while in captivity, and the other was released after spending two years in prison.[38]

The hardening of SLORC policy toward the Rohingyas was reflected in increased harassment, tighter immigration checks, forced labor programs, and the stationing of large numbers of additional military units in their part of the country; this provoked a new exodus of more than 250,000 Rohingyas to Bangladesh. In their wake, tension between Burma and Bangladesh led to military buildups on both sides of the border. The threat of warfare eased following a 1992 agreement between the two countries to allow the "voluntary and safe" return of refugees to Burma.[39] They also agreed to allow the UN High Commissioner for Refugees to monitor the returnees on both sides of the border and to open an office in Rangoon. By the end of 1995, 190,000 Rohingyas had returned; but, once inside of Burma, there was no international supervision of the treatment they received from government authorities or of their ability to recover their lands and resume normal lives.

In February 1996, a new exodus of Rohingyas started. The causes were similar to those in the past, although the government exercised even greater control over Rohingya activities and movements. According to Human Rights Watch/Asia, the government's classification of all Rohingyas as resident foreigners is clear from their inability to travel freely in the country: "there is no freedom of movement for Muslims in the Arakan State. Freedom of movement seemingly only exists out of Arakan and into Bangladesh, and even that is restricted."[40]

Prospects for the Future

If SLORC intends to alter or restate the government's ethnic policy, it most likely will do so after the new constitution is written and a government is elected under its authority. On the basis of the constitutional principles developed thus far, it appears that ethnic policy in Burma will not depart greatly from the course it has been on since 1962, when the military seized power. It will probably reflect several decisions that have already been made about political structures and processes.

First, Burma will be a unitary state in fact, but federal in form and name. Although a second chamber, *amyotha hluttaw* (the nationalities

---

38. Human Rights Watch/Asia, *Burma: The Rohingya Muslims*, p. 35.

39. *The Nation* (Bangkok), June 11, 1992.

40. Human Rights Watch/Asia, *Burma: The Rohingya Muslims*, p. 32.

parliament), will be added to the *pyidaungsu hluttaw* (the national parliament), with equal representation from all states and regions, real power will continue to reside in the *pyithu hluttaw* (the people's parliament), where representation will be based on the size of the populations in the states and regions.

The centralized nature of the system will be ensured through a dual system of control. The president will head a hierarchy of chief ministers in each state and region, and they, in turn, will have responsibility for ministers below them. Paralleling this hierarchy will be one headed by the commander in chief of the defense forces, who will also nominate one quarter of the members of all legislative and administrative bodies.[41]

Second, in addition to including seven states for the larger ethnic minorities and seven regions for predominantly Burman areas, the new state structure will include as many self-administered divisions and self-administered zones as necessary for indigenous minorities who do not receive states of their own. Self-administered areas are supposed to satisfy the desires of smaller, stateless ethnic groups, but, with real control at the center, little power will be given to these units. The central government will be able to control these areas through the two systems of authority under the president and commander in chief.

Third, there will be no right of secession under the new constitution.

Thus far, the National Convention has not reported any work on individual and community rights. SLORC made its position on such rights clear in the address given by General Myo Nyunt, the Chairman of the National Convention Convening Commission in January 1993:

for a genuine multiparty democracy to flourish . . . it [has] to practice democracy in a way which suits our Myanmar society. The most fundamental requirement in making use of democratic rights is the maintenance and observance of the law. Hence the practice of democracy in our country ought to be tempered with full cognizance of our traditional culture, values and ideas which are part and parcel of the society. In order to be worthy of democratic rights, it is necessary to stipulate the right preconditions for the fulfillment of duties and responsibilities as becoming of good citizens such as obedience of laws, rules and regulations, dutifulness, truthfulness, honesty and integrity. It may perhaps be necessary to link democratic rights with duties and responsibilities.[42]

---

41. "Chairman of the National Convention Convening Working Committee Clarification," *The New Light of Myanmar*, September 3–7, 1994. This should be read in conjunction with U Aung Toe's "Clarification and Final Compilation of Principles," in *The New Light of Myanmar*, April 9, 1994.

42. *Working People's Daily* (Rangoon), January 10, 1993.

Given that the convention is tightly controlled by SLORC and that all of the principles adopted, thus far, are consistent with SLORC's demands, it is very likely that the new constitution will specify no rights independent of duties and obligations, as was the case under the 1974 constitution. Although Burma was an original signatory of the UN Declaration of Human Rights when it was adopted in 1948 and never raised any questions about its universal applicability, SLORC's introduction of the idea that rights are qualified by the unique culture and traditions of a nation seems to be an excuse for ignoring its international obligations under the UN Charter and an attempt to deprive the people of their right to invoke these obligations in actions against the state. The National Convention's failure to discuss rights at any point in over three years of deliberations indicates the low priority SLORC assigns to this issue.

As far as SLORC is concerned, past promises about regional autonomy and constitutionally based rights, not subject to simple legislation, are dead. The trend that began when the military took power in 1962 continues in the direction of a unitary state, dominated by the military, with a single, primarily Burman national culture. The ascent will be slow for ethnic minorities in the military, administration, and the professions, and will depend on the degree to which they have assimilated into the common culture. So long as the military remains in charge, there is little or no likelihood that this will be reversed. For alien minorities, naturalization will continue to be an option, but one open to fewer and fewer people. The existing citizenship law, with its three-part classification scheme, is likely to remain in effect with little or no modification; while it provides for associate and naturalized citizens to see their descendants rise to full citizenship in a generation or two, few are likely to successfully run this tightly controlled administrative gauntlet.

Conclusions

The ethnic policies of the military have not worked, and there are no indications that they will work in the future. They do not address the issues that rose in the past and remain ascendant and unresolved. There are people in Burma who still remember the Panglong meeting, the promises of Aung San, and the first effort to build a federal system on the basis of equality, local autonomy, the coexistence of cultures, and constitutionally guaranteed individual and community rights. That said, the present generation does not want to set the clock back to 1947. Instead, it wants to correct the mistakes that led to warfare and disharmony while retaining the values and ideals of the nation's founders. It wants a modern, united country based on toleration for diversity, which it believes can only be achieved in a democratic environment. It is ready to work on these long-standing problems, but thus far it has not had the opportunity to do so.

If there is to be real change in ethnic policy in Burma, it must begin with fundamental changes in the country's political structure and the emergence of a new attitude on the part of those in power toward ethnic minorities.

The first change must be an end to dictatorial rule. So long as the military clings to the myth that "as SLORC is not a political organization, it has no reason to hold talks with any armed insurgent organization," there is no possibility of initiating a dialogue on any subject.[43] In its eight years of rule, SLORC has held talks only when doing so has suited its members—and always under terms it dictated. There should be little wonder that Burma has remained a divided and hostile society with no outlet for airing problems and discussing solutions.

The country's ethnic minorities have been calling for a dialogue since 1984, when, as the National Democratic Front—a coalition of ten ethnic groups then in revolt—they rescinded their demands for a right of secession and offered to begin discussions in good faith with the government in Rangoon. Daw Aung San Suu Kyi, the leader of the National League for Democracy, has also called for a dialogue on all issues, beginning with the seating of the elected members of the *Pyithu Hluttaw* and the peaceful transfer of power.

To hold a proper dialogue, all of its participants must be free and equal. The idea that the military stands above the state and its people is contrary to this most basic principle of political reconciliation. So long as the military continues the fiction that it stands outside and above politics, there can be no dialogue—no first step to change ethnic policies in Burma.

Second, there must be an end to the separation of Burmans from ethnic minorities, both at peace and at war. Restrictions on travel must end. When people and groups are isolated from each other, they cannot exchange ideas or solve deep-seated problems. Burmans and minorities must be able to visit and talk with each other, to learn firsthand how others live, and to listen to the complaints and solutions each offers. Until this happens, there can be no real airing of problems or consideration of alternative solutions.

Finally, there must be a new forum where Burmans, minorities, and the military can meet as equals, exchange ideas on ethnic policies, and look for ways to accommodate each other. SLORC's ideas are well known;

---

43. SLORC, *Announcement No. 1/90,* July 27, 1990, para. 10.

the ideas of the minorities and the National League for Democracy are not.

The Democratic Alliance of Burma (DAB), the organization of the National Democratic Front and Burmans who took refuge among the hill peoples after 1988, has drawn up a model constitution that incorporates its ideas about future ethnic policy. The DAB's successor is the National Council of the Union of Burma (NCUB). Central to the NCUB's thinking is the idea of equality: no group or class of individuals should be outside the law or above all others. Its second basic assumption is that power really is derived from the people and vested in elected officials and government according to the provisions of a constitution. A constitution, moreover, will be honored and upheld only if it is written by the elected representatives of the people. The third premise of the NCUB constitution is that Burma must have a true federal form of government. The NCUB wants the future union to be composed of eight states, one for each of the largest ethnic groups. Within the proposed state system, there would be national autonomous regions and special national territories within the states for indigenous ethnic groups that are too small to have states of their own. The NCUB wants these sub-units to have real power, especially in the areas of language, culture, and administration.

The NCUB constitution places great emphasis on human rights, for both individuals and groups. Indeed, its chapter on human rights is located at the beginning of the document. Some fifty-five rights are specified, and all are to be protected by a new human rights commission. Citizenship, according to the NCUB, should be open to all members of indigenous groups who were born in the territory of Burma as it was defined at the time of independence. Immigrants who were born in the federal union and have lived there continuously since 1948, or who are descendants of immigrant parents born in the federal union should, it is said, have a right to become full citizens through naturalization.

Finally, the issue on which the NCUB and SLORC are most widely divided is the role and place of the military in Burman politics. According to the NCUB, the military should be subordinate to civilian control. In addition, the leadership and personnel of the armed forces should come proportionally from the country's several states: there should be a chief of staff committee, composed of one commander from each state, with the office of chief of staff rotating between members of the committee.[44]

The ideas embodied in the NCUB constitution were born out of fifty years of political experience in Burma. They are offered both as solutions

---

44. National Council of the Union of Burma, *Federal Union of Burma Constitution* (draft), September 1995.

to old problems and the basis for forming a lasting and peaceful political community of Burmans and ethnic minorities.

There is, however, another alternative to SLORC's ideas on political and ethnic issues. On February 12, 1996, the anniversary of the Panglong Agreement, Daw Aung San Suu Kyi announced the National League for Democracy's platform on indigenous peoples. It proposed a national coordination convention of all indigenous groups to chart the country's future on questions of democracy, stability, unity, and the ethnic solidarity of the indigenous peoples. According to this line of thinking, the future Union of Burma should be based on equal rights and responsibilities for all indigenous ethnic groups. No group should have special privileges. In addition, all groups should work together to promote and preserve the sovereignty and unity of the country, and political, economic, social, educational, health, and regional development. Ethnic groups should be allowed to develop their own policies in political, economic, and administrative areas. Finally, each ethnic group should have the right to maintain and develop its culture, traditions, and language.[45]

A careful reading of this declaration shows that it includes many of the ideas of Aung San, as expressed at Panglong and later in public and party speeches and before the constituent assembly. These ideas and principles convinced many of Burma's minorities to join the new union in 1947. They are still valid in 1997 and could form the basis for ethnic policies that could rebuild national unity.

Although there are wide differences between the military and its opponents, the basis for a dialogue exists. Fifty years of failure cannot be overcome in a single meeting, of course. But nothing can be accomplished until that first step is taken.

---

45. *National League for Democracy Policy on Indigenous Peoples as Outlined in Daw Aung San Suu Kyi's Message at the 1996 Union Day Anniversary Held at Her House*, Rangoon, February 1996 (original in Burmese).

Chapter 5

Cultural Diversity and National Identity in Thailand

Charles F. Keyes

Thailand, a country of 55 million people located in the heart of mainland Southeast Asia, would appear from all censuses taken since the 1920s to have little ethnic diversity.[1] Census figures for 1970 and 1980 show that nearly 99 percent of the populace are citizens of Thailand, 97 percent speak Thai, and 94–95 percent adhere to Buddhism, the national religion of the country.[2] This appearance of cultural homogeneity is, however, deceptive. Those who have constructed Thai censuses have been discouraged from asking the kinds of ethnic self-identification questions asked in other countries, such as the United States.

Few in Thailand today would deny that the peoples of the country evince many contrasts in their cultural practices or that they are descendants of peoples who once followed very different cultural traditions. However, cultural diversity in and of itself does not generate ethnic groups. What makes cultural differences "ethnic" differences is a political setting that separates the stories—represented in art, rituals, plays, literature, folklore, and so on—that people tell about their heritage from the officially sanctioned stories that are told about the common heritage of those who are said to belong to the same nation.[3] Ethnic politics have

---

1. Only the first census in 1907 recognized significant ethnic and cultural divisions in the population.

2. See Charles F. Keyes, *Thailand: Buddhist Kingdom as Modern Nation-State* (Boulder, Colo.: Westview Press, 1987), p. 14.

3. For my approach to the study of ethnicity and the relationship between local cultural differences, ethnic differentiation, and national culture, see Charles F. Keyes, "Towards a New Formulation of the Concept of Ethnic Group," *Ethnicity*, Vol. 3 (1976), pp. 202–213; Keyes, "The Dialectics of Ethnic Change," in Charles F. Keyes, ed., *Ethnic Change* (Seattle: University of Washington Press, 1981), pp. 4–30; Keyes, "Who Are the Lue Revisited? Ethnic Identity in Laos, Thailand, and China" (Cambridge, Mass.: MIT, Center for International Studies, Working Paper, 1992); Keyes, "Who Are the Tai?

everywhere been shaped by how national communities have been envisioned and promoted by the structures of modern states. But these politics are not everywhere the same because modern states have adopted very different stances with respect to the significance of premodern cultural differences. The apparent relative absence of ethnic cleavages in contemporary Thailand is a consequence not of the absence of premodern cultural differences in what was formerly known as Siam but of the distinctive historical processes that have shaped how these differences have been situated within the framework of the Thai nation.

In the late nineteenth century, when Siam stood on the brink of modernization, the Siamese "empire"[4] included many different indigenous peoples and a very large immigrant population, largely from southeastern China, that differed markedly in cultural characteristics from the elite who ruled the empire from Bangkok. In this chapter I will trace the history of how most cultural differences came to be submerged under an inclusive vision of the Thai nation. Although some cultural differences still became politically salient ethnic differences and although there have been occasional outbreaks of ethnic violence in Thailand, the country has known remarkably little ethnic conflict.

Cultural Diversity in Premodern Siam

In 1792 General Chakkri—later known as King Rama I—founded a new dynasty in the Southeast Asian kingdom that had come in the West to be called Siam. The first three kings of the Chakkri dynasty, who ruled from Bangkok from 1782 to 1851, not only reasserted their rule over the territories that had constituted the previous Siamese state of Ayutthaya, but also extended their power beyond this core area of Ayutthaya. By the end of the third reign in 1851, principalities in what are today northern Thailand, Laos, the southernmost part of Yunnan, the sultanates of Patani, Kedah, Kelantan, and Trengganu on the Malay peninsula, and the kingdom of Cambodia had all been made vassals of Bangkok.[5] In the middle

---

Reflections on the Invention of Local, Ethnic and National Identities," in George DeVos and Lola Romucci-Ross, eds., *Ethnic Change*, 2d rev. ed. (Walnut Creek, Calif.: Alta Mira Press, 1995), pp. 136–160; Keyes, "Ethnicity, Ethnic Group," in Thomas J. Barfield, ed., *The Blackwell Dictionary of Anthropology* (Oxford: Basil Blackwell, in press); and Keyes, "Nation," in Barfield, *The Blackwell Dictionary of Anthropology*.

4. The term "empire" was used by Prince Damrong Rajanubhab, one of the prime architects of the modern Thai state. See Damrong, *Nithān bōrān khadī* (Historical Anecdotes) (Bangkok: Phrāē Phithayā, 1971 [1935]), p. 319.

5. See the map in Walter F. Vella, *Siam under Rama III, 1824–1851*, Association for Asian Studies Monograph IV (Locust Valley, N.Y.: J.J. Augustin, 1957), facing p. 108.

of the nineteenth century, the population of Siam proper also became markedly more diverse when tens of thousands of people living in what is today Laos were persuaded (sometimes involuntarily) to resettle in Siam, mainly in what is today northeastern Thailand.

Bangkok was forced to give up some territory in the late nineteenth and early twentieth centuries when the British and French extended their Asian empires to include territories to the west, south, and east of Siam. Nonetheless, by 1909, when the French and British ended their expansion into territories once controlled by Siam and after they had imposed the recognition of legal boundaries, represented by official maps, on the Siamese government, the "geo-body" of modern Siam/Thailand included large numbers of peoples who were not only culturally different from the elite in Bangkok but also had until quite recently lived in other political entities.[6]

SIAMESE, LAO, AND YUAN

At the end of the nineteenth century, when the boundaries of Siam were more or less fixed,[7] over three-quarters of the population spoke as their mother tongues languages belonging to the Tai (or Daic) language family.[8] However, differences among these languages were as great as those found in other language families; linguists recognize at least seven and perhaps as many as twenty mutually incomprehensible languages among the dozens of premodern dialects of Tai spoken in the country.[9] But while differences in spoken languages were locally important, they were not the primary basis for cultural differentiation in the country.

Far more important were the differences in written traditions. Tai-speaking peoples had developed a number of different orthographic systems based on models borrowed from various neighbors. These

---

6. Thongchai Winichakul has proposed the term "geo-body" to emphasize the way in which the drawing of territorial boundaries, as represented in maps, has served as one of the major elements of the construction of the modern state. Winichakul, *Siam Mapped: A History of the Geo-Body of a Nation* (Honolulu: University of Hawaii Press, 1994), especially pp. 16–17.

7. The country's current boundaries were set following the Franco-Siamese Treaty of 1907.

8. By convention, the term "Tai" is used as a label for the language family, while "Thai" is used only to refer to language and culture pertaining to Thailand.

9. See Marvin Brown, *From Ancient Thai to Modern Dialects* (Bangkok: Social Science Association of Thailand Press, 1965); and William A. Smalley, *Linguistic Diversity and National Unity: Language Ecology in Thailand* (Chicago: University of Chicago Press, 1994), especially pp. 362–363.

systems were employed for producing and reproducing Buddhist texts, for administering and documenting the activities of various courts, and, to a lesser extent, for creating poetry and other literary works. In premodern Siam, there were three major written traditions among Tai-speaking peoples, each associated with a different religious and political history: "Siamese," "Lao," and "Yuan."[10]

Those whom Westerners termed "Siamese" in nineteenth-century Siam and who called themselves "Thai" actually included speakers of many dialects associated with what linguists see as the distinctive languages of "Central Thai" and "Southern Thai." However, because ancestors of speakers of these different languages had long been under the authority of the Siamese state and because their monks used texts written in the same orthographies, they saw themselves as being the same people. In the late nineteenth century, the Siamese constituted approximately 30–35 percent of the total population of the Siamese empire and were located in plains centering on the Chao Phraya River and in the northern part of the Malay peninsula.[11]

Another 40–45 percent of the population of late nineteenth century Siam were also Tai-speaking peoples, but were seen by the Siamese as different. Although the Siamese used the term "Lao" to refer to all Tai-speaking peoples living in the northern and northeastern parts of the premodern empire as well as related peoples living beyond the borders of Siam, the peoples of what became northern Thailand and those of the northeastern region distinguished themselves from each other.

To the north of Siam proper were a congeries of principalities called *muang* that until the nineteenth century had been independent of Siam or, when not independent, had been under the suzerainty of one or another Burmese king. The most important of these *muang* was Chiang Mai, but in the nineteenth century another, Nan, was of almost equal

---

10. In fact, four different orthographic systems were used—the Siamese (derived from, but different from the Khmer), the Khmer (used by the Siamese for religious works), the "dhammic" or "Buddhist," derived from Mon (closely related to Burmese) and used in slightly variant forms by the Lao and Yuan (and others) for religious texts, and the Lao Wiang (or Vientiane) system used by the Lao for secular works. In practice, however, three traditions were recognized. The use of quotation marks around "Siamese," "Lao," and "Yuan" signifies that these terms had a different meaning in the premodern world than they have today.

11. It is difficult to make a precise estimate of the Siamese speakers in the population of the late nineteenth century. See David Streckfuss, "The Mixed Colonial Legacy in Siam: Origins of Thai Racialist Thought," in Laurie J. Sears, ed., *Autonomous Histories, Particular Truths: Essays in Honor of John R.W. Smail,* Center for Southeast Asian Studies Monograph No. 11 (Madison: University of Wisconsin, 1993), pp. 129–131; Keyes, *Thailand,* p. 16; and Smalley, *Linguistic Diversity,* p. 67.

Thailand.

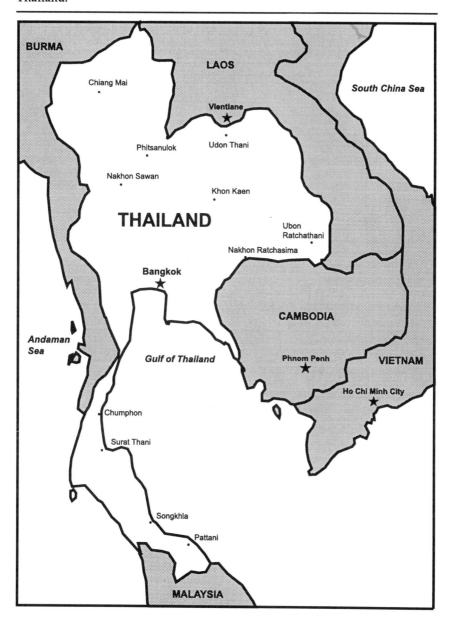

importance. The people of these *mɏang* called themselves *Khonmɏang*—people of the (northern) domains—and called their literary-religious tradition *Yuan*. Their religious tradition was also associated with a number of distinctive pilgrimage sites, mostly located in what is today northern Thailand, and with particular lineages of monks that were different from those of Siam. In the early nineteenth century, the Yuan were brought under Siamese rule, but the rulers of Chiang Mai, Nan, and even other smaller principalities retained some independence as vassal states of Bangkok until the late nineteenth century.

People living in other vassal states—the chief one being Luang Prabang—and dozens of feudalities found to the east of the Mekong River and on the Khorat Plateau (today, northeastern Thailand) followed traditions related to those of the Yuan, but were distinguished from the Yuan by a different political history and by some literary and religious practices. The rulers of these vassal states and feudalities traced their origin to the semi-legendary kingdom of *Lān Chāng*, the kingdom of a "million elephants." While peoples of these polities used essentially the same orthographic system as the Yuan for Buddhist texts and shared much the same Buddhist literary heritage, they used another writing system, closely related to the Siamese, for political and secular literary purposes. In addition, these people associated their religious tradition with lineages of monks that were not the same as those of the Yuan or the Siamese and with different pilgrimage centers.

During the nineteenth century, the Siamese court had encouraged (sometimes with force) the resettlement on the Khorat Plateau of Lao from territories to the east of the Mekong. By the end of the century, the Lao population in this region was eight or nine times larger than the Lao population living to the east of the Mekong. When the French first began their colonial conquests of the eastern part of mainland Southeast Asia, they were inclined to use the term "Lao" in much the same way as the Siamese did—that is, to include the Yuan as well. As they developed rationales for their political expansion, however, they came to apply this term only to those associated with the heritage of *Lān Chāng*. With the French conquest, the Lao were divided between Indochina and Siam, with those in Siam living primarily on the Khorat Plateau.

NON-TAI INDIGENOUS PEOPLES

While the *Khonmɏang* and the Lao constituted the largest groups that were differentiated from the Siamese in premodern Siam, there were many other indigenous peoples—making up a total of approximately 20 percent of the population—who were speakers of one or another non-Tai language and who followed quite different traditions. Some of these had also formerly belonged to a polity other than Siam.

Prior to the eleventh century, when Tai-speaking people first became historically significant, peoples speaking languages belonging to the Austroasiatic or Mon-Khmer language family were dominant in the area. This family includes not only the major languages of Mon and Khmer but also dozens of smaller languages. The Tai-speaking peoples who began settling in what is today central Thailand some time around the eleventh century acquired their civilization from the Mon and Khmer. Indeed, the Siamese tradition represents a fusion between the cultures of Tai, Mon, and Khmer; most Khmer and Mon assimilated linguistically to the Tai, while the Tai adopted Mon Buddhist culture and Khmer traditions of statecraft. On the borders of Siam, however, some peoples continued to speak Austroasiatic languages.

Of these, by far the greater number were speakers of Khmer dialects and dialects of the closely related Kui language. The inclusion of Khmer and Kui within the Siamese empire grew out of the Ayutthayan conquest of Angkor in the fifteenth century and the Siamese expansion into what is today Cambodia in the nineteenth century. Although the Siamese were compelled in a treaty signed in 1907 to cede control of territories today in Cambodia to the French, around 4–5 percent of the population living within the boundaries of Siam were still speaking Khmer or Kui dialects.

However, the influence of Khmer in Siam was far greater than this number would indicate. After the conquest of Angkor in the fifteenth century, the Siamese borrowed much from the Khmer. For example, almost all vocabulary in Thai for statecraft and religion is derived from Khmer adaptations of Sanskrit words. Indeed, Thai shares more of its vocabulary with Austroasiatic Khmer than it does with many Tai languages. Despite the close relationships between these traditions, the fact that there continued to be a separate Khmer land—Cambodia—meant that distinctions between Thai and Khmer could be politically significant. This political salience grew after 1862, when Cambodia became a protectorate of France.

Although the Mon had by the end of the nineteenth century almost disappeared as a distinct people in Siam as a result of the fusion of Mon and Siamese traditions, there were still several tens of thousands of Mon living in the western part of the country who were relatively recent refugees from lower Burma and who continued to speak the Mon language and follow distinctive customs. However, because Mon Buddhism was accorded high prestige by a Siamese royal monk, who in 1851 would leave the monkhood to become King Mongkut, and because most Mon were bilingual, the differences between Mon and Siamese had almost no political significance, and Mon continued to assimilate to the Siamese way of life.[12]

The largest number of indigenous peoples who were markedly different from the Buddhist Siamese and the other Buddhist peoples of premodern Siam were the Malay-speaking Muslims who lived in the Malay sultanates of Kedah, Kelantan, Trengganu, Perak, and Patani, and in areas bordering on Patani in what is today southern Thailand.[13] These sultanates had considerable autonomy and were connected to Bangkok primarily through tribute. During the late eighteenth century and at various times in the nineteenth century, Siam had been compelled to cede control to the British some parts of these Malay sultanates, and in 1909 all of the sultanates except Patani were transferred from Siamese to British rule as "the unfederated Malay states." The sultanate of Patani had already been abolished by the Siamese, who imposed a new administrative structure on the remaining area under its control and created the provinces of Narathiwat, Yala, and Pattani out of the former sultanate. Those who had lived under local rulers who shared their religion and language now found themselves directly under the alien rule of Siamese Buddhists.[14] Many of their descendants would look back fondly on the time when they lived within a relatively autonomous Patani. Others, however, would find more in common with non-Patani Malays or with Thai-speaking Muslims.

In the late nineteenth century, Siam also contained a small number of other non-Tai-speaking indigenous peoples, most of whom lived on the periphery of the empire in upland border regions. Most of these "forest" or "hill" peoples spoke Karen or Austroasiatic languages, although by the

---

12. This has continued to remain the case, although there are communities where Mon identity is locally recognized. See Brian L. Foster, "Ethnic Identity of the Mons in Thailand," *Journal of the Siam Society*, Vol. 61, No. 1 (January 1973), pp. 203–226, and Foster, "Changing Ethnicity and Social Resources in a Thai-Mon Village, 1971–81," in A. Terry Rambo, Kathleen Gillogly, and Karl L. Hutterer, eds., *Ethnic Diversity and the Control of Natural Resources in Southeast Asia*, Michigan Papers on South and Southeast Asia No. 12 (Ann Arbor: University of Michigan Center for South and Southeast Asian Studies, 1988), pp. 143–159.

13. I use "Patani" to refer to the sultanate and "Pattani" for the province in southern Thailand created after the abolition of the sultanate. The proponents of separatism or autonomy continue to prefer "Patani." See Che Man and Wan Kadir, "National Integration and Resistance Movements: The Case of Muslims in Southern Thailand," in Volker Grabowsky, ed., *Regions and National Integration in Thailand, 1892–1992* (Wiesbaden: Otto Harrassowitz, 1995), pp. 232–250.

14. Surin Pitsuwan, *Islam and Malay Nationalism: A Case Study of the Malay Muslims of Southern Thailand* (Bangkok: Thai Khadi Research Institute, Thammasat University, 1985), chap. 2.

end of the nineteenth century, some speakers of Tibeto-Burman (Akha, Lahu, and Lisu) and Miao-Yao (Hmong and Mien) languages had also moved into these areas. Because these peoples taken together constituted only about 1 percent of the population of the country and because they were located in remote areas, they held little interest to the Siamese elite of the period. However, they would later come to be seen in a different light.

CHINESE IMMIGRANTS

In addition to indigenous peoples, late-nineteenth century Siam had a rapidly expanding immigrant population. Even before the beginning of the nineteenth century, some Chinese and smaller numbers of peoples from other countries had settled in the country. During the nineteenth century and especially in the later part of the century, the immigrant population, especially the immigrant Chinese population, would expand exponentially.[15]

The rate of Chinese immigration began to increase in the early nine-teenth century following the shift of Siam's capital from Ayutthaya to Bangkok, a port city, where the Chakkri kings encouraged expansion of trade. The opening of the Siamese economy was greatly accelerated in 1855 with the signing of an agreement on trade between the British and the Siamese governments that was negotiated by Sir John Bowring, the governor of Hong Kong, and King Mongkut.[16]

Siam became a major exporter of raw materials—notably, rice, sugar, teak and other woods, tin, and, somewhat later, rubber—and an importer of goods manufactured in Britain and elsewhere in Europe. As a conse-quence, there was a marked increase in demand for labor to move these goods to and from the port of Bangkok. There were also increased oppor-tunities for middlemen, who purchased rice and other products from producers and resold them to exporting firms, as well as for those who

---

15. While vastly overshadowed by the Chinese, other immigrant groups—notably Vietnamese and Indians—also expanded in the nineteenth century. The Vietnamese community in Thailand would subsequently attract significant attention from Thai governments. The small Indian community, by contrast, remained almost invisible in the ethnic politics of the country. While the number of European immigrants was very small in the nineteenth century, their links to powerful colonizing states gave them roles greatly disproportionate to their numbers. Even so, not until the late twentieth century would European settlers, or, more precisely, Eurasians become recognized as a distinctive people within Thailand.

16. The Bowring Treaty is generally considered the point at which Siam started to become integrated into the Western-dominated global economy. See David K. Wyatt, *Thailand. A Short History* (New Haven, Conn.: Yale University Press, 1984), pp. 183–184.

made foreign goods available for purchase in local communities. These new laboring jobs and middlemen roles were filled overwhelmingly by Chinese immigrants and their descendants. Chinese also competed with Europeans for control of the credit associations and banks that facilitated the flow of capital in the country.[17]

By 1850, 15,000 new Chinese immigrants, mostly from southeastern China, were arriving in Siam each year, and they came in even larger numbers after the signing of the Bowring Treaty.[18] By 1900, Chinese peoples constituted 8.3 percent of the population of Siam. This percentage would increase even more in the first decades of the twentieth century, when Chinese migration expanded dramatically. By the middle of the twentieth century, approximately 12 percent of the population of Thailand were either Chinese-born or identified themselves as Chinese.[19]

Cultural Diversity and the Thai Nation

EUROPEAN EXPANSION AND THE ORIGINS OF THAI NATIONALISM

The diversity of cultures represented by both migrant and indigenous peoples had not posed problems for the rulers of the premodern Siamese empire. The threat of colonial expansion by European powers, however, radically changed this situation. The first moves by the British in the period from 1786 to 1826—the period that saw the founding of Penang and the conquest of the Tennaserim peninsula—had little impact on the Siamese court. But by the middle of the nineteenth century, the threat had become much more ominous. In 1851, as a consequence of the second Anglo-Burman War, London added lower Burma to the British empire. Shortly thereafter, in 1855, the British convinced the Siamese court to sign the Bowring Treaty. Then in the 1860s, the French persuaded the King of Cambodia to accept their "protection" and, following a war with the Vietnamese emperor, conquered southern Vietnam and made it into the colony of Cochin China. King Mongkut, the Siamese monarch from 1851 to 1868, recognized that the independence of his realm depended on understanding the mentality of those behind Western colonial expansion. He had already gained deep insights into this mentality through his

---

17. By far the best account of Chinese immigration to Thailand is that by G. William Skinner, *Chinese Society in Thailand* (Ithaca, N.Y.: Cornell University Press, 1957). Also see Suehiro Akira, *Capital Accumulation in Thailand, 1855–1985* (Tokyo: Centre for East Asian Cultural Studies, 1989).

18. See James C. Ingram, *Economic Change in Thailand, 1850–1970* (Stanford, Calif.: Stanford University Press, 1971), p. 7.

19. Skinner, *Chinese Society*, p. 183.

intensive interactions with Western missionaries during the quarter of a century when he had been a Buddhist monk. As king, he sponsored the introduction of Western subjects, especially French and English languages, mathematics, and science, at court, with instruction occasionally provided by Westerners.[20]

His son, King Chulalongkorn (1868–1910), was to carry this intellectual revolution much further.[21] Chulalongkorn had himself been educated in part by Western tutors and, as king, made a number of trips abroad—to Java in the Dutch East Indies and to British Malaya and Burma in 1871–72, to Singapore in 1890, to Dutch-ruled Java again in 1896, and finally to Europe in 1897.[22] By 1880 King Chulalongkorn had also replaced most of the old ruling elite with princes and nobles who had received part of their education in Western countries or who had received an education that incorporated Western knowledge.

The king and his advisers became acutely aware that the British and French were using as justification for the expansion of their empires in Southeast Asia the assumption that peoples who shared the same heritage should be under the same polity. The French in particular sought to use this "logic of race" as a justification for dismembering Siam and uniting Lao and Cambodians (Khmer) under French rule.[23] Charles Lemire, a French diplomat in Bangkok, put the case in its most extreme form in a work published in 1903. While his numbers were hardly accurate, they are symbolic of the French view of Siam as a country in which a minority group ruled over many other peoples. He wrote that of the six million inhabitants of Siam, only two million were Siamese. Of the rest, he claimed, 400,000 were Cambodians, one million were Lao, 600,000 were Malays, and two million were Chinese.[24]

The French took action based on the logic of race with the power of

---

20.   Anna Leonowens, whose memoirs inspired *The King and I*, was only one such instructor. Her romanticized account and the even more romanticized and fictionalized story as depicted in *The King and I* do little justice to the extraordinary intellectual revolution that King Mongkut began. For an account of this revolution, see Craig J. Reynolds, "Buddhist Cosmography in Thai History, with Special Reference to Nineteenth-Century Culture Change," *Journal of Asian Studies*, Vol. 35, No. 2 (May 1976), pp. 203–220.

21.   See David K. Wyatt, *The Politics of Reform in Thailand: Education in the Reign of King Chulalongkorn* (New Haven, Conn.: Yale University Press, 1969).

22.   Ibid., pp. 196–197.

23.   See Streckfuss, "The Mixed Colonial Legacy."

24.   Charles Lemire, *La France et le Siam* (Paris: A. Challamel, 1903), p. 12, as quoted in Streckfuss, "The Mixed Colonial Legacy," p. 130.

arms. In 1893, the French sent gunboats up the Chao Phraya River to Bangkok to compel the Siamese rulers to recognize the creation of a French Laos which had been conceived of through politically motivated research into the traditions and histories of peoples living in the middle Mekong region. Faced now with the very palpable possibility that the use of such a logic of race could result in the reduction of Siam to a very small polity or to its elimination altogether, King Chulalongkorn and his close associates began a process of transforming the Siamese empire into a Thai nation-state. The significance of premodern cultural differences was minimized, and a common heritage for most of those who lived under the jurisdiction of the Siamese state was developed.

The cultural differences of premodern Siam could not be simply defined away and a new national identity instituted by fiat alone. The vision of the Thai nation and its relationship to the modern Thai state conceived of by King Chulalongkorn and his associates have nonetheless shaped the politics of ethnicity in Thailand ever since.[25]

THE FOUNDATIONS OF THAI NATIONALISM

King Chulalongkorn died in 1910 and his son Vajiravudh (1910–1924) succeeded him. The new king, who had been educated in England, had been strongly influenced while there by the debates about nationalism that foreshadowed World War I. Almost immediately after ascending the throne, he had to confront the emergence of Chinese nationalism attendant to the 1911 revolution in China. The large Chinese immigrant community in Thailand, once seen in a positive light because of the contributions they made to the growth of the Thai economy, came to be seen as potential sources of ethnic problems.

The king wrote a highly influential essay, published in both English and Thai, entitled "The Jews of the East," which argued that the Thai nation was threatened by a division of labor in which people of another race/nation/ethnic group (the term *chāt* could mean any of these) dominated in certain sectors of the economy.[26] New laws were promulgated that required immigrants who sought to be citizens of Siam to forswear allegiance to any other state and to become subjects of the Thai monarch. New regulations also led to a significant slowing of immigration. In

---

25. See Charles F. Keyes, "Buddhism and National Integration in Thailand," *Journal of Asian Studies*, Vol. 30, No. 3 (August 1971), pp. 551–568.

26. The king's essay was first published in English by the *Siam Observer* in 1914. See Skinner, *Chinese Society*, pp. 164–165; and Walter F. Vella, assisted by Dorothy Vella, *Chaiyo! King Vajiravudh and the Development of Thai Nationalism* (Honolulu: University of Hawaii Press, 1978), pp. 193–194.

addition, the king and his advisers developed the principles for a compulsory education plan for the country that strongly discouraged instruction in any language but Thai; in the late 1930s, non-Thai schools were
banned altogether.[27]

King Vajiravudh's reflections on the differences between Thai and
Chinese *chāt* were central to his enunciation of what is considered to be
the first fully articulated ideology of Thai nationalism.[28] The king posited
that what the Thai people shared as a national heritage was a common
language (Thai), a common religion (Buddhism), and a common relationship to the Bangkok (Chakkri) monarchy. These three elements are the
main pillars of Thai nationalism even today, albeit with some modifications.

It was noteworthy that King Vajiravudh's nationalism stressed culture
over biology as the basis of what would later be called "Thai-ness"
(*khwāmpen Thai*). In marked contrast to the ways in which immigrant
Chinese were viewed in the early twentieth century in the colonial dependencies of Southeast Asia (and elsewhere, including the United
States), it was possible in Siam for immigrants (who were overwhelmingly Chinese) or those who were descendants of immigrants to change
their nationality and become Thai if they acquired fluency in standard
Thai, became adherents of Buddhism, and renounced any other citizenship in favor of becoming subjects of the Siamese monarch.

MAKING THAI NATIONALISM HEGEMONIC

Thai nationalism was construed differently by the military and bureaucratic elite who staged a successful coup in 1932 and brought the absolute
monarchy to an end. The 1932 coup was predicated on the premise that
sovereignty rested with the people rather than in the monarchy. The
question then became: who are the people? The leaders of the coup and
those who held power between 1932 and 1950, when the country was
without a resident adult monarch,[29] sought to instill in the populace a
sense of national identity that was not dependent on the monarchy. To
attain this end, they implemented a state compulsory education program

---

27. See Keith Watson, *Educational Development in Thailand* (Hong Kong: Heinemann
Asia, 1980), pp. 115–132.

28. See Vella, *Chaiyo!*

29. Soon after the coup, King Prajadhipok (1925–1935) went into exile in England; he
abdicated in 1935. His very young nephew, Ananda, became king but died in 1946
before he ever became an effective ruler. His younger brother, Bhumipol Adulyadej,
returned from being educated abroad and began to assume the role of active monarch
only in the 1950s.

centered on subjects—especially Thai language and history—that oriented students toward both the state and the nation.[30] The new government also created a number of national holidays that were given prominent attention in the expanding mass media—newspapers, films, and radio.

During this period, Thai did in fact become the "national" language because of the success of compulsory schooling. The official national historical narrative—one that emphasized the difference between Thai and Chinese—written by the very productive and influential Luang Wichit Watthakan, was made the basis of Thai history as taught in schools. Wichit's plays and the radio dramas staged by Prime Minister Phibun Songgram served to reinforce the new hegemonic nationalist ideology. One of the manifestations of this new ideology was the change of the name of the country from Siam to Thailand in 1939.

Luang Wichit Watthakan and Phibun Songgram also promoted pan-Thai-ism, a racialist interpretation of nationalism. They sought to expand the boundaries of Thailand to include other Tai-speaking peoples as well as Khmer, whom they deemed to share the same national culture but who were excluded from the Thai nation by colonial policies. Pan-Thai-ism provided the justification for the annexation in the early 1940s, with Japanese approval, of territories on the right bank of the Mekong River in French-ruled Laos, northwestern Cambodia, and Kengtung in the Shan states of British Burma. Although Thailand was forced to give up these territories after World War II, the precedent had been set for the promotion of militant nationalism. The Thai military would subsequently draw on this aggressive form of nationalism to justify the suppression of internal dissent.

Following World War II, Thailand rediscovered the monarchy. From 1932 until the early 1950s, the monarchy had been in disfavor, and for most of the period the two brothers who were successive kings were minors. In the early 1950s, however, King Bhumipol Adulyadej, who had ascended to the throne in 1946, began to redefine the monarchy through a series of public appearances throughout the kingdom. After Field Marshal Sarit Thanarat took power in a coup in 1957, the military dictators who controlled the Thai government until 1972 became strong supporters of an activist monarchy because they thought it would help legitimate their own role. During this period, the basic premises of Thai nationalism

---

30. See Charles F. Keyes, "The Proposed World of the School: Thai Villagers' Entry into a Bureaucratic State System," in Keyes, ed., *Reshaping Local Worlds: Rural Education and Cultural Change in Southeast Asia* (New Haven, Conn.: Yale University Southeast Asian Studies, 1991), pp. 87–138. On the creation of a national language, see Anthony Diller, "What Makes Central Thai a National Language," in Craig J. Reynolds, *National Identity and Its Defenders: Thailand, 1939–1989*, Monash Papers on Southeast Asia No. 25 (Melbourne: Monash University, Centre of Southeast Asian Studies, 1991), pp. 87–132.

that had first been articulated by King Vajiravudh were strongly promoted. The Thai nation, as every child learned in school and every adult heard repeated in a variety of contexts, was said to be based on three pillars: *chāt*, the (Thai) people; *sātsanā*, the (Buddhist) religion; and *phra mahākasat*, the monarchy. As with the Chinese in the reign of King Vajiravudh, any person could "become Thai" if he or she spoke Thai (even if they also spoke other languages), adhered to Buddhism, and accepted being subjects of the king. In short, this conception of Thai nationalism was highly tolerant of cultural diversity.

However, some who have wielded power or who have had significant influence on those in power have advocated a more constricted view of Thai nationalism. During the periods when there have been military-headed or military-backed governments (1957–72; 1976–87; 1991–92), some leading military figures have sought in the name of "Nation, Religion, and King" to suppress any challenge to their hold on power. Some officials have taken the premise that to be Thai is to be Buddhist as a rationale for forcing Muslims and Christians to act in ways—such as showing reverence for the Buddha in schools—that they find offensive or unacceptable. In the turbulent mid-1970s, a prominent Thai monk declared that Communists who rejected Buddhism were non-human and thus should be killed.[31]

Although some Thai leaders have embraced narrower conceptions of nationalism, most ruling elites in Thailand have consistently backed away from militant nationalism. King Bhumipol is to be credited with undermining the legitimacy of authoritarian military governments (notably in 1972 and 1992) and broadening the interpretation of *sātsanā* to include non-Buddhist religions. He has, for example, served as patron for Christian organizations and for the annual Koranic competition. In other words, King Bhumipol has sought to reassert the vision of a diverse nation defined by his predecessor, Chulalongkorn. The policies that have flowed from this vision, especially since it has been contested from time to time, have reflected a distinctive politics of ethnicity in Thailand.

Ethnic Politics and the Thai Nation-State

To fully understand the politics of ethnicity in Thailand, one needs to examine the policy stances taken with respect to the country's distinctive ethnic and ethnoregional minorities. (See Table 5.1.)

31. See Charles F. Keyes, "Political Crisis and Militant Buddhism in Contemporary Thailand," in Bardwell Smith, ed., *Religion and Legitimation of Power in Thailand, Burma, and Laos* (Chambersburg, Penn.: Anima Books), pp. 147–164.

Table 5.1. Ethnic and Ethnoregional Composition of Thailand.

Category	Location	Number	Percentage
Thai (speakers of Standard Thai, central Thai, and southern Thai, but not including Sino-Thai or Thai Muslims)	Throughout the country	29,700,000	49.5
Ethnoregionally distinctive Tai-speakers			
Northeastern Thai (Isan, Lao)	Northeastern Thailand	13,680,000	22.8
Northern Thai (Khon Muang, Yuan)	Northern Thailand	5,400,000	9.0
Religiously distinctive Tai-speakers			
Thai Muslims	Central and southern Thailand	1,200,000	2.0
Chinese and Sino-Thai			
Chinese (speakers of Chinese languages)	Bangkok and other urban areas	4,620,000	7.7
Sino-Thai (*lūk cīn*) (speakers of Thai)	Bangkok and other urban areas	2,160,000	3.6
Thai Malay	Southernmost provinces	1,140,000	1.9
Other distinctive indigenous minorities			
Khmer and Kui (Suai)	Borderlands with Cambodia	1,320,000	2.2
Hill peoples (*chāo khao*) (Karen, Hmong, Mien/Yao, Akha, Lahu, Lisu, Lawa, and others)	Mainly northern Thailand, with small numbers found elsewhere	600,000	1.0
Mon	Central Thailand	<60,000	<0.1
Other distinctive minorities (Vietnamese, Indians, Burmese)	Bangkok and northeastern Thailand	120,000	0.2
Total		60,000,000	100.0

NOTES: Thailand's population reached 60,000,000 in 1996. All percentages and numbers for each category are estimates and do not include refugees (in 1996, primarily from Burma), expatriates (from Europe, the United States, and other Asian countries), or illegal migrants (primarily from Burma, Laos, and southern China, whose number could have been as high as 200,000 in 1996). Most Sino-Thai and Thai-Muslims are also native speakers of standard Thai. It is possible that the estimate for Sino-Thai is too low and should include an additional number of those classified as "Thai."

SOURCES: This table is based on census data and on the following: Peter Kundstadter, ed., *Southeast Asian Tribes: Minorities and Nations* (Princeton, N.J.: Princeton University Press, 1967), pp. 397–400; United States Department of the Army, *Ethnographic Study Series: Minority Groups in Thailand* (Washington, D.C.: U.S. GPO, 1970); William A. Smalley, *Linguistic Diversity and National Unity: Language Ecology in Thailand* (Chicago: University of Chicago Press, 1994), Appendix B; G. William Skinner, *Chinese Society in Thailand: An Analytical History* (Ithaca, N.Y.: Cornell University Press, 1957), pp. 181–190 (for Chinese and Sino-Thai); and John McKinnon and Wanat Bhruksasri, eds., *Highlanders of Thailand* (Kuala Lumpur: Oxford University Press, 1983); and Paul and Elaine Lewis, *Peoples of the Golden Triangle* (London: Thames and Hudson, 1984) (for tribal peoples).

ETHNOREGIONALISM IN NORTHEASTERN AND NORTHERN THAILAND

One of the most dramatic consequences of politics promoting an inclusive nationalism was the disappearance of the "Lao" as a distinctive category in Thai society. Both the "Lao" of the Khorat Plateau and the "Lao" of the northern domains who called themselves *Khonmyang* and their tradition *Yuan*, became ethnoregional rather than ethnic minorities within the Thai state. By "ethnoregional," I mean that cultural differences have been taken to be characteristic of a particular part of the country rather than of a distinctive people.

The first efforts in the late nineteenth and early twentieth centuries to suppress potential ethnic separatism stimulated millenarian uprisings in both northeastern and northern Thailand.[32] But through the co-optation of the Buddhist clergy and subsequently through the implementation of compulsory education, expressions of ethnic distinctiveness were silenced.[33] This, however, contributed to the emergence of ethnoregionalism, especially in northeastern Thailand. By ethnoregionalism, I mean that resources and power were contested by people who saw themselves as disadvantaged by both their cultural differences and their geographical location relative to the center of the state.[34]

In the northeastern region, many of those who might have seen themselves as "Lao" have embraced an ethnoregional identity known as *khon īsān*. Isan, derived from a Sanskrit term meaning "northeast," was first introduced in conjunction with the provincial reorganization of the Thai state at the end of the nineteenth century. In contemporary Thailand, Isan is understood by both those who use it as an autonym and those who use it for others as pointing to cultural differences (most often

32. See Charles F. Keyes, "Millennialism, Theravāda Buddhism, and Thai Society," *Journal of Asian Studies*, Vol. 36, No. 2 (May 1977), pp. 283–302; Chatthip Nartsupha, "The Ideology of 'Holy Men' Revolts in North East Thailand," in Andrew Turton and Shigeharu Tanabe, eds., *Historical and Peasant Consciousness in South East Asia* (Osaka: National Museum of Ethnology, 1984), pp. 111–134; Ansil Ramsay, "Modernization and Reactionary Rebellions in Northern Siam," *Journal of Asian Studies*, Vol. 38, No. 2 (May 1979), pp. 283–298; and Shigeharu Tanabe, "Ideological Practice in Peasant Rebellions: Siam at the Turn of the Twentieth Century," in Turton and Tanabe, *Historical and Peasant Consciousness*, pp. 75–110.

33. See Michel-Rolph Trouillot, *Silencing the Past: Power and the Production of History* (Boston: Beacon Press, 1995). On the co-optation of the Buddhist clergy to promote national integration in northern Thailand, see Charles F. Keyes, "Buddhism and National Integration in Thailand," *Journal of Asian Studies*, Vol. 30, No. 3 (August 1971), pp. 551–568. On the role of compulsory education, especially in northeastern Thailand, see Charles F. Keyes, "The Proposed World of the School."

34. See Michael Hechter and Margaret Levi, "The Comparative Analysis of Ethnoregional Movements," *Ethnic and Racial Studies*, Vol. 2, No. 3 (July 1979), pp. 260–274.

associated with language, food, and music) and to economic underdevelopment and inequalities in wealth relative to Bangkok and central Thailand. Since over one-third of the population of the country resides in northeastern Thailand and since an overwhelming majority of the people of this region identify themselves as or could identify themselves as *khon īsān*, ethnoregionalism has been of major concern to the central government.[35]

Northeastern ethnoregionalism has its roots in the success of a number of regional politicians in gaining roles at the national level in the 1930s and 1940s.[36] The officially sponsored murder of several of these politicians in the 1950s and Laos's attainment of independence in 1954 created conditions that appeared conducive to the emergence of Lao ethnic separatism rather than Isan ethnoregionalism. In response, the government of Field Marshal Sarit Thanarat, who was prime minister from 1957 to 1963 and who identified himself as a *khon īsān* through his mother, initiated policies that were aimed at addressing what came to be known as "the northeastern problem." The government assumed that if there were significant improvements in the economy of the region, then support for ethnic separatism would disappear.

Since the Sarit-sponsored northeastern development plan of 1962, there have been many policy initiatives—mostly economic, some military—designed to ensure that the regional economy benefits at least to some degree from the expansion of the national economy and to dissuade people in the region from pursuing their grievances through separatist or other insurgency movements. However, the heavy-handedness of early government programs in the region tended to exacerbate such grievances. In the 1960s and 1970s, the Communist Party of Thailand (CPT) was able to build its largest base of support among rural people in the northeast. Even so, the CPT-led insurgency was never an ethnic separatist movement, since the CPT sought to capture state power rather than to unite the northeast with Laos, even after Laos came under communist rule in 1975. The CPT-led insurgency did, however, lead the government of Thailand to reconsider some of the programs directed at the region and

---

35. Approximately one-tenth of the population of northeastern Thailand are native speakers of Khmer or Khmer-related languages. A much smaller number are native speakers of Thai Khorat, a language closely related to Central Thai. Speakers of these languages rarely think of themselves as *khon īsān*.

36. See Charles F. Keyes, *Isan: Regionalism in Northeastern Thailand*, Southeast Asia Program Data Paper 65 (Ithaca, N.Y.: Cornell University, 1967); and Keyes, "Hegemony and Resistance in Northeastern Thailand," in Grabowsky, *Regions and National Integration*, pp. 154–182. Also see Harald Uhlig, "The 'Problem-Region' Northeastern Thailand," in Grabowsky, *Regions and National Integration*, pp. 130–144.

to create a number of new ones. When the CPT-led insurgency collapsed in the early 1980s because of the ideological rigidity of the party and because of a significant turn in Bangkok toward a more open political system, the northeast still remained the focus of particular attention.

In the late 1980s and especially after the popular rejection of an attempted reinstallation of military rule in 1991–92, elected politicians have controlled government power. Northeastern constituencies, which elect a larger percentage of parliamentarians than any other set of regional constituencies in the country, have attracted considerable attention from the major political parties. Northeastern members of parliament have been able, no matter what party has formed the government, to ensure that what has become the equivalent of an entitlement program for the northeast is funded in each budget. By the early 1990s, however, such "affirmative action" toward the northeast had begun to generate resistance among some politicians, notably those from Bangkok, who saw it as draining resources away from major urban problems such as infrastructure development, pollution abatement, and traffic control, which are seen as threats to Thailand's economic growth.

Ethnoregionalism has also been characteristic, to a much lesser extent than for the people of the northeast, of the relationship between peoples in northern Thailand and the center.[37] However, *phayāp*, the northern equivalent of *īsān*, did not become a label for a northern Thai regional identity. In official discourse since the late 1930s, the north is simply called *phāk nua* (the northern region) and its inhabitants, *khon phāk nua* (people of the north). There has been a greater effort to ignore the ethnoregional differences of peoples of the north because there is no other political community to which they might see themselves belonging. Even the terms "the north" and "northerners" entail an effort to deny ethnoregional status to the culturally distinctive people who call themselves *Khonmuang*, since these terms are also used for provinces in the north central plains where the population is culturally and linguistically different from the people of the upper north.

This said, northern Thai ethnoregionalism has still been manifest in a number of ways. Descendants of the old Chiang Mai princely family, a

---

37. See M.R. Rujaya Abhakorn and David Wyatt, "Administrative Reforms and National Integration in Northern Thailand," in Grabowsky, *Regions and National Integration*, pp. 68–81; Harold Uhlig, "Northern Thailand: The Natural Region and the Cultural Landscape," in Grabowsky, *Regions and National Integration*, pp. 22–45; Michael Rhum, "The Future of the Past in Northern Thailand," in Benedict R. O'G. Anderson, et al., *Southeast Asian Tribal Groups and Ethnic Minorities: Prospects for the Eighties and Beyond*, Cultural Survival Report 22 (Cambridge, Mass.: Cultural Survival, Inc., 1987), pp. 117–124.

number of leading monks and ex-monks, faculty at Chiang Mai University and other tertiary educational institutions, some tour companies, and even provincial officials posted to the region from Bangkok have promoted a number of activities to ensure that the distinctive cultural heritage of the *Khonmyang* is kept publicly visible. This was especially evident in 1996, when a number of events were mounted to celebrate the 700th anniversary of Chiang Mai. The age of the city was explicitly contrasted with that of Bangkok, which is only two hundred years old. For the 700th anniversary celebrations as in other ceremonial occasions, many middle- and upper-class women in the north wore clothing identified with Yuan, Lao, or Lue, the latter being another Tai people associated with the northern Thai tradition. While some of the efforts to perpetuate the distinctive cultural heritage of northern Thailand are blatantly commercial or are impelled by nostalgia for a less complex world—often by transplanted urbanites from Bangkok—others do contribute to the promotion of a distinctive northern Thai cultural identity.

Northern ethnoregionalism does not, however, have the political or economic salience of northeastern ethnoregionalism. Insofar as the government has developed affirmative action programs for the north, they have been targeted primarily at upland peoples rather than at those who identify themselves as *Khonmyang*. Development programs for the northern region also apply to provinces in the northern central plains populated by people who are not *Khonmyang*. Only very limited attention has been given to the very real grievances of many northern farmers, particularly those living in the Chiang Mai valley, who have seen their traditional modes of production undermined by the expansion of agribusinesses. Although the discontent that might fuel a more assertive northern Thai ethnoregionalism was relatively muted in the first half of the 1990s, the public attention given to the distinctive cultural heritage of the region continued to keep the potential alive for such assertiveness in the future.

HILL PEOPLES

The peoples of northern Thailand who have been subjected to policies that are explicitly based on a recognition of ethnic difference are those who have been labeled as "hill peoples" (*chāo khao*). Not all those so designated are found in the uplands of northern Thailand; some are also found in the western hills that border on Burma. But most in Thailand associate the hill peoples with northern Thailand.[38] While some of these

---

38. The following is drawn, with some changes, from Keyes, *Thailand*, pp. 127–130. For an overview of hill peoples in Thailand together with articles on each group, see John McKinnon and Wanat Bhruksasri, eds., *Highlanders of Thailand* (Kuala Lumpur:

peoples, such as some Karen,[39] feel a kinship with the *Khonmuang*, most are not in a position to make such a claim even if they wanted to do so. Until the 1950s, the Thai government effectively ignored the tribal peoples. Following Mao's successful revolution in China, the outbreak of tribal rebellions in Burma, and the growing conflict in Laos, tribal peoples from these neighboring areas began to immigrate in increasing numbers into northern Thailand. Some immigrants retained close relations with politically active tribal peoples in Burma, Laos, and China. The government of Sarit Thanarat (1957–63) determined that there was a "hill tribe problem," that is, that the hill peoples posed a threat to Thailand's internal security. In addition to the security question, the government also became increasingly concerned about the fact that most upland peoples engaged in swidden or shifting cultivation, a form of agriculture that was deemed damaging to the forests and watershed and inimical to economic development.[40]

The government tended to base the "hill tribe problem" on the assumption that all upland peoples were like the Hmong (referred to by the

Oxford University Press, 1983). A sequel, John McKinnon and Bernard Vienne, eds., *Hill Tribes Today: Problems in Change* (Bangkok: White Lotus-Orstom, Tri-Orstom Project, 1989), provides more attention to policy issues.

39. See David Marlowe, "In the Mosaic: The Cognitive and Structural Aspects of Karen-Other Relationships," in Charles F. Keyes, ed., *Ethnic Adaptation and Identity: The Karen on the Thai Frontier with Burma* (Philadelphia: ISHI [Institute for the Study of Human Issues], 1979), pp. 165–214; and Ananda Rajah, "Ethnicity, Nationalism, and the Nation-State: The Karen in Burma and Thailand," in Gehan Wijeyewardene, ed., *Ethnic Groups Across National Boundaries in Mainland Southeast Asia* (Singapore: Institute of Southeast Asian Studies, 1990), pp. 102–133.

40. For an excellent review of Thai government policies toward hill peoples, see Pinkaew Laungarmsri, "On the Discourse of Hill Tribes" (unpublished M.A. paper, University of Washington, 1995). Also see Robert G. Cooper, "The Tribal Minorities of Northern Thailand: Problems and Prospects," *Southeast Asian Affairs 1979* (Singapore: Heinemann Educational Books, 1979), pp. 323–332, and Anthony R. Walker, "In Mountain and Ulu: A Comparative History of Development Strategies for Ethnic Minority Peoples in Thailand and Malaysia," *Contemporary Southeast Asia*, Vol. 4 (1983), pp. 451–485. Several papers by Cornelia Ann Kammerer, while focused on the Akha, also provide significant insights into state-tribal relations: "Territorial Imperatives: Akha Ethnic Identity and Thailand's National Integration," in R. Guidieri, F. Pellizzi, and S.J. Tambiah, eds., *Ethnicities and Nations: Processes of Interethnic Relations in Latin America, Southeast Asia, and the Pacific* (Houston: Rothko Chapel, 1986), pp. 277–291; Kammerer, "Minority Identity in the Mountains of Northern Thailand: The Akha Case," in Anderson, et al., *Southeast Asian Tribal Groups and Ethnic Minorities*, pp. 85–96; and Kammerer, "Of Labels and Laws: Thailand's Resettlement and Repatriation Policies," *Cultural Survival*, Vol. 12, No. 4 (1988), pp. 7–12. For an examination of policy debates about swidden cultivation, see Peter Kunstadter, E.C. Chapman, and Sanga Sabhasri, eds., *Farmers in the Forest: Economic Development and Marginal Agriculture in Northern Thailand* (Honolulu: University of Hawaii Press, East-West Center Book, 1978).

Thai as the Meo). Although the largest number of new immigrants in northern Thailand were Hmong, Karen remain to this day the largest upland population in Thailand, numbering over half of the estimated 500,000–600,000 hill people in the country. Because of the focus on the Hmong rather than on the Karen or other hill peoples, the Thai government formulated policies that have seriously slowed official relations with upland groups. These policies have presumed that most hill peoples are recent illegal immigrants, that they cultivate opium poppies, and that they have few ties to Thai peoples. While these characteristics might be true of some, they are quite misleading when applied to the majority of upland peoples.

In the mid-1960s, the government decided that the hill peoples were sympathetic to if not outright supporters of the communist movements in Thailand and Laos. Direct military action was then taken against some upland communities. Napalm was used to destroy a number of Hmong and Mien villages, and members of many upland groups were forced to resettle in new areas determined by the government. Contrary to what the government intended, these actions stimulated certain groups, especially the Hmong, to support the communist-led insurrection. Thai military action against suspected tribal communist groups continued well into the 1970s, and only came to an end when the change of government in Laos in 1975 resulted in a large-scale exodus of Hmong and other tribal refugees into Thailand. Although the refugees from Laos showed the Thai government that all hill peoples were not communists, the government refused to permit these refugees to become permanent Thai residents—lest they create yet another "problem."

The concern that upland peoples posed a threat to national security led not only to armed conflict between Thai military forces and hill peoples deemed to be supporters of a communist-led insurrection, but also to programs designed to assimilate hill peoples into Thai society. In the mid-1960s, the Border Patrol Police were charged with establishing schools in upland villages. When these schools were considered to be functioning well, they were turned over to provincial educational authorities to be run as regular schools. Some upland village children were also brought by various government agencies as well as by Christian missionaries to study in schools in northern Thai towns. As a consequence of these educational programs, an increasing number of hill peoples have acquired literacy in Thai, and some have gone on to obtain secondary and even tertiary educations. This has been a mixed blessing in that educated hill peoples have become aware of their disadvantaged status.

A second program aimed at assimilating tribal peoples, also begun in the mid-1960s, entailed sending Buddhist missionaries into tribal communities.[41] The Buddhist missionary program was inspired by and competitive with long-standing Christian missionary work among tribal peoples. While some hill peoples have converted to Buddhism, the more significant consequence of the program has been to accentuate the distinction between Buddhist Thai and non-Buddhist hill peoples.

The Thai government has instituted policies designed to persuade hill peoples to give up swidden cultivation and especially to cease production of opium. The latter was strongly supported by the king under a "royal project," and by the 1990s opium production had been all but eliminated. It must be noted that crop substitution programs worked not only because of government policies but also because the dramatic growth in the Thai economy led to a substantial increase in the value of alternative crops, such as cabbage. The forced resettlement of hill peoples in non-swidden areas has, however, transformed some hill peoples into a rural underclass in northern Thailand.

Tourist interest in hill peoples has generated some new sources of income for some of these peoples.[42] Tribal handicrafts are marketed not only in northern Thailand but also in Bangkok and abroad. Some upland communities regularly host trekkers. While tourism has benefitted some hill peoples, it has also served to subordinate hill peoples to the Thai. Much of the packaging of upland cultures for tourists has been undertaken by Thai middlemen who assume that the hill peoples are "primitive." Even in its most benign effects, tourism serves to accentuate the distinctiveness of hill peoples within Thai society.

Since the mid-1960s, members of the royal family have become patrons of hill peoples. The king and queen and the late princess mother made well-publicized visits to upland communities to open schools, sponsor rice banks, and assist those who have suffered from various calamities. The craft work and especially the textiles of upland peoples have gained significantly in value because of royal projects and the use of tribal textiles in clothing worn by members of the royal family. There is no doubt that the patronage role played by the royal family has enhanced the image of hill peoples in Thai society. At the same time, it has served to underscore the fact that hill peoples occupy a distinctive place within the Thai system.

Hill peoples have not yet organized themselves into any pan-tribal groupings comparable to the American Indian Movement in the United

---

41. See Charles F. Keyes, "Buddhism and National Integration."

42. See Erik Cohen, "Hill Tribe Tourism," in McKinnon and Bhruksasri, *Highlanders of Thailand*, pp. 307–325.

States. However, by lumping different peoples into a common category—"hill peoples"—and by implementing policies based on a presumption that upland peoples are essentially the same, the government has created the basis for a pan-tribal organization. Many hill peoples, whatever their actual background, have now had common experiences in dealing with the government.

THAI MALAY AND THAI MUSLIMS

Since the 1960s, the peoples whose cultural differences have proven to be the greatest concerns to Thai governments have been those who follow Islam, and especially those Muslims who also identify themselves as Malay.

Thai-speaking Muslims in southern Thailand as well as Thai Muslims elsewhere (mainly in Bangkok and in areas around Bangkok) recognize that their religion makes them different from other Thai. However, they have tended to accentuate their "Thai-ness," as manifested in their language and their sense of shared traditions with other Thai, rather than their religion.[43] In the 1980s, however, some influenced by Islamic fundamentalism sought to gain greater recognition of their religious distinctiveness.[44] Although the premise that to be Thai is to be Buddhist has never been officially set aside, Muslim demands that they not be compelled to suppress their religious identity led in the 1980s and 1990s to a broadening of the interpretation of the "religious" pillar of Thai nationalism in a way that made a place for non-Buddhists.[45] The king has used his position to make Muslims and other non-Buddhists feel that they are indeed a part of the Thai nation. In recent years, the king has had many well-publicized meetings with Muslim leaders and has presented awards for study of the Koran to students from Muslim schools. Also indicative of the change in Thai attitudes is the rise to political prominence of a number of Thai Muslims, most notably of Surin Pitsuwan, who became deputy foreign minister in the early 1990s.

43. See Angela Burr, "Religious Institutional Diversity—Social Structural and Conceptual Unity: Islam and Buddhism in a Southern Thai Coastal Fishing Village," *Journal of the Siam Society*, Vol. 60, No. 2 (July 1972), pp. 183–216.

44. See, especially, Chaiwat Satha-Anand, "*Hijab* and Moments of Legitimation: Islamic Resurgence in Thai Society," in Charles F. Keyes, Laurel Kendall, and Helen Hardacre, eds., *Asian Visions of Authority: Religion and the Modern States of East and Southeast Asia* (Honolulu: University of Hawaii Press, 1994), pp. 279–300.

45. See Raymond Scupin, "Islamic Reformism in Thailand," *Journal of the Siam Society*, Vol. 68, No. 2 (July 1980), pp. 1–10; Scupin, "Thailand as a Plural Society: Ethnic Interaction in a Buddhist Kingdom," *Crossroads*, Vol. 2, No. 3 (1986), pp. 115–140; and

By far the strongest challenge to the dominant national ideology of Thailand has come from those who are both Muslims and Malay-speaking and who live in a geographically distinct area, the provinces in the far south that border on Malaysia.[46] Beginning in the 1960s, Thai governments began to focus more attention on the Thai Malays for a number of reasons. First, the granting of independence to Malaysia in 1959 raised the possibility of Thai Malay seeing themselves as members of another national community. In addition, the border area was deemed to be "insecure" because remnants of the Communist Party of Malaysia had taken refuge in the jungles along the border and because a number of "bandit" groups operated in the area.

Government programs instituted to deal with the border provinces in the south initially had the opposite effect of what was intended. These

---

Scupin, "Interpreting Islamic Movements in Thailand," *Crossroads*, Vol. 3, No. 2–3 (1986), pp. 78–93.

46. On the relationship of the Thai Malay to the state, see M. Ladd Thomas, *Political Violence in the Muslim Provinces of Southern Thailand*, Occasional Paper No. 28 (Singapore: Institute of Southeast Asian Studies, 1975); Astri Suhrke, "Irredentism Contained: The Thai-Muslim Case," *Comparative Politics*, Vol. 7, No. 2 (March 1975), pp. 187–204; Astri Suhrke, "Loyalists and Separatists: The Muslims in Southern Thailand," *Asian Survey*, Vol. 17, No. 3 (September 1977), pp. 237–250; Nantawan Haemindra, "The Problem of the Thai-Muslims in the Four Southern Provinces of Thailand," *Journal of Southeast Asian Studies*, Part One, Vol. 7, No. 2 (1976), pp. 197–225; Part Two, Vol. 8, No. 1 (March 1977), pp. 85–105; Ruth McVey, "Separatism and the Paradoxes of the Nation-State in Perspective," in Lim Joo-Jock and S. Vani, eds., *Armed Separatism in Southeast Asia* (Singapore: Institute of Southeast Asian Studies, 1984), pp. 3–29; Omar Farouk, "The Historical and Transnational Dimensions of Malay-Muslim Separatism in Southern Thailand," in Joo-Jock and Vani, *Armed Separatism in Southeast Asia*, pp. 234–260; Omar Farouk, "The Origins and Evolution of Malay-Muslim Ethnic Nationalism in Southern Thailand," in Taufik Abdullah and Sharon Siddique, eds., *Islam and Society in Southeast Asia* (Singapore: Institute of Southeast Asian Studies, 1986), pp. 250–281; Uthai Dulyakasem, "Muslim-Malay Separatism in Southern Thailand: Factors Underlying the Political Revolt," in Joo-Jock and Vani, *Armed Separatism in Southeast Asia*, pp. 217–234; Uthai Dulyakasem, "The Emergence and Escalation of Ethnic Nationalism: The Case of the Muslim Malays in Southern Siam," in Abdullah and Siddique, *Islam and Society in Southeast Asia*, pp. 208–249; Uthai Dulyakasem, "Education and Ethnic Nationalism: The Case of the Muslim-Malays in Southern Thailand," in Charles F. Keyes, ed., *Reshaping Local Worlds: Education and Cultural Change in Rural Southeast Asia* (New Haven, Conn.: Yale University Southeast Asian Studies, 1991), pp. 131–152; Surin Pitsuwan, *Islam and Malay Nationalism: A Case Study of the Malay Muslims of Southern Thailand* (Bangkok: Thai Khadi Research Institute, Thammasat University, 1985); Chaiwat Satha-Anand, *Islam and Violence: A Case Study of Violent Events in the Four Southern Provinces of Thailand, 1976–1981*, USF Monograph in Religion and Public Policy No. 2 (Tampa: Department of Religious Studies, University of South Florida, 1986); and Man and Kadir, "National Integration and Resistance Movements."

programs entailed the posting of more government officials, who were mostly Thai and Buddhist, in the region; Malay Muslims found themselves forced to deal with officials who almost never spoke their language and who not only did not understand Islam but were often hostile to it. In addition, schools in the far south, like schools throughout the country, provide instruction in the Thai language and present a Thai view of both the past and the present. Not surprisingly, schools in the Malay areas of southern Thailand have had among the lowest attendance rates of any in the country, and few Malay-speakers go beyond the compulsory primary grades. The government has also made use of coercive power in the far south to a more marked degree than almost anywhere else in the country, a policy that has been rationalized as necessary because of "banditry" in the area.

By the late 1960s, the intrusiveness of the Thai state in the southern border region had created conditions that fostered the creation of an ethnic insurgency. The alienation of Thai Malays in Thailand was most keenly felt among those living in Pattani Province, since Patani was once a semi-autonomous Malayan sultanate.[47] In the early 1970s, a separatist organization, the Patani United Liberation Organization (PALO), attracted considerable support from the local populace. The movement received outside aid from Libya and perhaps other countries as well. The conflict between PALO and the Thai government became very intense in the late 1970s, when a right-wing government took office in Bangkok.

Since the early 1980s, the situation has changed significantly. Thai governments have sought to tolerate political diversity rather than eliminate it. A concerted effort has been made to appoint officials who are sensitive to the cultural and religious distinctiveness of the area; this has also meant that a number of local officials are Thai Malay by origin. The Democrat Party, the dominant party in southern Thailand, has made a very public effort to recruit Thai Muslims as candidates for parliament. The Malaysian government, for its part, has gone out of its way to demonstrate that, despite the sympathies of some living in northern Malaya, it does not support Thai Malay separatism. At the same time, many Thai Malay, under the influence of Islamic fundamentalism, have come to emphasize their religious rather than their ethnic identity. With greater tolerance being shown by the Thai government toward Islam, even fundamentalist Muslims can find a place within the Thai nation.

There are limits to Thai tolerance, however. The public culture of

---

47. Worawit Baru (also known as Ahmad Idris), "Tradition and Cultural Background of the Patani Region," in Grabowsky, *Regions and National Integration*, pp. 195–210.

Thailand remains strongly influenced by Buddhism. Fundamentalist Islam has also stimulated a backlash among some Thai Buddhists who would like to return to the older premise that to be Thai is to be Buddhist. The potential thus remains for conflict to reemerge in response to the efforts of Thai Muslims, and especially Thai Malays, to retain their religious and ethnic distinctiveness.

THE SINO-THAI

Overseas Chinese communities have been a major source of ethnic conflict for many of Thailand's Southeast Asian neighbors. In Thailand those of Chinese descent dominate the economy and constitute a larger percentage of the population than in any Southeast Asian country save Malaysia. Thus the role they play in Thai society might be expected to be one of the country's major ethnic cleavages. To the contrary, by the 1990s many of this group were quite successfully seeking recognition for the critical role that they and their ancestors have played in developing the modern Thai nation.

The openness of Thai nationalism coupled with the restrictions placed on immigration and on Chinese-language schools led to widespread assimilation. Those who recognized their Chinese ancestry but had come to identify themselves as Thai—primarily because they had Thai ancestors on their mother's side, but sometimes simply because they became Thai citizens—acquired a new quasi ethnic status in Siam. They were *lūk cīn*, literally, "children of Chinese"; in English they are usually termed "Sino-Thai." The hybrid Sino-Thai identity has a counterpart in the economic sphere. Whereas prior to World War II, much of the commerce of Thailand—like that of many other Southeast Asian countries—was in the hands of those who were identifiably Chinese, in the postwar period most enterprises have also "become Thai" even though it is known that their owners are Sino-Thai. By this I mean that the Thai language is used as the primary means of communication within the organization and that capitalization has come primarily from Thai citizens.[48] Sino-Thai firms often show that they are Thai by inviting Buddhist monks to conduct rites at the openings of new plants or buildings. Prominent Sino-Thai

---

48. In dealing with the outside world, most companies today use English. However, there are some major companies—the huge conglomerate Charoen Pokphand, for example—with strong links to the PRC, Taiwan, or Hong Kong for which the use of a Chinese language is very important. That language tends to be Mandarin although very few Chinese immigrants to Siam/Thailand spoke a dialect of Mandarin as their native language.

enterprises have also attracted the patronage of the royal family, as in 1996 when Princess Sirindhorn officiated at the opening of a new office in Shanghai of Charoen Pokphand, the largest multinational enterprise in Thailand.

Because the Thai economy has grown so rapidly since the 1950s, there has been a dramatic increase in the size of the country's middle class. This burgeoning middle class, made up of not only Sino-Thai but also many from non-Chinese backgrounds, was at the forefront of the political movements of the 1970s, 1980s, and 1990s that succeeded in forcing the old military-bureaucratic elite to open the political system to wider participation. By the late 1980s, governments were more likely to be formed by the dominant political parties in parliament than by the military. Parties that have been successful have been so because of strong financial backing that has made it possible to buy votes in and extend patronage to constituencies. Because the wealthy backers of the parties have tended to be Sino-Thai, the Sino-Thai community gained significant political power in the late 1980s and 1990s. This has been troubling to the older elite, especially those in the military. A major reason given for a coup staged by the military in February 1991 was that the government of then Prime Minister Chatichai Choonhuwan was corrupt. A number of people in the government were said to be "unusually wealthy"—all were Sino-Thai. This accusation, which dissipated with the rejection of military rule in May 1992, was a thinly disguised attack on the dominance of the Sino-Thai in Thai affairs.

In September 1996, a challenge to the dominance of the Sino-Thai came from other members of parliament. In debate over a motion to censure Prime Minister Banharn Silpa-archa, a major issue was whether he had been born in China; if he had been, he would not by Thai law be eligible to be prime minister. Although he ultimately produced evidence that showed he had indeed been born in Thailand, this attack clearly pointed to a concern about the extent of "Chinese" influence in Thai politics. In the election that followed this debate, some parties made blatant appeals to voters of Sino-Thai background to reject those who had supported the challenge to Banharn.

This new debate about the Sino-Thai role in Thai politics occurred at a time when there had been a remarkable public resurgence of Chinese cultural practices in Thailand. With considerable disposable income available, many Sino-Thai began in the 1980s to build new Chinese shrines and refurbish old ones. By the early 1990s, the high level of investment in Chinese culture was conspicuous throughout urban Thailand. One leading scholar of Chinese descent has argued that it is essential to recognize the "cultural capital" controlled by Thai Chinese if Thai wish to understand how their economy has grown so rapidly.[49] Several scholars have argued that Thai history must include *chaek* history, that is, a history of the Sino-Thai; the use of the highly pejorative term *chaek* is meant to provoke.[50] The claim that "Thai-ness" must include a strong Chinese element is shocking to those whose knowledge of the Thai past is derived entirely from what they have learned in state schools. Yet the fact that such a claim has significant credibility reflects the fact that in the late twentieth century the descendants of those who were once deemed to pose a problem for the Thai nation now can see as problematic the absence of adequate recognition of the role of Sino-Thai in Thai society.

MAINTAINING THE GEO-BODY: IMMIGRANTS AND REFUGEES
Since World War II, legal immigration to Thailand has been very restricted. In marked contrast to immigration policies in the late nineteenth and early twentieth centuries that encouraged unskilled laborers to come to the country, immigration policies in the last half of the twentieth century have opened the country's doors only to those who have skills or capital and who can contribute to the country's economy. The few hundreds of legal immigrants allowed to settle in Thailand each year have mainly come from Taiwan, Hong Kong, Europe, and the United States. People from these countries, as well as from Japan, Korea, and (in much smaller numbers) the Middle East have also been given resident alien visas to permit them to work in multinational corporations located in the country. Today, in Bangkok and in some larger cities, there are enclave communities—some, like the Europeans and Japanese, with their own separate, legal schools—that strongly retain their cultural distinctiveness.

---

49. This term was promoted by Kasian Tejapira, a political scientist at Thammasat University who is widely known for his daily newspaper columns. See Tejapira, "The Postmodernization of Thainess," paper presented at the Sixth International Thai Studies Conference, Chiang Mai University, October 1996. Also see Tejapira, "Pigtail: A Pre-history of Chineseness in Siam," *Sojourn*, Vol. 7, No. 1 (February 1992), pp. 95–122. Whatever "cultural capital" the Sino-Thai may command, there is no question that they control most of the real capital in the country. See Akira, *Capital Accumulation in Thailand*.

50. The advocacy of *chaek* history was especially noteworthy in the discussions about the politics of history that took place at the Sixth International Thai Studies Conference in Chiang Mai, October 1996. The leading advocates are Charnvit Kasetsiri, a historian and former rector of Thammasat University; Niddhi Aeursrivongse, a historian at Chiang Mai University; and Kasian Tejapira. The story of the Chinese in Thailand has never been dampened as much as that of the Lao. In 1969, for example, a novel about the family of a Chinese immigrant and his Sino-Thai descendants, Botan [pseud.], *Letters from Thailand*, trans. Susan Fulop Morell (Bangkok: D.K. Book House, 1977), achieved wide popularity. It was subsequently made into a movie.

Save for the Chinese, these new immigrants have not, however, had any marked impact on Thailand's ethnic politics.

Of much greater significance has been the large number of refugees from neighboring countries who have sought asylum in Thailand. The first significant wave of refugees to enter Thailand were Vietnamese fleeing from the upheavals in their country from the time of World War II through the aftermath of the Geneva Agreements of 1954. By 1960, there were nearly 70,000 Vietnamese with refugee status in Thailand, although many had actually been born in the country. Because Thai governments in the 1950s and 1960s considered these refugees to be supporters of Ho Chi Minh and potential supporters of the illegal Thai Communist Party, very few were allowed to become legal residents. Even when it provided major U.S. military bases for operations in Vietnam, Thailand carried out negotiations with the government of the Democratic Republic of Vietnam to repatriate these refugees. By 1970, at least 15,000 had been repatriated, but with the reestablishment of diplomatic relations between Thailand and the Socialist Republic of Vietnam in the late 1970s, the issue of older refugees was quietly dropped; most of the remaining Vietnamese who had come before 1960 were allowed to stay in Thailand.[51] While Thailand has taken no official stance regarding these Vietnamese since the 1970s, they are often subject to negative stereotyping in popular culture.[52] Many descendants of Vietnamese have, nonetheless, like their counterparts among the descendants of Chinese, assimilated and become Thai.

The premise on which the earlier policy toward Vietnamese refugees was based was strongly reasserted when new waves of refugees began to flow into Thailand following the emergence of communist governments in Vietnam, Laos, and Cambodia in 1975, and subsequently in the late 1980s, following the violent confrontation between pro-democracy forces and the military government in Burma. In order to maintain the integrity of the Thai geo-body, those who entered the country illegally, even as refugees, were not allowed a place within the national community.

Several hundred thousand refugees from Cambodia and Laos lived for years in camps along the borders of the country, but almost none were granted permission to stay in the country permanently. This was also true

51. See Peter A. Poole, *The Vietnamese in Thailand: A Historical Perspective* (Ithaca, N.Y.: Cornell University Press, 1970); and Poole, "The Vietnamese in Thailand: Their Continuing Role in Thai-Vietnamese Relations," *South-East Asian Spectrum*, Vol. 4, No. 2 (1976), pp. 40–43.

52. See, for example, the contrasting images of Vietnamese and Chinese in northeastern rural society as depicted in the novel *A Child of the Northeast*, by Kampoon Boontawee, trans. Susan Fulop Kepner (Bangkok: Duang Kamol, 1988), pp. 52–62.

of the much smaller number of Vietnamese "boat people" who made it to Thailand, often through a gauntlet of Thai "pirates" whose actions initially were tolerated by local officials. Karen and Burmese who have fled Burma have not been given the status that Khmer, Lao, and Vietnamese refugees received under the aegis of the United Nations High Commission for Refugees because it is presumed that all refugees from Burma will eventually be repatriated to that country rather than resettled elsewhere.[53]

By the 1990s, thousands of illegal immigrants were living and working in Thailand. Some were refugees from neighboring countries, but others, including many from southern China, were drawn by Thailand's economic opportunities.

There have been some small-scale eruptions of violence when Thai authorities have attempted to enforce laws against illegal immigration. It can be anticipated that, until a new democratically based government emerges in Burma and until Laos, Vietnam, Cambodia, and southern China develop economies that are as dynamic as Thailand's, immigration and refugee problems will continue.

---

53. On Thai policies toward refugees in general, see S. Chantavanich and P. Rabé, "Thailand and the Indochinese Refugees: Fifteen Years of Compromise and Uncertainty," *Southeast Asian Journal of Social Sciences*, Vol. 18, No. 1 (1990), pp. 66–80; Supang Chantavanich and E. Bruce Reynolds, eds., *Indochinese Refugees: Asylum and Resettlement*, Asian Studies Monograph No. 39 (Bangkok: Chulalongkorn University, Institute of Asian Studies, 1988); Penny Van Esterik, "Thailand's Response to the Refugee Crisis," in Anderson, et al., *Southeast Asian Tribal Groups and Ethnic Minorities*, pp. 149–153. On Khmer refugees, see Lawyers Committee for Human Rights, *Seeking Shelter: Cambodians in Thailand* (New York: Lawyers Committee for Human Rights, 1987); United States Committee for Refugees, *Cambodians in Thailand: People on the Edge* (Washington, D.C.: American Council for Nationalities Service, 1985); and Michael Vickery, "Refugee Politics: The Khmer Camp System in Thailand," in David A. Ablin and Marlowe Hood, eds., *The Cambodian Agony* (London: M.E. Sharpe, 1990), pp. 293–331. On refugees from Laos, see W. Courtland Robinson, "Laotian Refugees in Thailand: The Thai and US Response, 1975–1988," in Joseph Zasloff and Leonard Unger, eds., *Laos: Beyond the Revolution* (New York: St. Martin's, 1991), pp. 215–240; and Lynellyn D. Long, *Ban Vinai: The Refugee Camp* (New York: Columbia University Press, 1993). On Thai pirates and the Vietnamese "boat people," see Nhat Tien, Duong Phuc, and Vu Thanh Thuy, *Pirates on the Gulf of Siam: Report from the Vietnamese Boat People Living in the Refugee Camp in Songkhla-Thailand* (San Diego, Calif.: Boat People S.O.S. Committee, 1981). Little analytical work has been done on refugees from Burma. One study deals with Karen refugees who came to Thailand before the 1988 political watershed in Burma: Roger P. Winter, "The Karens of Burma: Thailand's Other Refugees" (Washington, D.C.: United States Committee for Refugees, Issue Brief, 1986). An undetermined, but small, number of Lao refugees did settle in Thailand, often because they had relatives there.

REDISCOVERY OF CULTURAL DIVERSITY

In the period from the early 1950s through the mid-1990s, the Thai economy grew more rapidly than most economies in the world. This has led many rural peoples to move to the cities; by 1990, about 40 percent of the Thai population lived in cities, and by the year 2000, less than half of the population will live in rural areas. Urban middle-class culture, the culture that now dominates television and films, has been secularized and "globalized"—that is, it owes as much to popular culture in the United States, Japan, and other industrialized countries as it does to the folk cultures of Thailand itself. The Buddhist religion has been fragmented into a number of different movements. Many urban Thai have become disenchanted with the religion because of the corruption and materialism that has come to be associated with some prominent monks.

Affluence has provided the resources for exploring cultural roots and alternative modes of cultural being. In this context, there has been a striking move on the part of many urban Thai to rediscover the cultural traditions that their ancestors followed, or to find in the country's folk cultures a counterpoint to the alienating materialism of Bangkok and other urban centers. What were once considered "backward" or premodern cultures have now been given new value. Members of the elite actively seek to buy "authentic" craft work, especially textiles, of those who retain links with the premodern past. Tens of thousands of urban people travel upcountry each year to attend local festivals and visit some of the hundreds of local museums constructed in the 1980s and 1990s.

Among the cultural traditions that have been "rediscovered" are those of people living on the border between northeastern Thailand and Cambodia, whom the Thai have occasionally called Suai and who call themselves Kui and who are culturally and linguistically related to the Khmer. Although Kui and Khmer-speaking people together constitute a larger percentage of the Thai population than do the Thai Malay, they became all but invisible starting at the beginning of the century.[54] Because Kui and Khmer have long been able to speak Thai and are Buddhist, they have had no difficulty being taken as Thai when they have moved out of their home communities.

Beginning in the 1960s, this situation began to change when the Fine Arts Department, the state agency that has responsibility for conserving the cultural heritage of the nation as a whole, began to give attention to monuments in Thailand associated with the medieval Khmer kingdom of

---

54. See Paitoon Mikusol, "Social and Cultural History of Northeastern Thailand from 1868–1910: A Case Study of the Huamuang Khamen Padong (Surin, Sangkha and Khukhan)," Ph.D. dissertation, University of Washington, 1984.

Angkor. Many of these monuments are in areas of northeastern Thailand populated by Kui and Khmer. From the mid-1960s to the early 1990s, the Fine Arts Department invested heavily in the restoration and preservation of a number of prominent monuments on the presumption that the Hindu-Buddhist Angkorean traditions with which these monuments were associated were valued components of the Thai national heritage.[55] The Kui, more than the Thai Khmer, had traditions they felt should attract the attention of tourists—namely, their association with elephant hunting and their work with elephants. In the 1960s, they began to stage an "elephant round-up," and in the 1990s, two "elephant" museums were built.[56]

The Kui ethnic identity, expressed through "remembered" associations with elephants, has the approval of the state as represented by provincial officials because it is deemed to have benefits for the local economy. The same is true of a number of other rediscovered ethnic identities, as well as ones that previously were viewed more negatively. In the 1980s, the cultural heritage of the Lue of northern Thailand gained new attention after it became possible for Thai to visit the Lue homeland in southern Yunnan province. Although there is very little difference between the Lue and northern Thai traditions, Lue identity has been remembered in Thailand as distinctive because some see it as representing a "Thai-ness" that has been eclipsed by modernization. This remembering has been done through displays of textiles, the opening of cultural centers, and the convening of academic seminars.[57] In the 1980s, the ethnoregional name, *īsān*, became widely known in Bangkok and other urban areas as a popular cuisine.

The newly remembered cultural diversity of Thailand, coupled with the deracination of much of the urban population, has prompted deep questioning about what "Thai-ness" (*khwāmpen Thai*) means. Since the mid-1980s, a major debate has taken place at scholarly conferences, in many books, and in intellectual magazines on this issue. A growing number of Thai intellectuals have begun to question the premises on

---

55. See Charles F. Keyes, "The Case of the Purloined Lintel: The Politics of a Khmer Shrine as a Thai National Treasure," in Reynolds, *National Identity and Its Defenders, 1939–1989*, pp. 261–292.

56. I am indebted for this discussion of the Kui to the as-yet-unpublished work by Peter Cuasay and Komatra Cheungsatiansup, both doctoral candidates in anthropology, the former at the University of Washington and the latter at Harvard.

57. See Keyes, "Who Are the Lue? Revisited." A major event in the rediscovery of the Lue occurred in September 1994, when a seminar on the study of the Lue was held in Chiang Mai under the auspices of the Office of the National Cultural Commission. In conjunction with the seminar, a Lue cultural center was opened at Chiang Mai University and a display of Lue textiles was mounted.

which the geo-body of Siam was first founded.[58] This questioning prompted the government of Thailand to create a National Identity Board and a National Cultural Commission in the mid-1980s. The stage was set, thus, for a new moment in the ethnic politics of Thailand.

Conclusions

The widely held view that marked cultural differences with premodern roots lead inevitably in the modern world to ethnic conflicts cannot be sustained. The cultural differences of premodern Siam were as great as those found in the modern state of Yugoslavia. Indeed, one could argue that the immigrant Chinese population was more alien to Thai culture than any population, indigenous or immigrant, was in Yugoslavia. Yet, while Thailand passed through the twentieth century with remarkably little ethnic conflict, Yugoslavia degenerated into a Hobbesian state of war that conventional wisdom traces to centuries-old differences.

There have indeed been periods of ethnic tension and open conflict in Thailand; this is evident, for example, in the rebellions of Lao and Yuan at the beginning of the twentieth century, the demonstrations of Chinese in the 1920s, the rise of ethnoregionalism in northeastern Thailand in the 1950s and 1960s, the violence inflicted on communities of hill peoples in the 1960s and 1970s, and the insurrection of Thai Malay in Pattani in the 1970s. What is remarkable is that Thai leaders, in the wake of these problems, have turned away from policies that would have permanently silenced expressions of cultural diversity. Those with the power to shape nationalist ideologies in Thailand have rarely embraced the constricted nationalisms that have led in other societies to violent ethnic conflicts. While Buddhist values have contributed to this stance, Theravāda Buddhism (the dominant form of Buddhism found in Thailand) certainly did not prevent violent upheavals in Sri Lanka, Cambodia, or Burma. One must look to the origins of the Thai nation-state for the underlying vision that has shaped ethnic politics in the country.

Thailand is notable among Southeast Asian countries for never having been a colonial dependency. The first modern Thai state was created by Thai, not by foreigners. The leaders of this state never had to confront the problems of the colonial plural society found in two of Siam's neighbors, British Burma and the Dutch East Indies.[59] Most cultural diversity

---

58. See Charles F. Keyes, "Who Are the Tai?"

59. See J.S. Furnivall, *Netherlands India: A Study of Plural Economy* (Cambridge: Cambridge University Press, 1939), esp. pp. 446–469; and Furnivall, *Colonial Policy and Practice* (Cambridge: Cambridge University Press, 1948).

was, thus, not seen as fundamentally threatening. It became a premise of Thai nationalism from the very beginning, a premise that still continues, that Thai-ness incorporates diversity. It is possible to be Thai so long as one speaks the Thai language no matter what other language one speaks, so long as one is legally a subject of the Thai monarch (i.e., a legal citizen of the state) no matter where one was actually born, and so long as one adheres to a religion recognized or accepted by the state. While historically "religion" has meant Buddhism of some variety, by the 1980s adherents to Islam (and to Christianity) have also gained recognition as "good Thai."

The nationalism that evolved in Thailand has an important implication for the ethnic politics of the country. Few Thai governments since the emergence of the modern state in the late nineteenth century have instituted policies based on explicit recognition of ethnic differences. Many significant cultural differences have simply been ignored or subsumed within a vision of the country divided not by culture but by region. Even in the case of the Thai Malay, governments have been inclined to think in regional rather than ethnic terms. Citizenship laws and educational policies that goaded many Chinese into assimilating were not pointed at the Chinese alone. Only in the case of hill peoples have there been explicit ethnic policies.

Thailand thus stands in sharp contrast to many other societies that have officially reified ethnic differences and having done so are faced with managing ethnic relations. Thai governments have not been wholly tone-deaf to the social tensions that emerge from social interactions that are locally understood in ethnic terms. However, what these governments have avoided for the most part are policies that would ascribe to ethnic groups essentialist and timeless characteristics. The explicit ethnic policies adopted by a number of Thai governments toward hill peoples demonstrate well the negative consequences of overt efforts to effect social change through such policies. Future Thai governments would be well advised with regard to hill peoples to return to the tolerant vision that has long shaped government stances toward cultural differences within the country. Governments in other countries should learn from the Thai experience and avoid creating and emphasizing official ethnic categories that constrain policies and politics.

Chapter 6

Ethnic Policies and Political Quiescence in Malaysia and Singapore
Šumit Ganguly

Few multiethnic, postcolonial states have successfully formulated and implemented policies to stave off violent interethnic conflict. The reasons underlying the shortcomings of public policy in multiethnic states are complex. Significantly, however, the vast majority of these states emerged from colonial rule with weak and poorly developed political institutions. The existence of well-developed political institutions can enable a state to channel, mediate, and limit political demands that the forces of modernization unleash.[1] Robust political institutions do not, of course, guarantee ethnic peace. Institutions, unless maintained, can decline and lose their utility.

The states of Malaysia and Singapore stand in marked contrast to the many postcolonial and multiethnic societies that have been fraught with ethnic violence. Malaysia, which has three distinct ethnic groups—the Malays, the Chinese, and the Indians (see Table 6.1)—has been remarkably free of ethnic and communal violence.[2] The last major ethnic conflagration in Malaysia was the rioting that swept Kuala Lumpur on May 13, 1969. The absence of widespread interethnic violence is all the more remarkable in light of the systematic policies of ethnic preference that the government of Malaysia has pursued since 1970. There is little question that the minority Chinese and Indian communities in Malaysia have resented these policies of ethnic preference.[3] Yet, apart from a handful of

---

1. For the classic statement of this problem, see Samuel P. Huntington, *Political Order in Changing Societies* (New Haven, Conn.: Yale University Press, 1968).

2. In 1996, there were 8.5 million Malays, 4.5 billion Chinese, and 1.4 million Indians in Malaysia.

3. Rajakrishnan Ramasamy, "Racial Inequality and Social Reconstruction in Malaysia," *Journal of Asian and African Affairs*, Vol. 28, No. 3/4 (July–October 1993), pp. 217–229.

Table 6.1. Ethnic Composition of Malaysia.

Group	Number	Percentage
Malay	11,950,000	62.0
Chinese	5,290,000	27.0
Indian	1,500,000	8.0
Other	640,000	3.0
Total	**19,380,000**	**100.0**

SOURCE: Based on the census conducted in 1995 by the Government of Malaysia. See *Seventh Malaysia Plan, 1996–2000* (Kuala Lumpur: Government of Malaysia, 1996), p. 105.

Table 6.2. Ethnic Composition of Singapore.

Group	Number	Percentage
Chinese	2,311,300	77.4
Malay	423,500	14.2
Indian	214,900	7.2
Other	36,800	1.2
Total	**2,986,500**	**100.0**

SOURCE: Based on the census conducted in 1995. See *Singapore: Facts and Pictures, 1996* (Singapore: Ministry of Information and the Arts, 1996), p. 3.

sporadic incidents in 1987, these communities have not resorted to violent means to have their grievances redressed.

Singapore is a multiethnic society made up primarily of Chinese, Malays, and Indians.[4] (See Table 6.2.) It has pursued a set of ethnic policies markedly different from those of Malaysia, but has also successfully maintained ethnic peace. Unlike Malaysia, which has pursued explicit policies of ethnic preference, especially after 1969, Singapore has sought at least notionally to de-emphasize racial and ethnic differences. Instead, modern Singapore's preeminent leader, Lee Kuan Yew, has self-consciously sought to mold a distinctive Singaporean identity based on the concept of "multiracialism"—an acceptance of and respect for a variety of racial and ethnic groups.[5] Despite the commitment to this principle and the government's professed emphasis on meritocracy, its public policies

4. Ezra F. Vogel, *The Four Little Dragons: The Spread of Industrialization in East Asia* (Cambridge, Mass.: Harvard University Press, 1991), p. 74.

5. Beng-Huat Chua, *Communitarian Ideology and Democracy in Singapore* (London: Routledge, 1995), pp. 105–106.

have tended to strengthen the socioeconomic position of a segment of the dominant Chinese community.[6] Widespread political disorder has nonetheless not developed in Singapore.

What factors and policies have enabled Malaysia and Singapore to manage ethnic relations and forestall widespread ethnic violence? This question has enormous theoretical and policy significance. It is of theoretical interest because ethnic violence racks most multiethnic societies. Clearly, the particular political and economic arrangements that Malaysia and Singapore have developed have enabled them to fend off ethnic conflict. Our understanding of the factors that forestall ethnic violence and ensure political quiescence can be enriched through a careful examination of the policies that these governments have pursued. The policy significance of the success of Malaysia and Singapore in maintaining ethnic peace cannot be understated. Few policy issues are as vexing as the question of ethnic conflict, and multiethnic societies throughout the world are constantly grappling with the problem of ethnic violence. Many of these societies may be able to learn from the experiences of Malaysia and Singapore.

To answer this question, this chapter will first examine the impact of British colonial rule in forging and sharpening ethnic categories and distinctions in what are now Malaysia and Singapore. The chapter will then examine ethnic policies as they have evolved in Malaysia and Singapore since independence, concluding that constraints on political participation combined with economic growth and redistributive justice may forestall ethnic conflict in some multiethnic states.

Colonial Legacies in Malaysia

The three identifiable and mutually exclusive ethnic groups in Malaysia cannot be seen as primordial artifacts.[7] Their emergence as distinct, self-conscious groups stemmed in substantial part from the exigencies and priorities of British colonial policies.[8] Post-independence policies of ethnic preference have also enhanced group and ethnic solidarity. Furthermore,

---

6. Christopher Tremewan, *The Political Economy of Social Control in Singapore* (London: Macmillan, 1994), p. 125.

7. Charles Hirschman, "The Meaning and Measurement of Ethnicity in Malaysia: An Analysis of Census Classifications," *Journal of Asian Studies*, Vol. 46, No. 3 (August 1987), pp. 555–581; and Colin Nicholas, "The Original Champion," *Aliran Monthly*, Vol. 16, No. 8 (1996), pp. 28–30.

8. David Brown, "Malaysia: Class, State and Ethnic Politics," in David Brown, *The State and Ethnic Politics in Southeast Asia* (London: Routledge, 1994), pp. 216–217.

the policies that various Malaysian regimes have pursued since the country gained independence from Great Britain in 1957 have antecedents in the colonial period. Many present-day Malaysian policies can be linked to the legacy of British colonial policies.[9]

The British secured a foothold in Malaya in January 1874 with the signing of the Pangkor Treaty, which was pivotal in establishing formal relations between Great Britain and the Malay states. The British forged this relationship by arranging a truce between the warring Chinese secret societies and the Malay princes. The first formal symbol of British authority in Malaya was the acquiescence of Raja Abdullah, the sultan of Perak, to the appointment of a British Resident in his realm.

Over the course of the next several decades, British political control and commercial interests expanded across the Malay peninsula. The British set up an entire system of Residents; under the terms of the Pangkor Treaty, they were expected only to "advise" the ruler. However, for all practical purposes, the Resident could ensure that his advice was taken to heart and carried out.[10] Furthermore, the Residents were expected "to preserve the accepted customs and traditions of the country, to enlist the sympathies and interests of the people in our assistance, and to teach them the advantages of good government and enlightened policy."[11] Despite the seeming neutrality implied in this statement, British colonial administrators intruded into the realms of existing laws and customs as they deemed necessary. The effects of British rule were extensive and far-reaching. Some of the British intervention was beneficial, such as that which ended the practice of slavery. But many British policies had pernicious effects. For example, the British introduced a rule of property in Malaya that transformed the existing system of land tenure. To promote plantation agriculture, they introduced a system of individualized landholdings. Peasants were now allowed to hold land that they cultivated as long as they paid rent. All unused land, however, passed on to the

---

9. The terms Malay, Malaya, and Malaysia require some explication. An ethnic Malay, for all practical purposes, is any individual who professes Islam and is of Malay parentage. This definition is, nevertheless, problematic. One of the greatest exponents of Malay privilege, Mahathir bin Mohammed, is partially of Indian Tamil origin. The term Malaya was used to describe the British colonial possessions along the Malay Peninsula and North Borneo. The term Malaysia came about after the independence of Peninsular Malaya from the United Kingdom in 1957. In 1963, Singapore and the states of North Borneo, Sabah, and Sarawak joined Malaysia.

10. Barbara Watson Andaya and Leonard Y. Andaya, *A History of Malaysia* (London: Macmillan, 1982), p. 159.

11. Quotation from Frank Swettenham, in ibid., p. 172.

Malaysia and Singapore.

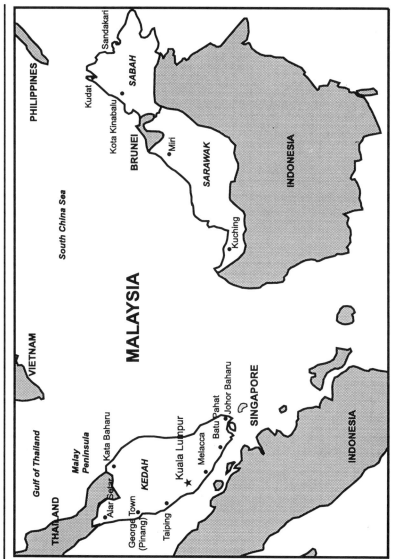

state and was made available for the development of a plantation economy.[12]

COLONIAL ETHNOGRAPHY

Despite the obvious intrusiveness of their colonial policies, the British continued to maintain the legal fiction that the Malays were the actual rulers of the country. This principle, obviously, only extended as far as the Malay aristocracy. Colonial ethnographers considered the vast majority of the population to be inherently lazy and unfit for governing. The British view of the Malay was aptly summed up by Frank Swettenham, a colonial administrator:

he is . . . lazy to a degree, is without method or order of any kind, knows no regularity or order of any kind, knows no regularity in the hours of his meals, and considers time of no importance. His house is untidy, even dirty, but he bathes twice a day, and is very fond of personal adornment in the shape of smart clothes.[13]

Although this characterization of the Malays suited the purposes of British colonial rule,[14] the Malays were far from innately unsuited for hard work. The majority were peasants engaged in rice cultivation. Not surprisingly, they were disinclined to move from their self-contained village communities. Nor were they especially desirous of working in the harsh conditions of the tin mines.

The Malays' reluctance to leave their traditional occupations and the extreme demand for labor led the British to allow Chinese immigrants into Malaya. To escape dire poverty, the Chinese willingly emigrated to Malaya to work in the burgeoning tin-mining industry. (See Table 6.3.) British colonial authorities considered the Chinese to be the very antithesis of the Malays.[15] The Chinese were seen as industrious, obedient, and productive laborers. It is easy to see how such an ethnic stereotype developed. The initial waves of Chinese workers toiled under the harsh tutelage of Chinese employers and secret societies. Simultaneously, the imperatives of survival in an alien land led them to create tightly woven

---

12. James V. Jesudason, *Ethnicity and the Economy: The State, Chinese Business and Multinationals in Malaysia* (Singapore: Oxford University Press, 1989), p. 28.

13. Quotation from Frank Swettenham, in Alvin Rabushka, *Race and Politics in Urban Malaya* (Stanford: Hoover Institution Press, 1973), p. 65.

14. See Donald L. Horowitz, *Ethnic Groups in Conflict* (Berkeley: University of California Press, 1985).

15. Andaya and Andaya, *A History of Malaysia*, p. 176.

Table 6.3. Ethnic Composition of Peninsular Malaysia, 1871–1957 (in thousands).

Date	Malays	Other Malaysians	Chinese	Indians	Others	Total
1911	1,221	152	695	240	35	2,342
1931	1,275	288	1,285	573	67	3,789
1957	2,803	323	2,334	696	124	6,279

SOURCE: Donald R. Snodgrass, *Inequality and Economic Development in Malaysia* (Kuala Lumpur: Oxford University Press, 1980), Table 2.1.

communities. The disinclination of the Malays to intermarry with the Chinese immigrant population further reinforced their distinctive identity.

As the British developed the plantation economy in Malaya, the need for labor expanded. The Chinese who were engaged in tin mining showed little inclination to work in the rubber plantations. To meet the growing demand for cheap plantation labor, the British allowed Indian migration into the Straits Settlements in 1872 and into the Protected States in 1884. The Indians who came to work in Malaya were primarily Tamils from Ceylon (now Sri Lanka) and Madras (now Tamil Nadu) on the eastern coast of India. Eager to escape their own grinding poverty, Indians came to work in Malaya in significant numbers. (See Table 6.3.) Divided by caste and occupational groups, the Indians proved unable to forge a common front to assert their shared interests. In turn, British colonial authorities ascribed the qualities of industriousness and docility to the Indian population of Malaya.

THE ORIGINS AND EFFECTS OF COLONIAL EDUCATIONAL POLICIES
Under British colonial rule, particular ethnic groups became associated with specific occupational categories. In this scheme, Europeans were to administer, the Chinese and the Indians were to work in the extractive industries, and the Malays were to be trained to work the land and fish. As Sir Richard Winstedt, a colonial administrator, pithily stated, "The purpose of Malay education is to make them better farmers and fishermen."[16]

Colonial educational policies quickly came to reflect this ethnic division of labor. At best, in the view of the British, a Malay elite could be

16. Quotation from Sir Richard Winstedt, in S. Jayasankaran, "A Degree of Success," *Far Eastern Economic Review*, Vol. 158, No. 51 (December 21, 1995), p. 27.

recruited and educated to perform the tasks of colonial administration and to staff the growing needs of European-controlled companies.[17] Consequently, little thought, effort, or money was expended to provide the commoners with modern, secular, and technical education.

The limited efforts that the British undertook to educate and develop a loyal, subservient Malay elite stemmed from the demands of the Malay aristocracy in the early part of the twentieth century. Sultan Idris of Perak, an articulate and able Malay ruler who had traveled to Great Britain, had become convinced of the necessity of modern education for social and economic advancement. Accordingly, he was keen on opening the ranks of the Malay Civil Service beyond mere token appointments, and he made this representation at the second Conference of Rulers in 1903.[18]

Considerations of expediency and morality shaped the British response to these demands. The British found it more economical to train and utilize Malay staff than to entice Europeans to relocate to Malaysia. Even though the hiring of expatriate staff was deemed to promote the virtue of administrative efficiency, fiscal considerations were of greater importance. The British moral conceit about creating a class of Malays suited to govern their country also came into play. After all, the British rationalized their presence in Malaya on the grounds that the rulers had invited them to teach a better form of administration.[19]

After some deliberation, the British created the Malay Residential School at Kuala Kangsar on January 2, 1905. Despite the democratic and egalitarian proclivities of R.J. Wilkinson, the recently appointed inspector of schools for the Federated Malaya States,[20] the initial recruits to this elite institution were drawn primarily from the ranks of the Malay aristocracy: twenty-six of the initial fifty-four boarders came directly from the royal houses of Malaya. Wilkinson's fond hope that the school would not only train the Malay elite but also be the principal training institution of Malay boys, regardless of origin, was soon dashed.[21] In 1906, Wilkinson was

---

17. Andaya and Andaya, *A History of Malaysia*, p. 222.

18. At the time of the Second Durbar or Conference of Rulers, only 2,636 Malays out of a population of 310,000 in the Federated Malay States were employed by the British. Of these, 1,175 were policemen. Andaya and Andaya, *A History of Malaysia*, p. 228.

19. William R. Roff, *The Origins of Malay Nationalism* (New Haven, Conn.: Yale University Press, 1967), pp. 98–99.

20. The Federated Malay States were created in 1896 with the consolidation of the four so-called Protected States. The town of Kuala Lumpur in the center of the tin-mining district was the capital, and a Federal Secretariat was created; it was headed by a Resident-General to whom all the residents were to report. See Andaya and Andaya, *A History of Malaysia*, p. 183.

21. Roff, *The Origins of Malay Nationalism*, pp. 102–103.

transferred to another posting. With his departure, any pretense that the school at Kuala Kangsar was not the exclusive preserve of the traditional Malay elite evaporated. His successors did not share his liberal temperament.

The creation of this school and the subsequent entry of English-educated Malays into the administrative services generated greater demands from the Malay community for the expansion of English-language schools. These demands produced only a partial response from the British. After initially expanding the scope of English-language education, in 1924 the British colonial authorities reaffirmed their elitist vision of education, stating that they had no desire to create any more English-educated natives than there were places in the government service.[22] Little effort was expended to develop secondary education in Malay. The handful of Malays who successfully finished primary education were sent to the Sultan Idris Training College, set up in 1921, or the Malay Women's Teacher Training College, founded in 1935.[23] The Malay commoner was expected to remain attached to the land.

The other two communities, the Chinese and the Indians, received an even less beneficent dispensation from the British. Until the time of colonial disengagement, the British maintained the fiction that both the Chinese and Indians in Malaya were only transient communities: having acquired a modicum of hard-earned prosperity, they would eventually return to their lands of origin. Consequently, the British felt little obligation to educate the members of these communities for professions other than those in which they were engaged.

THE INDIAN COMMUNITY

The colonial government followed what could most benignly be described as a laissez-faire approach to the education of the Tamil Indian community. It permitted the development of missionary schools, but did little to devise a common curriculum. Apart from these missionary schools (of varying quality), the Tamil population had to rely on the

---

22. In any case, until the creation of the junior Malay Administrative Service in 1910, the civil services were not open to Malays. The Malayan Civil Service continued to remain the preserve of Europeans. This pattern of ethnic recruitment meant that, as independence approached, Malays dominated the middle rungs of the civil service, Europeans held the politically sensitive upper rungs, and Indians and Chinese were in the technical and professional services. See Gordon P. Means, "Ethnic Preference in Malaysia," in Neil Nevitte and Charles H. Kennedy, eds., *Ethnic Preference and Public Policy in Developing States* (Boulder, Colo.: Lynne Rienner, 1986), pp. 95–118.

23. Tan Liok Lee, "The Development of Education in Malaysia," *Aliran Monthly*, Vol. 16, No. 1 (1996), p. 12.

schools of the coffee and rubber estates on which they were employed. Here their children received rudimentary education from either literate estate laborers or from clerks. Since the owners of the estates frequently employed adolescent children, they rarely saw reason to extend their education.[24] The colonial government did little to interfere with these arrangements. It was, after all, interested in ensuring the existence of a docile population with sufficient education to pursue only handicrafts and plantation agriculture. Finally, parents desirous of extending their children's education beyond the primary levels and vernacular training lacked the financial resources to send their children to English-medium schools.

THE CHINESE COMMUNITY

The Chinese community, like its Indian counterpart, also found it necessary to rely upon its own resources to educate its children. Initially, the Chinese relied on literate Chinese for this. Chinese education, also of widely varying quality, was heavily focused on the Chinese cultural and historical heritage. The British authorities did not object to this orientation because it suited their belief that the Chinese, like the Indians, were a transient community in Malaya. Only in the wake of the 1911 revolution in China, when Chinese education started to acquire a xenophobic and hyper-nationalistic streak, did British authorities start to pay serious attention to educational institutions within the Chinese community. Specifically, in 1919 the colonial government passed the School Registration Enactment, which was designed to curb political activities. This act did not have the desired effect, however; Chinese schools became centers of contentious argument between the supporters of the Chinese Communist Party and the Kuomintang. In 1929 the British again took action against the Chinese schools. It ensured that all xenophobic references were removed from Chinese texts, Chinese-born teachers were restricted, more government officials were designated to oversee Chinese schools, and British control was extended to Chinese schools through the use of federal grants.[25]

The goals of British colonial education were clear. Each community was expected to perform a particular economic function and not challenge corporate British interests. The creation of a substantial educated class could have pernicious consequences for British colonial interests. Such a

---

24. Andaya and Andaya, *A History of Malaysia*, p. 223.

25. Ibid., p. 225.

class could become the basis of a unified Malaysian nationalism, which, in turn, could challenge British dominance.[26]

Malaysia: Toward Independence

World War II, the flight of the British from Malaya, and the Japanese occupation from 1941 to 1945 had important consequences for the three major ethnic groups within the country. The Malays, for the most part, collaborated with the Japanese, who placed many of them in high administrative positions vacated by the British. The Japanese also encouraged Malays to develop a pan-Malaysian nationalism; many Malay intellectuals were drawn to this enterprise.

The Chinese and Indian communities fared quite differently under the Japanese occupation. The Japanese treatment of the Indians was mixed. To some extent, the Japanese maltreated the Indians, conscripting estate labor for Japanese war-related projects. On the other hand, the Japanese helped organize Subhas Chandra Bose's Indian National Army to fight against British rule in India.

There is little question that the Chinese suffered most from the harsh Japanese occupation policies. A significant section of the Chinese community had links with and was inspired by the Chinese Communist Party. Consequently, they chose to fight the Japanese occupation with vigor as part of a combined nationalist and communist enterprise. The Malaysian Communist Party (MCP), which had a substantial Chinese following, had organized both mining and estate workers during the Great Depression. It had successfully organized strikes and demonstrations and had created an enormous trade union, the Pan-Malayan Federation of Trade Unions.[27] The MCP also had developed an armed resistance wing, the Malayan People's Anti-Japanese Army (MPAJA), which had a following of around 10,000.[28] The Japanese moved to crush these organizations with considerable brutality. Furthermore, they encouraged interethnic hatred by promoting a Malay paramilitary force to fight against the predominantly Chinese MPAJA. When the Japanese occupation ended in 1945, members of the MPAJA turned against the Malay quislings, provoking further interethnic enmity.

When the British returned after the war, they refused to recognize the

---

26. See Tan, "The Development of Education in Malaysia," pp. 11–18.

27. Jesudason, *Ethnicity and the Economy*, pp. 40–41. For an overtly sympathetic account of the MCP and its activities against the Japanese, see Brown, "Malaysia," p. 221.

28. Brown, "Malaysia," p. 221.

MCP as a legitimate political entity even though it had played a vital role in opposing the Japanese occupation. The British hostility to the MCP stemmed primarily from Cold War considerations. As the MCP's tactics became more violent, the British turned against it with a vengeance. On June 18, 1948, the British declared a state of emergency throughout Malaya. This declaration permitted the colonial regime to draft men for the security forces, control employment, and closely regulate organizations.

The MCP scored some initial successes, including the assassination of Sir Henry Gurney shortly after his retirement. But the British authorities soon managed to outwit the MCP militarily and politically. British military success stemmed largely from the draconian laws that enabled the colonial authorities to act against the guerillas with impunity. By announcing their intention in March 1949 to grant Malaya independence, the British also undercut the communists politically. Furthermore, in early 1952, Lieutenant General Sir Gerald Templar, the newly arrived high commissioner, announced that it was the British government's immediate goal to form a unified Malayan nation. Within two years of that announcement, Templar proclaimed that national elections would be held in 1955.[29] The municipal elections of Kuala Lumpur foreshadowed the national elections. In these elections, the United Malay National Organization (UMNO), a Malay-dominated political party formed in 1946, joined a conservative Chinese party, the Malayan Chinese Association (MCA) against a Malay-led multiracial party, the Independence of Malaysia Party (IMP).[30] The UMNO-MCA combine, referred to as the Alliance, won the elections handsomely, taking ten out of a possible twelve seats. The IMP's defeat in the Kuala Lumpur municipal elections not only spelled its demise but also undermined the possibility of a party based on a multiracial alliance seeking to forge a common Malaysian identity. In 1954, the Malaysian Indian Congress (MIC) also joined the Alliance. This tripartite organization, which sought to represent the corporate interests of the three principal ethnic groups, won a dramatic victory in the 1955 general election. It captured 81 percent of the popular vote and won fifty-one out of the fifty-two seats it contested. The only other seat went to the Pan-Malaysian Islamic Party, a blatantly pro-Islamic party dedicated to establishing Islam as the cornerstone of a Malay-dominated state.[31]

With a relatively conservative government in place, one that would

---

29. Andaya and Andaya, *A History of Malaysia*, p. 261.

30. Harold Crouch, *Government and Society in Malaysia* (Ithaca, N.Y.: Cornell University Press, 1996), pp. 17–18.

31. Jesudason, *Ethnicity and the Economy*, p. 44.

not threaten British commercial and trading interests, and the dangers of a communist insurgency receding, the British made final preparations to leave Malaya. Before granting Malaya independence in 1957, the British helped fashion a constitution that sought to enshrine Malay privileges while granting the other communities citizenship rights.

Independence and "The Grand Bargain"

CONSTITUTIONAL ISSUES

As the time for their withdrawal approached after World War II, the British proposed the creation of a Malay Union, with several salient features. Within a unitary state, citizenship rights would be granted to all residents born locally as well as to residents of a specified duration. All citizens would have equal political status regardless of race. The nine sultans would be allowed to retain their positions, but sovereignty would pass to the British Crown.

This proposal met with stiff opposition from the Malay intelligentsia, who rapidly organized on a nationwide basis to scuttle it. They argued, with some force, that the scheme represented a British attempt to strip Malays of their privileges. In fact, varied Malay associations, clubs, and organizations merged to form the UMNO as they collectively organized to protest the creation of the Malayan Union. Faced with this bulwark of opposition, the British abandoned the Union scheme in 1948 in favor of the Federation of Malaya Agreement.[32]

The new British proposal called for a constitutional monarchy, with a head of state (*Yang Dipertuan Agong*) chosen from among the nine reigning sultans. It would also create a bicameral parliament. The Agreement, while promising citizenship to the Chinese and Indian residents of Malaya, also enshrined the special position of the Malays.

While this agreement found favor with the Malays, it understandably met with some opposition from the Indians and the Chinese. This opposition emerged from the middle-class, English-speaking sections of both communities and found institutional expression through the MCA and the MIC. Both organizations wanted citizenship for their constituents, a secular state, meritocratic appointments in the public and private sectors, and a laissez-faire economy. The Malays vigorously opposed most of these principles, and expressed fears of losing their political rights in an already Chinese-dominated economy.

The Malaysian Constitution of 1957 represented a compromise

---

32. Edmund Terence Gomez, *Political Business: Corporate Involvement of Malaysian Political Parties* (Townsville, Australia: James Cook University, 1994), p. 48.

among these competing positions. It accorded citizenship to all residents born in the federation after Merdeka (Independence) Day, August 31, 1957. Those born before Merdeka Day had to meet several qualifications. They had to register with the government and demonstrate that they had resided in the federation for five of the preceding seven years, that they intended to do so permanently, that they were of good character, and that they had a working knowledge of the Malay or English language. Within two years of Merdeka Day, more than two million non-Malays became citizens through this procedure.[33]

The Malays regarded their willingness to confer citizenship rights to non-Malays as a significant concession. In return, all the symbols of the state would be quintessentially Malay. Islam would be the state religion, but freedom of worship was guaranteed. Malay would become the national language after sharing equal status with English until 1967. The special position of the Malays was given explicit recognition. The government could provide a range of preferential services to Malays without specified time limits in higher education, government employment, and particular occupations.[34] These preferential arrangements were justified on two grounds. First, the Malays constituted the bumiputra (literally, "sons of the soil"), or the original inhabitants of the land. Second, these arrangements would compensate for the relative economic backwardness of the Malay community in comparison with the Chinese.[35]

DEVELOPMENT PROGRAMS

After independence, the UMNO lost little time in solidifying its electoral base through a series of rural development programs designed to

---

33. Donald R. Snodgrass, *Inequality and Economic Development in Malaysia* (Kuala Lumpur: Oxford University Press, 1980), pp. 45–47.

34. Milton J. Esman, *Ethnic Politics* (Ithaca, N.Y.: Cornell University Press, 1994), pp. 62–63.

35. Clearly there was ample evidence of the economically backward position of the Malays. As David Brown has written, "By 1957, 97.5 per cent of rice farmers were Malays, while 69 per cent of those in market gardening were Chinese; 48 per cent of Indians were involved in rubber production and they comprised 40 per cent of rubber estate labourers; 66 per cent of those in commerce and 72 per cent of those in mining and manufacturing were Chinese. In terms of occupational category, 62.4 per cent of administrative and managerial workers, 66.1 per cent of sales and related workers were Chinese, whereas 62.1 per cent of agricultural workers were Malays. . . . Finally, data on incomes show that in 1957 mean Chinese household incomes were perhaps twice as high as Malay incomes." Brown, "Malaysia," p. 218. Also see Just Faaland, J.R. Parkinson, and Rais Saniman, *Growth and Ethnic Inequality: Malaysia's New Economic Policy* (New York: St. Martin's, 1990), p. 17.

improve the lot of Malays. As the first post-independence prime minister, Tunku Abdul Rahman, stated,

The Malays required help in raising their standard of living, so in the first five-year development plan we agreed on extensive development because the people of the *kampungs* (villages) had been completely neglected by the British. To be fair, however, an equal area of land was given to the other communities with the government providing funds and facilities. Next, it provided economic help and business facilities for the Malays, though the government had to subsidize them as the Malays need time to learn commerce and business.[36]

The Tunku regime continued two rural development projects it had inherited from the colonial regime. They were the Rural and Industrial Development Authority, started in 1950, and the Federal Land Development Authority founded in 1956. Additionally, in 1959 the government created the new Ministry of Rural Development, headed by Deputy Prime Minister Tun Abdul Razak.

The new government's policies of limited socioeconomic restructuring were given a moderately strong endorsement in the first post-independence election of 1959. Since the election of 1955, the electorate had broadened substantially. In the 1955 election, Malays had constituted only 57 percent of the eligible electorate; in 1959 they constituted 84 percent. In this election, the Alliance (the consociational arrangement between the UMNO, the MCA, and the MIC, within which the UMNO was the dominant partner) saw its electoral base shrink. In the 1955 election, the Alliance had won 81.7 percent of the vote. In this election, it dropped to 51.8 percent. It nevertheless emerged with a comfortable majority, winning 74 out of a possible 104 seats in the parliament. Not surprisingly, the Alliance performed worst in the poor, Malay-dominated states of Kelantan and Trengganu, where it lost the state assemblies and won only two out of sixteen parliamentary seats.[37] Its moderate orientation toward questions of race and ethnicity obviously failed to appeal to poor Malays.

There were two major sources of opposition to the Alliance's moderate posture. One was a blatantly pro-Malay and Islamic party, the Parti Islam (PAS). The other was the Democratic Action Party (DAP), which

---

36. Quotation from Tunku Abdul Rahman, in Faaland, Parkinson, and Saniman, *Growth and Ethnic Inequality*, p. 20.

37. Snodgrass, *Inequality and Economic Development in Malaysia*, p. 48; and Gordon P. Means, *Malaysian Politics: The Second Generation* (Singapore: Oxford University Press, 1991), pp. 4–5.

had its origins in Lee Kuan Yew's People's Action Party (PAP) of Singapore. The DAP sought to represent non-Malay interests.

What did the government's policies of rural development yield? Between 1955 and 1960, Malay rice cultivators were important beneficiaries of the rural development programs. Irrigated rice land expanded from 270,000 acres to 390,000 acres. Other forms of rural infrastructure also expanded considerably. These included the creation of rural cooperatives, roads, new water supplies, and the extension of social services to the rural areas.

EDUCATIONAL POLICIES

Apart from attempting to improve the conditions of rural life, the government also made a concerted effort to expand educational facilities. In 1956 there were 767,000 students in primary schools and 89,000 in secondary schools. By 1965 the numbers had jumped to 1,252,000 and 345,000, respectively.[38] Given its commitment to preserving the "special position" of Malays, the government withdrew assistance to Chinese-language schools in 1961. Not surprisingly, the Chinese saw this action as a direct assault against their cultural institutions. Their ensuing resentment would continue to fester over the next several years and contribute to the ethnic tensions and rioting that erupted in Kuala Lumpur after the 1969 elections.

Singapore: The End of Colonial Rule over the "Lion City"

Singapore came under British control in 1819. Stamford Raffles, an official of the British East India Company, had sought to establish a British presence in Singapore because of the island's strategic location on the Straits of Malacca. The East India Company's presence on Singapore enabled it to suppress the pirates who had long preyed on commercial traffic in this region. In 1867 Singapore was formally transferred from the East India Company to the British Crown. Over the better part of the next century, thanks to its strategic location and British commercial policies, Singapore emerged as a major commercial hub in Southeast Asia.

Historical patterns of immigration explain most of Singapore's ethnic composition and the numerical dominance of the Chinese community there. As mentioned earlier, in the late nineteenth century, large numbers of Chinese migrated to Malaya to work in the tin-mining industry. An intermediary class of Chinese merchants in Singapore and Kuala Lumpur

---

38. Snodgrass, *Inequality and Economic Development in Malaysia*, p. 49.

controlled this labor supply. By the early part of the twentieth century, close to 75 percent of Singapore's population was ethnically Chinese in origin, brought there to supply labor for the Malaya peninsula.[39]

The origins of the Malay population of Singapore are complex. Some Malays were indeed inhabitants of the island when Raffles arrived in 1819. Subsequently, a wave of migration took place from Malacca, followed by waves of Javanese migrants in the mid-nineteenth century. Still later, during World War II, the Japanese brought substantial numbers of Javanese conscript laborers to Singapore.[40]

The composition of Singapore's Indian population stems largely from colonial labor policies. Most Indians in Singapore hail from South India and are Tamil, Malayalee, or Telegu in linguistic origin.[41]

During World War II, the Japanese occupied Singapore. After 1945, when the British returned to Singapore, they encountered increasing pressure from local nationalists to grant independence to Singapore. The first elections preparatory to Singapore's independence were held in 1955. Twenty-five of the thirty-two seats in the assembly were to be selected by the general electorate. No party won a clear-cut majority, however, and the governor invited David Marshall, the leader of the Left Front (LF), to form a coalition government. Ten elected LF members joined with the Alliance (a conglomeration of the UMNO, the MCA, and the Singapore Malay Union).[42] In 1957 Singapore obtained the right of self-government; foreign and defense policies, however, remained in British hands. Following the elections of 1959, it became an independent entity.

In the 1959 election, Lee Kuan Yew's People's Action Party emerged victorious, winning forty-three out of a possible fifty-one seats.[43] In the wake of its initial electoral victory, the PAP, under Lee's tutelage, quickly demonstrated an unwillingness to tolerate dissent. This attitude particularly affected the left-leaning faction of the PAP, which saw its position steadily undercut. The PAP retained repressive colonial laws, tried to control the radical trade unions, and allowed political detainees to languish in prison. Lee's hostility toward the PAP's leftists ultimately led to

---

39. Tremewan, *Political Economy*, p. 8.

40. Tania Li, *Malays in Singapore: Culture, Economy, and Ideology* (Singapore: Oxford University Press, 1989), pp. 94–95.

41. Lai Ah Eng, *Meanings of Multiethnicity: A Case Study of Ethnicity and Ethnic Relations in Singapore* (Kuala Lumpur: Oxford University Press, 1995), p. 16.

42. Chan Heng Chee, *The Dynamics of One-Party Dominance: The PAP at the Grass-Roots* (Singapore: Singapore University Press, 1976), p. 189.

43. Chua, *Communitarian Ideology*, p. 13.

a split within the party: in 1961, thirteen of the PAP Assembly members left the PAP to set up the *Barisan Sosialis* (Socialist Front). In 1962, as the issue of a merger of Singapore with Malaysia arose, the *Barisan* called for a boycott of the referendum. The electorate did not respond positively to this call: 71 percent of the eligible electorate voted for the merger.[44]

At one level, the split weakened the party: the PAP's leftists had constituted a significant section of its political base. On the other hand, the left's departure permitted the PAP to impose the full weight of the state's security apparatus on the *Barisan* and its supporters. To fully undermine the left's organizational strength, the PAP government chose a particularly harsh strategy: Operation Coldstore, launched on February 2, 1963, led to the arrest and incarceration of 111 opposition leaders. This sweep effectively decapitated the leftist opposition to the PAP.[45] In the 1963 elections, the PAP won 46.9 percent of the vote and the *Barisan* received 33.3 percent. The PAP has won every election since 1963, through policies that combine paternalism, widespread repression, the gerrymandering of electoral districts, and the pursuit of rapid economic growth.

A number of factors prompted the PAP leadership to seek a merger with Malaysia in the early 1960s. It looked like an excellent means to suppress the political left within Singapore, as Malaysia, still in the throes of confronting a communist insurgency, had retained the draconian colonial legislation directed against the left. Merger with Malaysia would also benefit Singapore's economy. Not only could the island-state sell its manufactured goods in Malaysia, but it would also have access to Malaysia's agricultural lands, tin mines, and rubber plantations. Malaysia, in turn, was interested in the merger because of Singapore's excellent natural harbor and its port facilities.[46]

Modern Malaysia

THE MALAYSIAN ELECTIONS OF 1964

Singapore's merger with Malaysia became one of the two key issues in the Malaysian election campaign of 1964. During this campaign, Lee Kuan Yew's PAP attempted to establish a political foothold in peninsular Malaysia.[47] Keen on breaking the MIC's hold over the Chinese community,

---

44. Ibid., p. 16.

45. Tremewan, *Political Economy*, pp. 27–29.

46. Clark D. Neher and Ross Marlay, eds., *Democracy and Development in Southeast Asia: The Winds of Change* (Boulder, Colo.: Westview Press, 1995), p. 131.

47. Singapore had been incorporated into the Malaysian Federation on September 16, 1963, as part of a larger plan that sought to bring together the former British colonies

Lee campaigned on the theme of "A Malaysian Malaysia." This campaign slogan was construed as an attack on the special rights of the Malays and generated considerable resentment against Lee in the Malay community.[48] The tensions that Lee's strategy generated ultimately contributed to Singapore's ouster from the Malaysian federation on August 9, 1965, only two years after the merger took place.[49] With Singapore ousted from the federation, Malay numerical dominance of Malaysia was all but assured.

The other prominent election issue was Indonesian President Sukarno's policy of "confrontation" with Malaysia over the creation of the Malaysian federation. Sukarno started a campaign of publicly bullying the Malaysian federation, calling it a neocolonial, imperialist plot. Sukarno's intimidation generated patriotic fervor in Malaysia and translated into support for the UMNO.[50]

In the 1964 election, the Alliance gained some of the ground it had lost in the previous election. It captured 89 seats out of a possible 104, and its share of the popular vote shot up from 51.8 percent to 58.5 percent. However, it still failed to take control of Kelantan state.

Buoyed by the returns of the 1964 election, the government launched the First Malaysia Plan, which continued to emphasize rural development and efforts to uplift the Malay population. Indeed, the government's commitment to agriculture almost doubled under this plan, climbing from $468 million between 1961 and 1965 to $900 million between 1965 and 1970. Interestingly enough, it made little or no effort to enter the traditional preserves of the Chinese community—mining, industry, and commerce. It remained content to pursue a regulatory role in these areas and. to extract revenue from them to redistribute among the Malay population.

The government also created a Malay bank (Bank Bumiputra) to break Chinese and foreign control over the banking industry. Furthermore, in an attempt to undermine the power of rural middlemen who exploited Malay farmers, the government created a Federal Agricultural Marketing Authority. These efforts notwithstanding, foreigners and the Chinese community continued to control large-scale commercial agriculture and all forms of non-agricultural enterprises.[51] Consequently, despite

---

of Sarawak, North Borneo, and Brunei. Eventually, Brunei chose not to join the federation.

48. The expression "A Malaysian Malaysia" was seen as a euphemism for a more pluralistic and meritocratic vision of Malaysian society.

49. Snodgrass, *Inequality and Economic Development in Malaysia*, p. 51.

50. Esman, *Ethnic Politics*, p. 67.

51. Snodgrass, *Inequality and Economic Development in Malaysia*, p. 52.

these government efforts to reduce rural, and in particular Malay, poverty, gaps in income distribution by ethnic group expanded during this period,[52] contributing to interethnic tensions, particularly between the Chinese and Malay communities. Despite the government's efforts to improve the lot of the Malay community, little appreciable change took place between 1957 and 1970 in terms of reducing aggregate family income disparities between the Chinese and the Malays; the average income of a Chinese household remained about twice that of a Malay household.[53]

The communal structure of politics in Malaysia, where few political parties offered a pluralistic vision seeking to unite all Malaysians through a common ideology, exacerbated interethnic differences. This growing reservoir of resentment and the consequent ethnic polarization taking place in Malaysia would manifest itself in the 1969 election campaign and its aftermath.

Two years before the election of 1969, the debate over a national language contributed to a worsening of communal relations within Malaysia. The 1957 constitution had called for the use of Malay and English for a period of ten years. In the wake of Singapore's expulsion from the federation in 1965, strong pressure developed from within the Malay community for the adoption of Malay as the national language when the ten-year period drew to a close on August 31, 1967. This campaign found support among many members of the UMNO, but was staunchly opposed by the MCA and the MIC. A number of non-Malay opposition parties also campaigned against the full implementation of the Malay language provisions. Tunku Abdul Rahman, the aristocratic and conciliatory prime minister, was instrumental in fashioning a compromise. In 1967, he managed to pass the National Language Act, which made Malay the sole national language but also envisaged a continuing role for English for official purposes. Non-Malays were satisfied with this compromise, but many Malays construed it as a sop to the non-Malay community. Some dissident members of the UMNO felt they could not longer rely upon Tunku to champion Malay causes.[54]

THE 1969 ELECTION

It was against this backdrop of steadily worsening communal relations that the 1969 election was held. In campaigning, the Alliance emphasized

---

52. K.S. Jomo, *Growth and Structural Change in the Malaysian Economy* (London: Macmillan, 1990), p. 10.

53. Snodgrass, *Inequality and Economic Development in Malaysia*, p. 82.

54. Crouch, *Government and Society in Malaysia*, p. 23.

its past achievements, promised to create a stable, liberal, and tolerant society, and insisted on its ability to contain communal discord. Although the Alliance continued to defend the special position of the Malays, it promised not to deny opportunities to non-Malays. However, important voices of dissent were emerging within the principal alliance partner, the UMNO; they argued that the old guard within the UMNO was incapable of defending Malay prerogatives.

Apart from the incumbent Alliance, the election was contested by the PAS, the DAP, and a new political party, the *Gerakan Rakyat Malaysia* (Malaysian People's Movement, founded in 1968). The PAS, as expected, took up the Malay cause, called for the expansion of the special rights that had been conferred on the *bumiputras*, and demanded that new policies be formulated to strengthen Islam. The DAP pushed a very different agenda. It called for the dismantling of the special rights, and argued that the *bumiputra* policies had not benefited Malays at large but had created a rapacious class of Malayan capitalists and had strengthened rural Malay elites. The *Gerakan* (as it was popularly called) was dedicated to social justice, human rights, and an open democratic system. It had a slender political base, primarily among the university-educated elites and in the urban areas of Penang and Kuala Lumpur.[55]

The election campaign was far more vigorous—and abrasive—than previous campaigns. Both the incumbent party and some of the opposition parties resorted to overt communal appeals to garner political support.[56] The elections were held throughout peninsular Malaysia on May 10, 1969, and were scheduled for the states of Sabah and Sarawak some two to four weeks later. The results of the election in peninsular Malaysia revealed a dramatic loss of support for the ruling party, which won a mere 48.8 percent of the vote and 66 of the 104 parliamentary seats. A substantial number of Malay voters shifted their allegiance from UMNO to PAS. Within the Alliance, the MCA proved to be the biggest loser. Twenty of the thirty-three candidates it put up for election lost. The disastrous performance of the MCA led its leader, Tan Siew Sin, to declare that it would not join the federal cabinet.[57] The Alliance performed even worse at the state level, losing control of Kelantan, Perak, and Penang.

The non-Malay opposition parties, the DAP and the *Gerakan*, were delighted with the electoral outcome. They had fallen considerably short

---

55. Much of this discussion has been drawn from Means, "Ethnic Preference in Malaysia," pp. 4–5.

56. Brown, "Malaysia," p. 230.

57. Means, "Ethnic Preference in Malaysia," pp. 6–7.

of victory at the national level. Nevertheless, they had succeeded in preventing the Alliance from achieving a two-thirds majority in parliament. Furthermore, they had been instrumental in toppling the Alliance from Perak and Penang.

THE ONSET OF RIOTING

Most scholars trace the origins of the riots that broke out in Kuala Lumpur on May 13, 1969, to the victory celebrations of some members of the Chinese community in light of the DAP and the *Gerakan* victories. Apparently, many of those attending the victory rallies taunted the Malays, leading to a Malay counterdemonstration.[58] Before long, the contending groups turned to violence. In these riots, some eight hundred individuals were killed and some six thousand were rendered homeless.[59]

There is some disagreement about the underlying sources of rioting, however. In one view, the riots were merely the manifestation of deep-seated ethnic grievances that had long been smoldering and were ignited by the callous behavior of the opposition parties.[60] In another view, the riots stemmed from fundamental economic grievances.[61] A third explanation suggests that the riots were neither "the expression of overt economic grievances [nor] of class animosities. Rather, in the atmosphere of crisis and with irrational mechanisms of crowd psychology, primal emotions surged into uncontrollable waves combining racial antipathies, anger, fear, hatred, and self-justifying rationalizations for barbarous behavior."[62] It appears, however, that two sets of factors, underlying and proximate, led to the rioting. There is little question that each ethnic group had long-standing grievances, real and imagined, against the others. At the same time, it seems clear that political leaders from every community helped to nurse these grievances. The Chinese demonstrations occasioned by the DAP and *Gerakan* victories and the Malay counterdemonstration organized by the *mentri besar* (chief minister) of Selangor, Datuk Harun Idris, were the proximate causes of the rioting.

---

58. William Case, "Aspects and Audiences of Legitimacy," in Muthiah Alagappa, ed., *Political Legitimacy in Southeast Asia* (Stanford: Stanford University Press, 1995), pp. 93–94.

59. Esman, *Ethnic Politics*, p. 68.

60. See Faaland, Parkinson, and Saniman, *Growth and Ethnic Inequality*, pp. 12–15.

61. See Brown, "Malaysia," p. 231.

62. Means, "Ethnic Preference in Malaysia," p. 7.

THE SUSPENSION OF PARLIAMENT AND THE NATIONAL OPERATIONS COUNCIL

Once the rioting was brought under control, both the constitution and parliament were suspended, a state of national emergency was declared, the elections for Sabah and Sarawak were postponed indefinitely, and the powers of governance were placed in the hands of a National Operations Council (NOC). The NOC, chaired by Deputy Prime Minister Tun Abdul Razak, was composed of the heads of the police, armed forces, public service, and foreign office, as well as three political leaders, Tun Abdul Razak of the UMNO, Tan Siew Sin of the MCA, and V.T. Sambanthan of the MIC. Although the cabinet continued to function under Prime Minister Tunku Abdul Rahman, for all practical purposes the real locus of power and decision-making shifted to the NOC.

In the wake of the rioting, Malay chauvinists took center stage in the political process. They contended that the previous government had been far too generous toward the Chinese and the Indian communities and that the lot of the Malays had been neglected. The bulk of their wrath, however, was directed against the Chinese. One of the most outspoken critics was a Malay physician from Kedah, Mahathir bin Mohammed.[63] Mahathir called for Tunku's resignation and wrote him a scathing letter, accusing him of giving the Chinese "too much face."[64] Tunku, who had been planning to retire anyway, felt compelled to step down in favor of his deputy, Tun Abdul Razak.

Faced with these waves of anger and resentment, the NOC decided to create several mechanisms to defuse the crisis. Specifically, it created a National Consultative Council (NCC), which was a forum designed to deal with interethnic problems. Although it was not vested with any formal powers, it served as a legitimating device for the NOC. The sixty-five members of the NCC was drawn from across the political spectrum. The government kept fifteen seats, and the combined opposition was given six. The remainder were drawn from the federal government, state governments, religious organizations, trade unions, and the press.

At a larger level, the NOC moved to fashion a new social contract to address what it believed were the underlying causes of the ethnic conflagration. In the view of the NOC, the roots of the 1969 crisis could be

---

63. Mahathir bin Mohammed subsequently was expelled from UMNO. He managed to rehabilitate himself, however, and in 1981 became the prime minister of Malaysia.

64. Gordon P. Means, *Malaysian Politics: The Second Generation*, p. 9.

traced to the continuing economic (and consequently psychological) backwardness of the Malay community. Accordingly, public policies had to be fashioned to deal with these underlying sources of tension and discord. Herein lay the beginnings of the New Economic Policy (NEP).

FORGING THE NEP

The members of the NOC met *in camera* and decided that a three-pronged approach was needed to restructure Malaysian society and politics. The preservation of ethnic peace, the NOC concluded, could only be accomplished through substantial social engineering and preferential policies. The three components of this strategy were a "national ideology," or *rukunegera*, which would define the norms of conduct within Malaysia; new educational and economic policies to redress the economic imbalances that existed between the Malays and the other two communities; and new legislation (which was passed by a reconvened parliament in 1971) to prohibit public challenge to the new order.[65]

The *rukunegera* called for the maintenance of a democratic society, respect for diverse cultural traditions, and the equitable sharing of wealth. The forging of this "national ideology" was little more than an exercise in symbolic politics. Nevertheless, it was an important undertaking in that it heralded the beginning of a new social contract.

The second component of the new strategy, the NEP, was undoubtedly the NOC's most significant initiative. Essentially, it had two facets: the elimination of the identification of race with occupation, and the eradication of poverty. No explicit quantitative targets were set for poverty alleviation, but a commitment was made to ensure that at least 30 percent of equity in the corporate sector would be shifted to Malay hands by 1990.[66] In an attempt to assuage the misgivings of the non-Malays, Prime Minister Tun Abdul Razak made clear that the expansion of Malay privileges would not come at the expense of other communities. In effect, there would be no expropriation of property, loss of jobs, or denial of the rights of non-Malays.[67]

The third and final component of the new strategy involved shrinking the terms of political debate within the country. New legislation was passed in parliament, when it reconvened in 1971, which specifically prohibited individuals or political parties from questioning a range of

---

65. Zakaria Haji Ahmed, "Malaysia: Quasi Democracy in a Divided Society," in Larry Diamond, Juan J. Linz, and Seymour Martin Lipset, eds., *Democracy in Developing Countries: Asia* (Boulder, Colo.: Lynne Rienner, 1989), pp. 362–365.

66. Snodgrass, *Inequality and Economic Development*, p. 60.

67. Means, "Ethnic Preference in Malaysia," p. 104.

policy provisions: Malay rights, citizenship (particularly that of the non-Malays), the royalty, and Malay as the national language. These were all deemed to be "sensitive issues," and challenging them was deemed to be seditious. Indeed, the constitution was amended in 1971 to extend the reach of this legislation to parliament itself.[68] The new prime minister forthrightly defended these restrictions on free speech and democratic procedures:

The Malaysian type of democracy is best suited to the needs of the country's unique multi-racial society. The Malaysian concept of democracy subscribes also to the need to balance individual interests against the general security of the State. . . . We recognize that each nation must develop . . . its own political and economic system and that the developing world has a special need of an articulated political system suitable to its own problems.[69]

IMPLEMENTING THE NEP

At its broadest level, the NEP involved a range of policies designed to improve the economic and political positions of Malays. To accomplish this, the NEP was folded into the Second Malaysia Plan (1971–75).[70] This plan affected such sectors as education, employment, business, and the administrative services.

In the early 1970s, the government introduced a number of sweeping changes in educational policy designed to benefit Malays. One of the key provisions of the new education policy was the conversion of English-language schools into Malay-language schools. In 1970 the first year of primary school was converted to Malay; each year another grade was converted until the process culminated in 1982. Universities were expected to follow suit by 1983. The National University of Malaysia (Universiti Kebangsaan Malaysia) was established in 1970 with Malay as the sole language of instruction.[71] Non-Malay resistance to these changes was

---

68. Crouch, *Government and Society in Malaysia*, pp. 82–83.

69. Quotation from Tun Abdul Razak, in Ahmad, "Malaysia," p. 365.

70. Faaland, Parkinson, and Saniman, *Growth and Ethnic Inequality*, p. 73. In 1990, the NEP was replaced by the National Development Plan (NDP). The objectives of the latter are not fundamentally different from those of the NEP. However, the NDP did reflect two shifts, one in terms of strategy and the other in terms of goals. The strategic shift involved an emphasis on privatization. Nevertheless, the benefits of privatization would be directed toward Malays and especially those with close connections with the UMNO. The other change involved a greater emphasis on redistributive goals. See Government of Malaysia, *The Sixth Malaysia Plan, 1991–1995* (Kuala Lumpur: National Printing Department, Government of Malaysia, 1991), esp. pp. 31–37.

71. Crouch, *Government and Society in Malaysia*, pp. 160–161.

largely ineffectual except at the level of primary education. Significant numbers of Chinese parents placed their children in Chinese-language schools, as the English-medium schools were converted into Malay-speaking schools.

In 1982, in addition to the switch in languages, the government primary schools placed a new emphasis on learning fundamental skills —reading, writing, and arithmetic. Much to the consternation of the Chinese community, even the Chinese-language schools were supplied with Malay texts. The government claimed that Chinese texts would eventually be provided.[72]

The Chinese community also protested the barriers they faced in higher education as a consequence of the government's ethnic preference policies. To increase the number of Malays in higher education, the government had set different standards for Malay and non-Malay applicants. The worsening prospects for non-Malay entrants to the universities led to repeated demands from the Chinese community for the creation of a Merdeka (Independence) University. The government repeatedly rejected this proposal. Eventually, under pressure from the MCA, it allowed the Chinese community to create the Tunku Abdul Rahman College, where the medium of instruction was English.

In another seeming concession to the Chinese and Tamil communities, in 1993 Prime Minister Mahathir announced that the government would allow the use of English in Malaysian universities for the purpose of teaching in the areas of science, technology, and medicine. In all likelihood, this change in policy was driven more by the imperative of competitiveness in an increasingly global economy than by the need to address the misgivings of minority communities. As Malaysia's economy continues to mature and moves into newer areas of high technology, the Mahathir regime and its successors may be forced to make further changes. Despite Malay opposition, universities may have to abandon their Malay-only policy. Indeed, Malaysia already faces a significant shortage of highly skilled personnel in science and technology.[73]

The Chinese community was not the only minority community in Malaysia to suffer from the preferential policies in education. The lack of government funding and the relative economic backwardness of the Indian community also hindered the educational prospects of that community. The 500 Tamil-language schools are among the worst in Malaysia; most are decrepit and short of teachers. The statistical evidence on the

---

72. Ibid., p. 161.

73. James Kynge, "A Shake-up on Campuses," *Financial Times*, June 19, 1996, p. iv.

poor performance of Indian students is damning. In 1991, only 19 percent of Tamils at the end of six years of schooling passed the composition test in Bahasa Malaysia, the national language. In comparison, 33 percent of Chinese and 72 percent of Malays passed the same examination. In technical subjects such as mathematics, their performance has also been distressing: only 50 percent of Tamils passed the mathematics examination, compared to 87 percent of Malays and 57 percent of Chinese. Only about 10 percent of the students entering Tamil primary schools complete eleven years of education, and a mere 3 percent go on to university.[74] The poor quality of Tamil-language education has hurt the prospects of Indians entering universities, especially in the technical areas. In 1988, the last year for which the Malaysian Ministry of Education provided race-based statistics, a mere 1 percent of students in technical colleges were of Indian origin.

The vast majority of Tamil-language schools are underfunded, due in part to the continuing poverty of much of the Indian (predominantly Tamil) population. According to one estimate, close to two-thirds of Malaysia's 1.4 million Indians remain mired in poverty.[75] Consequently, they have not been able to muster the requisite resources to improve the quality of their education. Obviously, the benefits of the NEP's educational successes have bypassed the country's Indian population.

The NEP's educational initiatives have dramatically improved the lot of the Malay population, however. This transformation began with the government devoting close to 6 percent of the gross domestic product (GDP) to education since the early 1970s. During this period, the GDP grew approximately six-fold in real terms.[76] Simultaneously, the government has instituted a range of preferential quotas and scholarships for the *bumiputra*, as well as generous scholarships and bursaries for pursuing higher education abroad. At the secondary school level, elite boarding schools were set up exclusively for Malays. In late 1995, close to 64 percent of the available positions at the university level were reserved for Malays.[77]

A battery of statistical evidence shows the results of these preferential policies. For example, in 1980, a decade after the beginning of the NEP,

---

74. Murray Hiebert, "Class Divide," *Far Eastern Economic Review,* Vol. 158, No. 42 (October 19, 1995), p. 33.

75. S. Jayasankaran, "Balancing Act," *Far Eastern Economic Review,* Vol. 158, No. 51 (December 21, 1995), p. 26.

76. S. Jayasankaran, "A Degree of Success," *Far Eastern Economic Review,* Vol. 158, No. 51 (December 21, 1995), p. 27.

77. Ibid.

1,164,980 Malays were enrolled in primary schools. Within five years, the number climbed to 1,336,922. More dramatic changes appeared in post-secondary education. For example, in the sciences, the numbers of Malay students increased from 5,111 to 12,110 during the same period.[78] The university-level statistics are even more striking. In 1980, 7,072 Malay students were enrolled in graduate and post-graduate science courses; by 1985 that number had shot up to 11,685.

Admittedly, this transformation in educational opportunities came at some cost. Apart from the racial inequities that it has perpetuated and, indeed, now exacerbated, the government's preferential policies have had other pernicious consequences. For example, it is widely held that race-based entry standards have lowered educational standards. Furthermore, non-Malays have faced widespread discrimination in terms of both university appointments and promotions.[79]

OCCUPATION AND EMPLOYMENT

One of the professed goals of the NEP was to disassociate occupation and race. From the preceding discussion, it is clear that the government embarked on a massive affirmative action program in the field of education. What steps did it undertake in the area of employment to achieve this goal?

Prior to 1969, Malaysia had already instituted a system of preferences in hiring. However, this system was confined to governmental services. With the adoption of the NEP, the system of preferences was extended to the private sector.[80] Quotas were set for the employment of Malays in commercial and industrial firms. Moreover, firms were asked to devise plans for the training and promotion of Malays to more skilled and upper management positions. Foreign corporations were expected to comply with these regulations. In fact, the contractual terms of investment in Malaysia were linked to the creation of quotas for Malays.

The systematic pursuit of these goals has yielded substantial results over the course of two and a half decades. Again, the statistical evidence

---

78. Government of Malaysia, *Fifth Malaysia Plan* (Kuala Lumpur: National Printing Department, Government of Malaysia), p. 493.

79. The evidence for this assertion is largely anecdotal. However, a range of interviews conducted with academics at the University of Malaya in Kuala Lumpur and Universiti Kebangsan in Bangi suggested that there was at least a kernel of truth to this assertion. One social scientist at the Universiti Kebangsan produced a copy of the faculty directory and stated, "See for yourself." Author interviews in Kuala Lumpur and Bangi, November 1995.

80. Means, "Ethnic Preference in Malaysia," p. 108.

Table 6.4. Employment in Malaysia by Occupation and Ethnic Group, 1957–1985.

Occupational group	1957			1970			1985		
	Malay	Chinese	Indian	Malay	Chinese	Indian	Malay	Chinese	Indian
Professional & technical	35.1	41.9	12.1	47.0	39.5	10.8	54.4	32.4	11.1
Administrative & managerial	17.5	62.3	12.3	24.1	62.9	7.8	28.2	66.0	5.0
Clerical	27.1	46.2	19.9	35.4	45.9	17.2	54.0	36.8	8.7
Sales	15.9	66.1	16.8	26.7	61.7	11.1	37.9	56.8	5.2
Service	39.7	33.3	12.8	44.3	39.6	14.6	57.9	31.2	9.7
Agricultural	62.1	24.3	12.8	72.0	N/A	9.7	73.5	17.2	8.3
Production	26.5	53.5	18.9	34.2	55.9	9.6	45.5	43.1	10.9

SOURCE: Adapted from K.S. Jomo, *Growth and Structural Change in the Malaysian Economy* (London: Macmillan, 1990), Table 4.2.

is compelling. For example, in 1970, 62.3 percent of Malays in peninsular Malaysia were engaged in some form of agriculture; by 1990, this number had dropped to 37.4 percent. Simultaneously, Malays had moved into middle-class occupations at an extraordinary pace, increasing from 12.9 percent to 27 percent between 1970 and 1990. For example, the proportion of *bumiputra* doctors rose from 4 to 28 percent, dentists from 3 to 24 percent, architects from 4 to 24 percent, engineers from 7 to 35 percent, and accountants from 7 to 11 percent.[81] Thanks to concerted efforts at social engineering, the widely held image of Malays as peasant cultivators underwent a dramatic transformation within the span of two decades. (See Table 6.4.)

Another stated goal of the NEP was the transfer of at least 30 percent of all equity holdings into Malay hands. This was a formidable task because in 1969 Malays owned a mere 1.5 percent of capital assets of limited companies. To accomplish its goal, the government acted on behalf of the Malay community, investing heavily in publicly owned corporations that were operated and managed by Malays. The government created a number of investment schemes to attract private Malay investment to these enterprises.

The government also adopted a highly interventionist posture in other areas of economic policy. For example, the Ministry of Works and Public Utilities, the principal contractor for government construction

81. Crouch, *Government and Society in Malaysia*, pp. 185–188.

projects, was required to reserve at least 30 percent of its contracts for Malay firms, that is, those with at least 51 percent Malay ownership.[82] In addition, the government established government-run banks—such as the Bank Rakyat and the Bank Bumiputra—to provide financial services to the Malay community.[83] Finally, the government created a number of development banks, such as Bank Pembangunan Malaysia Berhad (1973), Bank Kemajuan Perusahaan (1979), and Bank Islam (1979).

There is little question that the government has achieved some of its objectives. As a consequence of the creation of new banks, lending to the Malay community increased substantially. In 1968, 4 percent of the loans in Malaysia went to Malays; by 1980 this total had grown to 20.6 percent, and in 1985 it reached 28 percent.[84] However, even though the government mounted a concerted effort to create a Malay entrepreneurial class through extensive interventions in the market, the results have been distinctly mixed. A Malay economic elite has undoubtedly emerged. It is doubtful that this elite would have enjoyed a similar degree of success without the obvious benefits of steadfast governmental intervention on behalf of Malays.[85] At the same time, one government organization, the Council of Trust for the Indigenous People, which was created to promote entrepreneurship and provide credit to small businesses, reported in 1983 that of the 55,000 loans that had been given to Malay businesses, only 6,000 had been paid back. The bulk of the defaulters had either gone bankrupt or believed that the loans did not have to be paid back. Other evidence pointed to the difficulties of instilling the virtues of entrepreneurship. In 1980, for example, the Ministry of Public Works and Public Utilities announced that out of the 5,000 Malay contractors registered with it, only about 20 percent could be considered successful.[86]

The final component of the NEP is the government's efforts to eradicate poverty. At one level, it is difficult to gainsay the state's achievements in this area. In 1970, close to half the population in peninsular Malaysia lived in poverty; it is believed that the incidence of poverty in Sabah and Sarawak was even worse.[87] Fifteen years after the inception of the NEP, poverty had declined to 20.7 percent. By 1990, at the start of the National

---

82. Jesudason, *Ethnicity and the Economy*, p. 102.

83. Means, "Ethnic Preference in Malaysia," p. 110.

84. Jesudason, *Ethnicity and the Economy*, pp. 100–102.

85. S. Jayasankaran, "The Chosen Few," *Far Eastern Economic Review*, Vol. 158, No. 51 (December 21, 1995), p. 30.

86. Jesudason, *Ethnicity and the Economy*, p. 103.

87. Crouch, *Government and Society in Malaysia*, p. 189.

Development Plan (NDP), poverty had declined to 17.1 percent; the NDP projected a further decline to 11.1 percent by 1995.[88] The economic performance of the Malaysian economy exceeded the government's projections. By 1994, the poverty rate had declined to 8.8 percent, unemployment was around 2.9 percent, and the per capita income of the country was $3,406.[89] Much of this was made possible by the extraordinary dynamism of the Malaysian economy in the late 1980s and early 1990s. In 1995, the Malaysian economy registered its eighth consecutive year of growth at over 8 percent a year. Real growth of GDP amounted to 9.6 percent.[90] The reduction of poverty significantly improved the position of all three of the main ethnic communities in Malaysia, though the Malays, who were in the most dire situation prior to 1970, have been the greatest beneficiaries.

Beyond Economic Explanations

What other factors, beyond extraordinary levels of economic growth and the government's redistributive policies, have enabled Malaysia to maintain ethnic peace? After all, not all ethnic groups, most notably the Indian community, have enjoyed the rewards of economic growth to the same extent as the Malays or even the Chinese.[91]

Until the late 1960s, the consociational power-sharing arrangements embodied in the National Alliance succeeded in maintaining ethnic harmony. These arrangements obviously represented a tenuous peace because the electoral results of the 1969 elections served as a catalyst for ethnic violence. Apart from pursuing policies of growth and social justice, the Alliance and the *Barisan Nasional* (as the *Barisan Sosialis* was called after 1974) placed a number of curbs on personal rights, civil liberties, and press freedoms. Many of these limitations were put into force shortly after parliament was suspended and the state of emergency imposed. However, long after the state of emergency was lifted, these limitations on civil liberties have remained and in some cases, have even been strengthened.

This creeping authoritarianism has been made possible in part by the

---

88. Government of Malaysia, *Sixth Malaysia Plan, 1991–1995*, p. 32.

89. Mohamed Jawhar bin Hassan, "Malaysia in 1994: Staying the Course," *Asian Survey*, Vol. 35, No. 2 (February 1995), pp. 186–193.

90. Mohamed Jawhar bin Hassan, "Malaysia in 1995," *Asian Survey*, Vol. 36, No. 2 (February 1996), pp. 123–129.

91. Murray Hiebert, "Underclass Blues," *Far Eastern Economic Review*, Vol. 158, No. 42 (October 19, 1995), pp. 32–33.

structure of the Malaysian polity. The Malaysian Constitution is very susceptible to amendment. A mere two-thirds majority of parliament enables the ruling party (or coalition) to amend the constitution. Neither the Alliance nor the *Barisan Nasional* had much difficulty in mustering the requisite two-thirds majority. The opposition remained free to protest, but to little effect.

Other institutions of governance have bolstered the powers and prerogatives of the ruling regime. For example, except on rare occasions, the Malaysian judiciary has been remarkably pliant. In the early years of the Malaysian state, most Malay politicians came from the same social background as the judiciary. Consequently, they shared a consensus on a range of political and social issues. There is, in fact, some evidence that prime ministers even consulted the higher reaches of the judiciary before introducing legislation in parliament.[92]

The pliant judiciary in Malaysia has enabled various regimes to impose significant controls on the mass media. In 1974, parliament passed legislation that required Malay majority ownership for all newspapers. Soon thereafter, the principal political parties (UMNO, in particular) moved to control most major newspapers. By the 1980s, UMNO had direct or indirect control of the *New Straits Times*, *The Malay Mail*, *Berita Minggu*, *Utusan Melayu*, and *Utusan Malaysia*.[93] The government also controlled two of the three television channels and held 40 percent of the equity in the third.

Apart from ownership of the press and mass media, the government also possesses other legislative means to exercise control. The annual licensing requirements of the Printing Presses Ordinance of 1958 in conjunction with the Sedition Act of 1948 leave the threat of closure an ever-present possibility for any media outlet. The Sedition Act was amended over time to prohibit any discussion of Malay special rights, the privileges of the sultans and the royalty, the citizenship of non-Malays, or the government's language policy. The government has also moved to limit foreign publications that are deemed prejudicial to "public order, national interest, morality, or security."[94] In 1984, two more pieces of legislation that imposed further restrictions on press freedom were passed: the Printing Presses and Publications Act, and the Official Secrets Act. The first made it mandatory for foreign publications to provide large

---

92. Crouch, *Government and Society in Malaysia*, pp. 138–142.

93. Means, *Malaysian Politics: The Second Generation*, pp. 137–138.

94. Ibid., p. 138.

deposits, which would be forfeited if the publishers failed to appear in court following the publication of material detrimental to the national interest. The Official Secrets Act was equally insidious: under its terms, any information entrusted in confidence by one public official to another was deemed to be a secret. The penalties embodied in this act were nothing short of draconian. For example, the act called for five-year prison terms for government employees who failed to report to the police any requests for official information that they received from members of the public.[95]

In addition to this panoply of restrictions, a stunning array of legislation that curtails personal freedom has been passed and is invoked at will, including the Internal Security Act of 1960 (revised and amended in 1972 and 1975), under which the minister for home affairs can place an individual in preventive detention for a period of two years without trial. The Sedition Act of 1948 provides sweeping powers to the government to arrest individuals for "seditious" activities. If convicted, an individual can be imprisoned for up to three years.

Other pieces of legislation, passed after independence, have significantly reinforced the coercive powers of the state. Many of these were formulated during Malaysia's first state of emergency, during the communist-led uprising. Nevertheless, they have remained on the books and have been used by various regimes against members of the opposition. Two ordinances are of particular significance. The first, the Public Order (Preservation) Ordinance of 1958, permits the police to declare that certain areas are restricted. Once the ordinance is in effect, the police are empowered to regulate processions and meetings of more than five individuals, to search and arrest individuals at will, and to control firearms. Violations of this ordinance bring whipping and imprisonment for up to ten years. The other statute, the Prevention of Crime Ordinance of 1959, permits the police to detain individuals for up to twenty-eight days without showing cause.[96]

These dramatic restrictions on personal, press, and political freedoms have ensured that few inflammatory charges are made in the press, that politicians are hesitant to make overtly communal appeals, and that the dominance of the ruling regime remains largely unchallenged. The government has on occasion used these legislative powers not only to quell challenges from national opposition parties such as the DAP, but also to

---

95. Ibid., p. 139.

96. Much of this discussion has been derived from ibid., pp. 141–145.

discipline and punish challenges posed by the Islamist political party, PAS, particularly in the state of Kelantan.[97]

FEDERALISM

Has the federal structure of the Malaysian polity also assuaged the possibilities of ethnic conflict?[98] The evidence on this score is complex. For example, despite repeated efforts, the UMNO has made little headway in establishing a firm foothold in the Malay-dominated state of Kelantan. Much to the chagrin of the UMNO regime at the national level, the PAS, which has a stronghold in Kelantan, has sought to promote an Islamization program. PAS attempts to legislate Islamic values in the public sphere have frequently brought the PAS leadership into conflict with government authorities. However, the PAS commands so much support among Kelantan's predominantly Malay-Muslim population that the UMNO has not been able to oust it at the local level.[99]

The outcome of the PAS-UMNO competition, however, should not necessarily be taken as representative of the state of Malaysian federalism. The Mahathir regime has taken a much tougher stance in dealing with the state of Sabah on a range of contentious issues.[100] Sabah's multiethnic population and its physical distance from peninsular Malaysia may well account for the markedly different treatment it has received from the central government.

Modern Singapore

Unlike Malaysia, which has long pursued explicit preferential policies on behalf of Malays, Singapore has sought to downplay the dominance of its majority, the Chinese community. In its early years, it sought to de-emphasize its predominant Chinese identity because of widespread fears in Southeast Asia that expatriate Chinese communities could serve as potential "fifth columns" for the People's Republic of China.

Subsequently, the notionally democratic PAP regimes have promoted

97. S. Jayasankaran, "New Convictions," *Far Eastern Economic Review*, Vol. 159, No. 28 (July 11, 1996), p. 21.

98. B.H. Shafruddin, *The Federal Factor in the Government and Politics of Peninsular Malaysia* (Singapore: Oxford University Press, 1987).

99. David Camroux, "State Responses to Islamic Resurgence in Malaysia: Accommodation, Co-Option and Confrontation," *Asian Survey*, Vol. 32, No. 9 (September 1996), pp. 852–868.

100. Audrey R. Kahin, "Crisis on the Periphery: The Rift Between Kuala Lumpur and Sabah," *Pacific Affairs*, Vol. 65, No. 1 (Spring 1992), pp. 18–49.

a vision of a "multiracial" society where ethnic differences in the political arena are actively suppressed.[101] In this single-party state, the PAP, through an amalgam of rapid economic growth and a range of restrictions on political activity and personal freedoms, has maintained ethnic peace.[102]

Despite the government's professed commitment to racial equality and meritocracy, ethnic discrimination and dominance persist in Singapore. To prevent ethnic violence, PAP governments have pursued a range of educational and cultural policies, have developed and implemented particular notions of press freedom, and have confined the scope of independent judicial activity. As in Malaysia, two factors explain Singapore's political quiescence: rapid economic growth, and an extensive apparatus for political repression.

SOCIAL RESTRICTIONS AND OFFICIAL MORES

A variety of officially sponsored social restrictions and prohibitions circumscribe public life in Singapore. They include prohibitions on various forms of social behavior deemed undesirable, such as chewing gum, failure to flush toilets, and littering. Most of these activities are punishable under law and are actively prosecuted. These behavioral injunctions, though extraordinary, do not have explicit ethnic dimensions. The government also exhorts its citizens in a variety of ways to promote a particular civic vision. Accordingly, all citizens of the city-state are officially encouraged to take pride in Singapore's multicultural heritage, promote racial harmony, pursue religious tolerance, show care and concern, exercise a spirit of voluntarism, and recognize their common destiny.[103]

These efforts to instill a particular brand of civic consciousness and conformity among Singaporeans are often carried out via the state's extensive provision of public housing, one of the government's more striking achievements. The mandate of the government's housing agency, the Housing and Development Board (HDB) is to ensure that ethnic enclaves, such as those that had grown up under British colonial rule, are not allowed to develop. To this end, the government sets explicit quotas

---

101. Choo-Oon Khong, "Singapore: Political Legitimacy through Managing Conformity," in Alagappa, *Political Legitimacy in Southeast Asia*, p. 126.

102. For a succinct description and analysis of Singapore's strategy of economic growth, see Vogel, *The Four Little Dragons*.

103. Eng, *Meanings of Multiethnicity*, p. 43. Also see Hussin Mutalib, "Singapore's Quest for a National Identity: The Triumphs and Trials of Government Policies," in Ban Kah Choon, Anne Pakir, and Tong Chee Kiong, eds., *Imagining Singapore* (Singapore: Times Academic Press, 1992), pp. 69–96.

for Chinese, Malays, Indians, and "Others" in each neighborhood and each block of every public housing estate in Singapore. The government's public housing program is, by some standards, a remarkable success. Singapore's public housing projects accommodate some 80 percent of its population.[104] On the other hand, the extensive governmental role in the development and provision of housing amounts to a form of social control over Singapore's various ethnic groups. Furthermore, certain ethnic groups, especially the Malays, have expressed concerns about discrimination in predominantly Chinese settlements.[105]

EDUCATIONAL POLICIES

Singapore, like Malaysia, inherited colonial educational policies and institutions. During the long years of colonial rule, the British had done little to foster a system of universal education in Singapore. Missionary schools provided English-language education to a particular stratum of Singaporean society, which then found employment in the lower echelons of the British colonial administration. Only upon their return to Singapore in 1945, when they confronted a well-developed nationalist movement, did the British colonial authorities seek to control the Chinese schools that had developed in the 1930s under the tutelage of the Chinese Communist Party, and try to improve English-language education with a view toward co-opting an English-educated elite. English-educated Singaporeans were subsequently drawn into commercial and administrative positions while those with vernacular education (Chinese, Malay, and Tamil) were directed toward technical and vocational training.

As independence approached in 1955, the Legislative Assembly appointed a committee to review Singapore's education policies. Lee Kuan Yew was one of the members of this committee, and the roots of the PAP's educational policies can be traced to the committee's recommendations, which included the equal treatment of the four main language groups, the introduction of bilingual education in the primary schools and trilingual education in secondary schools, and the designation of Malay as the national language.[106] In making this last provision, the committee members had an eye on Singapore's geopolitical location and the strength of the indigenous Malay community within the city-state.

A major shift in educational policy occurred in 1980 in the wake of

---

104. Neher and Marlay, *Democracy and Development*, p. 139.

105. Eng, *Meanings of Multiethnicity*, p. 128.

106. R.S. Milne and Diane K. Mauzy, *Singapore: The Legacy of Lee Kuan Yew* (Boulder, Colo.: Westview Press, 1990), p. 18.

the "Goh Report," named after its author, Deputy Prime Minister Goh Keng Swee. The report had been prompted by unacceptably high dropout rates in Singaporean schools.[107] The report identified bilingualism as one of the key factors underlying these high attrition rates. Contending that large numbers of students were incapable of coping with the demands of bilingualism, it proposed that students be "streamed," based upon educational performance. The brightest students would be placed in superior schools with a more demanding curriculum, and weaker students would be directed towards monolingual and vocational education. Simultaneously, the report also called for incorporating moral education into the curriculum, to limit the penetration of "Western values." The government has subsequently sought to promote "Asian values," which in its view call for discipline and deference, as opposed to individualism, which it associates with Western decadence.[108]

Singapore's educational reforms have produced mixed results for the city-state's Malay and Indian communities. Malays continue to be the poorest performers in Singaporean schools. Their poor performance, in turn, has significantly affected their employment opportunities.[109] The response of the Singaporean government to the relative economic backwardness of the Malay and Indian communities has been less than benevolent. Instead of addressing historical and underlying factors that can inhibit educational performance, the government has blamed the victims. It has called for increased self-help efforts within the Malay community, and has suggested that Malay cultural traditions and habits may explain Malay educational failures.[110]

ETHNIC BACKGROUND AND ECONOMIC OPPORTUNITIES

Despite its professed commitment to multiracialism, the PAP government has actively discriminated against some of the city-state's ethnic communities. Malays, for example, are under-represented in the top ranks of the civil service. More to the point, they have been actively excluded from the military and the police services since the break with Malaysia in 1965. Even when Malay youth are called up for national service, they are given

---

107. Ibid., p. 19. The primary school attrition rate was about 29 percent when the government's new policy was instituted in 1980.

108. Neher and Marlay, *Democracy and Development*, p. 136. For a critique of Lee Kuan Yew's views, see Kim Dae Jung, "Is Culture Destiny? The Myth of Asia's Anti-Democratic Values," *Foreign Affairs*, Vol. 73, No. 6 (November/December 1994), pp. 189–194.

109. Eng, *Meanings of Multiethnicity*, pp. 156–157.

110. Ibid., p. 165.

menial duties and kept away from elite air force, commando, and tank units.[111]

In addition to encountering discrimination from the government and the state services, Malays report widespread discrimination in the private sector. Discrimination is most likely to take place in Chinese-controlled firms. This form of prejudice against Malays is rooted in the belief that, unlike the Chinese, the Malays are not industrious and reliable employees.[112] Although the existence of racial discrimination in the private sector cannot be directly attributed to government policies, the persistence of patterns of discrimination in an ostensibly multiracial and meritocratic society suggests that the government has not taken adequate steps to eradicate such practices.

CURBING DISSENT

Despite making notional commitments to democracy, PAP governments have systematically squelched political dissent in Singapore. Although elections are somewhat free and fair, the PAP has used the advantages of incumbency to undercut opposition forces. These repressive policies have also prevented the emergence of ethnic political mobilization. A battery of legislation limits free speech, civil liberties, and judicial review.

Significant curbs exist on press freedoms in Singapore. The government-controlled Singapore Broadcasting Corporation has a monopoly on all radio stations and television channels. Under pressure from foreign businessmen, the government has since 1993 allowed a Cable News Network channel in five-star hotels on in-room television sets only. All newspapers are published by Singapore Press Holdings, an organization with close ties to the PAP leadership. Local journals, fearing reprisals, engage in self-censorship.[113]

Much has been written about the pliant judiciary in Singapore.[114] Issues of judicial autonomy came to the fore in 1994 when Christopher Lingle, a visiting professor at the National University of Singapore, was charged with contempt after he published an article in the *International Herald Tribune*. In the article, he alleged that an unnamed Asian country had a "compliant judiciary." The *Herald Tribune* was forced to make a

---

111. Li, *Malays in Singapore*, p. 109.

112. Ibid., pp. 109–110.

113. Neher and Marlay, *Democracy and Development*, p. 136.

114. For a discussion that suggests that Western critiques of Singapore's legal regime may be overblown, see Diane K. Mauzy, "Consolidating the Succession," *Asian Survey*, Vol. 36, No. 2 (February 1996), pp. 117–122.

public apology.[115] This was not the first time that the executive branch of government in Singapore had sought to use judicial power to tame foreign publications.

Two important pieces of legislation that place significant curbs on political activity are the long-standing Internal Security Act and the more recent Maintenance of Religious Harmony Act. Both pieces of legislation have been relied upon extensively to curb any activity that the state sees as inimical to the preservation of ethnic peace. In 1987, for example, various church and social workers were arrested and imprisoned on charges of having organized a Marxist conspiracy. They were remanded under the Internal Security Act even though Prime Minister Goh Chok Tong admitted in parliament that he had reservations about the evidence against the group.[116] Although few individuals are still incarcerated under the Internal Security Act, it remains on the books.

Conclusions

Both Malaysia and Singapore have successfully maintained ethnic peace, in contrast to many postcolonial, multiethnic societies. However, this has entailed majority ethnic dominance and systematic political repression.

There is little that is transferable about Singapore's experiences in preserving ethnic peace; its experience is virtually unique. Admittedly, there is no gainsaying its striking economic achievements. But beyond its economic performance, its other accomplishments are hardly replicable in larger multiethnic societies. Much of Singapore's success rests on its extensively intrusive webs of social policies designed to maximize social control. However, the degree of social control that the Singaporean government exercises over its population could not be easily approximated in a significantly larger multiethnic society.

The Malaysian case, on the other hand, does have some useful policy implications. Extraordinary restrictions on political expression and personal freedom have helped to create a distinctively authoritarian political culture within the context of a seemingly democratic political framework.[117] These restrictions, coupled with a pattern of phenomenal

---

115. Diane K. Mauzy, "Singapore in 1994: Plus ça change, . . ." *Asian Survey,* Vol. 35, No. 2 (February 1995), pp. 179–185.

116. Milne and Mauzy, *Singapore,* p. 128.

117. See Crouch, *Government and Society in Malaysia,* pp. 236–247. Also see William F. Case, "Can the 'Halfway House' Stand? Semidemocracy and Elite Theory in Three Southeast Asian Countries," *Comparative Politics,* Vol. 28, No. 4 (July 1996), pp. 437–464.

economic expansion and moderately successful redistributive policies, have maintained a fragile ethnic peace. The Malaysian case also suggests that in the absence of powerful, robust political institutions for mediating ethnic conflicts, it may be useful to defer widespread political participation. The normative implications of this proposition may be quite unappealing to the adherents of liberal democratic values. Furthermore, from a practical standpoint, authoritarian institutions, once entrenched, are difficult to dismantle. Finally, ample evidence exists that authoritarian regimes do not necessarily promote economic growth, ensure social justice, and maintain ethnic peace. Consequently, authoritarian constraints on political participation alone are no guarantee of desirable political outcomes. Nevertheless, it needs to be borne in mind that political enfranchisement in most Western liberal democracies proceeded very gradually and in distinct stages. The rapid expansion of political participation in multiethnic societies has frequently given political entrepreneurs opportunities to stir imaginary grievances and generate ethnic violence.[118]

Finally, both the Singaporean and Malaysian cases underscore the signal importance of promoting economic growth in conjunction with a measure of redistributive justice. Ethnic tensions clearly lurk in both Singapore and Malaysia. The ability of governments in both states to promote rapid economic growth while providing economic security to all politically salient ethnic communities may well be the key to preventing a resurgence in ethnic conflict in this part of Southeast Asia.

---

118.   Jack Snyder and Karen Ballentine, "Nationalism and the Marketplace of Ideas," *International Security*, Vol. 21, No. 2 (Fall 1996), pp. 5–40.

Chapter 7

Coercion, Co-optation, and the Management of Ethnic Relations in Indonesia

R. William Liddle

The Republic of Indonesia is one of the largest and most ethnically diverse countries in the world. The former Netherlands India, it was founded in 1945 by nationalists of many different ethnic backgrounds who had been fighting against Dutch colonial rule since the 1920s. Seeing themselves as inheritors of the French, American, and Russian revolutionary tradition, they envisioned a modern society and a multiethnic nation-state based on popular sovereignty. They won independence in 1949, after a four-year struggle against a determined Dutch effort to regain power after World War II.

Since independence, cultural/regional, religious, and racial divisions have been major sources of political conflict in Indonesia. They contributed substantially to the breakdown of representative democratic institutions in the 1950s, and were not resolved during President Sukarno's presidential dictatorship from the late 1950s to the mid-1960s. Since 1966, ethnic policies have been formulated and implemented in the context of President Suharto's authoritarian New Order. Coercion has been the principal governmental instrument employed to settle disputes and respond to demands from groups outside the state, but ideological persuasion, the exchange of material goods and services, and co-optation have also been part of the policy equation. The result is a mixed record of policy successes and failures.

In the mid-1990s, conflict along three dimensions of ethnic cleavage—cultural/regional, religious, and racial—appears to be on the rise. By the beginning of the twenty-first century, if not before, Indonesia will likely enter a difficult period in its political life. President Suharto has been in power for more than thirty years, and turned seventy-five in June 1996. Growing ethnic conflict may be accompanied by a leadership crisis in a larger context of increasing vulnerability to international economic and political pressures and to the demands of new and more politically resourceful social groups in Indonesia as a result of economic development. Gradual democratization at the national level and devolution of authority from the center to the regions may be the best solutions to these problems, but there are few signs that Indonesian elites are prepared to adopt these reforms.

Sources of Ethnic Conflict

ETHNIC DIVISIONS

Indonesia is a multiethnic country in three senses: cultural/regional, religious, and racial. Its nearly 200 million people are divided into hundreds of distinct cultural groups living for the most part in regional homelands spread across nearly 4,000 miles of archipelago, from Aceh on the northern tip of Sumatra to Irian Jaya, the western half of the island of New Guinea.[1] Typically, the members of each group speak their own language or dialect and have a strong sense of their distinctiveness, in terms of customs and traditions, from other groups.

While useful as a guide to the size differences among cultural/regional groups, the actual numbers in Table 7.1 are undoubtedly too low. For example, most observers believe that the Javanese account for more than 90 million people or nearly half of all Indonesians, and the Sundanese for about 15 percent or close to thirty million people. The table does, however, correctly identify the Acehnese, Toba and Dairi Bataks, Minangkabau, Malays, and Lampung people of Sumatra, the Madurese of the island of Madura off the north coast of East Java, the Balinese, the Sasak of Lombok island in West Nusa Tenggara just east of Bali, the Banjarese of South Kalimantan, and the Buginese and Makasarese of South Sulawesi as important medium-size groups. In general, as one moves from western (Sumatra, Java, and Bali) to eastern Indonesia, group size diminishes while the number of groups increases. At the eastern end of the archipelago, Irian Jaya has fewer than two million inhabitants but more than two hundred distinct cultural groups.

Five religions—Islam, Protestantism, Catholicism, Hinduism, and Buddhism—are officially recognized by the Indonesian government. (See Table 7.2.) Most Hindus are Balinese, while Protestant and Catholic adherents are heavily concentrated among specific regional ethnic groups, such as the Batak of Sumatra or the people of Flores Island in eastern Indonesia. Most Buddhists are Sino-Indonesian, the descendants of

---

1. Joel C. Kuipers, "The Society and Its Environment," in William H. Frederick and Robert L. Worden, eds., *Indonesia: A Country Study* (Washington, D.C.: Federal Research Division, Library of Congress, 1993), pp. 69–136.

Table 7.1. Ethnic Composition of Indonesia.

Group	Location	Number	Percentage
Javanese	East and Central Java, Yogyakarta	70,000,000	41.5
Sundanese	West Java	25,000,000	14.8
Malay	Coastal and southern Sumatra	10,000,000	5.9
Madurese	East Java (Madura island)	9,000,000	5.3
Minangkabau	West Sumatra	7,500,000	4.4
Balinese	Bali	3,000,000	1.8
Buginese	South Sulawesi	2,500,000	1.5
Acehnese	Aceh	2,200,000	1.3
Toba Batak	North Sumatra	2,000,000	1.2
Banjarese	South Kalimantan	1,800,000	1.1
Makasarese	South Sulawesi	1,500,000	.9
Sasak	West Nusa Tenggara (Lombok island)	1,500,000	.9
Lampung	Lampung	1,500,000	.9
Dairi Batak	North Sumatra	1,200,000	.7
Other		30,175,000	17.8
Total		**168,875,000**	**100.0**

NOTE: These are rough estimates. As of the mid-1980s, Indonesia's population was estimated at 168,875,000.
SOURCE: Joel C. Kuipers, "The Society and Its Environment," in William H. Frederick and Robert L. Worden, eds., *Indonesia: A Country Study* (Washington, D.C.: Federal Research Division, Library of Congress, 1993), pp. 96–97.

Table 7.2. Religious Affiliation in Indonesia (as of 1985).

Religious Group	Number	Percentage
Muslim	146,752,375	86.9
Protestant	10,976,875	6.5
Catholic	5,235,125	3.1
Hindu	3,208,625	1.9
Buddhist	1,688,750	1.0
Other	1,013,250	.6
Total	**168,875,000**	**100.0**

SOURCE: *Statistik Indonesia/Statistical Handbook of Indonesia 1986* (Jakarta: Central Bureau of Statistics, 1987), pp. 168–169.

migrants from China in the nineteenth and twentieth centuries. While Muslims constitute the overwhelming majority of Indonesians at nearly 90 percent, they are themselves divided into several groups, including Javanese syncretists, traditionalists, and modernists or reformists.

Javanese syncretists (sometimes called nominal or "identity card"

Muslims by other Indonesians) are formal adherents to Islam whose real religious beliefs and practices mix traditional animistic, Hindu, Buddhist, and Islamic elements. The animistic elements are particularly strong among lower-class and village Javanese, while beliefs and practices derived from Hindu and Buddhist influences are more common among descendants of the traditional aristocratic upper class once centered in the courts of royal Java.

Muslim traditionalists adhere to the Syafi'i school of legal interpretation within Sunni Islam. In terms of political significance, the largest concentration of Muslim traditionalists is in eastern Java, although tens of millions live in central and western Java, Sumatra, Kalimantan, and Sulawesi. Most are small farmers or petty traders, living in villages and small towns. Islamic modernism or reformism is a movement that came to Indonesia from the Middle East in the last quarter of the nineteenth century; its current adherents, numbering tens of millions, reject all four of the traditional Sunni legal schools, preferring direct interpretation of the meaning of the Koran. While modernists live in every region, their political center of gravity has been in the islands outside Java, especially Sumatra and Sulawesi. Modernists also tend to be urban and to have been educated in Western-style schools, as opposed to the Koranic schools associated with traditional Islam.

The anthropologist Clifford Geertz was the first to analyze Indonesian, particularly Javanese, Islamic culture and society in terms of the distinction between syncretists, traditionalists, and modernists; he lived in eastern Java in the 1950s.[2] Geertz's position has since come under heavy attack both from scholars who claim that Javanese Islam never was syncretic and from those who argue that Indonesian Islam has become much more uniform since the 1950s.[3] The latter view holds that syncretic Muslims have become purer, or at any rate more like their Middle Eastern coreligionists, and that the modernist-traditionalist distinction is disappearing as a result of rapid urbanization and the spread of Western-style education. I believe that the second view has some merit, although there is still considerable evidence, as I shall show below, that syncretists, traditionalists, and modernists are all politically alive and well.

Indonesians recognize two kinds of racial difference. The first is the distinction between Sino-Indonesians (Indonesian citizens or long-time

---

2. Clifford Geertz, *The Religion of Java* (Glencoe, N.Y.: Free Press, 1960).

3. Mark Woodward, *Islam in Java: Normative Piety and Mysticism in the Sultanate of Yogyakarta* (Tucson: University of Arizona Press, 1989); and Robert Hefner, "Islamizing Java? Religion and Politics in Rural East Java," *Journal of Asian Studies*, Vol. 46, No. 3 (August 1987), pp. 533–554.

Indonesia.

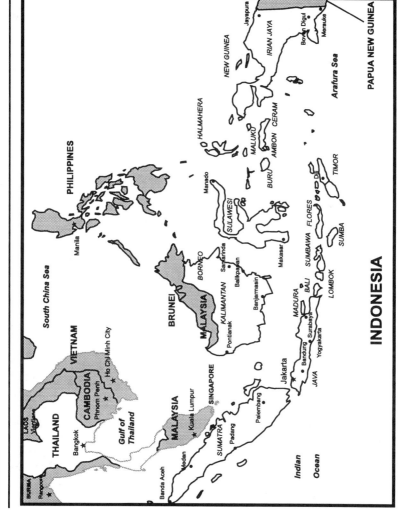

residents of Chinese ancestry) and indigenous Indonesians.[4] Chinese have been present in the archipelago for hundreds of years, but came in large numbers only in the nineteenth and early twentieth centuries, when the Dutch colonial government offered them both economic opportunity and a measure of personal security under colonial rule. Today they constitute about 4 percent of the population and live mainly in cities and towns.[5] They can be found in most urban occupations, from business tycoon to pedicab driver, but indigenous Indonesians typically meet them in the small shops that line the streets of all central business districts. Most indigenous Indonesians believe that the modern economy is dominated, if not controlled, by Sino-Indonesians. Few Sino-Indonesians have become Muslims, though many have converted to Christianity.

The second racial difference that Indonesians recognize is between the Indonesian-speaking (here in its linguistic meaning of four subgroups of the Austronesian language stock) people of western Indonesia, who constitute the large majority of all citizens of the Indonesian republic, and the Melanesian- and Papuan-speaking peoples of eastern Indonesia, particularly the province of Irian Jaya and adjacent islands.[6] Melanesian languages are an Austronesian subgroup, but Papuan languages are a totally unrelated group. Melanesian speakers tend to have very black skin and tightly curled hair, while Papuan speakers tend to have lighter skin and tightly curled hair, in contrast to the typically lighter-skinned, straight-haired Indonesian speakers of western Indonesia. A rough guide to the number of Melanesians and Papuans in Indonesia is the number of inhabitants of Irian Jaya province according to the 1990 census: 1,649,000, which is less than 2 percent of the total Indonesian population.[7] Like the Sino-Indonesians in western Indonesia, recent Indonesian-

---

4. For overviews of the Chinese in Indonesia, see Leo Suryadinata, *Pribumi Indonesians, The Chinese Minority and China*, 3d ed. (Singapore: Heinemann, 1992); Charles A. Coppel, *Indonesian Chinese in Crisis* (Kuala Lumpur: Oxford University Press, 1983); and J.A.C. Mackie, *The Chinese in Indonesia* (Honolulu: University of Hawaii Press, 1976).

5. "No reliable figures on the number of ethnic Chinese in Indonesia have been collected since the 1930 census; all later estimates . . . appear to be based on calculations that they still represent either 3 or 4 percent of the total population, although even that can be only an informed guess." Jamie Mackie, "Economic Systems of the Southeast Asian Chinese," in Leo Suryadinata, ed., *Southeast Asian Chinese and China: The Politico-Economic Dimension* (Singapore: Times Academic Press, 1995), p. 62, n. 14.

6. I am indebted to personal communication from Karl Heider for clarification of these terms.

7. *Indonesia 1996: An Official Handbook* (Jakarta: Department of Information, Republic of Indonesia, 1996), p. 301.

speaking migrants from western Indonesia predominate in the markets and central business districts of many eastern Indonesian towns.

ETHNIC DIFFERENCES AND POLITICAL CONFLICT

Since independence, cultural/regional, religious, and racial divisions have all been important sources of political conflict in Indonesia. Among cultural/regional groups, the main axis of conflict has been the relationship between the Javanese, who almost constitute a majority, and all the others, who have feared domination by the Javanese. Domination is defined both in terms of group interest (the competition among groups for scarce material and status rewards) and in broader cultural terms. The Javanese are perceived as wanting to impose "feudal" values of hierarchy and deference toward authority on traditionally more egalitarian non-Javanese cultures.

Tension between the Javanese and other groups has been exacerbated by the trend since the late 1950s toward centralization of power and decision-making in Jakarta. Both the population of the capital city and the personnel of the central government are multiethnic, but the sheer numbers of Javanese, and their physical proximity to the capital, make centralization seem equivalent to Javanization to many non-Javanese. Moreover, many, perhaps most, regions of the country experience miniature versions of this pattern of political tension and resulting conflict between larger and smaller, more and less advantaged groups. For example, in early 1997 an outbreak of ethnic violence in West Kalimantan between indigenous Dayaks and immigrant Madurese resulted in hundreds of deaths.

Three kinds of religious difference have been politicized in independent Indonesia. First, many Muslims and Christians are suspicious of one another. In colonial times, the small Christian minority was a relatively privileged group, more trusted by the Dutch and provided with more opportunities for modern education and employment. This gave them advantages over other groups, and is visible today in the disproportionate number of Christians who occupy high positions in the government and private sector. Many Muslims believe that Christian leaders conspire with each other and with syncretic Muslims to maintain their hold on these positions. They also believe that Christian proselytization, aided by foreign missionaries, is a serious threat to the Muslim community. For their part, many Christians fear that Muslims want to replace the current pan-religious constitution with an Islamic state, in which non-Muslims would be at best second-class citizens.

Second, there has been a sharp cleavage between syncretic and orthodox Muslims. Many syncretic Muslims identify with Javanist rather than

Islamic social and political beliefs and values, and are convinced that orthodox, especially modernist, Muslims are determined to "Arabize" Javanese culture. Orthodox Muslims tend to be dismissive of the syncretists, claiming that they have a poor understanding of their own religion or, alternatively, that they are trying to turn Hindu-Javanist philosophy (or superstitions) into a religion. Many Muslims also see the syncretists as pawns of the Christians, and indeed of Western governments, whose goal is to prevent Muslims from obtaining political power.

Third, Muslim modernists and traditionalists are political opponents. Urban, Western-educated modernists tend to regard themselves as more advanced, in religious as well as social and cultural terms, than the rural traditionalists, educated in Koranic schools. As a result, many modernist leaders claim, in the style of a Leninist vanguard, that they alone can express political views of the whole Muslim community. Traditionalists, on the other hand, resent what they see as the arrogance of modernist leaders and oppose the modernists' attempt to impose their particular interpretation of Islamic social and political philosophy both on the rest of the Islamic community and on Indonesian society as a whole.

All three of these religious cleavages have taken clear organizational form throughout the independence period. Muhammadiyah, the largest social and educational organization of Indonesian Muslim modernists (currently claiming over 20 million members), was founded in 1912. In response, traditionalists founded Nahdlatul Ulama (The Awakening of Traditional Religious Teachers) in 1926; it currently claims over 30 million members. There are also national-level organizations for both Protestants and Catholics. Syncretism is not an accepted religion, but an association represents the interests of Javanist spiritualist movements.

Indonesia's first political party system was organized in the 1940s primarily along religious and secondarily along class and cultural/regional lines. The four largest parties in the 1955 parliamentary election (the only free election in Indonesian history) were: the PNI (*Partai Nasional Indonesia*, or the Indonesian National Party), identified primarily with upper class syncretic Muslim Javanese; Masyumi (*Majelis Syuro Muslimin Indonesia*, or the Consultative Council of Indonesian Muslims), led predominantly by non-Javanese modernist Muslims; Nahdlatul Ulama, led by Javanese traditionalist Muslims; and the PKI (*Partai Komunis Indonesia*, or the Indonesian Communist Party), supported primarily by lower-class syncretic Muslims. The PNI, the largest of the four, received nearly 21 percent of the vote, while the smallest, the PKI, won over 16 percent. Most Christians voted for the PNI, the PKI, or the much smaller Protestant and Catholic parties. The PNI, the PKI, and Nahdlatul Ulama all received three-quarters or more of their votes from the two electoral districts of east and central Java, which represented just half of the voting population of Indonesia. Masyumi won only one-fourth of its votes in east and central Java, with the remaining three-quarters coming from districts inhabited mostly by groups other than the Javanese.[8]

The remnants of this party system are visible today in the two legal nongovernmental parties still permitted to contest elections. The PPP (*Partai Persatuan Pembangunan*, or the Development Unity Party) is a fusion of the Islamic parties, while the PDI (*Partai Demokrasi Indonesia*, or the Indonesian Democratic Party) incorporates the old PNI, two small nationalist parties, and the two Christian parties. The PPP and the PDI have become only minor players. At best they are very imperfect representatives of the religious, class, and regional communities for whose support they continue to compete, but under tightly restricted conditions.

Racial conflict has taken less explicit institutional form than has competition among religious or even regional groups. Sino-Indonesians, as individuals and organizationally, had some visibility in politics and government in the early years after independence, and a Sino-Indonesian political party managed to win 0.5 percent of the vote (one seat) in the 1955 parliamentary election.[9] In general, however, and especially since the mid-1960s, Sino-Indonesians have not participated directly or openly in either partisan politics or government. Many, perhaps most, indigenous Indonesians regard them as a pariah class, "foreigners" (regardless of their actual citizenship status) still loyal to China who have come to Indonesia only to make money. Breakdowns of law and order in Indonesia are often either caused or accompanied by the venting of anger toward Sino-Indonesians, in the form of attacks on Sino-Indonesians and destruction and looting of their property.

In response to this hostility, Sino-Indonesians have sought personal and communal security primarily by covertly giving money to powerful indigenous individuals and groups. In the 1950s and early 1960s, many Sino-Indonesians supported the Indonesian Communist Party, a rising force with ties to communist China. In the 1990s, they fund generals and high officials in the New Order government, although they also maintain connections with the PDI and other organizations and individuals opposed to militant Islam. This link is strengthened by the fact that many Sino- Indonesians are Christian.

Finally, the perceived racial difference between Melanesians/Papuans

---

8. Herbert Feith, *The Decline of Constitutional Democracy in Indonesia* (Ithaca, N.Y.: Cornell University Press, 1962), chap. 9.

9. The organization was Baperki (Consultative Council on Indonesian Citizenship). See Feith, *The Decline of Constitutional Democracy in Indonesia*, p. 435.

and other Indonesians is a factor that intensifies the sense of cultural distinctiveness of many eastern Indonesians, particularly the inhabitants of Irian Jaya. Many Melanesian- and Papuan-speakers believe that they are disdained as backward, even primitive, by western Indonesians. In Irian Jaya, pro-independence nationalists in the OPM (*Organisasi Papua Merdeka,* or the Free Papua Organization) base their demand for independence primarily on this perceived racial difference. Western Indonesians, on the other hand, define political Indonesian-ness not racially or linguistically but as a product of centuries of commonly experienced Dutch colonial rule. Some western Indonesians do in fact condescend to the Melanesians and Papuans, but many more are hardly conscious of the existence of their much less numerous, poorer, and geographically distant fellow citizens. Most western Indonesians therefore tend to accept uncritically whatever explanation the government offers for its repressive actions toward Irianese and other rebellious people in the east, such as the East Timorese.

Ethnic Conflict Management Before 1965

COLONIALISM AND NATIONALISM

As a modern nation-state, Indonesia is an indirect product of a long period of Dutch colonialism, starting with the first contact at the end of the sixteenth century, including a brief Japanese interregnum during World War II, and ending with the transfer of sovereignty to independent Indonesia at the end of 1949.[10] Colonial rule has had important effects on the management of ethnic conflict in the independence period.

Dutch colonialism literally created a state—both establishing the framework of modern administrative institutions and defining the territory and peoples it encompassed—that was to emerge in 1950 as the Republic of Indonesia. Indonesia is thus different from the contemporary mainland Southeast Asian states of Burma, Thailand, Vietnam, and even Malaysia, whose ethnic cores of Burmans, Thais, Vietnamese, and Malays predate the colonial state. It is more like the Philippines, where many territorially based ethnic groups were united by Spain. In Indonesia, however, the period of intense Dutch rule was briefer and had a shallower cultural impact than was the case in the Philippines, which endured centuries of Catholicization and Hispanicization (followed by decades of intense Americanization).

---

10. The best general account is M.C. Ricklefs, *A History of Modern Indonesia Since c. 1300* (Stanford: Stanford University Press), 1993.

Before the Dutch arrived, the peoples of the Indonesian archipelago interacted with each other through trade and other relations, and were variously influenced by outsiders from India, China, the Middle East, and Europe. Large traditional states, centered in Java, Sumatra, and Sulawesi, also existed, but were much more limited in extent than today's Republic of Indonesia. Dutch control gradually expanded during the seventeenth and eighteenth centuries, but it was only in the last quarter of the nineteenth century and the first decade of the twentieth that the basic structure of a modern bureaucratic state was put in place from one end of the archipelago to the other. Even then, in remote areas such as western New Guinea (Irian Jaya), the Dutch presence was minimal.

To staff the new state, called Netherlands India, the Dutch provided Western-style education to a select group of Indonesians, initially the children of traditional rulers, Christians, and other minorities from many parts of the colony. In short order, by the end of the second decade of the twentieth century, a small but significant portion of this new social group of Western-educated Indonesians had begun to think of themselves as the leaders of a nationalist movement whose ultimate goal was to capture the Dutch-created state.[11] In 1928, youth leaders from many parts of the archipelago met in the colonial capital to declare their allegiance to *satu nusa, satu bangsa, satu bahasa* (one homeland, one nation, one language).

The language they chose was Malay, a regional lingua franca in common use for centuries among traders, but the first language of very few Indonesians.[12] Renamed *bahasa Indonesia* (the Indonesian language), Malay became the primary language of anti-Dutch resistance and, after independence, the linguistic medium through which a modern Indonesian culture was built. Since the early 1950s, almost all public and private education, from elementary through tertiary level, has been in Indonesian. Most government and modern private-sector business is conducted in Indonesian, which is also the language of most newspapers, magazines, and books. In such a diverse country, without a prior history as a single society, it is hard to overestimate the importance for national unity of a language that is simultaneously common to its citizens, does not favor any one ethnic group, and erects a barrier between them and most of the outside world.

---

11. Robert Van Niel, *The Emergence of the Modern Indonesian Elite* (The Hague and Bandung: W. van Hoeve, 1960).

12. On the early development of the Indonesian language, see Ahmat B. Adam, *The Vernacular Press and the Emergence of Modern Indonesian Consciousness (1855–1913)* (Ithaca, N.Y.: Cornell Southeast Asia Program, 1995).

The role of *bahasa Indonesia* in creating national unity must be seen, however, in the context of what happened between 1928 and 1950.[13] For most of the 1930s, nationalism was repressed and its leaders were sent to jail or exile on remote islands, including the notorious malaria-infested prison camp at Boven Digul in southwestern New Guinea. (For many Indonesians today, Irian Jaya is irrevocably a part of Indonesia because of the suffering of early nationalists at Boven Digul.) During the Japanese occupation, most of these leaders were freed and allowed, within limits, to promote nationalist ideas. They included the charismatic half-Javanese half-Balinese syncretic Muslim engineer Sukarno and the highly intellectual modernist Muslim Sumatran economist, Mohammad Hatta, later to become first president and vice-president, respectively, of the Republic of Indonesia.

On August 17, 1945, two days after the Japanese surrender in the Pacific, Sukarno and Hatta declared independence in the name of the Indonesian people. Four years of revolution followed, marked by the spontaneous creation of armed guerrilla movements in many parts of the archipelago; the formation of a national army and civilian government, both of which were divided internally and in almost constant conflict with each other; the return of the Dutch, one of whose primary tactics was the creation of puppet states in regions they controlled; periods of negotiation and compromise followed by renewed hostilities; U.S. diplomatic intervention on behalf of the nationalists; the transfer of sovereignty in late 1949 from the Dutch to a federal Republic of the United States of Indonesia, comprising the Sukarno-Hatta-led nationalist Republic of Indonesia plus the Dutch-created states; and the absorption in 1950 of the federal states into the nationalist republic.

These events, like the American Revolution of 1776–82, forged a new national consciousness on the part of those who experienced it. In terms of ethnic relations, most politically aware members of most cultural/ regional groups came during the revolutionary period to identify the new Indonesian nation, not their particular group, as the ultimate or sovereign political community to which they would give their loyalty. Exceptions included some Acehnese, motivated by a powerful mix of ethnic pride and Islamic piety, some South Moluccan Christians fearful of incorporation into a majority Muslim state, and all Irianese, whose territory continued to be held by the Dutch until 1962.[14] Unfortunately, the revolution

---

13. The classic study of this period is George McT. Kahin, *Nationalism and Revolution in Indonesia* (Ithaca, N.Y.: Cornell University Press, 1952).

14. The 1949 agreement transferring sovereignty from the Netherlands to Indonesia did not include West New Guinea, which was left for future negotiations. The Dutch

did not resolve the question of the relationship between religion and the state, which has continued to disrupt national political life. Nor, despite the essentially non-ethnic character of the concept of Indonesian nationality (one homeland, one nation, one language), did it resolve the question of the relationship of Sino-Indonesians and Melanesians/Papuans to the Indonesian nation.

In addition to its role in creating the state that Indonesians turned into a nation, Dutch colonialism left four important specific legacies. First, unlike British India or the American Philippines, the Dutch colonial state was a heavily bureaucratic system that provided indigenous politicians with few opportunities to participate in the political process through elections and legislatures. Therefore, before independence, few nationalist politicians learned how to negotiate and compromise on ethnic or other issues.

Second, the Dutch bureaucratic apparatus was itself weak, both in the types of policies and programs it was capable of formulating and implementing and in the number of Indonesians it trained to assume high-level positions after independence. To an independent Indonesian government committed to social change, the state bureaucracy was more a hindrance than a help.

Third, the Dutch did not provide an appropriate model of central-regional bureaucratic relations for an ethnically diverse archipelagic nation-state. The colonial government prior to 1942 was highly centralized. To make matters worse, during the revolution the Dutch tried to reimpose their rule through a federal system of autonomous regions. While some type of federalism is probably the most suitable governmental structure for Indonesia, the association of federalism with Dutch puppet states made the idea anathema to nationalists. It remains unacceptable today.

Finally, it was in Netherlands India that the term "plural society" was coined to describe ethnic relations under colonialism.[15] In this racially defined caste system, Dutch governors and European big businessmen were at the top, with Chinese traders and medium-scale entrepreneurs in the middle, and the great masses of Indonesians, mostly farmers and laborers, at the bottom. The independence revolution and its aftermath expelled the Dutch and most other Europeans, replacing them, at least in government and politics, with Indonesians. But it did little to change the

---

proceeded to build up their presence in the territory until they were forced out in 1962 by a combination of Indonesian military and U.S. diplomatic pressures.

15. J. S. Furnivall, *Netherlands India: A Study of Plural Economy* (Cambridge: Cambridge University Press, 1939).

status of the Chinese as a group both apart from indigenous Indonesians and in control of much of the modern economy.

Ethnic Conflict Management under Representative Democracy, 1950–59, and Guided Democracy, 1959–65

From 1950 to 1965, Indonesia was governed by two regimes with fundamentally different approaches to ethnic conflict management. The basic principle of the representative democratic regime was to allow ethnic and other interests to express themselves through an open political system, in which parties competed in elections for seats in parliament, and governments were formed on the basis of parliamentary majorities.[16] The underlying assumption in this system was that ethnic and other demands would be articulated through the party system and conflicts would be settled through negotiation and compromise in the parliament.

In the Indonesian case, representative democracy had some successes. One example was the creation of a public education system designed to equalize opportunity to enter the modern world and to extend the national political culture to all citizens, through the Indonesian language and civics instruction.[17] This policy was continued under Guided Democracy but only fully realized in the 1970s, when the government for the first time earned enough revenue to build and staff schools throughout the archipelago. In general, however, the representative democratic system could not resolve the two major ethnic-related issues of the day: the relationship between Islam and the state, and the division of state authority between the center and the regions.

On the first issue, a constitutional assembly elected in 1955 came to a stalemate in 1959 when neither Masyumi, the main proponent of an Islamic state, nor the syncretic Muslim and non-Muslim parties, the main proponents of a pan-religious state, could find a middle ground.[18] On the second, a 1957 law devolved substantial authority to the provinces and districts, but was quickly superseded by local military-led rebellions in several regions.[19] The rebels were not separatists, but they demanded

---

16. See Feith, *The Decline of Constitutional Democracy in Indonesia*.

17. C.E. Beeby, *Assessment of Indonesian Education: A Guide in Planning* (Wellington: Oxford University Press, 1979).

18. Daniel S. Lev, *The Transition to Guided Democracy: Indonesian Politics 1957–1959* (Ithaca, N.Y.: Cornell University Modern Indonesia Project, 1966).

19. John D. Legge, *Central Authority and Regional Autonomy in Indonesia: A Study in Local Administration 1950–1960* (Ithaca, N.Y.: Cornell University Press, 1961).

changes in the armed forces command structure, the distribution of power between the central and regional governments, and central government policies discriminating against regions outside Java whose income was derived primarily from exports. The rebels were ultimately overcome by force, strengthening the national political position of the central armed forces leadership and of President Sukarno, with whom the armed forces were allied.

The parliamentary system was not well equipped to deal with these problems. First, the party system was politically weak. Its four major and many minor parties, divided along both ethnic and class lines, were unable to form lasting coalitions that might have provided a measure of executive strength and political stability. Second, the regime itself had little legitimacy because its institutions were borrowed from Europe. Since few party leaders had significant experience with or deep commitment to parliamentary politics, they were easily attracted to extra-parliamentary movements and solutions. Third, there was no place in the parliamentary system for either an activist president (the presidency being only a ceremonial office) or a politicized military (which was expected to take orders from a civilian and partisan minister of defense). From the early 1950s, both President Sukarno and military leaders continuously undermined the parliamentary leaders' efforts to find solutions to ethnic and other conflicts. Finally, the weakness of the bureaucracy was itself a major obstacle to effective management of ethnic conflict. It was easier for parliamentarians to pass a law than it was for ministry officials to implement it, and the former was generally far from easy.

In July 1959, President Sukarno, in alliance with the central leadership of the armed forces, decreed a return to the revolutionary constitution of 1945, under which the president was the dominant actor in the political system. Sukarno labelled his new regime Guided Democracy (the Indonesian term is *Demokrasi Terpimpin*, which translates more accurately as Democracy with Leadership) to indicate his intention to provide the leadership that had been lacking in the parliamentary system. Although Sukarno did not have unlimited power, the system was in essence a presidential dictatorship.[20]

Under Guided Democracy, Sukarno tried to deal with the demands of ethnic and other groups through a combination of coercion, persuasion, and co-optation. Applying *force majeure*, he settled, but only temporarily, the two most important ethnic-related conflicts in the 1950s: the relationships between Islam and the state and between regional rebels and the

---

20. Herbert Feith, "Dynamics of Guided Democracy," in Ruth McVey, ed., *Indonesia* (New Haven, Conn.: HRAF Press, 1963), pp. 309–409.

center. The decree returning to the Constitution of 1945 was itself an explicit rejection of the Islamic state, and in 1960 Masyumi, the political party most closely identified with the Islamic state idea (and also with regional rebels in Sumatra and Sulawesi), was banned. The regional rebels were defeated militarily. Other groups, such as traditional Muslims, syncretic Muslim nationalists, Christians, and communists, were both persuaded, through Sukarno's great skills as an orator and symbol-wielder, to accept Guided Democracy, and co-opted by being given status and a measure of influence within the regime.

As a form of government seeking to solve national problems, Guided Democracy had two fundamental weaknesses. First, it was not institutionalized as a system, and thus depended heavily on Sukarno's personal capacities and judgments for day-to-day decisions. From the mid-1950s until the end of Guided Democracy in 1965, much of the president's energy was taken up by two international campaigns: first, the ultimately successful struggle to win control over Dutch-ruled West New Guinea, and then, the quixotic crusade against the formation of Malaysia. These campaigns exacted high prices in terms of domestic economic growth and international good will. Second, Sukarno's two principal organized supporters, the army and the communist party, had been sworn enemies since the revolution. In the late 1950s, Sukarno was closest to the military. By the mid-1960s, however, he was turning more and more to the communist party, by that time the only political party capable of mobilizing mass support, as a counterweight to the army. It was only a matter of time before open conflict erupted between the army and the communists.

The break came in the early morning of October 1, 1965, when six senior army generals were kidnapped and assassinated by junior officers and soldiers of the presidential palace guard together with members of the communist party's youth organization. The assassinations were followed by an anti-communist pogrom, the repudiation of Sukarno, and the takeover of the government by the army, under the leadership of Major General Suharto. On March 11, 1966, President Sukarno signed an executive order effectively transferring power to Suharto. In March 1967, Suharto was named acting president by the People's Consultative Assembly, and in March 1968, he assumed the title of president, which he has held ever since.

The New Order, 1966–97

President Suharto's New Order is an authoritarian regime: the political actions of its ruler and his subordinates are in the final analysis arbitrary, based on personal control of the means of coercion and unconstrained by a system of laws. The regime consists of five main players and groups of players: a strong president who totally dominates the political process; armed forces, particularly the army, that constitute the president's principal organized power base; a strengthened civilian bureaucracy, which implements presidential policies in the country; a predominantly Sino-Indonesian business class, which generates wealth, part of which is redistributed through the political process; and foreign and international corporations, banks, and governments, which also supply wealth to Indonesia that is redistributed through the domestic political process.

GENERAL POLICIES

At the most general level, Suharto and other New Order leaders have chosen to deal with social conflict of all kinds through a political strategy that combines elements of coercion, persuasion, exchange, and co-optation. Adoption of this general strategy has had profound implications for ethnic conflict management. The regime has also adopted specific policies designed to contain or counter cultural/regional, religious, and racial conflict. The strengths and weaknesses, or successes and failures, of these specific policies must be seen in the context of the government's larger strategy of governance.

COERCION.   Arbitrary use of the means of coercion is the hallmark of any authoritarian regime, but there is variation in the degree of centralized control of coercion and the frequency, intensity, and pervasiveness (in relation to other instruments of power) of its use. The New Order army, in contrast to its representative democracy and Guided Democracy predecessors, is a well-disciplined organization whose officers do not challenge the orders of their superiors.[21] This hierarchy was for the most part constructed and has been maintained by President Suharto, who, though retired from the military for many years, is still closely involved in military promotions and appointments. The president appears to prefer other means to obtain compliance and to turn to coercion as a last resort, although force has often been the first instrument applied to solve a problem.

For example, the New Order was born in blood, with the slaughter of hundreds of thousands of communists and the incarceration of tens of

---

21. Ulf Sundhaussen, *The Road to Power: Indonesian Military Politics 1945–1967* (Kuala Lumpur: Oxford University Press, 1982).

thousands more from the mid-1960s to the late 1970s.[22] The government has put down student protests and labor uprisings on many occasions, and in the mid-1980s, even ordered army special forces to execute common criminals vigilante-style, without trial or even arrest. It employed coercion against opposition politicians and even ordinary voters in every parliamentary election from 1971 through 1992, in order to ensure that its own political party, Golkar (*Golongan Karya*, or Functional Groups) won an absolute majority of the popular vote. In 1996 it forcibly ousted Megawati Sukarnoputri, daughter of Indonesia's first president, from her position as head of the PDI. When Megawati refused to vacate party headquarters in central Jakarta, troops masquerading as PDI members stormed the building, sparking an urban riot that ended with five dead, almost one hundred and fifty wounded, and many buildings burned.[23]

Coercion has also been used to manage ethnic conflict. In Aceh, independence movements in the 1970s and 1990s were brutally crushed by army special forces, resulting in several thousand deaths.[24] East Timor was invaded by the Indonesian army in 1975, after a Timorese group declared independence from Portugal.[25] Over the next several years, an estimated 200,000 East Timorese lost their lives as a direct and indirect result of the Indonesian invasion and occupation. Many tens of thousands were killed in the initial invasion, many more pro-independence Timorese guerrillas and sympathetic villagers were executed, and thousands more starved to death as government resettlement policies denied sources of food to the guerrillas.

In Irian Jaya, tribal leaders were forced by the military to accept Indonesian sovereignty in the United Nations–mandated "Act of Free Choice" in 1969.[26] Since then, periodic uprisings by Irianese connected to the OPM have been put down by force. In 1996 alone, there were two incidents of kidnapping by OPM guerrillas, one of which involved several

---

22. Robert Cribb, ed., *The Indonesian Killings of 1965–1966: Studies from Java and Bali* (Clayton, Victoria, Australia: Monash University Centre of Southeast Asian Studies, 1990).

23. *Far Eastern Economic Review*, August 8, 1996, pp. 14–16.

24. Tim Kell, *The Roots of Acehnese Rebellion, 1989–1992* (Ithaca, N.Y.: Cornell Modern Indonesia Project, 1995).

25. For the early history, see Jill Jolliffe, *East Timor, Nationalism and Colonialism* (St. Lucia, Queensland, Australia: University of Queensland Press, 1978). More recent events are described in John G. Taylor, *Indonesia's Forgotten War: The Hidden History of East Timor* (London: Zed Books, 1991).

26. Robin Osborne, *Indonesia's Secret War: The Guerilla Struggle in Irian Jaya* (Sydney: Allen and Unwin, 1985), chap. 1.

foreigners and was widely reported in the international press.[27] In both of these cases, Suharto chose to use the army to solve the problem.

Armed force was also a prime instrument of choice for the suppression of Islamic militants, called the "extreme right" by the government. Many incidents occurred in the 1970s and early 1980s; in the most spectacular and the most traumatic for the Islamic community as a whole, well over one hundred Muslims were shot down during a protest in the Jakarta harbor area of Tanjung Priok in September 1984. In the 1990s, several social activists and ministers in Indonesia's largest Christian church, the HKBP (*Huria Kristen Batak Protestan,* or Protestant Batak Christian Church), have been detained and reportedly tortured by military authorities in North Sumatra, the HKBP's stronghold.[28]

Sino-Indonesians, physically distinctive, geographically concentrated in the central business districts of most Indonesian cities, and disproportionately wealthy, are a frequent target of popular or mob hostility in Indonesia. Seemingly small and localized incidents, such as the beating of an indigenous Indonesian servant in Surabaya, East Java, by a Sino-Indonesian employer, can trigger protests, looting, and burning as far away as Sumatra. When law and order breaks down for whatever reason, as in a protest against high ticket prices for a rock concert in Jakarta in 1994, Sino-Indonesian shops and vehicles serve as a handy outlet for mass anger. On these occasions, the police and military usually step in quickly to protect Sino-Indonesian lives and property. Government coercion with regard to the Sino-Indonesian problem runs in two directions, however: the same officials and officers who use it against the indigenous majority on behalf of the Sino-Indonesian minority also use it to extort protection money from Sino-Indonesians. While extortion is of course not formal government policy, neither civilian officials nor military officers make any attempt to stop it.

PERSUASION. Though authoritarian, the New Order leaders do not rely entirely on coercion to get their way. They have designed, constructed, and maintained an elaborate set of symbols to justify practices and institutions that channel and contain the demands of social groups. Most of these symbols and the practices and institutions associated with them date from before the New Order, but they have been reinterpreted and repositioned to meet the needs of a presidentially dominated military regime.

---

27. *Far Eastern Economic Review,* January 25, 1996, pp. 26–28.

28. For accounts of these incidents, see Human Rights Watch/Asia, *The Limits of Openness* (New York: Human Rights Watch, 1994).

A prime example is *dwi-fungsi*, the "twin functions" doctrine of the armed forces, which justifies military participation in civilian political life. The idea of *dwi-fungsi* is rooted in the relative autonomy the military had in relation to civilian politicians during the independence revolution in the late 1940s, and also in the struggle against civilian dominance and party intervention in military affairs in the 1950s.[29] General A.H. Nasution, the most prominent army politician of the 1950s and early 1960s, coined the phrase "middle way" to indicate that the Indonesian armed forces were seeking a role more interventionist than the Western model but not dominant as in Latin America and some other developing nations.

In the New Order, the *dwi-fungsi* doctrine has been interpreted to justify many practices and institutions. For example, in the name of national security, an official in the Department of Defense and Security routinely intervenes in the internal affairs of political parties and social organizations. That department maintains a nationwide system of ten territorial commands whose chief responsibility is to conduct surveillance of regional political activities and intervene when necessary. Moreover, active duty officers are routinely appointed to high positions in the state bureaucracy, including minister, director-general, secretary-general, and inspector-general, in departments that have no ostensible connection with military affairs.

In about half of the twenty-seven provinces, the governors are active-duty or retired military officers, and in the other half the vice-governor is from the armed forces. About forty percent of the heads of districts, the next administrative level below the province, are officers.[30] The armed forces also enjoy formal representation of about 20 percent in the Parliament or the DPR (*Dewan Perwakilan Rakyat*, or People's Representative Council), the MPR (*Majelis Permusyawaratan Rakyat*, or People's Consultative Assembly) or super-parliament that elects the president and vice-president, and regional legislatures at both the province and district levels. Retired officers hold many leadership posts in Golkar, where they act under direction from the Department of Defense and Security.

Dwi-fungsi is a central concept in a system of governance that the regime calls Pancasila Democracy. Pancasila, meaning Five Principles, is the core state doctrine of Belief in One God, Nationalism, Humanitarianism, Democracy, and Social Justice. The term democracy is of course borrowed from the modern West, and is intended to convince Indonesians

---

29. On the origins of *dwi-fungsi*, see Salim Said, *Genesis of Power* (Singapore: Institute of Southeast Asian Studies, 1992).

30. Interview with Home Affairs Minister Rudini, Jakarta, February 1993.

(and secondarily foreigners) both that "the people rule" in the most general sense and that the government is responsive to the wishes of individuals and groups in society. As a democracy, the New Order claims to adhere to a constitution, the revolutionary Constitution of 1945. It has held parliamentary elections every five years since 1971, after which it has convened the MPR to choose the president and vice-president for the next five-year term. It has also signed or otherwise indicated its acceptance of several international treaties and agreements upholding principles of democracy and human rights.

The adjective Pancasila in Pancasila Democracy was added to justify, on the ground of indigenization, departures from democracy as practiced in the West.[31] The argument is that Indonesian society is different from Western society and therefore needs democratic practices and institutions tailored to its own needs. *Dwi-fungsi* is one crucial part of the Pancasila half of this formulation. Another is the system of laws and regulations governing social and political organizations, which severely restrict political activity.

A key example of the latter is the law establishing a three-party system, consisting of Golkar, the state party (really just the political face of the armed forces and state bureaucracy), plus the two nongovernment (the word opposition is taboo) parties, the PDI and the PPP. The PDI and the PPP are forced fusions of nine pre–New Order parties, created in 1974 to "simplify" (the government's term) the party system and to make it easy to control. In the mid-1980s, the government pushed the process a step further by making the two nongovernment parties and then all social organizations incorporate Pancasila into their organizational charters.

Another example of an important New Order symbol is SARA, an acronym for the Indonesian words for ethnicity, religion, race, and "among groups," the latter generally taken as a reference to class conflict. The government has used the acronym since at least the late 1960s. It is meant to delineate the most sensitive political issues, those which may not be discussed in public, let alone serve as a basis for political mobilization and action.

What is the impact of New Order symbol-wielding on the management of ethnic conflict? It tightly limits the actions of individuals and groups with different conceptions of political community, or just different views on ethnic issues, from those of the government. At the most immediate level, regional complaints of excessive governmental centralization,

---

31. R. William Liddle, "A Useful Fiction: Democratic Legitimation in New Order Indonesia," in R.H. Taylor, ed., *The Politics of Elections in Southeast Asia* (Cambridge: Cambridge University Press, 1996), pp. 34–60.

Christian complaints of excessive Islamization, or indigenous Indonesian complaints about the growing economic gap between them and Sino-Indonesians are less likely to be voiced publicly. If voiced, they will probably be met with an official accusation that the boundary of permissible discussion has been crossed. This accusation has moral weight because behind it is the whole symbolic structure of Pancasila Democracy—according to state propaganda, a uniquely Indonesian but genuinely democratic form of government in which the military is empowered at its own discretion to suppress individual and group actions that it deems contrary to Pancasila.

To be sure, some Indonesians, including anti-government political activists, see these symbols as mere government propaganda, lies and distortions that carry no conviction. As such, they add little to the state's coercive capacities, the presidentially controlled armed forces hierarchy that possesses ample organization, personnel, and hardware to suppress ethnic-based or other opposition. Many other Indonesians, however, perhaps a majority, probably accept these symbols at something approaching face value. There are several reasons for this, not least of which is a history of successful economic development that predisposes many people—both sophisticated urbanites and uneducated villagers—to accept the political arrangements that have made development possible. Another important reason is Indonesia's relative isolation from the outside world, due in part to the focus on the development of *bahasa Indonesia* as a national language. This means that there are relatively few fluent speakers of English or other international languages who can explain the outside world to Indonesia (or Indonesia to the outside world).

A third reason is the relative success with which the New Order has presented itself as the legitimate heir to the nationalist movement of the pre-war period and the revolutionary generation of 1945 (of which, indeed, Suharto was a member). Within this tradition there are many values, beliefs, and attitudes, not all of which are consistent with each other, and many of which are the product of political manipulation by one government or another. One of the most powerful and deeply rooted of these beliefs is the conviction that in 1928 the founding fathers of the Indonesian nation, as individuals representing all parts of then Netherlands India, together declared their loyalty to "one country, one people, one language." This loyalty was reaffirmed in the 1945 declaration of independence, which claimed as Indonesian all of the previously Dutch-held territory, in the successful opposition to the Dutch-proposed federal union of the late 1940s, again in the defeat of regionalist challenges to central dominance in the 1950s and early 1960s, and finally in the withdrawal of the Dutch from New Guinea in 1962. Most of the regionalist movements were not separatist, but they were so labelled by President Sukarno and the leaders of the armed forces.

The implication of this history for the current management of ethnic conflict is to delegitimize, probably for most Indonesians, the independence movements in Aceh, Irian Jaya, and even East Timor. It is also to raise high the barrier to acceptance of even modest demands for regional autonomy in these three and other provinces. In the 1940s, the Acehnese played a leading role in the Indonesian independence revolution, for example, selling gold to buy the Indonesian air force's first plane. In the 1990s, the Acehnese independence movement called *Aceh Merdeka* (Free Aceh) is generally seen outside the province as a force led by a descendant of the traditional nobility that was massacred by revolutionary forces, who has been able to build a small following with Libyan money and gullible, fanatically Muslim, villagers. Acehnese are typically stereotyped by other Indonesians as backward fanatics. Until recently, few Acehnese have had an opportunity to receive a modern education, and they have been isolated from the more developed North Sumatran province by poor roads.

The campaign for the "return" of Irian Jaya (then West New Guinea) was the central obsession of Indonesian nationalists throughout the 1950s. The fact that the territory was ruled by the Dutch for an additional decade means—in the Indonesian popular mind—that the Dutch had an opportunity to create a time bomb, a pro-Dutch elite that would continue to do the imperialists' bidding. Even more than the Acehnese, ordinary Irianese are stereotyped as backward, indeed primitive. It is thus understandable that a small band of malcontents, still dreaming Dutch-planted dreams, can from time to time mobilize tribesmen angry over some minor and local transgression by individual government officials or corporate executives.

East Timor is a more puzzling case, since it was not a part of Netherlands India, and no national leader in the 1950s or, indeed, up to 1975, claimed that East Timor was or should become a part of Indonesia. Since 1975, the government has introduced a new legitimating theme in connection with East Timor: the idea that a single people long separated by Dutch and Portuguese colonialism have now been reunited. But it has been careful not to push this claim too hard, since most Filipinos, Malays, and Indonesians believe themselves to share a single racial and cultural ancestry. The existence of the independent states of Malaysia, Philippines, and Indonesia is widely recognized as a product of the same European imperialism that divided Dutch West Timor from Portuguese East Timor.

The more powerful metaphor, even though it contradicts historical reality, is that the East Timorese independence movement is separatist.

The government claims, and most Indonesians appear to accept, that East Timorese leaders requested assistance from Indonesia in late 1975, after a Marxist party unilaterally declared independence from Portugal. According to this logic, the pro-Indonesian Timorese leaders are like the Indonesian nationalists of the 1920s to 1940s, the Timorese Marxists are like the Indonesian communists who twice betrayed Indonesian nationalism (in 1948 during the independence revolution and again in 1965), and the Portuguese are like the Dutch. Indeed, the persistence of Portuguese support for the Timorese independence movement is widely taken in Indonesia as proof that the unrest in East Timor is mostly caused by external agitation.

Modest demands for regional autonomy, made by officials or politicians from any province, are met with great suspicion by the center. Certain provinces, such as West Sumatra, South Sulawesi, or Maluku, which have a history of rebellion, are particularly suspect, but there is a strong general prejudice against the devolution of authority from the center. This prejudice is partly interest-based, since the power, status, and even personal incomes of central government officials have grown exponentially since 1966 as the New Order has concentrated policymaking and implementation in Jakarta. It is also rooted, however, in the genuine fear that Indonesia might not survive as a nation-state; this fear has intensified since the dissolution of the Soviet Union and especially Yugoslavia, which is seen as more comparable to Indonesia. In this context, the government's extreme reluctance to modify its East Timor policy is based on a domino theory: if meaningful autonomy is given to East Timor, the center will also have to accede to similar demands from Irian Jayans, Acehnese, West Sumatrans, South Sulawesians, Moluccans, and so on. More extremist leaders will then seize the opportunity to mobilize support, and Indonesia will begin to slide down the slippery slope to its own destruction.

Despite these fears, there is also widespread recognition among policymakers in Jakarta that residents of the regions have legitimate complaints. They understand both that excessive centralization is bureaucratically inefficient and that it is reasonable for people to want to manage their own affairs. In the late 1980s, the home affairs minister (a former army chief of staff), proposed substantial decentralization to the districts and municipalities, the administrative level below the province.[32] In this scheme, the province, historically the level at which rebellions have been mobilized, would become a purely bureaucratic unit, losing even its

---

32. Interview with Home Affairs Minister Rudini, Jakarta, February 1993.

legislature, while the districts and municipalities would be given new policymaking responsibilities, large block grants of funds from the center, and their own tax bases. The proposed changes at the provincial level have been put on hold, but the district/municipality part of the plan is being implemented on a pilot basis in selected regions.[33] It remains to be seen whether this solution will be acceptable to most people in the regions.

EXCHANGE. The capacity of a government to coerce and persuade its citizens is closely related to its ability to generate a continuing stream of income. This income is used to build armed forces and a civil service, to train personnel, and to pay salaries. It is also used to educate the citizenry, to create, maintain, and regulate an economic infrastructure of banks, markets, transportation and communication systems, and to respond to the demands of specific groups in society with policies and programs that enable these groups to produce higher incomes both for themselves and for the government in the form of taxes. Finally, state income may be distributed covertly to particular individuals, key figures in the state and society, whose support for the government is regarded as crucial to political stability.

In all of these respects, the New Order has performed infinitely better than its predecessors.[34] Parliamentary leaders in the 1950s dissipated the windfall profits produced in the region by the Korean War boom and then pursued inflationary policies that slowed the economic growth rate. Sukarno's "Guided Economy" policies—which repeatedly sacrificed economic policy to political, especially international, causes—brought much worse inflation, a negative rate of growth, and a foreign debt that could not be paid. The New Order, by contrast, adopted market-oriented policies that slowed inflation, encouraged domestic and foreign private investment, and stimulated the manufacturing sector without neglecting agriculture.

The New Order government also borrowed heavily abroad, but on concessional terms and for projects that have produced an income stream that enables it to repay its loans. The result was an average 8 percent economic growth per year from the late 1960s through the early 1980s, when a sharp drop in the world oil price, then Indonesia's largest export, combined with a world recession to nearly flatten the growth rate. Since

---

33. Interview with Gunawan Sumodiningrat, Bappenas (National Development Planning Agency), August 1996.

34. Anne Booth, ed., *The Oil Boom and After: Indonesian Economic Policy and Performance in the Soeharto Era* (Singapore: Oxford University Press, 1992).

the mid-1980s, however, new government deregulation policies designed to diversify and expand exports have returned the growth rate to pre-recession levels. In regional terms, Indonesia has been for three decades a full participant in the East Asian "economic miracle."[35]

The government has used its vastly expanded revenues primarily to strengthen the state bureaucracy, including the military, and to improve basic services, such as education, health, transportation, and communications facilities, for the population as a whole. Although the New Order is a military regime, the armed forces have not been particularly favored financially. At just over 200,000 service men and women in a population of nearly 200 million, the army is comparatively small in the developing world. It is also not especially well equipped with modern weaponry, although it is treated much better than either the navy or the air force. After all, the army's main function, once publicly admitted by the armed forces commander, is to maintain domestic order, which has involved the use of infantry and special forces. There has been no perception in Indonesia of either domestic or foreign threats that might require it to develop a strong air force and navy.

The New Order's economic policies have had several implications for the management of ethnic conflict.[36] First, all regional governments, from the province to the village, have been heavily subsidized by the center since the mid-1970s. Most provinces and districts receive at least three-quarters of their budgets as central subsidies (the Special Capital Region of Jakarta is the only province-level government unit that comes close to being self-supporting). Through central government departments, Jakarta has also implemented a wide range of programs that directly affect the local level. Among these are the building of schools and health centers in every subdistrict, the repair of old and the construction of new roads and bridges, including such current massive projects as the trans-Sumatran and trans-Irian highways, and the rebuilding of irrigation systems for rice and sugar cultivation.

Some of these subsidies are determined by formulas based on population, which favor heavily populated Java, while others are based on administrative distinctions, which favor the less densely populated regions outside Java. As a result of these regionally targeted programs, combined with the general macroeconomic policies that have stimulated economic activity throughout the country, most people in most regions

---

35. World Bank, *The East Asian Miracle: Economic Growth and Public Policy* (New York: Oxford University Press, 1993).

36. A valuable overview is Anne Booth, "Can Indonesia Survive as a Unitary State?" *Indonesia Circle*, No. 58 (June 1992), pp. 32–47.

now live better than they did before. The World Bank reports that under the New Order the percentage of the population in absolute poverty has dropped from over 60 percent to less than 15 percent.[37] Although hard evidence is limited, most people in the regions appear to appreciate that they are better off now than they were in the 1960s or 1970s.

Second, economic development, especially when brought by large corporate investors, both foreign and domestic, has been responsible for unrest in several regions. In Aceh, for example, Mobil Oil built a massive liquefied natural gas plant in the 1970s; it currently earns tens of millions of dollars in royalties and taxes, all of which is paid to the central government, not to the provincial government. Many Acehnese object to what they see as Jakarta siphoning off wealth from their natural resource; they also claim that the plant provides few jobs for Acehnese while bringing in outsiders (including many non-Muslims) with undesirable life-styles.[38] In Irian Jaya, the U.S. corporation Freeport McMoRan has built one of the world's largest copper and gold mines, and in the process has seriously antagonized the people living nearby.[39] Like Acehnese, Irianese complain that the revenues generated for the central government by the foreign company in their midst far exceed the annual subsidies they receive from Jakarta. They also claim that tribal lands were seized without proper compensation, that there are few jobs for Irianese, and that the plant both destroys the land and pollutes it.

Large-scale logging in Kalimantan and other islands has aroused criticism from local people, who traditionally have obtained part of their living from forest products. Most of the logging companies are owned by Indonesian citizens, often retired generals (given concession rights for faithful service to Suharto) in partnership with experienced Sino-Indonesian business people. Most industry jobs go to outsiders, and the wood, exported to Japan as plywood, is a major foreign exchange earner. Pollution of local rivers is a serious problem in heavily logged areas. Indonesian law requires that forests be cut selectively and replanted, but there is little enforcement by forestry officials, whose job is to boost exports and who are also very protective of the industry.

Third, the central government's policy of "transmigration" (an Indonesian-coined word, despite its English appearance) has been a major

---

37. Frida Johansen, *Poverty Reduction in East Asia: The Silent Revolution* (Washington, D.C.: World Bank, 1993), p. 4.

38. Confidential interviews with Lhok Seumawe, Aceh, September 1986.

39. *Far Eastern Economic Review*, March 10, 1994, pp. 48–53; Confidential interviews, Jayapura, Irian Jaya, August 1996.

irritant in many provinces. Originally a Dutch policy but vastly expanded under the New Order thanks to large World Bank loans, transmigration is the resettling of poor Javanese and Balinese from their densely populated islands to less populous regions such as South Sumatra, Kalimantan, Sulawesi, and Irian Jaya. The goal has been both to reduce the pressure on the land in Java and Bali and to open up new agricultural land on other islands. The program provides settlers with cleared land suitable for agriculture plus some start-up money and provisions. In many cases, the land has turned out to be much harder to work than expected, and the settlers have soon moved to nearby towns and cities. Local people criticize both the taking of the land, which they claim is done without proper compensation or consideration of indigenous rights, and the unfair competition for jobs in the cities.

The World Bank no longer funds a massive transmigration program; instead the Indonesian government encourages "spontaneous transmigration," meaning migration with little direct government assistance. Spontaneous transmigration has also caused problems, however, especially in East Timor and Irian Jaya, where small traders from South Sulawesi now dominate local markets. In monolithically Catholic East Timor, the newcomers are especially disliked for their Islamic religion (Protestants are also resented) as well as for their sharp business practices. There have been several clashes and other incidents between Timorese youth and the newcomers; in 1995 several markets and mosques were burned.[40]

It is important to note that toward many regional complainants—the opponents of mining, logging, and transmigration—New Order leaders have tended to be rather trigger-happy, using force as a first rather than last resort. One reason for this shoot-first-discuss-later policy is that what happens in the regions ordinarily gets little attention in the national, let alone international, press. Another is that large amounts of money, especially foreign exchange, are at stake. Moreover, in Aceh, East Timor, and Irian Jaya, the government's view is that the integrity of the country is threatened by separatists.

Fourth, market-oriented, capitalist-style New Order development is widely perceived to have given an advantage to the "already strong" (as Indonesians put it) Sino-Indonesians over the "economically weak" indigenous Indonesians. There is indeed no question that Sino-Indonesians possess capital, organization, and entrepreneurial skills that have enabled them to succeed in business. Sino-Indonesians have also had the advantage (a result not of capitalism, but of New Order neopatrimonialism) of close personal links with Indonesian officials, starting with billionaire

---

40. *Far Eastern Economic Review*, October 26, 1995, pp. 22–23.

Liem Sioe Liong's forty-year relationship with President Suharto. Most officials prefer to do business with Sino-Indonesians, who are still not fully accepted as Indonesians and thus are politically vulnerable.

Almost all of the large "conglomerates" (holding companies for many individual businesses) that dominate the modern Indonesian economy at the national level are privately held, owned by Sino-Indonesian families. The major exceptions to this rule are companies owned by the children of President Suharto, which have themselves depended for their success on state favors and links with Sino-Indonesians. Since the adoption of economic liberalization policies beginning in the mid-1980s, the conglomerates have grown rapidly, leading many indigenous Indonesians to conclude that once again the strong have triumphed over the weak.

The reality appears to be more complex, since economic liberalization mainly created export opportunities, which were exploited by foreign investors and smaller domestic companies.[41] The big conglomerates have for the most part stayed with the import-substituting industries, such as motorcycle and automobile assembling, which have been their areas of comparative advantage since the 1970s. Nonetheless, the widespread perception among indigenous Indonesians is that New Order economic liberalization has favored large Sino-Indonesian companies.

One genuinely capitalist development that may help to reduce indigenous hostility toward Sino-Indonesians, or at least to keep it from destroying the Indonesian economy in the post-Suharto period, is the strengthening of the Jakarta stock market. The government has taken an interest in the stock market as a source of investment capital now that the state itself is less flush than when high-priced oil was Indonesia's principal export, and the royalties of foreign oil companies went directly into government coffers. New regulations and improved government supervisory capabilities have enlivened the once-moribund market, which now lists the shares of several conglomerates. When Suharto leaves the scene, there are bound to be populist demands to nationalize the assets of these companies or redistribute them to indigenous Indonesians. But Indonesia's next president (and his challengers) may be discouraged from giving in to these demands because of the consequences for economic stability and growth.[42]

Finally, an important side effect of the New Order's economic development policy has been an extraordinary growth in the number of pious

41. Hal Hill, "The Economy," in Hal Hill, ed., *Indonesia's New Order: The Dynamics of Socio-Economic Transformation* (Sydney: Allen and Unwin, 1994), pp. 54–122.

42. Interview with Syahrir, Yayasan Padi dan Kapas (Rice and Cotton Foundation), Jakarta, June 1995.

Muslims and in their role in modern Indonesian society and culture.[43] This change is in large part a consequence of the expansion of the educational system. Education for all is an old nationalist dream, and was one of the first programs adopted by the parliamentary cabinets of the early 1950s. Until the New Order, however, lack of funds hindered progress. Beginning in the early 1970s, as the first "oil shock" produced windfall revenues for oil-exporting Indonesia, the government spent heavily to build, equip, and staff schools throughout the archipelago. Within a decade, a village school was within the reach of nearly every Indonesian child, and the government began to shift its attention to junior and then senior secondary schools.

One implication of this policy was that millions of Muslim children in villages throughout the archipelago were given an opportunity, unavailable to their parents a generation earlier, to climb the educational ladder out of the village and into modern urban Indonesia. Equally important was the Islamic instruction provided to millions of children. Many Javanese families, as described above, are religious syncretists. Religion is a compulsory subject in all state and state-approved schools, a concession made by Sukarno to the devout Muslim community in the early 1960s and continued by Suharto as a means of vaccinating the young against the appeals of godless communism.

In order to receive religious instruction, first graders must declare a religious affiliation. Syncretist children of course chose Islam, and began a course of instruction in Islamic practices and beliefs that continued as long as they were in school. The result has been that modern Indonesian society and culture are now much more Islamic than they were in the 1950s and 1960s. There are prayer rooms in all government offices, including those of the armed forces, and in many private businesses. Perhaps most important, urban middle-class Muslims say that they no longer fear being regarded as backward villagers if they display their piety in public.

CO-OPTATION. The government has also attempted to control groups through organizational co-optation. The approach is similar to that of the former Soviet Union, though not as thoroughgoing; it is reminiscent of prewar fascist Europe and later Latin American authoritarianism.

Political parties were an early target of New Order co-optation.[44] Although Masyumi, representing modernist Islam, and the Indonesian

---

43. Robert Hefner, "Islam, State, and Civil Society: ICMI and the Struggle for the Indonesian Middle Class," *Indonesia*, No. 56 (October 1993), pp. 1–37.

44. David Reeve, *Golkar of Indonesia: An Alternative to the Party System* (Singapore: Oxford University Press, 1985).

Communist Party, representing lower-class workers and farmers, and several small parties had been banned either by Sukarno or by Suharto, nine parties remained and contested the first New Order parliamentary elections in 1971. Six of the nine represented religious groups: four Muslim parties, a Catholic party, and a Protestant party. None was restricted to particular regions, although one of the Muslim parties was strongest among the Javanese of east and central Java, the other three Muslim parties were strongest in other regions, and both the Catholic and Protestant parties drew substantial support from non-Javanese regions where Christians form majorities or large minorities. The remaining three parties, the Indonesian National Party and two small parties, were nationalist in political orientation.

In 1973 the nine parties were forced to combine into two, the PPP and the PDI. The PPP comprises the four Muslim parties. Some of Suharto's advisers had recommended combining all of the religious parties, to further reduce Muslim political influence, but they encountered strong objections from the Muslim party leaders. The PPP was not permitted to have a Muslim name, although for the next two elections its ballot symbol was the Kaaba, the Islamic shrine in Mecca. In 1984 it was forced to drop the Kaaba, in favor of a star, taken from the state's official Pancasila emblem, and to declare itself an open party, meaning that non-Muslims could also join. So far, however, none have done so. The PDI comprises the three nationalist parties plus the Catholic and Protestant parties. In official government descriptions of the party system, the PPP is said to represent the "spiritual aspirations" of the Indonesian people, the PDI the "material aspirations," and Golkar, the state party, the harmonious joining of the two.

The main purpose of the fusion was to make it easier for the government to limit partisan mobilization; given the decision to hold regular parliamentary elections, this represented the most serious potential threat to Suharto's and the armed forces' hold on the political system. New election and political party laws gave Golkar a predominant position and provided the government with many instruments to contain and control party activities. Election campaigning is limited to a period of a few weeks, and officials have considerable control over rallies and other public campaign activities. Party candidates for the regional and national legislatures are screened by a government committee. Officials intervene regularly in party congresses to make sure that acceptable leaders are chosen.

This system has been so successful that in five parliamentary elections Golkar has never won less than 62 percent of the vote nationally.[45]

---

45. See Blair A. King, "The 1992 General Election and Indonesia's Political Landscape," *Contemporary Southeast Asia*, Vol. 14, No. 2 (September 1992), pp. 154–173.

Moreover, in recent elections it has won a majority in every province (metropolitan Jakarta and Aceh were early holdouts) and almost every district. Despite this relative uniformity, Golkar's percentages are highest in the regions outside Java for at least four reasons: the absence of a credible successor in the PPP to Masyumi, in 1955 the most popular party outside Java; the fear, especially in once rebellious regions, of being considered hostile to the central government; the conscious decision by some regional leaders to use Golkar as their vehicle to obtain influential roles in the New Order; and the greater ease with which local officials can doctor the election results. In East Java and to some extent Central Java and Yogyakarta, traditional Islam is strong, and many voters identify with the PPP. These provinces are also the traditional heartlands of support for the Indonesian National Party, now the mainstay of the PDI. The PDI has also become identified, in both urban and rural areas of Java, as the party of protest for those who feel disadvantaged by government policies or officials' actions.

The government's tight control of the party system has only broken down once: in 1993, after a series of harrowing party congresses, Megawati Sukarnoputri, President Sukarno's daughter, was selected as the national chair of the PDI. The main cause of the breakdown was the inexperience of the recently appointed military leaders Suharto had assigned to "guide" the PDI leadership selection. Tactically skillful PDI politicians took advantage of this, aided by lower-ranking army officers opposed to the growing political influence of Islam. These younger generals were keen to keep the PDI afloat as a credible counter both to the PPP and to the ICMI (*Ikatan Cendekiawan Muslim Se-Indonesia*, the All-Indonesia Association of Muslim Intellectuals), which has become increasingly influential within both the government and the armed forces. In 1996, Suharto corrected his mistake by instructing more experienced senior generals to call a new PDI congress, where Megawati was replaced by a more pliable leader.

Most interest groups are also organized as monopolies in their respective areas of interest, with a leadership selected or at least approved by the government.[46] This is the case, for example, with organizations for labor, farmers, teachers, youth, students, women, lawyers, doctors, engineers, and journalists. The leaders of these organizations receive favored

---

46. Dwight King, "Indonesia's New Order as a Bureaucratic Polity, a Neo-Patrimonial Regime or a Bureaucratic Authoritarian Regime: What Difference Does it Make?" in Benedict Anderson and Audrey Kahin, eds., *Interpreting Indonesian Politics: Thirteen Contributions to the Debate* (Ithaca, N.Y.: Cornell Modern Indonesia Project, 1982), pp. 104–116.

treatment from the state, including funds for organizational activities, in return for political support, in many cases through organizational membership in Golkar. Some of these arrangements are contested—for example, there are competing organizations, unrecognized by the state, of journalists and private lawyers—but most have been accepted with little protest.

In addition to these interest groups, called mass organizations by the government and regulated by a law on mass organizations, there are thousands of private organizations broadly labelled Societal Self-Reliant Institutions or LSM (*Lembaga Swadaya Masyarakat*), a euphemism for non-governmental organizations.[47] Most LSMs are involved in village development work and are careful to avoid confrontation with the government, but others have been created expressly to oppose government policies or to change Indonesian society in ways not in conformity with government policy. Prominent examples are the Legal Aid Institute, active in legal defense and civil rights, the Indonesian Consumers' Institute, and the Forum of Environmental Organizations. Some of these LSMs were founded by religious groups, but for the most part they do not attempt to represent the interests of ethnic, religious, or racial groups.

The government has interfered much less in the affairs of purely religious organizations, such as Muhammadiyah and Nahdlatul Ulama and the Catholic and Protestant churches. There are probably several reasons for this. In general, since religious organizations have stayed out of politics, they are not threatening to the government. The major exception to this, Nahdlatul Ulama, was a part of the PPP until 1984, at which time it declared itself a non-political social and educational organization. Churches have strong international links, and the government may be sensitive to the prospect of protest from abroad. The government has intervened in the selection of the head of the HKBP, the largest Protestant church, but only after the church became socially active on behalf of causes that brought it into conflict with the government.

There are very few organizations in Indonesia representing purely ethnic interests, in the sense of regionally based cultural groups. In the 1950s, some ethnic political parties were formed but failed to win much support. Under the New Order, organizations have occasionally been founded to protect cultural traditions thought to be in decline, but the membership of these organizations has remained limited to cultural specialists who have only a narrow and mostly apolitical agenda.

Why this should be so is a puzzle, given the many cultural groups in

47. Philip J. Eldridge, *Non-Government Organizations and Democratic Participation in Indonesia* (Singapore: Oxford University Press, 1995).

Indonesia, their regional concentration (which should facilitate organization), the strong sense of ethnic solidarity within most groups, and the general pattern of suspicion or antagonism toward other groups. Two reasons may be the general sense that ethnic-based organization is un-Indonesian, combined with the availability of other outlets such as ecclesiastical organizations, both secular and religious political parties, and now the patron-client system of the state bureaucracy. For many non-Javanese ethnic groups, or at least their educated elites, Golkar—the political face of the state bureaucracy—is a main vehicle for representation.

SPECIFIC POLICIES

In addition to general policies of coercion, persuasion, exchange, and co-optation designed to maintain control over society, the New Order government has adopted a number of specific policies toward cultural/regional, religious, and racial groups.

POLICIES TOWARD CULTURAL/REGIONAL GROUPS. The New Order's cultural policy is reminiscent of the cultural policies of the former Soviet Union and other multiethnic communist countries. Ethnic difference is recognized, indeed celebrated, in the arts. Indonesian culture is said to be the combined "peak achievements" of the various regional cultures, and is supported in various ways. Regional artists and performers are subsidized by the provincial governors. They are brought out to entertain visiting dignitaries, whom they are meant to impress with the great cultural achievements of the region.

In Jakarta, the late Mrs. Tien Suharto, the president's wife, was the prime mover behind the construction of the popular amusement park *Taman Mini Indonesia Indah*, Beautiful Indonesia in Miniature. *Taman Mini* consists of dozens of buildings, museums, and performance halls, designed to look like traditional buildings "from Sabang to Merauke," that is, from one end of the archipelago to the other. There is also a Jakarta Arts Center, supported by the city government, which has an active program of inviting regional artists to perform or display their works. Regional singers and dancers regularly appear on state television. The rituals of Independence Day celebrations and other national occasions always include regional entertainment, plus a flag raising or proclamation reading by someone dressed in a Timorese or Irianese costume.

Tourism is of course one reason for the government's attention to the arts. Already a major foreign exchange earner, it is growing rapidly. Government officials recognize the extraordinary drawing power of Balinese culture for foreign tourists, and try to encourage artistic development that will attract tourists to other regions as well. Overall, however, the government's main reason for celebrating and subsidizing artistic culture is that it is a politically safe response to the desire of local groups to maintain their unique and separate identities and to have their collective interests recognized.

As described above, the government also tries to respond to regional interests in more material ways, by giving large annual grants to provinces, districts, and villages, and by carrying out many more centrally directed infrastructure improvement programs. However, it does not allow business people in most regions to establish regular trading networks outside the country. Most trade to and from Indonesia is conducted either through Jakarta's Tanjung Priok or through the port of Belawan, near Medan, North Sumatra, on the Straits of Malacca, and Tanjung Perak, the port of Surabaya, in East Java.

For example, Acehnese who wish to trade with Malaysia cannot do so directly; they must take their goods to Belawan for transshipment. The obvious political reason for this policy is to restrict the connections between a group like the Acehnese, who have a history of rebellion, and Malaysians, some of whom might be sympathetic to Acehnese independence aspirations. (There is indeed a small community of Acehnese in Malaysia.) To the Acehnese business community, however, it is a serious and continuing sore point in their relations with the center.[48]

POLICIES TOWARD MODERNIST ISLAM. For the first twenty years of the New Order, from the mid-1960s to the mid-1980s, modernist Muslim political activists were isolated and persecuted by the government as "extreme rightists." Their demands for specific reforms, such as an improved Islamic court system, Islamic banking, a marriage law based on the Koran, and permission for Muslim girls to wear a head scarf in state schools, were regarded as the opening wedge in a campaign to create an Islamic state. The hostile acts of a few militants, such as an attack on a police station in West Java or the bombing of the Borobudur temple, were interpreted as a broader conspiracy by modernist Muslims against the state.

The reasons for this attitude can be traced to the 1950s, when most modernist Muslims supported the Masyumi political party. Disproportionately urban, Western-educated, and non-Javanese, Masyumi leaders pressed insistently for a constitution that would recognize Islam as the state religion. Several Masyumi leaders also participated in one of the most prominent regional rebellions of the late 1950s, for which the party

---

48. Interviews with Acehnese businessmen, Banda Aceh, 1985–87.

was banned in 1960. In 1965–66, ex-Masyumi leaders plus a new generation of modernist activists supported the New Order, joining the anti-
Sukarno demonstrations and helping kill and arrest communists. Their
expected reward, the restoration of Masyumi, was denied to them by a
military leadership, headed by Suharto, unable to forgive or forget their
past sins. For the next twenty years, Suharto's position and especially that
of a succession of senior military officers seemed unchanged.

In the mid-1980s, Suharto unexpectedly began to embrace some of
the modernists' favorite issues.[49] The long-standing controversy over
girls' head scarves, which had pitted a secular and syncretist Department
of Education against devout Muslim parents of children in state schools,
was resolved in the Muslims' favor. New Islamic court and marriage
regulations were approved. A state lottery opposed by Muslims was
closed. A petition to found an Islamic bank was approved. A Catholic
journalist was jailed for insulting the Prophet Muhammad. The president,
nearly seventy years old at the time, and his family (Mrs. Suharto had
long been rumored to be a Catholic) made the pilgrimage to Mecca.

Perhaps most important, Suharto agreed to the creation of the ICMI,
a quasi political organization headed by his favorite subaltern, Research
and Technology Minister B.J. Habibie. Although Habibie himself had no
background in Islamic organizational life, the actual sponsor of the ICMI
was a coalition of modernist activists. By the mid-1990s, most Muslim
ministers, senior civil servants, and junior officials had joined the ICMI,
and the ICMI leaders were in control of the state party, Golkar. In a
reversal even more stunning than the president's own change of heart,
the new commander of the armed forces and the army chief of staff,
appointed in 1992, were also reported to be ICMI sympathizers.

There are at least two plausible, though contradictory, explanations
for Suharto's sudden shift in policy toward the modernists. One stresses
the growth in the number of pious Indonesian Muslims since the 1970s,
and suggests that Suharto has merely accepted a new political reality. The
other sees the change as a more calculated attempt by the president to
co-opt yet another constituency, and leaves open the question as to how
deep the modernists' support runs in the larger society. Both explanations
assume that modernists no longer advocate an Islamic state, but have
come to believe that they can live a pious life within the framework of
the New Order. Less plausible explanations assert that in old age Suharto
has become more devout, or that he needed to balance declining loyalty
from the military.

---

49. R. William Liddle, "The Islamic Turn in Indonesia: A Political Explanation," *Journal
of Asian Studies*, Vol. 55, No. 3 (August 1996), pp. 613–634.

POLICIES TOWARD SINO-INDONESIANS. Sino-Indonesians have been treated differently from other cultural groups in the New Order. As explained above, most Indonesians regard them as foreigners, even when they speak no Chinese, come from families that have lived in Indonesia for generations, and are Indonesian citizens. This position as national pariahs has had several consequences. On the one hand, it has made them reliable business partners of indigenous armed forces officers and state officials, because they dare not mobilize politically within the country against their patrons, as disgruntled indigenous business people might. It has also created problems for the government, which fears two developments. First is the possible consequence of popular anger among disadvantaged indigenous Indonesians against the alliance that oppresses them. Throughout the New Order, there have been many small- and medium-scale outbursts of violence against the Sino-Indonesians, in which officers and officials have also been targets, and many Indonesians believe that the tension between the indigenous population and the Sino-Indonesians is worsening. The second fear is that some Sino-Indonesians might become agents of Beijing or (less likely) of some other foreign Chinese-dominated government. This was a greater fear in the 1960s and 1970s, when Beijing was seen as an aggressive communist enemy, but it is still a matter of concern.

The New Order's long-term strategy for dealing with these problems is to assimilate Sino-Indonesians directly into the national Indonesian culture. That is, Chinese culture is not considered the equivalent of regional indigenous cultures, whose languages, artistic life, and great historical moments are celebrated within the nationalist political culture. Instead, specifically Chinese events, such as Chinese New Year, may be celebrated, but only in private. Chinese language schools were closed at the beginning of the New Order, and all school instruction must now be conducted in Indonesian and follow a government-approved curriculum. (In many regions, local languages may be used as the medium of instruction through second grade, and are taught as second languages after that.)

In the short term, the government—through army intelligence—keeps a close watch on the Sino-Indonesian community. There is now only one Chinese language newspaper, which is published by the armed forces; the military also sponsors a "liaison" organization to keep the Sino-Indonesians informed of government policy toward them. Its members include both prominent Sino-Indonesians and indigenous Indonesians, mostly retired officers and civilians completely trusted by the military.

No Sino-Indonesians have become ministers or generals, and few have joined the state bureaucracy or the military. There are some Sino-

Indonesian politicians in the PDI (including some prominent supporters of Megawati Sukarnoputri), but none in the PPP (although there is a small Sino-Indonesian Muslim community) or Golkar, at least not in high positions. Several prominent intellectuals and journalists, including a few who work for state research institutes, are Sino-Indonesian. For decades, the Indonesian government did not recognize the People's Republic of China, fearing that the Chinese embassy might organize a fifth column among Sino-Indonesians. The government also keeps a wary eye on the growing number of Sino-Indonesian business people who invest in China.

One of the most important policies toward Sino-Indonesians was introduced after independence and has continued to the present. The informal quota system for admission to the state universities—including the country's most prestigious general universities and technical colleges—keeps small the number of Sino-Indonesian students. In colonial times and even into the first decade of independence, university students were disproportionately Eurasian and Chinese. Currently most Sino-Indonesian students go abroad for university education (and even high school), if their parents can afford it, or study at one of the growing number of private universities in Indonesia. Ironically, those who go abroad receive a superior education; most return better prepared than indigenous Indonesians to compete for good jobs.

The effect of New Order educational policy, combined with the small number of new Chinese immigrants since independence, has been to assimilate the Sino-Indonesians. There are now many fewer Sino-Indonesians who speak mostly Chinese, and many more whose linguistic and cultural world is Indonesian. Even those young Sino-Indonesians who have spent several years studying abroad think of themselves as Indonesian and plan to return home when they finish their studies.

On the indigenous Indonesian side, however, less seems to have changed, for two reasons. First, indigenous Indonesians do not realize how much Sino-Indonesians have become assimilated. Second, the economic gap between the wealthiest Sino-Indonesians and most indigenous Indonesians is perceived to have widened during the New Order, but especially since the mid-1980s. There thus continues to be a very real possibility that indigenous Indonesians will direct more and greater violence against the Sino-Indonesian community.

Conclusions

Western observers rarely see merit in the authoritarian governments that have been so common in the developing world in the last half of the twentieth century. It seems obvious to Western observers that governmental coercion, the policy instrument of choice in authoritarian regimes, is more likely to worsen than to resolve or ameliorate conflict either among ethnic groups or between them and the state.

THE CASE FOR AUTHORITARIANISM

There is nonetheless a case to be made for authoritarianism. Indonesia, in fact, gives us three reasons to pause before recommending democratization as a solution to the problem of managing ethnic conflict, either in that country or generally. The first reason is Indonesia's unhappy experience with representative democracy in the 1950s, when ethnic conflict of two kinds, religious-based and cultural/regional-based, threatened to tear apart the infant republic. Both foreign observers and Indonesian scholars, intellectuals, and politicians disagree over just how serious and fissiparous either form of ethnic conflict was at that time. I am not sure what would have happened had democratic institutions been allowed to continue to develop and not been cut off by Sukarno's alliance with the army in the late 1950s. Indonesians who are opposed to democratization argue that in the 1950s, representative democracy caused more problems than it solved, and that social and cultural conditions in the 1990s differ little from the earlier period. In my judgment, their arguments carry considerable weight and should not be dismissed, as they tend to be, by outsiders and democratic activists.

The second reason is that authoritarianism as practiced by the New Order has involved much more than raw coercion. The New Order has certainly used persuasion, exchange, and co-optation, all important instruments of power in democratic political systems as well. Many Indonesians genuinely believe that the New Order is a "Pancasila Democracy" in which issues of SARA must be dealt with firmly by a strong government. Many are therefore willing to accept military dominance of that government. Many others are apolitical or have only shallow, partially formed, and therefore easily changed political views. Together these two groups may well constitute a majority of Indonesians, though we have no way of knowing for sure.

Economic development undoubtedly accounts for much of the positive support for the regime, as well as the lack of active resistance to it from members of many ethnic groups. This success may itself be attributable to New Order–style authoritarianism, which concentrated political power in the hands of a single individual who, as it happens, chose and stayed with economic policies that have led to thirty years of growth. The economic policy record—in terms of both substance and consistency—of the representative democratic regime of the 1950s does not give one confidence that a similar regime in the 1960–90 period would have been as successful.

The third reason to pause before recommending democratization is that the ethnic conflict management policies of the authoritarian New Order may be gradually transforming Indonesian culture and society, creating a new societal basis on which a future democratic regime can be built. There are three arguments worth taking seriously here. One is the view associated with modernization theory's analysis of European history: that capitalist economic development produces far-reaching changes in culture, social structure, and ultimately political life. If industrialization does not necessarily or smoothly lead to democracy, it at least creates social pluralism—a society comprising many groups with differing interests, particularly business and working classes—which in turn provides a base for political contestation within a democratic polity.[50]

In East Asia, South Korea, Taiwan, and Thailand are exemplars of this developmental pattern. Compared to these countries, Indonesia began its economic development with lower levels of per capita income, education, and industrial infrastructure. Moreover, most of Indonesia's successful entrepreneurs are Sino-Indonesian and thus unable to organize against the government, and even the indigenous entrepreneurs are so far content with their private arrangements with state officials, trading protection and favoritism for a share of business profits. What is important, however, is not Indonesia's current position on the modernization ladder, but the fact that it is steadily climbing upward. If current trends continue, in another twenty or thirty years Indonesia will have a much larger indigenous business community, in absolute terms larger than that of the Sino-Indonesians, who constitute only four percent of the total population.

The second argument in favor of the New Order as a vehicle of social transformation has to do with Islam. The government's education policies—including the expanded number of schools and the requirement to study religion—have unquestionably had a major impact in creating a more pious and, within the Muslim community broadly defined, a more uniformly Islamic culture. At the same time, the government has steadfastly held that all political and social organizations, and indeed all citizens, must subscribe to the official state ideology as the fundamental unifying principle of the nation. In the case of Islam, this means renouncing the aspiration for an Islamic state. If most Indonesian Muslims do not in fact harbor a desire for an Islamic state, it is clear that a critical cultural foundation has been laid for a less fissiparous society and that the New Order deserves much credit for this achievement.

---

50. Robert Dahl, *Polyarchy* (New Haven, Conn.: Yale University Press, 1971).

Third, the government's policies of bureaucratic and political centralization may have created the framework for a new pattern of post–New Order political conflict among the regions and between the regions and the center. Most regional elites have learned to articulate their interests through Golkar and the bureaucratic apparatus: the Department of Home Affairs and the various technical departments with provincial and district offices. In a democratic Indonesia they would be rid of military intervention in both the bureaucracy and Golkar (a great plus from their point of view), but they would have to cope with demands from a free people (a new experience for most of them). In a multiparty system, Golkar might well be able to turn itself into a broadly based party representing the developmental status quo, after the fashion of the Kuomintang in Taiwan or the former communist party in Hungary. From a regional perspective, it would become a multiregional coalition representing the interests of currently pro–New Order groups.

Finally, it is important to remember that behind the New Order's record of successful ethnic conflict management, to the extent it has been successful, are powerful unifying factors that the government controls either partially or not at all. Perhaps the most important of these are the common national language and the memory of the nationalist struggle culminating in the 1945–49 independence revolution. To foreigners who have travelled from one end of the archipelago to the other, it is obvious that nationalist ideals, in the sense of belief in the nation-state conceived by early leaders and realized by the 1945 generation, remain widely shared today. The Indonesian language is of course the means by which that belief is reproduced. More importantly, it provides the common vocabulary with which succeeding generations reassess and renegotiate their relationship to both nation and state.

THE CASE AGAINST AUTHORITARIANISM

A strong case can also be made for the proposition that the New Order's ethnic conflict management policies have failed, and that in many instances the reason for failure can be traced at least in part to the regime's authoritarianism. It is also worth noting that conflict along each of the three dimensions of ethnic cleavage—cultural/regional, religious, and racial—appears to be on the rise.

CULTURAL/REGIONAL CONFLICT. Cultural/regional conflict is of course most obvious in the three rebellious regions of Aceh, East Timor, and Irian Jaya. As of early 1997, Aceh has been quiet, but it was the scene of anti-government mobilization and brutal repression by the army as recently as the early 1990s. East Timor's rebels have never been quiet, and their movement appears to have been on an upward trajectory at least since 1991. With two sets of kidnappings in 1996, unrest in Irian Jaya seems to be worsening as well.

What is most troubling about the regions, however, is the extent to which the factors that are causing growing local discontent are characteristic of the country as a whole, or at least of many provinces. These include transmigration, both governmentally organized (an older problem, but still causing tension in many provinces) and spontaneous (a more important source of current anger), and the business activities of outside (both foreign and domestic) corporations, particularly those engaged in mining and logging.

Local complaints against the corporations are similar from place to place: their profits go elsewhere, they take land without compensation, they give jobs to outsiders, and they pollute the land, water, and air. Moreover, when local people protest, they are arbitrarily arrested or even murdered by the police and army, who many believe are in league with the companies. Under the Suharto regime, these disadvantaged people have little opportunity to voice their interests through Golkar, or even through the state bureaucracy. Their best hope for change would appear to be a policy of democratization combined with decentralization of authority to the provinces (but not to the districts, which are too small and financially weak to be able to negotiate with large corporations or with the central government).

RELIGIOUS CONFLICT. For the first two decades of the New Order, Islamic modernists were the most marginalized religious group in Indonesia. They complained bitterly of their harsh treatment at the hands of the government and stored up painful memories of instances of repression, including the 1984 killing of Muslim protestors at Tanjung Priok. Many modernists believed then and believe now that behind this mistreatment was a Christian conspiracy, led by General L.B. Moerdani, the Catholic army intelligence officer who rose under the patronage of President Suharto to become armed forces commander and then minister of defense and security.

Since the mid-1980s, Suharto has changed his political strategy to incorporate modernist Muslims and many of their religious as well as political interests. This has had two related consequences. First, many modernists have overreacted, seeking revenge against those who they believe repressed them in the early years of the New Order. For example, in 1992–93, they conducted a vocal campaign against Christians in the cabinet, asserting that the claims of the "majority" (meaning Muslims) should prevail over those of the "minority" (Christians). They succeeded in reducing from six to three the number of Christians in the new cabinet, which contains a total of about forty ministers.

In 1995, Amien Rais, an ICMI firebrand and the head of Muhammadi-yah, the principal social and educational organization of modernists, played a major role in turning East Timorese nationalist protests against immigrant traders into a national-level Muslim-Christian confrontation. In 1996, Amien spearheaded a short-lived campaign to open an investi-gation of the Tanjung Priok incident. (After about two weeks of modernist demands, the military commander said there would be no new investi-gation.) The clear target of such an inquiry would have been General Moerdani and, presumably, the "Christian conspiracy" behind him. In early 1997, Suharto forced Amien out of his position as chair of the ICMI's Council of Experts. This was taken as a sign that the president had grown tired of the stridency of Amien's rhetoric on this and other issues.

The second, related, consequence of the new incorporation of Islamic interests is the fearful, even desperate, reaction of many Christians. Chris-tians tend to hear only the shrillest and most communal Muslim voices, or at least to exaggerate the degree to which those voices represent the community as a whole. At the same time, they tend to deny entirely the validity of modernist claims that they were excluded and repressed dur-ing the first twenty years of the New Order. The gap in perceptions between Christians and modernist Muslims is enormous and widening.

The two groups also have a very different view of the impact of democratization. Many ICMI-associated modernists favor democratiza-tion (if not immediately, then at some point during the post-Suharto transition), because they believe they would win power in a free election. Many Christians agree with this assessment. They are accordingly turning for salvation not to democracy but to anti-Islamic elements in the army who might reconstruct an anti-modernist government like the early New Order.

The belief that a Muslim party led by modernists would win a majority in a democratic national election is almost certainly wrong. Ironically, it echoes the hopes and fears of modernists and Christians in the early 1950s, before the first national elections in 1955. As it turned out, Masyumi, the party of modernists at the time, won only 21 percent of the vote. In the first New Order election in 1971, before the Muslim parties were forced to combine into the PPP, Masyumi's successor Parmusi (*Partai Muslimin Indonesia,* or the Indonesian Muslims' Party) received only 5.3 percent. In contrast, the village-based traditionalist Islamic party Nahdlatul Ulama won 18 percent of the vote in both 1955 and 1971, de-spite army intervention on behalf of Golkar in the latter election. None-theless, the interplay of the exaggerated hopes and fears of modernists and Christians may help to prolong authoritarianism, or even to bring about a harsher, more militaristic, post-Suharto government.

RACIAL CONFLICT.   The increase in racial tension in Indonesia is an indirect result of the New Order's economic success, particularly the successful liberalization policies of the late 1980s and early 1990s. As argued above, the real cause of tension is not an actual widening of the economic gap between poor indigenous Indonesians and wealthy Sino-Indonesians. It is rather the general perception of a widening gap among educated indigenous Indonesians and apparently also among the urban lower and working classes. Most indigenous Indonesians also see that prominent officials and officers, including Suharto and his family, have personally benefited from connections with Sino-Indonesians.

The problem is further complicated by the widespread conclusion that the cause of the gap is economic liberalization—that is, a lifting of the previously heavy governmental hand. According to this logic, the obvious cure is a new set of regulations, a reimposition of governmental intervention. This conclusion is reinforced by a powerful belief in Indonesian political culture, rooted in the prewar nationalist movement's conception of Dutch imperialism, that capitalists are inherently greedy and must be controlled by a benevolent populist state.

For the future, the most effective redistributionist policy will probably be continuation of the market-oriented, World Bank–approved macroeconomic policies that have already facilitated thirty years of moderately high growth and steady improvements in distribution. Unfortunately, Indonesia's next government, whether authoritarian or democratic, may have to pay a high political price for the current disgust with Sino-Indonesian wealth and New Order favoritism toward Sino-Indonesian business people. The powerful and ambitious minister of research and technology, B.J. Habibie, together with at least some of his ICMI troops, favors state ownership of high-technology sectors of the economy, such as airplane manufacturing and shipbuilding.

Other ICMI forces and the nationalist/socialist core of the PDI want to use the state to redistribute wealth directly to the poor. The head of the national development planning agency, Ginanjar Kartasasmita, also a putative third president with support from influential retired military officers, is an economic nationalist who would adopt protectionist policies in support of private indigenous business people. It is thus possible that New Order authoritarianism, which established the political conditions for a thriving capitalist economy, may end ironically by creating the political conditions that destroy it.

RECOMMENDATIONS

How can ethnic conflict in Indonesia best be managed in the future? If present trends continue, two related sets of pressures are certain to have a powerful impact on Indonesian society and government. They are simultaneously creating new economic, social, cultural, and political groups while undermining the ability of authoritarian institutions and policies to contain or manage them.

One set of pressures comes from outside Indonesia and has both economic and political dimensions. The economic dimension is the pressure to conform to global free trade orthodoxy, to which Suharto's Indonesia has already acceded. If future Indonesian governments want to maintain Indonesia's economic growth rate, they will have to continue to encourage exports. This entails participation in the world economy on terms set by others, including monetary conservatism, an open foreign exchange regime, and strict limitations on assistance to exporting firms. It also means expanding and upgrading transportation networks and the telecommunications system, from telephones to facsimile machines to electronic mail, all prerequisites for conducting international business in the twenty-first century. Moreover, many more foreigners will come to Indonesia and many more Indonesians will study, work, and travel abroad on a regular basis.

The political dimension is the growing insistence of Western countries that governments in the developing world conform to international standards of human rights and democratic political participation. This pressure has a dynamic force of its own, driven by human rights groups and international nongovernmental organizations with specific concerns such as the environment, women's and children's rights, health care, the preservation of indigenous cultures, and so on. But it is strengthened by its links to economic interests in the developed world, which seek to end the comparative advantage of developing world economies in the use of slave, prisoner, and children's labor and to raise developing world labor costs in general by promoting higher wages, improved working conditions in export-oriented factories, and the formation of independent labor unions.

Both the economic and the political pressures, but especially the latter, are further strengthened by the revolution in communications technology. In Indonesia, activists in nongovernmental organizations across the archipelago now regularly use electronic mail to communicate with each other and with foreign donors and sympathizers. They also have access to on-line foreign and domestic media not under the control of the Indonesian government. The 1996 award of the Nobel Peace Prize to East Timor Bishop Carlos Belo and East Timor nationalist leader José Ramos-Horta is a powerful example both of the new external political pressure and of the way in which modern communications technology reduces the power of the authoritarian New Order to control both understanding and events. Belo and Ramos-Horta, and more importantly the East Timor independence movement, have been substantially empowered at the expense of the Jakarta government.

The second set of pressures on the Indonesian political system is domestic and is driven largely by sustained economic growth. Two groups—indigenous business people and the working class—are slowly emerging to challenge the military and state bureaucracy's hold on political power. One straw in the wind is the unprecedented 1994 victory of Aburizal Bakrie, one of the most successful indigenous businessmen, in a struggle to control the corporatist national association of business people, the KADIN (*Kamar Dagang dan Industri*, the Chamber of Industry and Commerce). Bakrie defeated Suharto's candidate, a retired general and former head of the state oil company and ambassador to the United States.[51] Another straw is the rapid growth in the early 1990s of the SBSI (*Serikat Buruh Sejahtera Indonesia*, the Indonesian Prosperous Labor Union), an independent labor union that challenged the monopoly of the government's own corporatist union F-SPSI (*Federasi-Serikat Pekerja Seluruh Indonesia*, the Federation-All Indonesian Workers' Union). The SBSI was suppressed after a massive labor protest in Medan, North Sumatra, in April 1994 turned into a riot against the Sino-Indonesians. But the number of localized wildcat strikes, particularly against companies producing for export, continues to grow.[52]

Given the impact of these external and internal pressures, the best course for a post–New Order regime to follow, if its leaders want to avoid massive political upheaval and even the ultimate breakup of the country, is democratization of the political system as a whole and decentralization of authority to the provinces. In a highly pluralistic world, with so many different economic, social, and ethnic (cultural/regional, religious, and racial) groups led by educated Indonesians, it is difficult to imagine a long-term future for a political system organized so tightly and controlled so completely by a tiny military elite. Eventually, many newly empowered groups will find this arrangement unacceptable and will make hard-to-deny demands for a greater share of power.

---

51. Adam Schwarz, *A Nation in Waiting: Indonesia in the 1990s* (Sydney: Allen and Unwin, 1994), p. 119.

52. Muhammad A.S. Hikam, "The State, Grass-Roots Politics and Civil Society: A Study of Social Movements Under Indonesia's New Order (1989–1994)" Ph.D. dissertation, University of Hawaii, Department of Political Science, 1995.

Indonesian democratizers and decentralizers are probably best advised to move slowly, however. They should also pay careful attention to the kinds of executive-legislative relationships, party and electoral systems, and local-central arrangements that will aggregate popular demands in ways that ensure both effective representation and political stability. The two pieces of advice go together. Indonesia is an enormously complex society with limited democratic experience, national or local, and even less sense for what kind of democratic institutions might work best in its particular circumstances.

A rapid opening would release a myriad of long-suppressed demands by aggrieved groups; these might destabilize the political system and lead to the reimposition of authoritarian rule. Similarly, a revival of Indonesia's only democratic experience—parliamentary rule with a party system comprising many small parties based in large part on ethnic cleavages and loyalties—is unlikely to produce a state executive leadership strong and stable enough to make and implement the best policies for the country as a whole. Instead of rushing to democratize, therefore, it might be prudent for Indonesian political intellectuals and activists to conduct, through the media already available to them, a grand debate on the executive-legislative relationships, party and electoral forms, and local-central arrangements most suitable for the new democracy to which they aspire.

Chapter 8

Ethnicity and Public Policy in the Philippines

R.J. May

For the Philippines, as for most of the world, contemporary ethnic problems are the product of a long history of the movement and interaction of peoples, particularly in the period since European colonization.

The prehistoric settlers of the Philippine islands were ethno-linguistically diverse, though mostly of a common linguistic stock. Subsequently, there was a small influx of traders and settlers from China and from Malaysia, India, and the Arab world. The latter initiated a process of conversion to Islam, a process that both brought together ethno-linguistically diverse groups and drew a distinction between Muslim and non-Muslim Filipinos. With the coming of Spanish colonialism in the sixteenth century, Muslim identity was reinforced by confrontation with the Spanish colonizers, and a new set of ethnic identities—Christian *indio*, non-Christian *indio*, and mestizo—was created. Spanish colonialism also helped to define Chinese and Chinese mestizo identities, though Chinese mestizo identity progressively blended into the emerging Filipino (Christian *indio* and Spanish mestizo) national identity.

These distinctions continue to compose the four predominant ethnic cleavages in contemporary Philippine society. (See Table 8.1.) First, the "Filipinos" or "Christian Filipinos," people of predominantly Malay stock and Christian religion, constitute around 92 percent of the Philippines population of some seventy million and retain separate subnational ethnic identities (Tagalog, Ilocano, Cebuano, Bicolano, Pampagno, and so on) but in most contexts constitute a cohesive "super ethnie." Second, the "tribal Filipinos" or "indigenous cultural communities" (or Lumads and Highlanders/Uplanders), people of the same ethnic stock, and Negritos, who resisted Christianization and colonial rule and largely maintain their traditional (pre-Islamic, pre-Hispanic) cultures comprise some forty-odd ethno-linguistic groups, representing about 3 percent of the national population, which are concentrated in Mindanao and the Cordilleras of

Table 8.1. Ethnic Composition of the Philippines.

Group	Number[a]	Percentage
Christian Filipinos	65,100,000	92.0
Muslim Filipinos	3,200,000	4.5
Tribal Filipinos[b]	2,100,000	3.0
Chinese Filipinos[c]	400,000	0.5
Total	**70,800,000**	**100.0**

NOTES: [a] These figures are rough estimates based in part on the 1980 Philippines Census, projected onto a 1996 figure for total population.
[b] Other estimates put the figure for tribal Filipinos much higher. See "Ethnographic Survey of Ethnic Groups," *Tribal Forum*, Vol. 6, No. 5 (September/October 1986), pp. 13–16.
[c] This figure is a conservative estimate based on Charles J. McCarthy's figure of "600,000 people, either entirely or partly speaking Chinese dialect at home or among themselves, and observing Chinese cultural manners and social patterns." See McCarthy, "The Chinese in the Philippines Today and Tomorrow," *Fookien Times Philippines Year 1975*, p. 348. Many scholars believe that younger people of Chinese descent are losing Chinese linguistic abilities and cultural affinities.

northern Luzon.[1] Third, Muslim Filipinos (or Philippine Muslims), also of the same ethno-linguistic stock but differentiated over several centuries by religion and the impact of Islamic social institutions, include thirteen ethno-linguistic groups, representing about 4–5 percent of the population, and are concentrated in central and western Mindanao, the Sulu Archipelago, and Palawan. Chinese Filipinos (Filipinos of ethnic Chinese ancestry) and Philippine Chinese (citizens and non-citizens of the Philippines who identify with China rather than the Philippines) constitute a fourth broad group, but relative to other Southeast Asian countries, they have enjoyed a high degree of integration and have not posed a major line of ethnic cleavage. Apart from the Chinese, the main lines of ethnic cleavage in the Philippines have been defined by religion (and in the case of the Chinese, integration was achieved primarily by marriage and conversion to Christianity).

1. For a detailed analysis of who the tribal Filipinos are, see Herbert W. Krieger, *Peoples of the Philippines*, Smithsonian Institution War Background Studies No. 4 (Washington, D.C.: Smithsonian Institution, 1942); R. Fox and E. Flory, "The Filipino People" (map) (Manila: National Museum of the Philippines, 1974); *Tribal Forum*, Vol. 2, No. 7 (September–October 1981), pp. 2–5; and B. Rudy Rodil, "Ancestral Domain: A Central Issue in the Human Struggle for Self-determination in Mindanao," in Mark Turner, R.J. May, and Lulu Turner, eds., *Mindanao: Land of Unfulfilled Promise* (Quezon City: New Day Publishers, 1992), pp. 233–247.

The Pre-Colonial and Colonial Heritage

The early arrivals in the Philippine islands have generally been classified into two principal groups, the Negritos and the Malays. The Negritos were probably the first to settle, and they mostly retreated into the hinterlands following the arrival of the Malays, whose cultures were technologically and socially more advanced. Their descendants include the Aetas of Zambales, the Dumagats of the Sierra Madres, the Agtas of Bicol, the Atis of the western Visayas, the Isinai of Benguet, and the Mangyans of Mindoro. The Malays, who communicated in a variety of Austronesian languages and practiced traditional (or animist) religions, mostly settled along the coast in politically autonomous small communities, termed *barangays*, and are regarded as the "basic stock" of today's Filipinos.

There is archaeological evidence that the people of the Philippine islands were trading with China late in the pre-Christian era, and by the ninth century A.D. the Philippines had become something of an entrepôt for trade north to China and west to India. Chinese merchants had settled in the Philippines by the tenth century; during the Ming Dynasty (1368–1644), China briefly exercised "some sort of nominal suzerainty over certain parts of the Philippines,"[2] and trade and migration from China flourished. By the thirteenth century, extensive commercial relations between the Philippine islands and the Islamic world to the west had developed, and foreign Muslims had established settlements in the south. Within the space of three hundred years, Islam had taken root in the Sulu Archipelago, where a powerful sultanate was established in the fifteenth century; had spread to Mindanao; and was expanding north to Luzon. With Islam came the creation of larger political units and integration, through marriage and commerce, into the wider Islamic community in Southeast Asia.

In 1565, the Spanish arrived as colonists in the Philippines, with a mission to establish commerce and to convert the *indios* to Christianity. Encountering their old religious adversary, the Moro, less than seventy-five years after the defeat of the Moors at Granada, the Spaniards effectively transported the Crusades to Asia. In 1578, the Spanish governor instructed the commander of the first expedition against the Moros in Sulu and Mindanao: "You shall order them not to admit any more preachers of the doctrine of Mahoma, since it is evil and false, and that of the

---

2. Antonio S. Tan, "The Emergence of Philippine Chinese National and Political Consciousness," Ph.D. dissertation, University of California, Berkeley (Ann Arbor, Mich.: University Microfilms, 1970), p. 14.

Christians alone is good. And you shall burn or destroy the house where that accursed doctrine has been preached, and you shall order that it be not rebuilt."[3] Having defeated Filipino and Bornean Muslim forces in Luzon, Mindoro, and the Visayas, the Spanish, aided by Christianized *indios*, embarked on a series of military campaigns against the Muslim south, which continued over the next three centuries. In the process, Muslim and *indio* settlements were destroyed, thousands were killed or carried off into slavery, and the basis for one line of continuing ethnic conflict was firmly entrenched in the Philippines.

Elsewhere, particularly in the mountainous interior of northern Luzon, where Spanish expeditions were sent in search of gold, other indigenous groups also successfully resisted the Spanish incursion. Until well into the Spanish colonial period, the peoples of the Cordilleras of Luzon, collectively referred to as *Igorrotes*, were termed *tribus independientes*.

The Spanish regime, in its dealings with the indigenous peoples, thus created an ethnic hierarchy: at the top were the *Peninsulares* (Spaniards from Spain) and *Filipinos* (initially a term for Spaniards born in the Philippines); below them, in descending order, were the Christianized *indios*, the non-Christianized peoples variously referred to as *infieles*, *paganos*, or more generously, *tribus independientes*, and the Moros. Intermarriage between Spaniards and *indios* created a growing intermediate class of Spanish mestizo. Chinese and Chinese mestizo constituted another sub-group. In time (and particularly after the cession of the Philippines to the United States in 1898 following the Spanish-American War), the Spanish population mostly either intermarried or left. The indigenous population became known as Filipino, a term that was progressively applied also to Chinese as well as Spanish mestizo. But the categories of Moro and *infieles* (which under U.S. administration became "wild tribes" or "non-Christian tribes") persisted, and it is these ethnic identities that pose the major issues in contemporary ethnic relations.[4]

---

3. Quoted in Cesar A. Majul, *Muslims in the Philippines*, 2d ed. (Quezon City: University of the Philippines Press, 1973), p. 68.

4. This paper does not consider questions of ethnic relations among the Christian Filipino population, which have not been a subject of significant political debate. Such questions have received passing scholarly attention. See Cynthia Enloe, *Ethnic Soldiers: State Security in a Divided Society* (Harmondsworth: Penguin, 1980); Hirofumi Ando, "A Study of Voting Patterns in the Philippine Presidential and Senatorial Elections, 1945–1965," *Midwest Journal of Political Science*, Vol. 13, No. 4 (November 1969), pp. 567–586; and F.V. Magdalena, *Politics, Ethnicity and Modernization in the Philippines, 1957–1969*, URC Professional Paper No. 2, Series 1981 (Marawi City: University Research Center, Mindanao State University).

The Philippines.

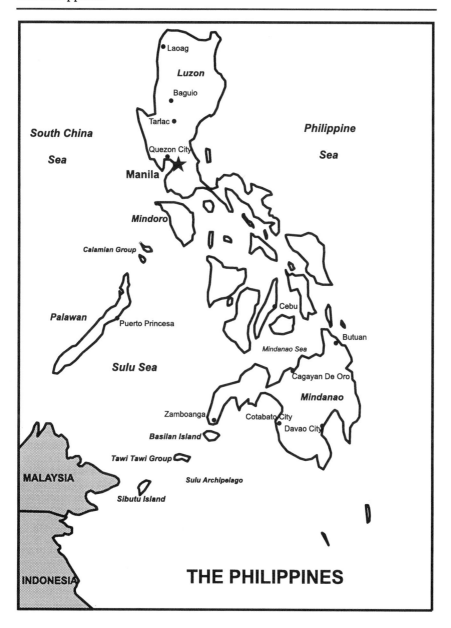

THE PHILIPPINES

Chinese Filipinos and Philippine Chinese

When the Spanish came to settle in the Philippines, the Chinese were already well entrenched among the local population. They were traders, artisans, and skilled workers, and they had intermarried with the indigenous population. The Spanish government saw them as serving a useful role in the colonial economy; as one of Spain's early administrators observed, "the colony cannot exist without the Chinese as they are the workers of all trades and business, and are very industrious and worked for small wages."[5] The Spanish even encouraged Chinese immigration; the estimated number of Chinese resident in the Philippines rose from 150 in 1571 to 30,000 in 1603.[6] By the late sixteenth century, the Catholic Church in the Philippines was encouraging the growth of a Chinese *indio*-mestizo (*mestizo de sangley*) Christian community, from which it hoped to recruit missionaries for its work in China.

However, Spanish attitudes towards the Chinese were ambivalent. The history of Sino-Spanish relations, as one scholar put it, "alternated between tolerance and extermination, the latter policy being adopted every time the Chinese population grew to what was considered a dangerous size."[7] From 1581, fearful of political collaboration between the Chinese and the *indios*, the Spanish administration in Manila segregated the Chinese into the *Parian*, an area outside the city walls and in the sights of the Spanish artillery. In 1603, suspecting an uprising against the Spanish government, the Spaniards attacked the Chinese enclave in Manila, killing an estimated 25,000. Soon after, facing a shortage of skilled workers, the Spanish government again encouraged Chinese migration, but further massacres and deportations of the Chinese continued to occur throughout the seventeenth and eighteenth centuries. In 1686 and again in 1709, the Spanish king ordered the expulsion from the Philippines of all Chinese who had not converted to Christianity. The effect of this, in part, was to encourage further intermarriage between Chinese and Christianized *indios* and to foster the growth of the Chinese mestizo population, which, increasingly, blended with the *indio* and Spanish mestizo populations. Unlike the situation that developed in Indonesia and

---

5. Antonio de Morga, cited in Eufronio M. Alip, *Ten Centuries of Philippine-Chinese Relations (Historical, Political, Social, Economic)* (Manila: Alip Sons, Inc., 1959), p. 12.

6. Ibid., p. 12.

7. Tan, "The Emergence of Philippine Chinese National and Political Consciousness," p. 21.

Malaysia, "the Chinese mestizo in the Philippines was not a special kind of local Chinese. He was a special kind of Filipino."[8]

In 1762 the Chinese supported the short-lived British invasion of Manila. Spanish authorities responded with a further massacre of Chinese and another round of expulsions, which lasted for over two decades. This was the last mass expulsion of the Chinese. However, ethnic discrimination against Chinese persisted in the form of restrictions on movement (though the Manila *Parian* was destroyed in 1790), higher taxes,[9] restrictions on occupation, and discrimination in legal and administrative processes.[10]

From the early days of Spanish settlement, the Chinese had played the role of intermediaries between Spanish merchants and the native population. With the expulsion of many Chinese in 1776 and the restrictions placed on those who remained, there was an expansion of the economic role played by Chinese mestizos: they became provisioners to the colonial authorities and to the foreign community in Manila; they acquired a large share of the wholesale and retail trade in Manila and in the provinces; and they entered the import-export business. Following the opening of Manila to international trade in the 1840s, Chinese immigration resumed and the new immigrants largely displaced mestizos in the wholesale and retail trade. During the eighteenth and early nineteenth centuries, the Spanish administration made several attempts to direct the Chinese into agriculture. In 1804, for example, artisans and those engaged in agricultural pursuits were the only Chinese permitted residency in the Philippines. Such policies had only limited success; but with increased competition in wholesale and retail trade and the progressive shift in Philippine agriculture from subsistence to export production, many Chinese mestizos became landowners and played a major role in the cultivation and marketing of export crops. There was increasing intermarriage

---

8. Edgar Wickberg, *The Chinese in Philippine Life, 1850–1898* (New Haven, Conn.: Yale University Press, 1965), p. 31.

9. In 1741 the population was divided, for tax purposes, into five ethnic categories: Spanish, and Spanish mestizos, who paid no tax; indios, who paid a basic tax; Chinese mestizos, who paid twice the indios rate; and Chinese, who paid four times the basic rate. See Antonio S. Tan, "Chinese Mestizos and the Formation of Filipino Nationality," in Theresa C. Cariño, ed., *Chinese in the Philippines* (Manila: China Studies Program, De La Salle University, 1985), p. 52; and Tan, "The Emergence of Philippine Chinese National and Political Consciousness," chap. 6. The requirement that ethnic origin be stated on certificates of taxation was finally rescinded in 1884.

10. For a fuller account, see Tan, "The Emergence of Philippine Chinese National and Political Consciousness"; and Wickberg, *The Chinese in Philippine Life.*

with the Filipino elite, and Chinese mestizos acquired wealth, education, and social status; in the provinces, they took office as mayors and *gobernadorcillos*. On Negros, the development of the sugar industry in the 1850s brought in Chinese workers, some of whom in time became *hacenderos*, traders, mill owners, and financiers, eventually marrying "the landed native ladies" and becoming "leading figures in the history of the province [Negros Occidental]."[11] Elsewhere, the expansion of tobacco, abaca, indigo, and timber production had similar effects.

These developments paved the way for the emergence of a Filipino middle class that was a blending of *indio*, Chinese mestizo, and Spanish mestizo, drawn together by a common religion and a shared, predominantly hispanic, culture.[12] Towards the end of the nineteenth century, this middle class became a vehicle for Filipino nationalism, and Filipinos of Chinese descent (such as national hero José Rizal) played a prominent part in the revolution against Spanish rule.

Due to substantial Chinese immigration in the second half of the nineteenth century, the number of Chinese in the Philippines rose from around 6,000 to over 50,000. This expansion, and the economic success enjoyed by many Chinese immigrants, sparked a revival of anti-Chinese sentiment in the last two decades of Spanish rule, but without the violence that had characterized relations in earlier years. In turn, anti-Chinese sentiment encouraged the growth of a range of Chinese ethnic community organizations.[13]

Under U.S. rule, policies towards the Chinese were generally less discriminatory, though the early extension to the Philippines of the U.S. Exclusion Act, which precluded Chinese immigration, caused resentment in the Philippine Chinese community, especially insofar as it effectively prevented resident Chinese from moving outside the Philippines and in that similar restrictions were not placed on Japanese immigration. There was also resentment towards a series of economic nationalist measures

---

11. Modesto P. Sañonoy, "The Chinese in Negros Occidental," in Aileen S.P. Baviera and Teresita Ang See, eds., *Chinese Across the Seas: The Chinese as Filipinos* (Quezon City: Philippine Association for Chinese Studies, 1992), p. 72.

12. For a fuller discussion of this, see Wickberg, "The Chinese Mestizo in Philippine History," *Journal of Southeast Asian History*, Vol. 5 (March 1964), pp. 62–100, and Wickberg, *The Chinese in Philippine Life*, chaps. 1, 5; Tan, "The Emergence of Philippine Chinese National and Political Consciousness," and Tan, "Chinese Mestizos"; and Jesus Merino, "The Chinese Mestizo: General Considerations," in Alfonso Felix, ed., *The Chinese in the Philippines*, Vol. 2 (Manila: Solidaridad Publishing House, 1969), pp. 45–66.

13. See Wickberg, *The Chinese in Philippine Life*, chap. 7; and Liu Chi Tien, "The Chinese Point of View," in Felix, *The Chinese in the Philippines*, pp. 205–252.

pursued by various Filipino groups during the 1920s and 1930s, including demands for nationalization (that is, Filipinization) of retail trade. This economic nationalism was embodied in provisions of the Commonwealth Constitution of 1935,[14] which, in its preamble, also made pointed reference to "the Filipino people," rather than, as proposed by some, "the people of the Philippines."

Racial antipathies, instilled during the Spanish period and reinforced by the obvious prosperity and economic power of some Chinese merchants, continued to be manifested in violent incidents, such as the anti-Chinese riots of 1919 and 1924, but generally the Chinese community prospered during the U.S. colonial period, further immigration took place from the 1920s on, and descendants of Chinese immigrants were assimilated into Filipino society.

Following World War II, economic nationalist policies were implemented by the independent Republic of the Philippines in several fields, including nationalization of import trade (1952), retail trade (1954), and the rice and corn industries (1960); adoption of a "Filipino First" policy with respect to certain government contracts; and restriction of noncitizens from certain professions. Also, the annual immigration quota for Chinese, which at the end of the U.S. colonial period stood at 500, was in 1949 reduced to zero. Under the Marcos administration (1966–86), there was support for the "assimilation and integration" of ethnic Chinese, particularly the group of so-called "overstaying Chinese."[15] A series of presidential decrees and letters of instruction in the 1970s lifted the immigration quota to allow "overstaying Chinese" to remain in the country and to facilitate the acquisition of citizenship by Chinese residents; by 1980 some 26,000 had been naturalized. In the field of education, the 1973 (martial law) constitution prohibited the establishment of schools "exclusively for aliens," and the government sought a Filipinization of curricula, teaching staff, and management in Chinese schools.[16] At the same time, without formally abandoning the policy of economic nationalism, Ferdinand Marcos used his executive authority to facilitate and encourage Chinese participation in a range of economic activities. In a 1981 study of Philippine policies towards the ethnic Chinese, it was observed that, as a result of policy changes under President Marcos, the Chinese had moved

---

14. See, for example, Tan, "The Emergence of Philippine Chinese National and Political Consciousness," chap. 9.

15. In 1966 the Bureau of Immigration listed 180,674 aliens, of whom 115,501 were Chinese. See Tien, "The Chinese Point of View," p. 205.

16. There were, in 1973, 154 Chinese schools in the Philippines, with an enrollment of over 58,000.

into land acquisition and development, farming, and other economic activities and occupations, which previously were largely the preserve of Filipinos.[17] Specifically, having been excluded from importing and retail trade, many Chinese turned to import-replacing manufacturing.

Following the overthrow of Marcos, the question of "overstaying Chinese" was raised again in 1988, with Immigration and Deportation Commissioner Miriam Defensor-Santiago (generously) estimating the number of illegal aliens at 100,000. A subsequent executive order gave these people twelve months to register and apply for naturalization, but following a legal challenge the program was suspended.[18]

While the issue of "overstaying Chinese" remains a delicate one, the integration of Chinese into the "native" population has probably proceeded further in the Philippines than in any other country in Southeast Asia. In 1966, in a speech to the Federation of Filipino Chinese Chambers of Commerce and Industry, President Marcos said: "I have Chinese blood in me . . . and I am not ashamed to admit that perhaps the great leaders of our country all have Chinese blood."[19] This is certainly true of his next two successors, President Corazon Aquino and President Fidel Ramos. Racial stereotyping and resentment of the prosperity enjoyed by some Chinese Filipinos certainly still exist—in response to a recent spate of kidnappings, Interior Secretary Robert Barbers was reported as saying that affluent Chinese-Filipinos are easy prey because "they have more money [and] are also easily scared."[20] But having begun the process of cultural and religious integration at an early stage and having established their nationalist credentials during the revolution against Spain, the "Chinese" in the Philippines have been substantially assimilated, and have not been a subject of significant policy concern.

"Tribal" Filipinos

As discussed above, the category of "tribal Filipino" was an artifact of the Spanish colonial period. The term *infieles* described those Filipinos who remained outside the control of the Spanish administration; as a corollary,

---

17. Arturo G. Pacho, "Policy Agenda of the Ethnic Chinese in the Philippines," Ph.D. dissertation, Kent State University, 1981 (Ann Arbor: University Microfilms International, 1984), p. 139.

18. See Theresa C. Cariño, "Issues in Philippine-China Relations," in Baviera and Ang See, *China Across the Seas*, p. 22.

19. Ferdinand Marcos, Presidential Speeches 1978: I, pp. 104–105, quoted in Pacho, "Policy Agenda of the Ethnic Chinese," p. 103.

20. Reuters report, August 25, 1996.

one can scarcely talk of Spanish policies towards tribal Filipinos, except to the extent that attempts to bring such groups under Spanish influence constituted, in themselves, a "policy." At the turn of the century, the United States inherited the categorization of the Philippine population into Christian, Moro, and (other) non-Christian ("pagan") peoples, and in 1901 a Bureau of Non-Christian Tribes (BNCT) was created to take responsibility for the latter two groups.[21]

The BNCT was given the task of investigating the boundaries, languages, social organizations, beliefs, manners, and customs of the "pagan and Mohammedan tribes" with a view "to determining the most practicable means for bringing about their advancement and material prosperity."[22] There was a presumption that the U.S. experience of administering its own "non-Christian tribes" would provide a model for the BNCT, but its first director was of the view that "the policy of the United States in dealing with the American Indian contains little that can be followed in governing backward races here."[23] Specifically, he recommended that "the employment of the reservation system should be avoided" (some were later established, and proved to be short-lived) and that the teaching of English should be pursued. Two years after its establishment, the BNCT was renamed the Ethnological Survey of the Philippines. The task of governing the "non-Christian tribes," however, was left with the secretary of the interior, who attempted to exercise his authority through a number of "special provinces."[24] In the south, the non-Christian tribes of Mindanao and Sulu, including the Muslim communities, were administered by U.S. Army officers until 1913, and policy was generally aimed at integrating the non-Christian peoples under a single administrative system. In the north, where the U.S. administration had been extending political control throughout the Cordilleras, a single Mountain Province was created in 1908, and administration of the region was reorganized so

---

21. In a 1926 decision concerning the Mangyans of Mindoro, the Philippine Supreme Court argued that the term non-Christian referred not to religious beliefs but "more directly to the natives of the Philippine Islands of a low grade of civilization." Quoted in Violeta B. Lopez, *The Mangyans of Mindoro: An Ethnology* (Quezon City: University of the Philippines Press, 1976), p. 107.

22. Quoted in Peter G. Gowing, *Mandate in Moroland: The American Government of Muslim Filipinos 1899–1920* (Quezon City: Philippine Center for Advanced Studies, University of the Philippines System, 1977), p. 67. The work of the Bureau of Non-Christian Tribes is discussed in Gowing, and also in Lopez, *The Mangyans*, chap. 5.

23. David Barrows (1902), cited in Gowing, *Mandate in Moroland*, p. 68.

24. Lopez describes how these arrangements worked for the Mangyans, concluding that the Americans' efforts to organize Mangyan settlements turned out to be a total failure. See Lopez, *The Mangyans*, pp. 110–114.

that, as a contemporary commentator observed, "the wild tribes were safely removed from the field of insular politics" and effectively placed under the control of the U.S. administration.[25]

Around this time, there were growing demands for the administration of non-Christian tribes to be left to Filipino provincial and municipal officials. Such a move was opposed by Secretary of the Interior Dean Worcester, who argued that, despite their "common racial origin," the gap between the Filipino, the Igorot, and the Moro was very great, and "to turn the control of the non-Christian tribes over to the Filipinos would speedily result in disaster."[26]

Notwithstanding Worcester's prediction, a new policy was instituted in 1914, which sought to achieve "a more rapid spread of civilization" by reducing the isolation of the non-Christian tribes and "cultivating confidence and goodwill between the non-Christians and their Christian neighbors."[27] Overall responsibility for non-Christian peoples was delegated to an officer under the secretary of the interior, but in fact was exercised increasingly by provincial and municipal authorities. The same year, a Department of Mindanao and Sulu was created under a resident governor.

Within three years, however, dissatisfaction with the new system had led to the reconstitution of the BNCT. Under a new mandate, the BNCT was directed to continue to work for the moral, material, economic, social, and political development of the non-Christian regions, but with a new injunction, "always having in view the aim of rendering permanent the mutual intelligence between and complete fusion of all the Christian and non-Christian elements populating the Provinces of the Archipelago."[28] In 1920 the Department of Mindanao and Sulu was abolished and its

25. Dean Bartlett, cited in Howard T. Fry, *A History of the Mountain Province* (Quezon City: New Day Publishers, 1983). A history of Spanish and American activity in the Cordilleras may be found in William Henry Scott, *The Discovery of the Igorots: Spanish Contacts with the Pagans of Northern Luzon*, rev. ed. (Quezon City: New Day Publishers, 1977), and Scott, "The Creation of a Cultural Minority," in Scott, ed., *Cracks in the Parchment Curtain* (Quezon City: New Day Publishers, 1985), pp. 28–41; Fry, *History of the Mountain Province*; and Frank L. Jenista, *The White Apos: American Governors on the Cordillera Central* (Quezon City: New Day Publishers, 1987). Also see Felix M. Keesing, *The Ethnohistory of Northern Luzon* (Stanford: Stanford University Press, 1962).

26. *Report of the Philippine Commission, 1909–1911* (Washington, D.C.: U.S. Government Printing Office [U.S. GPO], n.d.), pp. 75, 81. Quoted in Lopez, *The Mangyans*, p. 113.

27. *Report of the Philippine Commission to the Secretary of War* (Washington, D.C.: U.S. GPO, 1915), p. 39. Quoted in Lopez, *The Mangyans*, p. 114.

28. *Report of the Governor-General of the Philippines to the Secretary of War, 1917* (Washington, D.C.: U.S. GPO, 1918), p. 29.

responsibilities assumed by the BNCT. The emphasis on assimilation was to be endorsed in subsequent policy initiatives.

During this early period, there was little in the way of a coherent "policy" concerning tribal Filipinos, other than that they be progressively integrated into the larger Christian Filipino society, an enterprise in which the objectives of the state were supported by the work of Christian missions. This became increasingly the case as political authority was passed on to the Philippine legislature; indeed, one of the first actions of the National Assembly, following the declaration of the Commonwealth in 1935, was to abolish the BNCT. Administration of non-Christian peoples was left to the Department of the Interior, though in recognition of the particular circumstances in the south, a Commission for Mindanao and Sulu was appointed. Meanwhile, though some communities in remote areas remained virtually untouched, in many parts of the country internal migration from the populous lowlands into relatively undeveloped frontier areas—in some cases sponsored by the national government—encroached on tribal lands, not infrequently resulting in violent confrontations.[29]

Land has always been a critical issue in relations with tribal Filipinos. Under royal doctrine, the Spanish crown had "acquired" most ancestral lands (though a Royal Decree of 1754 recognized *indio* rights to ancestral lands), and in 1898 these lands passed to the U.S. government. The U.S. administration's control over land was consolidated under the Land Registration Act (1902) and the passage of the Public Land Act (1903). In 1909, the U.S. Supreme Court (in *Cariño v. Insular Government*) upheld the constitutional right of indigenous Filipinos to their ancestral lands, "by native custom and by long association," and this decision has since been reaffirmed on several occasions. Nevertheless, land rights were often violated, and many Muslim and tribal Filipinos lost their traditional land rights to outsiders who exploited their ignorance of the legal system.[30]

---

29. Lopez refers to conflicts on Mindoro in the 1920s posed by Christian land grabbers. See Lopez, *The Mangyans*, p. 116. Stuart Schlegel, in *Tiruray Subsistence* (Quezon City: Ateneo de Manila University Press, 1979); and E. Arsenio Manuel, *Manuvu Social Organization* (Quezon City: Community Development Research Council, University of the Philippines, 1973) report similar data for, respectively, the Tiruray and the Manuvu (Manobo). Also see R.J. May, "The Wild West in the South: A Recent Political History of Mindanao," in Turner, May, and Turner, *Mindanao: Land of Unfulfilled Promise*, pp. 125–146.

30. For a discussion of the land question and tribal Filipinos, see Owen J. Lynch, "Tribal Land Law: A Mechanism for Upland Participatory Development," *Sandugo*, 2nd Quarter, 1982, pp. 24–30, 4th Quarter, 1982, pp. 14, 16, 18, 20; Rodil, "Ancestral Domain"; *Tribal Forum*, Vol. 2, No. 7 (September–October, 1981); and Jaime Dumarpa, "An

In the post-independence period, the incidence of unrest resulting from encroachment on tribal lands increased—especially in Mindanao. In 1957, following an investigation into "the Moro problem" by a special committee of the Philippine House of Representatives, a Commission on National Integration (CNI) was created to address the problems of unrest in Muslim and tribal areas. The broad purpose of the CNI was indicated in the title of its enabling legislation: "An Act to Effectuate in a More Rapid and Complete Manner the Economic, Social, Moral, and Political Advancement of the Non-Christian Filipinos or National Cultural Minorities and to Render Real, Complete, and Permanent the Integration of All Said National Cultural Minorities Into the Body Politic." To achieve this advancement and integration, the CNI was given extensive powers: to engage in business and agriculture; to establish schools and assist in training and employment; to provide scholarships for study locally or abroad; to provide credit facilities; to provide legal aid and assist minorities in land disputes; to help landless minorities secure homesteads or move to resettlement areas; and to promote the community life of minorities. However, the CNI was given a modest budget, many of its powers were never exercised, and its achievements, especially in relation to tribal peoples, were at best slight.[31] In 1975 it was abolished.

The philosophy of integration continued to dominate approaches to tribal Filipinos (and, to a slightly lesser extent, Muslim Filipinos) throughout the 1950s and 1960s. However, little was achieved in the way of tangible policy benefits for cultural minorities, and often the rhetoric of integration provided a cover for loggers, miners, agribusiness, and migrant settlers to exploit tribal lands.

During the Marcos era, the situation of tribal Filipinos deteriorated significantly. In 1968, the Private Association for National Minorities (PANAMIN) was created by a wealthy Marcos crony, Manuel Elizalde; in the previous year Elizalde had been appointed presidential adviser on national minorities and subsequently given cabinet status. Following the abolition of the CNI in 1975, PANAMIN was given formal responsibility for non-Muslim minorities. The activities of PANAMIN became one of the scandals of the Marcos regime. Among other things, Elizalde was widely accused of using his power to give access to tribal lands to loggers, miners, and agribusinesses. In addition, PANAMIN became involved in

Exploratory Study of Maranao Muslims' Concepts of Land Ownership: Its Implications for the Mindanao Conflict," *Dansaian Quarterly*, Vol. 6, No. 1 (October 1984), pp. 5–78.

31. Lopez goes further: "The CNI representatives sent to work in Mindoro will surely be remembered by the Mangyans, not as agents of good but of exploitation." Lopez, *The Mangyans*, p. 126.

the forcible relocation of people from Muslim and communist areas and in the employment of tribal Filipino groups in counterinsurgency operations.[32] In 1983 Elizalde left the Philippines; in 1984, amid rumors of financial irregularities, PANAMIN was dissolved. Its functions were transferred to the Ministry of Muslim Affairs, which was renamed Office of Muslim Affairs and Cultural Communities (OMACC). Like its predecessors, OMACC was given a range of economic, social, and cultural responsibilities, but little financial or administrative capacity. It also inherited from PANAMIN a counterinsurgency program.[33]

More generally, increasing migration into Mindanao and the spread of lowland settlers into the interior of Luzon, Mindoro, and Palawan, encroachment on ancestral lands by government-supported corporations, and proposed land alienation for national development projects provoked increasingly militant responses from some tribal groups. This was particularly so in the Cordilleras.[34] In the early 1970s, a Chico River Basin Development Project (CRBDP) envisaged the construction of a series of

---

32. See Joel Rocamora, "The Political Uses of PANAMIN," *Southeast Asian Chronicle*, No. 67 (October 1979), pp. 11–21; Chip Fay, *Counter-insurgency and Tribal Peoples in the Philippines: A Report by Cultural Survival USA* (Washington, D.C.: Survival International USA, 1987); P. Bion Griffin, "National Policy on Minority Cultural Communities: The Philippine Case," *Southeast Asian Journal of Social Science*, Vol. 16, No. 2 (1988), pp. 5–16 (Special Issue on National Policy and Minority Cultures in Asia, edited by David Y.H. Wu); Jonathan Y. Okamura, "The Politics of Neglect: Philippines Ethnic Minority Policy," *Southeast Asian Journal of Social Science*, Vol. 16, No. 2 (1988), pp. 17–46; and Thomas N. Headland, ed., *The Tasaday Controversy: Assessing the Evidence*, AAA Scholarly Series Special Publication No. 28 (Washington, D.C.: American Anthropological Association, 1992).

33. For a commentary on the work of the OMACC, see Griffin, "National Policy," pp. 25–29.

34. A good deal has been written on this, though much of it is somewhat ephemeral. *Tribal Forum* (published by the Catholic Church's Episcopal Commission on Tribal Filipinos) and *Sandugo* (published by the People's Action for Cultural Ties) report regularly on tribal and Muslim Filipino issues. Other useful references include ICL Research Team, *A Report on Tribal Minorities in Mindanao* (Manila: Regal Printing, 1979); Anti-Slavery Society, *The Philippines: Authoritarian Government, Multinationals and Ancestral Lands*, Indigenous Peoples and Development Series No. 1 (London: Anti-Slavery Society, 1983); "Tribal People and the Marcos Regime: Cultural Genocide in the Philippines," *Southeast Asian Chronicle*, No. 67 (October 1979), Special Issue; Griffin, "National Policy"; Okamura, "The Politics of Neglect"; Rodil, "Ancestral Domain"; R.J. May, "Muslim and Tribal Filipinos," in R.J. May and Francisco Nemenzo, eds., *The Philippines After Marcos* (London: Croom Helm, 1985), pp. 110–129; R.J. May, "A Perspective from Mindanao," in Peter Krinks, ed., *The Philippines Under Aquino* (Canberra: The Australian Development Studies Network, 1987), pp. 71–84; May, "The Wild West in the South"; and various publications from the Cordillera Research Center, University of the Philippines College Baguio.

dams and the flooding of ancestral land of the Kalinga and Bontoc peoples. In 1975, the affected communities joined in a traditional peace pact (*bodong*) to oppose the CRBDP. PANAMIN officials were called in, and a Kalinga Special Development Region was declared. But the issue also attracted progressive political support for the tribal people; from around 1976, the Communist New People's Army (NPA) became increasingly active in the region. The government responded by increasing military deployments, including the deployment of frequently ill-disciplined Civil Home Defence Force (CHDF) units. Among a number of violent incidents was the much publicized murder of Kalinga leader and anti-CRBDP spokesman Macli-ing Dulag in 1980. To the north of the Chico River basin, a major hydroelectric development proposal threatened the ancestral lands of the Isneg people, and in other parts of the region the Isneg, Bontoc, Kalinga, and Tingguian peoples were resisting the logging operations of a multinational company that held concessions over some 200,000 hectares in four provinces.

As early as 1979, the leftist National Democratic Front (NDF) had proposed the formation of a Cordillera Peoples Democratic Front to assert demands for regional self-determination at a time when regional antagonism towards the government was mounting. In 1984, a Cordillera Peoples Alliance (CPA) was formed, which claimed to have the support of some 120 groups representing 25,000 members;[35] although it denied having links to the NDF, the CPA employed much the same rhetoric as the underground left. By 1984 the demands for regional autonomy had resulted in legislation being introduced into the national parliament. Events, however, were overtaken by the People Power Revolution of 1986.

By 1986 Cordillera politics had become very complex. Among the prominent local actors was the renegade former priest, Conrado Balweg, who had left his parish to join the NPA. In the wake of the People Power Revolution, Balweg split from the NPA to form a Cordillera Peoples Liberation Army (CPLA), and he subsequently entered into negotiations with the Aquino government over the creation of an autonomous Cordillera state based on indigenous institutions. These negotiations resulted in the signing of a *bodong* in late 1986.

Meanwhile, to the south—in Zambales and Bataan, in Mindoro, and across Mindanao—other tribal groups became politically mobilized in opposition to land grabbing by cattle ranchers, agribusinesses, and settlers, who were frequently backed by government security forces. In the mid-1970s, for example, central Mindanao became something of a battle-

---

35. Alan Robson, "The Politics of Cordillera Autonomy," unpublished manuscript.

ground between tribal Filipinos, lowland settlers, fanatical gangs, NPA units, and the military (including the CHDF).[36] PANAMIN was also involved, introducing an amnesty program, establishing PANAMIN reservations, and resettling tribal people displaced (or forcibly relocated) in the ongoing conflict—but it was generally seen as an agent of the central government and regarded with deep distrust by tribal people.

In 1977, church groups on Mindanao organized the first convention of tribal communities on Mindanao. This initiated a process of joint consultation among tribal communities, from which the term "Lumad" emerged and which in 1983 led to the first Lumad Mindanao General Assembly. Three years later Lumad-Mindanao, a coalition of local and regional all-Lumad organizations, was created to campaign for indigenous rights, especially in relation to ancestral domains.

Thus in 1986, when the incoming Aquino government began drafting a new constitution, the demands of tribal Filipinos were firmly on the agenda. The 1986 constitution recognized these demands in several provisions. It declares that "the state recognizes and promotes the rights of indigenous cultural communities within the framework of national unity and development." In addition, the constitution provides that the state "shall protect the rights of indigenous cultural communities to their ancestral lands" and that Congress "may provide for the applicability of customary laws governing property rights or relations in determining the ownership and extent of ancestral domain." Furthermore, it guarantees "the rights of indigenous cultural communities to preserve and develop their cultures, traditions, and institutions." However, the protection of minorities' ancestral land rights is "subject to the provisions of this Constitution and national development policies and programs." Provision was also made in the constitution for Congress to create a consultative body, comprising a majority of members from cultural minorities, to advise the president on policies that affect indigenous cultural communities. Community rights to ancestral domains were constitutionally excluded from agrarian reform.

More significantly, the 1986 constitution provides that "there shall be created autonomous regions in Muslim Mindanao and in the Cordilleras" and that "the President shall exercise general supervision over autonomous regions." The constitution listed eight areas of legislative jurisdiction (administrative organization; sources of revenues; ancestral domains and natural resources; personal, family, and property relations; urban and rural planning; economic, social, and tourism development; educational

---

36. See May, "The Wild West in the South."

policies; preservation and development of cultural heritage; and "such other matters as may be authorized by law for the promotion of the general welfare of the people of the region"), as well as providing that "the preservation of peace and order within the regions shall be the responsibility of the local police agencies."

Administratively, the government signaled its good intentions by dividing the existing Office of Muslim Affairs and Cultural Communities into separate offices—of Muslim Affairs, Southern Cultural Communities, and Northern Cultural Communities. The mandate of the latter two bodies is to coordinate the activities of government agencies dealing with cultural communities, and to assist development by providing livelihood programs, loans, training programs, cultural projects, and assistance in formulating land use plans for ancestral landholders.

Another important initiative of the Aquino administration was the reorganization of the Department of Environment and Natural Resources (DENR), in part with the objective of making it "less a regulatory agency and more . . . a developmental one."[37] Under Marcos, the Bureau of Forestry Development was generally seen as an opponent of cultural minority interests, particularly insofar as it gave outsiders access to ancestral lands (through timber license agreements) for logging, and prohibited traditional practices of *kaingin* (slash and burn) agriculture. Within the new DENR, which was headed by a prominent human rights activist, an Indigenous Communities Affairs Division was created and serious attempts were made to promote sustainable development, including the National Forestation Program and an Integrated Social Forestry Program. Among other measures, "Uplanders" were offered twenty-five-year certificate-of-stewardship contracts that gave security of tenure to forest land and provided agro-forestry technology, conditional upon their undertaking reforestation and soil conservation activities. Between 1987 and 1991, over 146,000 certificates were issued for areas covering about 431,000 hectares. The department also reduced the number of timber license agreements from 143 to 33 over the same period.

In 1989, an Ancestral Domain Bill was drafted within the DENR to give effect to the intentions of the 1986 constitution, and in 1991 the bill was put before Congress. Meanwhile, "preparatory steps toward the recognition of ancestral domains"[38] were taken through the issuing of certificates of ancestral domain claims (CADCs) to indigenous cultural

---

37. For details, see *The Aquino Administration Record and Legacy (1986–1992): President Corazon C. Aquino and her Cabinet*, U.P. Public Lectures, Vol. 1 (Quezon City: University of the Philippines Press, 1992), chap. 17.

38. *The Aquino Administration*, p. 221.

communities. These initiatives have been sustained under the administration of President Fidel Ramos, who took office in 1992. By March 1996, CADCs covering over 500,000 hectares had been issued. Eventually, recognized ancestral domains will cover a minimum of two million hectares across the country. However, as of early 1997, the Ancestral Domain Bill, introduced in 1991, has yet to be passed.[39]

The DENR has also been conducting informal consultations with local and foreign mining companies concerning a series of proposed revisions to the implementing rules and regulations of the Mining Act of 1955. Liberalization of the mining industry has led to a resurgence of exploration and mine development, much of it impinging on the ancestral domains of cultural minorities. The chairman of the DENR committee drafting these revisions has announced that mining companies have agreed to respect the rights of indigenous peoples and have accepted a provision identifying areas closed to exploration and mining.[40] However, there has been some disagreement over the definition of "ancestral lands"; moreover, mining companies have objected to paying proposed royalty fees (set at a minimum of 1 percent of gross output) to indigenous peoples for the exploitation of mineral resources on their land.[41] Cultural communities have also been targeted for poverty alleviation programs under the Ramos government's Social Reform Agenda, and cases involving ancestral land rights of tribal Filipinos have been brought before the Philippines Human Rights Commission.

In the Cordilleras, following the 1986 peace pact, an Interim Cordillera Regional Administration was established, and a regional consultative commission was created under the terms of the constitution to draft the necessary organic law for the proposed Cordillera Autonomous Region. However, this process ran into considerable political turbulence; the CPA and the CPLA adopted opposing positions, and groups such as the Cordillera Broad Coalition (CBC) and traditional politicians from the region attempted to occupy the middle ground. When the organic law was submitted to a plebiscite in the five provinces and one city in the region in 1990, only one province (Ifugao) voted in its favor.[42] Consequently, the

---

39. According to Dr. Socorro Reyes, the director of the Center for Legislative Development in Manila, the bill has been, literally, lost in a congressional committee; personal communication.

40. *SEAsian Business World* (Philippines) report, October 4, 1996.

41. Malou L. Sayson, Philippine News Agency report, October 1, 1996.

42. For a more detailed examination of the Cordillera autonomy issue, see Rollie Buendia, "The Case of the Cordillera: An Unresolved National Question," *Philippine Journal of Public Policy*, Vol. 31, No. 2 (April 1987), pp. 157–187; Robson, "The Politics

Cordillera Administrative Region remains in existence. An organic law is to be resubmitted to a future plebiscite.

Therefore, since 1986 greater consideration seems to have been given to the position of cultural communities in policymaking, and there is evidence of a shift away from the long-standing commitment to integration as the government's broad policy objective. Notwithstanding this, cultural communities, whose ancestral lands are typically on the frontiers of development, remain threatened by proposed dam and tourism development projects, by logging and mining, and by continued settler migration.

The "Moro Problem"[43]

Although Spain never did achieve effective sovereignty over the Moros,[44] in 1898 Mindanao and Sulu were included in the territory ceded to the United States, which set about overcoming Moro resistance to colonial rule. Following a series of frequently brutal military encounters, by 1913

---

of Cordillera Autonomy"; Maximo B. Garming, *Towards Understanding the Cordillera Autonomous Region* (Manila: Friedrich Ebert Stiftung, 1989); Steven Rood, *Issues in Creating an Autonomous Region for the Cordillera, Northern Philippines*, CSC Working Paper No. 11 (Baguio: University of the Philippines College Baguio, Cordillera Studies Center [CSC], 1989); CSC, *Issues on Cordillera Autonomy: General Summary*, CSC Working Paper No. 18 (Baguio: University of the Philippines College Baguio, CSC, 1991); and Alex B. Brillantes, "Managing the Ethnic Problems in the Philippine Cordilleras," in Harold Crouch, Stephen Henningham and R.J. May, eds., *Managing Ethnic Diversity in Asia and the Pacific* (forthcoming).

43. This section draws on my earlier writing on the subject. R.J. May, "The Philippines," in Mohammed Ayoob, ed., *The Politics of Islamic Reassertion* (London: Croom Helm, 1981), pp. 211–232; May, "Muslim and Tribal Filipinos," pp. 110–129; May, "A Perspective from Mindanao," pp. 71–84; and May, "The Moro Movement in Southern Philippines," in R. Stewart and C. Jennett, eds., *Politics of the Future: The Role of Social Movements* (Melbourne: Macmillan Australia, 1989), pp. 321–339. See also P.G. Gowing, *Muslim Filipinos: Heritage and Horizon* (Quezon City: New Day Publishers, 1979); T.J.S. George, *Revolt in Mindanao: The Rise of Islam in Philippine Politics* (Kuala Lumpur: Oxford University Press, 1980); Nagasura T. Madale, *The Muslim Filipinos: A Book of Readings* (Quezon City: Alemar-Phoenix Publishing House, 1981); Michael O. Mastura, *Muslim Filipino Experience: A Collection of Essays* (Manila: Ministry of Muslim Affairs, 1984); C.A. Majul, *The Contemporary Muslim Movement in the Philippines* (Berkeley, Calif.: Mizan Press, 1985); and Wan Kadirbin Che Man, *Muslim Separatism: The Moros of Southern Philippines and the Malays of Southern Thailand* (Singapore: Oxford University Press, 1987).

44. The term Moro was imported from Spain and for a long time had a derogatory connotation. In the late 1960s, however, Philippine Muslims adopted the term to describe their collective identity.

the Moros had been subdued, and the administration of Mindanao and Sulu passed from the U.S. army to civilian authorities.[45]

Generally, U.S. officials displayed greater religious tolerance than their colonial predecessors, and they made some attempt to accommodate Muslim Filipino customs and Islamic law. Nevertheless, U.S. policy was essentially aimed at assimilating the Moros into the larger Christian society. From 1914, integration was pursued through what was referred to as a "policy of attraction"; substantial government spending on roads, schools, hospitals, and other services took place in Muslim areas; education was made compulsory, and scholarships were provided for Muslims to study in Manila and in the United States; and Muslims began to participate in the emerging political system. The U.S. administration also encouraged migration to Mindanao from the populous northern islands of Luzon and the Visayas through the provision of timber and mining concessions and land for plantations and cattle ranches. Between 1903 and 1939, the population of Mindanao, estimated at around 500,000 at the end of the Spanish period, had grown by 1.4 million. Increasingly, the new settlers encroached on ancestral Muslim and tribal lands.

In 1920, control of Mindanao and Sulu passed from the U.S. administration to the Philippine legislature, and in 1935 to the newly established Commonwealth. In the latter year, a group of 120 Moro *datus* from Lanao petitioned the U.S. president, repeating earlier requests either to give the Moros political independence or to let them remain under U.S. rule. Christian Filipinos, they claimed, discriminated against Muslims and treated them abusively.[46] Under an administration dominated by Christian Filipinos, the policy of attraction did indeed lapse, and there was an increasing incidence of clashes between Muslims and Christian settlers.[47]

Following World War II and Philippine independence, there were further large movements of settlers into Mindanao. Of seven provinces nationally that more than doubled their populations between 1948 and 1960, six were in Mindanao; this pattern continued during the 1960s. By

45. For accounts of the U.S. colonial administration of Mindanao and Sulu, see Gowing, *Mandate in Moroland,* and Gowing, *Muslim Filipinos;* and H.F. Funtecha, *American Military Occupation of the Lake Lanao Region, 1901–1913* (Marawi City: University Research Center, Mindanao State University, 1979). Also see S.C. Miller, *Benevolent Assimilation: The American Conquest of the Philippines, 1899–1903* (New Haven, Conn.: Yale University Press, 1982).

46. See Gowing, *Muslim Filipinos,* pp. 169–170.

47. See Samuel K. Tan, *The Filipino Muslim Armed Struggle, 1900–1972* (Manila: Filipinas Foundation, 1977).

the end of the 1960s, disputes over land between the Muslim population, tribal peoples, and Christian settlers were becoming more frequent and more violent, and the growing number of settlers was threatening the electoral base of many Muslim politicians.

As early as 1954, a special committee of the Philippine Congress was set up to report on "the Moro problem," especially with regard to peace and order in Mindanao and Sulu. Largely as a result of this, the Commission on National Integration was established in 1957, as discussed above. But apart from providing scholarships to Muslim students, the CNI achieved little before it was abolished in 1975. The CNI was, moreover, generally regarded with suspicion and hostility by Muslim Filipinos, who resented being referred to as a "national minority" and saw the real objective of the commission as the destruction of Philippine Muslim identity.[48]

In 1963 and 1971, a Senate Committee on National Minorities produced reports, respectively, on "The Problems of Philippine Cultural Minorities" and "The Deteriorating Peace and Order Conditions in Cotabato," identifying migration and land grabbing as the major sources of conflict in Mindanao. However, these reports brought about no real change in policy; the solution to the problem continued to be cast in terms of social and political integration and economic development.

During the 1960s, under the pressure of continuing migration and coincident with a resurgence of Islamic consciousness in Mindanao and Sulu,[49] the distrust and hostility that had characterized relations between Muslim and Christian Filipinos for four hundred years intensified. In 1968 tensions were heightened by an incident in which a number of Muslim recruits to the armed forces were executed for alleged mutiny, and in the same year a Muslim (later Mindanao) Independence Movement was established on Mindanao. The incidence of disturbances subsequently increased, and by 1971, Muslim Mindanao and Sulu were in a state of rebellion. A government task force was sent to Mindanao in an attempt to mediate between the conflicting groups, but had little success. By the end of the year, official sources acknowledged that over 1,500 people had been killed in clashes between Muslim and Christian groups and the military.

By the early 1970s, the armed separatist movement had come under

---

48. For a critical assessment of the work of the CNI, specifically in relation to Muslim Filipinos, see Filipinas Foundation, *An Anatomy of Philippine Muslim Affairs* (Makati: Filipinas Foundation, 1971).

49. See May, "The Philippines."

the leadership of the Moro National Liberation Front (MNLF). The MNLF was headed by Nur Misuari, a young man from Sulu who had received guerilla training in West Malaysia in the late 1960s. The international Islamic community had also become involved in the conflict, supplying arms and finance to the MNLF, sending two fact-finding missions to Mindanao, and accusing the Marcos government of genocide. When martial law was declared in 1972, the situation in the south was cited as one reason for the government's action.

While clearly intent on a military victory over the MNLF, in 1973 President Marcos arranged a meeting of Filipino Muslim leaders and announced a package of social and economic measures. These included the establishment of a Muslim Amanah Bank; removal of restrictions on the historic barter trade between Mindanao-Sulu and Malaysia; creation of an Institute of Islamic Studies within the University of the Philippines; proclamation of Muslim holidays; and a commitment to the codification of *Shari'a* (Islamic law), though this was not promulgated for another four years. Several economic projects were initiated, and a Presidential Task Force for Reconstruction and Development of the Southern Philippines was created to coordinate the efforts of the agencies involved (though it was not clear how much of the Task Force's program represented new initiatives or how much the projects envisaged were specifically intended to benefit the Muslim population). The following year, under increasing pressure from the Organization of Islamic Conference (OIC), a consultative council of Muslim leaders was created by the Marcos government, and a conference in Marawi City, nominally sponsored by the Federation of the Royal Houses of Mindanao and Sulu but in fact orchestrated by the government, recorded a vote of confidence in Marcos's leadership and endorsed a list of socioeconomic policy proposals intended to address some of the grievances of Philippine Muslims. Shortly after this, Marcos announced the creation of a Southern Philippines Development Authority, the establishment of two new regional offices headed by Muslims, and the commissioning in the armed forces of twelve former rebel leaders.

These measures, however, did little to address the fundamental grievances of the Moros, whose demands were for a separate *Bangsa Moro* (Moro homeland) and the return of lands now occupied by Christian Filipinos. Those who saw a solution to "the Moro Problem" in terms of social and economic reforms designed to integrate Muslims into the larger (Christian-dominated) Philippine society failed to recognize the extent to which historical circumstances created a long-standing sense of religious and cultural separateness among Muslim Filipinos, who thus saw integration as a first step towards assimilation and the loss of Muslim identity.[50]

Amid numerous reports of surrenders by Moro fighters in the mid-1970s, the Philippine government also began a series of negotiations for a peace settlement with the MNLF, with the mediation of the OIC, the Islamic Conference of Foreign Ministers (ICFM), and Libya's Colonel Muammar Qaddafi. These talks culminated in the signing of an agreement in Tripoli in December 1976, which provided for a cease-fire and put forward tentative provisions for a broader political settlement. The latter included Muslim-dominated political autonomy in thirteen provinces of Mindanao, Sulu, and Palawan, which the MNLF considered Moro homeland, with separate legislatures, administrations, legal systems, security forces, schools, and financial and economic systems, but with the right to participate in the national government.[51] Further talks were scheduled for early 1977 to discuss the details of implementation, but negotiations collapsed and the cease-fire was abandoned before further progress could be made.

The main sticking point in negotiations in 1976–77 (and ever since) concerned the geographical boundaries of Moro autonomy. By 1980, as a result of heavy migration, the proportion of Muslims in Mindanao, which had been estimated at 76 percent in 1903, had fallen to 23 percent; of the twenty-three provinces in Mindanao and Sulu, only five (and on Mindanao only two) still had a Muslim majority. Having modified its earlier claim to the whole of Mindanao, Sulu, and Palawan (MINSUPALA), the MNLF nevertheless insisted that the area of autonomy should include the thirteen provinces of traditional Muslim dominance. In 1977, Marcos proposed to put the issue of Muslim autonomy to a plebiscite in the thirteen provinces. Realizing that this would produce a negative vote, the MNLF rejected the idea of a plebiscite and accused the government of violating the Tripoli Agreement; it was supported in this by the ICFM, Qaddafi, and subsequently the OIC. Notwithstanding this, Marcos went ahead to proclaim an autonomous region, appoint a provisional government, and organize a referendum to determine the form of autonomy. The MNLF rejected an invitation to participate in the provisional government and boycotted the referendum, which predictably rejected the MNLF/ICFM plan (by a vote of 2,744,000 to 38,600) and endorsed a more limited form

---

50. Ibid., p. 229.

51. The Tripoli Agreement, together with several commentaries on its implications, is reproduced in International Studies Institute of the Philippines (ISIP), *Papers on the Tripoli Agreement* (Quezon City: ISIP, UP Law Complex, University of the Philippines, 1986).

of autonomy put forward by the Marcos government. Subsequently, autonomous regions were created in Regions IX (western Mindanao and Sulu) and XII (central Mindanao), and elections were held for the two regional assemblies in 1979. But with the majority of Muslims and the major local non-Muslim opposition group boycotting the elections, the Commission on Elections reported "a general public apathy and apprehension over the credibility of the political exercise," which resulted in a victory for Marcos-backed candidates. The regional assemblies were largely ineffective, and were generally regarded with a great deal of cynicism by the people of the regions.

Meanwhile, the MNLF was seriously weakened in the latter half of the 1970s by a number of surrenders and by a three-way split in the movement along personal, ethnic, and ideological lines. The split created three groups: the Misuari-led MNLF, recognized by the OIC, whose ideology was socially progressive and whose geographical support base was centered in Sulu; the more religiously oriented Moro Islamic Liberation Front (MILF) led by Hashim Salamat, a Maguindanaon from western Mindanao; and the MNLF-Reformist Group (MNLF-RG), comprising mainly Maranao people and led by Dimasangcay Pundato. A fourth group, the Bangsa Moro Liberation Organization, a socially conservative, mostly Maranao group headed by Macapantan Abbas, also emerged in this period. Although fighting continued, the government's preoccupation with the "Moro problem" seems to have diminished in the early 1980s. A Ministry of Muslim Affairs was created in 1981, but its activities appear to have been largely devoted to organizing Koran reading competitions and the annual *haj*, accrediting *madaris*, and supporting the implementation of *Shari'a*.

Prior to the elections of 1986, Marcos's opponents held talks with MNLF leader Misuari, promising to address Muslim demands if the MNLF joined the opposition forces. After Corazon Aquino's victory in the elections, peace talks were initiated with the MNLF in Mindanao, and the demand for autonomy was recognized in the new constitution, as discussed above.

In September 1986, Misuari returned to the Philippines and met with President Aquino in Sulu. Subsequently an agreement was signed between Misuari and representatives of the Philippine government at a meeting in Jeddah, held under OIC auspices, to continue discussions on autonomy through a joint commission. The MILF and MNLF-RG were invited to join the talks; the MILF rejected the invitation and soon after launched a series of attacks on government installations, while the MNLF-RG played some part in later negotiations. Misuari's demands included the extension of autonomy arrangements to all twenty-three provinces in

Mindanao and Sulu (this was more than envisaged in the Tripoli Agreement); incorporation of the MNLF's Bangsa Moro Army into the Armed Forces of the Philippines (AFP); withdrawal of the AFP from the south; fiscal autonomy; and control over mineral exploration in the region. These demands were considered unreasonable by the government's negotiating panel. Several meetings were held during 1987, but despite the urgings of some OIC members that Misuari accept a compromise, the talks collapsed in mid-year. By this time, however, the Philippine government was committed to implementing the constitutional provisions for autonomy.

Procedurally, the constitution provided that "the congress shall enact an organic act for each autonomous region with the assistance and participation of the regional consultative commission composed of representatives appointed by the president from a list of nominees from multisectoral bodies." In fact, at least in the case of the Autonomous Region of Muslim Mindanao (ARMM), the implementation of this provision was deeply flawed.

The deliberating body contained twenty-six Muslims, eighteen Christians, and nine representatives of "Highlander" cultural minorities (some of whom were Christian); in a consultative committee to deliberate on a Muslim Mindanao, Muslims were in a minority. Moreover, the committee was supported by a secretariat drawn largely from the (Christian) Ateneo de Manila University in Manila, and one of its first and most intense debates was over whether its duty was to formulate provisions for an Autonomous Region of Muslim Mindanao or simply for a Mindanao Autonomous Region. The proceedings were marked by frequent acrimonious debate, and the outcome was seen by most Muslims as a poor compromise.[52] In 1989, an organic act was drafted and put to a plebiscite in thirteen provinces and nine cities in central and western Mindanao and Sulu, on the basis that only those provinces and cities voting yes would become part of the autonomous region. In the event, only four provinces (Lanao del Sur, Maguindanao, Sulu, and Tawi-Tawi) and no cities voted in favor of the proposition. An assembly for the ARMM, representing these four provinces, was subsequently established, though the various Moro factions again boycotted the poll. As with the earlier regional assemblies established under Marcos, small budgets, restricted authority,

---

52. For an insider critique of the process, see Nagasura T. Madale, *Autonomy for Muslim Mindanao: The RCC Untold Story* (B-lal Publishers, 1989); and Madale, "The Organic Law for the Autonomous Region in Muslim Mindanao: Contrasting Views," in Turner, May, and Turner, *Mindanao*, pp. 169–183.

and a widespread perception among the community that the ARMM lacks real legitimacy have rendered it largely ineffective.

Although the Aquino government failed to resolve the conflict in the south—and indeed was criticized by many for having given a boost to Misuari's flagging political fortunes—a cease-fire with the MNLF was maintained (albeit with occasional violations), and the OIC formally recognized the efforts of the Philippine government to find a peaceful solution to the conflict. The Office of Muslim Affairs and Cultural Communities was dismantled by executive order in January 1987 and replaced by a new Office of Muslim Affairs and separate offices for northern and southern cultural communities (as discussed above), but apart from placing more emphasis on ancestral land matters, there was little evidence of new policy initiatives in the area of Muslim affairs. It is perhaps significant that in a review of the Aquino administration's record and legacy almost no mention is made of Muslim Filipinos, except in the context of national defense and security.[53]

Following the election of Fidel Ramos in 1992 and his visit to Libya in the same year, new attempts were made to negotiate a settlement with the MNLF. In June 1996, a series of discussions between Philippine government representatives and Nur Misuari, brokered by the OIC, culminated in the signing of an agreement on points of consensus.[54] The principal element of this agreement was a decision to establish, as "Phase 1 of the Implementation of the Tripoli Agreement," a Southern Philippines Council for Peace and Development (SPCPD), within a Special Zone of Peace and Development in the Southern Philippines, which is to include the (now) fourteen provinces covered by the Tripoli Agreement (and all the cities therein). The SPCPD is to have a chairman and vice-chairman and three deputies (representing respectively the Muslims, Christians, and Lumads); and it is to be appointed by the president upon recommendation of the MNLF and in consultation with "the various leaders and sectors in the Southern Philippines." The SPCPD will be assisted by a *Darul Iftah* (religious advisory council) created by the SPCPD chairman, and there will be a Consultative Assembly of eighty-one members, including forty-four members of the MNLF. The powers of the SPCPD are described as being "derivative and extensions of the powers of the President," and the funding for the SPCPD and the assembly are to come from

---

53. *The Aquino Administration.*

54. *The 8th GRP-MNLF Mixed Committee Meeting With the Participation of the OIC Ministerial Committee of Six: Points of Consensus,* Davao City, June 21–23, 1996.

the Office of the President. Local government units in the region, including the ARMM, will continue to operate. Misuari accepted an appointment as chairman of the SPCPD, and in September 1996, with the backing of President Ramos's Laban ng Demokratikong Pilipino (Laban) party, he also gained election as governor of the ARMM.

It is anticipated that the special zone will be the focus of energetic peace and development efforts. Indeed, a substantial commitment of funds from the National Economic and Development Authority (NEDA) has already been made for infrastructure, social services, and environmental protection in Mindanao over a three-year period. Promises of investment from OIC countries, including Malaysia and Indonesia, have also been made. Following the formal signing of the SPCPD agreement in Indonesia in October 1996, the AFP has announced that some three thousand MNLF fighters, two thousand MILF, and five hundred others have been accepted for integration into the AFP, and the *Bangko Sentral* has offered to establish an Islamic banking unit.

However, one must also note that the creation of the SPCPD was bitterly opposed by a number of Christian groups and members of Congress, and the president's commitment was challenged in the Supreme Court as unconstitutional. The MILF, moreover, denounced the initial agreement and vowed to continue the armed struggle for an Islamic state.

Various aspects of the new arrangements are still unclear—particularly aspects relating to the relationships between the SPCPD and Consultative Assembly, and the ARMM; the scope of the SPCPD's authority;[55] and the implications of the final provision that "Phase 2" will involve a change to the ARMM, through congressional action and plebiscite. However, the Ramos government has taken a bold step, and although the prospects of a new outbreak of Muslim-Christian conflict (and an escalation of Muslim-Muslim conflict) cannot be ruled out, it does appear in early 1997 that the government's action may have provided the basis for a period of relative peace and development in the south.

Conclusion

In an introduction to a multi-authored report on Southeast Asian tribal groups and ethnic minorities some years ago, Benedict Anderson commented that although the Philippines contains far more ethno-linguistic

---

55. Point 5 of the *Consensus* says: "Appropriate agencies of the government that are engaged in peace and development activities in the area [it specifically identifies the Southern Philippine Development Agency] shall be placed under the control of the Council."

groups than Burma, "ethnicity as such has played only a minor role in Philippine politics."[56] If one excludes the Moro rebellion (and it is not clear why one should[57]), this is probably roughly true.

Although there was quite heavy Chinese migration into the Philippines in the nineteenth century, the Chinese had been in the Philippines well before the Spanish arrived and, at times encouraged by Spanish policies, had integrated into Filipino society, intermarrying with the indigenous *principales* and contributing to the growth of an increasingly nationalistic Filipino middle class in the years leading up to Philippine independence. Apart from the occasional question of "overstaying Chinese," although people of Chinese descent are generally perceived as being disproportionately wealthy, the blending of indigenous Filipinos and Chinese immigrants has been so thorough that few prominent families are without Chinese ancestry and Chinese ethnicity has not been a significant political issue.

On the other hand, the indigenous communities that resisted Spanish and later U.S. colonial rule, either by force of arms or by retreating into the interior, have remained politically marginalized and, especially in the second half of the twentieth century, have suffered as economic development has pushed back the frontiers of settlement and resource exploitation. In this, they have shared the fate of indigenous communities elsewhere. Since the mid-1980s, however, tribal Filipinos have become politically mobilized, and there is some evidence of a national government commitment to addressing their demands—even though the constitutional provision for regional autonomy has so far been rejected.

The issue of Moro separatism appears to be more intractable, notwithstanding more than two decades of negotiations by three national administrations. To date, the Moro leadership has insisted on recognition of territorial rights over an area which is now, after decades of Christian settlement, unrealistic. It is possible that the developments of 1996 will bring about a settlement that will at least reduce the level of armed conflict, but the underlying problem in Mindanao remains.

Over the centuries, there have been gradual changes in the definition of ethnic categories and in concepts of ethnic identity in the Philippines. In recent years, developments in international Islam have probably tended to strengthen Philippine Muslims' identification with Islam over

---

56. Benedict Anderson, "Introduction," in *Southeast Asian Tribal Groups and Ethnic Minorities: Prospects for the Eighties and Beyond,* Cultural Survival Report No. 22 (Cambridge, Mass: Cultural Survival, Inc., 1987), p. 9.

57. Anderson argues, somewhat opaquely, that "the Muslim minorities were mishandled, not as ethnicities, but as religious deviants." See ibid.

their identification as Filipinos. On the other hand, partly as a result of the experience of martial law, at least some Christian (and communist) Filipinos have come to see "tribal" Filipinos more as part of the same nation, rather than as *infieles*, "wild tribes," or uncivilized people. But given the robust nature of its democratic system and the strength of its parochial politics, there seems little prospect of the Philippines achieving the sort of assimilationist integration that was the preoccupation earlier in the century and that is implicit in the nationalist state ideologies of some of its neighbors. Rather, within a dominant Christian and heavily Westernized country, steps are being taken to accommodate the demands of the minority Muslim and tribal communities. Recent developments in negotiations with the MNLF and in recognizing the ancestral domain of tribal Filipinos, as well as the continuing discussion of proposals for regional autonomy in the Cordilleras, suggest that the national government is at least willing to address important issues.

Chapter 9

Assimilation and Accommodation in China

June Teufel Dreyer

Under Mao Zedong, Chinese policies toward ethnic minorities alternated between accommodation to and assimilation of minority languages, traditions, and other characteristics. Whether they were accommodative or assimilative, Mao's policies had the effect of creating strong ties between central party and government institutions and areas inhabited by ethnic minorities. Beijing's writ was heard and generally obeyed, even in the remote areas where many of China's minorities live. The channels of mobility for minorities were created and defined by party and government. Fluency in Mandarin was crucial to one's ability to rise within those channels. Moreover, the economies of minority areas were firmly linked with those of Han China. Despite the proximity of several minority nationality areas to foreign countries, external contacts with and influences from abroad were minimized, often to the point of being effectively eliminated.

Deng Xiaoping reversed many of these policies. In an effort to rapidly modernize China, he decentralized economic power and replaced Mao's redistributive policies with measures that channeled investment into areas where economic gains would be greatest. Almost invariably, these areas were on China's coast. Deng's policies worked: the economies of these areas boomed. However, the reforms left inland provinces, and in particular the areas inhabited by ethnic minorities, far behind. To redress this imbalance and assuage minority feelings that they were being exploited by the majority Han group, minorities were permitted to trade across borders. Tourism from abroad was encouraged as well. Foreign contacts brought foreign influence and created new channels through which minorities could express their grievances. They also created new economic linkages, which weakened the ties between minority areas and Han China. Centrifugal forces in minority areas were further encouraged by a resurgence of Islamic fundamentalism, as well as ethnic nationalist forces unleashed by the disintegration of the Soviet empire.

These centrifugal forces are strongest in the case of Tibetans, several minorities who adhere to the Muslim faith, and Mongols. There have also been attempts by ethnic Koreans to emigrate to South Korea, and some Dai (Thai) have had their sense of ethnicity heightened through contact with citizens of Thailand. These latter cases have involved attraction to the cultures and systems of more prosperous states that border China.

Although the central government has been able to suppress most manifestations of ethnic discontent, it has not been able to prevent their regular recurrence and growth in strength and organization. As China enters the post-Deng era, it is not clear what policies might be successful in dealing with these grievances. A return to the culturally assimilationist and centralized economic policies of the past would surely provoke more resistance. However, granting more autonomy to minorities could have the effect of encouraging demands for still more freedom from Beijing's control.

China's Minorities in the Pre-1949 Period

China's dominant ethnic group, in both numerical and political terms, is the Han. Silk producers and rice cultivators for millennia, the Han spread gradually from a small area in what is now northwest China. By the fifth century before the birth of Christ, Confucius had articulated long-held beliefs concerning respect for one's ancestors, the obligations between rulers and ruled, and the importance of music and ritual in maintaining the social order. This system of beliefs was later officially adopted as the state philosophy. Confucianism remained the definitive statement of Han Chinese norms and values until the twentieth century.

Since the Han were sedentary agriculturists, they tended to migrate southward and along river banks rather than toward the north, with its cold and arid climate. In the course of this lengthy migration, the Han naturally encountered occupants as they entered new areas. Proud of their own culture and technology, the Han tended to consider other groups to be barbarians; they showed little interest in learning about or from them, unless a group posed a direct military threat to their survival. In the words of an American missionary, "The Chinese have never taken a great deal of trouble to find out about the history of these different tribes, and while willing that the aboriginals shall come to them, learn of them, and share their privileges, they have never been keen on learning from the aboriginals."[1]

Some ethnic groups were pushed from their original homes into mountainous terrain or other areas unsuitable for cultivation. Other groups were sinicized and assimilated to Confucian principles, though rarely because of any conscious effort by the Han Chinese state.

Barbarian groups were dealt with on an ad hoc basis. The traditional leaders of smaller groups were often given lower-level titles in the Chinese bureaucratic hierarchy, preceded by the character "tu," meaning earth, to denote their separate (and inferior) status. The leaders of some large and potentially troublesome barbarian groups were given imperial titles in return for pledges of peace. The court also tried to play one ethnic group against another, but this did not always work. China had several dynasties that were not Han, most notably the Mongol (Yuan) dynasty of the thirteenth century and the Manchu (Qing) dynasty, which ruled from the seventeenth through the twentieth centuries. As long as the rulers of China were guided by Confucian principles, they were accepted as legitimate.

The growth of nationalism in Europe in the nineteenth century was echoed in China. The younger generation of politically aware Chinese was acutely conscious of the humiliations visited on their country by the Western powers and Japan. One of these Chinese nationalists, Sun Yat-sen, blamed both the Manchu dynasty and Confucian philosophy for the weakness of the state; he built the 1911 revolution around the idea of replacing them with a republic led by Han Chinese. Sun believed that, to create a strong state, the government "must facilitate the dying out of all names of individual peoples inhabiting China, i.e., Manchus, Tibetans, etc. . . . we must satisfy the demands of all races and unite them in a single cultural and political whole."[2] This consciously assimilationist aim contrasted sharply with the essentially pluralistic attitudes of the Confucian system. His successor, Chiang Kai-shek, carried forward these assimilationist ideas, but his Kuomintang (KMT) government did not have the strength to apply them effectively. Outer Mongolia became independent, and Tibet, although it did not formally declare its independence, severed its ties with the Chinese state. A sinicized Yi ruled Yunnan, and Muslim warlords held sway in several northwestern provinces. In Xinjiang, a Han

---

1. Samuel Pollard, *In Unknown China* (Philadelphia: J.B. Lippincott, 1921), p. 56.

2. Sun Yat-sen, *Memoirs of a Chinese Revolutionary* (Taipei: China Cultural Service, 1953), p. 180.

Chinese general presided over a coalition of ethnic groups under the protection of the Soviet Union.

The Communist Party's Minority Policy

When the Chinese Communist Party (CCP) came to power in 1949, one priority was to institute specific policies toward China's ethnic minorities. The major world powers were hostile toward the communist government, and the security of China's borders was a concern. Since most of China's minorities lived on these far-flung borders, winning their loyalties, or at least their grudging acceptance of CCP rule, was important to the continued existence of the party and the new state, the People's Republic of China (PRC), that it had founded.

Although the official media issued strident propaganda about sinister plots against the ancestral land by rapacious capitalist-imperialist states, China's communist leaders were keenly aware that not all the threats to its borders came from such states. Boundaries divided many minority groups arbitrarily, and irredentism and pressures for reunification were strong in several areas, including Xinjiang and Mongolia. Moreover, China's ostensibly friendly socialist neighbor, the Soviet Union, clearly had designs on Chinese territory. The Soviet Union administered several counties in China's Xinjiang province in the far northwest. Xinjiang's ever-restive Turkic Muslim majority had ethnic ties to several Soviet republics, which, the Chinese elite feared, could be used to goad China's Turkic Muslims into rebellion. Moscow had already helped Mongolia attain its independence from China, and it exercised considerable influence over the Chinese Eastern Railway and in the northeastern port of Luxun, known in the Soviet Union as Port Arthur. China also had unresolved border issues with several other neighbors; the most important involved India. China's claim to administer these areas would be directly affected by the actions of minority groups in border regions.

Carefully devised policies toward ethnic minorities were also essential for economic reasons. China's economic capacities had been crushed by decades of war, both against Japan and in the civil war between Chiang Kai-shek's bourgeois nationalist KMT and Mao Zedong's CCP. Most of China's meat- and milk-producing animals were raised in minority areas, which also contained important hydroelectric and mineral resources. Because minority areas tended to be less densely populated than lands inhabited by the Han, these areas could also be used to absorb Han settlers. Migration would alleviate pressures in seriously overcrowded areas while boosting economic development in minority areas. Han

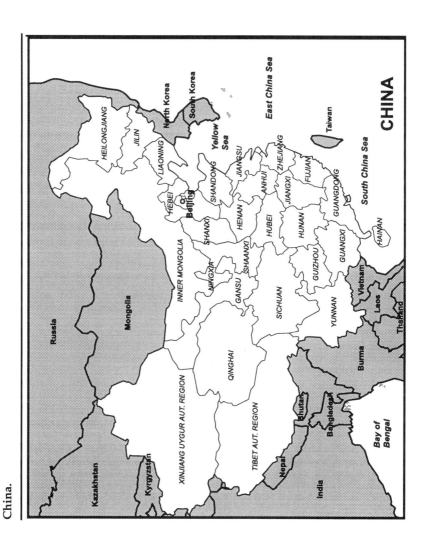

China.

migration would also dilute the concentration of minorities in border regions and help to bring these areas more firmly under Beijing's control.

As a communist movement, the CCP took seriously its ideological mentors' admonition to bring the socialist message to all of mankind; thus it wished to emancipate the other peoples of the world as well. This desire was reinforced after the increasingly public estrangement of relations with the Soviet Union, which Mao had come to regard as betraying Marxism-Leninism. If China's minorities could be portrayed as satisfied, productive members of the PRC, the Chinese model of socialism could be portrayed as superior to that of the Soviet Union.

In short, practical considerations were reinforced by ideological ones. Karl Marx believed that ethnic and national splits were a function of exploitative economic systems. Under communism, the toilers of the world would be given equal access to the products of their labor. They would come to realize that their common interests were far greater than their differences, which had been manipulated by exploitative capitalists in order to stay in power. It was argued that a common proletarian culture would gradually and naturally come into existence, based not on forced assimilation into the language and culture of the dominant group but on a mutually acceptable amalgam of the strong points of the component parts.

The Early Years, 1949–56

Power politics, economic concerns, and ideology thus dictated the careful formulation of policies for a relatively small percentage of the population. It is impossible to get accurate demographic information on China for the immediate postwar period, since tens of millions of people had died in conflict and many more simply did not want to be counted. However, it is estimated that ethnic minorities constituted six percent of the PRC's population at the time.[3] Put differently, China's minority groups contained 35–40 million people, equivalent to the population of a medium-sized European state.

The new government in Beijing was not naive about the difficulty of the task it faced. During its legendary Long March to escape annihilation by KMT forces in 1934–35, the CCP passed through several areas populated by minorities. The Yi had looted what few possessions the marchers had been able to bring with them. Tibetans had rolled boulders down at the communists as they attempted to traverse narrow mountain passes,

---

3. See A. Doak Barnett, *China on the Eve of Communist Takeover* (New York: Praeger, 1963), p. 209.

and shot at them from behind tall grass. Hui (Chinese Muslim)[4] cavalry had charged at them with swords. Some members of minority groups had been converted to the communist cause, but they were relatively few in number. And there were dozens of minorities about whom the communists knew little or nothing.

Even if the CCP had been inclined to pursue assimilationist rather than pluralist policies toward non-Han ethnic groups during the late 1940s and early 1950s, it simply did not have the capacities to impose uniform or rigidly ideological policies on the minorities. To be sure, coercion was used on occasion. The Muslim warlords of the northwest were defeated in battle; they subsequently escaped to Taiwan or Saudi Arabia. Xinjiang surrendered to communist armies when its collective leadership realized that victory was impossible. Individuals who dissented, most notably the Kazakh warrior Osman Bator, were hunted down and killed.

Tibet was successfully invaded in 1950. Having belatedly declared its independence and cut its telephone link with China, Tibet's inhabitants remained more interested in spirituality than the martial arts. Indeed, they prepared for the Chinese invasion by staging an impressive prayer festival. Nonetheless, Tibet's ill-trained, poorly equipped, and badly outnumbered army fought bravely for nine days before surrendering. Ngapo Ngawang Jigme, the emissary of Tibet's secular and spiritual leader, the Dalai Lama, signed an agreement proclaiming Tibet an integral part of China and stating that the Lhasa government would welcome the deployment of the People's Liberation Army (PLA) in Tibet in order to consolidate national defense. The Chinese central government agreed that the Lhasa government would retain control of Tibet's domestic affairs and that its existing political system would be maintained. Reforms would not be instituted until the masses demanded them.[5] Ngapo could scarcely have avoided capitulating, but Tibetan nationalists denounced him as a collaborator because he seemed to convert instantly to communism.

Force was not the Chinese government's preferred solution to ethnic problems. The government's Common Program, which the Chinese People's Political and Consultative Conference passed in 1949 to serve as a constitution until a more formal document could be devised, declared

---

4. This group is different from the Turkic Muslims or Tajiks, whose language is closely related to Farsi. Hui are Mandarin speakers, although they typically incorporate a number of Arabic words into Mandarin.

5. *Xinhua*, May 27, 1951, in *China and Tibet, 1950–1967* (Hong Kong: Union Research Publications, 1968), p. 20.

that party and government would cooperate with those minorities who would cooperate with it. Traditional leaders would remain in power, and the new government in Beijing would respect the beliefs of all those who agreed not to oppose it. A "united front of patriotic bourgeois upper strata" of minority nationalities was proclaimed. Greater concessions were made to members of these upper strata than to Han in comparable positions. This was necessary, it was explained, because ethnic minorities had "special characteristics," including economic and political backwardness. These were defined in terms of poorly developed class differentiation, which meant the party's theme of class struggle would have to be muted in minority areas. The main goal of political education in this period would be inculcating a spirit of patriotism and a sensed unity among nationalities. The period of growing together was envisioned as a long one, with reforms being made gradually, "in conformity with the wishes of the masses."[6]

The Common Program also proclaimed the equality of the PRC's nationalities in terms of both rights and duties. It became illegal to discriminate against or oppress minorities, but it also prohibited "national splittism"—that is, any effort by ethnic groups or nationalities to leave the PRC. Minorities were given the right to have what the party described as autonomous governments in areas where they were concentrated, and minorities were guaranteed a number of representatives on other government bodies proportional to their numbers. They were free to preserve dialects, languages, customs, habits, and religious beliefs. The People's Government was charged with the task of helping the masses of minority groups to "develop their outlook on politics, economics, culture, and education."[7] To carry this out, the consultative conference created the Government Administration Council, forerunner of the State Council, which in turn created ministry-level entities, including the Nationalities Affairs Commission.

In nationality work, as in other matters, government agencies received direction from, and interacted with, party organs. The party organization most deeply involved in minority work was the United Front Work Department of the Party Central Committee. The department was charged with formulating broad guidelines for minority policy in accordance with the decisions of the party's Politburo. These guidelines were

---

6. Common Program of the Chinese People's Political Consultative Conference, Article 9, in *Minzu chengce wenxian* (Documents on nationality policy) (Beijing, n.d.), p. 1.

7. Ibid., Article 51, p. 1.

then sent to the Nationalities Affairs Commission, which was responsible for implementing them.

In 1951, the Central People's Government issued instructions to ban or change all names, place names, inscriptions and the like that discriminated against or were insulting to ethnic minorities. Strong feelings of Han superiority developed over millennia had spawned many pejorative terms. For example, Yi were commonly referred to as "Lolo," a derisive reference to the spirit boxes they wore around their necks. The ideographic rendering of the names of many minority groups included an element meaning "animal," implying that the members thereof were sub-human. These were to be eliminated or replaced by less objectionable ideographic elements such as that for "man." Place names that indicated pacification by the Han or an acceptance of the Han variant of civilization were also to be changed. Hence "Guisui" formally became Huhhot and "Dihua" became Urumqi, the names by which their respective Mongol and Turkic Muslim inhabitants had traditionally known them. On the other hand, in some areas, traditional names were replaced with more politically acceptable ones. Wangyemiao, the site of the temple of a Mongol prince, was re-named Ulanhot, or "Red City." And the term "bator," or hero, would henceforth be awarded to heroes of socialist labor rather than, as in the past, to nomadic warriors who had distinguished themselves in battle.

Cadres, as the officials of the new regime were called, were told to "do good and win friends" for party and government. Much of this work was done by the PLA. In some cases, emissaries of the new government were welcomed by people who appreciated PLA help in digging irrigation ditches and harvesting crops. For example, the all-but-completely assimilated Manchus did not present many problems, nor did the Koreans, whose educational and income levels actually exceeded those of the Han. Other minorities, including the Bai of Yunnan province and China's largest group, the Zhuang of Guangxi, had long since accommodated to Han ways.

A number of minorities, however, regarded the Han with great suspicion, and greeted with utmost skepticism any efforts to convince them that communists were different from and superior to the Han they had previously known—if in fact the locals would talk to them at all. Some cadres told how people would simply walk away or run off rather than listen to their presentations. There was worse. Yunnan's Wa minority believed that their crops grew better if fields were fertilized each year with a fresh Han head. Several other minorities, such as the Yi, also objected to the Han. Resisters would wait until nightfall, when the cadres gathered around a camp fire to warm themselves. Silhouetted against the flames, the Han made excellent targets for snipers.[8]

Medical teams were dispatched to many minority areas with the aim of curing diseases as well as teaching local people how to prevent sickness. Medical personnel were instructed to tell their patients that their treatment came from the party and Chairman Mao. Fees corresponded to the patient's ability to pay, except for venereal disease, which was treated free of charge. Venereal disease was a particular problem in Tibet and Inner Mongolia, where a significant part of the male population lived in what were supposed to be celibate monasteries. Medical workers also received mixed receptions. Minorities, including the Miao, Tibetans, and Bai, often stubbornly clung to traditional remedies that were medically useless or even dangerous. People who believed that their gods resided in the swamps were reluctant to believe that malaria also came from swamps and adamantly resisted advice to drain them. Given the government's promises to respect the traditions and cultures of minorities, this often put medical teams in difficult positions.

RESEARCH ON MINORITIES

Meanwhile, the government was attempting to fill the lacunae in its knowledge of ethnic minorities. It attached considerable importance to this effort, naming as its head Fei Xiaotong, one of China's most eminent anthropologists. In addition to amassing knowledge and winning friends for party and government, Fei's organization was charged with the daunting task of determining how many ethnic minorities China actually had. Several hundred groups in China believed themselves to be separate ethnic entities. The official list was finally pared to fifty-four, after considerable controversy. For example, reasonable persons could—and did—disagree on how different the speech patterns of two groups needed to be before they were declared two distinct minorities speaking two different languages, as opposed to one minority speaking a language with two distinct dialects. There were also cases where members of minority groups had become geographically separated from one another and developed quite differently over time. In other cases, Han soldiers sent to guard the country's ancient borders had intermarried with local women; the distinctive culture that evolved was neither Han nor that of the original minority group.

---

8. See Alan Winnington, *Slaves of the Cool Mountains* (London: Lawrence and Wishart, 1959), p. 203; and Stuart and Roma Gelder, *The Timely Rain: Travels in New Tibet* (London: Hutchinson and Co., 1964), p. 46.

Having pledged to help minorities preserve and develop their languages and cultures, the government was generally more comfortable with fewer groups rather than many. On the other hand, the well-assimilated Manchus, only a handful of whom could still speak their native language, seem to have been declared a minority simply because the government thought they should be. The Chinese-speaking Hui differed from Han Chinese mainly in terms of their Muslim faith. Buddhists and Christians were not considered to be ethnic minorities; Hui appear to have gained minority status because most believed so firmly that they *were* an ethnic minority—a stand not taken by Buddhists or Christians. In addition, the Chinese government knew that the Hui could cause considerable trouble if denied separate status. A fifty-fifth nationality, the Jinuo of Yunnan, was added in 1979;[9] there have been no changes to the list since then. According to the 1953 census, the PRC's minority population totaled 40 million, ranging from 7,780,000 Zhuang to the 600 Hezhe of Heilongjiang.[10] By the 1990 census, China's minorities numbered 91 million, or 8 percent of the total population. (See Table 9.1.)

EDUCATIONAL POLICIES

In 1952, an All-China Minority Nationalities Education Conference was held. It stressed that training cadres from minority groups would be the main goal of education policy. Six nationality academies and one minority nationality institution of higher learning, the Central Institute of Minorities in Beijing, had already been founded and more than four thousand individuals, some Han and some from minority groups, were being trained to serve in minority areas. The children of Ngapo Ngawang Jigme, whom Tibetans considered a traitor to their cause, were among those enrolled in these institutes, as were the children of other compliant minority leaders. In addition to training personnel to introduce and develop the party's programs in ethnic minority areas, the institutes conducted research on minority histories, cultures, and languages. Several dictionary projects were begun.

---

9. Beijing Radio, September 28, 1979, in United States Technical Information Service, *Foreign Broadcast Information Service Daily Report, Volume 1: China* (hereafter, FBIS-CHI), September 28, 1979, p. Q/1.

10. *Renmin shouce* (People's handbook) (Beijing, 1965), except for Loba, listed in *Xinhua shudian* (Beijing: New China News Agency Books, 1971), p. 1. Tibetans consider the Loba and the Monba, another small group in the Tibet Autonomous Region, to be Tibetans. They believe that the decision to recognize these people as separate groups is another manifestation of the PRC's "divide and rule" policy.

Table 9.1. Ethnic Composition of China.

Group	Location	Number	Percentage
Han	Throughout	1,026,050,400	91.94
Zhuang	Guangxi, Yunnan	15,489,630	1.34
Manchu	Liaoning, Jilin, Heilongjiang	9,821,180	.88
Hui	Ningxia, Gansu	8,602,978	.77
Miao	Guizhou, Hunan, Yunnan	7,398,035	.66
Uygur	Xinjiang	7,214,431	.65
Yi	Sichuan, Yunnan	6,572,173	.60
Tujia	Hunan, Hubei	5,704,223	.51
Mongol	Inner Mongolia, Liaoning	4,806,849	.43
Tibetan	Tibet, Sichuan, Qinghai	4,593,330	.41
Bouyei	Guizhou	2,545,059	.23
Dong	Guizhou	2,514,014	.23
Yao	Guangxi, Guangdong	2,134,013	.19
Korean	Jilin, Liaoning, Helongjiang	1,920,597	.17
Bai	Yunnan	1,594,827	.14
Hani	Yunnan	1,253,952	.11
Kazakh	Xinjiang, Qinghai	1,111,718	.099
Li	Hainan	1,110,900	.099
Dai/Thai	Yunnan	1,025,128	.092
She	Fujian	630,378	.056
Lisu	Yunnan	574,856	.051
Gelao	Guizhou	437,997	.039
Lahu	Yunnan	411,476	.037
Dongxiang	Gansu	373,872	.033
Va/Wa	Yunnan	351,974	.032
Sui	Guizhou	345,993	.031
Naxi	Yunnan	278,009	.025
Qiang	Sichuan	198,252	.018
Tu	Qinghai, Gansu	191,624	.017
Xibe	Xinjiang	172,847	.015
Mulam/Molao	Guangxi	159,328	.014
Kirghiz	Xinjiang	141,549	.013
Daur	Inner Mongolia, Heilongjiang	121,357	.011
Jingpo	Yunnan	119,209	.011
Salar	Qinghai, Gansu	87,697	.008
Biang/Bulang	Yunnan	82,280	.007
Maonan	Guangxi	71,968	.006
Tajik	Xinjiang	33,538	.003
Primi/Pumi	Yunnan	29,657	.0027
Achang	Yunnan	27,708	.0025
Nu	Yunnan	27,123	.0024
Ewenki	Inner Mongolia	26,315	.0024
Gin/Jing	Guangdong	18,915	.0017
Jino	Yunnan	18,021	.0016
De'ang/Benglong	Yunnan	15,462	.0014
Uzbek	Xinjiang	14,502	.0013

Table 9.1. *continued*

Group	Location	Number	Percentage
Russian	Xinjiang	13,504	.0012
Yugu	Gansu	12,297	.0011
Bonan/Baoan	Gansu	12,212	.0011
Monba	Tibet	7,475	.0006
Orogen	Inner Mongolia	6,965	.0006
Derung/Dulong	Yunnan	5,816	.0005
Tatar	Xinjiang	4,873	.0004
Hezhen	Heilongjiang	4,245	.0003
Gaoshan	Taiwan	2,909	.0002
Lhoba	Tibet	2,312	.0002
Total		**1.116 billion**	**100.0**

NOTE: According to the Chinese government's 1990 census data, minorities numbered 90,447,552, constituting 8.0592 percent of the total population. As of 1996, China's population was estimated at 1,210,476,000.
SOURCE: Census data, 1990.

ECONOMIC REFORMS

Since most minorities lived in rural areas, economic policies concentrated on preparations for land reform. This had the potential to bring the party's economic reforms into conflict with its promise to maintain a united front with patriotic upper strata. Reform efforts therefore had to be carried out with utmost care. Members of minority groups who were receptive to the party's explanations about economic exploitation and the need for change were considered to be good candidates for admission to the new minority institutes. It was anticipated that, after training, they would return to their native areas and form the vanguard for further reform. At this point, the Common Program's clause that no reforms would be implemented until the masses demanded them would be activated: led by communist-trained cadres of their own ethnic group, "the masses" would demand reform. State-sponsored trading organs were also set up in minority areas with the aim of selling useful commodities such as needles and cooking pots at fair prices. In very poor areas, the state trading organs often supplied badly needed items such as salt and tea even if that meant operating at a loss. Han traders had in the past charged exorbitant prices for such goods; the new policy attempted to emphasize the differences between communist Han and other Han.

THE GOVERNMENT'S EVALUATION OF ITS WORK

In 1952, the Nationalities Affairs Commission reviewed its work with ethnic minorities and found most of it satisfactory. The investigators believed that the problems they did find were due much more to short-comings among government cadres than to the minority groups them-selves. The report acknowledged the existence of "numerous mistakes," including continued Han chauvinism and the mechanical application of Han experiences in minority areas. For example, cadres had tried to turn a traditional Yao trysting place into a cabbage patch. Other officials, appalled by the wasteful Tibetan practice of burning butter as incense, had tried to get them to stop.

Although the report considered Han chauvinism a more serious prob-lem than ethnic nationalism, it is questionable whether the "mistakes" it mentions were genuinely the result of misunderstandings by lower-level cadres. Party policy could also be regarded as overtly tolerant while covertly engaged in low-level harassment. For example, in 1952 the gov-ernment summoned Hui prayer leaders in Henan province to a meeting. At the end, they were invited to perform ritual ablutions in a very dirty bath. Those who refused were criticized as "too stubborn" to accept new ideas. They came away with the distinct impression of having been deliberately entrapped.[11]

THE 1954 CONSTITUTION

The results of this investigation were incorporated into the 1954 Chinese Constitution. Whereas the Common Program had been essentially a state-ment of intent with regard to minority areas, the constitution was more explicit about aims and policies. For example, it warned that there should be no mechanical application of Han experiences in minority areas. As for reforms, the state promised to pay full attention to the special circum-stances of different groups, while giving minorities time to think over reform proposals; decisions would be made in accordance with their wishes.[12]

The constitution also granted "limited powers to adapt the laws, regulations, and decisions of higher authorities to the requirements of the particular nationality," with the stipulation that central authorities must approve the regulations drawn up by local authorities. The state promised that all nationalities would have the right to use their own spoken and written languages in court proceedings and that courts would be required to provide interpreters for any party unacquainted with the spoken or written languages commonly used in the area. Court hearings were to be

---

11. Kao Han-jen, *The Imam's Story* (Hong Kong: Dragonfly Press, 1953), p. 21.

12. Constitution of the People's Republic of China, *Preamble* (Beijing: Foreign Lan-guages Press, 1954).

conducted in the languages commonly used there, and judgments, notices, and all other court documents were to be promulgated in that language.[13]

In actuality, the Chinese Constitution should be understood as a statement of intent rather than a guarantee of specific rights and protections. As we will see, when party leaders revised their opinions on policies toward ethnic minorities, constitutional provisions that ran contrary to these new policies became irrelevant.

DEVELOPMENT OF THE AUTONOMOUS AREA SYSTEM

Part of the party's promise to minorities was that in the new China they would be allocated specially designated areas in which they could practice a limited form of self-government. Local languages, customs, religions, and other traditional practices would be allowed. The party made it clear that Beijing would control foreign relations, and would tolerate no opposition to communist principles; secession was prohibited.

Eventually there would be five autonomous regions, each equivalent to a province. In recognition of the party's early work there, the first, Inner Mongolia, had been founded in 1947, two years before the PRC was established. The Xinjiang Uygur Autonomous Region was formed in 1955, followed by special areas for the Guangxi Zhuang and Ningxia Hui autonomous regions in 1958. Tibet attained autonomous region status in 1965. There was considerable opposition to the founding of both the Guangxi and Ningxia autonomous regions, since each area had a substantial Han majority population.[14] Twenty-nine autonomous prefectures were also established over time, as were sixty-nine autonomous counties and several hundred autonomous townships.

Although the Han resented being included in autonomous areas, minorities were not necessarily satisfied by these arrangements. The overwhelming majority of the land area of Qinghai, a province neighboring Tibet, is composed of Tibetan autonomous prefectures; in Sichuan, another neighboring province, several Tibetan autonomous prefectures and counties are directly contiguous to the territory of the Tibet Autonomous Region. Tibetans consider these areas to be part of Tibet—their provinces of Amdo and Chamdo, respectively. The CCP's decision to incorporate them into other provinces is seen as a "divide and rule" effort, and is bitterly resented.

---

13. Ibid., Article 77.

14. Han constituted about two thirds of the total population in each case. The Mongol population of Inner Mongolia was even smaller, but it was established before the founding of the PRC and in the midst of the civil war between KMT and CCP; thus there was little opportunity for public opinion to mobilize against the decision.

The Anti-Rightist Campaign and the Great Leap Forward

In 1956, the Nationalities Affairs Commission undertook a second examination of the government's minorities work. Its findings echoed those of 1952: insufficient attention had been paid to training cadres from minority groups and promoting them to leadership positions; there had not been enough support for devising and promoting written minority languages; there were restrictions on the rights of minority peoples to manage their own businesses; and Han cadres had usurped the work of local cadres.[15]

Shortly thereafter, however, a virulent attack against dissenting views—known as the Anti-Rightist Campaign—was launched throughout China. During the summer of 1957, the Nationalities Affairs Commission decided to include minority work in one of its forums. Minorities who had spoken out against government policies soon came to regret their frank words. The torrent of criticism against minorities revealed what had never been disclosed before: separatist movements among the Uygurs, Kazakhs, and Hui.

Other minorities, who were not accused of having secessionist impulses, were criticized for wanting to expel all Han from their areas. A persistent local complaint, corroborated by convincing information, was that the party and the government were using both covert and overt means to assimilate minorities. They were also exploiting minority areas for the benefit of the Han. Local cadres were branded as traitors, and the practice of autonomy was denounced as a sham. Many minority leaders spoke out against collectivization as being incompatible with their groups' culture and traditions. And many claimed that the true leaders of minority groups were their traditional leaders; in other words, local critics did not accept the legitimacy of party-appointed officials.

The individuals who spoke out in these terms were subsequently purged. However, the party also tried to deal with the substance of some of these complaints. In a forerunner of his later policies, Deng Xiaoping, who was then Secretary-General of the CCP, stressed that criticism of local nationalisms must not be made too hastily, and should have the support of most party members and nonparty activists from minority groups.[16] Responding to charges of exploitation, the party pointed out that it had frequently supplied seed, grain, and tools to needy areas, and had under-

---

15. Ulanhu, "Preliminary Report on Minorities Work," translated in United States Consulate General, Hong Kong, *Current Background*, No. 418 (1956), p. 18.

16. Deng Xiaoping, Report on the Rectification Campaign to the Third Enlarged Plenary Session of the Eighth Central Committee of the CCP, translated in *Current Background*, No. 477 (1957), p. 43.

written Xinjiang's budget, for example, for three years. It argued that the Han sought no more than a fair exchange for their generosity and superior technology: some of the products of the minority areas. New regulations were announced in June 1958, giving autonomous areas all revenues from certain taxes that had previously been shared between central and local governments.

This modest gain proved short-lived. In August 1958, the party launched an unprecedented China-wide leveling experiment known as the Great Leap Forward. Born of dissatisfaction with the results of gradual reform and of rebellion against the Soviet path to socialism, the party mandated immediate and sweeping changes. Minority areas were quickly swept into the maelstrom. Their inhabitants were said to be besieging the government with requests for reforms. Class struggle, it was said, did indeed exist in minority areas.

According to the official media, ethnic minorities, even those who had not already undergone land reform, were eager to be included in communes. They were portrayed as delighted to participate in this daring socioeconomic innovation in which virtually everything, including nomads' animals, would be subject to collective ownership. Herdsmen were said to be convinced that the land on which they grazed their animals would be more productively used if sowed with grain and vegetables. Other minorities were said to have realized that their traditional costumes were not conducive to efficient labor in the fields, and also wasted cloth. Hence, the wide sashes of the Dai were replaced with leather belts, and the Gansu Tibetans substituted standard cotton Mao caps for their cumbersome turban-like headgear. With the money saved, they supposedly vowed to buy wheelbarrows. Tibetan lamas, who would normally spend their days in prayer and contemplation, allegedly clamored to take part in productive labor. And the Hui, whose aversion to eating pork or even being anywhere near it had previously led the government to provide them with separate restaurants and butchering establishments, were now described as enthusiastic about joining multinational communes and eating in mess halls where they would be treated like everyone else. Minorities would no longer receive favored treatment; their special privileges were deemed to be manifestations of local nationalism. There was even an attack on the autonomous area system.

Suddenly, again according to the media, everyone wanted to read and write the Han language. They were also eager to welcome young Han immigrants into their areas, the better to learn from them. Intermarriage, even between Han and Hui, was reportedly becoming fashionable. The leveling process of the Great Leap Forward also extended to entertainment. Minority song and dance troupes began to sing revolutionary songs in the Han language. The compilation of dictionaries for local languages and other scholarly research projects related to ethnic issues were halted: there was simply no longer any need for such "bourgeois scientific objectivism."

It soon became obvious that the attitudes of minorities toward these reforms were vastly different from the situations described in the official media. The party had undertaken this drive in order to increase economic production. However, it had precisely the opposite effect. Tremendous anger and resentment generated by the party's blatant reversal of its promises on minority rights led to a drastic decrease in production. Herdsmen slaughtered their animals instead of turning them over to communes. Grazing areas turned out to be unsuitable for raising crops, just as herdsmen had argued. Hui were in fact livid at being forced to use what they considered to be unclean dining and bathing facilities.

Several small rebellions occurred, as well as major ones in Tibet and Xinjiang. Ironically, the first major upheaval caused by the Great Leap Forward occurred in an area that had felt few of its effects. Ethnic Tibetans from provinces outside the Tibet Autonomous Region had fled into the region bearing tales of the horrors that the reforms had caused. Many believed that the region would soon suffer the same fate. Tensions reached a breaking point in March 1959, when Chinese authorities in the region chose an unusual and demeaning way to invite the Dalai Lama to a theatrical performance. Rumors spread that the Chinese intended to abduct the Tibetan leader and incarcerate him in Beijing to reduce resistance to the reforms. The rebels fought bravely, being much better armed and trained than they had been in 1950 due to help from sympathetic outside powers (including India, the United States, and Taiwan). But their efforts were doomed. The Chinese rushed in troops from outside the region and effectively ended the uprising within a few weeks.

Sixty thousand Tibetans, including the Dalai Lama, fled to northern India and Nepal, where they were well positioned to cause trouble for the PRC. In their own monthly magazine and in other publications, exiles charged the Chinese party and government with committing genocide through sterilization, and assimilation through compulsory intermarriage. They also described the destruction of temples and scriptures, forced labor, and the seizure of food and other resources. It is difficult to prove the first two allegations. Since the population of the Tibet Autonomous Region has continued to grow and remains mostly Tibetan, it may be assumed that if sterilization and forced intermarriage have occurred, they have not been widespread. The latter allegations have been confirmed by successive waves of refugees, investigations by Western human rights organizations, and photographic evidence.

In Xinjiang, armed opposition to reforms emerged in several places during 1958 and 1959, but was sporadic and uncoordinated. Disgruntled residents of the region had another option: emigration to the Soviet Union. During the brief Sino-Soviet honeymoon in the early 1950s, the boundary between the two countries had been dubbed "Friendship Border," and herdsmen frequently crossed back and forth seeking seasonal pasturage for their animals. The estrangement of the late 1950s did not, however, result in an immediate tightening of border controls.

A larger revolt occurred in Xinjiang in 1962, which the Chinese blamed on "external forces," meaning the Soviet Union.[17] As a direct result of this rebellion, 70,000 Uygurs and Kazakhs fled across the border and into the Soviet Union. They took along their herds, or what remained of them, thereby exacerbating already existing food shortages in China. Some of the émigrés simply overwhelmed border checkpoints; others had been provided with passports by helpful Soviet consular officials. The refugees were welcomed by Soviet leaders, who immediately enlisted them in the propaganda war that had developed between Moscow and Beijing. Refugees' complaints against the Chinese party and government were broadcast into the PRC, along with commentaries on how much better life was in the Soviet Union.

China's leaders soon realized that the Great Leap Forward had been a mistake. However, rather than publicly acknowledge the fundamental flaws in the reforms, they placed the blame for problems on low-level cadres who allegedly provided their superiors with misleading information on the way reforms were being received. Losses of animals were blamed on poor weather or the activities of a small number of unreformed herdsmen. The party again portrayed itself as the protector of minority cultures, although this must surely have been unconvincing to minorities. In any case, the special characteristics of minority groups were once again acknowledged, and many of the exemptions and affirmative action privileges they had enjoyed before were reinstituted. The canceled dictionary and research projects were revived. The government did admit that the exclusive emphasis on class struggle in minority areas had been harmful, and it promised minorities that the reform of nationality habits and customs would henceforth be carried out according to the free will of the masses. In the words of Wang Enmao, the Han party leader of Xinjiang, the thoughts of Chairman Mao would be integrated with the actual

---

17. Zhou Enlai made this charge in his Report on the Work of the Government, speech to the first session of the Third National People's Congress, December 30, 1964, in United States Consulate General, Hong Kong, *Survey of the China Mainland Press*, No. 3370 (January 1965), p. 12.

situations in minority areas. As official sources noted, hasty actions had caused it to lose the trust of minority nationalities. What it did not say but must have known is that trust once lost is difficult to regain. The three years of famine and widespread starvation that followed the Great Leap Forward did not help in this regard.

The Cultural Revolution

This respite from assimilative pressures was brief. With the advent of the Cultural Revolution, party and government reversed course once more. One of the earliest admonitions Mao Zedong gave to the Red Guards he delegated as the vanguard of the Cultural Revolution in 1966 was to "destroy the four olds": old ideas, old customs, old cultures, and old habits. These were particularly salient in minority communities, partly because the party had specifically promised that minorities would be allowed to retain their traditional ways. The Red Guards sprang eagerly into action. They ripped down pictures of the Dalai Lama from the walls of Tibetan homes and replaced them with pictures of Chairman Mao. The heretofore complaisant Panchen Lama, Tibet's second-ranking spiritual and secular leader, disappeared after he allegedly refused to denounce the Dalai Lama and instead called for an end to the oppression and religious persecution of his countrymen.[18]

Lhasa's central temple was desecrated, as were a number of lamaseries. So were many mosques. Wearing of traditional dress became dangerous, as did the performing of folk dances, even those based on such apparently innocuous themes as bringing in the harvest. Since traditional celebrations of successful harvests implied that prosperity predated the communist revolution, performing them was said to denigrate the importance of the communist revolution. Broadcasting and publishing in minority languages all but ceased.

Attacks went beyond the destruction of buildings and icons, however, and focused on the entire structure of the party's minority work. The United Front Work Department was castigated for capitulating to the decadent upper strata of minorities. A number of Han officials who worked in minority areas were denounced on these grounds as well. Wang Enmao's statement that the thoughts of Mao would have to be

---

18. Although the Cultural Revolution did not formally begin until 1966, the purge of the Panchen Lama and several other radical-instigated moves occurred in 1964. The purge of the Panchen Lama surprised foreign analysts; he had been raised under Chinese (KMT) tutelage and gave every indication of being completely compliant with the wishes of the communist government.

integrated with the realities of the areas in which they were applied was now considered heretical. The autonomous area system came under attack for the same reason.

Mao Zedong's statement that "national struggle is in the final analysis class struggle," dating from the 1950s and never before applied to minorities, suddenly became in an exaggerated form the sole criterion for judging policy in that sector. China's president, Liu Shaoqi, was attacked for having stated that "national problems are *linked with* class problems"; a true Maoist would surely have said that they *were* class problems. Once having accepted the connection between nationality problems and class problems, the correct direction for policy was to end peaceful reform, since it represented the negation of class struggle.

Localized rebellions occurred, although nothing on the scale of those during the Great Leap Forward. The most serious seems to have been in Xinjiang, where provocations included the desecration of mosques, public burning of the Koran, and forcing Muslims to eat pork. Many of those who resisted were heavily armed, having stolen their weapons from military storage sites or having been equipped by the Soviet Union. The rebels tried, as their forebears had done several times in the past under other Chinese governments, to establish an independent East Turkestan Republic. In another case, the inhabitants of an entire Uygur commune simply disappeared across the border into the neighboring Soviet Kirghiz Republic. There were also tales of Kazakh guerrilla bands with thousands of members being supported by the Soviet Union. Ethnically based armed resistance to the Cultural Revolution also occurred in Liaoning, Gansu, the Ningxia Hui Autonomous Region, Tibet, and Yunnan.

An unintended benefit to minority areas was a consequence of Mao's directive to Red Guards to "exchange revolutionary experiences." While some young people chose to enter ethnic minority areas, their number was quite small compared to those who had arrived earlier and now opted to leave. Beginning about 1956, young city dwellers had been sent, generally involuntarily, from their homes to places such as Inner Mongolia, Qinghai, and Xinjiang. This was part of Mao's effort to alleviate population pressures in crowded cities such as Shanghai and Beijing, while diluting the concentration of ethnic minorities in outlying regions. Life in these regions was harsh; even those who had "gone to the countryside" with great enthusiasm found the adjustment to rural life quite difficult.[19] Under normal circumstances, return would have been unthinkable. However, given the opportunity by no less than Mao himself,

---

19. The movement was known as *xiafang* or *xiaxiang* in Mandarin, and sometimes translated as "rustication." Tens of millions of young people took part; not all went to

these stalwart young revolutionaries chose to exchange revolutionary experiences by visiting the nation's capital, or by returning home to their families.

In 1968, Mao decreed an end to the violence of the Cultural Revolution. The chaos within China had gone beyond what he had envisioned, and the Soviet Union, having invaded Czechoslovakia in the name of restoring true socialism, was believed to be contemplating doing the same to the PRC. It was therefore seen as necessary to strengthen China's border defenses. Since many minorities lived near the borders, it made sense to adopt policies that were less provocative toward these groups.

Much damage had already been done: religious institutions had been looted and destroyed; individuals had been tortured and killed; and antagonisms between the Han and minorities had been exacerbated. One institution that survived was the autonomous area system; this was curious in light of radical attacks on it as capitulation to decadent feudal forces, as well as dissident minority insistence that it did not provide them with meaningful self-government. Although the system as a whole survived, a portion of Inner Mongolia that contained a large Han majority was transferred to a contiguous province. And at least one minority autonomous prefecture in Yunnan was abolished. A draft constitution circulated at the end of 1970 confirmed the existence of autonomous areas by noting their inalienability, but reduced their rights. Although it affirmed the right to use minority languages, the draft constitution made no mention of retaining customs or habits, as had the 1954 constitution. In addition, the latter's clause forbidding discrimination on account of nationality was omitted from the new draft constitution.[20]

Most other aspects of minority policy were in shambles. Experienced

---

minority areas. See June Teufel Dreyer, "Go West Young Han: The *Hsia-fang* Movement to China's Minority Areas," *Pacific Affairs*, Vol. 48, No. 3 (Fall 1975), pp. 353–369.

20. This document appeared in mimeographed form in Hong Kong in the fall of 1970, where it was made available to me. An appended note explained that the draft had been approved at the Second Plenum of the Ninth Central Committee, which met between August 23 and September 6, 1970. It was being circulated so that the masses could study it and make comments. I was unable to confirm its authenticity. However, the document has striking similarities to the constitution that was actually adopted nearly five years later, on January 17, 1975. First, both contain thirty articles, as opposed to the 106 in the 1954 constitution. Second, each describes China as a socialist state of the dictatorship of the proletariat, whereas the 1954 constitution terms the PRC a democratic state. Third, although the 1954 constitution provides for a chairman of the PRC, neither the 1970 draft nor the 1975 constitution mentions this office. The most salient difference between the 1970 and 1975 documents is that the earlier one names Lin Biao as Mao Zedong's successor. He was purged in 1971.

administrators of both Han and minority nationalities had been purged, and the institutions they served had been discredited as well. The United Front Work Department had ceased to exist, as had the State Council's Nationality Affairs Commission. Moreover, there were no formal statements as to what government policy toward minorities should be.

Xinhua, the official news agency, occasionally reported that a traditional festival, such as the Muslim celebration of Corban, had been observed. But minorities were scarcely mentioned otherwise. On the rare occasions when they appeared, they were parts of a chorus that uniformly sang the praises of the latest party or government pronouncement. Thus, when a statement was issued condemning alleged Soviet plots against China, a worker in Shanghai, a peasant from Fujian, and a Kazakh herdsman were quoted as saying "do not let them take a blade of grass or a shrub of China's sacred soil." In other words, minorities were portrayed as Han in terms of their language, costume, and political outlook.

Policy Liberalization, 1971–79

This policy on minorities began to change when Chairman Mao's heir apparent, Lin Biao, began his slide from power in 1971. Although these changes appeared gradually, without the strident rhetoric and sloganeering that had characterized previous policy shifts, they were nonetheless cumulatively significant. Personnel changes put less radical individuals in charge of minority areas. In Xinjiang, for example, the first party secretary, a Fourth Field Army associate of Lin Biao, was replaced with a Uygur. This was the first time that a civilian or a Uygur had held such a position in the Xinjiang Uygur Autonomous Region.[21] In Tibet, another radical was replaced with someone who had been repeatedly criticized as conservative during the Cultural Revolution.[22] There was an abrupt end to the effort to eliminate people accused of "sabotaging the unity of nationalities and using religious superstitions in a vain attempt to restore the feudal system." Pictures of Mao were replaced by pictures of the Dalai Lama.

Radio stations resumed or expanded programming in minority languages. Han cadres working in ethnic minority areas were again enjoined to study the languages of those areas. There was also a renewed effort to

---

21. See June Teufel Dreyer, "The PLA and Regionalism in Xinjiang," *Pacific Review*, Vol. 7, No. 1 (Winter 1994), pp. 41–55.

22. In this case, both were members of Lin's Fourth Field Army. Tibet has yet to have a first party secretary who is Tibetan.

train more minorities as cadres. The number of schools specifically for minority students, and presumably using their languages, increased. The Central Institute of Minorities reopened in January 1972 with a class of seven hundred representing forty-six of the then-recognized fifty-four nationalities; by October, there were 1,100 students representing forty-eight nationalities. Teachers reportedly spoke their native languages in class.[23]

Just as it had after the Great Leap Forward, the party, having only recently played the role of destroyer of minority cultures, recast itself as their protector and nurturer. Official media announced that research efforts were under way to enable Tibetans to grow and process the particular variety of tea they favored.[24] Party and government sources also expressed concern about providing minorities with items used in traditional activities: hunting knives, felt boots, brocade, and beads, for example. Since these were described as being produced by factories in Han areas such as Shanghai and Wuhan, the vaunted magnanimity of the party's concern for minorities seems to have had a more self-serving additional effect: bringing the economies of the minority areas more firmly under central government control. However self-serving the motives and despite the lack of any explicit statement on the matter, the special characteristics of minorities had been re-legitimized, as had their separate status.

The official gloss notwithstanding, these years were not without their problems. In 1974 and 1975, several Muslim groups in Yunnan in the extreme south and Xinjiang in the far northwest rebelled. It was rumored, and later confirmed, that the riots broke out after Muslims were told to work on Friday, their holy day. A Western reporter who visited the Yunnan area, Shadian, fifteen years later was told that communist officials had tried to force Muslims to raise pigs. The army had been sent in, and several hundred people were reportedly killed.[25]

Moreover, while there was a tacit acknowledgment that minorities did have special characteristics, no formal protection was accorded to them. The new constitution, ratified in January 1975, omitted the 1954 constitution's statement on respecting the special features of nationalities. The lengthy guarantee of the right to use minority languages found in

---

23. *Xinhua* (Beijing), December 13, 1972.

24. *Beijing Review,* January 21, 1972, p. 4.

25. In this relatively sparsely populated area, several hundred deaths constituted a major conflict. Sheryl Wu Dunn, "The Perfect Union Still Eludes China," *New York Times,* March 28, 1990, p. A4.

the earlier document was reduced to the terse statement that "all the nationalities have the freedom to use their own spoken and written languages." The right to autonomous self-government was reaffirmed, but again in a much briefer form.[26]

One should not overemphasize the importance of the Chinese Constitution: the guarantees of the 1954 document were theoretically in force during the Anti-Rightist Campaign, the Great Leap Forward, and the Cultural Revolution—when they were regularly violated with impunity. Notwithstanding the limited nature of the rights given to minorities by the 1975 constitution, the actual situation resembled 1954 in important respects, as discussed earlier.

By the time Mao died in September 1976, minorities appeared to have acquiesced to the rule of the Communist Party and their inclusion under the jurisdiction of the PRC. Rebellions might succeed in winning some concessions, albeit at considerable human cost, but the party and the government had made it clear that independence was not an option. While the right to use one's native language was theoretically unchallenged, minorities had come to appreciate the value of being fluent in the Han language. The party and the institutions it had created were the major channels of social mobility, not the traditional leadership patterns that had existed before 1949. The educational systems of minority areas were controlled by the central government, as were their economies. This would soon change.

Mao's death was quickly followed by the arrest and incarceration of the Gang of Four, who were subsequently blamed for most of the abuses that minorities suffered during the Cultural Revolution. However, policies had become much more accommodative toward minorities following Lin's downfall in 1971, which would seem to indicate that Lin rather than the Gang of Four was primarily responsible for these assimilationist policies. Nonetheless, policies toward minorities eased still further under Hua Guofeng, who succeeded Mao.

A new constitution introduced in January 1978 and ratified by the National People's Congress two months later proclaimed the equality of all of China's nationalities and enjoined them to help and learn from each other. Discrimination against or oppression of any nationality was expressly forbidden; so was the commission of any act that would undermine the unity of nationalities. Both Han chauvinism and local-nationality chauvinism were to be opposed. All nationalities were given

26. The entire text of the 1975 constitution may be found in *Beijing Review*, January 24, 1975, pp. 12–17.

the freedom to use and develop their own spoken and written languages, and to preserve or reform their own customs and ways.[27]

The constitution affirmed the principle of regional autonomy, and organs of self-government were empowered to draw up specific regulations that reflected the political, economic, and cultural characteristics of their areas and submit them to the Standing Committee of the National People's Congress for approval. These organs would use the spoken and written language or languages commonly used by the nationality or nationalities in the region in question. Each nationality was entitled to "appropriate" representation in the organs of self-government.[28]

Almost simultaneously, the United Front Work Department was reconvened; it had not met since 1964.[29] One of the delegates was the Panchen Lama.[30] His presence, and hence rehabilitation, indicated the official return to what Cultural Revolution radicals had called pandering to the traditional upper strata of the minorities. The Nationalities Affairs Commission was also resuscitated at this time.[31] These changes took place under the aegis of Mao's chosen successor, Hua Guofeng. Deng Xiaoping, who had been purged twice—once during the Cultural Revolution and again in 1976—had been rehabilitated a second time in July 1977, but does not seem to have risen to the dominant but informal position of "paramount leader" until late 1978. It is, of course, still possible that Deng's views played a part in the changes in minority policy that took place before 1978.

Official sources stated explicitly that "China's modernization was . . . in pressing need of the participation of the minority nationalities,"[32] as was its border defense.[33] Therefore, the party and the government were drawing up a series of measures to help minorities develop their economies and cultures. It was decided that minority nationalities would not simply disappear, and that solutions to nationality problems were long-term matters. Class struggle was decoupled from questions involving

---

27. The Constitution of the People's Republic of China, Article 4, *Beijing Review*, March 17, 1978, pp. 6–7.

28. Ibid., Articles 38 and 39, pp. 12–13.

29. Fox Butterfield, "China Calls Meeting With All Minorities, The First Since 1964," *New York Times*, February 25, 1978, pp. 1, 3.

30. Carey Winfrey, "Tibetan Spiritual Leader: The Panchen Lama," *New York Times*, February 25, 1978, p. 3.

31. *Xinhua*, June 9, 1979, in FBIS-CHI, June 13, 1979, p. L/18.

32. Ibid., p. L/17.

33. Beijing Radio, January 26, 1980, in FBIS-CHI, January 31, 1980, p. L/13.

minorities; it was explained that Lin Biao and the Gang of Four had distorted a statement by Mao in support of American blacks and applied it to China's minorities.[34] This explanation is difficult to believe. Among other problems, it does not explain why the chairman himself made no attempt to correct this "distortion" of his intent, since it had such devastating policy consequences.

Han-minority tensions were now assumed to be a function of the economic backwardness of minority areas rather than, as Cultural Revolution radicals had argued, being rooted in class struggle. Hence, economic development of those areas would help solve minority problems; it would also assist in Deng's Four Modernizations program for China. State investment for capital construction and subsidies to minority areas were to be increased "by a big margin."[35] How much of a net increase over pre–Cultural Revolution practice this represented is uncertain, since it was revealed elsewhere that state subsidies to minorities had been cut by one third between 1968 and 1975.[36]

In any case, vehicles, tractors, and rolled steel were to be allocated to minority areas. Provinces and cities in the interior were to make manpower, matériel, and technical support available to them.[37] Herdsmen were to be allowed to keep more animals for private use and set aside more land for growing their own fruit trees;[38] later, these would become completely privatized. The head of the Nationalities Affairs Commission warned cadres against forcing minorities to raise pigs if they believed that pork was unclean, and added that "no administrative decree is allowed to enforce reform."[39]

Minorities also received whole or partial exemptions from the PRC's stringent new family planning regulations. While Han couples faced heavy pressure to have just one child, even minorities who lived in crowded areas were permitted two children. This applied, for example, to Manchus, Koreans, and Zhuang who lived in urban areas. Nomadic Kazakhs and rural Tibetans could have as many as four children. In practice, such groups could often ignore family planning regulations altogether.

---

34. Commentator, "Make a Success of Nationalities Work and Strive to Realize the Four Modernizations," *Renmin Ribao*, June 19, 1979, p. 4.

35. FBIS-CHI, June 13, 1979, pp. L/17–L/18.

36. Liu Xianzhao and Wei Shiming, "On the Protracted Nature of the Nationalities Problem in the Socialist Period," *Renmin Ribao*, April 6, 1979, p. 3.

37. FBIS-CHI, June 13, 1979, pp. L/17–L/18.

38. *Xinhua*, June 4, 1979, in FBIS-CHI, June 7, 1979, p. T/6.

39. *Xinhua*, October 28, 1978, in FBIS-CHI, November 3, 1978, pp. L/10–L/11.

Territorial adjustments that were beneficial to minorities were also made. The portion of the Inner Mongolian Autonomous Region that had been detached during the Cultural Revolution was returned.[40] An autonomous prefecture that had been abolished during the Cultural Revolution was revived,[41] and several new autonomous areas were created.[42] The autonomous township system, defunct since the Great Leap Forward, was re-created. A fifty-fifth nationality, the Jinuo, was officially recognized.[43]

In March 1979, the capitulationist labels that had been applied to those involved in minority work were removed.[44] Minority literature and art were also rehabilitated, it being explicitly stated that this would be useful in establishing cultural exchanges with other countries.[45] There was also renewed interest in educational work in minority areas: it was recognized that economic backwardness could be attributed at least in part to poor schools. The Ministry of Education announced that six junior colleges in minority areas would become four-year institutions in order to train more medical personnel and teachers for work in these areas.[46] The state vowed to expand minority education and education in a minority child's own language. Liaoning province announced the establishment of new elementary and secondary schools for Mongols and Koreans, respectively;[47] a standard Yi script was introduced in Sichuan; and a newly developed alphabet for the Tu of Qinghai was tried out.[48]

Not all the news about and from minorities was positive. There were rumbles of unrest in Xinjiang, with the provincial radio station complaining that "certain people, catering to the needs of an adverse current, have been obstructing the normal order of society, production, and work," thus

---

40. Beijing Radio, July 20, 1979, in FBIS-CHI, July 20, 1979, p. R/4.

41. Kunming Radio, October 17, 1979, in FBIS-CHI, October 18, 1979, p. J/2.

42. For example, Yunnan's Mojiang County became the Mojiang Hani Autonomous County on July 30, 1979. Kunming Radio, October 17, 1979, in FBIS-CHI, October 23, 1979, p. Q/3.

43. *Xinhua*, September 28, 1979, in FBIS-CHI, September 28, 1979, p. Q/1. The Jinuo, who live in the Xishuangbanna Dai Autonomous Prefecture, were described as having a population of 10,000.

44. Li Weihan, "On the New Stage and New Task of China's United Front: Rereading Comrade Zhou Enlai's Government Work Report at the CPPCC Session in 1962," *Renmin Ribao*, September 18, 1979, p. 2.

45. Mao Dun, speech to Fourth National Congress of Writers and Artists of China, Beijing, October 30, 1979, in FBIS-CHI, November 2, 1979, p. L/20.

46. *Xinhua*, October 19, 1978, in FBIS-CHI, October 20, 1978, p. E/22.

47. Shenyang Radio, September 24, 1979, in FBIS-CHI, September 26, 1979, p. S/4.

48. *Xinhua*, January 8, 1980, in FBIS-CHI, January 23, 1980, p. L/5.

showing that "class struggle has not died out." The new focus of party work "does not mean that class struggle has been abandoned and the dictatorship of the proletariat abolished . . . we must be ready to smash any subversion, sabotage, and invasion by imperialism [a code word for the United States], social imperialism [a code word for the Soviet Union], and big and small hegemonism."[49]

In the Tibet Autonomous Region, the Han were being evacuated due to severe food shortages. These were caused not by natural disasters but by human folly: the government had forced Tibetans to grow wheat rather than the barley that formed the staple of their traditional diet. After a few years of promising results, the soil became depleted and grain had to be sent into the region to avert famine. Han occupation had brought the region to the brink of ecological disaster. The army had slaughtered huge numbers of yaks—animals crucial to the economy—apparently for sport, and forests had been cut down indiscriminately. In Yunnan, problems arose over land and water rights. For example, in the course of setting up rubber plantations, state farms had taken land and the rubber trees thereon away from the minority nationalities. The situation was apparently deemed sufficiently serious that Hu Yaobang, who was about to become China's first party secretary, made an inspection visit to the area.[50]

Efforts to develop industries in minority areas apparently made little progress. At the end of 1979, *Xinhua* proudly announced that China was producing television sets in every province except Tibet, Xinjiang, Qinghai, and Ningxia—three of the five autonomous regions and one province whose territory is overwhelmingly composed of autonomous prefectures.[51] A subsequent effort to privatize the economies of minority areas by replacing state subsidies with loans also caused problems, since people in these areas did not know how to make good use of them.[52]

Other policies devised for Han areas caused problems for minority communities. For example, a ban imposed on recruiting cadres from rural areas had the unintentional effect of negating the party's promise to recruit more cadres from ethnic minorities, since very few of them lived

---

49. Urumqi Radio, May 9, 1979, in FBIS-CHI, May 24, 1979, pp. T/1–T/2.

50. Liu Qian, "Comrade Hu Yaobang Asked About Xishuangbanna," *Renmin Ribao*, March 29, 1985, p. 4. Hu's first inspection tour was in 1981; he returned in 1985 as first party secretary.

51. *Xinhua*, November 14, 1979, in FBIS-CHI, November 28, 1979.

52. Wang Rong, "Drive Helps Minorities Adjust to the Market," *China Daily*, October 27, 1992, p. 1.

in urban areas.[53] Because Deng Xiaoping's effort to raise educational standards in the PRC included the establishment of a difficult examination for admission to universities, the number of minority students in universities dropped precipitously.[54]

In his zeal to modernize the PRC, Deng Xiaoping reversed Mao Zedong's redistributive policies, whereby wealth was siphoned out of prosperous cities and provinces to help poorer areas. Investment was now made where it would produce the best return on capital. Typically, this was in coastal areas, and in the same cities that had prospered before the communist party took over: Guangzhou, Shanghai, Tianjin, and Wuhan. Meanwhile, minority areas fell behind.

A long-term communist party member of Mongol nationality, Ulanhu, complained that cadres were not implementing minority rights safeguards and that "some of the communist party members hardly sound like Marxists on the question of minority nationalities." Part—but only part—of the reason was that they feared the new policies might be reversed. This had happened several times in the past, and the cadres who implemented the new policies were criticized and often punished severely for what they had done.

Development and Disquiet in the 1980s and 1990s

REFORMING THE REFORMS, 1980–84

Efforts were made to solve the problems that emerged in the 1970s. Tibet was exempted from certain taxes. Apologies were made when Han writers produced books or plays portraying minorities in an offensive manner. An affirmative action program was instituted to facilitate minority admission into universities: quotas were established to ensure that a fixed (but unspecified) number of minority students were able to enter college. In addition, the minimum entrance standards were lowered for minorities. Several new nationality institutes were established, and remedial classes were set up to help minorities who had graduated from senior middle school prepare for university entrance examinations.[55]

Border minorities were urged to develop their economies through cross-border exchanges. Hence, Tibetans could trade with Nepal or India,

---

53. Li Jiguo and Qian Zhixin, "Leading Comrades of Minority Nationality Areas in Yunnan Call for Selecting and Promoting Minority Nationalities Cadres," *Renmin Ribao*, November 8, 1979, p. 4.

54. *Xinhua*, December 4, 1979, in FBIS-CHI, December 13, 1979, p. P/4.

55. Ibid., p. P/5.

Yunnan minorities with Laos and Burma, Inner Mongolian Mongols with the Mongolian People's Republic, and Kazakhs and Uygurs with the peoples of the Soviet Union. Foreign investment in minority areas was welcomed. When considered solely on the basis of return on capital, these were not the best options for foreign investors. However, there was hope that investors could be induced to help for non-financial reasons. Wealthy foreign Muslims might, for example, want to help their co-religionists in Ningxia or Xinjiang. The government also welcomed soft loans from international development agencies to minority areas.

At Fei Xiaotong's suggestion, tourism was encouraged as well. A number of minorities inhabit areas of great scenic beauty. This, plus colorful traditional costumes and folk arts, would make them popular with foreign visitors who would, it was hoped, contribute to the prosperity of minority areas by spending large sums of money there. Chinese travel agency brochures quickly began to feature expensive side excursions to standard Beijing-Shanghai-Guangzhou itineraries. One could arrange to spend a night in a modified Mongolian tent, dine on yakburger in Lhasa, or examine the exotic flora and fauna of the Xishuangbanna Dai Autonomous Prefecture in southern Yunnan.

In 1982, the PRC's fourth and current constitution was promulgated. On matters pertaining to ethnic minorities, there were no startling changes from its 1978 predecessor. All nationalities of the PRC were declared equal; discrimination against and oppression of any nationality were prohibited, as were any acts that undermined the unity of the nationalities. However, a new phrase prohibiting acts that would instigate secession was added. The 1978 constitution's guarantee that all nationalities had the freedom to use and develop their own spoken and written languages and to preserve or reform their own customs and ways was carried over verbatim. A new paragraph added that the state would "help areas inhabited by minority nationalities to speed up their economic and cultural development in accordance with the peculiarities and needs of the different minority nationalities."[56]

In 1984, a law on regional autonomy went into effect. In essence, the new law was an enlarged version of the rights conferred by the constitution with minor additions. One was that the administrative head of an autonomous area should be a citizen of the nationality or nationalities exercising regional autonomy in the area concerned. While this would be of some benefit to the exercise of self-government, there were no comparable stipulations for party leadership in autonomous areas. The latter

---

56. See *Beijing Review,* December 27, 1982, pp. 12, 23, 27.

was by far the more powerful position. A second addition gave autonomous areas the power to administer local finances, though adding that "revenue and expenditure of the national autonomous areas are determined in accordance with the principle of the State Council."[57]

Although problems were occasionally mentioned, the party and government appeared to be pleased with the results of their policies toward ethnic minorities. That the total minority population had grown to 67 million was taken as proof of the wisdom of these policies. In 1984, minorities constituted 6.2 percent of those taking university entrance examinations, which was fairly close to their 6.7 percent share of the population as a whole.[58] In administrative terms, the autonomous area system was well developed, with five autonomous regions, thirty-one autonomous prefectures, eighty-three autonomous counties, and more than eight hundred autonomous townships.

NEW PROBLEMS, 1985–96

Shortly thereafter, a note of alarm began to creep into official announcements on minority questions. A number of new problems had arisen, many of them direct consequences of earlier reforms. Reform efforts notwithstanding, the economies of minority areas continued to fall further behind those of coastal China. This contributed to minorities' sense of exploitation by the Han, whether or not the facts bore out their perception. A few areas, including Xinjiang, had set up economic blockades against goods coming in from elsewhere in China.

Tibetans complained that the benefits of tourism were not going to Tibetans but to Han immigrants to the Tibet Autonomous Region. This was frequently true. The new arrivals, often young people from impoverished areas of nearby Sichuan province, flooded into Lhasa to profit from the tourist trade and take advantage of the preferential taxes that had been given to the Tibet Autonomous Region. Most tourists probably had no idea that the peddlers they were buying trinkets from were not Tibetans, but the locals knew and resented it. A group of Tibetan-speaking Americans discovered that the waitresses at Lhasa's Holiday Inn spoke no Tibetan despite the traditional costumes they wore. Others, who interviewed workers constructing Dai-style buildings in different sectors of the capital of the Xishuangbanna Dai Autonomous Prefecture, found that

---

57. "Law on Regional Autonomy for Minority Nationalities of the PRC," *Renmin Ribao*, June 4, 1984, pp. 1, 2; English translation in FBIS-CHI, June 14, 1984, pp. K/3– K/13.

58. *Xinhua*, July 7, 1984, in U.S. National Technical Information Service, Joint Publications Research Service (JPRS), *China: Political and Social Report*, August 15, 1984, p. 61.

there were no minorities or even any permanent residents of the area among the work crews.

That many Han were moving freely to minority areas is ironic in view of the strong resentment Mao's forced transfer of the Han to minority areas had engendered. The perception that economic opportunities existed in these areas provided the impetus for this new wave of voluntary migration. Minorities resented the Han influx regardless of their reasons for coming.

Tourism also brought locals into contact with foreigners who heard about minority grievances and reported them to international human rights organizations. Videos and audiocassettes detailing human rights abuses were smuggled out. While most tourists had no ulterior motives, others were supporters of separatist movements, foreign intelligence agents, or members of terrorist groups. This fact posed a particular problem in Muslim areas of northwest China. Despite decades of directives admonishing Han cadres who worked in minority areas to learn local languages, few had actually taken the time to do so, and locals could often speak frankly with visitors even in the presence of party "minders."

In addition, China's minorities were attracted by the lifestyle of fellow ethnics who lived abroad. The Xishuangbanna Dai Autonomous Prefecture became a popular destination for tourists from Thailand. The Dai took note of their fellow ethnics' stylish clothing, expensive cameras, and freedom to express themselves politically and culturally. This reinforced their ethnic consciousness, and some Dai began to emulate the Thai. Chinese officials became apprehensive about this and refused to allow Royal Thai Air to fly directly from Chiang Mai in northern Thailand to Jinhong, the capital of Xishuangbanna.[59]

The prospect of economic gain was a main reason why ethnic Koreans who are Chinese citizens have tried to emigrate to the Republic of Korea. South Korean officials have had to deal with Korean "tourists" from China who simply disappeared from Seoul hotel rooms; with fishing boats loaded with illegal Chinese Korean immigrants attempting to enter Pusan Harbor; and with a country-wide marriage-for-money scam that enabled thousands of ethnically Korean Chinese "brides" to obtain residency in South Korea.[60]

Foreign investment brought similar problems. International lending

---

59. I am indebted to Professor Charles Keyes, Department of Anthropology, University of Washington, for this information.

60. See "ROK Police Catch 126 Korean-Chinese Trying to Enter ROK," *Korea Times*, April 7, 1996, p. 3; and "ROK, PRC to Jointly Crack Down on 'Disguised Marriages'," *Yonhap*, May 7, 1996, via internet.

agencies sometimes consider a country's human rights record when deciding whether or not to approve a grant request. Businesspeople often make donations directly to mosques or to the charitable foundations of minorities, thus giving those entities more autonomy from the central government. It is difficult for Beijing to object if a foreigner gives large sums of money to build a school or a mosque. What is taught and preached in those edifices is often objectionable to the government, although authorities do not have an easy time finding out the exact content of the messages being imparted, again, because of language barriers that the government has never overcome.

Cross-border trade has added to these problems. Searching every person and vehicle coming through busy checkpoints would inhibit the commerce that the trade routes were set up to encourage. Bombs and firearms have entered Xinjiang, scriptures and proscribed pictures of the Dalai Lama have come into Tibet, and drugs from the Golden Triangle have passed into Yunnan. Chinese Wa, Hui, and others have bought land in the Wa foothills of Burma, where they have raised poppies.[61] The opium they have produced has been sold in Yunnan and transported by Muslim traders with extensive distribution networks to buyers in northwest China and Hong Kong.

Nor was the burgeoning minority population the blessing it first seemed. Alarmed demographers pointed out that, if trends continued, the minority population would constitute 587 million people, or 28.5 percent of China's total, by the year 2048.[62] If population continued to increase at this rate, it would be impossible to raise living standards in minority areas: part of the reason for the gap between the living standards in Han and minority areas was rapid population growth in the latter. In addition, respect for minority customs was impairing the quality of life in minority areas: Yi, who by tradition marry cousins, and Hui, who practice same-surname and intralineage-group marriage, have had higher than average incidences of birth defects.

Not all of the increase in minority populations was due to high birth rates. Although the 1990 census showed twenty-four million more minorities in China than the 1982 census, for a total of ninety-one million, only ten million of these represented a natural increase in population. The other fourteen million were people originally listed as Han who had since

---

61. "Pull of the Land," *Far Eastern Economic Review,* September 5, 1996, p. 12.

62. Yan Tiansan and Jin Cao, "Concern over Negative Population-Selection Phenomenon: Economic Considerations of the Impact of Family Planning on Population Growth," *Renkou Yanjiu* (Beijing), September 29, 1992, pp. 36–41.

registered as minorities. The authorities were convinced that individuals were seeking permission to re-register less because of their minority ancestry and more because minority status was a way to circumvent the one-child policy and could ease the path of their children into higher education. More stringent standards were subsequently imposed on the re-registration process, but they could be circumvented. For example, between September 1994 and May 1995, the nationality bureau of Luchuan county in Guangxi province made almost 80,000 yuan (about $10,000—a large sum in this impoverished area) by selling minority nationality registration certificates.[63]

These trends, set in motion by the government's reforms, were exacerbated because of the backdrop against which they played out: a disintegrating Soviet Union, a rising tide of Islamic fundamentalism, increasing concern with human rights in the West, and Deng Xiaoping's failing health. Borders were more porous, and directives from party and government could more easily be ignored.

The party and government responded by becoming more intransigent. For example, pro-Tibetan independence activists had been making impressive and generally successful efforts to draw international attention to their cause. In June 1988, despite angry protests from Beijing, the Dalai Lama was invited to address the European Parliament in Strasbourg. He chose this occasion to offer a compromise to China. More specifically, he proposed that Beijing would be responsible for Tibet's foreign policy; Tibet would be governed by its own constitution or basic law; the Tibetan government would be composed of a popularly elected chief executive, a bicameral legislature, and an independent legal system; and Tibet would become a demilitarized zone, with China retaining the right to maintain military installations in Tibet for defense purposes only, until Tibet's neutrality had been internationally established.[64]

The Chinese accused the Dalai Lama of trying to internationalize the issue of Tibet, and called for negotiations on terms that they must have known would be unacceptable to him. Persons within Tibet believed to be sympathetic to the Dalai Lama were arrested, and in September 1988, a large police and military contingent was moved into the region and paraded though the streets of Lhasa. Soldiers were sent to monasteries on inspection tours. Tibetan opposition to compromise subsequently stiffened. Demonstrations took place in December 1988. In January 1989, the normally accommodative Panchen Lama stated publicly that although

---

63. "Nationality Identity Can Be Bought," *China Focus*, February 1996, p. 4.

64. "Tibet's Leader Outlines Plan," *South China Morning Post*, June 16, 1988, p. 1.

there had been progress in Tibet since 1950, it had come at too high a price.[65] Four days later, it was reported that the otherwise healthy fifty-one-year-old lama had died of a heart attack. Suspicious Tibetans concluded that he had been executed for speaking out. Given the paucity of details available, it is impossible to either confirm or refute this hypothesis. More important, perhaps, is the fact that many Tibetans believed that the Panchen Lama had been murdered, and they became more inclined than ever to protest Chinese policy.

By the time pro-democracy demonstrations began in Beijing and elsewhere in China during the spring of 1989, Lhasa was already under martial law. It remained so for more than a year, after which anti-government activities quickly resumed. In the interim, the Dalai Lama had been awarded the Nobel Peace Prize. In addition, the son and namesake of Ngapo Ngawang Jigme, who had signed Tibet's surrender to the Chinese communists four decades before, had emigrated to New York where he became active in the Tibet independence movement.

Uygur and Kazakh demonstrations in Xinjiang in the spring of 1989 went almost unnoticed by the international community, whose attention was riveted on the events unfolding in Tiananmen Square. Although the protesters in Xinjiang had a long list of grievances and some sought independence, the proximate cause of the demonstration was the publication of a book in Shanghai that contained material offensive to Islam. According to official sources, the protesters attacked Communist Party headquarters in Xinjiang's capital city of Urumqi with rocks and steel bars, destroying 40 vehicles and injuring 150 police.[66]

Beijing authorities soon agreed to ban the book, although they must have been aware that the outburst in Xinjiang was merely the latest manifestation of underlying discontent in various parts of the country. Concurrent with the protests in Tiananmen Square and Urumqi, there were Hui demonstrations in Gansu and Qinghai, which had nothing to do with the allegedly salacious book. Qinghai Hui, for example, were upset because a Hui had not been appointed vice-governor. According to government sources, a "small handful" had been inciting public opinion against party, government, and military. Their attacks on trains had caused several suspensions of service on the Gansu-Qinghai rail line.[67]

---

65. *Zhongguo Xinwen She* (Beijing), January 24, 1989, in FBIS-CHI, January 25, 1989, p. 56.

66. See Xinjiang Radio, May 26, 1989, in FBIS-CHI, June 2, 1989; and Carl Goldstein, "Letter from Xinjiang," *Far Eastern Economic Review*, August 9, 1989, p. 37.

67. Beijing Radio, June 10, 1989, in FBIS-CHI, June 12, 1989, p. 90.

In June 1989, Xinjiang officials published a "most-wanted" list that suggested that local protesters had received cross-provincial help: the first four of the seven names on the list were Gansu Hui; the other three were local Uygurs. One of the latter regularly traveled outside Xinjiang as an acrobat. A central government delegation headed by China's public security minister visited Xinjiang in August and concluded that the demonstrations there had not been inspired by those at Tiananmen Square. It argued that the problems in Xinjiang had been instigated by unnamed foreign supporters of separatism.[68]

There were also major protests in Inner Mongolia in May and June 1989, blamed on a "small number of [minority] people . . . exploiting ethnic issues to stir things up in a vain attempt to destroy national solidarity and the unity of the motherland."[69] In fact, Mongols in Inner Mongolia were attracted by the burgeoning democracy movement in the Mongolian People's Republic. Some wanted to emulate its example, and others to unite the two Mongolias.

Although the crackdown on demonstrators in Tiananmen Square seemed to end the public manifestation of discontent in the major cities of Han China, demonstrations in several minority areas worsened. Party and government efforts to end what the media referred to as "splittist sentiments" consequently intensified. The official media simply did not report what was happening in the Mongolian People's Republic, where a popular movement ousted the communist government and established a democratic republic. Nonetheless, many people in China found out what was happening in Mongolia. An inspection team from Beijing visited Inner Mongolia in 1990, after which the province's governor announced that although "on the whole" relations among ethnic groups were good, "all our work should be focused on the effort to maintain stability." A major replacement of personnel at the top levels of Inner Mongolia's leadership was carried out, presumably with that in mind, in that year. However, the governor himself, a Mongol and the son of long-term party stalwart Ulanhu, remained in place.

In 1991, provincial authorities arrested the members of two organizations that described themselves as dedicated to researching and promoting traditional Mongolian culture and identity. Officials accused the groups, which had tried to register legally with the government, of being "splittist" and "subversive" and of promoting the secession of Mongol

---

68. Xinjiang Radio, August 26, 1989, in FBIS-CHI, August 30, 1989, pp. 70–71.

69. *"Jinxin Dongpo De 56 Tian"* (56 Soul-Stirring Days) (Beijing: State Education Commission, 1989), cited in Human Rights Watch/Asia (HRW/A), *Crackdown in Inner Mongolia* (New York: HRW/A, 1991), p. 7.

areas and the disintegration of China.[70] Interestingly, many of the leaders of these movements were educated in institutions that had been created to disseminate the party's message.[71]

Agitation in Inner Mongolia is not as serious a problem for the government as turmoil in Xinjiang or Tibet, since there are only four million Mongols in a total population of some twenty-two million in the Inner Mongolian Autonomous Region. Some of the dissidents in Inner Mongolia have indicated, moreover, that neither independence nor re-unification with Mongolia is likely: they would settle for genuine regional autonomy.[72] Unrest continues, however. Local complaints reflect both cultural and environmental concerns: the central government's policy of increasing the human and cattle population of the grasslands is said to be causing serious land erosion.[73] In 1992 Human Rights Watch/Asia reported ethnic unrest in six Inner Mongolian cities, including gun battles between local herders and Chinese military forces.[74] In December 1995, government authorities detained dozens of protesters, many of them university students, carrying posters of Chinggis Khan.[75]

In Tibet, protests escalated as well. In May 1993, more than one thousand people demonstrated in the streets of Lhasa in the first large-scale protest since 1989. Moreover, whereas the protests of the previous four years had been led mainly by monks and nuns, in 1993 most of the demonstrators were lay people. Another noteworthy development was the emergence of protests in rural areas of the Tibet Autonomous Region as well as in Tibetan areas of Qinghai province. In 1994 it became clear that government authorities would no longer tolerate the expression of even economic grievances. They had previously allowed limited protests on economic issues so long as demonstrations did not address overtly political matters.[76]

---

70. HRW/A, *Crackdown in Inner Mongolia*, p. 1.

71. See ibid., pp. 22–26.

72. Nicholas Kristof, "Restlessness Reaches Mongols in China," *New York Times*, July 7, 1992, Sect. 4, p. 3.

73. A scholarly explanation of this issue is provided in Didi Tatlow, "Government Policy Said To Destroy Grasslands," *Eastern Express* (Hong Kong), July 1–2, 1995, p. 10. Research institutes in Inner Mongolia have become increasingly critical of the effect of central government policies on their province.

74. Human Rights Watch/Asia, *Continuing Crackdown in Inner Mongolia* (New York: HRW/A, 1992), p. 5.

75. "Mongolia Protest Is Halted," *New York Times*, February 2, 1992, p. A4.

76. See Robert Barnett, *Cutting Off the Serpent's Head: Tightening Control in Tibet, 1994–1995* (London: Tibet Information Network and New York: HRW/A, 1995), pp. 6–8.

Tibetans were further angered in 1995 when the boy whom the Dalai Lama had selected as the reincarnation of the Panchen Lama disappeared and was replaced by a child of Beijing's choosing. Dissidents included not only clerics and students but eminent individuals who had theretofore been accommodative. By the spring of 1996, official sources openly admitted that party and government officials in Tibet were not carrying out Beijing's directives. They had "failed to act firmly on the issue of banning the Dalai Lama's portrait" and some even had pictures of him in their own homes. Furthermore, some officials maintained lavish shrines in their homes for the performance of religious rituals. A number of Tibetan cadres whose children attended schools run by the Dalai Lama outside of China had refused a party directive to bring them back. The influence of monks and monasteries consequently grew, and they became the focal points of separatist activities.[77]

The situation in Xinjiang deteriorated as well. Twenty-seven secret organizations were said to be operating in the province in the mid-1990s. One, the "Tigers of Lop Nor,"[78] claimed credit for killing nine Han officials in a car bombing in February 1996. Foreign visitors to several different cities reported separatist-inspired street fighting. In late April, the Chinese government hosted a meeting in Shanghai of high-level representatives of Russia, Kazakhstan, Kyrgyzstan, and Tajikistan to gain their assent to clamp down on the movement of terrorists into and out of Xinjiang. However, less than two weeks later a seventy-three-year-old imam was brutally attacked by assailants who regarded him as being too supportive of the government.

Here again the central government's lack of control over its own officials is manifest. In late May, the provincial newspaper issued a call to

sternly deal with party members and cadres, especially leading cadres, who continue to be devout religious believers despite repeated education; instill separatist ideas and religious doctrines into young people's minds; publish distorted history; [issue] books or magazines advocating separatism and illegal religious ideas; or make audio or video products propagating such ideas.[79]

---

77. Ni Banggui, "Paying Attention to Politics Should Be Closely Linked with Tibet's Reality," *Xizang Ribao* (Lhasa), May 13, 1996, p. 4, in FBIS-CHI, June 3, 1996, pp. 35–39.

78. "Lop Nor" means "Dry Lake" in Mongolian and is the PRC's nuclear testing site. Xinjiang natives have been openly protesting the use of their territory for these tests since 1985.

79. "Regional Discipline Inspection Commission and Regional Supervision Department Call on Discipline Inspection and Supervision Organs Across Xinjiang to Strictly Enforce Political Discipline and Maintain the Stability of the Overall Situation," *Xinjiang Ribao* (Urumqi), May 22, 1996, p. 1, in FBIS-CHI, June 7, 1996, pp. 82–84.

Although communist ideology had faded as the party's reason for being, the party remained as an institution. Many of those who joined it did so in order to use its legitimizing features for their own purposes. In minority areas, these purposes included furthering the interests of minorities and their cultures. The party had, in essence, been infiltrated by people who were inclined to ignore or subvert its directives. Individual manifestations of dissent and demonstrations were quelled, but protest, both passive and active, had become endemic.

Conclusions

Under Mao Zedong, China's policies toward its ethnic minorities alternated between periods of accommodation to minority languages, cultures, and traditions and strident attempts to obliterate them in favor of complete assimilation. One theme ran through all these periods: an effort to link minority economies firmly with that of Han China and to consolidate the locus of decision-making with regard to minority policy in central party and government organizations in Beijing. Neither policy worked well enough to satisfy party and government leaders: accommodation kept alive languages and cultures that officials usually regarded as inferior and perhaps decadent. It also lengthened the period of "growing together" that officials believed was the path to a strong, unified Chinese state. On the other hand, assimilative policies intensified ethnic resolve to cling to languages and cultures and frequently led minorities to rebel against the central government.

Mao's demise occurred during a period of accommodation that had begun in 1971. Deng Xiaoping extended this policy and introduced a number of measures that were still more accommodative to minorities. In addition, he decentralized economic decision-making throughout China and reversed Mao's redistributive economic policies, which had attempted to siphon wealth from prosperous areas in order to alleviate poverty in poorer ones.

These policies left local economies in minority areas lagging behind those of coastal areas, and threatened to exacerbate Han-minority tensions. In response, government policies changed to allow minorities to trade across borders and encouraged tourism to the areas in which they lived. These changes took effect at a time when Islamic fundamentalism was gaining power, the Soviet Union and its Eastern European empire were dissolving into smaller ethnically based states, and more attention was being paid in the West to the protection of human rights and the rights of minorities. The net effect of these developments was to reverse the centripetal trend established by Mao and create centrifugal forces that threatened to spin off various parts of the Chinese empire.

While government policy in principle treats ethnic minorities uniformly, various minority groups have in fact had different histories and have varied in their levels of accommodation toward the Chinese government. Most of the minority peoples who had become comfortable with Han culture and norms before 1949 did not wish to secede. Other minorities, including some who had not willingly accepted Han culture, simply desired a more meaningful form of autonomy than Beijing has thus far been willing to permit. However, Xinjiang, Tibet, and, to a lesser extent, Inner Mongolia have generated separatist movements that are quite determined.

Maintaining the present accommodative policy or liberalizing still further would risk encouraging current centrifugal trends. By the early 1990s, the central authorities had begun to take a harder line with regard to public manifestations of ethnic grievances. At the same time, they attempted to discourage foreign governments from giving aid or succor to dissident minorities. These policies have had only modest success. Official media continue to rail against foreign interference in China's domestic affairs, and military and public security personnel are able to quell demonstrations when they break out. But the authorities do not seem to be addressing the underlying causes of ethnic discontent, and the gap between the economic development of minority areas and that of coastal China continues to widen.

China's ethnic problems are likely to worsen in the future. The post-Deng leadership is overwhelmingly composed of Han, who are apt to regard their group as the core of China's national identity and to view manifestations of other ethnic identities as subversive. They are concerned that granting true autonomy would lead to calls for further concessions by minorities and, eventually, demands for independence. The central government may therefore be tempted to tighten controls further over minorities, to bring minority areas more firmly under central control. This is liable to provoke violent reactions, comparable to those during the Great Leap Forward and the Cultural Revolution, and after the Tiananmen crackdown. In minority policy as in other areas of Chinese policy, forceful responses will become more common as the Chinese government's crisis of political legitimacy deepens. The leadership's options are limited. As shown by past experience, liberalization, accommodation, and repression are all apt to cause problems—albeit different sorts of problems.

Part III
Australia and the Asia-Pacific Region

Chapter 10

Federalism and Indigenous Peoples in Australia

Christine Fletcher

Australia differs from its neighbors in the Asia-Pacific region in three respects: the migratory background of its multicultural population, the ancient culture of its indigenous peoples, and the predominance of its federal form of government. Australia is positioned on the edge of Southeast Asia. Its nearest neighbors to the north are the Indonesian province of East Timor—less than 120 miles away—and Papua New Guinea. With some exceptions, most of Australia's Asian neighbors were colonized by Europeans.[1] Many communities in the region were tribal societies at the time of colonization. When they finally gained independence, they had to reconstruct social and political order out of the ruins of their own traditional structures and those that were abandoned by the departing Europeans.

Australia was also colonized but, unlike most countries in the Asia-Pacific region, its European colonizers—the British—never left. The British declared their formal occupation of the country in 1788, and for more than two centuries, the original native peoples—Aborigines and Torres Strait Islanders[2]—have experienced the consequences of this occupation. Within forty years of their arrival in the late eighteenth century, the settlers had carved Australia into several colonies and claimed virtual ownership of the entire continent. Throughout the first half of the twentieth century, Australian governments exercised unconditional authority

---

1. Thailand, for example, was never colonized by Europeans.

2. Only recently have Australian governments begun referring specifically to the Torres Strait Islanders, who own the islands to the north of Australia. Until the late 1980s, they were identified only as Aborigines—a term which, they argued, denied them their own identity as saltwater people, rather than land people. Governments now refer to the indigenous peoples of Australia as Aborigines and Torres Strait Islanders. However, the terms *indigenous* and *Aboriginal* are also used.

over the country's indigenous peoples. Those with light skin—the so-called "part" Aborigines—were rounded up and moved across the country to reserves and missions under an assimilation policy.[3] Assimilation policies were designed to integrate Aborigines into the wider Australian community and remove the embarrassing stigma of native peoples, thereby solving the Aboriginal "problem."[4] Officially, the aim was to elevate their standard of living by integrating them into white society—on the assumption that assimilation would provide Aborigines with access to good housing, health care, and education.[5] However, with cultural and tribal practices radically different from those of white society, the Aborigines suffered under this assimilationist onslaught.

"Ethnicity" is a term generally reserved in Australia for immigrants, or Australians born overseas; it is not applied to indigenous peoples. This is reflected in the fact that the Australian governments have rarely attempted to make a policy connection between immigrants and indigenous groups. For decades, non-white immigrants were excluded from Australia; the now-disgraced White Australia policy was in force from 1901, when the Australian federation was formed, until 1969.[6] In the decades of non-discriminatory immigration policies since 1969, Australian society has become more multicultural in composition; by the mid-1990s, one in every four Australians was born overseas. The concept of ethnicity is only a problem when politicians meddle in racial issues. The indigenous peoples, unfortunately, face volatile economic and political circumstances: their communities continue to be isolated and underprivileged, their cultural claims are still discredited, and their access to mainstream resources remains restricted.

These issues form the background to this chapter as it explains how Australian government policy in Aboriginal and Torres Strait Islander affairs has evolved since the 1950s. There are two main parts to the chapter. The first examines the distinct nature of Australia's indigenous societies and describes how Australia's federal system of government

---

3. See Christine Fletcher, *Aboriginal Politics: Intergovernmental Relations* (Melbourne: Melbourne University Press, 1992).

4. Assimilation was also practiced in Canada and the United States during an earlier period. See Paul Tennant, *Aboriginal Peoples and Politics: The Indian Land Question in British Columbia, 1849–1989* (Vancouver: University of British Columbia Press, 1990).

5. See Paul Hasluck, *The Policy of Assimilation: Decisions of Commonwealth and State Ministers at the Native Welfare Conference, Canberra, January 26 and 27, 1961* (Canberra: Government Printers, 1961).

6. J.H. Collins, "Migrants: The Political Void?" in H. Mayer and H. Nelson, eds., *Australian Politics: A Fifth Reader* (Melbourne: Longman Cheshire, 1980), pp. 485–497.

Table 10.1. Ethnic Composition of Australia.

Country of Birth	Number	Percentage
Non-Aboriginal Australia	13,514,700	75.7
Aboriginal Australia	265,000	1.5
Europe and Former Soviet Union	2,377,300	13.3
Southeast Asia	446,800	2.5
Oceania and Antarctica	372,900	2.1
Northeast Asia	243,400	1.4
Middle East and North Africa	208,100	1.2
South Asia	136,000	.8
Sub-Saharan Africa	112,400	.6
South America, Central America, and the Caribbean	83,800	.5
North America	83,000	.4
Total	**17,843,400**	**100.0**

NOTE: In 1994, Australia's population was estimated at 17,843,400.
SOURCE: *Estimated Resident Population by Country of Birth, 1994* (Washington, D.C.: Embassy of Australia Library, 1994).

operates. The second section traces the evolution of government policy at various levels from the 1950s to the 1990s.

The Demographic, Historical, and Political Setting

Aboriginal peoples and Torres Strait Islanders number almost 300,000 in an overall population of some 18 million. (See Table 10.1.) In the two centuries since the British established the first Australian colony, the indigenous community has been traumatized in ways not unlike those experienced by the native peoples of the United States and Canada. The current relationship between the indigenous peoples of Australia and the country's multilayered governments reflects a history of cultural misunderstanding and political struggle.

The Australian federation is comprised of six states and several territories, two of which are part of the mainland and have state-like powers. Three other territories with self-governing powers are islands off the east and west coasts of the Australian continent: Norfolk Island, Christmas Island, and the Cocos (Keeling) Islands.[7] The Northern Territory has the largest percentage of Aboriginal and Torres Strait Islander peoples per

---

7. Christine Fletcher, "The Australian Territories: Diversity in Governing," *Australian Journal of Political Science*, Special Issue on Federalism, Vol. 27 (September 1992), pp. 159–176.

capita. The Northern Territory had been part of the state of South Australia, which decided it was too remote and too costly to maintain. In 1911 the South Australian government handed authority for that area over to the national, or commonwealth, government. Several decades later, that transfer gave the commonwealth powers to legislate on behalf of the Aborigines in that region.

Government policies towards Aboriginal peoples and immigrants have always been developed separately; from an Australian perspective, they are unrelated. However, some of the principles—such as assimilation—that governments applied to keep non-white immigrants from entering Australia during the first half of the twentieth century originated in Aboriginal affairs policy. More importantly, until the late 1960s, Australia's pro-white immigration policy and its reluctance to embrace a non-discriminatory policy intensified the Anglo-Celtic dimension of Australia's culture. British and European ideas about democracy influenced the free development of civil society in Australia—free association, unions, parties, and other democratic organizations—and thus had an obvious influence on the development of a stable nation.[8]

The indigenous peoples, however, have a history of ideas derived from a totally different source from those of Western societies. Dating their arrival in Australia back to well before biblical times, Aborigines see themselves as the exact opposite of immigrants, and quite rightly resist being bundled into a category that includes immigrants. There is no evidence of any cultural alliance between Aborigines and immigrants. Various ethnic communities unite to resist the erosion of their rights in times of racial crisis, but immigrant groups have little if anything in common with the indigenous community.[9] In addition, until the late 1960s, Aborigines were denied citizenship under the Australian Constitution.

As if to emphasize the distinction between immigrants and other Australians, immigrants, particularly those in the postwar wave from Europe, were known as "New Australians." They were the first non-British settlers to arrive in Australia under a policy designed to rebuild the country after the war and encourage settlement in sparsely populated or newly developing areas. These areas included rural and industrial

---

8. Christine Fletcher, "Trapped in Civil Society: Aborigines and Federalism in Australia," Discussion Paper No. 4 (Darwin: North Australia Research Unit, Australian National University, 1996).

9. Robert Birrell, "The Dynamics of Multiculturalism in Australia," in D. Lovell, I. McAllister, W. Maley, and C. Kukathas, eds., *The Australian Political System* (Melbourne: Longman, 1995), pp. 634–641.

Australia.

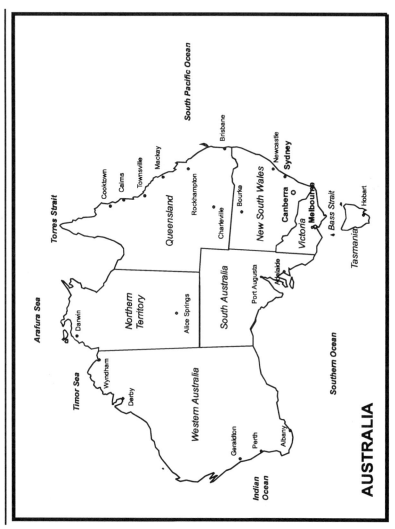

regions in the most populated states, New South Wales and Victoria; areas in the most isolated states, Western Australia, the Northern Territory, and Queensland; and areas in South Australia where manufacturing and pastoral activities were to be promoted.

PROFILE OF A PEOPLE: ABORIGINES AND TORRES STRAIT ISLANDERS

Recent archaeological evidence—rock-dating in the remote Kimberley region of northwestern Australia[10]—suggests that Aboriginal occupation of the continent dates back at least 116,000 and perhaps 176,000 years. Aboriginals identify themselves as Australia's "first" peoples. Their traditional society is governed by a culture recognized as among the world's most ancient "living" cultures. Aboriginal knowledge of the country helped the white settlers secure a foothold on the continent—and ultimately become entrenched. Aborigines were experienced travellers and expert hunters; they knew where to find water and how to predict the weather. They also understood the significance of land management practices and the importance of sustaining indigenous local economies.[11] Today, approximately 40 percent of Australia's indigenous peoples live in traditional and remote communities. Many others, although they live in urban, metropolitan circumstances, acknowledge that they are strongly tied to their indigenous roots by the cultural traditions of their Aboriginal ancestry.[12]

By the turn of the twentieth century, most of the colonial governments had passed legislation discouraging Aborigines from living near towns and villages. On the coastal plains and more fertile regions of the country, Aborigines were pushed to the fringes of white settlement areas, whereas in the more remote regions of northern and central Australia, Aborigines were marginalized by pastoralists who erected fences on Aboriginal land and who used the Aborigines as unpaid labor.

Aboriginal and Islander trade routes, which had linked the north of the continent to the south, east, and west for thousands of years, were

---

10. The Australian Museum's September 1996 announcement that ancient Aboriginal rock paintings and implements were discovered in northwestern Australia will prompt a revision of Australian history.

11. Andrew Lawson, President of the Ngaanyatjarra Council, Warburton, 1995. See also S. Zimran and Christine Fletcher, "Indigenous Peoples and Problems of Fiscal Reform in Australia: Not Getting Our Fair Share," in Christine Fletcher, ed., *Equity and Development Across Nations: Political and Fiscal Realities* (New York: St. Martin's, 1996).

12. See Marcia Langton, "Indigenous Self-government and Self-determination: Overlapping Jurisdictions at Cape York," in Christine Fletcher, ed., *Aboriginal Self-Determination in Australia* (Canberra: Aboriginal Studies Press, 1994), pp. 131–138.

disrupted by the middle of the twentieth century.[13] Local community life was severely dislocated, often intentionally. Legislation was passed to subsidize white settlers who wanted to take up government offers of land, while other settlers were encouraged to build towns, schools, and businesses. Meanwhile, new legislation restricted the movement of Aboriginal peoples in these newly settled areas. Pastoral activities and mining became the basis of development in most areas, and Aboriginal peoples faced widespread dispossession in every state. As the settlers moved in, the indigenous population was moved out—either by the settlers or the police. The arbitrary nature of white settlement meant that the colonial boundaries cut across the ancient jurisdictions that had governed Aboriginal society for centuries.[14]

The Australian colonies federated in 1901; boundaries and jurisdictions were further complicated with the addition of another level of government—the commonwealth. The six colonies had been advancing Western development across Australia for almost a century, and each colonial government had its own constitution, bicameral parliament, and administration before they federated.[15] Local governments, modelled along those in the British system, were established in each state, mostly for the purpose of building roads and enforcing health regulations.

Because white Australian settlers wanted to keep Aboriginal peoples away from their towns and out of their white schools, they passed laws that enabled them to jail Aborigines or throw them out of towns. Other laws enabled authorities to remove Aboriginal children from their families and put them into public institutions, where they were renamed and sent to other institutions, missions, and private homesteads. Separated from their traditional lands, sources of income, and even their families, Aboriginal peoples became trapped in a cycle of poverty, unpaid labor, and misery. Today, this is reflected in the comparatively high percentage of Aboriginal peoples in prison and in the poor quality of life of many Aboriginal peoples and Torres Strait Islanders—particularly the condition of their health.[16] Many Aboriginal-specific laws passed by the state

---

13. See Kim Ackerman, "Material Culture and Trade in the Kimberley Today," in R.M. Berndt and C.H. Berndt, eds., *Aborigines of the West: Their Past and Their Present* (Perth: University of Western Australia Press, 1980), pp. 243–251.

14. Langton, "Indigenous Self-government and Self-determination."

15. See Paul Finn, *Law and Government in Colonial Australia* (Melbourne: Oxford University Press, 1987); and Fletcher, *Aboriginal Politics*.

16. Australian Bureau of Statistics, *National Aboriginal and Torres Strait Islander Survey 1994* (Canberra: Australian Bureau of Statistics, 1995).

legislatures were couched in protectionist language, but if the Aborigines needed protection, it was protection from these very state governments.[17]

Most state governments were prepared to quarantine their pastoral and resource industries from the Aboriginal peoples, even after it became known that the Aborigines had lived on the land for tens of thousands of years. In Western Australia, some Aboriginal peoples were shipped to island prisons from which they could never escape; others were marched across country and incarcerated in "reserves." Many Aboriginal peoples died of disease and mistreatment. Such was their alienation that, as late as the 1960s, government responsibility for Aboriginal peoples in Western Australia fell within a government portfolio for native fauna and fisheries.

The Aborigines were not the only people to be mistreated by Australian settlers and governments. At the turn of the nineteenth century, Queensland had a booming sugar industry but was one of the continent's least populated states. To solve their labor problems, cane farmers kidnapped South Sea Islanders and brought them to Australia to work the cane farms as slave labor. Known by the derogatory term, *Kanakas*, they came from eighty or so islands in the Pacific, mainly Vanuatu and the Solomon Islands. Between 1863 and 1904, up to 60,000 South Sea Islanders were brought to Queensland in this manner.[18] After Australia federated in 1901, they were the first and only people to be deported en masse under the new White Australia policy; deportation took place between 1902 and 1904.[19] Approximately one thousand islanders evaded deportation and another 1,400 were exempt; their descendants are still trying to come to terms with their special status in Australian society. In 1977, when anti-discrimination laws were being enacted, the commonwealth government created a royal commission to examine race relations in Australia. That inquiry revealed that many Australians regarded South Sea Islanders as Aborigines. Since they were not, however, they could receive none of the special benefits designed for Aboriginal peoples—unless they identified themselves as indigenous to Australia.[20]

---

17. See, for example, proceedings of the Conference of Commonwealth and State Ministers on Aboriginal Welfare, Darwin, 1963.

18. Australian Human Rights and Equal Opportunity Commission, *The Call for Recognition: A Report on the Situation of Australian South Sea Islanders* (Canberra: Australian Government Printing Service [AGPS], December 1992).

19. See ibid.

20. See ibid.

FEDERALISM AND THE AUSTRALIAN CONSTITUTION

To understand the vulnerability of the Australian indigenous peoples and the ambiguities of governmental jurisdictions, we must first recognize that Australian governments are preoccupied with constitutionalism: as federalism is based on shared jurisdictions, it tends to generate competition for resources and conflict over which government has the constitutional authority to exercise power.[21] In the late nineteenth century, Australia's colonial governments found it virtually impossible to negotiate a form of government based on national unity until they reached agreement on sharing constitutional authority. The finer points of the agreement included maintaining their own semi-sovereign positions within the federation, arranging to share power with each other and with the newly formed commonwealth government, and, most importantly, building constraints into the constitution to protect them from the very commonwealth government they were creating.

As a consequence, there is no clear central authority within Australia. Jurisdictions over certain policy areas are shared according to such considerations as which government has taxing powers and which areas of public policy impinge on others. Land, for example, falls under the jurisdiction of the states, whereas indigenous affairs fall under the authority of both state and commonwealth governments. By the same token, decisions that influence land policy—on housing, service delivery, Aboriginal title, and roads, for example—affect a number of jurisdictions simultaneously. The constitution has therefore had a major impact on policy outcomes and, in the more recent past, on people's expectations of their rights and entitlements.

In the Australian federation, policy decisions can only be implemented if different levels of government can achieve consensus. Governments themselves have difficulty comprehending their own limitations within the Australian federal system, and in public debates the constraints within the system sometimes provoke hostility within pockets of the general public. After every national election in Australia, the new incoming government promises to sort out the roles and responsibilities of government; they rarely understand that shared jurisdictions are a fundamental part of the nature of federalism.[22] Without shared jurisdictions,

---

21. A.V. Dicey, *Introduction to the Study of the Law of the Constitution*. (London: Macmillan, 1885).

22. See Christine Fletcher, "Altered States? Federalism, Sovereignty and Self-Government," Discussion Paper No. 22, Federalism Research Centre, Australian National University, Canberra, October 1992.

the system would not be federal—it would be simply a collection of states with some sort of confederal agent employed to perform a strictly limited number of continental functions, such as providing for defense of the country. Under such a system, true nationhood and civil society would not exist. The colonial governments spent most of the 1890s deciding how powers should be distributed to the different levels. The federation they eventually formed was based partly on the British parliamentary system and partly on the American federal system. The Australian national government, known officially as the commonwealth government, emerged with substantial financial powers. To add to the confusion, the commonwealth government is also often referred to as the federal government because national elections are known as federal elections.

Most of the debates in Australia over how power is actually shared are dominated by politicians and by High Court decisions. Some constraints are historical: none of the original colonies had any intention of relinquishing its power and handing responsibility over to another government to make decisions on its behalf. On many important constitutional issues, the states are only able to reach agreement with each other in principle—a fact of life in many federations. When the federal constitution came into affect in 1901, laws enacted by the six separate colonies—five on the mainland plus the island of Tasmania—became state laws. From a territorial perspective, state jurisdictions remained unaltered but the balance of power and authority between different levels of government has shifted over time in favor of the commonwealth. The commonwealth owes much of its political advantage to its revenue-raising power under the Income Tax Act of 1942 and the High Court's interpretation of the relationship between the commonwealth and the states. Several decades passed, however, before the commonwealth's financial advantage over the states also became an advantage for the Aboriginal population.

COMMONWEALTH JURISDICTION

Although the commonwealth government has jurisdiction over all ten Australian territories, the Northern Territory and the Australian Capital Territory have a relatively strong form of self-government. Others, such as the Territory of Norfolk Island, are self-governing, though less powerful. Most of the Australian territories are small island communities. Formally, they exercise a form of self-determination but are enclaves within the federation, and the Cocos (Keeling) Islands and Christmas Island territories exercise governance through contractual arrangements with other states and territories.[23] All ten Australian territories are governed

23. See Fletcher, "The Australian Territories."

by commonwealth legislation, but some depend on states for essential services and infrastructure development. Unlike Native Canadians or the Maori of New Zealand, Aboriginal people in Australia are in no position to exercise self-government. A very limited form of self-government is emerging in the Torres Strait Islands due to commonwealth legislation. Those islands, however, fall within the jurisdiction of the state of Queensland, and this type of self-government has not yet been supported by the type of revenue or expenditure powers that legitimize other types of territorial governments within the federation—for example, the Territory of Norfolk Island or the Australian Capital Territory. As yet, no constitutional provisions recognize the right of indigenous peoples to self-government at any level of government.[24]

State and territory governments regard the commonwealth as intrusive and centralist, and are highly suspicious of its motives. Jurisdictional ambiguities further complicate the situation. Aside from its exclusive powers, the commonwealth government has concurrent powers with the states (and with the Northern Territory and the Australian Capital Territory) under the provisions of the constitution. In addition, a 1967 referendum gave the commonwealth jurisdiction over Aboriginal and Torres Strait Islander peoples. However, commonwealth power does not automatically replace the jurisdiction of the states, which sometimes causes confusion and resentment. For example, in the Northern Territory, two key pieces of legislation govern Aboriginal land rights: the commonwealth Aboriginal Land Rights (Northern Territory) Act of 1976, and a bill passed in the Northern Territory legislature. Although commonwealth legislation overrides that of the states, in the case of land rights, the commonwealth act has a sunset clause—meaning it could eventually be superseded. Also, political decisions tend to dominate public debate whenever questions of Aboriginal rights converge with resource development; the territory government will quite likely alter the land rights legislation to weaken Aboriginal control of land and resources. At the same time, this peculiar constitutional status of the territories has enabled Aboriginal communities to gain access to resources within the system, by allowing the commonwealth to create special institutional frameworks for them. Few states have taken a similar line; they have generally managed to resist pressure from the commonwealth—except when it came with substantial financial incentives.[25] In short, constitutional and

24. Mick Dodson, *Office of the Aboriginal and Torres Strait Islander Social Justice Commission, Second Report* (Canberra: AGPS, 1995).

25. See, for example, Commonwealth and Northern Territory, *Agreement for the Provision and Management of Housing and Related Infrastructure for Aboriginal and Torres Strait Islander People in the Northern Territory,* 1995.

jurisdictional ambiguities have blurred the position of the indigenous peoples in Australia. This in itself has become an issue in the 1990s.

Moreover, the silence of the Australian Constitution on many major policy issues has led to confusion over responsibility for delivery of services.[26] Any government can formulate public policy, but not every government has the power or the financial resources to implement policy. In a federal system, it is virtually impossible for any one government to implement policy and deliver a service entirely on its own. Each state also has its own constitution. For governments that want to sort out roles and responsibilities and for Aboriginal peoples who want access to government resources, the principle of divided authority can be difficult to resolve.

Significantly, no state constitution makes any mention of Aboriginal rights or even acknowledges their status as the country's original inhabitants. Indeed, no state constitution even mentions the existence of Aboriginal peoples.[27] Of the original colonial constitutions, only two—those of Western Australia and South Australia—referred to the indigenous peoples.[28] Western Australia inserted a clause in its colonial constitution at the insistence of the British Parliament; the clause empowered the colonial government to transfer one percent of total revenue—or £10,000—to the Aboriginal population in the colony. However, when gold mining began to boom, revenues soared, and the clause was removed after a decade of spasmodic debate in the Western Australian legislature. Following federation, the commonwealth constitution made only two references to Aboriginal peoples. One of those, repealed by the referendum in 1967, prohibited the commonwealth government from counting or recognizing Aborigines in the national census. For most of the twentieth century, the fortunes of the indigenous peoples have been determined by political decisions and legislation rather than by constitutional reform.

The Evolution of Government Policy

POLICY IN POSTWAR AUSTRALIA

After World War II, Australian governments came to rely on assimilation as a solution to the Aboriginal "problem" and as a way of integrating

26. *The Constitution* (Canberra: Government Publishers, 1968).

27. Wes Lanhupuy, "Marine Management for 40,000 Years: A Yolngu View of Sea Rights," in Law Faculty, Northern Territory University, *Turning the Tide: Conference on Indigenous Peoples and Sea Rights, July 14–16, 1993: Selected Papers*, Darwin, Australia.

28. Sessional Committee on Constitutional Development, *Recognition of Aboriginal Customary Law* (Darwin: Northern Territory Legislative Assembly, 1992).

immigrants into mainstream Australian society. Immigrants chose to nurture their own cultural, social, and economic enclaves in suburban Australia; since governments could not force their assimilationist policies on immigrant communities, they abandoned the policies. In any event, these policies are examples of how misleading perceptions about different cultures affect the quality of peoples' lives. Governments had no idea how the new immigrants would fit into Australian society.[29]

Assimilation policies with respect to Aboriginal peoples were officially introduced in 1951, just as postwar immigration got under way. At the time, it was widely believed that the Aboriginal population faced extinction, though there was no direct evidence to support the idea: the Aboriginal peoples had never been counted in the Australian census. Ironically, at the same time that activists were wringing their hands over how to "save" the "natives," federal and state governments were pursuing policies that would speed up the process of Aboriginal cultural and social disintegration.[30] The best one can say about Australia's assimilation policies is that they were based on the naive idea that Aborigines would benefit if they led a life-style similar to that of white Australians. Commonwealth and state governments remained stoically supportive of assimilation for years, arguing that it was the best way to standardize living conditions for all Australians.[31] In fact, government behavior towards Aboriginal peoples was at best highly discriminatory, and at worst devastating.

By the end of the 1950s, when it was clear that assimilation was not achieving the results that governments had expected with respect to either immigrants or indigenous peoples,[32] the White Australia policy was officially denounced and the process of normalizing immigration policy began. Policies towards Aborigines began to change as well.

CITIZENSHIP, SELF-DETERMINATION, AND CONSTITUTIONAL REFORM
IN THE 1960s

In the early 1960s, Australian citizenship, in its original Anglo-Celtic form, came under pressure from "outsiders"—Aborigines and non-British immigrants. Although labor shortages threatened to slow economic growth,

---

29. See A. Marcus and M.C. Ricklefs, eds., *Surrender Australia: Essays in the Study and Uses of History* (Sydney: Allen and Unwin, 1985).

30. See Daisy Bates, *The Passing of the Aborigines: A Lifetime Spent Among the Natives of Australia* (London: John Murray, 1938).

31. See Hasluck, *The Policy of Assimilation*.

32. T. Long, "The Development of Government Aboriginal Policy: The Effect of Administrative Changes, 1829–1977," in Berndt and Berndt, *Aborigines of the West*.

immigration from Asia was relatively slow and those who did come were not encouraged to apply for Australian residency or citizenship. Indeed, Australia's Constitution did not anticipate non-British citizens: there is nothing in the constitution about the rights of non-British subjects, and it contains no Bill of Rights. The commonwealth has limited jurisdiction over immigration and over related legislation affected by Australia's international treaty obligations.

On issues concerning citizenship, the commonwealth did have a say in how the law was applied to immigrants: for example, under the Australian Citizenship Act of 1948, immigrants were forced to pledge allegiance to God. Since many immigrants were not Christians, this posed a problem. On the other hand, Aborigines had very little choice about becoming citizens. In certain states, such as Western Australia, an Aborigine had to secure a certificate from the local magistrate and promise to disassociate from other Aboriginal people in order to become a citizen. According to the Natives (Citizenship Rights) Act of 1944, a person could become a citizen only if he or she were "deemed to be no longer an Aborigine." The Act was amended in the 1950s and 1960s, largely to ensure that Aboriginal children could become citizens. Changes to the Act in 1964 brought Western Australia more in line with commonwealth legislation passed in the 1960s to enfranchise Aborigines to vote in federal elections without first having to deny their place in Aboriginal society. The commonwealth act, however, had little impact on the status of Aborigines as citizens under state legislation. In fact, state legislation encouraged people to deny their status as Aborigines; once an individual was no longer classed as an Aborigine, he or she would have the same voting rights as anyone else.

Aborigines had none of the benefits of citizenship. They were denied freedom of association, and laws even limited their movements in and around some towns and cities: such a law survived in Western Australia until 1971. In Queensland, state laws prevented indigenous Palm Island peoples from returning to their island homes if they dared to venture onto the mainland.[33] The laws on electoral and citizenship issues were extremely ambiguous even within the commonwealth's own regional jurisdictions. For example, electoral regulations in the Northern Territory stated that "no aboriginal native of Australia . . . shall be entitled to have his name placed on or retained on any Roll or to vote at any election unless . . . he is not a ward as defined by the Welfare Ordinance 1953–1960

---

33. See Bill Rosser, *This Is Palm Island* (Canberra: Australian Institute of Aboriginal Studies, 1978).

of the Territory; or is or has been a member of the Defence Forces."[34] In the Aboriginal population of the Northern Territory, estimated at around 17,000, only eighty-nine Aboriginal individuals were classified as ordinary citizens, that is, not declared to be wards. The most liberal states in this regard were New South Wales, Victoria, and South Australia. Those with the most repressive legislation were Queensland, Western Australia, and the Northern Territory. In Tasmania, the official policy was that all Aborigines had been exterminated in the nineteenth century.

In Aboriginal affairs policy, 1967 is considered to be the turning point. In that year, the heads of state and commonwealth governments met for a serious discussion of Aboriginal policy. They decided that the commonwealth government, with more resources to devote to these issues, was in a much better position than the states to support developments in Aboriginal affairs. The governments also decided to hold a referendum on the issue of constitutional reform. In regions with a history of cruelty towards the indigenous people, mainly regions with a relatively substantial Aboriginal population, a majority voted against change.[35] But metropolitan areas and areas where Aboriginal peoples were less visible recorded a high "yes" vote. Over 92 percent of those who voted in the referendum approved the reform: all Aborigines would now be counted in the Australian national census, and the commonwealth government would be authorized to enter the jurisdiction of the states to make laws relating to the Aboriginal population.[36] Many anti-federalists believed that the referendum would reduce the jurisdiction of state governments because powers over indigenous peoples would shift to the commonwealth. Broadly speaking, the commonwealth's authority did increase in subsequent years, but that was due as much to its revenue-raising power and its expanding bureaucracy as anything else.[37] Overall, the states maintained their strong positions in Australia's federal system.

---

34. House of Representatives, *Report*, from the *Select Committee on Voting Rights of Aborigines* (Canberra: Parliament of the Commonwealth of Australia, 1961).

35. Prior to 1967, under the terms of the Australian Constitution, the commonwealth had no power to make laws on behalf of indigenous people.

36. See Scott Bennett, "The 1967 Referendum," *Australian Aboriginal Studies*, Vol. 2, No. 1 (1985), pp. 26–31; and Don Aitkin, "Australia," in D. Butler and A. Ranney, eds., *Referendums: A Comparative Study of Practice and Theory* (Washington, D.C.: American Enterprise Institute, 1978), pp. 123–137.

37. Aboriginal and Torres Strait Islander Commission (ATSIC), *Recognition, Rights, and Reform: Report to Government on Native Title Social Justice Measures* (Canberra: ATSIC, 1995).

EQUITY, REFORM, AND ABORIGINAL LAND RIGHTS IN THE 1970S

Compared to the more general area of immigration and ethnic affairs, Aboriginal and Torres Strait Islander issues have remained on the edge of mainstream decision-making. Until well into the 1980s, the administrative organization dealing with indigenous affairs was small, inept, and not taken very seriously by governments. In the 1970s, Australia became a signatory to international treaties on human rights, and Aboriginal land rights gained a limited degree of support.[38] Several positive decisions were made in the 1970s; in 1975, the commonwealth passed the Racial Discrimination Act (RDA), designed to reduce discrimination. The RDA was used to reinforce diversity and to protect people from discrimination because of ethnicity, gender, age, sexual preference, and so on. The Act endured: in 1993, it was used to shield the Native Title Act of 1993 from governments and others who were working to undermine the principles of native title. In 1976, the commonwealth parliament passed the Aboriginal Land Rights (Northern Territory) Act, the first Aboriginal land rights legislation giving Aboriginal peoples access to their own land in the Northern Territory. But even while the Gurindji Aboriginal people were negotiating for the return of the first parcel of land, the Supreme Court of the Northern Territory was undermining the strength of indigenous history by reinstating the doctrine of *terra nullius*.

Terra nullius refers to vacant or unoccupied land. In 1971 Justice Blackburn, judge of the Supreme Court, decided that the courts should endorse Aboriginal dispossession: when the Europeans arrived, he declared, Australia was *terra nullius*.[39] Defining the country as vacant land had enormous implications for the Aborigines: if Australia was declared to be unoccupied when the settlers first arrived, governments could deny any responsibility to compensate them for dispossession. If the country had, in reality, been vacant, then European land practices could proceed unhindered. The Blackburn decision placed an already policy-weary indigenous society into an even more vulnerable position. It strengthened European, rather than Aboriginal, dominance of the land and its resources. Aboriginal peoples and Torres Strait Islanders found themselves in the ridiculous position of having no officially recognized history before white settlement.

By the late 1970s, it was clear that the commonwealth had virtually

---

38. Frank Brennan, *Sharing the Country: The Case for an Agreement between Black and White Australians* (Victoria: Penguin, 1991); and Frank Brennan, *One Land, One Nation* (St. Lucia: Queensland University Press, 1995).

39. J. Blackburn, *Supreme Court of the Northern Territory: Milirrpum v. Nabalco Pty. Ltd. and the Commonwealth of Australia* (Sydney: Law Book Company, 1971).

no administrative connections with the Aboriginal and Torres Strait Islander population. The first set of policy guidelines issued by the Department of Aboriginal Affairs (DAA) emphasized three key areas of commonwealth involvement: making intergovernmental grants, gathering information about Aboriginal society, and coordinating policy. It saw the allocation of commonwealth funds to the states as an incentive for state governments to use "state machinery" to deliver services. Since the commonwealth was engineering the grants, it was assumed that the states would use the funds to compensate for the extra costs involved in delivering services to Aboriginal communities through existing administrative structures—including the system of local government. Local government thus became a crucial link in the service delivery chain between commonwealth and state governments and Aboriginal communities—particularly communities in remote parts of the country.

All state governments were on a learning curve in making policy for Aboriginal and Torres Strait Islander peoples. Most of the intergovernmental agreements signed during the 1970s had emphasized a much greater financial role for the commonwealth than the states, but the central objective was to emerge with a workable process for delivering basic essential services. Most states agreed to give the commonwealth control over their Aboriginal affairs administration; they found it too costly to deliver services to people in remote areas of the continent. Indeed, the Western Australian government seemed almost eager to hand over administration for Aboriginal affairs; it put its entire resources, including office space, at the commonwealth's disposal.[40] Queensland, by comparison, absolutely refused to recognize that the Aboriginal and Torres Strait Islander peoples had any special needs; it dismissed as irrelevant any agreement with the commonwealth.[41]

Self-determination was, and always has been, the principle for reform.[42] It was used to sweep away the trappings of assimilation and, as an administrative principle, it was linked closely to decentralization—an attempt to move away from strong central control. When the Department of Aboriginal Affairs (DAA) first appeared in the 1970s, it did not

---

40. Fletcher, *Aboriginal Politics.*

41. Patricia Turner, "From Paternalism: The Role of the Commonwealth in the Administration of Aboriginal and Torres Strait Islander Affairs Policy," Masters of Public Administration thesis, University of Canberra, 1994; also see Turner, "Intergovernmental Relations," paper presented to Public Policy Program, Australian National University, October 1995.

42. Mick Dodson, *Office of the Aboriginal and Torres Strait Islander Social Justice Commissioner, Fourth Report* (Canberra: AGPS, 1996).

exactly embody self-determination, but it was the first serious attempt to support indigenous community development in remote areas. The DAA was the first national organization to liaise with the states, territories, and local governments, and with other commonwealth agencies. But there were no provisions to include Aboriginal peoples in the decision-making process, nor any way that they could have their say in community development. These factors largely explain why the DAA became redundant in the late 1980s, to be replaced by the Aboriginal and Torres Strait Islander Commission (ATSIC). The 1980s witnessed a burgeoning of intergovernmental agreements between the commonwealth and the states.

PUBLIC ADMINISTRATION IN THE 1980S

Public administration in the area of indigenous affairs is striking as both a source of weakness—in the policy relationship between government and indigenous communities—and a source of great strength—in accountability procedures. On one side, modern management principles produce benchmarking methods and performance indicators, which connect outputs with outcomes, making public sector managment highly sophisticated. Unfortunately, the same modern principles fail miserably in dealing with the indigenous social and political institutions on which Aboriginal cultures depend. Indeed, experience shows that the system will only work if indigenous and non-indigenous societies can learn to lean towards each other without either side losing sight of the origins of its principles for decision-making.

The Aboriginal and Torres Strait Islander Commission emerged out of the old Department of Aboriginal Affairs. ATSIC was designed to be different from other government departments. Its primary aim was to lever government resources quickly and directly into areas where they were most needed—at the community level. To meet this aim, the organization itself was designed as a peculiar form of administrative democracy. ATSIC is composed of two distinctly different elements: First, its administrative structure resembles a normal government department with a central office in Canberra, the national capital, and agencies in all of the states and territories. Second, its Aboriginal and Torres Strait Islander constituency elects representatives to the thirty-six regional councils within its regional council structure. In theory, the councilors are supposed to translate the needs of their constituents directly into the system through the administrative arm of the organization. This complex structure is a commonwealth organization—ATSIC was established under commonwealth legislation in 1989—and runs parallel to mainstream local government.

This very structure embodies a contradiction. For ATSIC to serve its

Aboriginal constituents, it has to challenge the integrity of its own accountability principles, an idea unacceptable to many people outside of the organization, Aborigines and others. ATSIC's own Aboriginal constituencies have different views of accountability, and ATSIC, targeted for being different, has had to take responsibility for the burden of conflict among its own constituents. Moreover, as Aboriginal society has advanced its own cultural strengths, ATSIC's skills in resolving differences have increasingly been seen as political. Governments in Australia meticulously avoid discussions of divided sovereignty, even as a principle.

By the mid-1980s, Aboriginal peoples had slowly begun to return to their tribal and ancestral lands, a move endorsed by the commonwealth government's Return to Country policy.[43] Policies were to be based much more realistically on a set of circumstances that emphasized quality of life considerations. Some communities found that their lands had been devastated by decades of excessive grazing and mining. Aboriginal outstations began to emerge in response to the rhetoric of self-determination, beginning as small settlements and expanding as entire families began returning to their traditional lands. These outstations became the home of many Aboriginal peoples, often hundreds of miles from where they had been forced to relocate decades earlier. In some regions where Aboriginal land is extremely remote from towns and cities, service delivery problems multiplied. Through this process, Aboriginal peoples began to rediscover their past. The Hawke government of the 1980s and the Keating government of the 1990s recognized these changes as the start, rather than the end, of a process of justice. Recognition came from abroad, too, as problems facing the Aboriginal community began to receive more widespread exposure at the United Nations. By the end of the 1980s, it was clear that the system of government was not responding adequately to the needs of the Aborigines. Despite increased funding, Aboriginal and Torres Strait Islander health had barely improved. It was time to address systemic neglect, the lack of empowerment, poor infrastructure, and general social and economic malaise. Efforts to do so ranged from calls for constitutional recognition of indigenous rights to some form of self-government. Aborigines themselves agitated internationally for urgent reform.

They also faced a deepening crisis at home: Aborigines were dying in police custody at an alarming rate.[44] In 1988, at the insistence of the

---

43. House of Representatives Standing Committee on Aboriginal Affairs, *Return to Country: The Aboriginal Homelands Movement in Australia* (Canberra: AGPS, 1987).

44. Royal Commission into Aboriginal Deaths in Custody, *National Report*, Vol. 1 (Canberra: AGPS, 1991).

Aboriginal and Torres Strait Islander communities, the commonwealth government set up a Royal Commission into Aboriginal Deaths in Custody. It found that lack of basic service delivery was a major factor in the deteriorating circumstances facing most Aboriginal peoples; public inquiries revealed connections between the increasing number of Aboriginal deaths in police custody and the cultural alienation that resulted from the assimilation policies of the past. Of the ninety-nine Aboriginal people who died in custody between 1980 and 1989, forty-three had been officially removed from their families.[45] Unfortunately, the rate of Aboriginal deaths in custody increased by record numbers in 1995.[46] The position of the Aboriginal peoples within state criminal justice systems reflects their deprivation and inequality in the larger society. There is not a thriving relationship between the institutions of Aboriginal and Torres Strait Islander societies and those of Western governance, nor have policy reforms been helped by general community attitudes toward the indigenous population.

Aborigines are not the only Australians to face discrimination. However, discrimination against Aborigines has been institutionalized, whereas public racism against immigrants tends to occur in fits and starts. Also, concerted public attacks against indigenous peoples began to spill over into the territory of other non-white groups. Hostility against Aborigines quite openly takes the form of resentment about the level of funding they receive, whereas discrimination against Asians is surrounded by debates about acceptable levels of immigration.[47] A more virulent form of racism broke out in the 1990s, targeting both Asians and Aborigines. Pauline Hanson, the owner and operator of a Queensland fish-and-chip shop, was elected to the commonwealth parliament on the Liberal Party ticket. She rode to victory on a wave of vicious attacks on Asians, Aborigines, and homosexuals—an attack the prime minister himself foolishly endorsed as a form of "free speech." Like many before her, Hanson targeted the most vulnerable and perhaps most visibly different groups in Australian society. Following Hanson's parliamentary speech, Phillip Ruddock, minister for immigration, defended Australia's intake of

---

45. Ibid., p. 44.

46. According to Amnesty International; reported in *The Australian*, June 19, 1996.

47. In the 1980s, the Asian population was the target of public controversy when Geoffrey Blainey, a well-known historian speaking to a group of Rotarians, claimed that Australia's immigration policy was stacked in favor of Asians. The issue divided the Australian community; in a letter to the *Melbourne Age*, twenty-four of Blainey's colleagues from the University of Melbourne disassociated themselves from what they argued was the path of intolerance. See Marcus and Ricklefs, *Surrender Australia*.

Asian immigrants. The Aboriginal population, however, was less fortunate. Their federal minister would not defend even the most basic Aboriginal human rights; he appeared to be totally ignorant of their needs and unsympathetic to their historical position in Australian society. Completely abandoned by their own minister, the Aborigines were left to defend themselves.

THE MABO JUDGEMENT, LAND, AND "NATIVE TITLE" IN THE 1990S

Questions of rights and representation depend on many factors, including the culture and nature of civil society. Most demands by indigenous peoples in Australia relate to land and property; since 1992, the issue of indigenous rights, particularly claims of native title rights over existing pastoral property leases, has become a major and somewhat divisive question in Australian society. The concept of native title grew out of a 1992 High Court decision known as *Mabo v. Queensland*, which legitimized an ancient relationship between a group of Torres Strait Islanders and their land. The Court found in favor of Eddie Mabo, a Torres Strait Islander seeking access to his ancestral lands, who challenged the Queensland state government. The judgment in *Mabo* was based on historical evidence of unbroken ties between indigenous people and their land. Since Aboriginal peoples have no written histories, it was crucial to provide documented evidence of how they had managed their land in the century before federation.

Many argue that the principle of native title is essential to black and white reconciliation. With such high stakes, native title has become something of a benchmark for judging Australia's social and political maturity. It can also be a significant source of conflict in commonwealth-state relations. Even when the commonwealth does have powers concurrent with the states, there is no guarantee that it can use its power to affect outcomes. Legislation can be costly to politicians; in some states, the commonwealth tries to avoid confrontation with powerful constituent groups, particularly the pastoral and mining lobby groups. This was clearly the case in the Western Australian land rights debates of the mid-1980s. During a 1984 election campaign, the government of that state promised to initiate Aboriginal land rights in a deal involving the enactment of a uniform commonwealth land rights law. The deal was derailed when opposition to land rights gathered momentum; the commonwealth quietly withdrew its support and refocused its powers on heritage issues instead. As a consequence, national land rights for Aboriginal people have never materialized.

Aboriginal land rights have had limited success in some states, with the most gains in the Northern Territory under the Aboriginal Land Rights (Northern Territory) Act. The Native Title Act has produced virtually no recognition of Aboriginal rights. Governments, pastoralists, and a new generation of Aboriginal and Torres Strait Islander political leaders are battling over the survival of native title on pastoral leases and, ultimately, the survival of access rights to traditional Aboriginal lands. The Act demands serious scrutiny of government itself and of the nature of rights in Australia.[48]

The commonwealth Native Title Act was finally passed in 1993 to legitimate the High Court judgment of the previous year; passage of the legislation was torturous. Some state governments—notably those with powerful resource and pastoral industry constituencies—orchestrated campaigns to defeat it, and over three hundred conditional amendments reflected the demands of various senators. The legislation passed, amid speculation that colonial occupation may have extinguished the right to claim native title. The controversy continues. Constant and ongoing battles between indigenous groups and others to weaken, abolish, strengthen, and, from the Aboriginal organizations, quarantine the Native Title Act from interference, are now regular features of Australian national and state politics. In 1993, the Racial Discrimination Act of 1975 prevented the Native Title Act from erosion but, at one point in the debates, the commonwealth government actually considered suspending the Racial Discrimination Act to facilitate adjustments to the Native Title Act. That was seen as a major breach of trust between the government and the people and a breach also of Australia's international treaty obligations. The government's intentions outraged some Australians, particularly Aborigines and Torres Strait Islanders.

The Native Title Act establishes a Native Title Tribunal through which individuals can lodge native title claims. The Act is administered by the commonwealth Office of Indigenous Affairs and falls within the authority of the Department of Prime Minister and Cabinet. The Tribunal falls within the authority of the commonwealth attorney general. One of its key tasks is to decide whether pastoral leaseholds have extinguished native title. In practice, the Tribunal's main clients have been representatives of the mineral and pastoral industries. Claims and counterclaims concerning the workability of the Act have polarized sections of both the non-indigenous and the indigenous communities. Meanwhile, given the contentious nature of land title, the issue reaches into the

---

48. The Australian High Court found in favor of the Wik people when they appealed, claiming that native title can coexist with pastoral leaseholds. See *The Australian*, December 23, 1996.

structures of public administration, influencing policy expectations, financial decentralization, and the political agenda at large.

Native title has had a remarkable impact in only a few years. At one level, it can be argued that native title has quickened the pace to constitutional reform by highlighting the vulnerable position of the Aboriginal and Torres Strait Islander populations in relation to the Australian Constitution. At another level, it has served to broaden debates over issues such as rights, native sovereignty, and self-determination—meanwhile ensuring that the indigenous population can secure a place at the negotiating table. The general bureaucracy is also beginning to understand the concept and its association with rights; ideally, this should lead public administrators and state and local governments to better fulfill their obligations to provide basic services to their Aboriginal constituents. Despite interpretations by the courts in Australia, the government has yet to recognize that as a political concept, native rights predate the application of Western property rights. This is understood in Canada, where, in contrast to Australia, the courts have interpreted indigenous rights within Section 35 of the Canadian constitution as "inherent rights."[49] Inherent rights are not "given"; rather, they are rights that the courts recognize as having existed well before the arrival of the colonial settlers. Since Aborigines currently lack constitutional protection, "rights" have been treated as an element of public policy; they are generally used to promote the needs of indigenous communities under such strategic government frameworks as social justice, access and equity, and reconciliation. For native title to affect the future of Aboriginal and Torres Strait Islander affairs will require greater, more positive attempts toward institutional reform within the federation. Within that process, cultural issues also require greater attention, as does the empowering of Aborigines in every form.

Despite all efforts to improve relationships between stakeholders, the Aboriginal and Torres Strait Islander peoples have no formal authority within the organization of any territorial or state government structure. A weak sort of indigenous empowerment has developed at the level of local government, but not enough to enable communities to raise revenue or determine long-term future directions for expenditure. Local governments have always had a strong influence on the welfare of the Aboriginal and Torres Strait Islander peoples, but because local governments vary across Australia according to state and territory laws, policy outcomes are inconsistent and standards are difficult to set. Compared to those in

---

49. Peter H. Russell, *Constitutional Odyssey: Can Canadians Become a Sovereign People?* 2d ed. (Toronto: University of Toronto Press, 1993).

unitary systems in Britain or New Zealand, local governments in Australia are at the mercy of the state, rather than the national government; with limited revenues, local government is a weak structure. Moreover, while local government has helped to empower indigenous peoples in some states and territories, it also has created circumstances which disempowered them in other places.

Conclusions

There are no simple solutions to the problems raised in this chapter. As the twentieth century draws to a close, bureaucracies and governments lurch erratically from one set of policy reforms to another in an effort by non-Aborigines to "settle" the Aboriginal "problem." Moreover, the relationship between indigenous communities and governments varies considerably across the Australian federal system, mostly because different types of legislative regimes and political cultures have evolved over time in each of the states and territories, shaping the way policy is implemented. As indigenous peoples continue to press their demands onto the local political scene, the economic, social, and political landscapes in each region will continue to evolve. At the end of the day, community satisfaction depends on whether or not governments are responsive; since the Australian Constitution subscribes to the principles of a federal liberal democracy, one would anticipate that governments would try to meet their constituents' expectations. As this chapter illustrates, governments are likely to be far less responsive to their indigenous constituents than to other Australians.

There is little evidence that Aboriginal health or quality of life is improving significantly. Given the increased level of awareness and expenditure since the referendum of 1967, these outcomes are disgraceful. The reasons for this policy failure center around lack of local autonomy, limited opportunities for indigenous peoples to take part in decision-making, and ineffective administration of their affairs. Lack of attention to cultural differences and the way people identify with their way of life is another major hurdle.

The value of Aboriginal culture has not been considered in Australian decision-making processes, despite the obvious differences in the paradigms that govern Western and indigenous societies. The cultural distance between the two societies was, and still is, enormous, often so great that governments have no idea how to interpret indigenous needs. Thus the legal and administrative framework of the governing system is saturated with principles that are likely to be at odds with indigenous principles,[50] leaving Aboriginal peoples isolated by almost every aspect of the system—administration, political institutions, and economic structures.

For all of these reasons, many now see "outsiders" as a problem. It is presumptuous and ethnocentric to make recommendations without negotiating with the indigenous peoples in the area of indigenous affairs. Doing so perpetuates the existing problems of non-indigenous patronage, which continue to beleaguer the Aboriginal and Torres Strait Islander communities in Australia today. Given past disasters, it is no longer considered acceptable for non-indigenous peoples to make policy on behalf of, or for, indigenous peoples. Anyone can suggest reforms, of course, provided that indigenous peoples have negotiating status within the decision-making process.

Governments in Australia must sharpen their focus and take new directions in indigenous affairs. First, they need a new public policy paradigm: policy relationships cannot be simply "settled" or "terminated" according to a "final" agreement. Making policy "for" indigenous peoples and then demanding adherence to goals that might be ineffective, irrelevant, and destabilizing is costly both in both human and monetary terms. Part of the solution lies in constructing relevant negotiating forums, preferably on a regional basis, through which indigenous communities and governments can meet and negotiate the best way to establish a level of decision-making autonomy within each region.

Such autonomy, however, will be threatening to Australian governments, which have a history of rejecting devolution to Aboriginal communities, particularly if it concerns money. One way to approach this problem is to establish a process, in the context of regional forums, for setting up a committee system composed of people drawn from communities in each region. Aboriginal community members who are respected as decision-makers would form a committee for each particular policy area, such as health policy, housing, education, schools, and roads. Each committee member would define the policy deficiencies in his or her region. This would allow government to devolve authority for expenditure to the community in order to clearly target critical areas. The real benefit that would flow from this sort of devolution is self-determination. Such a working process, midway between community self-government

---

50. James Crawford, "Legal Pluralism and the Indigenous Peoples of Australia," in Oliver Mendelssohn and Upendra Baxi, eds., *The Rights of Subordinated Peoples* (Delhi: Oxford University Press, 1994).

and policy devolution, would also enhance the principles of account-ability, which are fundamental to the operations of government.

The culture of Western bureaucracy models itself on a set of principles that makes it difficult to recognize demands that emanate from different paradigms. Now that these different paradigms are widely recognized, Australian governments must respond. The views of indigenous peoples, and the demands that follow, must be incorporated into mainstream public administration. A more coordinated and transparent process of accountability is crucial, as are more creative links between indigenous structures and governments. This will involve changes in the very culture of government, and some will resist. However, cultural change is a natu-ral part of life. Culture has an important role to play in the process of adjustment when societies must cope with political, social, and economic upheavals in order to survive. Substantial evidence suggests that through-out the two centuries of white settlement, Aboriginal and Torres Strait Islander societies managed to sustain their traditional systems, broadly defined, through the use of culture. Despite enormous suffering and dislocation, those systems survive today, alongside the institutions of modern government. It is not too late to recognize the importance of maintaining equity in that relationship.

Chapter 11

Civil Rights, Amelioration, and Reparation in New Zealand

Andrew Sharp

Figures from New Zealand's 1991 census showed its nearly 3.4 million inhabitants to display an ethnic composition of the following order: New Zealand European, or Pakeha (75.1 percent), New Zealand Maori (9.7 percent), Pacific Island Groups (5 percent), Europeans from Britain, Ireland, Australia, and the United States (3.2 percent), Chinese (1.34 percent), and Indian (0.92 percent).[1] There were also several smaller groups deriving mainly from Southeast Asia and other Asian locations, and the Maori total might in fact be expanded to around 14 percent if one employed a more expansive method of interpreting "Maori" to include a further census category—"European ethnicity with Maori Ancestry." Trends in immigration since 1991 will yield changes in the as yet unreported 1996 census, especially in the Chinese and Indian categories that will have enlarged; but enough has been said to indicate the general distribution of ethnic groups in New Zealand. (See Table 11.1.)

As is only partly suggested by these figures, however, any discussion of government policy with respect to ethnic issues must focus on the relationships between the Crown and the descendants of the aboriginal inhabitants of the land—the Maori. It has been the confrontation between the Maori and the Crown that since the mid-1970s has dominated government policy. Their disputes have also colored the way in which all ethnic groups in New Zealand have seen themselves and have acted. To add insult to injury in a volume devoted to studies focused on the widest range of ethnic matters, it must be added that the very language of ethnicity does not find easy domicile in New Zealand—which does not

---

1. Statistics New Zealand (SNZ), *New Zealand Official Yearbook* (Wellington: Department of Statistics, 1995), p. 129; and *New Zealand Official Yearbook* (1996), Section 6.3. This series of yearbooks, henceforth *NZY*, contains the best brief description of New Zealand's geography, history, demography, economics, and politics.

Table 11.1. Ethnic Composition of New Zealand.

Group	Number	Percentage
New Zealand European (Pakeha)	2,488,509	75.1
Single New Zealand Maori	323,493	9.7
Pacific Island Ethnic Groups	167,073	5.0
European Ethnicity with Maori Ancestry	111,330	3.34
British, Irish, Australian, Canadian, American	107,388	3.2
Chinese	44,793	1.34
Indian	30,609	.92
Southeast Asian Ethnic Groups	16,642	.50
Other Asian Ethnic Groups	7,673	.23
Other	7,839	.24
Not Specified	28,113	.43
Total	**3,333,462**	**100.0**

NOTE: Unless otherwise stated, figures include those who listed two or more identifications as well as single ethnicity for each ethnic category. Some 4.3 percent of the total population identified themselves as members of two or more ethnic groups. As of late 1996, New Zealand's population was estimated at 3,561,000.

SOURCES: 1991 Census of Population and Dwellings, Department of Statistics, 1992: *National Summary, Population Overview, Population Structure, New Zealand Maori Population and Dwellings, Iwi Population and Dwellings, Pacific Island Population and Dwellings; Cook Island People in New Zealand,* Statistics New Zealand, 1995; *Fijian People in New Zealand,* Statistics New Zealand, 1995; *Niuean People in New Zealand,* Statistics New Zealand, 1995; *Samoan People in New Zealand,* Statistics New Zealand, 1995; *Tokelauan People in New Zealand,* Statistics New Zealand, 1995; *Tongan People in New Zealand,* Statistics New Zealand, 1995; Barbara Thomson, *Ethnic Groups in New Zealand: A Statistical Profile,* Department of Internal Affairs, 1993.

mean, of course, that an outside observer may not well find it illuminating to apply it to the inhabitants of New Zealand.[2]

It must be said at the outset that whatever the obsession with the Maori and the relative consequent weakness of government policy as to other groups, Maori-state relations and interethnic relations in New Zealand can only be described as good on any realistic scale of measurement. Since the mid-1970s (which because of the centrality of Maori issues from then on will be the focus of this chapter), ethnic conflict has indeed occurred. Most of it has been carried on within the established legal, bureaucratic, and political systems. The Maori have been very adept at this. Some of the contestation, though, has been physical: in land occupations,

2. For more discussion of the issues touched upon in this chapter, see Andrew Sharp, *Justice and the Maori: Maori Claims in New Zealand Political Argument in the 1980s,* 2d ed. (Auckland: Oxford University Press, 1997).

demonstrations, and the like.[3] But although some minor injury and damage have been done to persons and property, Pakeha sympathizers have as often been implicated as their Maori friends, no one has been killed, and only a handful of buildings has been burned. It remains rational for Asian immigrants in the 1990s—the butt of considerable criticism by opposition politicians and sections of the population—to give as one of their predominant reasons for wishing to come to the country, that "racial harmony prevails."[4]

A 1994 poll on "Groups you wouldn't like for Neighbours" illustrates more than heaped-up examples could just how the issue of ethnic relations sits in New Zealand in relation to other matters. Asked who they would not like as neighbors, an ethnically balanced cross-section of the population answered in percentage terms (highest to lowest) thus: criminals (42.2), heavy drinkers (41.9), emotionally unstable persons (35.7), religious cults or sects (27.8), right-wing extremists (25.3), left-wing extremists (24), wouldn't mind any (21), homosexuals (14.3), Polynesians (11.9), students (9.7), people of a different race (9.1), Maori (9.1), large families (8.9), immigrants/foreign workers (7.7), Pakeha/Europeans (7.4), unemployed persons (5.5), and unmarried mothers (5.4).[5] Ethnic prejudice in New Zealand is, it may be seen, not great; and if interethnic harmony is to be taken as an index of the success of government policies, New Zealand governments have performed well.

On the other hand, the governments' objectives can be criticized as too narrow in focus and not enough concerned with the long-term consequences of their allowing, since the mid-1980s, the growth of inequalities in a society that has been traditionally markedly egalitarian. Maori and Pacific Island immigrants in particular (the latter described as the "Polynesian Group" of the 1991 Census) have remained worse off than the rest of the population, in ways which will later be described. The Maori "problem" (this is my description, not the government's or the Maori's)[6] will also certainly persist. The "problem" is this: when the Maori have felt themselves to have been denied reparative justice for past

3. Geoffrey W. Rice, *The Oxford History of New Zealand*, 2d ed. (Auckland: Oxford University Press, 1992), chap. 19.

4. Manying Ip, "Chinese Settlers: Old Settlers and New Immigrants," in Stuart Greif, ed., *Immigration and National Identity in New Zealand* (Palmerston North: Dunmore Press, 1995), pp. 161–199 at p. 194.

5. Listener/Heylen Poll, *New Zealand Listener*, April 20, 1994, p. 18.

6. Andrew Sharp, "The Problem of Maori Affairs, 1984–89," in Martin Holland and Jonathan Boston, eds., *The Fourth Labour Government: Policy and Politics in New Zealand*, 2d ed. (Auckland: Oxford University Press, 1990), pp. 251–269.

wrongs done by the settler Pakeha, when they have contemplated their disadvantaged situation in society, and when they have seen their right to express themselves culturally in danger, they have tended to demand various kinds of self-rule. On those recurring occasions, they have depicted themselves as a separate people—in fact, as a series of separate peoples—who will insist on dealing with a sovereign government as if they were its equals.

It may well be that Maori will continue to claim varieties of self-rule even if their demands for reparative, distributive, and cultural justice were to be as fully met as can be imagined, because they have distinct grounds for doing so. And what any governmental policy can or should do about that must remain a moot point on both empirical and normative grounds. Rather, what this chapter will concentrate on are the three areas of policy on which governments since the mid-1970s may more reasonably be judged as to their management of ethnic affairs: on their performance, first, in the area of protection of civil and human rights; second, in providing by ameliorative policies better lives for the worst-off in the population; and, third, in providing reparations to the Maori for past wrongs and in allowing them degrees of autonomy. After an introductory section that sets the scene, the following sections of the chapter will deal with each of those three areas. The argument, in brief, is that the governments' records as to civil and human rights have been exemplary. However, their ameliorative policies—a marked feature of governments from the 1970s until 1984—have since then taken a new, more market-oriented and individualistic form and have not as yet been markedly successful. Finally, their management of the problem of reparations and the related claims to Maori autonomy has been (as perhaps it has had to be) reactive and ad hoc.

The Ethnic, Historical, and Political Setting

New Zealand is a sparsely populated state about the size of Japan or Great Britain.[7] Like Japan and Great Britain, it is an archipelago. It consists of two main islands and their outliers situated in the South Pacific Ocean at the southwestern extreme of Polynesia. Maori and Pakeha name the two main islands (and the outliers) differently: for instance, the North Island is Aotearoa; the South Island is Te Waipounamu; and New Zealand itself is usually called Aotearoa, which reflects the fact that 94 percent of Maori live on the North Island.

---

7. SNZ, *NZY* (1995), p. 1.

New Zealand.

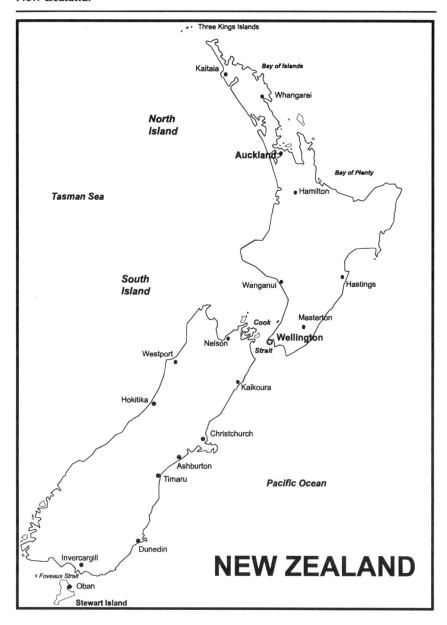

Location, cultural affinity, and economic considerations have provided New Zealand with its means of self-description and other-comparison. The country is about a three-hour plane trip from Australia to the west and to its closest Pacific neighbors—Western Samoa, the Cook Islands, Tonga, and Fiji—to the north. The country has always had the closest of political and economic relations with Australia; these developed further from the 1970s through the 1990s. Because its economic, military, and sentimental ties with Britain, the "mother country," were vastly weakened during the same period, official policy from 1984 until the early 1990s was to regard New Zealand as part of "the Pacific" on geographical and cultural grounds. But since the early 1990s, its policy has rather been to depict itself as part of the "Asia-Pacific region" in the light of its desire to expand commercial and financial relations with China, Japan, Taiwan, and Southeast Asia in particular. Finally, the country prides itself on being a developed country—part of the "first world." It continually compares its economic and social policy ranking with those of the OECD (Organization for Economic Cooperation and Development) countries.

The ancestors of the Maori settled the islands first about a thousand years ago, from unknown Pacific islands to the north and east. The ancestors of the Pakeha came next, beginning at the end of the eighteenth century; they came predominantly from England, but also in numbers from Ireland and Scotland. The two peoples—Maori and Pakeha—interacted in a complex of political, familial, and military (1863–72) encounters characterized by great mixing and intermingling on all those levels, as well as by the typical disasters visited on a native people by more technologically developed colonizers who brought new physical and moral diseases with them.[8] They were well entrenched when Pacific Islanders began to immigrate in the late 1940s to fill a demand for cheap labor in an expanding economy. The other settlers have a history, beginning with the Chinese being brought over (also as cheap labor) in the 1860s, and continuing through a series of minor, mainly Dutch and Dalmation migrations, to a large influx of immigrants from North Asia (notably Hong Kong and Taiwan) since the late 1980s.[9]

---

8. James Belich, *Making Peoples: A History of the New Zealanders from Polynesian Settlement to the End of the Nineteenth Century* (Auckland: Allen Lane Penguin Press, 1996); and Rice, *The Oxford History of New Zealand*, chaps. 1, 6, 11, and 19.

9. Patrick Ongley, "Immigration, Employment and Ethnic Minorities," in Paul Spoonley, ed., *Nga Patai: Racism and Ethnic Relations in Aotearoa/New Zealand* (Palmerston North: Dunmore Press, 1996), pp. 13–34; Ravi Arvind Palat, "Curries, Chopsticks and Kiwis," in Spoonley, *Nga Patai*, pp. 35–54; Alexander Trapeznik, "Recent European Migration to New Zealand," in Greif, *Immigration*, pp. 77–96; and Raj Vasil and Hon-Key Yoon, *New Zealanders of Asian Origin* (Wellington: Institute of Policy Studies,

More than 85 percent of the population live in the five main urban areas and sixteen provincial towns. More than 26 percent live in the largest city, Auckland, which boasts around one million people and lies in the north of the North Island.[10] The Maori, a largely rural and tribal people in the early 1940s, began to move in the 1950s to the cities in search of employment and enjoyment. They are now 80 percent an urban people, though some, mainly older and younger people, remain in (or have returned to) the tribal heartlands. They retain many characteristic social and political organizations,[11] but they are racially extremely mixed with Pakeha, so that many of Maori ancestry now think of themselves as Pakeha and very few claim to be "full-blooded." In the 1991 Census, 511,278 people claimed Maori ancestry. Of those, 22.1 percent did not know their tribal affiliations and 4 percent explicitly denied having any. Of those who did not know their tribal affiliations, over half (55.2 percent) described their ethnicity as "European," 28 percent described themselves as "Maori," and 16.8 percent described themselves as both "Maori" and "European." Of those who denied having a tribal affiliation, 60 percent described themselves as "European," 17.5 percent as "Maori," and 16 percent as "Maori-European."[12] Longer-settled Asians, notably "New Zealand Chinese" and "New Zealand Indians," are much more widely scattered than the more recent arrivals. They retain their links with each other rather than with recent immigrants from their areas of origin, and the New Zealand Chinese are intermarried, almost as much as the Maori, especially with Pakeha.[13] Post-1980 Asian immigrants have congregated in the larger cities, especially Auckland. They tend to cluster in better-off, often newly developed localities, but they congregate and act in distinct language, clan, and national groups. Fijian Indians remain a distinct group. Pacific Islanders live mainly in the poorer parts of the larger cities; they divide into six main island groups and can also display marked differences between the generations as the children come to live less traditional lives, often losing their family's native tongues.[14]

Victoria University of Wellington, 1996), chap. 3. Gross figures on the ethnic composition of the country from 1858–1986 are in SNZ, *NZY* (1990), p. 158.

10. SNZ, *NZY* (1996), chap. 5.

11. Rice, *The Oxford History of New Zealand*, chap. 19.

12. J.D. Gould, "Socio-Economic Differences between Maori Iwi," *Journal of the Polynesian Society*, Vol. 105, No. 2 (June 1996), pp. 166–167.

13. Vasil and Yoon, *New Zealanders of Asian Origin*, p. 14. See also SNZ, *Asian New Zealanders* (Wellington: Department of Statistics, 1995).

14. See the following SNZ publications (all published in Wellington by the Department of Statistics in 1995): *Cook Island People in New Zealand; Fijian People in New*

New Zealand was proclaimed a Dependency by Britain in 1840. In law then and now, the proclamation in the *London Gazette* established British sovereignty, but negotiations with a little over five hundred heads of mainly northland *hapu* (the sub-tribal effective operating group of Maori) had produced what is called in English The Treaty of Waitangi and in Maori *Te Tiriti o Waitangi*. The Maori still claim that the Treaty was neither simply an instrument to pacify "numerous dispersed, and petty tribes,"[15] nor a treaty of cession, but was and remains the constitutional foundation of a partnership between two peoples. The British (and continued New Zealand governments') view has been that it was simply a *politique* prelude to the Crown's assuming sovereignty by proclamation, and if not simply that, then an instrument of cession.

The texts provide ample scope for both claims. In Article 1 of the English language version, the Crown was granted "sovereignty" by the Maori. In the Maori version (signed by all but thirteen of their leaders), the Crown had been granted only *"kawanatanga"*: a power to govern for strictly limited purposes, certainly not that supreme power that "sovereignty" suggests to the British mind. In exchange for whatever it was the Maori ceded, in the third article, which differs little in the two languages, the Maori were guaranteed the "same rights" under law as all other New Zealanders. But the crucial article with respect to reparations and claims to constitutional independence was the second. There, in the English version, the Crown guaranteed the Maori, in exchange for sovereignty, the "full exclusive and undisturbed possession of their Lands and Estates Forests and Fisheries and other Properties so long as it is their desire to do so." In the Maori version, though, they were guaranteed *"te tino rangatiratanga"* (full chieftainship; sovereignty) in their lands, habitations, and *"ratou taonga katoa"* (all things highly prized). By the mid-1980s, Maori were plausibly able to begin arguing, increasingly publicly, that in ceding *kawanatanga* they had given up only *some* of their right to rule themselves; moreover, since the Article 2 guarantees of the Treaty had clearly not been kept, it was arguable that by that default they retained their entire *tino rangatiratanga*, or sovereignty over everything they treasured.

The Treaty/*te Tiriti* was, over most of its history, a time bomb waiting to explode. Constitutional development went on, oblivious of its presence and its continuing appeal, especially to the Maori north of Auckland.

Zealand; Niuean People in New Zealand; Samoan People in New Zealand; Tokelauan People in New Zealand; and *Tongan People in New Zealand.*

15. Claudia Orange, *The Treaty of Waitangi* (Sydney: Allen and Unwin, 1987), p. 30.

From the 1840s, New Zealand underwent a process of becoming increasingly independent of Britain. For all intents and purposes it is now autochthonous. As it became more independent, its political culture and institutions became increasingly liberal and democratic, innocent of the Treaty claims that were to emerge.[16] New Zealanders now live under a unitary government (separately legislating provinces were abolished in 1865), the main policymaking powers of which are exercised by a cabinet chosen from the majority party elected on universal adult suffrage to a single chamber parliament (a legislative chamber was abolished in 1951). Until 1996, Members of Parliament (MPs) were elected on a First-Past-the-Post (FPP) system: a simple majority of votes in one of the electorates gained a seat in the House of Representatives. This has meant that since the late nineteenth century, governments in Wellington, the capital, though controlled by laws and conventions and by public opinion, could nevertheless act swiftly. They were unhindered by the checks and balances of a federal system, a second house (which was never other than a rubber stamp), or the necessity to keep a coalition of parties together in parliament.

It was while these political arrangements were in force that two successive Labour governments (1984–90) and two successive National governments (1990–96) freed up the economy, reorganized the administration of government, and greatly weakened the welfare state in the teeth of public opinion. However, the politicians unleashed forces they could not control. Since the 1993 election, although the National government was elected—as was quite usual under FPP—on a minority vote not much larger than its traditional more leftward-leaning Labour Party rival, it governed under the shadow of a proportional representation system (called Mixed Member Proportional, or MMP) due to come into play in the election of October 1996. The people had decided to punish all politicians for their unpopular reforms and to make them more accountable to the electorate.[17] Consequently, a fundamentally two-party system, which had been normal for the country since the turn of the century, gave

---

16. The best introduction to New Zealand's political system is Richard G. Mulgan, *Politics in New Zealand* (Auckland: Auckland University Press, 1994). It is being revised for publication in late 1996 to take account of new developments.

17. For an idea of the scope of the reforms, their consequences, and their possible further consequences, see Jonathan Boston, John Martin, June Pallot, and Pat Walsh, eds., *Reshaping the State* (Auckland: Oxford University Press, 1991); Andrew Sharp, ed., *Leap Into the Dark: The Changing Role of the State in New Zealand since 1984* (Auckland: Auckland University Press, 1994); and Jane Kelsey, *The New Zealand Experiment: A World Model for Structural Adjustment?* (Auckland: Auckland University Press/Bridget Williams Books, 1995).

way to a multiparty system as politicians sought to adjust themselves to the new regime. Both parties spawned rivals to their left and right, and from their religious and populist elements. There were three main newcomers. To Labour's left there had already emerged the Alliance Party. It was to become a major player in the 1996 elections. To National's right appeared the Association of Citizens and Ratepayers, a neo-liberal party. The other newcomer was New Zealand First, led by a Maori, Winston Peters, who had been a National government Minister of Maori Affairs in 1990–91. His populist appeal was directed particularly towards the Maori and to an older, conservative electorate, infuriated by the neo-liberal reforms of both established parties.

It might be said that the New Zealand Constitution, having long been liberal, democratic, and inclined to treat all its peoples in the same way, has been entering a "post-imperial" phase in which the "strange multiplicity" of its peoples was being recognized.[18] This would be suggested by the upsurge of Maori constitutional demands and their demands for cultural recognition together with the change in the electoral system. It would be suggested even more by an accelerating change from governmental policies of racial assimilation towards the recognition and support of cultural, "ethnic" difference since the 1960s.

Over most of the state's short history, New Zealand governments recognized "race" problems—in particular a "native problem" and a problem with "race aliens," notably the few Chinese and Indians. The Chinese were a minor irritant, combated until the early 1950s with restrictive immigration laws, denial of nationality, and poll taxes.[19] The Indians suffered almost as much under what was an unstated white New Zealand immigration policy, even though such a policy contradicted imperial policy.[20] It was the Maori who mattered. Although the country prided itself on being British (as well as white), the official ideal until 1960 was to meld the Maori and British "races" so that a culturally and (perhaps surprisingly to a foreigner) genetically undifferentiated nation would emerge over time. As early as the 1890s, it was thought that education, miscegenation, and the pursuit by governments of sociopolitical equality

---

18. James Tully, *Strange Multiplicity: Constitutionalism in an Age of Diversity* (Cambridge: Cambridge University Press, 1995).

19. Tom Brooking and Roberto Rabel, "Neither British nor Polynesian," in Greif, *Immigration,* pp. 23–49; and Ip, "Chinese New Zealanders: Old Settlers and New Immigrants," in Greif, *Immigration,* pp. 161–199.

20. Jacqueline Leckie, "South Asians: Old and New Migrations," in Greif, *Immigration,* pp. 133–160.

would bring about assimilation. Thus in 1946, Leslie Lipson, a distinguished U.S. scholar, could write:

There is no such gulf in the standard of personal capacity between the white and colored New Zealanders as between the white Australian and the aborigine. Race equality for the Maori people has thus become a cardinal principle in this Dominion, formalized into constitutional law and proclaimed in the perorations of statesmen. Miscegenation has been fairly common and has seldom carried with it a social stigma. Maoris possess equal voting rights, receive special representation in Parliament, and take office as ministers of the Crown.[21]

This view almost perfectly captured mainstream thought among the political elite, though it did not perhaps quite respect enough the widespread feeling that good Maori customs might be allowed, even encouraged, to survive.

By the early 1970s, the wider public began to hear the Maori more energetically asserting their cultural distinctiveness. Maori leadership found allies in (mainly Pakeha) anti-racist groups, impressing on governments the necessity of thinking in terms of culture and ethnicity as proper descriptions of the elements of national society; they insisted that since culture and ethnicity were worth preserving and fostering, respect for ethnic difference should be the normative basis for policy. "Monoculturalism" and monocultural policies would no longer do. But the language of ethnicity was a foreign import, arising from the disciplines of sociology and social anthropology[22] rather than from the common opinions of New Zealanders. It did not and still does not sit easily in the national consciousness. It was not that there was not widespread agreement that the language of race was to be avoided, but it was not until 1982, in a publication called *Race Against Time,* that the Race Relations Office committed itself and government agencies to the guiding policy principle of "multiculturalism," and thus to the language of ethnicity.

This hesitancy in conception and consequently in action was largely due to a long-settled propensity among the great majority of individuals in the population not to think of themselves as members of an "ethnic group" at all: if distinctions *had* to be made among groups, then racial distinctions seemed more natural. Most Pakeha seem to have thought of themselves as a "race" when they undertook invidious racial discrimina-

21. Leslie Lipson, *The Politics of Equality: New Zealand's Adventures in Democracy* (Chicago: University of Chicago Press, 1948), p. 3.

22. Ivan Hannaford, *Race: The History of an Idea in the West* (Baltimore: Johns Hopkins University Press, 1996), pp. 385–401.

tion against Maori, Pacific Islanders, or Asians. But they did not much like being called "Pakeha." For one thing, it was a Maori word. For another, while it was alleged by the Maori to mean simply "white New Zealander," many Pakeha harbored the suspicion that it meant something more insulting; moreover, they considered themselves to be simply "ordinary New Zealanders" and to have no marked "cultural" characteristics.[23] For their part, the Maori also thought of themselves both as a race (and they were not about to admit their race was inferior) and as New Zealanders (how could they not be?).

Nor did the Maori easily think of themselves as simply an ethnic group like other ethnic groups. It is true that they asserted a separate and valuable culture and that they described themselves collectively as *"te iwi Maori"* (Maori originally meaning: "ordinary, normal people") over and against *"te iwi Pakeha."* But the notion of their being *te iwi Maori* and thus something like an ethnic group was not by any means the end of their self-description. They were, they claimed, *tangata whenua*—the people of the land. They were its aboriginal inhabitants. They had a unique, spiritual, and inalienable relationship with it—*whenua* means "womb" as well as "land." Their identity as well as their livelihood was derived from their relationship with it. They were a "first nation," an "indigenous people"— an ethnic group maybe, but only incidentally to that primary status. And in fact, as well as seeing themselves as one people, they often saw themselves as forty-three to sixty separate *iwi* (tribes),[24] all claiming *tino rangatiratanga* (full chieftainship), each against each other and each against the Crown. At times, even *hapu* (sub-tribes) have claimed *tino rangatiratanga* against the rest of their *iwi* and against other *hapu* within the same *iwi*—for it was leaders of *hapu* who had signed the Treaty of Waitangi. Each locality had its *tangata whenua.*

Despite their complex self-perceptions, the Maori were well able to adopt the language of ethnicity and culture when national politics demanded it. In the 1970s, the idea of New Zealand being a "multicultural society" was first mooted by anti-racist groups. It was then adopted as policy in at least some official circles in the early 1980s. At that point, the Maori successfully protested that New Zealand was rather a "bicultural society," made up fundamentally of Maori and Pakeha, in which both "cultures" were native to the land and to be valued equally, and in which

---

23. See Avril Bell, "'We're Just New Zealanders': Pakeha Identity Politics," in Spoonley, *Nga Patai*, pp. 144–158.

24. The number of *iwi* is not known. Forty-three are members of the tribal collective, the Maori Congress, founded in 1990, but other groups also claim *iwi* status.

government was to be shared between the Maori and the Crown.[25] They argued that "multiculturalism" was a Pakeha method of denying them their rights, and they largely succeeded in promoting the bicultural perspective. Maori became an official language. New Zealand nationalist ideology changed. It became a matter of depicting a "Pacific nation" forged from two heritages, Maori and Pakeha.

This bicultural understanding of things was both unstable and inimical to the development of a clear and persistent idea of New Zealand's being made up of a wide collection of ethnic groups, and of being multicultural. It was unstable because *no* language incorporating ethnicity and culture appealed to the Pakeha. Nor, as has been seen, did the Maori unambiguously think of themselves as an ethnic group: they were as likely to think of themselves as a race or else as *Ngapuhi, Ngati Whatua, Waikato-Tainui, Ngati Kahungunu, Ngai Tahu,* or some other *iwi* or even *hapu.* Only members of non-Maori and non-Pakeha minority groups (Asians and Pacific Islanders mainly) had a stake in speaking of ethnic groups, their nature and their rights, for they wished to promote the policy perspective that there were many ethnic groups in New Zealand who deserved, in various ways, differentiated but equal treatment. However, non-Maori minority ethnic group claims could only be advanced at the expense of the Maori case for special treatment.[26] Not surprisingly, when they pushed their claims, they met fierce opposition.

It was under these political circumstances that governments and officials in New Zealand attempted over the period from about 1973 to 1993 to frame and execute not just the settled anti-discrimination policies discussed in the following section, but new policies designed to recognize ethnic groups and to protect and foster their interests, and to expunge the very notion of race from the population's consciousness. An index of the process of change over the long run can be observed in the descriptions of persons sought in the quinquennial censuses. From 1945 until 1971, the censuses used criteria of race to distinguish persons; from 1976 until 1986, they used ethnic "origin"; since 1991, they have used ethnic "group," and

---

25. Useful studies of elite use of bicultural rhetoric and policy starting in the mid-1980s are Richard Benton, "Biculturalism in Education: Policy and Practice under the Fourth Labour Government," in Holland and Boston, *The Fourth Labour Government,* pp. 192–212; and the essays in Margaret Wilson and Anna Yeatman, eds., *Justice and Identity: Antipodean Practices* (Wellington: Bridget Williams Books, 1995).

26. For a recent statement of Asian positions, see Vasil and Yoon, *New Zealanders of Asian Origin,* chap. 4.

have also asked Maori-identifiers to specify if they can and will which *iwi* (the word is both singular and plural) they "affiliate" with.[27]

In introducing these and other changes to the gathering of statistics, officials were from the beginning attracted by Anthony Smith's criteria of ethnicity and consequently of the grounds of group classification. An ethnic group would be defined as those who shared a sense of common origins, history, destiny, and solidarity, and possessed "one or more dimensions of cultural individuality." An individual's categorization would not be an imposed one or one based on race, but one chosen in accord with their actual sentimental and practical lives. The upshot of the attempt at a new policy of naming was, however, much less Smithian. It was expressed in the *Standard Classification of Ethnicity* published in 1993.[28] A five-tier classificatory system was adopted, expanding from four "ethnic" groups at level one (Pakeha/European, New Zealand Maori, Pacific Island Groups, and Other) to over 220 groups at level five. A vanishingly small proportion of the groups so named at any level are much like Smithian ethnic groups, yet the system is appropriate for New Zealand, and the result of a complex politics of naming. Geographical origin and racial origin were in the event evidently taken as markers, as was ethnic identification.

The Maori case will suffice as an illustration. The Maori were categorized as a racial rather than an ethnic group, and a racial group whose components were to be distinguished each from each, not by ethnicity but by tribal affiliation. There were good reasons for this, but the reasons were not entirely based on a commitment to Smithian categories. It was found indeed by study that most people who identified themselves as Maori claimed Maori ancestry and those who did not so identify did not. But the main reasons for insisting on ancestry as the criterion for being Maori were legal and bureaucratic. During the 1970s, the statutory definition of Maori had become "a person of the Maori race, and includes any descendant of such a person."[29] Even though the main idea was to avoid

---

27. Terry Papps, "Issues Regarding Ethnic Statistics," *The New Zealand Statistics Review* (September 1994), App. 1, pp. 26–29.

28. A record of the development of naming and measurements is in P.G. Brown, "An Investigation of Official Ethnic Statistics," *Department of Statistics, Occasional Paper No. 5* (Wellington: Department of Statistics, 1983); Department of Statistics, *Report of the Review Committee on Ethnic Statistics* (Wellington: Department of Statistics, 1988); and Department of Statistics/Te Tari Tatau, *New Zealand Standard Classification of Ethnicity 1993* (Wellington: Department of Statistics/Te Tari Tatau, 1993).

29. Maori Affairs (Amendment) Act, 1974. The Electoral (Amendment) Act of 1975 added after "person," "who elects to be considered as a Maori for the purposes of this Act"; but the Electoral (Amendment) Act of 1980 removed those added words.

questions posed on earlier censuses as to what precise degree of Maori "blood" the respondent had, the criterion of genetic descent still remained embedded in the law. There was good reason for this: there was a separate Maori voting system, and various welfare and development programs were targeted at the Maori. Not just anyone should be allowed to claim to be Maori. So the race criterion remained. The *Standard Classification* did not itself distinguish tribes; but the 1991 Census Form was altered so as to elicit that information from those stating that they had Maori ancestry. Thus were the self-identification needs of the Maori met. They were to be seen rather more as a race and as a series of tribes than as an ethnic group.

These difficulties of nomenclature (which expresses the practical reality) aside, what have been the main lines of "ethnic" policy in New Zealand, and how effective have they been?

Civil and Political Rights

New Zealand governments' management of the civil and political rights aspects of ethnic relations is widely and rightly respected on the world scene. This happy reputation has only been disturbed in 1995–96 by an unpleasant public reaction to an influx of Asian migrants, but there is little reason to think it will not be restored.

The main reason for this, besides the country's having a tolerant political and social culture, is a human rights–inspired system of legal protections against invidious discrimination, which has been well entrenched since the early 1970s, together with a political system that allows the full participation of all. New Zealand governments adopted human rights policies early on, and soon gave them institutional form. In 1971, a Race Relations Office was set up, headed by a Race Relations Conciliator. This was followed in 1977 by the establishment of a Human Rights Commission. The Race Relations Act, which established the Race Relations Office, made it unlawful to discriminate invidiously on the grounds of "colour, race, ethnic or national origins" in matters of access to public places, vehicles, and facilities, and in the provision of goods and services, employment, and the occupation and ownership of land and housing. Advertisements which suggested that any discrimination might occur were also declared unlawful. The Conciliator's main role was initially that of mediator; however, with the creation of the Human Rights Commission, he (no women have held the office though there have been Maori, Pakeha, Jewish, and Indian Conciliators) might take a case to an Equal Opportunities Tribunal, a section of the Human Rights Commission, for enforcement.

The Race Relations Office has recorded the number, source, and means of resolution of client complaints it has received on these matters over its nearly twenty-five years of existence.[30] From 1972 to 1993, the annual number of complaints varied from 25 to 142, and they came from all ethnic groups. The record demonstrates that discrimination does indeed manifest itself, but there has also been a reasonably successful series of attempts at mediating particular cases.

Over its life, the Race Relations Office has operated to the satisfaction of most people. However, it has attracted its share of public controversy, notably from 1980 to 1990 and again from 1993 onwards, when the numbers of client complaints and the level of public controversy both increased. There were two sets of reasons for public complaint: one was legal, relating to the statute under which the office operated; the other was political, connected with the upsurge in Asian immigration beginning in the late 1980s.

The controversies of the 1980s were engendered when, in 1977, a new series of unlawful acts was brought into the Race Relations Conciliator's purview by an amendment to the office's establishing statute (Section 9a): "threatening, abusive or insulting language . . . likely to excite hostility or ill-will against, or bring into contempt and ridicule any group of persons." The idea was that there ought to be freedom of speech, but that all public speech should be subject to legal scrutiny. When the conciliator on more than one occasion found that such acts on a *marae* (a meeting place of local *tangata whenua*) were acts in private and not in public and therefore outside the jurisdiction of his office, public outrage ensued. (One Maori, for instance, had said on a *marae* that it was a good idea to "kill a white.") The offending section of the statute was ultimately removed in 1989. But legislation against public denigration was soon felt to be necessary again. In 1993, an amended Human Rights Act replaced the lapsed Section 9a of the Race Relations Act with prohibitions on "incitement to racial disharmony" (Section 61) and "racial harassment" (Section 63). In every year when either Section 9a or Sections 61 and 63 were in force, over half the complaints to the office have concerned words said in public—and almost all the public criticism of the office was to the effect that it was not prosecuting inflammatory language enough, or that the office was itself being inflammatory. In 1996, for instance, when the new legislation was in force, the Race Relations Conciliator was widely condemned for encouraging and defending the publication of a cartoon

---

30. This section is based on the series of reports of the Human Rights Commission to Parliament, 1989–95. They are called *Report of the Human Rights Commission and the Office of the Race Relations Conciliator . . . 1989 [etc.]* and are printed as Appendix E.6 to the *Journals of the House of Representatives*.

comparing the brain sizes of Maori, Pakeha, and Asian (all the same size) with that of a Racist (about one-third the size).

It was the issue of Asian immigration that had brought the "Racist" with the small brain to prominence and that caused an upsurge of client complaints (and public controversy) from 1993 to 1995. From June 1991 to June 1992 and from June 1992 to June 1993, there were, respectively, 135 and 131 complaints. From June 1993 to June 1994 and June 1994 to June 1995, there were 272 and 587. The 1993–94 figure had only been attained once before in the history of the office; the 1994–95 figure was quite unprecedented. What had happened? Labour had begun in 1987 a push towards encouraging those with entrepreneurial skills and with capital to come into New Zealand, especially people from New Zealand's rich and economically expansive Asian "neighbors." What Labour had begun, National continued. In 1982 only 11.9 percent of those gaining residence permits were Asian. By 1987, the figure was 20.4 percent; and by 1988, 28.4 percent. The sudden change came in 1989 (47.2 percent); after that, Asian immigrants began to top the 50 percent mark.[31] The trend continued into 1995, amid great publicity, not least stirred by the anti-immigration campaign of Winston Peters, leader of New Zealand First. Peters put considerable emphasis on the government's policy of increasing immigration in general; but he could with some reason have been interpreted as being anti-Asian, because the fact was that the increasing proportion of immigrants was Asian, and that opinion polls taken from October 1994 showed Asian immigrants to be much less popular than those from Australia and Great Britain—the traditional sources of most immigrants. Even white South Africans were more popular, though the new Asians were more welcome than Pacific Islanders.[32]

The central problem for the government was not one of managing the new immigrants or even of ensuring them of their civil rights: it was managing the votes of the settled population. Anti-Asian sentiment was being tapped by New Zealand First: around 57 percent of those who thought there were "too many" Asian immigrants had decided to vote for New Zealand First. Perhaps with this in mind, the government changed the rules of entry, and Asian immigration plummeted in 1996, clearing the way for the October election. The 1996 election campaign was

---

31. Unpublished Immigration Permit Information, SNZ, tabulated in Palat, "Curries, Chopsticks and Kiwis," p. 49. See also Ongley, "Immigration, Employment and Ethnic Minorities," and Vasil and Yoon, *New Zealanders of Asian Origin*, chap. 3.

32. "The National Business Review–Consultus Poll," *National Business Review* (Wellington), April 19, 1996, p. 14; and "Public Says No to Asians, Islanders," *National Business Review*, September 13, 1996, p. 16.

characterized by every other party attacking New Zealand First's "racism" in questioning immigration policy, and Winston Peters' defense of himself and his party against the charge. To play the "race card" in New Zealand politics is to expose a weak flank to attack.

Overall, it seems most likely that the new Asian immigrants will settle in New Zealand with as few problems as their predecessors have experienced (at least since the late 1940s, when remaining legislation that was disadvantageous to them was removed). They will be subject to minor and irritating discrimination, but little more. Their aims, like those of their predecessors, are overwhelmingly to fit into New Zealand society in as uncontroversial a way as possible, while insisting on the preservation of their cultures and demanding that they not be discriminated against.[33]

It remains to record the civil and political rights of all ethnic groups. All have equal protection of the law, which an unentrenched Bill of Rights (1990) protects.[34] Freedom of association is guaranteed in the Bill of Rights and has in any case never been challenged since labor disputes in 1951. Communist groups suffered minor persecution during the Cold War era, but ethnic groupings have never been threatened. There are innumerable Maori groups devoted to political, social, and economic action; Asians, Dalmations, Jews, and many other groups are not so devoted to political action but retain lively cultural contact, and, through a federation of Ethnic Councils, maintain policy input into governing circles. All citizens and permanent residents have equal rights to welfare benefits, with no chance of political actions undermining them. The action of ethnic groups has rather been to alert governments to their special needs.

Citizens and residents of a year's standing are fully enfranchised with respect to the election of their political representatives. (They must enroll in national electorates but need not vote; they may enroll and may vote in local elections.) The Maori are a special case.[35] From 1867 to 1993, there were four Maori MPs (of a growing total of seventy-four to ninety-nine MPs) representing four Maori electorates. The electoral law since 1975 has stated that people with Maori ancestry may elect, via a triennial "Maori

---

33. Yongjin Zhang, "The Chinese Community and Political Parties: What Can the Polls Tell Us?" in Y. Zhang and Manying Ip, eds., *The Chinese Community and New Zealand Politics* (Auckland: Department of Political Studies and Asian Languages and Literature Department, 1996), pp. 59–66.

34. Paul Rishworth, "Civil Liberties," in Hyam Gold, ed., *New Zealand Politics in Perspective*, 3d ed. (Auckland: Longman Paul, 1992), pp. 143–157.

35. Waitangi Tribunal, *Maori Electoral Option Report* (Wellington: The Tribunal WAI 413, 1994), Sections 2.1–2.3; and *Report of the Royal Commission on the Electoral System: Towards a Better Democracy* (Wellington: The Commission, 1986), App. B.

Roll Option," to be on the separate Maori Electoral Roll for the purposes of electing the Maori MPs. If they so elect, then they may not be on the General Roll; if they do not so elect, then they are placed on the General Roll. In 1986, the Royal Commission on the Electoral System, which advocated an MMP system, also advocated the abolition of the Maori seats on grounds that, captured since the late 1930s by the Labour party, the Maori MPs could not bring their influence to bear across the party spectrum. In fact, Labour lost its grip on the four Maori seats in the 1993 election; one of the Maori seats went to New Zealand First. In any case, many Maori objected to the abolition of their separate seats on grounds that, inadequate as that representation was, they at least represented a vestige of *tino rangatiratanga*. Therefore, though the MMP system was in fact legislated into existence in 1993, the established Maori Option was retained and the number of Maori seats was boosted to five, with the effect that the mainstream parties in 1996 would as usual contest the Maori as well as General Seats. With this change in prospect, Maori voters continued to choose in greater numbers to be on the General Roll than on the Maori Roll,[36] and Maori politicians were to be found in all the parties. No significant separate special interest Maori or minority ethnic party emerged.[37] They were too diverse in their interests, and in any case the numbers of non-Maori ethnic groups were too small to attain the 5 percent of votes needed to attain a list seat, let alone the much greater number needed for a constituency seat.[38]

A question to be asked of the 1996 elections was whether the new MMP system would increase Maori and other ethnic minority representation in parliament. For minority ethnic groups other than Maori, the answer was yes. Only one member of a minority ethnic group (a Samoan) had ever been elected under the FPP system. This was in the 1993–96 Parliament, which was made up of ninety-nine MPs, all elected by simple majorities in their constituencies. In October 1996, four minority ethnic group MPs were elected to a parliament of 120 (one Asian and three Pacific Islanders). The Maori did even better. Generally, from the 1970s on, both major parties have had two or three Maori MPs elected to General seats; and in the last FPP parliament of 1993–96, there were four

---

36. After the 1991 Census, when the Maori were given an option, 126,723 chose the General Roll, 87,652 chose the Maori Roll, and 72,965 of those who were eligible (and required) to enroll did not enroll at all. See Waitangi Tribunal, *Maori Electoral Option Report*, Sect 2.3.

37. There were some small ones: Mana Maori; te Tawhara; Asia-Pacific United; and the Ethnic Party. Their share of the vote was negligible.

38. Zhang, "The Chinese Community and Political Parties."

Maori MPs besides those who represented the Maori constituencies. There were, therefore, eight Maori to ninety-one Other. Under MMP in 1996, besides the five Maori MPs elected by the Maori electorates, two Maori were elected in constituencies and six were elected from party lists—the new party list system had made it imperative for the major parties to include Maori candidates near the top of their lists. More startlingly, Peters's New Zealand First captured the five Maori seats, had two Maori elected from constituencies, and found itself in a crucial bargaining position between National and Labour. The Maori had come to occupy a pivotal position in New Zealand party politics.

Ameliorative Policies

The Maori and Pacific Islanders have long suffered from relative deprivation. Changes in government policy since 1984 have worsened that deprivation in some crucial but not all respects. Nevertheless, insofar as the exercise of cultural rights is essential to well-being, there has been great improvement; and long-term improvements in their standards of living, which were set in motion in the 1940s and 1950s, have either continued or may well resume.

With the first Labour government of 1935, New Zealand consolidated a pervasive tradition of being a redistributive, egalitarian state. This resulted in great improvements in Maori and Pacific Islander standards of living and life-expectancy, which are recorded in the *Official Yearbooks* and Census reports until the mid-1980s. It was in line with this tradition that, in 1988, a Royal Commission on Social Policy reported to the government. Following the precise wording of the Social Welfare Act of 1972, it suggested that policies should be pursued that would enable each person to achieve "a standard of living sufficient to . . . participate in and have a sense of belonging to the community." It added (echoing the bicultural, multicultural, and gender-conscious discourse of its own day) that "all people, of whatever age, race, gender, social and economic position or abilities" should have a "genuine opportunity" to develop "their own potential." "Dignity and self determination" of "individuals, families and groups" should be fostered, together with "acceptance of the identity and cultures of different peoples within the community, and understanding and respect for cultural diversity."[39] Special attention should be paid to the needs of Maori, Pacific Islanders, other minority

---

39. The Royal Commission on Social Policy/*Te Komihana A Te Katauna Mo Nga Ahuatanga-A-Iwi*, *The April Report*, Vol. 2 (Wellington: The Commission, 1988), pp. 3–23.

ethnic groups, and women: positive discrimination was allowed by the Human Rights Act and social equity demanded it.

That was in 1988. A new policy community, centered on the Treasury in alliance with the Labour government's minister of finance, had come to power since 1984 and was already exercising overriding influence on the new government. That policy community stressed the need to rely on international markets for the creation and distribution of wealth, the disincentive effects of excessive provision of social welfare, the error of government's providing what could better be provided by private enter- prise, the importance of government's distinguishing the policymaking and policy-delivery functions, and the danger of policymaking being captured by interest groups professionally or personally concerned with the outcome of policy. As to the citizenry, they were to be considered primarily as a collection of individuals, each reacting to market signals, most particularly as workers allocating their efforts in line with the labor market, and as consumers of services. If and when they were members of groups, they were to be considered so because of their individual choice. They might well choose to act together for their mutual benefit; they would and should, especially if encouraged to do so, by being freed from central government controls and empowered to act for them- selves as government devolved the delivery of services. The thrust of policy—at a time of high national debt, an unfavorable balance of trade, and a poorly educated work force—was to create wealth in the most efficient way and to distribute wealth as a market reward. Provision of social welfare by way of unemployment benefits, health and housing benefits, and superannuation payments should be not universal but tar- geted, and should be a safety net—to allow each person to achieve that "standard of living sufficient to . . . participate in and have a sense of belonging to the community," which the Royal Commission had recom- mended. The ameliorative, equalizing function of the state was to be much reduced. And so it was by both Labour and National governments from 1984 to 1996.

The institutional history of the provision of Maori amelioration since 1984 has been one of central governments twice reforming the Ministry of Maori Affairs so as to make it a policy ministry with greatly reduced service functions. Provision of Maori welfare benefits was "main- streamed" through other departments, chiefly through the Department of Social Welfare. Similarly mainstreamed were education and employment. Overall spending on Maori-specific purposes was reduced with the im- plementation of "mainstreaming."

The Ministry of Maori Affairs (by 1992 called *Te Puni Kokiri*, the Ministry of Maori Development) also lost much of its service-provider power not only to government ministries and other agencies, but to its own constituency, the Maori people. The process began as early as 1978 with Maori approval. They wished to run their own affairs and were eager to have economic development devolved to pan-Maori and to local organizations. *Kohanga reo*, early childhood Maori language immersion centers, which had been set up in the early 1980s entirely without government funding, were allowed to expand and were encouraged by government grants; a series of *matua whangai* (extended family groups) aimed at the rehabilitation of Maori youth were also encouraged, funded by the departments of Maori Affairs, Justice, and Social Welfare. The Department of Maori Affairs' welfare functions had accordingly already begun to lapse. But the department, together with such pan-Maori organizations as the New Zealand Maori Council, the Maori Women's Welfare League, and the Maori Wardens, continued to work closely together, the pan-Maori organizations reliant on the department for a good deal of their funding. Finally, various attempts were made to pool and use Maori capital, mostly generated by the proceeds of land-management programs. Those attempts centered on the department were attended with failure, with the consequence that any further attempts were to be independently mounted. Economic advancement and social equality were the aims; Maori cultural renaissance, self-help, and self-delivery were the means.

Those aims meshed well with the neo-liberal policies of successive governments. By 1987, a series of *kokiri* (work training) centers had been established in the localities, funded by the department, but free from strict central control. By 1990, the Labour government legislated a transition period during which the department would oversee the legal registration of *iwi runanga* (legal representatives of iwi); they would be groomed for service delivery based on traditional Maori organization devoted to Maori development; and the department would evolve in the direction of a policy ministry. In 1992 the National government statutorily turned its back on *iwi* delivery on the grounds that many Maori did not see *iwi runanga* as either traditional or as representing the 70–80 percent of urban Maori who were cut off from their *iwi*. *Te Puni Kokiri* would be further downsized until it became a ministry devoted to giving policy advice to the government and to monitoring the activities and outputs of the other government departments and agencies in relation to the Maori. In the event, the process of change took exactly that form.[40]

Such were the trends in ameliorative policy formulation and delivery

---

40. See Te Puni Kokiri, *Summary of the Establishment and Achievements of Te Puni Kokiri (January 1, 1992 to October 13, 1995)* (Wellington: Ministry of Maori Development, 1995).

of services to the Maori. In the course of a similar process of devolution affecting Pacific Islanders, Island Affairs, once a subdepartment of Maori Affairs, was set up in 1992 as a stand-alone ministry; it became the Ministry of Pacific Island Affairs, with policy and monitoring functions similar to those of *Te Puni Kokiri*. The ministry was very small, and was charged with "encouraging other government agencies to take responsibility for meeting the aspirations of Pacific Island people," rather than with delivering services to them.[41] It may be added that in 1992 an Office of Ethnic Affairs was established, first as a conduit through which the government might hear the concerns of non-Maori and non–Pacific Island groups. Initially, the tiny office—located in the Department of Internal Affairs and staffed by only one professional policy analyst—played an advocacy role for the Federation of Ethnic Councils and concentrated on the collection and dissemination of information to its clients. Under continual government pressure, it was being forced by 1996 to act as a policy-development agency, and government funding to the Federation of Ethnic Councils was declining.[42] Client capture was to be avoided there just as it was by *Te Puni Kokiri* and the Ministry of Pacific Island Affairs. Devolution of responsibility to the "communities" and avoidance of central control (and funding) was to be practiced.

It is a moot point whether these institutional developments have done more harm than good. For one thing, the performance of the departments to which special Maori responsibilities were handed is hard to assess. For another, they occurred during a period when the governments of 1984–96 also pursued economic policies[43] that they knew would have deleterious effects on Maori and Pacific Islanders, at least in the short term. They knew that the divesting of state ownership and control of railways, the post office, forests, fisheries, electricity supply, and public works (1986–92) would affect most heavily unskilled and semi-skilled workers, which the Maori and Pacific Islanders tended to be.[44] They knew there would be higher structural unemployment. They knew that the lower-paid would suffer most as a result of labor market reforms in the Employment Contracts Act (1990) aimed at de-unionizing the work force. They knew that

---

41. SNZ, *NZY* (1995), pp. 165–166.

42. Vasil and Yoon, *New Zealanders of Asian Origin*, p. 17; and unpublished papers by Kate McMillan, Department of Politics, Victoria University of Wellington.

43. Summarized in SNZ, *New Zealand System of National Accounts* (Wellington: Department of Statistics, 1995), App. 2.

44. Spoonley, "Mahi Awatea? The Racialisation of Work in Aotearoa/New Zealand," in SNZ, *Maori* (Wellington: Department of Statistics, 1995), pp. 39–42.

the reductions in welfare benefits (1991) and in income taxes on higher earners (1996) would have the same effect.[45] They knew that refusing benefits to illegal immigrants would affect Pacific Islanders very severely.[46] Yet it must be said that although they do not seem to have persuaded the general population of this,[47] both governments believed that in the longer term their policies would benefit disadvantaged groups, and that the pain of restructuring would result not only in greater national wealth overall but in improvements in the well-being of the worst off, and opportunities for the more energetic among them.

How is one to judge the success of this change in policy-setting and organization? It is not easy. From the point of view of ameliorative policies, Maori and Pacific Islanders were in and before the mid-1980s worse off than all other ethnic groups in terms of unemployment, income, education, health, housing, and imprisonment rates. Much evidence attested to this. One test of the ameliorative effect of the new policies would be to compare relative positions before the new policy direction was clearly in motion (that is, around 1986) and up to the present time. The best crude indicator of the changes, because most other social disadvantage flows from it, is the record of employment of ethnic groups. The record of long-term unemployment (March to March figures) does not look good.[48] (See Table 11.2.)

It is clear that the neo-liberal thrust of government policy disadvantaged Maori and Pacific Islanders much more than other groups (the figures for "Other" largely represent new Asian migrants, and will probably reconverge with Pakeha over the next decade).

Other indicators of Maori and Pacific Islander relative deprivation tend to point to the same conclusion. According to the latest figures, the two groups had in 1993, as they had before 1986, lower incomes. In 1986, males of "sole Maori origin" enjoyed 76.9 percent of the New Zealand population's average income; females enjoyed 85.6 percent. Males of Maori origin or descent enjoyed 78 percent, females 86.7 percent. By 1991

45. SNZ, *Maori*, p. 48.

46. For the results, see Cluny Macpherson, "Economic and Political Restructuring and the Sustainability of Migrant Remittances: The Case of Western Samoa," *Contemporary Pacific*, Vol. 4, No. 1 (Spring 1992), pp. 109–135, esp. pp. 113–118; and Macpherson, "Economic and Political Restructuring and the Sustainability of Migrant Remittances: The Case of Western Samoa," *Pacific Studies*, Vol. 17, No. 3 (September 1994), pp. 83–116.

47. Kelsey, *The New Zealand Experiment*, pp. 324–325.

48. The source is SNZ, *Labour Market 1994* (Wellington: Department of Statistics, 1995), p. 92, updated with internet information from the department.

Table 11.2. Unemployment Rate in New Zealand By Ethnic Group, 1986–96.

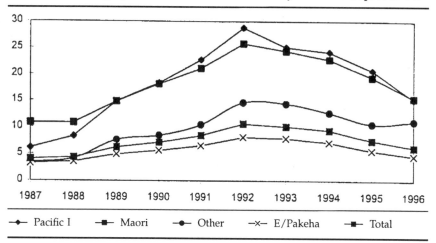

(after cuts in social welfare payments had been instituted), things had got worse. Males of "Maori sole ethnic group" enjoyed 69.1 percent, females 82.6 percent; males of "Maori ethnic group" enjoyed 70.9 percent, females 83.4 percent; males of "Maori ancestry" enjoyed 74.9 percent, females 87.6 percent. Pacific Islander incomes, while better than Maori from 1985 to 1987 (Maori incomes rose in 1988–89), dropped to the same low levels thereafter.[49] Maori continued to have more alcohol problems, higher suicide rates, and shorter lives; together with young Pacific Island males, they continued to be imprisoned more often than members of other ethnic groups. Maori women, too, continue to make up the highest proportion of solo mothers and therefore continue to live in near poverty made worse by the social welfare cuts of 1991.[50]

Nevertheless, although both groups continued to have less education, worse mental and physical health, and worse housing, it must be said that their growing (and perhaps temporary) relative deprivation is not the result of an *ethnic* policy, but rather of general policies that have had deleterious effects on the worst off as a whole.[51] And indeed, improve-

49. Brian Easton, "Distribution," in Alan Bollard, R. Lattimore, and B. Silverstone, eds., *A Study of Economic Reform: A Case Study of New Zealand* (forthcoming).

50. Kelsey, *The New Zealand Experiment*, pp. 283–296, lists and gives sources for many of the indicators of relative deprivation, as does SNZ, *New Zealand Now: Maori* (Wellington: Department of Statistics, 1994).

51. Te Puni Kokiri, *Trends in Maori Mental Health: A Discussion Document* (Wellington: Department of Statistics, 1993); and Public Health Commission, *Our Health Our Future* (Wellington: Department of Statistics, 1993), pp. 60–67.

ments in their life expectancy and educational attainments have continued through the 1980s and 1990s. Maori death rates have continued a long-term improving trend. From 1985–87, Maori males could expect to live 67.4 years compared with non-Maori's 71.4; females, 72.3 compared with 77.4. These figures have been converging since the 1950s and appear to be continuing to do so. Vital statistics for Pacific Islanders follow the same trends.

It must also be said that in the face of public opinion, which tends to oppose positive discrimination,[52] governments did take initiatives designed to benefit Maori and Pacific Islanders and which were against the more general thrust towards decentralization and market-driven distributions. The initiatives are too many to discuss in detail,[53] but they include a Cabinet instruction to government agencies in 1986 to practice positive discrimination in hiring, and a State Sector Act (1988) and an Education Act (1989), which stressed that equity in hiring, promotion, and work conditions was to include attention to questions of equity across ethnic groups. The provisions in these Acts that governed public service—typically including the injunction to be a "good employer" and to respect and attend to the needs of Maori and ethnic minorities—were extended to private enterprise in, for instance, amendments to the State-Owned Enterprises Act, as well as the Employment Contracts Act (1991), the Disability Commissioner Act (1994), and the Radio New Zealand Act (1995). These initiatives seem to have had some effect, though government departments and agencies have varied widely in their attention to the matter and in their reporting standards; the now semi-private state-owned enterprises are not much better.

In education, the qualifications gained by Maori and Pacific Island schoolchildren have shown some improvement. Maori preschool attendance, mostly at *kohanga reo*, has doubled since 1983; Maori (and to a lesser degree Pacific Island) participation in tertiary study certainly has increased.[54] By 1993, 10 percent of tertiary enrollments were Maori.[55] The Maori language is (only just) holding its own in the face of fears that it might die out; Maori-language primary and secondary schools have been instituted; by 1998 there will be two Maori universities. New Zealand–

---

52. Kelsey, *The New Zealand Experiment*, pp. 324–325; and David Novitz and Bill Willmot, eds., *New Zealand in Crisis* (Wellington: GP Publications, 1992), pp. 117–129.

53. See Spoonley, "Mahi Awatea? The Racialisation of Work in Aotearoa/New Zealand," pp. 73–76.

54. SNZ, *Maori*, chap. 4.

55. SNZ, *NZY* (1995), p. 241.

born Pacific Islanders were attaining higher qualifications than their island-born parents and grandparents. A network of local Maori radio stations was developed in the 1990s, and a funding body was established for Maori television programming. There is much more limited coverage in Pacific Island and Asian languages in the media and in the schools, though—with no government aid—recent immigrants from China have set up an array of eight newspapers. Maori and Pacific Island under-employment has also received attention. In 1995, the National government made these employment problems the focus of policy attention:[56] the Community Employment Group of the Department of Labour was instructed to give high priority to Maori and Pacific Islands communities to assist with strategic planning; Job Action Workshops[57] were to be contracted out to Maori and Pacific Island providers; pilot programs designed to improve the employability of the young were to be instituted; various educational initiatives were to be taken;[58] and Job Plus subsidy schemes[59] were to be administered more flexibly to allow temporary work on the development of Maori-owned assets. The Maori initiatives would cost $19 million over three years; the Pacific Island initiatives, $6.5 million.[60] Clearly, these initiatives have not yet borne much fruit, and there are no signs in government strategic thinking that ethnic, as opposed to Maori issues, figure in the long term. They are simply not on the agenda in the strategic plans in various policy areas that were developed from 1993 to 1996. The danger of this, if danger it is, could be that of a growing coincidence between being Maori or being a Pacific Islander, and being a member of an underclass.

Reparations for Past Wrongs and Claims to Autonomy

Complaints about the relative deprivation of the Maori have been made ever since the 1930s. Starting in the mid-1970s, Maori public claims on

---

56. The Prime Minister's Office, *Focus on Employment. The Government's Response to the Employment Task Force and the Multi-Party Group Memorandum of Understanding* (Wellington: The Prime Minister's Office, October 1995).

57. This is a program of individualized assistance in job searching, self-esteem, communication skills, and motivation.

58. This is in addition to a separately conceived draft plan for Pacific Islanders under development by the Ministry of Education.

59. Under this scheme, employers are subsidized to take on job seekers to train them for a potential vacancy.

60. All dollar figures are New Zealand dollars; as of early 1997 the NZ dollar was worth U.S. $0.71.

governments began to take a new turn. They claimed to be a separate and a wronged people; they claimed reparation for past and present wrongs; and when reparations were not forthcoming, they claimed, in varying ways, the right to rule themselves in their own way and not to be subject to a government they found difficulty in recognizing as legitimate. Under the Labour government of 1984–90, a process of institutional, legal, and constitutional change began that neither it nor the National government of 1990–96 succeeded in controlling. The agenda was set by the Maori, and governments have not been successful in wresting the initiative back. Both governments attempted to deal with the issues raised with a mixture of legal and formal devices, on the one hand, and by direct political negotiation, on the other. Both found the law (to which they had turned to keep the issues from being inflamed in parliamentary and public debate) to be a two-edged weapon. In attempting to bring the question of reparation under the aegis of normal legal process, they discovered that profound constitutional issues and costly settlements were entailed. Both found political negotiation more difficult than they had perhaps imagined. It has been this area of policy and activity that has most gripped the public imagination and that lies at the heart of New Zealand's obsession with the Maori.

It was the new (Fourth) Labour government of 1984 that first felt the brunt of a new pan-Maori unity with respect to claims to reparation. By 1984, the *iwi* had joined together under the aegis of the Treaty of Waitangi, claiming that the document asserted their already-existing rights to rule themselves and provided a standard against which past wrongs could be measured. One of the reasons for the growing emphasis on the Treaty— previously, Maori activists had tended to dismiss it simply as "a fraud," and many tribes had not felt themselves attracted to or bound by it in any case—was that there was already in existence an institution whose role in the politics and policy of reparation and *rangatiratanga* was to be crucial at least until 1990. This was the Waitangi Tribunal. It had been set up during the dying gasp of the Third Labour government in 1975, and had scarcely been of much interest to the succeeding National government of Robert Muldoon (1975–84), perhaps because its powers were not very great. It was empowered by the Treaty of Waitangi Act, and its purpose was "to provide for the observance, and confirmation, of the principles of the Treaty of Waitangi by establishing a Tribunal to make recommendations on claims relating to the practical application of the treaty and to determine whether certain matters are inconsistent with the Treaty." The Tribunal's powers were to "hear and enquire into" "claims of prejudice" by any "Maori" or "group of Maori" in regard to "acts or omissions" on the part of the Crown or its agents. It could report and make recommendations to the government. It could indeed suggest ways of ameliorating the prejudice, but it could not legally bind a government to action. It had no power of legal determination whatsoever, except, within the ambit of the statute that erected it, "exclusive authority to determine the meaning and effect of the Treaty" in its two languages. It could not retrospect beyond 1975. One would not have thought the Tribunal an instrument well-designed to address questions of wrongs going back to 1840. Yet it was this institution to which the Maori turned and whose work was soon to publicize among Pakeha the huge extent of Maori dispossession of all their treasured things over the 150 or so years of white settler rule; and it was this institution that, together with the dexterity of Maori politicians, drove government policy and began a legal (and perhaps constitutional) revolution in New Zealand.[61]

The Maori had reason to take their grievances to the Tribunal, and they did. Counting claims is not a greatly useful exercise. They are too diverse and have been too badly reported. It is enough to say that governments acted slowly and not as generously as the claimants would have wished, thus causing them to see the Tribunal as a broken reed.[62] Maori claims nevertheless mounted. There was a modest backlog of fourteen claims at the end of 1984. By October 1996, there was a backlog of 618 claims, 70 of which had been made over the previous year.[63] One thing is clear: whatever their dissatisfaction with the Tribunal's speed of action and its effect in persuading governments, the Maori had turned to and would continue to use the Tribunal.

Whatever its shortcomings as a deliverer of reparations, the Tribunal has had a powerful educative function for the Maori (who have taken their research to it and who have had research done by it) and to the Pakeha (who have heard the results). It was not until 1985 that the Fourth Labour government enlarged the Tribunal from three to seven members

---

61. For the story until 1992, see Andrew Sharp, "The Treaty, the Tribunal and the Law: Recognising Rights in New Zealand," in Gold, *New Zealand Politics in Perspective*, pp. 123–141. For a rather less government-friendly account, which takes the story to 1995, see Jane Kelsey, "From Flagpoles to Pinetrees," in Spoonley, *Nga Takai*, pp. 175–201.

62. Te Puni Kokiri, *Report on the Implementation of Waitangi Tribunal Recommendations and Agreements Negotiated by the Crown* (Wellington: Ministry of Maori Development, n.d. [about November 1992]); Minister of Maori Affairs, *Implementation of Waitangi Tribunal Recommendations and Agreements Negotiated between Maori Claimants and the Crown: 1994* (Wellington: Ministry of Maori Development, 1995); and D.J.D. MacDonald, *The Settlement of Claims Under the Treaty of Waitangi: Report of the Controller and Auditor-General* (Second Report for 1995, September 12, 1995).

63. *Sunday Star-Times*, October 6, 1996, p. A3.

and empowered it to retrospect back to 1840. Even so, especially in the *Manukau* and *Orakei* reports, it succeeded: in the *Manukau* case in exposing an unjust war and confiscations against the country people of the Waikato (1863–66); and in the *Orakei* case, exposing the workings of the legal system over an extended period up to the present, as it individuated the communal title of *Ngati Whatua* in Auckland to enable land sales of doubtful validity, and as it empowered governments to take land for public purposes in a way it did not from Pakeha. In the *Te Reo Report*, the history of the Maori loss of language was related in such a way as to cast blame for it on the education policies of governments dating back to the 1880s. Naturally, after retrospection was introduced such reporting continued. There was a report with major legal implications as to the ownership of fisheries (*The Muriwhenua Fisheries Report* of 1987). In 1988, the Tribunal membership was increased from seven to seventeen, and reports continued to flow. There were reports concerning huge tracts of land (most of the South Island) illegally taken (the *Ngai Tahu* reports of 1991–93). There was a report—more are in process—on land wrongly confiscated after an unjust war (*The Taranaki Report* of 1996). There were also reports that were less far-reaching in implication or that concerned much smaller tracts of land and water, but that nevertheless stirred the localities, were widely publicized, and often resulted in corrective legislation.

One effect of all this reporting was the polarization of public opinion. Another was lowering Pakeha resistance to Maori claims. Maori and Pakeha opinions on most matters of general interest are strikingly similar, but as to whether the Treaty should be respected (or put into law) and as to whether the Tribunal has been a useful institution, opinion is split along a Maori-Pakeha axis.[64] This has meant that whatever reparative measures governments were to take had to take into account the dangers of losing votes and worsening race relations. Nevertheless, so far did the Tribunal's success in public education extend that there was no effective opposition to the remarkable preamble to the National government's statutory settlement with Waikato-Tainui in 1996. In the preamble, in both English and Maori, the Crown acknowledged that:

its representatives and advisers acted unjustly and in breach of the Treaty of Waitangi . . . in sending its forces across the Mangataawhiri in July 1893 and in unfairly labelling Waikato as rebels. . . . The Crown acknowledges that subsequent confiscations of land and resources under the New Zealand Settlements Act . . . were wrongful, have caused Waikato to the present time

---

64. See the opinion polls in "Attitudes and Values," Royal Commission on Social Policy, *The April Report*, Vol. 1, Appendix.

to suffer feelings in relation to their lost lands akin to those of orphans, and have had a crippling impact on the welfare, economy and development of Waikato.

The Crown therefore expressed its "profound regret and apologies unreservedly for the loss of lives . . . arising from its invasion, and at the devastation of property and social life which resulted." It would now seek "on behalf of all New Zealanders to atone for these acknowledged injustices," by making reparation for past wrongs. When the Tribunal's *Manukau Report* had first brought these wrongs to public attention in 1984, there had been a public outcry of denial. It is evidence of the impact of a new historical consciousness, largely brought about as a result of the Tribunal's educative activity, that in 1996 these wrongs were scarcely denied.

More important even than its educative function perhaps, the Tribunal's intimate legal relationship with the Treaty made it a central policy player in what was until 1989 almost exclusively a game for lawyers. The Tribunal's empowering statute was the first to approach the incorporation of the Treaty into municipal law: until then, the Treaty had simply not been part of the municipal law. After that, while still not law, it was at least being considered by a statutory tribunal.[65] As it turned out, because the Tribunal succeeded in educating the politicians as to transgressions of the principles of the Treaty, it appeared that the implications of the precedent might be followed as a means of writing Maori rights into law and the constitution. It appeared so especially to Geoffrey Palmer, the architect of the Labour government's treaty policy. From 1985 to 1990, he unsuccessfully tried to have the Treaty incorporated in an entrenched Bill of Rights. Although he failed in that particular attempt, from 1986 to 1991, several statutes were passed embodying requirements that Treaty rights be respected or that "regard" be had to the Treaty and its principles, thus definitely incorporating it into law.[66] In two of the statutes, the State Owned Enterprises Act (1986) and the Conservation Act (1987), *priority* was given to Treaty principles. It was this priority, crucially in the State Owned Enterprises (SOE) Act, which set off a train of events that

---

65. The Treaty in both language versions was attached as a schedule to the Treaty of Waitangi Act (1975), and schedules, unless otherwise specially provided, "are not part of the municipal law." See Philip A. Joseph, *Constitutional and Administrative Law in New Zealand* (Sydney: Law Book Company, 1993), p. 59. See also Kenneth Keith, "The Roles of the Treaty, the Tribunal, the Courts and the Legislature," *Victoria University Law Review*, Vol. 25, No. 2 (July 1995), pp. 39–53.

66. Joseph, *Constitutional and Administrative Law in New Zealand*, pp. 59–62; and Margaret Wilson, "Constitutional Recognition of the Treaty of Waitangi: Myth or Reality," in Wilson and Yeatman, *Justice and Identity*, pp. 1–17.

complicated the legal situation immensely, made the Tribunal a central player in a largely unforeseen unfolding of law and policy, and opened up an as yet largely unexplored vista of constitutional change. None of this was much to the taste of government policymakers who, in empowering the Tribunal, had merely wished to remove Maori issues from the heat of partisan debate in parliament and public.

The SOE Act, in the course of providing for the divestment of Crown property to private companies—which, it was envisaged, would act for profit but with due regard to social imperatives—laid down in Section 9 that "nothing in this Act shall permit the Crown to act in a manner that is inconsistent with the principles of the Treaty of Waitangi." The New Zealand Maori Council, a pan-tribal organization, took a case to the Court of Appeal, claiming that divestment to private owners would render reparation for past wrongs far more difficult, and would therefore contravene Section 9. In the epoch-making case, *The New Zealand Maori Council v. the Solicitor General* (1987), the judges agreed. They thus set the precedent for a long series of still-continuing cases concerning the ownership and control of land, forests, and broadcast frequencies, together with natural resources such as electricity, coal, and geothermal power. The government could not divest itself of these without going through the courts.

The issues that absorbed the judges in the cases were to provide, where necessary, a legal elaboration of the "principles" of the Treaty, and to require the contending parties to negotiate a court-approved settlement of their differences according to those principles. They generally tried to avoid directly imposing their own views as to what the details of a reasonable settlement would be, but they decided that the principles expressed in the Treaty must govern any settlement. These were fundamentally the principles of "partnership" and "trust" between the two peoples and between the Crown and the Maori. The partners had "responsibilities analogous to fiduciary duties" to each other, and the Crown in particular had a duty of "active protection" of Maori interests. The principle that Maori were understood to have ceded sovereignty was upheld; nevertheless, full consultation on all matters of Maori interest was required of the Crown. Moreover, it was suggested by the president of the Court of Appeal that the principles of the Treaty might be part of the country's "supreme law" (New Zealand has no written constitution)—and as such cannot be abrogated by statute. Governments were losing control of policy formulation and execution in an unprecedented way.

As important as its role in elaborating and publicly arguing the principles of the Treaty was the Tribunal's role as a collector of evidence. For here the spheres of the quasi legality of Treaty jurisprudence and strict legality of common law came nearly to coincide. The Tribunal's collecting and recording, while primarily designed to assist it in its own deliberations, nevertheless had great bearing on the settlements that governments might make. This first became starkly evident in regard to the right to commercial fishing, as the issue was contested from 1987 onwards. In the course of preparing its findings and recommendations for the *Muriwhenua Fishing Report*, the Tribunal collected massive evidence of Maori pre-Treaty participation in the "business and enterprise" of fishing. The evidence clearly showed that against their will, Maori had been reduced to minor players in the industry. Little need have followed from that conclusion: while the Maori claimed they still owned all the fisheries, since they had never agreed to their alienation, the Treaty under which such a claim was made did not legally bind the government. In the normal run of things, the Crown would have had wide discretion in interpreting Treaty "principles" for itself and in deciding how to act on them.

However, two sets of legal developments made the Tribunal's findings on lost fisheries highly preemptive of government discretion. First, new fisheries legislation contemplated what was in effect privatized ownership of the rights to commercially fish certain species. This would make restitution of fisheries to the Maori much more difficult for the Crown; the same issues were raised as had been under the SOE legislation, and the government could expect to undergo a similar court-superintended negotiation to settlement. This in itself would be limiting enough on governments. But second, the courts had begun to recognize the doctrine of "aboriginal title," and had suggested that it was still a live title with respect to fisheries. That doctrine, to the effect that the aboriginal inhabitants of a colonized land retain a right to their possessions unless some explicit act of the Crown extinguishes them, was inapplicable to Maori land. Separate Maori title to land had been extinguished; all the Maori held their land in fee from the Crown. But no such extinguishment had occurred with respect to fisheries. Indeed, Section 2 of the Fisheries Act (1982) held that "nothing in this Act shall affect any Maori fishing rights." It was clearly arguable from the evidence that the Tribunal had collected for other purposes that Maori owned *all* the fisheries on grounds of aboriginal title. Thus, whatever (lesser) settlements might be suggested by Treaty principles along SOE settlement lines, here the legal case seemed to be that the government, without extinguishing aboriginal title, which would be politically very difficult, could neither resist the Maori claim nor reorganize fisheries management along privatized lines. The government would have to negotiate from a position of weakness.

Therefore, from 1988 on, it became increasingly evident that governments could find themselves hamstrung—hostages to Maori demands as interpreted by the Tribunal and the courts. Since no government could contemplate this, settlements would have to be "political" rather than "legal." The attempts to routinize the problem of Maori affairs and take it out of politics had failed. As a consequence, Labour employed an old National Party policy, one that had preceded the setting up of the Tribunal in 1975: direct negotiation with claimant tribes. It also encouraged the Tribunal to make findings and not recommendations. It set up its own official office for researching and negotiating Treaty claims, and by mid-1989, it stated its own version of the principles on which it would negotiate: the government would have the right to make laws; all New Zealanders were equal under the law; the *iwi* would have the right "to organize as iwi, and, under law, to control their resources as their own"; "both the Government and the iwi are obliged to accord each other reasonable cooperation on major issues of common concern"; and the government was "responsible for providing effective processes for the resolution of grievances in the expectation that reconciliation can occur."[67]

The National government, which came to power in November 1990, continued and extended the policy of direct negotiation and assertion of Crown sovereignty. It would turn to direct negotiation rather more than the reactive policy of waiting for Waitangi Tribunal advice. The government further strengthened official research and negotiating capacities at the expense of the Tribunal's. It finished the fisheries negotiations, which Labour had begun in 1988. In so doing, it succeeded in expunging Maori legal rights to commercial fisheries, though not in helping the Maori commissioners it appointed to work out how to divide the proceeds of a complex deal involving about $170 million worth of fishing quotas and a fishing company. Labour had begun direct negotiations with the Waikato-Tainui over their war confiscation claims. In 1995 National brought them to a successful conclusion;[68] this settlement was also worth about $170 million. This settlement came to be seen as part of what was by then an overall settlement plan. For, advised by the Treasury, the government had developed from 1991 to 1994 a proposed "settlement envelope" of $1 billion to reach "full and final" settlements of all "historical" claims over "about" the following decade. A land bank of surplus Crown land, which had been set up to meet Treaty claims, would be replenished, but conservation estate lands would be used only sparingly in settlements.

---

67. *Principles for Crown Action on the Treaty of Waitangi* (Wellington: Government Printer, July 1989).

68. *Heads of Agreement between HM the Queen and RTK Mahuta and the Tainui Maori Trust Board* (Wellington: Office of Treaty Settlements, Department of Justice, December 21, 1994).

Claims to natural resources not exploited by the Maori in 1840 would not be met; when claims to natural resources *were* met, only use and not ownership rights would be granted. A procedure for negotiation would be introduced: to get onto a "work programme," claims would have to be fully researched and proved; claimants would have to produce a "deed of mandate" from those whom they represented so that settlements could not be disputed by rival claimants. Procedures were put in place for ensuring that beneficiaries were defined, and that benefits would be passed in trust to appropriately constituted legal bodies. As settlements progressed, the jurisdiction of the Waitangi Tribunal and the courts would be wound down. In December 1994, the government published these *Crown Proposals for the Settlement of Treaty of Waitangi Claims*[69]—and in so doing, demonstrated that the problem of Maori affairs had not been solved.

There was an immediate Maori outburst over these proposals. Land occupations immediately followed, in which claims to *tino rangatiratanga* were aired.[70] A series of consultative *hui* (meetings) roundly rejected the proposals in early 1995, concentrating on their not having been previously negotiated with the Maori "partner," and on government efforts to set a "fiscal cap" and a time limit on what must be an open-ended process, continuing into the indefinite future. While the controversy raged, the government, like its predecessor, continued to proclaim Crown sovereignty over and against the *tino rangatiratanga* or any kind of Maori independence,[71] and in its last days it persisted with its policies. In October 1996, it reached agreement with a small North Island east coast tribe for a settlement of $40 million, and it approached a settlement with the South Island Ngai Tahu for $170 million in lands, forests, and cash. At the end of its term, it was enmeshed in negotiations with other east coast tribes and with the large North Island war confiscation claims of the Taranaki tribes. Meanwhile, the courts and the Waitangi Tribunal were dealing with a number of cases in which various *iwi* and *hapu* struggled among and within themselves as to who would be the beneficiaries of settlements and who would represent the beneficiaries; the pan-Maori

---

69. *Crown Proposals for the Settlement of Treaty of Waitangi Claims* (Wellington: Office of Treaty Settlements, Department of Justice, December 8, 1994).

70. The most convenient place to find a range of views as to what Maori sovereignty and *tino rangatiratanga* might mean are in twin publications: Hineani Melbourne, *Maori Sovereignty: The Maori Perspective* (Auckland: Hodder Moa Beckett, 1995); and Carol Archie, *Maori Sovereignty: The Pakeha Perspective* (Auckland: Hodder Moa Beckett, 1995).

71. See *Maori Law Review* (May 1995), p. 10.

beneficiaries of the fishing settlement were in their fourth year of litigation and inter-*iwi* politics with respect to the division of spoils.[72]

As could be said of Labour's position at the end of its term, so it could be said of National's as it approached the election of 1996: the central problem of Maori affairs had not been solved. Nor have the Treaty settlements been (as they were always thought to have been) well targeted as ameliorative acts. There is the problem of deciding just who the beneficiaries of settlements will be. And even when that problem is settled, distribution might not relate to need. Waikato-Tainui, the second poorest of the largest eighteen *iwi* and the worst-hit by Pakeha injustice, are certainly benefiting and need to benefit from their $170 million settlement. But Ngai Tahu, the beneficiaries of a similar-sized settlement, are the best-off Maori in the country.[73] Nevertheless, it must be said that although governments have not succeeded in controlling the process of reparation as much as they would have liked to, Maori-Crown relations have improved rather than deteriorated since 1975, and that both the Maori and the Pakeha have been educated to withstand the frustrations, delays, and apparent injustices that the process of reparation inevitably produced. The Pakeha, at the beginning of the process, greatly fearful of the consequences to the state purse and obsessed with the injustice of the Maori being treated "differently" and not under "one law," have become resigned to the fact that the Maori were owed reparation, if not autonomy. Only a tiny vote supported Mana Maori, a Maori independence party standing in the October 1996 elections.

Conclusions

New Zealand governments' management of ethnic relations has been carried out by way of legal protections for all groups, by way of ameliorative policies designed for the less well-off, and by way of a legal and political process of negotiation with the Maori. However much the ameliorative policies have been weakened by neo-liberal purposes since the late 1980s, they have continued to bear fruit. However much the processes of negotiation and settlement with the Maori have tended to slip from government control, they have been carried out in reasonable peace and with some effect. It may be thought that the reasons for these successes lie in political and legal arrangements that guarantee civil and political rights to all people, and in a culture that respects those arrangements.

---

72. *Maori Law Review*, October and November 1994, December–January 1995–96, and May 1996.

73. Gould, "Socio-Economic Differences between Maori Iwi."

Chapter 12

Culture and Conflict in Fiji, Papua New Guinea, Vanuatu, and the Federated States of Micronesia

Stephen Levine

Much of the scholarly literature on ethnic issues focuses on political relationships in Europe. By contrast, ethnic complexities in the Asia-Pacific region have been overlooked. Within the Asia-Pacific region, moreover, perhaps no group of states has been more neglected by Western scholars than the island states of the central and southern Pacific. Although many of these countries are small in land area, population, and resources, their absence from scholarly work which is intended to be conceptually comprehensive deprives political studies of unique insights drawn from their experiences.

This chapter analyzes developments in several Pacific Island states, some of them quite diminutive, far from major population centers, and generally remote from the concerns of strategic analysts and scholars alike. Each of the countries on which this chapter will focus has had the task of developing government institutions and making policy against often formidable obstacles. These include a lack of infrastructure, a very small governing elite, and in some cases a weak and fragile commitment among the population to national unity and the concept of a nation-state.

From the perspective of ethnicity and politics, the principal difficulties faced by nation-builders in the four countries considered here—Fiji, Papua New Guinea (PNG), Vanuatu, and the Federated States of Micronesia (the FSM)[1]—are the centripetal tendencies found in each one of them. Two of the countries examined in this study, Vanuatu and the FSM, are typical of other Pacific Island entities: they are multi-island polities, their peoples scattered across distant atoll groups, politically and culturally separate from one another notwithstanding the acquisition of a common citizenship amid a variety of shared political symbols. The other two,

---

1. These are the four main states in the Pacific that are both politically independent and ethnically heterogenous.

Fiji and PNG, are perhaps the major Pacific Island states, important players on a distant stage. Each faces serious challenges to national unity, attributable in large part to ethnic differences. Military coups in Fiji and a secessionist rebellion on the PNG island of Bougainville are reminders of the difficulties faced by island states seeking to maintain territorial stability and institutional legitimacy in the face of severe and in some cases tragic divisions of interest and outlook.

This chapter reviews the goals and policies of the aforementioned four island states against the wider background of political and cultural change in the contemporary Pacific. Across the Pacific, from one island group to the next, indigenous peoples have been reemphasizing the relevance and value of their history, culture, and traditions, in the process influencing domestic law, inter-state relations, and government priorities. These increasingly conspicuous developments reflect a continuing (if in some respects delayed) reaction against Western colonial rule, only recently brought to an end in most (though not yet all) island entities. The ethnic tensions arising out of what might be called indigenous empowerment have their beginnings in what proved to be a Pacific-wide colonial experience, and it is from that background that this analysis will begin. Subsequently, the chapter will examine political and constitutional developments within Fiji, PNG, Vanuatu, and the FSM. Following this country-by-country discussion, the chapter identifies several common themes with respect to ethnicity and politics in the four island states and the wider Pacific. Contrasts in experiences among the four countries will also be examined in order to suggest policy options available to promote harmonious relationships among their diverse peoples.

The Colonial Legacy and the Political Setting

Although the Pacific Island states may play only a small role in Western scholarship, they have at times loomed large in Asia-Pacific affairs. As a region, the islands have more often been objects than subjects of history, acted upon by outside powers during the past two centuries rather than acting forcefully and autonomously either individually or collectively.[2] In a sense they may be categorized as "victim states"—that is, as entities

---

2. There are several very thorough histories of the Pacific Islands. See, for example, Glen Barclay, *A History of the Pacific from the Stone Age to the Present Day* (London: Sidgwick and Jackson, 1978); I.C. Campbell, *A History of the Pacific Islands* (Christchurch: University of Canterbury Press, 1989); C. Hartley Grattan, *The Southwest Pacific to 1900* (Ann Arbor: University of Michigan Press, 1963); and C. Hartley Grattan, *The Southwest Pacific Since 1900* (Ann Arbor: University of Michigan Press, 1963).

defined and shaped to some degree by suffering and exploitation. The nineteenth century, for instance, brought European "discoverers" and "explorers" to the islands, generally bringing in their wake disease, enslavement, and cultural dislocation. Ultimately, few islands were able to preserve a genuine sense of self-reliance or self-government; from one end of the Pacific to the other, indigenous ethnic groups long accustomed to managing their own affairs found their capacities to maintain political and economic order eroded as a consequence of European imperialism.

The twentieth century brought new forms of political, social, cultural, and economic upheaval to the Pacific. For some islands, World War I—so decisive for the European powers—simply exchanged one group of non-indigenous rulers for another. The first unconditional surrender of the war took place in the Pacific when a New Zealand expeditionary force (on behalf of the British Empire) defeated the German forces in Western Samoa. For the Samoan population, this event did not "liberate" them from German rule; rather, it prolonged their experience as an ethnic group defined by Europeans as incapable or undeserving of self-government. For Pacific Islanders, Western colonialism—an example of the governance of one ethnic group by another—was as damaging as it proved to be for many other peoples. The ultimately futile international instrument fashioned out of the postwar Versailles peace settlement, the League of Nations, excluded Pacific Island peoples from the otherwise universal reach of the ideology of national self-determination. New Zealand's occupation and governance of Western Samoa, which in pre–League of Nations terms might have been presumed to have rested on superior military power, was legitimated in the prevailing ethics of the international community when the League granted New Zealand a "mandate" over Western Samoa.

Further north, through the islands of Micronesia, the League of Nations came to a comparable decision of more wide-ranging significance. Notwithstanding the rhetoric of ethnic rights to self-government, the peoples of a vast array of islands went unconsulted when the League awarded a mandate over Micronesia to the Imperial Japanese Empire. This fateful decision led in due course to Japanese fortification of the islands and enslavement, deportation, torture, and death for many islanders. The sacrifices made by the U.S. armed forces in capturing Japanese-held islands during World War II may also be attributed to the League's decision not to apply the principle of national self-determination to Pacific Islanders. Among the often overlooked casualties of the Pacific war were many islanders themselves: when Japanese and U.S. forces collided, islanders inevitably perished in the ensuing struggle.

At the end of the war, none of the islands captured from the Japanese was granted independence. For the Micronesian peoples, governance by one non-indigenous ethnic group (the Japanese) was brought to an end with the arrival of yet another non-indigenous ethnic group, the Americans. Similarly, the "four freedoms" and other principles of the Atlantic Charter brought to fruition in the Charter of the United Nations were given a circumscribed application. The peoples of the islands of Micronesia were not consulted about their political destiny, as the United Nations awarded "trusteeship" over the islands to the United States—a unique "security" trusteeship, moreover, which gave the U.S. government greater powers over its vast multi-island trust territory than were held by any other trusteeship power in the history of the UN organization.[3]

External rule by non-indigenous powers lasted later into the twentieth century in the Pacific than in any other region. The persistence of formal colonial arrangements no doubt reflects the relative invisibility of the Pacific Islands in international terms. Generally neglected by the international news media, Pacific Islanders themselves have often had few resources with which to demand changes to their political status. At a time when the "winds of change" brought colonial rule virtually to an end in Asia, the Middle East, and Africa, the peoples of the Pacific remained almost entirely without any contemporary experience of independence. In the eventual move to a new political status, Western Samoa again led the way. New Zealand had its dominion over the islands of Upolu and Savai'i (Western Samoa) relegitimated by the United Nations, which brought the territory under the International Trusteeship System provided for in the UN Charter. Sensitive to criticism at the United Nations of its stewardship over the territory, New Zealand moved to grant Western Samoa independence, an option approved in a referendum held in Western Samoa in 1961. Samoan independence on New Year's Day 1962 was followed by similar moves in other Pacific Island entities. Fiji gained independence in 1970; Tonga regained its full independence that same year, and Papua New Guinea achieved independence in 1975. Many islands have found, to their disappointment, however, that the achievement of political independence does not inevitably lead to either economic advancement or the restoration of cultural integrity.

Although decolonization came late to the Pacific region, the region is now constituted almost entirely of island entities that are either fully

---

3. Studies of Pacific trusteeship and the U.S. stewardship over Micronesia include A.H. McDonald, ed., *Trusteeship in the Pacific* (Sydney: Angus and Robertson, 1949); David Nevin, *The American Touch in Micronesia* (New York: W.W. Norton, 1979); Donald F. McHenry, *Micronesia: Trust Betrayed—Altruism vs. Self-Interest in American Foreign Policy* (New York: Carnegie Endowment, 1975); and Harold F. Nufer, *Micronesia Under American Rule: An Evaluation of the Strategic Trusteeship (1947–77)* (Hicksville, N.Y.: Exposition Press, 1978).

Fiji, Papua New Guinea, Vanuatu, and the Federated States of Micronesia.

independent (in a formal political sense), or are self-governing "in association" with a metropolitan power whose people are ethnically distinct from the islanders themselves. In only a few islands do political arrangements fall short of either independence or full self-government. There is a continuing French presence in New Caledonia, Wallis and Futuna, and French Polynesia. The United States maintains sovereignty over American Samoa, Guam, and the Commonwealth of the Northern Mariana Islands. New Zealand governs the three atolls of Tokelau as a dependent territory, while Niue and the Cook Islands, though internally self-governing and with a recognized right to declare full independence, remain linked to New Zealand through "free association" arrangements. Much more elaborate "free association" documents link the United States to Palau, the Marshall Islands, and the Federated States of Micronesia.[4]

This diversity in political status is matched by a diversity in forms of governance. Here too the legacy of colonialism is evident: those entities that experienced U.S. rule generally employ a presidential model of government, while islands exposed to British, Australian, or New Zealand tutelage tend to utilize Westminster, or cabinet, forms of government.

The region is also diverse in ethnic terms (see Table 12.1.), and this complex ethnic picture has political ramifications. Even within island states—and particularly in multi-island entities—shared ethnic characteristics compete with loyalties to particular islands within the larger polity. Thus, for example, in the Cook Islands or in French Polynesia, it is sensible to speak of a hierarchy of overlapping and generally compatible identities; islanders identify themselves in terms of their island of birth, upbringing, or ancestry—as Aitutakians as well as Cook Islanders, as Marquesans as well as French Polynesians—while broader cultural affinities, enabling Cook Islanders and French Polynesians to regard one another as "Polynesians," are also apparent. Such multiple identities are found throughout the Pacific. Tokelauans, for instance, are discovering the political meaning in identifying themselves as "one people" as they move towards self-government and a more clearly defined political status. But this evolving political identity complements more fundamental self-definitions as peoples of one or other of Tokelau's atolls: Atafu, Faka'ofo, and Nukunonu. There are only a few single-island entities in the Pacific—Guam, Niue, and Nauru—and even these are not entirely homogeneous when ethnicity is viewed in cultural terms and from the perspective of islanders' self-perceptions.

---

4. The United Nations, whose membership is limited to countries that are fully independent, admitted the Marshalls and the FSM in 1991 and Palau in 1994. Neither Niue nor the Cook Islands has applied for UN membership.

Table 12.1. Ethnic Compositions of Fiji, Papua New Guinea, Vanuatu, and the Federated States of Micronesia.

Fiji's Composition (by ethnic group)		
Group	Number	Percentage
Fijians	382,690	49.7
Indians	348,810	45.3
Others (Chinese, Europeans, other Pacific Islanders)	38,500	5.0
Total	**784,000**	**100.0**

Papua New Guinea's Composition (by province)		
Province	Number	Percentage
Morobe	381,000	10.1
Western Highlands	337,000	8.9
Southern Highlands	318,000	8.4
Eastern Highlands	301,000	8.0
East Sepik	255,000	6.8
Madang	254,000	6.7
Enga	236,000	6.2
National Capital District	196,000	5.2
East New Britain	186,000	5.0
Chimbu	184,000	4.9
Milne Bay	159,000	4.2
Bougainville (North Solomons)	156,000	4.1
West Sepik	143,000	3.8
Central	141,000	3.7
West New Britain	131,000	3.5
Western	112,000	3.1
Northern (Oro)	97,000	2.6
New Ireland	88,000	2.3
Gulf	69,000	1.8
Manus	33,000	.8
Total	**3,777,000**	**100.0**

Vanuatu's Composition (by ethnic group)		
Group	Number	Percentage
Ni-Vanuatu	139,475	97.9
European	1,474	1.0
Asian	597	.4
Other Pacific Islanders	521	.4
Other/Unknown	352	.3
Total	**142,419**	**100.0**

(continued)

Table 12.1. *continued*

State	Number	Percentage
Chuuk	49,150	49.0
Pohnpei	33,550	33.0
Yap	11,050	11.0
Kosrae	7,450	7.0
Total	**101,200**	**100.0**

Composition of the Federated States of Micronesia (by state)

NOTES: Up-to-date census data for each of the four countries discussed in this chapter are not available. Population totals are based on the most recent census information or informed estimates (see sources below). Census data are seldom broken down by ethnicity (apart from Fiji). State populations in the FSM broadly correspond to the most significant ethnic divisions. Figures for Vanuatu on religious affiliation and language would further complicate the ethnic portrait given above: 'Ni-Vanuatu' is a term encompassing indigenous Melanesians (citizens of Vanuatu) found across 66 islands (on which over 130 different languages are spoken). Similarly, census data from Papua New Guinea only summarize provincial divisions (some of them, such as Chimbu, Enga, Sepik, and Madang correspond to meaningful ethno-regional boundaries). A genuine ethnic census of Papua New Guinea would provide figures for well over perhaps one thousand distinct groups.

SOURCES: Population totals: UN Department for Economic and Social Information and Policy Analysis, *World Population Prospects: The 1994 Revision*, Annex tables; Vanuatu: 1989 census data provided by South Pacific Commission, November 1996; Fiji: 1992 estimates, *The Far East and Australasia, 1995*, 26th ed. (London: Europa Publications Ltd., 1994); Papua New Guinea: 1990 census data and estimates, South Pacific Commission, November 1996; Federated States of Micronesia, *The Far East and Australasia*.

While questions of identity and culture are commonplace in Pacific Islands discourse, both among non-indigenous academic observers and among islanders themselves, this chapter examines these topics by looking at the policies instituted to cope with ethnic diversity by the elites of four very different countries.

Fiji

Fiji is an important regional actor in Pacific affairs. In its capital, Suva, are the headquarters of the South Pacific Forum and the main campus of the Pacific's principal multiethnic tertiary institution, the University of the South Pacific. Fiji has also experienced the region's most turbulent ethnic conflict, leading in 1987 to the overthrow of its elected government—the Pacific's sole experience to date of a military coup,[5] and the first and only

---

5. In 1996, the Vanuatu military briefly abducted the president and the acting prime minister in a (successful) attempt to resolve a pay dispute.

time that a Pacific Island state's independence constitution has been replaced through extra-legal means. When complex electoral system arrangements failed to maintain a Fijian-dominated polity, the military—with the support of at least one segment of the indigenous Fijian elite—took matters into its own hands.

COLONIAL LEGACIES

All protagonists agree that the seeds of contemporary ethnic conflict in Fiji were planted during colonial times. The first European contact with Fijians was made by Great Britain in 1791. Although there were subsequent conflicts between Europeans and Fijians, trade developed during the early nineteenth century. In 1858, fearing invasion from Tonga or annexation by the United States, the Fijian chief, Cakobau, offered to cede the islands to Great Britain.[6] In this instance Britain proved to be a reluctant colonialist, and cession was not achieved until 1874, the Foreign Office having initially taken the view that the expenses associated with administering the islands would outweigh the gains.[7] Financial considerations (the attempt to make possession of the islands economically worthwhile) led within a few years to a decision to introduce indentured plantation labor from India. Fiji's first Governor, Sir Arthur Gordon, was apparently determined that the indigenous Fijian people would not be "exploited" (as had happened to other peoples in the British Empire), and he sought to preserve the lands, traditions, and customs of Fijians. Although Gordon's policies protected Fijians from exploitation as plantation workers, a determination to develop the colonial economy led to the introduction of Indian labor and the creation—almost unwittingly—of an ethnically variegated Fiji. What the British apparently failed to consider were the consequences of the decision subsequently taken by most indentured Indians to remain in Fiji, to settle there permanently, and to raise families whose birthplace, and home, was Fiji—not India.

Indian immigration to Fiji began in 1879, and tensions between the two communities hampered the development of self-government through-

6. Stephanie Lawson points out that at the time "there was no sense in which a 'national' polity existed in Fiji," so that Cakobau's move concentrated power among a group of chiefs (who remain pre-eminent to this day). The absence of unity among indigenous Fijians (and, for that matter, among the Indo-Fijian population) further complicates the country's ethnic politics. See Stephanie Lawson, *Tradition Versus Democracy in the South Pacific: Fiji, Tonga, and Western Samoa* (Cambridge: Cambridge University Press, 1996), p. 45.

7. See Ronald A. Derrick, *A History of Fiji* (Suva: Government Printer, 1946).

out the twentieth century.[8] In 1945, the colonial government issued the Fijian Affairs Ordinance, which reaffirmed the special status of indigenous Fijians in regard to land ownership and matters of custom. Thus the original objectives of Fiji's first British governor remained intact. Indeed, the entire "problem" around which Fiji's ethnic politics continue to revolve has to do with the tension between the lines of policy originally laid down by the colonial government—providing for a constitutionally preeminent position for indigenous Fijians—and the more egalitarian imperatives associated with contemporary democratic norms and practices.

CONSTITUTIONAL FRAMEWORKS AND POLITICAL DEVELOPMENTS

Fiji's independence was achieved peacefully, but not without conflict. There were protracted and difficult negotiations in London involving the British and representatives of Fijian and Indo-Fijian political parties. Only when agreement was reached on the terms of a new constitution was Fiji allowed to achieve independence.[9] The basic problem was clear enough: how to build a system in which two peoples, more or less comparable in numbers, could live together in harmony. The solution drew on both traditional and democratic perspectives.

THE 1970 CONSTITUTION. Fiji's independence constitution of 1970 emphasized the special place of the indigenous population. It is clear from the document's first lines that sovereignty was originally in the hands of Fijians and no one else: "Whereas on 10th October 1874 Cakobau, styled Tui Viti [High Chief of Fiji] and Vunivalu, and other High Chiefs signified their loyalty to Her Most Gracious Queen Victoria" and, as a result, entered into a "Deed of Cession" with "the representative of Her Majesty."[10] A similar "Deed of Rotuma Cession" was also entered into by "the Chiefs" of a distinct but comparable indigenous ethnic group on the island of Rotuma (which lies within sovereign Fiji territory). The constitution goes on to make a broad commitment to democracy, equality, and unity:

---

8. See Brij Lal, *Girmityas: The Origins of the Fiji Indians* (Canberra: Journal of Pacific History, 1983); and K.L. Gillion, *The Fiji Indians: Challenge to European Domination 1920–1946* (Melbourne: Oxford University Press, 1977).

9. An account of the 1970 London conference (and the submissions made to it by the different communities in Fiji) is provided in *Report of the Fiji Constitutional Conference* (Suva: Legislative Council of Fiji, 1970).

10. All quotations from Fiji's independence constitution are from "The Constitution of Fiji," in *Pacific Constitutions: Independent States of Melanesia and Micronesia* (Suva: Institute of Pacific Studies and Port Vila: Pacific Law Unit, 1983), pp. 1–83.

Whereas many persons of all races and creeds have come from [diverse] countries and have desired peace and prosperity under the precepts and principles of such Cessions; And Whereas all the peoples of Fiji have ever since acknowledged their allegiance to the Crown . . . and Whereas those peoples have become united under a common bond . . . Now, therefore, the people of Fiji do affirm their allegiance to Her Most Excellent Majesty Queen Elizabeth II, Her heir and successors, their reverence for God and their unshakeable belief that all are entitled to fundamental human rights and freedoms based upon and secured by the rule of law.

The extent to which Fiji's peoples were "united under a common bond" was tested prior to and at the constitutional conference, however, and has remained the most persistent and troublesome issue in Fijian politics.[11] Not surprisingly, Fiji's constitution was unable to resolve the tensions between universalistic norms (based on the equality of all persons irrespective of ethnic origins) and the concept of an indigenous people having a primordial primacy over the land and its political institutions, re-asserting its inalienable rights and privileges upon regaining sovereign control. For the British left behind more than buildings, sporting and political traditions, and the English language. Could the descendants of the Indian workers brought in to work the sugar plantations simply be "repatriated" back to an India that few had ever seen? For those Fijians who resented the Indo-Fijians' presence and economic success, this was a Fijian "problem," but one caused by British action: the Indian workers, after all, had been brought into the country without Fijian consent. With the British gone but the Indian population still present, it was perhaps inevitable that there would be difficulties, recriminations, and frustrations. The result of so divided a legacy was a complicated constitutional architecture designed to protect each ethnic group from the ambitions of the other.

The Indian population was to be protected from a Fijian-dominated

---

11. There is a substantial literature on the political consequences of Fiji's ethnic divisions. See, for instance, Michael C. Howard, *Fiji: Race and Politics in an Island State* (Vancouver: University of British Columbia Press, 1991); Brij Lal, *Broken Waves: A History of the Fiji Islands in the Twentieth Century* (Honolulu: University of Hawaii Press, 1992); Stephanie Lawson, *Ethnic Politics and the State in Fiji* (Canberra: Australian National University, 1993); Alexander Mamak and Ahmed Ali, *Race, Class and Rebellion in the South Pacific* (Sydney: George Allen and Unwin, 1979); Robert Norton, "The Mediation of Ethnic Conflict: Comparative Implications of the Fiji Case," *Journal of Commonwealth and Comparative Politics*, Vol. 19, No. 3 (November 1981), pp. 309–328; Robert Norton, *Race and Politics in Fiji*, 2d ed. (St. Lucia: University of Queensland Press, 1990); Ralph R. Premdas, *Communal Politics in Fiji* (Port Moresby: University of Papua New Guinea, 1977); and William Sutherland, *Beyond the Politics of Race: An Alternative History of Fiji to 1992* (Canberra: Australian National University, 1992).

government through a series of detailed and elaborate guarantees found in the lengthy chapter on "Fundamental Rights and Freedoms of the Individual" in the 1970 constitution. At the same time, the Fijian population was also presumed by the British and by the Fijian political elite to need protection from the more assertive and economically competitive Indian community; as a result, ethnic Fijians were given wide-ranging, ethnically defined constitutional advantages.

The Fiji Constitution did make clear the repugnance of laws and administrative arrangements that were "discriminatory"—a term that meant "affording different treatment to different persons . . . wholly or mainly [due] to their respective descriptions by race, place of origin, political opinions, colour or creed." Nevertheless, a range of important policy areas was exempt from legal challenge based on prohibitions against discrimination. Among them were government spending and the awarding of "any privilege or advantage" based on ethnic criteria.

PARTIES, ELECTIONS, AND COUPS.   Independent Fiji was governed from 1970 onwards by the Alliance Party under its leader, Ratu Sir Kamisese Mara, who continued many of the policies and perspectives introduced by the colonial administration. In 1974 a Fijian member of parliament (MP), Sakeasi Butadroka, was expelled from the party because he advocated constitutional changes that would have given indigenous Fijians control of most governmental activities. In October 1975, Butadroka placed before parliament a motion calling for all Fijians of Indian descent (Fiji citizens as well as residents) to be returned to India. His motion was rejected, but his policies became the basis for a new political force in Fiji, the Fijian Nationalist Party (FNP).

The 1977 elections saw the FNP (with its platform of "Fiji for the Fijian") capture 25 percent of all Fijian votes. Butadroka was the only FNP MP elected, but his party's share of the vote, as well as a decline in Indian support for the Alliance (which fell from 24 percent in 1972 to 16 percent), contributed to the governing party gaining only twenty-four parliamentary seats. The National Federation Party (NFP), the party of the Indian community, gained a slight majority—twenty-six seats. Unprepared for its own success, the NFP missed the opportunity to take office, and the governor-general invited Mara to form a minority government.[12] New elections were held, and in these—the second elections of 1977—the FNP received only 15 percent of the Fijian vote, which gave the Alliance

---

12. See Ahmed Ali, "The Fiji General Election of 1977," *Journal of Pacific History*, Vol. 12, No. 4 (1977), pp. 189–201; and David J. Murray, "The Governor-General in Fiji's Constitutional Crisis," *Politics*, Vol. 13, No. 2 (November 1978), pp. 230–238.

thirty-six seats and the NFP (which was weakened as a result of leadership rivalries) only fifteen.[13]

In 1981, ethnic Fijians were further divided when another Fijian political party, the Western United Front (a party appealing to Fijians on the western part of the country's main island, Viti Levu), was formed. The 1982 elections saw the Alliance win twenty-eight seats (52 percent of the vote). The NFP/WUF opposition won twenty-four seats (twenty-two for the NFP, and two for the WUF). Butadroka's FNP did not win any seats. However, voting was increasingly polarized along ethnic lines. Less than 1 percent of ethnic Fijians voted for the Indian-led NFP, and only 16 percent of the ethnically Indian population voted for the Alliance Party, notwithstanding its ostensible commitment to multiracial politics.[14]

Fiji's politics were complicated still further when the Fiji Labour Party was formed in 1985. The party was committed to non-racial politics, putting economic or class issues above ethnic and racial divisions. Labour appealed to younger, urban Fijians, those living in towns and cities away from the traditional chiefly leadership in the villages. In 1987 the Labour Party was able to further divide the ethnic Fijian vote and, with the NFP, denied the Alliance a further electoral victory.[15] A Labour-NFP coalition government took office briefly until being overthrown in May 1987, when a military force led by a Fijian army officer, Sitiveni Rabuka, entered parliament and arrested government MPs.[16]

Although many explanations have been offered for the Fijian coup,[17] it is clear that ethnic issues were major factors. The coup gained support among Fijians deeply disturbed by the prospect of Fiji being governed by

---

13. See Ralph R. Premdas, "Elections in Fiji: Restoration of the Balance in September 1977," *Journal of Pacific History*, Vol. 14, No. 4 (1979), pp. 194–207.

14. See Brij Lal, "The Fiji General Election of 1982: The Tidal Wave That Never Came," *Journal of Pacific History*, Vol. 18, No. 2 (April 1983), pp. 134–157.

15. See Victor Lal, "The Fiji General Election of 1987," *Electoral Studies*, Vol. 6, No. 3 (December 1987), pp. 249–262.

16. Rabuka's account of the coup is given in Eddie Dean and Stan Ritova, *Rabuka: No Other Way: His Own Story of the Fijian Coup* (Sydney: Doubleday, 1988). See also Roderic Alley, "The 1987 Military Coups in Fiji: The Regional Implications," *Contemporary Pacific*, Vol. 2, No. 1 (Spring 1990), pp. 37–58; Victor Lal, *Fiji: Coups in Paradise—Race, Politics and Military Intervention* (London: Zed Books, 1990); and Deryck Scarr, "Evidence, Ideology and Miscalculation: Public Opinion and the 1987 Military Coups in Fiji," *Journal de la Société des Océanistes*, Vols. 92–93 (1991), pp. 69–88.

17. For a thorough analysis, see Rory Ewins, *Colour, Class and Custom: The Literature of the 1987 Fiji Coup* (Canberra: Australian National University, 1992). See also John Overton, "Coups and Constitutions: Drawing a Political Geography of Fiji," *New Zealand Geographer*, Vol. 48, No. 2 (October 1992), pp. 50–58.

a cabinet dominated by Indo-Fijians, Fijians from western Fiji, and "commoner" Fijians opposed to the chiefly establishment. Following the ouster of the elected government, the governor-general of Fiji, Ratu Sir Penaia Ganilau, established a sixteen-member Constitutional Review Committee to receive proposals for changes to Fiji's constitution. It was assumed, in other words, that the "problem" of Fiji's divided polity could be "solved" by changing the rules of the political game. Multiparty talks proved sufficiently successful for an interim Council of State to be established, comprised equally of representatives from the Alliance and the Labour/NFP coalition. On September 25, however, shortly before the governor-general was to announce the composition of the Council of State in a national address, Rabuka staged a second military coup, reassuming executive authority "to preserve the ideals of the May coup" and "to prevent the country's further descent into racial violence." Three days later, Rabuka announced that the 1970 constitution had been revoked; subsequently, he published a "Fiji Constitution Revocation Decree," which was then declared invalid by then chief justice Sir Timoci Tuivaga. Rabuka subsequently announced that the position of governor-general had been abolished and that he had replaced the queen as head of state, ruling by decree until a new constitution could be promulgated. In a broadcast address on October 7, Rabuka formally announced the reconstitution of Fiji as a republic. New Supreme Court justices were appointed on October 28 to replace those dismissed following the second coup; the position of chief justice was left vacant.

Civilian rule was reinstated in December, with the former governor-general, Ratu Ganilau, appointed as Fiji's first president and with Ratu Mara as interim prime minister. A draft constitution was issued in September 1988, and a multiracial committee was appointed to review public opinion and make recommendations. Mara advised that few significant changes would be permitted, however, and in October 1989, the constitutional draft review committee endorsed the government's proposed constitution. However, the document was not one which could win multi-ethnic support. A conference of delegates from Indian organizations denounced the draft, referring to it "as an instrument of oppression and grave injustice." Nevertheless, the newly proclaimed Sovereign Democratic Republic of Fiji came into existence on July 25, 1990, with the promulgation of a new constitution.

THE 1990 CONSTITUTION. The challenge was difficult: to establish elements of consistency between democratic precepts, the needs of a plural society, and the special interests of indigenous Fijians. In the 1990 constitution, the source of authority for Fiji's supreme law was not "we, the people" but rather the Great Council of Chiefs, the guardians of Fijian tradition and collectively the inheritors of sovereignty over the lands and waterways of Fiji.[18] In other respects, Fiji's 1990 constitution represented less of a break from pre-existing policy than is often assumed. Like its predecessor, the 1990 constitution sought to insulate Fiji from the consequences of ethnic diversity and competition. It had as its inspiration and aim the preservation of the pre-eminent position of the traditional leadership of indigenous Fiji islanders. All other values and practices—including those associated with democracy, the rule of law, and equality of treatment—came in a very distant second place.

Like the 1970 constitution revoked by Rabuka, the 1990 constitution began the history of the Fijian state with the cession to Queen Victoria. It went on to say that "the people of Fiji have expressed the desire to have a new Constitution for the advancement of their beliefs, rights and freedoms and accept that it is desirous that the 1970 Constitution be replaced so that the will of the people may be truly set forth and their hopes, aspirations and goals be achieved and thereby enshrined."[19] However, the constitution refused to surrender altogether the idea of reconciling Fijian paramountcy with democratic practices: "they reconfirm that Fiji is a democratic society in which all peoples may to the full extent of their capacity play some part in the institutions of national life and thereby develop and maintain due deference and respect for each other and the rule of law." There was also a concession towards religious tolerance, important for Fiji given its ethnically derived religious diversity. Thus, while the constitution went on "to affirm and respect" the role played by Christianity "in the lives of the indigenous Fijians and the enduring contribution it has had," there was an acceptance of "the rights of other religious groups to practice their own religion." Complementing this gesture towards religious pluralism (for the Hindu and Muslim Indo-Fijian citizens and residents)—and complicating the task for Fiji policy-

---

18. See "Constitution of the Sovereign Democratic Republic of Fiji (Promulgation) Decree 1990," reprinted in Albert P. Blaustein and Gisbert H. Flanz, eds., *Constitutions of the World* (Dobbs Ferry, N.Y.: Oceana Publications, 1990).

19. All quotations are from ibid. For different perspectives on the 1990 constitution, see Ralph R. Premdas and Jeffrey S. Steeves, "Fiji: Problems of Ethnic Discrimination and Inequality in the New Constitutional Order," *Round Table*, No. 318 (April 1991), pp. 155–170; Roger A.R. Barltrop, "Notes on Premdas and Steeves," *Round Table*, No. 318 (April 1991), pp. 170–172; and Ratu Sir Kamisese Mara, "Fiji's Constitution: Product of a Complex History," *Parliamentarian*, Vol. 72, No. 4 (October 1991), pp. 273–277.

makers intent on preserving indigenous Fijian political power—were twin (and in some ways competing) commitments to both indigenous rights and the possibility of a multicultural society.

Although those elements of the Fijian elite who supported the coups sought to entrench Fijian dominance while establishing the conditions for Fiji-Indian communal harmony, the 1990 constitution identified the *Bose Levu Vakaturaga* (the Great Council of Chiefs) as the main source of political power and authority on Fiji. By definition, this was a group neither accountable to nor representative of non-ethnic Fijians. Its special powers and privileges transformed a multiethnic parliamentary democracy into a very different polity.

The 1990 constitution was supposed to be reviewed within seven years of promulgation, and subsequently every ten years. However, the first elections held under it (in 1992) failed to achieve the results the coup makers and constitutional designers had planned. Once again, the Fijian community split, and so even with the additional advantages provided to it under a new electoral system, power via the ballot box was not entirely guaranteed. In order to become prime minister, Rabuka entered into an agreement with the party whose government he and his forces had overthrown—the Fiji Labour Party—and, in exchange for its support, agreed that the constitution would be reviewed.[20] In 1994 a constitution review commission was established, which received recommendations and proposals from a large number of organizations, parties, and ethnic groups.[21] Subsequently a three-person committee (comprised of a former New Zealand governor-general, a Fijian, and an Indian) was authorized to receive further submissions on possible alternatives to the 1990 constitution. The committee issued its report in 1996, and this report is being considered by a parliamentary committee (chaired by Prime Minister Rabuka). It is likely, therefore, that Fiji will see further constitutional changes as attempts are made to reconcile the idea of paramountcy for indigenous Fijians with wider expectations about social justice and egalitarian values.

PARLIAMENTARY PROTOCOLS

One of the principal instruments for preserving indigenous Fijian rule is the country's electoral system. Fiji's bicameral legislature was established

---

20. See Ralph R. Premdas, "General Rabuka and the Fiji Elections of 1992," *Asian Survey*, Vol. 33, No. 10 (October 1993), pp. 997–1009.

21. See *Report on Consultation on Fiji's Constitution Review* (Suva: International Alert, and School of Social and Economic Development of the University of the South Pacific, 1994).

in the 1970 constitution on an entirely ethnic basis. The fifty-two-member House of Representatives was elected through a complex voting system. Separate electoral rolls were kept for Fijians, for Indians, and for those "who are neither Fijians or Indians." In addition, all voters were placed on a "national" roll. Twenty-two members of the House were elected "from among persons who are registered on the roll of voters who are Fijians": twelve of them by voters registered on the Fiji voters' roll, and a further ten by voters registered on the national roll. Similarly, twenty-two members of the House were elected from among those on the Indian voters' roll: twelve by Indian voters themselves, and the remaining ten by all voters. The balance—numerically and politically—was held by eight MPs who were neither Fijians nor Indians, three of them elected by their own roll and five elected by voters on the national roll. Thus, at independence the country's system of parliamentary government—affirmations of non-discriminatory treatment and the unity of a common bond notwithstanding—was predicated on permanent ethnic divisions. The British and Fijians fully expected that the non-Indian residents—both European and Asian—would side with the Fijians when it came to matters of politics and parliamentary government. The Indians, for their part, expected the same: for that reason, they favored a simpler "one person, one vote" majoritarian system, under which they might contemplate the possibility of eventually winning national elections and so forming a government.

Neither group has been disappointed. An unbroken sequence of elections saw ethnic Fijian and Indian parties opposed to one another, with European voters providing the Fijian "side" with electoral and parliamentary support. As noted earlier, this came to an end briefly in 1977, when a Fijian nationalist party—which opposed existing arrangements and "understandings" giving Fijians control over politics and Indians considerable dominance in the economy and professions—campaigned on a platform openly antagonistic to the Indian community. The split among Fijians nearly ended Fijian control over the government; however, post-election maneuvering deprived the Indian parliamentary leadership of its opportunity to form a government, and so Indian political aspirations were deferred until the 1987 elections. In 1987, a further split among Fijians gave the election to the multiracial Fiji Labour Party. A government comprised of both Fijians and Indians came to power, albeit briefly.

The overthrow of that government represented a breakdown of the policies of ethnic accommodation in Fiji. The post-coup leadership devoted itself to the elaboration of a new set of electoral and parliamentary rules with the same goal as the independence constitution: ensuring ethnic Fijian dominance within a political system at least superficially committed to values and procedures recognizably democratic in form.

Fiji's independence constitution also provided for a second legislative chamber, the Senate, which like the House used ethnic criteria as the basis for representation. The twenty-two-member Senate consisted of eight persons "appointed by the Governor-General acting in accordance with the advice of the Great Council of Chiefs," and one person appointed "in accordance with the advice of the Council of Rotuma." A further seven senators gained office on appointment "in accordance with the advice of the Prime Minister." Thus at least nine members of the Senate served (in effect) as nominees of Fiji's traditional leadership—not an ethnically neutral category, since the membership of the Great Council of Chiefs and the Council of Rotuma was and is exclusively indigenous Fijian. Furthermore, if the House of Representatives electoral system worked as intended—with the government chosen by the House (and accountable to it) led by a Fijian prime minister—it was expected that sixteen seats of the twenty-two-seat Senate would be perpetually under ethnic Fijian control.

The 1990 constitution preserved bicameralism and separate communal electoral rolls. The parliamentary distribution was altered, however, in an attempt to ensure that an Indian-dominated government could not win a subsequent election. Thirty-seven members of the House would henceforth be elected "from among persons who are registered on the roll of voters who are Fijians"; twenty-seven MPs were to be elected from persons on the Indian voters' roll, one member from the Rotumans, and five more from the remaining roll. Of the thirty-seven Fijian representatives, thirty-two were allocated to fourteen constituencies "in accordance with the provincial boundaries constituted and prescribed under the Fijian Affairs Act." Five more were reserved for five urban constituencies. Electorates for the remaining MPs were to be determined by a Constituency Boundaries Commission. The effect of these provisions was to strengthen traditional Fijian positions and to weaken the voting power of urban Fijians—those less likely to vote in accordance with chiefly strictures.

The composition of the Senate was also modified by the 1990 constitution. Membership would henceforth consist of twenty-four Fijians "appointed by the President on the advice of the Bose Levu Vakaturaga," one Rotuman "appointed by the President on the advice of the Rotuma Island Council," and nine members "appointed by the President in his own deliberate judgment from other communities: Provided that the President shall in appointing the members from other communities take into consideration the special interests of the minority communities." This was an exercise in constitutional mathematics designed to entrench chiefly Fijian dominance over indigenous Fijians and the political system more generally.

The 1996 committee report did not do away with the ethnic basis of Fiji's political system; it did, however, recommend changes in the allocations of House and Senate seats. The House of Representatives would still have seventy seats, but they would be distributed in the following way: twelve for Fijians and other Pacific Islanders; ten for Indo-Fijians; one for Rotuma; two for "other races"; and a further forty-five seats, open to any person from any group, with three persons elected from each of fifteen "all race" constituencies. The new parliamentary system—if approved and implemented—would make it possible for either Fijians or Indians to gain a majority of seats in the House and so form a new government.

Similarly, the committee's recommendations for the Senate would do away with Fijian dominance. There would be twenty-eight elected provincial representatives, one elected Rotuman member, and six other members appointed by the president. These recommendations were in line with other changes proposed by the committee, all of which were designed to scale back Fijian dominance of the country's political system. For instance, Fiji's independence constitution did not specify any ethnic qualifications for government positions. One of the central grievances of the coup makers was that an Indian could become prime minister. The 1990 constitution consequently included an ethnic qualification for that position: "The President, acting in his own deliberate judgment, shall appoint as Prime Minister the Fijian member of the House of Representatives who appears to him best able to command the support of the majority of the members of that House." The 1996 proposals for constitutional reform would remove this provision, allowing any member of the House to become prime minister.

Similar changes—though more symbolic, given the much more limited power of the office—were proposed for the presidency. The establishment of a Fijian republic had made the previous position of head of state obsolete. Where there had been a governor-general appointed by the queen on the advice of the cabinet, there was instead "a President and Commander-in-Chief" appointed by the *Bose Levu Vakaturaga* for a five-year term. This provision ensured that the Great Council of Chiefs would have absolute control over the choice of president (and the commander in chief of Fiji's armed forces, which are comprised almost entirely of ethnic Fijians), and guaranteed that Fiji's head of state—the symbol of the country, above politics and partisan divisions—would invariably be an ethnic Fijian.[22] The 1996 report, however, while preserving Fiji's republican status, recommended that the president only be nominated by the

---

22. See R.R. Nayacakalou, *Leadership in Fiji* (Melbourne: Oxford University Press, 1975).

Great Council of Chiefs. To be confirmed, the nominee would also have to be elected by both the House and the Senate. Although the report proposed that the president would have to be an ethnic Fijian, it insisted that the vice president (currently nominated by the president) be a non-Fijian elected by both houses of parliament. However, the vice president (being a non-Fijian) would not be able to become president, should the latter office become vacant.

LANDS, CUSTOMS, AND LANGUAGES

Concern over the status of Fijian lands represents another element of policy continuity from colonial times to the present. Loss of land, language, and culture by indigenous peoples elsewhere—in Hawaii and New Zealand, for instance—represents both a lesson and a warning for Fijian policymakers. The colonial administration protected Fijian-held land from encroachment by Europeans and Indians alike. At independence, the overall sovereignty of parliament was nevertheless circumscribed by provisions requiring extraordinary majorities for certain categories of legislation, each of which was constitutionally entrenched through procedural hurdles that no Indian-dominated government (even if one could emerge) could have expected to surmount. Several such acts—all having to do with Fijian lands—were given special protection: the Fijian Affairs Act, the Fijian Development Fund Act, the Native Lands Act, the Native Land Trust Act, the Rotuma Act, the Rotuma Lands Act, the Agricultural Landlord and Tenant Act, the Banaban Land Act, and the Banaban Settlement Act. In each case, any bill altering any of their provisions would have to be "supported at the final voting thereon . . . by the votes of not less than three-quarters of all the members of the House." But even that majority would be insufficient to change these laws, which protect Fijian land-holdings and virtually exclusive land ownership rights, in the event of "any provision that affects Fijian land, customs or customary rights." In such circumstances, the law shall not be deemed to have been altered unless the amending legislation "is supported at the final voting . . . by the votes of not less than six of the members of the Senate" representing the members of Fiji's Great Council of Chiefs. These protections were extended under the 1990 constitution. Furthermore, Fiji's ombudsman was explicitly barred from investigating any complaints made against the Great Council of Chiefs, or against any of the various bodies having control over Fijian lands (the Native Lands Commission, the Native Fisheries Commission, the Native Land Trust Board, and the Rotuma Island and the Banaban Island councils).

The 1990 constitution limited parliamentary sovereignty in other ways, too. Ethnic traditions were not to be dismissed as irrelevant by an elected House and Senate: "Parliament shall have particular regard to the customs, traditions, usages, values and aspirations of the Fijian people." As for Fiji's judiciary—already somewhat constrained given the reliance on a British legal inheritance—the courts were reminded that "Fijian customary law shall have effect as part of the laws of Fiji." Fiji has its own "common law"; as elsewhere in the Pacific, these are the customs, traditions, habits, and values practiced by the indigenous population. This was particularly important for Fijians, who were anxious about their capacity to retain control of their lands in the face of challenges from expatriate investors and Indo-Fijian planters and entrepreneurs. They wanted the courts to understand that "the opinion or decision of the Native Lands Commission on—(a) matters relating to and concerning Fijian customs, traditions, and usages or the existence, extent, or application of customary laws; and (b) disputes as to the headship of any division or sub-division of the Fijian people having the customary right to occupy and use any native lands, shall be final and conclusive and shall not be challenged in a court of law."

Fiji's 1990 constitution also endeavored to consolidate traditional chiefly leadership—a long-standing objective of those who supported prevailing authority relationships in Fiji's villages. There were constitutional provisions for "Fijian courts" with "such jurisdiction and powers as may be prescribed by Parliament." Indigenous Fijian villages are organized along traditional lines of authority, which the Great Council of Chiefs in particular has sought to strengthen. Exceptions in the constitution's guarantees against "slavery and forced labour"—excluding from its prohibitions "any labour reasonably required as part of reasonable and normal communal or other civic obligations"—are to be understood as attempts to reinforce chiefly authority in traditional Fijian surroundings.

Rights to freedom of expression in Fiji are also circumscribed in the interest of traditional values. Thus, legislation narrowing rights to communicate "ideas and information" may be constitutionally valid when it has been enacted "for the purpose of protecting the reputation, the dignity and esteem of institutions and values of the Fijian people, in particular the Bose Levu Vakaturaga and the traditional Fijian system and titles or the reputation, dignity and esteem of institutions and values of other races in Fiji, in particular their traditional systems." Similarly, other "fundamental rights and freedoms of the individual" may be overridden when parliament considers it necessary to do so "with the object of promoting and safeguarding the economic, social, educational, cultural, traditional and other interests of the Fijian and Rotuman people."

Concerns for the protection of language rights have been much less evident in Fiji. The 1990 constitution stipulated that English would be the official language of parliament, but it granted the right to "any member of either House" to speak "in Fijian or Hindustani." Although this provision values the indigenous Fijian language, it is an important concession for Indian representatives; elsewhere, minority legislators have experienced difficulty in securing a right to give speeches in their own native languages.

CITIZENSHIP AND ETHNICITY

Citizenship in Fiji is defined in ethnic terms; so, too, are voting rights, given the existence of separate communal electoral rolls. At independence, a person was regarded "as a Fijian if . . . his father or any of his earlier male progenitors in the male line is or was the child of parents both of whom are or were indigenous inhabitants of Fiji or any island in Melanesia, Micronesia or Polynesia." Similarly, a person was to be regarded "as an Indian if . . . his father or any of his earlier male progenitors in the male line is or was the child of parents both of whom are or were indigenous inhabitants of the sub-continent of India." In either case, "where the identity of the father of any person cannot be ascertained, the male progenitors of that person may instead be traced through that person's mother."

These definitions were also employed in the 1990 constitution.[23] The 1996 report on the constitution proposed that citizenship and ethnicity be framed along less sexist lines: citizenship would be an entitlement if either parent were a citizen of Fiji, and would be open to any person married to a Fiji citizen. Registration on the ethnically separate voter rolls would be a matter of choice: a prospective voter could choose to register on a voting roll associated with the ethnic affiliation of either parent.

The issue of "who is a Fijian" remains central to the ethnic conflict in Fiji. There is an important relationship between terminology and the capacity of the polity to accommodate multiple claims to citizenship from different ethnic groups. Remarkably, Fiji does not have a normatively neutral term for a citizen of Fiji. "Fijian" does not refer to a citizen of Fiji. Rather, it denotes a person who qualifies as one of the indigenous peoples of the island. Efforts by Rabuka, as prime minister, to broaden the meaning of this term to encompass Fiji citizens of Indian ancestry provoked a sharp response from some ethnic Fijians. Until the word "Fijian" (or an equivalent) can be claimed equally by all Fijians, irrespective of ethnic or

---

23. To the qualifications for citizenship by naturalization, the 1990 constitution added the following: "no person shall be qualified to apply for the grant of a certificate of naturalisation, unless he satisfies the Prime Minister that . . . he has been assimilated into the way of life of the people of Fiji."

national background, the country's problems of ethnic management will remain latent even at the best of times.

Papua New Guinea

Papua New Guinea is so much larger than any of the other Pacific Island states that it is difficult to regard it as an "island." It dwarfs all the other such states in its size, population, resources, and ethnic diversity. If ethnic communities are understood to be groups possessing a distinctive language, customs, and memories—traits that give its members a sense of unity and cause them to distinguish themselves from (and be distinguished by) others—then PNG may have more than one thousand such ethnic groups within its borders.[24] PNG has also experienced significant ethnic violence—it has the only ongoing secessionist rebellion in the region—even while making good faith efforts to deal constructively with the realities of ethnic heterogeneity. Constitutional solutions to the separatist tendencies latent in this incredibly diverse ethnic mosaic have not always brought about desired outcomes, however.

COLONIAL LEGACIES AND THE CHALLENGE OF NATION-BUILDING
PNG occupies the eastern half of the island of New Guinea, as well as a number of other islands to the north of New Guinea (including Bougainville, New Britain, and New Ireland). This territory came to form a single political entity through a series of colonial encounters. In 1884, the southeastern territory of the island of New Guinea (that is, Papua) was annexed by Great Britain, while the northern section of New Guinea came under German control. New Guinea was taken by Australia in 1914 and came under an Australian-governed mandate following World War I. Japan occupied parts of both Papua and New Guinea during World War II. After the war, the two entities were joined for administrative purposes, and New Guinea was classified as a UN trust territory.

Australia initially did little to prepare PNG for self-government: colonial decision-making and administration were monopolized by Australian and British citizens until the 1960s. Many villages had little contact with the colonial government, and Australia was criticized by the United

---

24. Tony Deklin, "Culture and Democracy in Papua New Guinea: Marit Tru or Giaman Marit?" in Ron Crocombe et al., eds., *Culture and Democracy in the South Pacific* (Suva: Institute of Pacific Studies, 1992), p. 36. Deklin writes, "PNG is a land of many cultures and, if we take the number of languages in the country as a rough criterion, there are some 1,000 cultures. . . . The nation is at present held together by tolerance of the cultural differences and sharing of common cultural values. . . . Culture is indigenous and the term democracy is imported."

Nations over its performance in this regard. This led to several constitutional initiatives: a House of Assembly was established in 1964, with forty-four of sixty-four members elected by indigenous voters. The country's first political party (the Pangu Pati) was established in 1967; a nationalist, pro-independence party, it came to power in 1972 under the leadership of Michael Somare. Somare formed PNG's first indigenous government, and independence was achieved peacefully (if somewhat abruptly) in 1975.

The problems of forging a nation among the peoples of Papua, New Guinea, and the country's offshore islands were well understood by Somare: "In New Guinea, we have no common enemy and people have no sense of being part of one great country . . . [a] Niuginian is more interested in his own tribe."[25] Notwithstanding the arbitrary character of PNG's political boundaries—the product of colonial arrangements and historical accident more than anything else—the PNG political and administrative elite has repeatedly affirmed its overriding commitment to national unity. Thus, clear lines of policy link the response to earlier secessionist movements in the New Guinea Highlands and Papua to the Bougainville rebellion, which has been raging since December 1988. While there may be room for discussion about devolution and administrative autonomy, the national unity of PNG—its sovereignty over the entire territory inherited from Australia—appears to be non-negotiable.

CONSTITUTIONAL AND NATIONAL PRINCIPLES

The strong commitment to political unity was emphasized in the opening lines of the PNG Constitution, a lengthy and detailed document that constituted the country's first "national plan": "We, the people of Papua New Guinea—united in one nation."[26] At the same time, the constitution hints at underlying tensions between the realities of ethnic diversity and the much more artificial character of PNG nationhood. Thus the legitimacy of the PNG "nation" ultimately rests on fidelity to a multiplicity of indigenous ethnic values and perspectives: we "pay homage to the memory of our ancestors—the source of our strength and origin of our combined heritage; acknowledge the worthy customs and traditional wisdoms of our people—which have come down to us from generation to

25. Michael Somare, "Problems of Political Organisation of Diversified Tribes in Papua New Guinea," in M. Ward, ed., *The Politics of Melanesia* (Port Moresby: University of Papua New Guinea, 1970), p. 470.

26. All quotations from the Papua New Guinea Constitution are from "The Constitution of the Independent State of Papua New Guinea," in *Pacific Constitutions: Independent States of Melanesia and Micronesia*, pp. 85–223.

generation; pledge ourselves to guard and pass on to those who come after us our noble traditions and the Christian principles that are ours now." The multiethnic character of the country was also acknowledged in other language intended to validate the national constitution: "By authority of our inherent right as ancient, free and independent *peoples*, we, the people, do now establish this sovereign nation."[27]

Independence was accompanied by a commitment to a set of "National Goals and Directive Principles," among which was a commitment to build a single nation in which the rights and privileges of all ethnic groups would be given equal respect. At the same time, there was a commitment to "Papua New Guinean ways," an affirmation of the worth and ongoing relevance of traditional practices and outlooks.

We declare our . . . goal to be to achieve development primarily through the use of Papua New Guinean forms of social, political and economic organization. We accordingly call for . . . a fundamental re-orientation of our attitudes and the institutions of government, commerce, education and religion towards Papua New Guinean forms of participation, consultation, and consensus, and a continuous renewal of the responsiveness of these institutions to the needs and attitudes of the People.

It was contended that "the cultural, commercial and ethnic diversity of our people" is a strength. A call was made to foster "a respect for, and appreciation of, traditional ways of life and culture, including language, in all their richness and variety."

Thus, the framers of the PNG Constitution rejected the concept of a nation-state built around the vision of a melting pot of indigenous peoples and cultures. This commitment to ethnic continuity and diversity had important implications for development strategies, because it would not be possible to preserve ethnic communities unless they were given further support. The constitution recognized the need to keep PNG citizens in remote and rural areas of the country in order to preserve ethnic traditions: "traditional villages and communities [must] remain as viable units of Papua New Guinean society, and active steps [must be] taken to improve their cultural, social, economic and ethical quality." This outlook contrasted with the notion that development would require the progressive depopulation of rural areas in favor of large-scale urbanization, which would transform residential patterns and create new relationships that cut across traditional ethnic lines. Nevertheless, ethnic groups from different parts of PNG have migrated, especially to Port Moresby, the

---

27. Ibid., emphasis added.

capital, where they have come to live and work in proximity to one another—not always with happy results. The consequences—ethnic conflict, social dislocation, violence—suggest that the commitment to village development might well have been designed (at least in part) to keep PNG together by keeping many of its peoples apart.

THE BOUGAINVILLE IMBROGLIO

The Bougainville rebellion represents the most serious challenge to PNG's national unity.[28] From the outset, Bougainville resisted becoming part of PNG. It was incorporated into German New Guinea in 1899, its separation from the Solomon Islands a consequence of British-German rivalry. Bougainville sought to secede when PNG became independent in 1975, but the movement faltered in the face of opposition from PNG (and Australia) and various government concessions (including the establishment of a provincial government in Bougainville). These efforts have done little to transform the people of Bougainville into a citizenry whose primary loyalties are to a wider nation. That they are ethnically distinct from most other Papua New Guineans seems undeniable:

its people have no significant traditional links with other parts of Papua New Guinea and, indeed, may easily be distinguished from their compatriots by skin colour. Whereas the bulk of the Papua New Guinea population are dark brown in complexion (and contemptuously called 'red skins' by the Bougainvilleans) those of Bougainville, including its small neighbour Buka, are of a hue that approaches black: throughout Papua New Guinea the word 'buka' has come to denote 'black.'[29]

Joseph Kabui, speaking on behalf of Bougainville secessionism, places great emphasis on the ethnic basis of the rebellion: "Bougainvilleans feel

---

28.   There is a very substantial literature on events in Bougainville. See Peter Larmour, *Legitimacy, Sovereignty and Regime Change in the South Pacific: Comparisons Between the Fiji Coups and the Bougainville Rebellion* (Canberra: Australian National University, 1992); Hugh Laracy, "Bougainville Secessionism," *Journal de la Société des Océanistes,* Vols. 92–93 (1991), pp. 53–59; Stephanie Lawson, "Ethno-nationalist Dimensions of Internal Conflict: The Case of Bougainville Secessionism," in Kevin Clements, ed., *Peace and Security in the Asia Pacific Region: Post–Cold War Problems and Prospects* (Tokyo: United Nations University, 1993); Ronald J. May and Matthew Spriggs, eds., *The Bougainville Crisis* (Bathurst, New South Wales: Crawford House, 1990); Eugene Ogan, "The Cultural Background to the Bougainville Crisis," *Journal de la Société des Océanistes,* Vols. 92–93 (1991), pp. 61–67; and Terence Wesley-Smith, "A Legacy of Development: Three Years of Crisis in Bougainville," *Contemporary Pacific,* Vol. 4, No. 2 (Fall 1992).

29.   Laracy, "Bougainville Secessionism," p. 53.

. . . that Bougainville is totally different from Papua New Guinea. Geographically, culturally, it's been a separate place since time immemorial."[30]

Against this background of perceived ethnic distinctiveness—of coerced participation in a larger national entity, first under colonial administration and then under rule from the Papua New Guinea mainland—rebellion broke out largely as a result of the environmental destruction brought about by the Panguna copper mine. The mine has had a devastating impact on the local environment, destroying villages and polluting river systems; there have also been ethnic tensions between local residents and landowners, and migrant workers. Mine workers "usually speak a different language and come from a very different culture; they earn much higher incomes than local people."[31] Bougainville's grievances also include complaints about how revenues from mining ought to be shared, with demands for compensation increasing steadily over the 1988–96 period, eventually transforming into a demand that the mine (which has been responsible for a significant proportion of PNG's exports and the government's income) be closed altogether.

Ultimately, the demands of the Bougainville Revolutionary Army give negotiators little with which to work. Rebels maintain that ancestral lands provide the basis for ethnic continuity, identity, and pride: "Land is marriage—land is history—land is everything. If our land is ruined our life is finished."[32] Giving any land over to mining is therefore seen as threatening to group survival. In the face of such sentiments, the government (through several changes of prime minister and party composition) in Port Moresby—considerably distant from Bougainville—has repeatedly sought a negotiated settlement, only to be frustrated. Exasperated, the government has on several occasions opted for a military solution to the conflict: through search-and-destroy missions, a naval blockade, and armed pursuit (involving incursions into Solomon Islands territory). Some of these operations have had limited success, but even these efforts have largely been temporary. At the same time, the PNG military has suffered heavy casualties. Efforts to win over the hearts and minds of the

---

30. Quotation from Joseph Kabui in R.J. May, "The Ethnic Factor in Politics," *Pacific Viewpoint*, Vol. 31, No. 2 (October 1990), p. 6.

31. C. O'Faircheallaigh, "The Local Politics of Resource Development in the South Pacific," in R. May and S. Henningham, eds., *Resources, Development and Politics in the Pacific Islands* (Bathurst: Crawford House, 1992), p. 274. See also Jill Nash and Eugene Ogan, "The Red and the Black: Bougainvilleans' Perceptions of Other Papua New Guineans," *Pacific Studies*, Vol. 13, No. 2 (March 1990).

32. Quotation in R.J. May, "Papua New Guinea's Bougainville Crisis," *Pacific Review*, Vol. 3, No. 2 (1990), p. 174.

Bougainvillean people have failed because of the hardships brought about by the blockade (loss of government services, including medical supplies) and the consequences of military activity (civilian casualties, refugees, and restrictions such as curfews). This has been complicated further by ethnic friction, as members of the PNG military are viewed (and indeed often conduct themselves) as "outsiders."

The people of Bougainville are themselves not easily viewed as "one people." The island is comprised of several distinct ethnic groups, among them the Nasioi, Buka, Banoni, and Siwai. As one analyst observes, "The inhabitants of Bougainville would never have traditionally recognised themselves as Solomon Islanders or even Bougainvilleans. People's horizons would have rarely extended beyond the immediate district in which they lived."[33] The development of a "Bougainvillean identity" is thus in many respects as recent and as artificial as the effort to inculcate a wider PNG identity. The rebellion in Bougainville shows that affirmations about national unity may be difficult to harmonize with efforts to protect and promote the value of individual ethnic traditions—especially when deepening animosities and high financial stakes complicate the picture. Under these conditions, neither side feels able to compromise.

ETHNIC POLITICS AND POLICIES

Thus far, the Bougainville rebellion has not encouraged other ethnic groups in PNG to rise up against the government. To the contrary, the years of carnage in Bougainville—the ruthlessness on both sides, the well-publicized atrocities, the enormous suffering of the Bougainville population—may have discouraged other groups from following suit.

The Bougainville rebellion aside, PNG has experienced surprisingly little ethnic separatism. The PNG government has carried out few if any explicitly "ethnic" policies, which suggests that the national "experiment" has been relatively successful. If "ethnic politics" is not high on the PNG political agenda—Bougainville excepted—this is evidence that PNG has had some success in establishing itself as a multiethnic polity. But this assessment must be qualified: PNG has been independent only since 1975—scarcely a generation—and the development of self-determination movements may require more time, a greater degree of politicization, and a greater awareness of political options and possibilities. Furthermore, it is difficult to describe the absence of explicit ethnic policies in PNG as an unqualified success for a multiethnic vision. In many respects, the PNG state is failing: its economy is collapsing (in part because of the loss of

33. Matthew Spriggs, "Alternative Prehistories for Bougainville: Regional, National or Micronational," *Contemporary Pacific*, Vol. 4, No. 2 (Fall 1992), p. 292.

mining receipts from Bougainville), law and order is deteriorating, and the government is increasingly irrelevant, scarcely able to extend its authority over Port Moresby, let alone distant islands such as Bougainville. Thus the absence of policies to advance ethnic diversity and promote interethnic harmony may more reasonably be viewed as evidence of the general incapacity of the PNG state, and of a government lacking in resources, cohesion, and leadership.

Although the PNG government may have few explicitly ethnic policies, aspects of the PNG political system have important ethnic implications. These include an electoral system that guarantees all regions of the country minimal levels of representation in parliament. PNG has held elections at five-year intervals since independence, and there have been several transitions from one government to the next.[34]

Perhaps the principal feature of PNG elections has been the fluidity of party lines. Many MPs stand for office as independents, and post-election developments involve many changes of allegiance, so that fluid coalition arrangements are by no means uncommon. The parliamentary atmosphere is such that national perspectives on politics are confined to a relatively small elite. Local attachments are strong, and the numerous candidates for election to parliament (and the high turnover at elections) suggest that MPs are more akin to "ambassadors" to Port Moresby from their own village, clan, or ethnic group than lawmakers within a national legislative body. Thus, parliamentary and electoral arrangements reflect the primacy of local and communal ties as opposed to genuinely integrative national ideologies and perspectives.

PNG has had a controversial experience with provincial government. Provincial governments are subordinate to the national government, which has retained (and used) broad powers to suspend provincial governments in connection with a wide variety of administrative defects. These powers have in fact been used with some frequency, and considerable dissatisfaction with the character and efficiency of PNG's provincial government led the government of Prime Minister Julius Chan to make major changes in 1995 (with parliamentary approval) to the entire system. Elected governments were subsequently overturned throughout PNG, and administrations appointed from Port Moresby were established in their places. Several provinces threatened to secede—which led to

---

34. See David Hegarty, ed., *Electoral Politics in Papua New Guinea: Studies on the 1977 National Elections* (Port Moresby: University of Papua New Guinea Press, 1983); Peter King, ed., *Pangu Returns to Power: The 1982 Elections in Papua New Guinea* (Canberra: Australian National University, 1989); and Michael Oliver, ed., *Eleksin: The 1987 Election in Papua New Guinea* (Port Moresby: University of Papua New Guinea, 1989).

counter-threats from the government—but no secessionist movements were launched.

Below the provincial level, there is a system of local government that is also clearly subordinate in power and authority to the national government in Port Moresby. The existence of these local and provincial institutions is further evidence of the importance of local attachments in PNG. However, these formal institutions exist side by side with traditional arrangements, which, in effect, allow ethnic groups to govern themselves. Largely left alone by the central government, these groups strive to maintain their cultures and traditions and—more tangibly—their land.[35]

LAND, LANGUAGE, CITIZENSHIP, AND TRADITION

Land rights are not spelled out in the PNG Constitution, notwithstanding the broad commitment to the values of custom and tradition (in which attachment to ancestral lands is generally pre-eminent). The constitution's commitment to economic self-reliance and national sovereignty was more of a statement against neocolonialism and the dangers of foreign investment capital than a statement in favor of any particular land policy.

However, grievances over land and environment problems have been politically salient and contentious. As noted above, the tremendous environmental damage brought about by mining operations has been a source of great unrest.[36] The long-running insurrection in Bougainville has among its beginnings a deeply felt view that the people of the island had lost control over their land and rivers, and over the island's future. Elsewhere in PNG, group rights with respect to control of their land are assumed to be inherent—the land is held to be literally "inalienable" (owned by all, it may be sold by none)—a perspective that clearly militates against large-scale resource exploitation by foreign corporations even when sanctioned by the PNG government.

Next to land—the guarantee of livelihood and the basis for identity—the preservation of an ethnic group's language is its most important communal objective. However, more languages are spoken in PNG than in any other country—over 1,000. While Tokpisin (pidgin) was originally the country's lingua franca, it has effectively become the national language, permitting members of various ethnic groups to communicate

---

35. See Ronald J. May, *National-Provincial Government Relations in Papua New Guinea* (Canberra: Australian National University, 1982); and Ronald J. May, ed., *Micronationalist Movements in Papua New Guinea* (Canberra: Australian National University, 1982).

36. See Terence Wesley-Smith, "The Politics of Access: Mining Companies, the State, and Land Owners in Papua New Guinea," *Political Science*, Vol. 42, No. 2 (December 1990), pp. 1–19.

with one another. The constitution makes a number of references to language issues. Applicants for citizenship are advised that among "the matters that may be taken into account" in deciding on such applications are the applicant's knowledge of either Tokpisin or "a vernacular of the country." Furthermore, one of the national goals enshrined in the constitution is for all citizens to be literate in either Tokpisin, English, or one of the local languages.

The PNG Constitution does not define citizenship in explicitly ethnic terms. However, ethnic ties to neighboring Melanesian states are evident in constitutional language providing for citizenship for persons born in PNG prior to independence with two grandparents who were born either in PNG "or an adjacent area"—defined as the Solomon Islands, the Torres Strait Islands, or "the Province of the Republic of Indonesia known as Irian Jaya" (that is, the western half of the island of Papua New Guinea). Indigenous sensitivities are apparent, too, in provisions making eligibility for naturalization dependent in part on applicants having "a respect for the customs and cultures of the country."

Ethnic diversity is found not only in village and tribal government, but also in terms of leadership expectations. In this respect, PNG's many ethnic groups each retain their own leadership traditions. In general, traditional "chiefly models" remain important, often providing a template for behavior in Western-influenced legislative and bureaucratic settings.[37] At the national and provincial level, no specific ethnic criteria are associated with any government position. It is noteworthy that—notwithstanding some initial controversy—Papua New Guinea has had a head of government of mixed ancestry (Prime Minister Julius Chan), and, unlike some other island states that have become independent of British rule, the queen remains head of state. She is represented, however, by a governor-general (in practice, an indigenous Papua New Guinean) who is constitutionally required only to be "a mature person of good standing who enjoys the general respect of the community."

Few have challenged the idea that the many peoples and communities of PNG have an ongoing entitlement to the preservation and expression of their distinctive cultures. The PNG Constitution gives "recognition" to ethnic custom, declaring that (subject to its being consistent with "the general principles of humanity") "custom is adopted, and shall be applied and enforced, as part of the underlying law." It would be virtually impossible for the PNG government to act against custom in any comprehensive way, although there have been conflicts between some cus-

---

37. See Richard Scaglion, "Chiefly Models in Papua New Guinea," *Contemporary Pacific*, Vol. 8, No. 1 (Spring 1996), pp. 1–32.

tomary practices (such as cannibalism and the killing of "sorcerers") on the one hand, and human rights and the rule of law, on the other. There have also been government restrictions on certain kinds of activity—logging, mining, tourism, and even anthropological fieldwork—in an attempt to prevent cultural damage arising from external encroachments.

In addition, especially since the 1970s, the government has pursued policies designed to promote indigenous culture. For example, a National Cultural Council was established, providing grants to regional cultural groups, and the government has supported involvement by PNG groups in various Pacific Islands arts meetings, festivals, and entertainments. There has also been controversy, however, over the use of indigenous culture for tourist purposes. PNG's "mud people," for instance, have found their traditions featured in advertisements by various Western companies. Concerns about the ability of ethnic groups to withstand sustained external exploitation—whether from Western investigators or commercial groups—is not peculiar to PNG, but it has emerged as a sensitive issue.

Vanuatu

The Melanesian population of Vanuatu (formerly the New Hebrides) encountered French and British traders and missionaries during the nineteenth century. The islands were jointly administered by Britain and France from 1906 through 1980. In 1957, the two countries established an Advisory Council, with four British, four French, and four indigenous appointees nominated jointly by the French and British resident commissioners. By 1964, half the members were being elected by local councils, and ten years later a Representative Assembly was set up. Elections in 1975, 1977, and 1979 were accompanied by ethnic rivalries and conflicts, and in due course the Assembly effectively collapsed.

Thus Vanuatu owes much of its ethnic and political complexity to multiple accidents of history. It is a multi-island state in which (by definition) its various communities share citizenship and nationhood. It is the only state in the region (indeed, in the world) that had to struggle for independence simultaneously against two colonial rulers, Great Britain and France, which ruled the country after agreeing to share sovereignty over the islands. The residents, however, were not consulted about this plan; nor had they ever before been grouped together in a single political entity. Vanuatu was thus defined as a nation by two non-indigenous powers, and the separate legacy of each left behind a people already divided by geography with further divisions based on language, religion, laws, educational experience, and political party allegiance.

The Vanua'aku Party won the 1979 elections promising to "continue the struggle for freedom until the day Britain and France leave [our] shores."[38] Vanuatu achieved independence as a united country only after a secessionist rebellion in 1980 was suppressed through the intervention of PNG forces, invited in by Walter Lini, the prime minister at the time. The rebellion was centered on the northern island of Santo, but it also involved a number of other islands (including Tanna, Malekula, and Aoba). Although Vanuatu's constitution sought to reassure French-speaking islanders (who are in the minority) and to safeguard the position of traditional chiefs, the attempt to establish a separate state of "Vemerana" was made by ethnic communities uncertain of the value of constitutional protections and uneasy about the prospect of exchanging French and British dominance for rule by English-speaking Melanesians.

As noted, the acquisition of sovereignty in Vanuatu followed a struggle against two colonial powers, Britain and France, the latter much more reluctant to surrender control lest it be interpreted as a precedent for Vanuatu's Melanesian neighbor, New Caledonia, and for French Polynesia. That the effort to achieve independence was led by an English-speaking party, headed by an Anglican priest, Father Walter Lini, perceived to be anti-French in outlook and politics, made the goal of an independent and unified Vanuatu state an ethnic rather than a clear-cut national aspiration.

The legacy of the anti-colonialist experience is expressed in the values invoked in Vanuatu's constitution: "We the people of Vanuatu, proud of our struggle for freedom, determined to safeguard the achievements of this struggle."[39] As in PNG and Fiji, Vanuatu's fundamental law opens with an explicit acknowledgment and embrace of the island state's ethnic, linguistic, and cultural diversity. At the same time, the constitution enunciates a commitment to build a single nation-state within which all ethnic groups may feel comfortable. Thus the value of unity is affirmed: "mindful at the same time of our common destiny, [we] hereby proclaim the establishment of the united and free Republic of Vanuatu founded on traditional Melanesian values, faith in God, and Christian principles."

There are no parallels in Vanuatu to the complexities of Fiji's various electoral systems. Vanuatu has a unicameral parliament whose members are elected on the basis of universal franchise. Vanuatu's electoral system was designed to accommodate ethnic diversity and ease communal con-

---

38. Quotation in James Jupp, "Elections in Vanuatu," *Political Science*, Vol. 35, No. 1 (July 1983), pp. 1–15.

39. All quotations from Vanuatu's Constitution are from "The Constitution of Vanuatu," in *Pacific Constitutions: Independent States of Melanesia and Micronesia*, pp. 305–325.

cerns by introducing some disproportionality in an effort "to ensure fair representation of different political groups and opinions." More specifically, the country's electoral system has been configured so as to guarantee adequate parliamentary representation to diverse ethnic groups on the country's many islands. Vanuatu's Council of Ministers (that is, its cabinet) is accountable, therefore, to a parliament designed at least in principle to be ethnically diverse and nationally representative.

Vanuatu's Constitution does not set down any ethnic criteria for the country's most important political positions: the prime minister, other cabinet ministers, the speaker of parliament, or MPs. A more ethnically nationalistic stance is taken with respect to the head of state, however. The principal function of the president of the republic is to "symbolise the unity of the nation." Reflecting the country's rocky road to independence, Vanuatu's constitution makers decided that it would be unseemly for the nation to be symbolized by a visibly foreign individual (irrespective of his or her citizenship). Therefore, Vanuatu's head of state can be neither foreign nor resident overseas; this precludes the British monarch from being Vanuatu's head of state. Nor can the position be filled by naturalized citizens or citizens whose ethnic origins are predominantly European. Vanuatu's constitution stipulates that any "indigenous Vanuatu citizen qualified to be elected to Parliament shall be eligible for election as President of the Republic."

Leadership of Vanuatu's government has alternated between English-speaking and French-speaking prime ministers. Father Lini was succeeded very briefly by Donald Kalpokas, who lost power in the 1991 elections. The victory of the francophone Union of Moderate Parties allowed Maxime Carlot Korman to take office. Intra-party divisions among Anglophone parties and political personalities brought about a further victory for French-speaking MPs in November 1995. These changes of leadership have had foreign as well as domestic policy implications, making possible warmer relations between Vanuatu and France, which were effectively frozen under Lini's government.

In Vanuatu, formal government institutions overlie strong village-based traditional leadership systems. This is recognized to some extent in Vanuatu's constitution, which provides for a National Council of Chiefs "composed of custom chiefs elected by their peers." The council "has a general competence to discuss all matters relating to custom and tradition and may make recommendations for the preservation and promotion of [indigenous] culture and languages." The constitution also specifies that the council be "consulted on any question, particularly any question relating to tradition and custom, in connection with any bill before Parliament"—a provision that has led some traditional leaders to complain that they are not being asked for their views on matters where it would be appropriate for parliament to do so. Vanuatu's judicial system also provides "for the establishment of village or island courts with jurisdiction over customary and other matters," and it is stipulated that there shall be a "role [for] chiefs in such courts."

Indigenous values are recognized elsewhere in Vanuatu's constitution. The constitution states, for example, that every person has "fundamental duties" (as well as "fundamental rights"), among which are duties "to protect Vanuatu and to safeguard the national wealth, resources and environment." An entire constitutional chapter deals with land; most importantly, it is stated that "all land in the Republic belongs to the indigenous custom owners and their descendants." Furthermore, the "rules of custom shall form the basis of ownership and use of land" and "appropriate customary institutions or procedures" are to be used "to resolve disputes concerning the ownership of customary land." It is possible for land transactions to be made "between an indigenous citizen and either a non-indigenous citizen or a non-citizen," but only with government consent, which may be granted only if doing so would not be "prejudicial" to the interests of the custom owner and "the community in whose locality the land is situated." The government was also given powers to "buy land from custom owners for the purpose of transferring ownership of it to indigenous citizens or indigenous communities from over-populated islands," although in this instance, too, government action must "give priority to ethnic, linguistic, customary and geographical ties."

As noted above, language issues in linguistically divided Vanuatu have been an issue of concern to both French- and English-speaking communities. Stipulating Bislama, a form of pidgin, as the "national language," the Vanuatu Constitution intended it to be a unifying force across ethnic lines. However, the constitution also provides for several "official languages"—Bislama, English, and French—and states that two are "principal languages of education": English and French. This was a concession to ethnic realities, but at the same time a policy likely to ensure that the polity remained divided along linguistically definable ethnic lines for many years to come. Linguistic diversity is also accommodated in government policies towards the news media as well as education. Vanuatu's newspapers and broadcast media are generally trilingual. Attempts by the owner of one newspaper to publish only in English led the government to threaten him with deportation if he persevered with his plans.

Most residents of Vanuatu have some fluency in several languages. In addition to either English or French (as a result of formal schooling) and Bislama (as a lingua franca allowing English- and French-educated residents to communicate with one another), many speak a language peculiar to their own customary or cultural group. In addition, other languages are used by immigrants from Asian countries, who are often active in commercial enterprises in Vanuatu's towns and its capital city, Port Vila. Vanuatu's linguistic heterogeneity is further recognized, and protected, in the constitution: "The Republic shall protect the different local languages which are part of the national heritage."

As elsewhere in the Pacific, citizenship in Vanuatu is also largely a matter of ethnic definition. At independence, persons whose parents or grandparents were indigenous to the islands of Vanuatu and who were not foreign nationals automatically became citizens of Vanuatu. Other ethnically indigenous residents of Vanuatu who had foreign citizenship were given the opportunity to become naturalized citizens of Vanuatu.

Like its Melanesian neighbor, PNG, Vanuatu faced and overcame a secessionist rebellion at independence. Unlike PNG, there have been no subsequent secessionist moves, although ethnic divisions based on overlapping cleavages of language, religion, residence, and political affiliation continue to exist. In Vanuatu, the absence of ethnic policies from the national agenda represents a reluctance on the part of the governing elite to devote significant resources to matters not seen as threatening to the state.

The Federated States of Micronesia

The islands that constitute the Federated States of Micronesia have been bracketed together as a result of colonial contact. Over the centuries, indigenous cultures in Micronesia have struggled to survive against a succession of colonial rulers. Spain gained nominal control over the area of the Caroline Islands (part of Micronesia) starting in the late 1600s. Germany purchased the islands from Spain but lost them to Japan in 1914. U.S. armed forces took control of the area following heavy fighting during World War II.

The FSM is one of four entities that emerged from the U.S.-governed Trust Territory of the Pacific Islands (TTPI)—a trusteeship established by the United Nations in 1947. District congresses were established in 1959, and a bicameral Congress of Micronesia was set up in 1964. Lengthy negotiations begun in 1969 between leaders of the Congress of Micronesia and U.S. State Department representatives left both sides exasperated.[40]

---

40. See Roger W. Gale, *The Americanization of Micronesia: A Study of the Consolidation of U.S. Rule in the Pacific* (Washington, D.C.: American University Press, 1979); and Robert C. Kiste, "Termination of the U.S. Trusteeship in Micronesia," *Journal of Pacific History*, Vol. 21, No. 3 (July 1986), pp. 127–138.

In the mid-1970s, the United States entered into a separate agreement with representatives of what was to become the Commonwealth of the Northern Mariana Islands (north of Guam, which is the southernmost island in the Marianas chain). With the Northern Marianas separated from the TTPI, the administrative center of the group was moved from Saipan (in the Northern Marianas) to Ponape (later "Pohnpei," in accordance with local tradition). The Marshall Islands and Palau subsequently split away from the TTPI, depriving the abortive federation of the three groups of islands (the Marianas, Marshalls, and Palau) with the most valuable resources and the most Westernized populations. The United States eventually signed documents (each known as a "Compact of Free Association") with the Marshalls, Palau, and the FSM.

In 1982, the United States and the FSM signed a compact that was approved in a referendum in the FSM on June 21, 1983. The constitutions of the four states making up the FSM were approved in 1983–84. Approved by the U.S. Congress on January 14, 1986, the compact came into effect on November 3, 1986, at which time U.S. President Ronald Reagan informed the United Nations that the trusteeship agreement had been terminated. The United Nations Security Council approved a resolution terminating trust territory status for the FSM in December 1990.

The FSM is the only federation in the Pacific. Both the name of the country and its political structure reveal U.S. influence.[41] While the original vision of a "United States of the Pacific" (in permanent partnership with the United States) may have faded, the four-state FSM (comprising Yap, Chuuk, Pohnpei, and Kosrae) still represents a characteristically U.S. perspective and design, as distinct communities with legitimate aspirations for limited self-government strive to balance these loyalties against a larger attachment to a more transcendent (yet somewhat abstract) national entity. An examination of the FSM's experience with ethnic relationships is at the same time an assessment of its elite's capacity to implement a U.S.-inspired vision of unity in diversity.

THE FEDERAL CONSTITUTION

The Constitution of the FSM finds "we, the people of Micronesia" addressing—rather hopefully—the ethnic diversity of their new state: "With this Constitution, we affirm our common wish to live together in peace and harmony, to preserve the heritage of the past, and to protect the promise of the future. To make one nation of many islands, we respect the diversity of our cultures. Our differences enrich us. The seas bring us

---

41. See Norman Meller, *Constitutionalism in Micronesia* (Laie, Hawaii: Institute for Polynesian Studies, 1985).

together, they do not separate us. Our islands sustain us, our island nation enlarges us and makes us stronger."[42]

There is no doubting the tragic history of the islands and peoples comprising the FSM, and their relative powerlessness in regional and world affairs. The FSM Constitution provides a summary account: "Our ancestors, who made their homes on these islands, displaced no other people. We, who remain, wish no other home than this. Having known war, we hope for peace. Having been divided, we wish unity. Having been ruled, we seek freedom." The goals of the new state are clear: "Micronesia began in the days when man explored seas in rafts and canoes. The Micronesian nation is born in an age when men voyage among stars; our world itself is an island. We extend to all nations what we seek from each: peace, friendship, cooperation, and love in our common humanity. With this Constitution we, who have been the wards of other nations, become the proud guardian of our own islands, now and forever."

As noted above, the FSM's birth was a protracted and difficult one. Indeed, the state was very nearly stillborn. From its troubled history—its flag, like that of the United States, depicts each state as a star; unlike the U.S. banner, the number of stars on the FSM flag has fallen over the years—it is not surprising to see a concern for unity among its diverse (and widely separated) peoples placed in a paramount position. Even the "General Provisions" of the constitution include "the solemn obligation of the national and state governments to . . . advance the principles of unity upon which this Constitution is founded."

STATE CONSTITUTIONS

The FSM's four state constitutions also articulate important values, foremost among them the need for unity and respect for traditional values. The Yap Constitution, for instance, emphasizes the desire for peace and harmony and concern for neighbors and the environment. It recognizes the value of traditional heritage and villages, along with modern technology and institutions. Yap, the FSM's most traditional state, seeks to harmonize the unavoidable consequences of progress with the inherited values and outlooks preserved and practiced in village life.

The FSM's least traditional (and smallest) state is Kosrae, itself formed out of a distinctive sense of ethnic identity, having successfully seceded from what was then the Ponape district of the TTPI on the basis

---

42. All quotations from the FSM Constitution and from the constitutions of its four states are from Albert P. Blaustein and Phyllis M. Blaustein, eds., *Constitutions of Dependencies and Special Sovereignties* (Dobbs Ferry, N.Y.: Oceana Publications, 1996).

of being a distinct people with its own culture and values. Kosrae is also the most ethnically homogenous of the FSM's four states. Its constitution declares, "As a people, in our language, in our traditions, and in our common habitation and love of this island, we are one," in an almost defiant statement of ethnic distinctiveness and the right to a separate political identity.

There is a strong traditional leadership on Pohnpei, and adherence to tradition is established forthrightly in its constitution: "to serve as the guardians of our people and islands, both now and in the future; to protect and uphold the inalienable rights of our people; to protect and maintain the heritage and traditions of each of our islands; to protect and promote the harmony and prosperity of all the people of Pohnpei." Pohnpei identifies the protection of the multi-island state's distinctive traditions as the state's raison d'être and the only genuine basis for constitutional legitimacy. The idea of diversity is emphasized in positive terms: "We acknowledge the strength that comes from the union of our individual cultural pasts; we are united by a common sea; and we freely express our desire to live and work together in peace and harmony for the common good of the people of Pohnpei and all mankind." The Chuuk (formerly Truk) state's constitution also declares its authors' "solemn dedication" to be "guided by law, custom and tradition, now and forever."

Each state possesses considerable autonomy; by contrast, the federal government on Pohnpei is relatively weak. What authority it has derives largely from its position as a conduit for U.S. financial and technical assistance as provided for under the Compact of Free Association with the United States. Some have questioned whether the FSM could survive as a political entity if U.S. aid declines significantly, particularly given the artificial nature of the FSM "union" and the strong ties to local culture, traditions, land, and language found in each of the four states (and on the islands within the three multi-island states, Yap, Chuuk, and Pohnpei).[43] However, it is possible that a sense of nationhood and the perceived benefits of "unity" may be growing.

POLITICAL INSTITUTIONS
As a federal republic, the FSM Constitution recognizes the existence of different levels of government (national, state, and local) and to some extent allocates powers among them. Indeed, by its federal character, the

---

43. See Glenn Petersen, *Ethnicity and Interests at the 1990 Federated States of Micronesia Constitutional Convention* (Canberra: Australian National University, 1993).

FSM seeks to maintain national unity without dissolving any of its component island states.

Federal legislative power is vested in a unicameral Congress that comprises, however, members apportioned according to two different representational principles. The FSM is not large or wealthy enough to provide for two legislative chambers (in addition to those found within the four member states). Thus, both "the people" and the four states are represented in a single-chamber federal Congress, which "consists of one member elected at large from each state on the basis of state equality, and additional members elected from congressional districts in each state apportioned by population." Those elected to the FSM Congress as state representatives have four-year terms, while other members are elected for two-year periods. The congressional districts within the states have to accommodate ethnic realities, and must be "approximately equal in population after giving due regard to language, cultural, and geographic differences."

State legislatures also have to meet district requirements intended to accommodate intra-state ethnic diversity. For instance, in Yap state there are districts for "Yap Islands Proper," with other constituencies reserved for Yap's outer islands. Similar arrangements are found in the other states. The Pohnpei legislature, for example, has representatives from "each local jurisdiction," and the electoral districts include eleven different local governments, some on Ponape Island and some from other islands.

LAND, LANGUAGE, AND CITIZENSHIP

Various statutes in the FSM demonstrate a strong commitment to sequestering scarce island lands from outside control. These laws distinguish rights to land use and ownership through ethnic criteria. In Yap state, for instance, there is a fifty-year limit on any "agreement for the use of land where a party is not a citizen of the [FSM] or a corporation not wholly owned by such citizens." In addition, title to land "may be acquired only in a manner consistent with traditions and customs." There are other constitutional strictures as well, reflecting the interrelationship between the strength of traditional attachments generally and attitudes towards land. Thus the "State recognizes traditional rights and ownership of natural resources and areas within the marine space of the State, within and beyond 12 miles from island base lines. No action may be taken to impair these traditional rights." There are limitations elsewhere in the FSM as well. On Pohnpei, for instance, land leases may not exceed twenty-five years, and land may not be purchased by anyone who is not both a Pohnpei citizen and an indigenous Pohnpeian.

The FSM also provides for the preservation of indigenous languages, while encouraging the learning and use of English. The Yap Constitution establishes the state's indigenous languages and English as official languages. Kosraean is the official language of that state, but English may also be used in government business. The constitution states that Kosraean and English are "of equal authority," although where there is "irresolvable conflict" between them "the English language expression prevails." All laws are published in both Kosraean and English, with English again controlling in the event of a conflict. Similarly, the official languages of the Pohnpei government are both Pohnpei and English; in Chuuk, all laws and resolutions are to be published in both the English and Chuukese languages.

Unlike in Fiji, rights of citizenship in the FSM are available on a gender-neutral basis: "A person born of parents one or both of whom are citizens of the Federated States of Micronesia is a citizen and national of the Federated States by birth." Indeed, the FSM's constitution incorporates a "Declaration of Rights" based on ethnic impartiality: persons may not be denied "the equal protection of the laws" and equal protection of the laws "may not be denied or impaired on account of sex, race, ancestry, national origin, language, or social status." FSM citizens were also given explicit and important rights to "travel and migrate within the Federated States," notwithstanding ethnic differences that represent barriers to full acceptance for migrants who exercise these rights and take up permanent residence in a state other than their own. Similar laws on citizenship are found in the FSM state constitutions. In Pohnpei, for instance, citizenship is available to persons resident on Pohnpei only "if either of his parents at the time of his birth was a citizen [and of indigenous ancestry]." Thus, the tendency for Pacific Island states to define themselves and their citizens in largely ethnic terms virtually precludes ethnically neutral policies pertaining to immigration, naturalization, and the rights and privileges associated with citizenship status.

LEADERSHIP, TRADITIONS, AND CUSTOMS

As in the United States, in the FSM the head of state and the head of government are the same person: the president. In the FSM, the president "is elected by Congress for a term of four years by a majority vote of all the members." Presidents can serve no more than two consecutive terms. Presidential qualifications are few: the officeholder must be a member of the FSM Congress elected for a four-year term, a citizen of the FSM by birth, and a resident of the FSM for at least fifteen years.

Prior to 1995, the presidency rotated from one state to the next. Thus the first president, Kuniwo Nakayama, was from Chuuk; the second, John Haglelgam, was from Yap; and the third, Bailey Olter, was from Pohnpei.

When it came to the fourth presidential election, in 1995, the pattern of rotation was altered: Olter sought and received a second successive term, with the other states acceding to his candidacy to avoid precipitating a possible withdrawal by Pohnpei from the FSM.

Ethnic criteria for leadership are also found in the FSM state constitutions. The elected governor of Chuuk state must be both a citizen by birth and an indigenous Chuukese. Furthermore, recognizing ethnic differences within the state, the Chuuk Constitution specifies that if the governor is a resident of one particular region, then the lieutenant governor must be a resident of another. A comparable attempt to achieve ethnic balance is found in Yap: "if the Governor is a resident of Yap islands Proper, the Lieutenant Governor shall be a resident of the Outer Islands," and vice versa. Kosrae has a directly elected governor who must be a citizen of the FSM and "a Kosraean by birth." Similarly, the head of government in Pohnpei state is a directly elected governor who must be "a citizen of Pohnpei by birth."

Sweeping constitutional protections for individual rights are often followed in non-Western settings by precepts drawn from other cultural sources. The FSM Constitution's broad guarantees to individuals are followed by a section on "Traditional Rights," which declares: "Nothing in this Constitution takes away a role or function of a traditional leader as recognized by custom and tradition, or prevents a traditional leader from being recognized, honored, and given formal or functional roles at any level of government." The constitution also states that statutes may be written to protect the "traditions of the people," and if they are challenged as "violative of" the Declaration of Rights, then "protection of Micronesian tradition shall be considered a compelling social purpose warranting such governmental action."

The FSM Constitution also permits the national Congress to "establish, when needed, a Chamber of Chiefs consisting of traditional leaders from each state having such leaders, and of elected representatives from states having no traditional leaders." Furthermore, state constitutions may "provide for an active, functional role" for traditional leaders in those states that have them. This injunction sits in an ultimately uneasy relationship with language requiring the states of the FSM to have "a democratic constitution." States are also permitted to "set aside" one of their elected congressional seats "for a traditional leader who shall be chosen as provided by statute for a 2-year term." The importance of custom and tradition is also acknowledged in the FSM's judicial system. Its courts must uphold not only the national constitution, the laws enacted by Congress, and those regulations lawfully introduced by the government. For there are other criteria for judges to consider as well:

"Court decisions shall be consistent with this Constitution, Micronesian customs and traditions, and the social and geographical configuration of Micronesia."

Similar gestures towards custom, tradition, and customary leaders are found in the FSM's states. Each of Pohnpei's eleven local governments may have its own constitution; such constitutions "may provide a functional role for traditional leaders." In Chuuk, special councils of traditional leaders, "composed of one recognized traditional chief from each of the election districts," have been established to "ensure by all traditional means" the resolution of any civil disturbances; to "enforce tradition and custom as recognized and practiced in each place, island or group of islands"; and to "preserve all tradition, custom, language and everything of historical value peculiar to life and living in Chuuk." The Chuuk Constitution also specifies that due recognition "shall be given to traditions and customs in providing a system of law" for Chuuk, and that "nothing in this Constitution [or the Bill of Rights] shall be construed to limit or invalidate any recognized tradition or custom." Nor are the two Chuuk councils expected to play only a ceremonial or symbolic role. The councils of traditional leaders have a right to read and consider every bill that passes in the legislature. They "have the power to disapprove a bill which concerns tradition and custom or the role or function of a traditional leader as recognized by tradition and custom. The Councils shall be the judge of the concerns of such a bill." Bills vetoed by the councils may be amended and then returned to them for further consideration. Only when approved by the councils do bills go to the elected governor for consideration (and a possible further veto, one which may, however—unlike that of the two councils—be overridden by the elected legislature).

In Pohnpei, too, a special constitutional article is devoted to "Tradition." It states that the Pohnpei Constitution "upholds, respects, and protects the customs and traditions of the traditional Kingdoms in Pohnpei." Thus, the government must "respect and protect the customs and traditions of Pohnpei" and may enact statutes for that purpose. No such statute can be disallowed in court "upon proof of the existence and regular practice of the custom or tradition and the reasonableness of the means established for its protection." In addition, the Pohnpei government's responsibilities include conservation of resources, development, education, health services, public safety, and "history and culture," the latter involving the preservation and administration of historic and culturally important sites.

The Kosrae state constitution also has a declaration protecting individual rights, but one modified to ensure respect for communal concerns: individuals have these constitutionally protected rights except "when a tradition protected by statute provides to the contrary." Court decisions must be consistent not only with the constitution, but with "State traditions and customs, and the social and geographical configurations of the State."

In short, traditional patterns of leadership and local customs are protected by an array of constitutional safeguards in the Federated States of Micronesia.

Ethnicity and Politics: Some Common Themes

In each of the four island states discussed in this chapter, as indeed elsewhere in the Pacific, the tasks of contemporary governance are exercised by both "modern" and "traditional" rule-making authorities. These introduced and indigenous institutions function side by side—they often involve the same people taking up different roles depending on circumstance. A similar synthesis is taking place in the judicial arena. As one scholar has observed, "Most Pacific Island states are now developing modern legal systems that to some degree incorporate elements of indigenous customary law into the formal Western-style systems imposed during the colonial era."[44]

Formal constitutional solutions to a variety of challenges—among them, ethnic diversity—were first developed by colonial rulers uneasy about the consequences of their departure. Some of this work was rather patronizing. Could democratic institutions survive in the islands without the rulers who had introduced them being present? Could Pacific Islanders remember how the institutions of government (from which they were excluded for so long) actually worked without the rules and conventions by which they operate being written down?

A new "tradition" of constitution-making spread throughout the Pacific from the 1960s onward. In most cases, colonial powers would not leave until a written constitution was in place. For Fiji, PNG, Vanuatu, and the FSM, written constitutions satisfactory to external and indigenous actors were a necessary precondition for the achievement of independence. Constitutions have since come to be seen in the Pacific, as they are at times elsewhere, as important, even necessary, parts of the processes by which peoples identify themselves politically. In Fiji—perennially preoccupied with its ethnic divisions—the constitution is seen as both cause and effect, a source of ethnic conflict and a document on which prevailing

---

44. David Weisbrot, "Custom, Pluralism, and Realism in Vanuatu: Legal Development and the Role of Customary Law," *Pacific Studies*, Vol. 13, No. 1 (November 1989), pp. 65–97.

power relationships among Fijians and Indo-Fijians are inevitably inscribed. Elsewhere, constitutions provide frameworks for policies that impinge on matters of ethnic integrity (such as land, language, and citizenship), and serve as instruments for recognizing and affirming the complementary ideals of unity and ethnic distinctiveness.[45]

Language disputes are also often central to political conflict in societies finely balanced along ethnic lines. Through the effects of education systems and the media, English has become the language of both government and business in PNG, Fiji, and the FSM. Only in Vanuatu can English not play an integrative role in overcoming communal barriers; its acceptance there as a "natural" bridge between different ethnic groups would imply the domination of one group (the English-speaking, non-Catholic population) over the other (the French-speaking, Catholic communities). While Vanuatu's separate education systems (which perpetuate linguistic and religious barriers) represent a challenge for leaders committed to a common national identity, language policies in all four countries serve to deepen cross-cultural ties while at the same time preserving indigenous cultures.

A less obviously integrative role has been taken up by political parties. Unlike constitutionalism, the idea that political parties are fundamental to government and politics has been viewed with some skepticism. Where political parties do exist, they do not always play a role in promoting national cohesion. In ethnically divided societies, political parties often act as catalysts for conflict. During the colonial period, the political parties that existed in the Pacific often mobilized indigenous populations in their struggles to free themselves from governance by outside powers. Parties active in movements for independence thus had ethnic beginnings when they were juxtaposed against colonial administrations.

In the independent Pacific, political parties provide opportunities for individuals and groups to compete for political power. Political parties in Fiji and Vanuatu are defined largely by ethnic criteria. Thus, in Fiji there are Fijian parties and Indo-Fijian parties; in Vanuatu, anglophone and francophone parties (each associated at least informally with particular communities and churches) vie for power. From time to time, particularly in Fiji, claimants to a multiethnic (or non-ethnic) outlook emerge—the Alliance, at the outset, and the Fiji Labour Party—but these aspirations have either failed or led to catastrophe.

---

45. The scholarly literature on Pacific Island constitutions includes Yash H. Ghai, ed., *Law, Politics and Government in the Pacific Island States* (Suva, Fiji: Institute of Pacific Studies, University of the South Pacific, 1988); and Peter Sack, ed., *Pacific Constitutions* (Canberra: Australian National University, 1982). In addition, an entire special issue of *Pacific Perspective*, Vol. 13, No. 2 (n.d.) is devoted to this topic.

In PNG, political parties also played a role in the move to independence. As noted previously, the electoral success of Michael Somare's Pangu Pati helped the country gain independence earlier than one might have expected. Since independence, some political parties in PNG have been ethnic in character—parties representing the Papuan people, for instance, or those on the country's island provinces (Bougainville, New Britain, and New Ireland)—but in general PNG's parties have had limited strength or stability. As for the FSM, no political parties have managed to unite voters across four states separated by thousands of miles of ocean.

The absence of an overriding and explicit ethnic agenda on most island states suggests that, in the Pacific, ethnic politics is less a matter of interethnic aggressiveness than a by-product of positive attitudes people hold towards their own community's beliefs about itself, its customs, and its traditions. In all four island states—and indeed elsewhere in the Pacific—concerns among indigenous peoples have increasingly come to focus on matters of culture, tradition, land, language, and political power. This chapter confirms that there may be "problems of fit between the Western model of ethnicity and the perception and organization of cultural differences in the Pacific." An approach that emphasizes cultural differences (as opposed to "descent, innate characteristics, and unchanging boundaries") may correspond more closely to the self-images and images of others found among Pacific Islanders and their governments.[46]

Scholars have noted how "cultural issues are salient in the negotiation of local and national identities."[47] In this respect, there has been a "politicization of culture," with ethnic authenticity—called *kastom* in PNG and Vanuatu—playing an important role in nationalist movements and aspirations. These micro-nationalist sentiments at times exist side by side with pan-Pacific perspectives, which come to the fore when outside powers are seen as infringing on Pacific peoples and their rights (as with respect to

---

46. Jocelyn Linnekin and Lin Poyer, "Introduction," in Jocelyn Linnekin and Lin Poyer, eds., *Cultural Identity and Ethnicity in the Pacific* (Honolulu: University of Hawaii Press, 1990), p. 5.

47. See Jocelyn Linnekin, "The Politics of Culture in the Pacific," in Linnekin and Poyer, *Cultural Identity and Ethnicity in the Pacific*, pp. 149–173. For a further elaboration of this perspective, see Margaret Jolly, "Custom and the Way of the Land: Past and Present in Vanuatu and Fiji," *Oceania*, Vol. 62, No. 4 (June 1992), pp. 330–354; Margaret Jolly and Nicholas Thomas, "Introduction: The Politics of Tradition in the Pacific," *Oceania*, Vol. 62, No. 4 (June 1992), pp. 241–248; Jocelyn Linnekin, "On the Theory and Politics of Cultural Construction in the Pacific," *Oceania*, Vol. 62, No. 4 (June 1992), pp. 249–263; and Deryck Scarr, "Authentic Identities—False Colours—False Steps in Politics," *Journal of Pacific History*, Vol. 28, No. 2 (December 1993), pp. 204–232.

nuclear testing or proposals for islands to be used as nuclear waste dumps).

Thus, matters are still in a state of flux in the Pacific: "We have in Oceania the possibility of seeing people struggle for the first time with who they are—their cultural identity—in an increasingly complex social world."[48] A Pacific policy review took note of the strength of indigenous culture throughout the region, describing "culture and religion" as the "driving forces behind economic, social, and political development."[49] Culture, however, is a double-edged sword. It remains to be seen if multiethnic states—and multi-island states, in particular—will develop the common bonds they need to form true, durable national identities.

Conclusions

When Pacific Island states began to recover their sovereignty in the 1960s and 1970s, the idea of a "Pacific Way" was put forward, most visibly by Fiji Prime Minister Ratu Mara.[50] The idea of a distinctively Pacific approach to politics, more committed to consensus and unity (in contradistinction to a majoritarian politics based on confrontation), seemed more inclusive and more appropriate, particularly to small island societies where "winners" and "losers" may be friends, neighbors, and relatives, and will in any case need to go on working and living together irrespective of electoral outcomes.

The "Pacific Way" is little heard of these days, and seems an especially unfortunate formulation given subsequent events in Fiji itself. Its diminished use as a descriptive phrase for Pacific Island decision-making is on balance a good thing. The Pacific has inspired many myths about island "paradises," and the idea of a virtually conflict-free political process seems to have been one more attractive illusion. If in time a genuinely consensual "Pacific Way" does emerge, it will no doubt be based on the extension of values of empathy and social harmony found in some island cultures to the ethnically distinct yet native-born "newcomers" in their midst.

---

48. See Alan Howard, "Cultural Paradigms, History, and the Search for Identity in Oceania," in Linnekin and Poyer, *Cultural Identity and Ethnicity in the Pacific*, pp. 259–279.

49. See *Towards a Pacific Island Community: Report of the South Pacific Policy Review Group* (Wellington: Government Printer, 1990).

50. See Ron Crocombe, *The Pacific Way: An Emerging Identity* (Suva: Lotu Pasifika, 1976).

In any case, Pacific Island states have not dealt with the consequences of multiple ethnicities in any single "way." The island states of the Pacific are sufficiently dissimilar (in history, political institutions, economic circumstances, demography, and political culture) for them to resist one overall approach. Thus far, Vanuatu appears to have been most successful in accommodating ethnic diversity, once resistance at independence was overcome. Any appraisal of PNG's claims to multiethnic comity must acknowledge the inability of the central government to resolve differences with the people of Bougainville. The FSM, by contrast, exists only because its members had neither the will nor the capacity to enforce constitutional claims to three island groups: the Northern Marianas, the Marshall Islands, and Palau. As for Fiji, it remains a polity defined by a sense of "racial" grievance.

One approach to accommodating different ethnic aspirations for autonomy and self-expression is to provide the maximum opportunity for such groups to govern themselves. Many see federalism "as a means of accommodating the spreading desire of people to preserve or revive the intimacy of small societies, and the growing necessity for larger combinations to mobilize the utilization of common resources better." But federal arrangements are entered into when there is both a need "to integrate new polities while preserving legitimate internal diversities" and a desire "to link established polities for economic advantage and greater security."[51] The FSM (for instance) is neither an "established polity" nor one whose union provides its members "greater security" (at least in the current international environment). Nor is it evident that the Micronesian federation is becoming deeply integrated. In due course, its component states may conclude that their "legitimate internal diversities" can as easily be promoted by each going their separate ways, preserving forms of government consistent with their own customs and traditions or already devised in their own state constitutions.

Federal forms of government are often unstable, reflecting as they do a set of compromises designed to strike some sort of balance between the need for unity and the desire to remain separate. Other forms of multiethnic political association may also be precarious. The enforced union (in the Gilbert and Ellice Islands Colony) of the people of Kiribati and Tuvalu—a Micronesian and a Polynesian people, respectively—seemed "natural" to neither, and appealed to the less numerous of the two (the Tuvaluans) even less. Contemplating a post-colonial future in which they

---

51. Daniel J. Elazar, ed., *Federal Systems of the World: A Handbook of Federal, Confederal and Autonomy Arrangements*, 2d ed. (Essex: Longman, 1994), p. xv.

exchanged rule by one external ethnic group (the British) for another (the people of Kiribati), the people of Tuvalu opted to secede.[52] Where a union involves peoples geographically separated from one another (most obviously on different islands), secession becomes a more plausible alternative. There may well be no long-term future for the FSM; it may go the way of the Gilbert and Ellice Islands Colony. This would not necessarily be a tragic outcome, so much as a confirmation of the fact that superpower-inspired designs for distant peoples do not always come to fruition even when population numbers are relatively low and available aid monies relatively high.

Although not a federation, Papua New Guinea has sought to promote the sorts of goals associated with such systems. PNG has provincial governments, local and village administrations, and village courts. Provincial policymaking (either on its own or in conjunction with the central government) encompasses most areas of governmental activity: education, development projects, health care, public works programs, agricultural projects, forests and fisheries, tourism, transport and communication, labor, and employment. The failure of the provincial system to work effectively, however, complicates efforts to maintain a unified state. While greater provincial autonomy may at this stage only encourage separatist tendencies (and may bring about further inefficiencies in the delivery of services), a looser union may be the only way to avoid further tensions and a reprise of the Bougainville experience.

Vanuatu has also sought to achieve some of the advantages of devolution without introducing the complexities of a federal system.[53] Its local governments carry out many important governmental functions, in accordance with agreements completed between them and the national government, while the exercise of traditional authority in villages and the establishment of island courts are further signs that national unity is predicated upon an acceptance of considerable regional autonomy. Although parliamentary politics in the capital is at times divisive, Vanuatu appears to have developed a formula for unity based on ethnic groups from its many islands continuing to develop their own traditions. At

---

52. See Barrie MacDonald, "Secession in Defence of Identity: The Making of Tuvalu," *Pacific Viewpoint*, Vol. 16, No. 1 (May 1975), pp. 26–44; and Barrie MacDonald, "The Separation of the Gilbert and Ellice Islands," *Journal of Pacific History*, Vol. 10, No. 4 (1975), pp. 84–88.

53. See Howard Van Trease, ed., *Melanesian Politics: Stael Blong Vanuatu* (Christchurch: Macmillan Brown Centre for Pacific Studies, 1995) for an overview of Vanuatu politics and culture written mainly by indigenous Vanuatu.

the same time, the example of military force being used to crush the one genuine attempt at secession remains in the background to warn any group seeking to move beyond relative autonomy towards independence.

Prospects for federalism (or devolution) would seem to have least relevance for Fiji. While Fiji's policymakers continue to explore the implications for both Fijians and Indo-Fijians of moves towards a more recognizably democratic polity, outside the cities Fijians and Indians continue to live in separate communities. However, the two ethnic groups are not sufficiently separated geographically for each to be granted a separate state or for any federal plan (even if the concept were to be acceptable) to be practical. Both communities already have considerable control over their own affairs, however, and it is largely a shared sense of nationhood that continues to elude both the public and policymakers. Progress may need to await what are superficially non-political developments: further contact between members of all communities; a shared sense of national self-esteem following such phenomena as sporting achievements by Fijian citizens and national teams; and, at the same time, further developments among indigenous Fijians themselves, as their own communal "unity" becomes less politically salient as a consequence of education, travel, and secularization in attitudes and life-style.

There are many signs of faith in Pacific Island societies, and, given their exposure to catastrophes both human and climatic, there is no doubt good reason for it to play so important a role in island affairs. Constitutionalism has (with Christianity) become one of the introduced "traditions" of the region, and serious problems consequently tend to attract constitutional solutions. This is so even where there is something of an inherent tension in such an approach, as predominantly oral cultures seek to enshrine "custom and tradition" by inscribing a promise to protect them within an untraditional written document.[54] In any event, proposals for constitutional change are on the agenda in many, if not most, Pacific Island states. Where these originate out of ethnically defined problems, their chances for success seem related to the number of ethnic communities involved and their geographic dispersal.

---

54. For analyses of the conflict between democratic perspectives and traditional values, see Ron Crocombe, Uentabo Neemia, Asesela Ravuvu, and Werner vom Busch, eds., *Culture and Democracy in the South Pacific* (Suva, Fiji: Institute of Pacific Studies, University of the South Pacific, 1992); Lawson, *Tradition Versus Democracy in the South Pacific*; and Bernard Narakobi, *Lo Bilong Yumi Yet: Law and Custom in Melanesia* (Suva, Fiji: Institute of Pacific Studies, University of the South Pacific, and Melanesian Institute for Pastoral and Socio-Economic Service, Goroka, Papua New Guinea, 1989).

Pacific Island countries can be depicted as falling along a continuum of ethnic diversity. While there are special problems for a state (such as PNG) with a large number of ethnic groups, these seem manageable when compared with the issues facing states whose politics revolve around a struggle between only two peoples. Multicultural societies, in other words, may more easily lend themselves to the civilizing qualities of pragmatism and tolerance than bicultural societies.

Statist solutions still loom large in Pacific polities. There may be another way forward, however. Public-choice thinking (premised on a reduced role for the state) has thus far had little impact in the region, notwithstanding the fact that leaving matters to individuals and families (rather than to the government) would appear to be consistent with island traditions and practices. Furthermore, Pacific Island governments are generally not well endowed; those with especially abundant and market-able resources have had them depleted (Nauru's and Banaba's phos-phates), plundered (the Solomons' rain forests), or transformed into a source of environmental degradation and political strife (copper mining in PNG).

Where Pacific Islands were once self-reliant, their economies now frequently rely on externally funded development programs and remit-tances sent home by nationals living and working abroad. Economic dependence on so large and seemingly permanent a scale suggests that some independent or self-governing island states may well be unsustain-able unless an outside power makes an ongoing financial commitment to them. The breakup of the FSM, for instance, could well leave some of its remnant states without any visible means of support, and their popula-tions facing difficult choices: emigration (a right that would be restricted without links to a larger entity); a return to simpler life-styles (an option fraught with difficulty, particularly for younger islanders); or a search by leaders for a new protector, with all that that might entail.

Some island governments have already experienced economic and budgetary problems arising out of the disproportionately large size of their public bureaucracies. A dependence on external aid goes against trends elsewhere. It also has consequences for ethnic relationships: Fiji's Indian population, for example, regards infusions of outside aid as sup-port not only for a Fijian-dominated government, but for ethnic Fijians as well (as the recipients of much governmental assistance). In the FSM, devising a formula for distributing U.S. aid among the four states contin-ues to be a source of ethnic tension and rivalry. Similar suspicions and jealousies occur in Vanuatu and PNG with regard to the distribution of external aid to islands and provinces. At the same time, one of the criteria that citizens often use to assess government performance is the capacity of leaders to generate additional economic assistance either from established aid donors or from new sources. In the long term, healthy relationships among ethnic groups in bicultural and multicultural societies may require a reduced role for the state, and the emergence of a self-sustaining economic infrastructure capable of providing employment, services, and hope for all their peoples.

Part IV
Conclusions

Chapter 13

The Impact of Government Policies on Ethnic Relations

Michael E. Brown

In this book, we have sought to advance understanding of ethnic problems by analyzing government policies with respect to ethnic groups, ethnic issues, and ethnic conflicts in Asia and the Pacific. With this broad goal in mind, we have traced the evolution of government policies in sixteen countries: India, Pakistan, Sri Lanka, Burma, Thailand, Malaysia, Singapore, Indonesia, the Philippines, China, Australia, New Zealand, Fiji, Papua New Guinea, Vanuatu, and the Federated States of Micronesia. More specifically, we have identified the main policy initiatives that have been undertaken, examined the ways in which policies have changed over time, and analyzed the effects these policies have had on ethnic relations in the countries in question. We have tried to determine how governments have fared in promoting peace, order, and stability, on the one hand, and political, economic, and social justice, on the other.

In this concluding chapter, I draw on the foregoing descriptive and analytical foundation, look at government policies with respect to ethnic relations from a broad comparative perspective, develop a framework for thinking about these issues, and put forward some analytical generalizations and policy recommendations.

First, I make some general remarks about the different kinds of effects government policies can have on ethnic groups, issues, and problems. The main point to be made in this regard is a simple but important one: government policies almost always have significant effects on the course and trajectory of ethnic relations in the country in question. Misguided or malicious policies can aggravate ethnic problems and turn potentially violent situations into deadly confrontations. Comparatively benign policies can help to hold together countries under difficult circumstances. When thinking about how government policies influence ethnic problems, one should keep in mind that governments formulate both general policies aimed at the country as a whole and specific policies targeted at specific ethnic issues. Governments also influence ethnic issues both by design and by accident. In addition, governments influence ethnic relations through inaction, which can be caused by neglect or insufficient governmental capacities. Because governments have effects on ethnic problems, one has to look at how problems and policies evolve over time, and consider the interactions between the two. To do this, we need to analyze three sets of factors: policy settings, broad policy parameters, and specific policy areas.

In the second section of this chapter, I focus on policy settings—the arrays of ethnic problems and challenges with which governments have to contend. I show how different kinds of ethnic settings pose different kinds of problems for governments and leaders. In particular, I illustrate how some settings are comparatively benign while others are more problematic. Five main sets of factors frame the ethnic setting in any given country: demographic patterns and ethnic geography; pre-colonial and colonial legacies; the histories, fears, and goals of ethnic groups in the country; economic factors and trends; and regional and international influences. I argue that demographic factors and ethnic geography, group fears and goals, and economic developments and trends, in particular, should not be thought of as immutable facts of life but as dynamic factors that are influenced to a significant degree by governmental initiatives and policies. The relationship between governmental action and inaction, on the one hand, and group fears and goals, on the other, is especially important. Governments are often indifferent to or unable to respond effectively to the concerns, needs, and demands of ethnic minorities. In the worst cases—and these are all too common—governments respond to group demands with repression and coercion. When governments respond unconstructively or belligerently to group demands, groups often become radicalized and conflicts become militarized. These radicalization and militarization processes are dangerous and difficult to reverse, but governments often push ethnic groups and conflicts in these directions.

In the third section of this chapter, I turn to four broad parameters that shape government policies with respect to ethnic issues: policy goals; policy instruments; policy patterns with respect to different ethnic groups; and generic policy problems (timing problems, implementation problems, and political dilemmas with which governments have to contend). I argue that governments generally have one of two basic ethnic visions of their countries: a unicultural vision, where the policy goal is assimilation; or a multicultural vision, where the policy goal is maintenance of political unity while preserving cultural diversity. Unicultural visions are often favored because central authorities see assimilation as the key to promoting political unity and thereby protecting national security. Unicultural visions are also favored because they serve parochial interests: they reso-nate well with large ethnic constituencies, they provide politically pre-sentable rationales (promoting political unity and protecting national security) for strong central rule, and they provide excuses to crack down on ethnic and other dissidents. This leads to the instruments governments employ to translate their ethnic visions into reality. In broad terms, we can distinguish between policies based primarily on coercion and policies based primarily on inducement. Coercion and military force are often favored as policy instruments in the ethnic arena because central authori-ties believe that forceful actions will produce quick and permanent solu-tions to ethnic problems. However, the track record suggests that coercion often leads to radicalization and escalation: military clashes with ethnic minorities often become bloody conflicts that last for decades.

Drawing on these distinctions, I suggest that governments have four basic policy options: forced assimilation (where governments rely on coercive instruments in the pursuit of unicultural visions); induced as-similation (where governments emphasize persuasive instruments in the pursuit of unicultural visions); benign accommodation (where govern-ments employ persuasive instruments in the pursuit of multicultural visions); and "toleration with attitude" (where governments use military force to keep multicultural countries intact). Forced assimilation is the most problematic of the lot. Assimilation is in itself a highly contentious undertaking because it threatens ethnic minorities with political dimin-ishment and cultural extinction. Utilizing coercive policy instruments compounds the threat, radicalizes minorities, and stiffens resistance. Un-less overwhelming military force is used against small, weak minorities, long-term military conflicts are likely to result. One of the troubling conclusions that flows from this analysis is that if governments do indeed tend to favor both unicultural visions and coercive instruments, then there is a tendency for governments to favor forced assimilation—the most violence-prone and arguably most unsuccessful policy option—over other policy packages.

In the fourth section of this chapter, I examine initiatives and pro-grams in eight specific areas: democratic and authoritarian political sys-tems, federal and centralized political systems, citizenship policies, civil and minority rights policies, policies on religion and religious groups, language policies, education policies, and economic policies. I identify initiatives and programs that have had significant effects—good or bad—on ethnic relations and problems, and account for these policy successes and failures. Because policies that work well in one place at one particular point in time do not necessarily work well under other conditions, I specify the conditions under which policies succeeded and failed in terms of the criteria that have guided this inquiry: peace, order, and stability; and political, economic, and social justice. Drawing on this empirical and analytical record, I develop policy recommendations in each of these areas. My overarching recommendation is that governments should try to dampen ethnic tensions by trying to depoliticize ethnicity. In practical terms, this means establishing and maintaining the rule of law; favoring civic over ethnic conceptions of citizenship; favoring broad civil rights protections over specific minority rights initiatives; favoring secularism over the establishment of official state religions; respecting linguistic diversity and promoting multilingualism; and building broad-based consensus for preferential and affirmative action policies in the educational and economic arenas. Obviously, authoritarian regimes are unlikely to champion the rule of law, and leaders who have ethnic axes to grind are unlikely to favor ethnically neutral policies. However, leaders who want to address ethnic problems constructively—that is, in a way that will promote both stability and harmony between and among ethnic groups—should endeavor to depoliticize ethnicity.

Next, I develop two sets of broader policy recommendations: one for national leaders who have to contend with ethnic issues and problems in their own countries; and one for international actors who are concerned about the promotion of ethnic harmony elsewhere. National leaders should keep in mind, first of all, that the only thing worse than having no ethnic vision is having a bad ethnic vision—that is, a vision that lacks broad-based support and that consequently cannot be sustained over time. Unicultural visions and assimilationist agendas can be successfully implemented, but they are generally problematic because they threaten ethnic minorities and therefore lack broad support. Multicultural frameworks usually do a better job of depoliticizing ethnicity and thereby promoting stability. Second, national leaders should be wary of relying on coercive policy instruments: escalation is easy, de-escalation is hard, and the radicalization of ethnic groups is extremely difficult to reverse. It is hard to switch from coercive to persuasive approaches because it is hard to convince minorities, after they have been treated harshly, that governments can be trusted partners. Third, national leaders should not neglect ethnic problems, hoping they will go away. Ethnic problems rarely go away on their own; to the contrary, they almost always get worse if ignored. Instead of waiting for a crisis—when ethnic groups are agitated, problems are mounting, and institutional capacities are strained—leaders should try to take advantage of windows of opportunity and take action when things are going comparatively well: this is when the odds of success are greatest. Fourth, dramatic pronouncements and bold policy initiatives have to be followed by energetic implementation efforts.

Declarations and pronouncements are insufficient by themselves, and they can be counterproductive if talk is not followed by action and if raised expectations are replaced by cynicism. Fifth, national leaders have to recognize that, since ethnic conflict is inherent in multiethnic societies, ethnic problems cannot be eliminated—only managed.[1] There are no quick or permanent fixes for ethnic problems and conflicts. Leaders and governments should therefore prepare themselves for the long haul.

International actors (distant states, regional organizations, international organizations, and nongovernmental organizations) should appreciate that their interests are often affected by ethnic conflicts in other countries—even far-off lands. Few ethnic conflicts are hermetically sealed, and most pose threats to regional peace and security. Ethnic conflicts are also important because they undermine regional and international organizations, international law and norms of behavior, and international order in general. These costs are difficult to measure, but they are real and they are significant. International actors should also note that, although ethnic problems are often horrible, they are not always hopeless. Ethnic diversity does not have to lead to violence, and ethnic violence is not always intractable. International actors, therefore, should not despair and refuse to become engaged on these issues. International actors, moreover, should not be allowed to use the "ethnic conflicts are intractable" argument as an excuse for staying on the sidelines: it is analytically indefensible. International actors will be able to influence events in many countries. They should focus, in particular, on governmental actors as sources of leverage in intra-state ethnic conflicts. Governments are discrete and identifiable actors, and international actors almost always have at least some influence over them.

The Importance of Government Policies

This book's main conclusion can be stated in simple and straightforward terms: government policies almost always have a significant impact on the course and trajectory of ethnic relations in the country in question. Ethnic differences do not have to lead to violence—Thailand, Malaysia, and New Zealand, for example, have experienced little ethnic violence in the last few decades of the twentieth century—and government policies are often decisive in determining whether ethnic problems, which are inherent in multiethnic societies, are resolved peacefully and equitably. This might seem obvious, but scholars have tended to focus on other

---

1. See Milton J. Esman, *Ethnic Politics* (Ithaca, N.Y.: Cornell University Press, 1994), p. 261.

factors—economic developments, the impact of modernization, patterns of social and cultural discrimination, historical grievances, inter-group politics and security concerns, and pernicious regional influences—in their analyses of ethnic issues and problems.[2]

Government policies are of course not the whole story. Other factors—domestic, regional, and international—constitute the settings within which government policies are formulated and implemented. If these settings are highly problematic, it will be difficult even for well-formulated and well-executed policies to cope with ethnic problems. The Federated States of Micronesia, for example, contains ethnic groups that live on widely dispersed islands and that had, prior to colonial rule, never been linked politically. This federation could disintegrate in the future even though its leaders have demonstrated gifts for ethnic tolerance and political compromise. Papua New Guinea contains over one thousand distinct ethnic groups, many of which have no experience with modern forms of governance. Papua New Guinea's government officials consequently face extraordinarily formidable challenges. By the same token, if policy settings are comparatively benign, governments can get away with controversial and even confrontational programs and actions. Malaysia has remained peaceful even though ethnic minorities bitterly resent the government's campaign to favor the Malay majority. Although ethnic minorities have serious political grievances in Malaysia, they do not want to rock the boat and destabilize systems that have generated much economic prosperity. The Indonesian government has been able to get away with brutal crackdowns in Aceh, East Timor, and Irian Jaya in part because years of economic growth have given it political room to maneuver. In short, government policies are only one part of the ethnic equation, although they constitute an important part of the overall equation.

Government policies can influence ethnic relations in a variety of ways. At the most fundamental level, they can push countries towards violent conflict, on the one hand, or stability, on the other. Misguided or malicious policies can aggravate ethnic problems and turn potentially violent situations into deadly confrontations. In Sri Lanka, for example, decades of discriminatory government policies with respect to citizenship, language, religion, education, and government employment alienated and radicalized the country's Tamil minority, and ultimately led to open rebellion and civil war. In Pakistan, the government's favored treatment of Punjabis in West Pakistan precipitated East Pakistan's secession

---

2. For an overview of the scholarly literature on the subject, see Michael E. Brown, "Introduction," in Brown, ed., *The International Dimensions of Internal Conflict* (Cambridge, Mass.: MIT Press, 1996), pp. 12–26.

in 1971. The Burmese government's assimilationist agenda, its refusal to grant real autonomy to minorities in outlying regions, its anti-democratic impulses, and its heavy reliance on military force are the main reasons why Burma has experienced ethnic violence throughout most of its post-colonial history. By invading East Timor in 1975 and subsequently killing over two hundred thousand East Timorese, the Indonesian government initiated an ethnic clash and brought another ethnic problem into a country already vexed by ethnic diversity. In the Philippines, the government actively sought to assimilate the country's Muslim minority, the Moros, and consolidate control over Moro regions. Decades of policies aimed at cultural assimilation, economic exploitation, and political domination led to the emergence of a militant Moro opposition and armed rebellion. The Chinese government's often brutal efforts to assimilate and subjugate Muslim and Tibetan minorities have radicalized ethnic relations in China in ways that will be difficult to reverse. In all of these cases, government decisions, actions, and programs played key roles in aggravating ethnic problems and generating violent confrontations.

In other cases, comparatively benign policies have helped to hold countries together under extraordinarily difficult circumstances. Perhaps the best example of this in Asia is India, a country with a large population and tremendous ethnic diversity. Although the policies of the Indian government have not always been well conceived, well executed, or non-violent in nature, the country's democratic traditions and the government's comparatively temperate policies with respect to religious issues, language issues, education, and regional autonomy have undeniably played key roles in dampening ethnic tensions and keeping a potentially fragile country from disintegrating.

Changes in government policies have helped other countries turn the corner with respect to ethnic problems. In New Zealand, authorities turned away from assimilationist policies in the early 1970s, and began to accept, and even nurture, cultural distinctiveness. An elaborate and effective system of legal protections was set up to safeguard civil and political rights, and steps were taken to address long-standing economic and social problems in minority communities. Although change has in some respects come slowly and grudgingly, the ethnic situation in New Zealand in the 1990s is much better than the situation that existed in the 1960s, and more enlightened government policies are largely responsible for this improvement. A similar turn of events has taken place in Australia, where years of vicious, constitutionally sanctioned discrimination towards and ferocious assimilation of Aborigines started to come to an end in the late 1960s. Much remains to be done, but there is a good case to be made that Australia has turned the corner in its treatment of

Aboriginal peoples. In the Philippines, the government of Fidel Ramos took a bold step in 1996 and offered a regional autonomy and economic development package to Moro leaders that previous governments had been unwilling or politically unable to extend. Key leaders of the Moro community subsequently entered into negotiations with the government, and the prospects for peace and development in the southern part of the country are consequently greater than they have been for decades. In all of these cases, policy initiatives from governments brought about fundamental changes for the better in ethnic relations in the countries in question.

When thinking about how government policies influence ethnic relations, three additional sets of distinctions should be kept in mind. First, governments influence ethnic relations through both general policies aimed at the country as a whole and specific policies targeted at specific ethnic issues. The former include basic decisions about political structures (such as democratic versus authoritarian systems and federal versus centralized arrangements) as well as decisions about broad economic policies (such as planned versus market systems). "General" policies almost always have important ethnic effects and these effects are often anticipated by decision-makers, but it is nonetheless useful to distinguish between these general actions and policies targeted more specifically at ethnic issues and problems. The latter include citizenship policies, civil rights and minority rights policies, policies on religion and religious groups, language policies, education policies, and economic policies aimed at improving the lot of one group or another.

Second, governments influence ethnic relations both by design and by accident. In some cases, governments make deliberate, well-intentioned efforts to address ethnic problems, improve the positions of ethnic minorities, and promote better ethnic relations. In India, for example, language policies have been carefully crafted to address the concerns of ethnic minorities and to create a sustainable framework for harmonious ethnic relations. Since the early 1970s, governments in New Zealand have implemented a wide range of policies designed to protect Maori culture, safeguard minority rights, address economic and social problems experienced by minority peoples, and make reparations for past injustices. These policies have had significant, positive results.

In all too many cases, however, leaders and governments make deliberate efforts to promote the interests of some ethnic groups over others and to discriminate politically and economically against ethnic minorities. This often grows out of a political need to take care of ethnic constituencies, which can be the key to getting in or staying in power. This has been one of the driving forces behind pernicious ethnic policies in Pakistan and

Sri Lanka, for example. In other cases, the driving forces behind pernicious policies are economic: governments exploit minority groups and minority regions because there is money to be made—and these profits frequently find their way to private, overseas bank accounts. In the Philippines, for example, tribal and Moro areas were exploited for decades by non-native loggers, miners, ranchers, and farmers, who in turn rewarded governmental authorities in Manila for their support of these endeavors. In the most extreme cases, leaders and governments promote ethnic turmoil for political purposes. This can be an effective way of mobilizing ethnic supporters, dividing ethnic opponents, and creating rationales for repressive measures and the use of force. This, in turn, can pave the way for self-interested individuals to get or stay in power. Politicians in Sri Lanka have often made blatant ethnic appeals to the Sinhalese majority and launched rhetorical ethnic attacks on the Tamil minority in order to mobilize support, intensifying ethnic animosities along the way. Military leaders in Pakistan have supported extremist ethnic factions, which they were subsequently unable to control, in order to divide opposition movements. Governments in Burma, China, and Indonesia have repeatedly cracked down on secessionist ethnic movements, fomenting further ethnic strife and using these problems as rationales for nationwide political repression.

It has been said that 90 percent of what appears to be maliciousness in the policy arena is really the product of incompetence. This figure is unquestionably high as far as ethnic affairs are concerned, but there is no doubt that many of the effects of governmental actions on ethnic relations are accidental. For example, governments can inadvertently aggravate ethnic problems by being grossly incompetent and prone to pursuing policies that have unintended consequences. For example, chronic mismanagement of the economy clearly contributed to ethnic strains in the Philippines during the reign of Ferdinand Marcos in the late 1960s, 1970s, and early 1980s.

Third, in addition to the actions governments take—general and specific, intended and unintended—governments influence ethnic relations through inaction. Here, one should distinguish between inaction caused by neglect and inaction caused by insufficient governmental capacities. Governments often neglect ethnic problems, in some cases believing the problems are trivial, in others believing that the groups in question are politically unimportant, in still others hoping or believing that ethnic problems will eventually go away. Even when governments are inclined to act, insufficient capacities may prevent governments from taking action. Newly independent countries often lack both institutional capacities and financial resources for major initiatives. Countries plagued by low levels of economic development and economic growth also lack robust capacities for action. Most of the countries of Asia and the Pacific have been hobbled by resource constraints of one kind or another at various points in the last half of the twentieth century. Burma, India, Indonesia, Malaysia, Pakistan, the Philippines, Singapore, and Sri Lanka attained independence in the late 1940s and 1950s; Fiji, Papua New Guinea, Vanuatu, and the Federated States of Micronesia followed suit only in the 1970s and 1980s. Most of these countries, as well as China and Thailand, have experienced severe economic hardships at one time or another. The parts of Southeast and East Asia that are examined in this volume began to boom economically only in the late 1970s, and some countries—Burma, for example—continue to struggle in the 1990s. In addition, countries that have been or are still involved in wars generally have limited institutional and economic resources for ameliorative policies towards ethnic minorities; China was torn by invasion and civil war in the 1930s and 1940s; India and Pakistan have gone to war three times since 1947. Many countries in these regions—Burma, India, Indonesia, Pakistan, Papua New Guinea, the Philippines, and Sri Lanka—have had to contend with ethnic civil wars. One of the sad ironies of ethnic conflicts is that once ethnic problems escalate into prolonged, violent confrontations, governments inevitably have fewer resources to devote to underlying ethnic problems.

Because governments have effects on ethnic problems, one has to look at how problems and policies evolve over time, and the interactions between the two. How do ethnic problems affect government attitudes and actions? And how, in turn, do government policies change ethnic problems? To address these questions, we need to consider three interconnected sets of factors: policy settings, policy parameters, and policy areas. (See Table 13.1.) My framework for analyzing government policies with respect to ethnic relations has these three main elements.

Policy Settings

The starting point for analyzing government policies has to be a consideration of policy settings—the array of ethnic problems and challenges with which governments have to contend. Policies, after all, are not formulated or implemented in vacuums. Different governments have to contend with different kinds of ethnic problems and challenges, and these problems change over time, both in response to whatever governments do and do not do, and in response to other domestic, regional, and international developments. In this section, I show how different kinds of

---

Table 13.1. Government Policies and Ethnic Relations.

Policy Settings
Demographic Patterns and Ethnic Geography
Pre-colonial and Colonial Legacies
Group Histories, Fears, and Goals
Economic Factors and Trends
Regional and International Influences

Policy Parameters
Policy Goals
Policy Instruments
Policy Patterns
Policy Problems

Policy Areas
Democratic versus Authoritarian Systems
Federal versus Centralized Systems
Citizenship Policies
Civil and Minority Rights Policies
Policies on Religion and Religious Groups
Language Policies
Education Policies
Economic Policies

---

ethnic settings pose different kinds of problems for governments and leaders. In particular, I explain how some settings are comparatively benign while others are comparatively problematic. Then, I identify and discuss some of the main ways ethnic settings and government policies interact over time.

Five main sets of factors frame the ethnic setting in any given country: demographic patterns and ethnic geography; pre-colonial and colonial legacies; group histories, fears, and goals; economic factors and trends; and regional and international influences.

DEMOGRAPHIC PATTERNS AND ETHNIC GEOGRAPHY
Three main factors have to be taken into account when one analyzes the impact demographic patterns and ethnic geography have on a country's ethnic setting. First, one needs to determine the ethnic composition of the population—in particular, the number and size of ethnic minorities. Second, one has to look at the way in which ethnic groups are distributed geographically—whether they are concentrated in particular regions or dispersed widely over the territory of the country. Third, one needs to determine if cross-border ethnic affinities create regional complications.

The main features of the ethnic geography of the sixteen countries studied in this volume are summarized in Table 13.2.[3]

Some countries are ethnically unipolar in character, while others are bipolar and still others are multipolar. For the purposes of this discussion, a country can be categorized as ethnically unipolar if one ethnic group constitutes 90 percent or more of the total population: by this measure, China and the Philippines can be described as being unipolar. Countries can be categorized as bipolar if two groups compose 90 percent or more of the total population: Fiji, New Zealand, Singapore, and Sri Lanka can therefore be described as being ethnically bipolar. Countries can be categorized as multipolar if no two ethnic groups taken together make up 90 percent or more of the total population of the country in question: Burma, the Federated States of Micronesia, India, Indonesia, Malaysia, Pakistan, Papua New Guinea, and Vanuatu are ethnically multipolar.

These differences are significant because countries with different demographic settings face different kinds of problems when it comes to forging national identities and maintaining political stability. The good news for countries with unipolar settings is that forming national identities is comparatively easy and nationwide ethnic wars are less likely to develop. The bad news is that countries that are dominated numerically, politically, economically, and culturally by one ethnic group are prone to discriminate against ethnic minorities because the latter are small and weak. This has been a problem for minorities in China and the Philippines, for example, as it has for Aborigines in Australia, who constitute only 1.5 percent of the country's total population. The good news for countries with bipolar settings is that they generally have to contend with only one major ethnic cleavage. The bad news is that these countries lack the cross-cutting cleavages that are generated by the presence of large numbers of politically significant ethnic groups. As a result, confrontations between the two dominant groups can become zero-sum competitions. These confrontations can become violent, as we have seen in Fiji and Sri Lanka. The good news for countries with multipolar settings is that cross-cutting cleavages make nationwide ethnic war unlikely. The bad news is that creating national identities is difficult and fragmentation is often a worry. For India, Indonesia, and Papua New Guinea, for example, piecemeal disintegration is the main concern.

The geographic distribution of ethnic populations is key. Groups that are concentrated geographically are more likely to seek regional autonomy arrangements, and groups that are concentrated near international

---

3. For more details on specific ethnic groups, see the tables found in chapters 1–12 of this volume.

Table 13.2. Demographic Patterns and Ethnic Geography.

Country	Ethnic Composition[a]	Ethnic Distribution[b]	Cross-Border Problems
Australia	Unipolar[c]	Dispersed	No
Burma	Multipolar	Regional Concentrations	Yes
China	Unipolar	Regional Concentrations	Yes
Federated States of Micronesia	Multipolar	Regional Concentrations	No
Fiji	Bipolar	Dispersed	No
India	Multipolar	Regional Concentrations	Yes
Indonesia	Multipolar	Regional Concentrations	Yes[d]
Malaysia	Multipolar	Regional Concentrations	Yes[e]
New Zealand	Bipolar[f]	Dispersed	No
Pakistan	Multipolar	Regional Concentrations	Yes
Papua New Guinea	Multipolar	Regional Concentrations	Yes[d]
Philippines	Unipolar	Regional Concentrations	No
Singapore	Bipolar	Dispersed	Yes
Sri Lanka	Bipolar	Regional Concentrations	Yes
Thailand	Multipolar[g]	Regional Concentrations	Yes
Vanuatu	Multipolar	Regional Concentrations	No

[a] Countries are categorized as unipolar if 90 percent or more of the population consists of one main ethnic group. Countries are categorized as bipolar if 90 percent or more of the population is composed of two main ethnic groups. Countries are categorized as multipolar if no two ethnic groups taken together make up 90 percent or more of the total population.

[b] Even when ethnic populations are dispersed and intermingled to a great degree, groups will cluster to a certain extent.

[c] Australia was demographically unipolar until immigration policies were changed after World War II and again in the late 1960s. By the mid-1990s, one in four Australians was born overseas. Although ethnic groups are dispersed and intermingled to a significant degree, many Aborigines live together in remote, rural locations.

[d] The OPM (Free Papua Organization) in Irian Jaya makes occasional forays into Papua New Guinea. In addition, the Indonesian government's annexation of East Timor in 1976 has not received international diplomatic recognition.

[e] Malaysia has had cross-border problems with both Thailand and Singapore.

[f] New Zealanders with European, Maori, or mixed European-Maori backgrounds together constitute approximately 90 percent of the total population.

[g] Thailand was ethnically heterogeneous in the late nineteenth century, when European encroachments in Southeast Asia compelled the Thai monarchy to begin forging a Thai national identity. The country's minorities have since been assimilated into the mainstream Thai culture to a significant degree.

SOURCES: See the tables and case studies in chapters 1–12 in this volume.

borders are more likely to develop secessionist movements. Secessionist tendencies are even more likely to develop if groups concentrated near international borders have ethnic compatriots living on the other side of the borders in question; these tendencies are likely to be especially pronounced if ethnic compatriots run a neighboring state. Due to the arbitrary ways in which many borders were drawn in Asia, cross-border ethnic complications of this type are common. Most of the sixteen countries examined in this volume contain regionally concentrated ethnic groups: only Australia, Fiji, New Zealand, and Singapore can be described as having intermingled ethnic populations. Several countries have regionally concentrated ethnic groups that receive material and moral support from ethnic compatriots living in neighboring states. For example, Burma's rulers have had to contend with Karen rebels, some of whom use bases in Thailand as sanctuaries. The Chinese government worries about secessionist movements among Muslims in Xinjiang, which now abuts an independent Kazakhstan. The Indian government has had to contend with a secessionist movement in Kashmir that has received support from Pakistan. Tamil rebels in Sri Lanka have received support from ethnic compatriots in the Indian state of Tamil Nadu. The good news for countries with regionally concentrated ethnic populations is that regional autonomy arrangements and federalism are potential solutions to some ethnic problems. However, central authorities are generally reluctant to go down this path because they are worried about encouraging secessionist movements. Governments in Burma, China, Indonesia, and Pakistan have favored highly centralized political systems for these and other more self-serving reasons; governments in India, the Philippines, and Sri Lanka have proposed regional autonomy packages only grudgingly.

In general, demographic patterns and ethnic geography change slowly, but they do change. This further complicates the picture because changes in ethnic geography almost always aggravate existing ethnic tensions. Many changes in ethnic geography are simply the products of birth and death rate differentials between and among ethnic groups, and responses to patterns of labor migration that are, in turn, shaped by economic problems and opportunities in different parts of the country in question. Demographic patterns and ethnic geography also change in response to deliberate government policies. "Ethnic flooding" programs are always highly contentious: minorities correctly conclude that, as they lose control over their lands, they are in danger of being weakened politically and extinguished culturally. For example, the Chinese government has encouraged Han Chinese to settle in Muslim and Tibetan areas. Governments in the Philippines have encouraged Christian Filipinos to settle in tribal and Moro areas. The Sri Lankan government has provided economic incentives for Sinhalese to relocate to Tamil areas. These kinds of programs are usually driven by both economic and political motivations: in addition to promoting economic development, central authorities are keen to solidify control over minority areas by changing the demographic balances in these regions. In sum, one should not think of demographic patterns and ethnic geography as immutable facts of life, but as dynamic factors that can be influenced to a significant degree by governmental initiatives and policies.

PRE-COLONIAL AND COLONIAL LEGACIES

Pre-colonial and colonial legacies constitute another set of factors that help to set the stage in many countries. Some countries had a pre-colonial national identity and existed in pre-colonial times as viable political entities. Among the countries studied in this volume, Burma, China, and Fiji fit this description. Many others, however, do not have these pre-colonial traditions. Not surprisingly, the latter generally have had a more difficult time forging post-colonial national identities.

Obviously, colonial experiences varied significantly from place to place. Thailand, for example, never fell under colonial rule, while many other countries in Asia and the Pacific did.[4] Some countries were subjected to colonial rule for longer periods of time than others. Some countries have been independent for decades, while others have been independent for comparatively short periods of time. In addition, different colonial powers—Australia, France, Germany, Great Britain, Japan, the Netherlands, Portugal, Spain, and the United States—ruled in different parts of the region at different times.

In general, colonial experiences have been tremendously important in Asia and the Pacific, as they have been in other parts of the world. Five political legacies stand out. First, colonial rulers defined political borders, and they often did so in ways that generated ethnic complications. In some cases—Indonesia, the Philippines, the Federated States of Micronesia, Papua New Guinea, and Vanuatu, for example—colonial powers brought together peoples who had theretofore never been part of the same political entity. As a result, after independence, some ethnic groups found themselves situated in political entities with which they did not

---

4. The colonial era had a big impact on Thailand even though it was not formally colonized by and placed under the direct rule of imperial powers. Thai rulers launched a concerted effort to forge a Thai national identity in the late nineteenth century, fearing that European powers would take advantage of the country's ethnic heterogeneity and chip away at the territories then under Thai control.

wish to be associated. The peoples of Bougainville, for example, were not and are not enthralled at the prospect of being part of Papua New Guinea. In other cases, colonial powers drew borders in ways that left ethnic groups divided by arbitrary lines.

Second, colonial powers often changed ethnic demographics by encouraging European settlement in the region and by bringing in foreign laborers from other parts of the region. British settlers consequently came to dominate political and economic life in Australia and New Zealand. In other parts of Asia and the Pacific, British colonial rulers opened up territories to immigration (often from China and India), and they brought in foreign laborers to work on plantations or in mines. As a result, large numbers of Tamils were brought from Tamil Nadu in India to Sri Lanka, large numbers of Indian workers were brought to Burma and Fiji, and Indian and Chinese workers were brought to Malaysia and Singapore. These influxes were of course resented by those with deeper roots in the areas in question. In some cases, post-independence authorities have taken radical steps to try to turn back the clock demographically and to ensure that colonial-era immigrants do not upset the local balance of power. In Sri Lanka, the post-independence government denied citizenship to many "Upcountry" Tamils who had come to the island during British colonial rule, and it took steps to force these immigrants to return to India. Since independence, Burmese governments have periodically pressured Indian immigrants to leave the country. The Fijian military seized power in a coup in 1987, fearing that an Indian-dominated cabinet was about to assume office. Since 1969, the Malaysian government has openly and aggressively worked to boost educational and economic opportunities for the country's Malays, who had come to be overshadowed economically by the Chinese minority.

Third, colonial powers had important effects on ethnic identities in the territories they ruled. For example, Spanish colonists arrived in the Philippines in the sixteenth century, bringing their crusade against Islam and the Moors with them. Their discovery of more "Moros" in the Philippines led to a three-hundred-year campaign that forged a Moro identity that had theretofore not existed in a sharply defined way. The arrival of British colonists in New Zealand ultimately led Maori to think of themselves as a group, not just disparate *iwi* (tribes).

Fourth, colonial powers also had important effects on inter-group relations in the lands they governed. Colonial rulers almost always favored some ethnic groups over others, which created grievances, intensified divisions, and begat problems with which post-colonial governments have had to contend. More specifically, colonial powers routinely employed "divide and rule" tactics that facilitated colonial administration and simultaneously fueled ethnic antagonisms. In some cases—Sri Lanka, for example—minorities were placed in positions of influence in order to help keep majorities in check. In Burma, colonial rule sharpened differences between the center and the periphery. In what eventually became Pakistan, Punjabis were placed in dominant positions in the military and in civilian bureaucracies. In the Philippines, Spanish authorities polarized religious differences and created rigid ethnic hierarchies. Inevitably, groups that thought they had received unfair treatment during colonial times sought redress after independence; they were especially eager to turn the tables if they were in the numerical majority. However, in Sri Lanka and Burma, for example, minorities became accustomed to being treated better than or at least as well as majorities; they were consequently not inclined to accept second-class status in the post-independence era. Finally, at a more general level, colonial rule tended to make political discourse more confrontational in character and more ethnic in orientation. Colonial rule generated anti-colonial movements that came to think in "us versus them" and ethnic terms; this way of thinking persevered after independence and came to be applied to in-country ethnic relations. As a result, ethnic politics became more combative.

Fifth, colonial rule brought new political systems and institutions to the territories they ruled, and in some places these systems and institutions have endured (albeit in modified form). This is not to say that Western political institutions now hold sway in every country once subjected to colonial rule; clearly, they do not. However, the rule of law—manifested in constitutions, bills of rights, and independent judiciaries—has taken root in some places, such as India, Sri Lanka, the Philippines, Papua New Guinea, and Vanuatu. From my parochial Western perspective, this is a positive development. At the same time, it is uncontestably true that colonial powers often left newly independent countries with weak political institutions, limited bureaucratic capacities, and insufficient numbers of proficient legislators, administrators, and judges. This is a pernicious colonial legacy that has undercut the ability of many governments to deal effectively with ethnic problems.

GROUP HISTORIES, FEARS, AND GOALS

Although governments play key roles in domestic political debates, they are of course not the only participants in these exercises. Different ethnic groups, which enjoy varying degrees of representation in governmental circles, bring their own histories, fears, and goals to these discussions.[5]

---

5. Studies that analyze the importance and dynamics of inter-group ethnic politics include Joseph Rothschild, *Ethnopolitics: A Conceptual Framework* (New York: Columbia

Over long periods of time, often dating back centuries, ethnic groups develop histories that include recollections and reconstructions of events; these include, in particular, recollections of interactions with other groups. As a general rule, groups glorify their own histories, and they tend to demonize former adversaries.[6] These historical legacies continue to influence group identities, attitudes, and policy agendas. Although many scholars have correctly argued that one should not rely entirely on "ancient hatreds" explanations of contemporary ethnic phenomena, there is no doubt that group histories, which are rarely filtered by dispassionate scholarship, play important roles in shaping contemporary perceptions.[7]

These group histories are particularly influential when governments weaken and individual groups begin to take steps to provide for their own security. Under these conditions, group histories provide frameworks for interpreting current events and for making extrapolations about uncertain and potentially difficult futures. When group histories are mutually antagonistic, as they often are, group decisions are likely to be based on worst-case ethnic scenarios. This can lead to military build-ups, which may be seen by others as offensive even if these steps are taken for defensive reasons. This, in turn, can lead to further escalatory actions and spirals of conflict. Security concerns based in part on historical references and in part on uncertain circumstances can lead groups to take steps that make difficult situations even worse.[8]

Even under comparatively stable circumstances, different ethnic groups have different goals and agendas. These goals and agendas constitute important parts of the ethnic settings with which governments, well-meaning and otherwise, have to contend.[9] Some groups have largely apolitical agendas; they simply seek religious freedom and an environ-

---

University Press, 1981); Donald L. Horowitz, *Ethnic Groups in Conflict* (Berkeley: University of California Press, 1985); Ted Robert Gurr and Barbara Harff, *Ethnic Conflict and World Politics* (Boulder, Colo.: Westview Press, 1994); Stephen Van Evera, "Hypotheses on Nationalism and War," *International Security*, Vol. 18, No. 4 (Spring 1994), pp. 5–39; Esman, *Ethnic Politics*.

6. See Jack Snyder, "Nationalism and the Crisis of the Post-Soviet State," and Barry R. Posen, "The Security Dilemma and Ethnic Conflict," both in Michael E. Brown, ed., *Ethnic Conflict and International Security* (Princeton, N.J.: Princeton University Press, 1993), pp. 79–101, 103–124; Van Evera, "Hypotheses on Nationalism and War."

7. For more discussion of the limitations and proper role of "ancient hatreds" theorizing, see Brown, "Introduction," in Brown, *The International Dimensions of Internal Conflict*, pp. 12–13, 20–22.

8. See Posen, "The Security Dilemma and Ethnic Conflict."

9. I would like to thank Steven Miller for suggesting this characterization of the problem.

ment in which their cultural survival will not be endangered. Others, more ambitiously, seek to end established patterns of social, economic, and political discrimination. Still others, frustrated by the inability of existing governmental bodies to address their needs and demands, seek more political autonomy. Groups that were brought under the control of central authorities against their will often seek a greater measure of self-government or outright political independence. Groups whose agendas include more regional autonomy, a higher degree of self-government, or secession pose inherent challenges to central authorities, and debates about autonomy questions are always contentious.

Group goals are not set in concrete. They evolve over time, in conjunction with the personal ambitions of group leaders who are often malignant characters and in response to the decisions, actions, and policies of the governments with which they are associated. In some cases, governmental actions are responsive to the concerns, needs, and demands of individual groups, and relations between the governments and groups in question stabilize and even improve. This seems to have happened, for example, in parts of India, where reorganizations of states, the devolution of more power to states, and progressive language laws have addressed concerns of groups in many parts of the country.[10] In Thailand, King Bhumipol has de-emphasized the Buddhist character of Thai nationalism, thereby making it easier for the country's Muslims to feel that they are indeed part of the Thai nation. In New Zealand, governments have taken steps to preserve Maori culture, address economic and social problems in the Maori community, and make reparations for past injustices.

In all too many cases, however, governments are indifferent to or unwilling to respond to the concerns, needs, and demands of ethnic minorities. In some cases, central authorities are unwilling to grant more autonomy to ethnic minorities because they fear that this will lead to secessionism and because they fear that other ethnic groups will be inspired to make similar demands. In other cases—and these are far from rare—governments respond to group demands with deliberate and sustained campaigns of discrimination and repression. This is a fair characterization, for example, of the Burmese government's policies toward the Karen, the Chinese government's policies toward Muslim and Tibetan minorities, Indonesian government actions in East Timor, and the Sri Lankan government's policies toward Tamils. When governments respond unconstructively or destructively to group demands, the outcome almost inevitably is the radicalization of group agendas. Groups become

---

10. The Indian government's policies towards Kashmir have been notably less successful.

increasingly convinced that their political, economic, and cultural needs cannot be met within the existing political order. Secession becomes the goal, and means become more violent. This is precisely what happened in Sri Lanka, where decades of government discrimination radicalized elements of the Tamil community and led the country into civil war. In 1995, the Liberation Tigers of Tamil Eelam (LTTE) rejected a proposal from the government that would have granted substantial amounts of regional autonomy to Tamil areas; the LTTE had become radicalized to a point where nothing short of complete political independence would be acceptable. One of the tragedies of this story is that, if the Sri Lankan government had been more willing to adopt such policies in the 1950s, 1960s, and 1970s, war almost certainly would not have broken out.

In short, governments play key roles in determining whether ethnic groups are likely to be radicalized or placated. Radicalization is dangerous and difficult to reverse, yet governments often push groups in this direction.

ECONOMIC FACTORS AND TRENDS

Economic factors and trends also shape ethnic settings, creating varied problems for governments along the way.[11] For starters, colonial rule is generally disruptive economically. Colonial governments introduce new forms of agriculture, start new industries, bring in foreign labor, and create new commercial and financial classes, which often break down along ethnic lines. These economic changes often intensify existing ethnic tensions and create new ones. In addition, colonial rulers do not always bequeath robust economies and strong economic infrastructures to post-independence leaders. Post-independence governments, therefore, generally have to cope with troublesome colonial economic legacies.

Obviously, countries at different stages of economic development have to contend with different kinds of economic problems. In industrialized countries or regions, public dissatisfaction can intensify even if economies are growing, if they are not growing as fast as they once were or fast enough to keep pace with societal demands. Countries in the process of making transitions from centrally planned to market-based systems usually have to contend with a host of economic problems, ranging from high levels of unemployment to rampant inflation. Countries that are in the process of modernizing have to contend with migra-

---

11. See S.W.R. de A. Samarasinghe and Reed Coughlan, eds., *Economic Dimensions of Ethnic Conflict* (London: Pinter, 1991). For a discussion of the economic sources of turmoil in South Asia, see Sandy Gordon, "Resources and Instability in South Asia," *Survival*, Vol. 35, No. 2 (Summer 1993), pp. 66–87.

tion, urbanization, and other social and economic dislocations. In addition, growing public demands and expectations in modernizing countries can overwhelm the capacities of political institutions to respond.[12] In multiethnic countries, these kinds of economic problems invariably have ethnic reverberations. Economic problems, regardless of their source, can aggravate existing ethnic tensions or generate new tensions, especially if they take place in a context where different ethnic groups have unequal economic burdens, different standards of living, and different economic opportunities, which is almost always the case. These tensions are often compounded by domestic elites, who, in campaigns designed to either preserve or enhance their own political positions, blame ethnic minorities for whatever economic difficulties their country may be experiencing.

Although economic booms can dampen ethnic tensions and reduce the potential for ethnic violence—as seen in Malaysia, Indonesia, Singapore, and Thailand, for example—economic growth is not a panacea. Indeed, economic booms can generate ethnic problems of their own. In Thailand, for example, the country's growing economy has attracted illegal immigrants from Burma, where good jobs are scarce. In Indonesia, the Chinese minority, which heads the business community, has benefitted disproportionately from the country's economic upswing. This has generated a great deal of resentment in other ethnic quarters. The economic boom in China has benefitted some regions more than others: coastal areas have prospered much more than remote interior areas, many of which are minority regions. This, of course, is resented in these minority areas. China's economic boom, moreover, was sparked by economic decentralization, which has led to a reduction in the center's control over remote minority areas. This has led to relaxed border controls, which have allowed outside money and arms to stream into minority areas. As a result, some minorities along China's periphery have growing capacities for independent action. The net effect of China's economic boom,

---

12. See Samuel P. Huntington, *Political Order in Changing Societies* (New Haven, Conn.: Yale University Press, 1968); Ted Robert Gurr, *Why Men Rebel* (Princeton, N.J.: Princeton University Press, 1970); Walker Conner, "Nation-Building or Nation-Destroying?" *World Politics*, Vol. 24, No. 3 (April 1972), pp. 319–355; Walker Conner, *Ethnonationalism: The Quest for Understanding* (Princeton, N.J.: Princeton University Press, 1994). For an overview of this literature, see Saul Newman, "Does Modernization Breed Ethnic Conflict?" *World Politics*, Vol. 43, No. 3 (April 1991), pp. 451–478; and Jack A. Goldstone, "Theories of Revolution: The Third Generation," *World Politics*, Vol. 32, No. 3 (April 1980), pp. 425–453. For critiques of this approach, see Charles Tilly, "Does Modernization Breed Revolution?" *Comparative Politics*, Vol. 5, No. 3 (April 1973), pp. 425–447; Rod Aya, "Theories of Revolution Reconsidered: Contrasting Models of Collective Violence," *Theory and Society*, Vol. 8, No. 1 (July 1979), pp. 1–38.

therefore, is that many of China's minorities are both more dissatisfied with the central government and more capable of pursuing their own political agendas.

Although economic factors and trends help to construct the ethnic settings within which governments operate, they should not be thought of as immutable facts of life. Governments make decisions about the kinds of economic systems that will be put into place as well as specific economic policies. Governments also make decisions about whether or not they will try to mitigate the impact of economic problems on affected ethnic communities. In sum, this is yet another area where governments have considerable influence over ethnic settings and how these settings evolve over time.

REGIONAL AND INTERNATIONAL INFLUENCES

Ethnic settings are also shaped by a range of regional and international factors. Regional influences are generally disruptive.[13] Ethnic groups often straddle international borders, which means that ethnic groups in borderlands can be agitated by developments in neighboring states—if ethnic compatriots are being persecuted, for example—and they can receive material and moral support from ethnic compatriots in neighboring states. For example, Karen rebels in Burma have received support from their ethnic kin in Thailand, and Muslims in China's Xinjiang province have received support from compatriots in Kazakhstan.

In addition, problems in neighboring states can generate refugee flows and trigger military incursions, which in turn can destabilize border regions. Refugees from Afghanistan have contributed to instability in parts of Pakistan, for example, and the Burmese military has made occasional forays into Thailand to root out Karen military bases and sanctuaries. Regional powers often meddle in the ethnic politics of other states for opportunistic reasons. India and Pakistan have a long history of doing this; Pakistan has supported insurgents in the Indian state of Kashmir, and the Indian government has supported rebels in Pakistan's Sindh province, the protestations of both governments to the contrary.

Stabilizing regional influences, such as mediation efforts and peace operations, are comparatively rare. India sent troops to Sri Lanka in the late 1980s in an effort to bring the civil war there to an end. This effort failed. India's motivations were not entirely altruistic, in any event; the

---

13. For more discussion of the regional dimensions of ethnic problems, see Michael E. Brown, "The Causes and Regional Dimensions of Internal Conflict," in Brown, *The International Dimensions of Internal Conflict,* pp. 590–601.

Indian government was worried that continued warfare in Sri Lanka could lead Tamils in the southern Indian state of Tamil Nadu to become radicalized. Papua New Guinea carried out a more successful operation to keep people in Santo from seceding from Vanuatu in 1980. But here, too, the intervenor's motivations were not entirely selfless; facing turmoil of its own in Bougainville, the Papua New Guinean government wanted to reinforce the idea that secession would not be tolerated in that part of the world.[14]

Although distant international powers and international organizations such as the United Nations are generally in a better position to marshall resources for economic and political development programs, mediation efforts, and peace operations, they often fail to do so. Leading international military powers—the United States, in particular—have been averse to direct involvement in ethnic conflicts in distant lands, and international peace operations, when they have been undertaken, have an uneven record.[15] Indeed, some of the steps that have been taken by international actors in the 1980s and 1990s, such as imposing economic and political conditions on financial assistance, have weakened state structures and undermined stability in many parts of the world.[16]

In short, regional influences on ethnic problems are generally pernicious, and the actions of more distant international actors can cut both ways.

INTERACTIONS BETWEEN SETTINGS AND POLICIES

Although the new governments of countries that are coming out from under colonial rule are in effect presented with an array of ethnic problems and challenges—an ethnic setting—these settings begin to change immediately in response to what governments do and do not do and in response to other internal and external developments. One should not

---

14. A study of the West African peacekeeping operation in Liberia shows that regional peacekeeping efforts are inherently problematic because the motivations of intervenors will always be suspect. See Herbert Howe, "Lessons of Liberia: ECOMOG and Regional Peacekeeping," *International Security*, Vol. 21, No. 3 (Winter 1996/97), pp. 145–176.

15. For more details on international peace operations in the first half of the 1990s, see Chantal de Jonge Oudraat, "The United Nations and Internal Conflict," and Michael E. Brown, "Internal Conflict and International Action," both in Brown, *The International Dimensions of Internal Conflict*, pp. 489–535, 603–627.

16. For a discussion of how international financial institutions have affected stability in Africa, see Stephen John Stedman, "Conflict and Conciliation in Sub-Saharan Africa," in Brown, *The International Dimensions of Internal Conflict*, pp. 235–265.

think of either settings or policies as static. Indeed, it is important to look at how they evolve and, in particular, how the two interact over time: settings influence policies, which in turn influence ethnic geography, group fears and political agendas, economic trends, and so on.

Among the most important processes to analyze are the ways in which governments precipitate the radicalization of group agendas. In many countries, groups that once had apolitical goals have come to adopt political agendas and to favor political autonomy and self-government as the solutions to their problems. In addition, as group goals have become more ambitious and contentious, groups have often become more willing to use violent means to realize their ends. Governments have enormous influence over the evolution of group agendas—through the broad policy goals they pursue, the policy instruments they employ, the policy patterns they create over time, the policy problems they fail to address, and the specific initiatives they launch in particular policy areas. It is to these policy parameters and policy areas that we now turn.

Policy Parameters

With these situational factors in mind, we can analyze four broad parameters that frame government policies with respect to ethnic issues: policy goals, policy instruments, policy patterns, and generic policy problems. I identify and distinguish between different kinds of policy goals, instruments, patterns, and problems; categorize actions that governments in Asia and the Pacific have taken; and analyze the impact these actions have had on ethnic relations in the countries in question.[17]

POLICY GOALS

National governments generally have the overarching goal of maintaining the political unity and territorial integrity of their countries.[18] However, different governments have very different ideas about the amount of ethnic diversity that can be tolerated in the short term, and they have very different visions of how their countries should be constituted ethnically in the long term. Governments generally have one of two basic ethnic visions of their countries: a unicultural vision, where the policy goal is assimilation and the creation of an ethnically grounded national

---

17. The policy recommendations that flow from this analysis will be presented at the end of this chapter.

18. Czechoslovakia's peaceful dissolution in 1993 is a notable exception in this regard.

identity;[19] or a multicultural vision, where the policy goal is maintenance of political unity while preserving ethnic and cultural diversity.[20]

Unicultural visions are often favored for a combination of demographic, strategic, and parochial political reasons. Countries that are dominated demographically by one ethnic group are often guided by governments with unicultural visions; China and the Philippines are examples. Some governments argue, often with justification, that their countries face external threats to national security that behoove them to forge a strong national identity and a common front. For example, British and French colonial expansion in Southeast Asia in the late nineteenth century was the impetus behind the Thai monarchy's drive to create a Thai national identity. The Chinese government argued in the 1950s that external security threats obligated it to adopt assimilationist policies, especially with respect to minorities in border regions. Governments often argue that national identities have to be created and assimilationist agendas have to be adopted in order to forge national identities, maintain political unity, and preserve the territorial integrity of their states. This has been the main justification for assimilationist policies in Pakistan, Burma, and Indonesia, for example. Some governments have unicultural visions that seem to be based mainly on preponderant majorities acting out of a sense of entitlement. Authorities in Australia pursued unicultural visions and assimilationist policies until the late 1960s, and governments in New Zealand did the same until the early 1970s. Since the late 1960s, the Malaysian government has worked energetically to forge a national identity based on Malay linguistic, religious, and cultural traditions. Governments in the Philippines had assimilationist agendas until the mid-1980s (with respect to hill peoples) and until the 1990s (with respect to the Moros). Governments in Sri Lanka embraced unicultural precepts until the mid-1990s. The government of Singapore claims to have a multicultural and multiracial vision of the country, but its assimilationist

---

19. The term "unicultural" is admittedly problematic in this context. Some governments are willing to allow ethnic groups to preserve some cultural traditions even though central authorities are determined to form ethnically grounded national identities through assimilationist policies. Governments in Thailand, for example, have worked since the late nineteenth century to forge a Thai national identity; at the same time, they have allowed ethnic minorities to preserve some aspects of their cultures as long as the groups in question do not pursue political agendas of their own.

20. Categorizing the ethnic visions and broad goals of governments is easy in some cases. In others, this kind of exercise is more difficult: the goals of some governments do not fit easily into either category; some governments have different goals with respect to different ethnic groups; and their visions and goals change over time. These problems should be kept in mind, but they are not barriers to analysis.

policy agenda is shaped by the fact that the Chinese community dominates political and economic life in the country.[21]

Unicultural visions are also favored because they serve parochial political interests. Many governments are run by one or more ethnic groups who want to stay in power, which means keeping other groups out of power; who want and need to maintain the support of their ethnic constituents; and who do not care about or want to help other ethnic groups or minorities.[22] Unicultural visions resonate well with such governments; many of Pakistan's regimes, for example, fit this description. Unicultural visions also provide politically presentable rationales—protecting national security and promoting political unity—for strong central rule, and they provide excuses to crack down on ethnic and other dissidents. Governments in Burma, China, Indonesia, Malaysia, Pakistan, and the Philippines have embraced unicultural visions for these reasons. In each of these cases, unicultural precepts worked to the political advantage of central authorities who wanted to maintain their hold on power.

Other governments, however, are either more tolerant of ethnic diversity or more resigned to diversity as a fact of life in their countries. Some go far to preserve cultural and ethnic diversity. Some are aware of and sensitive to ethnic problems, and are interested in making good-faith efforts to promote political, economic, and social justice. One could say that such governments have multicultural visions of their countries. Governments in India, the Federated States of Micronesia, Papua New Guinea, and Vanuatu have embraced this view. Other governments, over time, began to abandon unicultural visions and adopt multicultural orientations: Australia beginning in the late 1960s; New Zealand beginning in the early 1970s; the Philippines with respect to hill tribes beginning in the mid-1980s and with respect to Moros beginning in the mid-1990s; and Sri Lanka beginning in the mid-1990s.

Ethnic visions and broad policy goals changed in four of the sixteen countries studied in this volume: unicultural visions were abandoned in Australia, New Zealand, the Philippines, and Sri Lanka. In only one of these cases, Australia, can the policy shift be traced to major changes in ethnic demographics; due to labor shortages, Australian governments began to relax immigration laws after World War II. This led to an influx

---

21. Since the military takeover in 1987, the main goal of the Fijian government has been to keep Fijians in power politically and thriving culturally. The government therefore shares some priorities with hard-line uniculturalists, although cultural assimilation per se is not a top priority.

22. I would like to thank Ron May for suggesting this characterization of the problem.

of non-British immigrants and ultimately transformed a largely homogeneous society into a much more heterogeneous one. In each of the other three cases, unicultural visions were abandoned because leaders came to realize that unicultural agendas were politically unsustainable or unjust. In the Philippines and Sri Lanka, the inability of central authorities to quell rebellions among Moros and Tamils, respectively, ultimately led new central governments to pursue fundamentally different ethnic visions and policy goals.

Decisions about ethnic visions are obviously influenced by situational factors such as ethnic geography. However, the correlation between ethnic geography and ethnic visions is far from perfect. Many countries with high levels of ethnic diversity (Burma, Indonesia, Malaysia, Pakistan, Sri Lanka) have governments that have embraced unicultural visions for long periods of time. Political leaders play key roles in deciding on ethnic visions and shaping specific policy goals. Their perceptions of external threats to national security, internal threats to political unity, and long-term national needs—in conjunction with their own political ambitions and agendas—are often decisive in determining the ethnic visions they will embrace and the policy goals they will pursue.

POLICY INSTRUMENTS

We can now turn to governmental actions—the plans governments make and the instruments they employ to translate ethnic visions into reality. In broad terms, we can distinguish between policies based primarily on coercion and policies based primarily on inducement.[23]

Coercive instruments include legal prohibitions, political repression, the use of economic repression, the imposition of martial law, and the use of military force. Australian governments relied heavily on coercive instruments in their treatment of Aborigines, at least until the late 1960s; Aboriginal land was confiscated, laws on association and movement were put into place, and Aboriginal families were forcibly broken up. Governments in Burma, civilian and military, have relied on the use of military force in their dealings with the Karen and the Shan, in particular, and Rohingyas (Indian Muslims living mainly in Arakan) have been harassed into fleeing to Bangladesh on several

---

23. Categorizing policy instruments is easy in some cases. In others, this kind of exercise is more difficult: all governments employ combinations of coercive and persuasive instruments; some government employ different instruments with respect to different ethnic groups; and governments favor different types of instruments at different times.

occasions.[24] Communist Chinese governments, being fundamentally authoritarian in character, have depended on coercion as a basic instrument of governance in all aspects of domestic affairs, but especially in their handling of Muslim and Tibetan minorities and areas. The authoritarian regimes in Indonesia, Malaysia, and Singapore have also depended on coercion as a matter of course; the Indonesian government's crackdowns on ethnic groups in Aceh, East Timor, and Irian Jaya stand out even against this coercive backdrop.[25] Governments in Pakistan and Sri Lanka have repeatedly used military force in disputes with ethnic minorities. India has used military force against rebels in Kashmir, the Northeast, and Punjab; Papua New Guinea has done the same in Bougainville; and governments in Manila relied on economic coercion and military force in their dealings with hill tribes and the Moros. The military coup in Fiji in 1987 marked a shift in that country to policies based on coercion.

Policies based on inducement rely primarily on persuasion, co-optation, and the extension of political, economic, and educational opportunities. As a general rule, inducement has been relied on by governments in the Federated States of Micronesia, New Zealand, Thailand, and Vanuatu. It has also been favored in India and Papua New Guinea (with the exceptions noted above), and it has been the main mode of engagement in Australian policy with respect to Aborigines since the late 1960s and in Philippine policy towards hill tribes (since the mid-1980s) and the Moros (since the mid-1990s).

Coercion is often favored as a policy instrument in the ethnic arena. Authoritarian regimes, by definition, depend on the use of coercion and force, and they are rarely hesitant to use it against what they see as ethnic troublemaking. Even in non-authoritarian settings, coercion and military force are often seen as quick and permanent solutions to ethnic problems, especially when problems drag on or intensify. The track record suggests, however, that coercive instruments rarely produce quick or permanent settlements to such problems. Military clashes with ethnic minorities often degenerate into slugfests that last for decades: Burman governments have been fighting Karen rebels since the late 1940s; Philippine governments fought Moro rebels from the early 1970s until the mid-1990s; and

---

24. The Burmese government's treatment of other groups (the Arakanese, Chins, and Mon, for example) has been more of a mixed bag. The government has sought to seek accommodation with some groups so that it could concentrate its coercive energies on the Karen and the Shan.

25. R. William Liddle points out that the Indonesian government has also utilized co-optation and persuasive policy instruments in its treatment of some ethnic groups. The Indonesian case is not clear-cut. See his chapter on Indonesia in this volume.

civil war has raged in Sri Lanka since the early 1980s. In addition, whenever governments employ coercive instruments, ethnic groups become more radicalized, and the prospects for political accommodation and conflict resolution consequently dim. Sadly but inevitably, governments usually take a long time to admit publicly that their highly expensive (in financial, political, and human terms) coercive efforts have failed. Indeed, many governments are never able to take this step: it often takes a change in government—such as Fidel Ramos's ascension to power in the Philippines in 1992 or Chandrika Kumaratunge's electoral victory in Sri Lanka in 1994—before mistakes can be acknowledged, sunk costs can be set aside, and peace initiatives can be launched.

POLICY PATTERNS

Drawing on the foregoing, we can link policy goals and policy instruments in an integrated framework—which can be depicted as a two-by-two matrix—and we can categorize actions that governments in Asia and the Pacific have taken with respect to ethnic issues and groups.[26] (See Table 13.3.) We can then go on to analyze the impact these actions have had on ethnic relations in the countries in question.

Governments that (a) have unicultural visions of their countries and (b) rely primarily on coercive policy instruments, can be characterized as engaging in forced assimilation. By and large, these policies have failed to accomplish what governments had hoped they would accomplish: cultural assimilation, social integration, and political stability. Decades of aggressive assimilationist efforts in Pakistan have led to secession in the east and continued turmoil in the west. Burmese leaders fought Shan and Karen rebels for decades and failed to bring them to their knees; the government struck a deal with drug warlord Khun Sa and the Shan rebels in 1995, but the war with the Karen is moving towards its sixth decade. The Indonesian government has failed to stamp out rebellions in Aceh, East Timor, and Irian Jaya. The central government in China has flooded Tibet and Xinjiang with large numbers of Han Chinese, bringing these provinces more into Beijing's orbit in some respects, but true assimilation has not taken place and political instability in these regions is likely to increase as China moves into the post–Deng Xiaoping era. Successive

---

26. Categorizing policies is easy in some cases. In others, it is more difficult. Some governments (Fiji, for example) pursue policy goals that are difficult to capture in this framework, and all governments employ combinations of coercive and persuasive instruments. In addition, as noted above, governments often have different policies for different ethnic groups, and policies change over time. Some of these distinctions are reflected in the entries in Table 13.3. A similar analytic framework is developed in Esman, *Ethnic Politics*, pp. 259–260.

Table 13.3. Policy Patterns.

	Persuasive Instruments	Coercive Instruments
Unicultural Goals	*Induced Assimilation*	*Forced Assimilation*
	Australia (immigrants)	Australia (Aborigines,
	Burma (Mon, Arakanese)	until 1960s)
	New Zealand (until 1970s)	Burma (Karen, Shan)
	Philippines (Chinese immigrants)	China (Tibetans, Muslims)
	Thailand	Indonesia
		Malaysia
		Pakistan
		Philippines (hill peoples
		until mid-1980s; Moros
		until 1996)
		Singapore
		Sri Lanka (until 1994)
Multicultural Goals	*Benign Accommodation*	*Toleration with Attitude*
	Australia (Aborigines, since 1960s)	India (Kashmir)
	Federated States of Micronesia	Papua New Guinea
	India (on religion, language)	(Bougainville)
	New Zealand (since 1970s)	
	Papua New Guinea	
	Philippines (hill peoples since mid-	
	1980s; Moros since 1996)	
	Sri Lanka (since 1994)	
	Vanuatu	

governments in the Philippines tried to flood Moro areas with Christian Filipinos and crush Moro rebels militarily. This decades-long effort failed to either eliminate rebel forces or win over Moro hearts and minds. In the end, the government changed course and offered the Moros a regional autonomy package. Similarly, the Sri Lankan government failed to defeat Tamil rebels after more than a decade of civil war. In the end, it, too, changed course and offered insurgents a political settlement that featured regional autonomy arrangements. Australian governments never faced a sustained, armed uprising from Aborigines, but decades of cruel assimilation policies failed to produce true assimilation. In fact, these policies compounded many of the social and economic problems in Aboriginal communities that assimilation was supposed to solve.[27] In sum, assimilation is, by itself, a highly contentious undertaking that threatens ethnic

27. Malaysia and Singapore have not had to contend with full-blown ethnic rebellions, but minorities remain deeply dissatisfied with the assimilationist policies that have been imposed on them.

minorities with political diminishment and cultural extinction. Utilizing coercive policy instruments compounds the problem by radicalizing minorities and stiffening resistance. Coercion also radicalizes ethnic majorities and makes compromise more difficult; many Sinhalese opposed the peace initiatives launched by Sri Lankan leader Chandrika Kumaratunge in the mid-1990s. Unless overwhelming force is used against small, weak, isolated minorities (Tibetans, Aboriginal Australians), long military conflicts are likely to result. To be successful, assimilationist policies ultimately have to be based on political accommodation; the use of coercive instruments makes accommodations harder—not easier—to obtain.

Governments that (a) have unicultural visions of their countries and (b) rely primarily on persuasive policy instruments, can be characterized as engaging in induced assimilation. By and large, these policies have been much more successful than their coercive counterparts in bringing about cultural assimilation, social integration, and political stability. Thailand has been successful in forging a strong national identity while allowing for a measure of non-political cultural diversity. Burmese governments have successfully co-opted many ethnic minorities (Mon and Arakanese, for example), which shows that even autocrats are capable of pursuing comparatively constructive policies. Although Chinese immigrants to the Philippines were often treated harshly under Spanish colonial rule, Chinese Filipinos have now assimilated into the Philippine mainstream to a very great degree. Immigrants to Australia have also assimilated into mainstream political, economic, and social life. In sum, policies based on induced assimilation have a comparatively good track record in bringing about high levels of assimilation and in keeping political violence to low levels. There is a case to be made that induced assimilation is more effective than forced assimilation both in the short run and in the long run.

Governments that (a) have multicultural visions of their countries and (b) rely primarily on persuasive policy instruments, can be characterized as engaging in benign accommodation. These policies have been largely successful in striking a balance between the preservation of cultural diversity, on the one hand, and maintaining national unity and political stability, on the other. The Indian government's sustained commitment to conciliatory policies on religion and language, in particular, have been successful in dampening many potential ethnic conflicts. The Indian government's track record is far from perfect and post-independence India's history has had tumultuous periods, to be sure, but one can safely say that India's history would have been far more tumultuous—and might have already come to a cataclysmic end—if these policies had not been pursued. Although the jury is still out on whether or not the Federated States of Micronesia, Papua New Guinea, and Vanuatu will survive in their current forms, their governments' conscientious tolerance of ethnic diversity has maximized their chances for survival while keeping political violence to comparatively low levels. The shifts away from efforts to assimilate indigenous people in Australia and New Zealand in the late 1960s and early 1970s, respectively, have already produced significant, positive results. The many social and economic problems that plagued Australian Aborigines and New Zealand Maori are now being addressed more seriously than in times past. It is still too early to tell if the dramatic policy shifts in Sri Lanka and the Philippines—from forced assimilation to benign accommodation of Tamils and Moros, respectively—will bring to an end the violent conflicts that have torn these countries for many years. The signs are encouraging in the Philippines, where government overtures and regional autonomy proposals have been accepted by leading figures in the Moro community. In Sri Lanka, the government's new, accommodationist posture constitutes a major step that could lead to a reconciliation between the Sinhalese and moderate Tamil communities. Whether or not Tamil extremists can be co-opted or defeated on the battlefield remains an open question. The key to successful accommodationist policies seems to be a serious, sustained effort on the part of the government in question. Durable cultural, economic, and political accommodations cannot be reached overnight, especially in countries that have legacies of ethnic discrimination or ethnic violence. India's long-standing commitments to secularism, multilingualism, and political devolution, and Australia's and New Zealand's decades-long efforts to establish better relations with their indigenous peoples are good examples of the kinds of sustained efforts that governments have to make if they want to reach true and durable accommodations with minority peoples.

Finally, governments that (a) have multicultural visions of their countries and (b) occasionally rely on coercive policy instruments, can be characterized as pursuing "toleration with attitude." At first glance, this combination of policy goals and policy instruments might seem to be incompatible. How can governments pursue a multicultural vision, which implies toleration of ethnic diversity, and utilize coercive policy instruments at the same time? How can toleration and coercion coexist? The answer is that governments in some countries—India and Papua New Guinea, for example—are deeply committed to multicultural precepts but they are also deeply committed to maintaining viable states. If necessary, they are willing to use force to keep ethnic groups from seceding, which could trigger a chain reaction and lead other groups to secede.

Such a process could lead to the disintegration of the state. It is largely because of such fears that Port Moresby is determined to keep Bougainville in Papua New Guinea and New Delhi is determined to keep Kashmir in India. New Delhi is particularly adamant about keeping Kashmir in India, because India was founded on the idea that it would be and could be a multiethnic, secular state. If Kashmir were to secede, one of the founding principles of the Indian state would be undercut. The main problem with pursuing "toleration with attitude" is that, even in countries committed to multicultural visions, the use of military force is highly problematic. It radicalizes the minorities who are being coerced when accommodation is what is needed in the long run. Even in settings such as these, the use of force compounds existing ethnic problems and makes long-term political accommodation more difficult.

One of the troubling conclusions that flows from this analysis is that if governments do indeed tend to favor both unicultural visions (for national unity reasons as well as parochial political reasons) and coercive instruments (because of authoritarian impulses or misguided beliefs about the efficacy of force), then there is a tendency for governments to favor forced assimilation—the most violence-prone and arguably most unsuccessful policy option—over other policy packages.[28]

POLICY PROBLEMS

Government policies with respect to ethnic issues are often plagued by three sets of generic problems: timing problems, implementation problems, and political dilemmas that undercut the effectiveness of government action.

TIMING PROBLEMS. Governments are often slow to respond to ethnic problems because leaders are preoccupied with other matters, because leaders believe that ethnic problems are not pressing, or because the ethnic groups in question are not politically influential. Thai governments paid comparatively little attention to hill tribes in the north and northeast until external security problems focused their attention in the 1950s. Governments in Australia and New Zealand neglected problems faced by indigenous communities for decades. Governmental neglect of ethnic problems in Pakistan led to secession in 1971 and continued ethnic turmoil in what remained of the Pakistani state. Similarly, governmental

---

28. This should be thought of as a hypothesis that requires further investigation. The set of cases examined in this volume is too small to constitute a definitive test of this proposition.

mistreatment of and unresponsiveness to Tamils in Sri Lanka ultimately led to ethnic radicalization and violence. Governments in China and Indonesia have mainly been worried about holding their countries together and consolidating control over peripheral areas; assuaging minority groups in remote areas has not been a priority. Since the late 1960s, Malaysian governments have been focused on elevating the economic and educational status of the country's numerically dominant Malay population; pacifying the country's Chinese and Indian minorities has been, at best, a secondary concern. Even India, which has a good track record in many respects, has been slow to respond to some regional and religious problems. In short, getting governments to pay attention to and engage on ethnic issues is a widespread problem.

Governments are most likely to act on ethnic problems only when they have to act. External security threats, real and imagined, can focus the attention of policymakers on the need to consolidate control over peripheral areas. This was one of the driving forces behind the Chinese government's actions in Tibet and Xinjiang in the 1950s, and, as noted, it impelled Thai governments to pay more attention to hill tribe areas in the north and northeastern parts of the country in the 1950s. Economic problems can also motivate governments to address long-standing but theretofore neglected ethnic problems. Authorities in New Zealand, for example, stepped up efforts in the 1980s to settle Maori claims to resource-rich lands, forests, fisheries, and even broadcasting frequencies because these unsettled claims interfered with government efforts to sell off government assets and privatize the economy. More commonly, governments wait until ethnic crises develop. Unfortunately, in times of crisis—when fears are great, groups are radicalized, time is short, economic resources are limited, and political institutions are weak—mistakes are more likely, options are more limited, governments are more likely to resort to force, and the probabilities of success are consequently lower. Put another way, governments are most likely to address ethnic problems when they are most likely to fail.

Conversely, governments are least likely to act when ethnic problems are small and comparatively solvable.[29] When state institutions are strong, central authorities do not feel threatened by ethnic problems. When economies are booming, ethnic groups are often quiescent because they do not want to rock the economic boat. Under these conditions, governments rarely feel compelled to tackle difficult, latent ethnic problems. As a result, governments often miss windows of opportunity created by

---

29. See Horowitz, *Ethnic Groups in Conflict*, p. 684.

robust institutional capacities and periods of economic growth. The governments that can afford to address ethnic problems are also the governments that can afford to ignore them.

Continued neglect, however, usually leads to worse ethnic problems and the radicalization of ethnic groups, which in turn leads governments to act coercively when they finally get around to acting. Conflicts then escalate. Governmental neglect and delay are often the precursors of ethnic violence.

IMPLEMENTATION PROBLEMS. Implementation problems are, of course, common in all policy areas. As far as ethnic issues are concerned, three main implementation problems stand out.[30] First, leaders and governments are often insincere when they express concern about ethnic problems and when they launch policy initiatives, often with great fanfare, to address these problems. In cases such as these, leaders and governments are only interested in creating the impression that they care about ethnic problems, hoping to mollify domestic or international audiences. Their hope is that rhetorical flourishes and grandiose pronouncements will substitute for real action. Burmese and Chinese governments have made repeated, solemn pledges to respect minority rights, for example, but their actions belie their words.

Second, even when intentions are sincere, policy initiatives often fail to receive sustained, high-level attention. Without sustained engagement on the part of top officials, policy initiatives usually flounder. For example, after the fall of Ferdinand Marcos in the Philippines in 1986, new constitutional provisions designed to provide more regional autonomy to and protect the ancestral homelands of tribal peoples were passed; in 1989, enabling legislation was drafted, but in 1996 it was still languishing, unpassed, in a congressional committee. Tribal Filipinos, who constitute only three percent of the total population, were unable to keep high-level attention focused on this issue.

Third, even when high-level attention is focused on the issue at hand, limited institutional capacities and resource constraints can undercut implementation efforts. In countries coming out from under colonial rule and struggling to develop politically and economically, cases of institutional and resource constraints abound. One example from the Philippines will suffice for our present purposes. In 1957, a Commission on National Integration was set up and given powers to, *inter alia*, set up schools for and provide financial assistance to Moros and tribal peoples.

---

30. Implementation problems in specific policy areas will be discussed later in this chapter.

However, the commission was given only a small budget, and it consequently accomplished little. It was disbanded in 1975.

When policy initiatives are not implemented, partially implemented, or implemented in a delayed fashion, the ethnic problems they were meant to address fester and the ethnic groups they were meant to pacify become more resentful and radicalized with the passage of time. Equally important, implementation problems undermine governments' credibility, which is hard to reconstitute once lost. As a result, governments are even less able to engage ethnic groups constructively later on.

POLITICAL DILEMMAS. In multiethnic societies, governments are never ethnically neutral policy machines. Governments are constituted of individuals who have ethnic affiliations, and the composition of any given government may or may not reflect the ethnic composition of that country's population as a whole. Along with ethnic affiliations come ethnic constituencies. One of the most difficult political dilemmas faced by governmental leaders in multiethnic societies is the tension that almost always exists between the need to serve and reward constituents, on the one hand, and the needs and demands of other ethnic groups, on the other.[31] Leaders and governments are generally preoccupied with the former, which is the key to staying in power, at the expense of taking steps to deal equitably and effectively with other ethnic groups and other ethnic problems. As a result, short-term political preoccupations can generate and aggravate long-term ethnic problems, which become increasingly formidable as time goes by.

Inevitably but unfortunately, when leaders and governments do turn their attention to ethnic problems, they favor what they hope will be quick fixes to these problems: solemn declarations of concern, grand pronouncements, dramatic policy initiatives, and the use of coercive policy instruments, including military force. As discussed above, the use of coercive instruments and military force is often counterproductive: in addition to failing to provide the desired quick and permanent fix to existing ethnic problems, it intensifies and prolongs ethnic confrontations. The usual outcome is not political order and social harmony, but continued, violent strife. Leaders and governments often find out, to their dismay, that escalation is easy and de-escalation is hard—especially in the arena of ethnic conflict. Thoughtful leaders and governments discover, more generally, that there are no quick fixes to most ethnic problems. Therefore, if governments are serious about addressing ethnic problems,

---

31. I would like to thank Sidney Jones for suggesting this characterization of the problem.

they need to make sustained efforts and long-term, even open-ended, policy commitments. This, however, is incompatible with the short-term political priorities of leaders and governments.

In sum, the political dilemmas inherent in multiethnic societies—the tension between the need to serve ethnic constituents and the need to address the problems of other ethnic groups; the tension between the appeal of short-term solutions and the requirement to address ethnic problems through sustained, long-term action—help to explain why governments often fail to address ethnic problems effectively.[32]

Policy Areas

With this general framework in mind, we turn to government policies in eight specific areas: democratic and authoritarian political systems, federal and centralized political systems, citizenship policies, civil and minority rights policies, language policies, policies on religion and religious groups, education policies, and economic policies. I identify the policy initiatives and programs in each area that have had significant effects—good or bad—on ethnic relations and problems, and account for these policy successes and failures. Because policies that work well in one place at one particular point in time do not necessarily work well under other conditions, I describe the conditions under which policies succeeded and failed. I also put forward some policy recommendations in each of these areas as this section of the chapter unfolds.

My overarching recommendation is that governments should try to dampen ethnic tensions by trying to depoliticize ethnicity. In practical terms, this means establishing and maintaining the rule of law; favoring civic over ethnic conceptions of nationalism and citizenship; favoring broad civil rights protections over specific minority rights initiatives; supporting secularism over the establishment of official state religions; respecting linguistic diversity and promoting multilingualism; and building broad-based consensus for preferential and affirmative action policies in the educational and economic arenas. Obviously, authoritarian regimes are unlikely to promote the rule of law, and leaders who have ethnic axes to grind are unlikely to favor ethnically neutral policies. However, leaders who want to address ethnic problems constructively—that is, in a way that will promote both stability and harmony between and among ethnic groups—should strive to depoliticize ethnicity.

---

32. As Donald Horowitz observes, when it comes to dealing effectively with many ethnic questions, "the problems are not intellectual but political." See Horowitz, *Ethnic Groups in Conflict*, p. 684.

DEMOCRATIC VERSUS AUTHORITARIAN SYSTEMS

Although we would like to think that all good things go together, democracies often do a poor job of managing ethnic tensions in multiethnic societies.[33] Fiji and Sri Lanka have been deeply troubled democracies. Although India has strong democratic traditions, its post-independence history has not been trouble-free. The democratically elected government in Papua New Guinea was unable to prevent a rebellion in Bougainville from breaking out, and it has been unable to bring the rebellion to an end. Democratically elected governments in Australia caused and then ignored terrible problems in Aboriginal communities. Democratically elected leaders in New Zealand were slow to respond to widespread social and economic problems in Maori communities.

There is no doubt that democracies have weaknesses when it comes to addressing ethnic problems. When ethnic groups are small, weak, and not prone to violence, they can be mistreated and their grievances can be ignored by authorities for very long periods of time. This is what happened to Aborigines in Australia and Maori in New Zealand, for example. Another problem is that elections often generate incentives to play "the ethnic card," which in turn can polarize societies. Politicians make overt appeals to particular ethnic groups, promising to advance specific ethnic agendas. This can lead to bidding wars between and among politicians, each trying to outdo the other and win the support of the groups in question. Since promises to one group frequently work to the detriment of other groups, polarization results. This is what happened in Sri Lanka in the 1950s, 1960s, and 1970s. Bidding wars among politicians desperately seeking Sinhalese votes led to the Sinhalese agenda being pushed ever more aggressively and at the expense of Tamil concerns. The result was ethnic polarization, radicalization of the Tamil community, and ultimately civil war. In some cases, ethnic minorities are singled out and

33. For thoughtful discussions of the problems experienced by democracies in multiethnic societies, see Arend Lijphart, *Democracy in Plural Societies* (New Haven, Conn.: Yale University Press, 1977); Horowitz, *Ethnic Groups in Conflict*, especially chaps. 7–10; Larry Diamond and Marc F. Plattner, eds., *Nationalism, Ethnic Conflict, and Democracy* (Baltimore, Md.: Johns Hopkins University Press, 1994); Human Rights Watch, *Playing the "Communal Card": Communal Violence and Human Rights* (New York: Human Rights Watch, 1995); Saul Newman, *Ethnoregional Conflict in Democracies* (Westport, Conn.: Greenwood Press, 1996), especially chaps. 1, 7; Timothy D. Sisk, *Power Sharing and International Mediation in Ethnic Conflicts* (Washington, D.C.: U.S. Institute of Peace Press, 1996), especially chap. 3. See also Donald L. Horowitz, "Making Moderation Pay: The Comparative Politics of Ethnic Conflict Management," and Arend Lijphart, "The Power-Sharing Approach," both in Joseph V. Montville, ed., *Conflict and Peacemaking in Multiethnic Societies* (Lexington, Mass.: Lexington Books, 1990), pp. 451–475, 491–509.

blamed for whatever ills the country may be experiencing: politicians play to and fan ethnic fears as a way of winning electoral support. In India, for example, Hindu extremists raise the specter of Islamic hordes besieging the country on all sides. Some Fijian politicians play to Fijian fears of their country being taken over, ironically, by Indian immigrants. These kinds of ethnic appeals can be troublesome in the short term, but more importantly, they can lead to ethnic polarization, radicalization, and violence in the long-term.[34]

However, the track record for democracies in dealing with ethnic problems is quite good in important respects. Democracies provide mechanisms for ethnic groups, large and small, to participate in the formation of governments, be represented in decision-making circles, and to have influence over policy. Democracies can thereby address ethnic concerns and reduce the likelihood that ethnic groups will conclude that they have to resort to violence. In India, for example, democratic and secular traditions have helped to keep Hindu-Muslim tensions to manageable levels most of the time. Democratic forms of governance have clearly helped to dampen latent ethnic tensions in the Federated States of Micronesia, Papua New Guinea, and Vanuatu. In the Philippines, the return of democracy made a settlement with the Moros possible: regional autonomy arrangements were more likely to produce true autonomy, which the Moros demanded, if democracy and the rule of law were in place in the country as a whole. Democracies also provide mechanisms for people to express their displeasure with policies that are failing and to chart new, more constructive policy courses. In Australia and New Zealand, public pressure helped to bring about changes in policies towards indigenous peoples. In Sri Lanka, public exhaustion with war led to elections in 1994 and a new government committed to negotiating with Tamil rebels; the new government subsequently launched a peace initiative. At a more general level, democracies are comparatively transparent systems, which means that the fear of the unknown is reduced for ethnic minorities. Democracies also have high levels of public debate and political interaction between and among ethnic groups; this provides mechanisms for conciliation and conflict resolution.[35]

Authoritarian regimes, on the other hand, are often able to repress and control ethnic dissidents in the short run. Malaysia and Singapore,

---

34. These problems—ignoring weak minority groups, making ethnic appeals, and blaming minorities for economic and social problems—are not unique to democracies; authoritarian leaders also engage in this kind of political behavior. I would like to thank Chantal de Jonge Oudraat for making this point.

35. I would like to thank Stephen Stedman for suggesting this point.

for example, have been comparatively placid even though they have been governed by authoritarian regimes for decades. Some Asian officials have argued that the "Asian way," which values social order over individual liberty and which therefore features strong central rule, is one of the reasons why many countries in the region have been comparatively peaceful and prosperous. Critics would respond that this is simply a smokescreen for authoritarian rule; that many countries in the region (Burma, China, Indonesia, Pakistan, the Philippines) have experienced high levels of violence not just in spite of but because of strong central rule; and that authoritarian systems have structural problems that create serious stability problems in the long run. Authoritarian systems, by definition, keep some groups from the corridors of power and, again by definition, they rely heavily on repression, coercion, and the use of force to maintain domestic political hegemony. As discussed above, repression and suppression lead ethnic groups to adopt radical agendas and militant postures. Radicalization and militancy are very difficult to reverse, which means that suppressed groups generally lash out when central authorities weaken and action becomes possible.

In China, for example, economic decentralization has already led to weaker border controls and a rise in ethnic activism in Muslim and Tibetan areas. Centrifugal forces could intensify as the post–Deng Xiao-ping era unfolds. Suharto's authoritarian regime has maintained order in Indonesia since 1966, but there are signs that ethnic conflict is on the rise, and not just in chronic troublespots such as Aceh, East Timor, and Irian Jaya. Suharto's embrace of Islam has aggravated tensions between Mus-lims and Christians, and there is widespread disenchantment with the regime's favoritism towards Sino-Indonesians, who have benefitted dis-proportionately from the country's economic boom. These problems will probably intensify when Suharto passes from Indonesia's political scene, especially if economic growth rates plummet from the high altitudes at which they have flown for many years. Malaysia is another country where authoritarian rule has benefitted from economic pacifier effects. It is a safe bet that the country's Chinese and Indian minorities, who have born the brunt of the government's aggressive, pro-Malay affirmative action poli-cies, will be more outspoken in their criticism of the government if and when the boom busts. In short, even if authoritarian systems successfully suppress ethnic problems in the short run, they only compound them in the long run. To paraphrase Winston Churchill, democracy is the worst possible form of governance in multiethnic countries—except for all the others.

Although a systematic discussion of the trials and tribulations of democratic and authoritarian systems is beyond the scope of his book, two additional issues merit attention: the importance of constitutional frameworks, and the relative merits of consociational and integrative institutions in multiethnic, democratic settings.

CONSTITUTIONAL FRAMEWORKS. In theory, constitutions frame and guide governmental behavior. In many countries, of course, constitutions have little or no impact on governmental actions. Authoritarian regimes create constitutional documents mainly for public relations purposes. In countries where military coups have taken place (Fiji, Pakistan, and Thailand, for example) constitutional provisions have been in effect only intermittently. In short, constitutions are often of little consequence. There is frequently a huge gap between theory and practice.

Constitutions can make a difference, however. Countries with strong constitutional and rule-of-law traditions have generally done a good job of maintaining ethnic peace and harmony. The Federated States of Micronesia, Papua New Guinea, New Zealand, and Vanuatu all have strong constitutions and, with the exception of the Bougainville rebellion in Papua New Guinea, all have been islands of ethnic tranquility. Australia began to turn the corner in its treatment of indigenous peoples in the late 1960s, when its constitution was changed to extend citizenship to Aborigines and to count Aborigines in the national census. Similarly, the Philippines began to turn the corner in its treatment of tribal peoples in 1986, when Ferdinand Marcos was ousted and a new constitution more protective of tribal peoples was drafted. Although India's track record in dealing with ethnic problems is far from perfect, there is a good case to be made that the country's strong constitutional traditions and its respect for the rule of law has contributed in important ways to its constructive handling of ethnic issues.[36]

Leaders interested in developing effective and durable constitutions should keep three guidelines in mind. First, constitutions should be based on extensive negotiations involving representatives of all major political and ethnic groups. Creating broad-based political support at the outset is key. This might seem obvious, but it is not always done. Constitutions often come out of discussions involving only selected elites, and these constitutions frequently experience problems later on. Sri Lanka's first post-independence constitution, for example, was framed by British and Sinhalese leaders; representatives of the country's Tamil community participated only in the final stages of this process. Similarly, the Karen

---

36. This is not to say that India's constitutional track record is itself unblemished; Indira Gandhi imposed emergency rule and governed by decree during her tenure in office.

National Union did not participate in the discussions that led to the creation of Burma's first post-independence constitution in 1947. Tamils and Karen later questioned the legitimacy of these constitutional frameworks and ultimately went to war with their respective central governments.

Second, constitutional provisions and safeguards are meaningless if they are not implemented, and they are often implemented poorly or not at all. As noted above, governments in the Philippines have been slow to pass legislation that would activate constitutional provisions designed to provide more regional autonomy to tribal peoples. A failure to follow through with effective implementation, which involves creating strong courts, passing enabling legislation, and appropriating funds to the appropriate bodies, will eventually undermine the constitution's credibility. Creating strong, independent courts is especially important. Courts are needed to interpret constitutional provisions, which are often deliberately ambiguous, help resolve disputes between and among ethnic groups, and (as we have seen in Australia and New Zealand) spur governments into taking action.

Third, once a constitution is discredited, it is difficult to build trust in a new one. In China, for example, the 1954 constitution contained provisions to protect minority languages and cultures. These constitutional safeguards did not protect minorities during the Great Leap Forward and the Cultural Revolution in the late 1950s and 1960s, when a concerted effort was made to assimilate minority groups. These groups subsequently had little faith in the protections that were enshrined in China's new constitutions in 1975 and 1978. New constitutions were put into place in Pakistan in 1956, 1962, and 1973, the last of which, in particular, has been suspended during periods of military rule. Many people in Pakistan, therefore, have little faith in the efficacy or durability of constitutional frameworks. Thoughtful leaders will therefore be extremely careful about scrapping or undercutting constitutional frameworks once they are in place. Many leaders, of course, will do whatever is necessary to get or stay in power—even if this involves undermining their country's long-term political stability.

CONSOCIATIONAL AND INTEGRATIVE INSTITUTIONS. One of the great debates in scholarly circles is over the relative merits of consociational and integrative approaches to ethnic conflict management in democratic settings.[37] Advocates of both approaches start from the premise that, in

---

37. The term "integrative" is from Sisk, *Power Sharing and International Mediation in Ethnic Conflicts*, chap. 3.

multiethnic, democratic countries, political power must be shared between and among ethnic groups. This is the key to creating political systems that are just, effective, stable, and durable. However, scholars disagree about the best way of doing this.[38]

Some scholars favor consociational systems, which have four main characteristics.[39] First, in consociational systems, representatives of all major groups participate in governmental bodies, especially in the executive branch of government. "Grand coalitions" that cut across ethnic lines are formed after elections. Second, proportionality is the guiding principle behind high-level government appointments, parliamentary representation, civil service appointments, and allocations of public funds: ethnic groups are represented in government and taken care of by government in proportion to their size. Third, minority groups have vetoes to protect their vital interests. Fourth, minority groups are given sufficient autonomy to address issues that are of concern only to themselves.

The great strength of consociationalism is that it ensures minority participation in governmental deliberations. Indeed, minority groups can veto governmental actions that would be detrimental to their interests. However, consociationalism also has several weaknesses.[40] First, to be successful, consociational systems depend on elites, who have to be willing and able to cooperate between and among themselves: they have to be willing to form broad-based coalitions after elections, and they have to be able to bring their followers along with them. This does not always happen. Second, consociational systems rely on quotas, constraints, and vetoes, rather than positive incentives to cooperate. Interethnic dialogues therefore tend to be competitive rather than cooperative in character. Third, consociational systems intensify and perpetuate ethnic identifications: being part of an ethnic group is the mechanism through which individuals participate in the political process and benefit from government services.

Other scholars favor integrative approaches, which aim to de-emphasize ethnic identifications and promote interethnic cooperation by "making moderation pay."[41] In democratic settings, this means devising

---

38. For a concise summary of this debate, see ibid.

39. See Lijphart, *Democracy in Plural Societies;* and Lijphart, "The Power-Sharing Approach."

40. See Sisk, *Power Sharing and International Mediation in Ethnic Conflicts,* chap. 3.

41. See Donald L. Horowitz, "Democracy in Divided Societies," in Diamond and Plattner, *Nationalism, Ethnic Conflict, and Democracy,* pp. 35–55; Horowitz, "Making Moderation Pay," especially pp. 471–474; and Horowitz, *Ethnic Groups in Conflict,* especially chaps. 7–10, 14–15. For an analysis of the integrative approach, see ibid.

electoral inducements for politicians to reach out to more than one ethnic group for support. This, in turn, gives politicians positive incentives to moderate their rhetoric and their policy positions. As one scholar put it, the idea is to "offer *reasons* for politicians and divided groups to behave moderately, rather than *obstacles* aimed at preventing them from pursuing hegemonic, defeat-the-other aims."[42] In practical terms, this means devising systems that fragment support for ethnic parties, encourage parties to form pre-election pacts with other parties, and, ideally, encourage the formation of broad-based multiethnic parties and coalitions.[43]

The debate over consociational and integrative approaches to ethnic conflict management will not be resolved in this volume, which focuses more on policy initiatives than political institutions. However, I am more sympathetic to the integrative approach, which aims to de-emphasize ethnic identifications and create incentives for political moderation. In later sections of this chapter, I will discuss how various governments have taken steps in different policy areas to depoliticize ethnicity and thereby dampen ethnic tensions.

FEDERAL VERSUS CENTRALIZED SYSTEMS

Many scholars believe that the adoption of regional autonomy arrangements and federal political systems is an effective way of addressing ethnic problems in countries where ethnic groups are concentrated in clusters. Indeed, several of the contributors to this volume favor the adoption or extension of regional autonomy arrangements in the countries they studied.[44]

---

42. Sisk, *Power Sharing and International Mediation in Ethnic Conflicts*, p. 41; emphasis in original.

43. See Horowitz, *Ethnic Groups in Conflict*, p. 632.

44. See Kanti Bajpai's chapter on India; Samina Ahmed's chapter on Pakistan; Amita Shastri's chapter on Sri Lanka; and Josef Silverstein's chapter on Burma, all in this volume. Arend Lijphart and Donald Horowitz, who strongly disagree about the relative merits of consociationalism and integrative approaches to ethnic conflict management, do agree on the virtues of regional autonomy arrangements and federalism. See, for example, Lijphart, "The Power-Sharing Approach," p. 494; Horowitz, "Making Moderation Pay," pp. 471–472. For more on the strengths and weaknesses of regional autonomy and federal arrangements, see Murray Forsyth, ed., *Federalism and Nationalism* (New York: St. Martin's Press, 1989); Hurst Hannum, *Autonomy, Sovereignty, and Self-Determination: The Accommodation of Conflicting Rights* (Philadelphia: University of Pennsylvania Press, 1990); Alexis Heraclides, *The Self-Determination of Minorities in International Politics* (London: Frank Cass, 1991); Michael Burgess and Alain-G. Gagnon, eds., *Comparative Federalism and Federation: Competing Traditions and Future Directions* (Toronto: University of Toronto Press, 1993); Graham Smith, ed., *Federalism: The Multiethnic Challenge* (London: Longman, 1995); Karen Knop, Sylvia Ostry, Richard

The case studies in this volume do not conclusively demonstrate that federal systems are superior to centralized systems in their handling of ethnic problems, but they do offer some evidence in support of this proposition. Two of the countries studied in this volume have federal or semi-federal systems defined along ethnic lines: the Federated States of Micronesia and India, respectively. (Australia's federal system is not defined in ethnic terms.) It seems clear that federal arrangements have helped to keep the component parts of the Federated States of Micronesia together, but the country has existed as an independent entity only since 1986. The jury is still out on its long-term prospects. The Indian case provides stronger evidence in support of regional autonomy and federal approaches to ethnic conflict management. India consists of ethnically and linguistically defined states, to which considerable power has been given; it is often described as having a semi-federal system. The creation of these ethnically defined states has addressed the desires of many ethnic groups for political structures with which they can identify. It has also given ethnic groups more control over their political, economic, and cultural destinies. In short, these regional autonomy arrangements have helped to balance ethnic and national needs, and to balance state and central power. There is a good case to be made that they have helped to dampen ethnic tensions in Tamil Nadu, Punjab, the Northeast, and elsewhere, and to keep the country together. Contrary to what leaders in many countries argue, usually for self-serving reasons, regional autonomy arrangements do not necessarily lead to secession and political disintegration. Indeed, such arrangements can help to dampen secessionist impulses.

Several of the countries studied in this volume have experienced ethnic wars precisely because the leaders of these countries insisted on maintaining tight control over highly centralized political systems. The perpetuation of centralized political arrangements contributed mightily to ethnic dissatisfaction in Burma, Pakistan, the Philippines, and Sri Lanka. Significantly, in the Philippines, the government's 1996 offer to give the Moros more autonomy in the south led to the signing of a peace settlement. This supports the view that centralized political systems handle some ethnic problems poorly, and that regional autonomy and federal arrangements can be effective compromise solutions to some ethnic conflicts.

Simeon, and Katherine Swinton, eds., *Rethinking Federalism: Citizens, Markets, and Governments in a Changing World* (Vancouver: UBC Press, 1995); and Ruth Lapidoth, *Autonomy: Flexible Solutions to Ethnic Conflicts* (Washington, D.C.: U.S. Institute of Peace Press, 1996).

Federalism is not a panacea, however. As Australia's experience with federalism shows, federal systems give the country's component states the ability to pursue their own, often misguided, often discriminatory policies towards ethnic minorities. In addition, federal systems can have overlapping and confused jurisdictions. Policy implementation can be difficult because it usually depends on the cooperation of two or more levels of government. In addition, because governmental capacities are divided between central, state, and local governments, marshalling the resources for major policy initiatives can be complicated.

The use, misuse, and non-use of regional autonomy and federal arrangements in the countries studied in this volume suggest six guidelines for policymakers who are contemplating adopting such measures in response to ethnic demands. First, act sooner rather than later. Central authorities are generally reluctant to propose federal or regional autonomy arrangements early in a conflict because decentralization involves a diminution in their power and because they fear that decentralization will lead to secession. However, after ethnic conflicts become violent, reconciliation is much more difficult and ethnic rebels are much less likely to find any sort of accommodation acceptable.[45] For decades, Sri Lankan leaders refused to give Tamils significant amounts of regional autonomy; civil war broke out in the early 1980s. In the mid-1990s, government leaders offered Tamils a regional autonomy package but Tamil rebels, who had become radicalized by years of mistreatment and fighting, refused to accept anything short of complete political independence. As noted above, if this offer had been extended in the 1950s, 1960s, or 1970s, war probably would not have broken out.

Second, be prepared for highly contentious negotiations. Ethnic demographics always change over time, often because members of majority groups settle in minority areas. Central authorities and ethnic groups are therefore bound to disagree over a deeply sensitive issue: the definition of the areas that are to be placed under minority control. This issue stymied negotiations between the central government of the Philippines and the Moros in the 1970s and 1980s. At one point in the mid-1980s, Moro leaders demanded autonomy for all twenty-three provinces of Mindanao and Sulu, even though Muslims no longer constituted a majority in eighteen of these regions. The 1996 agreement between the government and the Moros covered fourteen provinces.

Third, build a broad base of political support at the center for autonomy initiatives. Changing a centralized system into a comparatively de-

---

45. See Chaim Kaufmann, "Possible and Impossible Solutions to Ethnic Civil Wars," *International Security*, Vol. 20, No. 4 (Spring 1996), pp. 136–175.

centralized one involves changes in the domestic distribution of power. To put it bluntly, ethnic minorities win, central authorities lose, and the latter are never happy about this turn of events. To see this process through, the central government's leadership has to have a strong base of support among moderates. In Sri Lanka, Chandrika Kumaratunge's 1995 proposal to give more regional autonomy to the Tamils has been opposed by Sinhalese extremists, members of the Buddhist clergy, and opportunistic political opponents. Whether she will be able to sustain this initiative remains to be seen.

Fourth, take steps to implement regional autonomy agreements. This means giving regional and local bodies real decision-making authority and control over significant financial and economic resources. Several governments in Asia—in Burma, China, Malaysia, and Pakistan—are practitioners of "phony federalism": regional autonomy arrangements exist in one form or another on paper, but they have little or no impact on the conduct of political and economic affairs in the regions in question. Phony federalism does not fool anybody, least of all the minorities such arrangements are supposed to placate.

Fifth, remember that regional autonomy and federal arrangements are not panaceas: they are complicated and inefficient; they give regional authorities more opportunities to pursue discriminatory policies of their own; and they strengthen ethno-regional identifications. Regional autonomy and federal arrangements might be the best available responses to ethnic demands for more control over their own affairs, but they have steep costs. The way they intensify ethnic identifications and politicize ethnic relations is particularly problematic.

Sixth, because ethnic demographics and ethnic politics are always changing, central authorities should think of negotiations with regionally based ethnic groups as ongoing undertakings. It is unlikely that any regional autonomy settlement will constitute a permanent solution to the problem at hand.

CITIZENSHIP POLICIES

Citizenship policies are profoundly important because they help to define a country's political identity: they determine who has a right to live in and participate in the political life of the country in question. They always have important ethnic ramifications, and they are, therefore, almost invariably contentious.

As discussed above, colonial legacies complicated the ethnic pictures in many of the countries studied in this volume. British colonial rule brought large numbers of foreign laborers to Burma, Fiji, Malaysia, Singapore, and Sri Lanka, as well as waves of European immigrants to

Australia and New Zealand. As a result, debates about citizenship have been heated in many of these countries. Burma's 1947 constitution contained a liberal definition of citizenship—that is, a definition of citizenship that made it relatively easy for most of the country's residents, including comparatively recent arrivals, to become full-fledged citizens of the country. However, parliament passed a citizenship law in 1948 that made it harder for Indians to become citizens. After the military took over in 1962, the government declared that Rohingyas would no longer be considered citizens. At various points in the 1960s, 1970s, and 1980s, the military took steps to drive Rohingyas out of the country. The junta also created three classes of citizenship (full, associate, and naturalized) that was designed to make some minorities—Indians, Karen, and Shan, in particular— literally second-class citizens. In Sri Lanka, the post-independence government took steps to deny citizenship to Upcountry Tamils, who had originally been brought to the country by the British to work on plantations. Over half of the Upcountry Tamils were subsequently repatriated to India.[46] In Australia, Aborigines were not recognized as citizens until the late 1960s.

Colonial legacies aside, citizenship policies revolve around one critical issue: whether citizenship should be defined in narrow, ethnic terms or broader civic terms. In the case of the former, citizenship is based mainly on ethnic identification. Citizenship in Australia, for example, was defined primarily in ethnic terms until the 1960s. Aborigines were not and could not become citizens; for decades, the only way Aborigines could become citizens was to be classified as non-Aboriginal. Burma and Sri Lanka have emphasized ethnic criteria in framing citizenship laws, as noted above.[47]

When citizenship is defined in civic terms, citizenship is open to anyone born in or a permanent resident of the country, as long as he or she meets certain residency criteria, has an understanding of the laws of the land, and is willing to declare political loyalty to the country in question.[48] Australia, for example, has embraced a civic conception of citizenship since the 1960s. India and Thailand have long had civic defini-

---

46. In 1947, Upcountry Tamils constituted twelve percent of Sri Lanka's total population; by the 1980s, they composed less than six percent of the population. In the late 1980s, the Upcountry Tamils who remained in Sri Lanka were given citizenship.

47. In Europe, Germany stands out as an example of a country that defines citizenship in ethnic terms.

48. See Snyder, "Nationalism and the Crisis of the Post-Soviet State," p. 81. For more discussion of these issues, see Will Kymlicka, *Multicultural Citizenship* (Oxford: Oxford University Press, 1995), especially chap. 2.

tions of citizenship. India was founded on the premise that it would be a secular, multiethnic state. Thai nationalism is based on the idea that one can "become" Thai by learning the Thai language and declaring one's loyalty to the Thai state.[49] New Zealand and Papua New Guinea also base citizenship on civic criteria. China and Indonesia have civic conceptions of citizenship because their governments have been worried about maintaining the territorial integrity of their states; Beijing considers Tibetans, for example, to be citizens of China, whether the Tibetans like it or not.

Policies based on ethnic definitions of citizenship are inherently problematic. They discriminate against ethnic minorities and immigrants, and they therefore intensify ethnic identities and tensions in the country in question. Minorities might conclude that, if they are going to be discriminated against on such a fundamental issue, they will always be treated unfairly by central authorities; when this happens, secessionist movements are more likely to develop. Citizenship policies based on civic criteria dampen many of these inter-group tensions, but they should not be thought of as panaceas. Ethnic majorities inevitably feel threatened when their dominant places in national life are eroded by new immigrants and new cultures. Moreover, in some places—China with respect to Tibet, Indonesia with respect to East Timor and Irian Jaya, for example—liberal citizenship policies are employed in service of governments with expansionist agendas. However, citizenship policies based on civic criteria are more likely than their ethnic counterparts to depoliticize ethnicity and dampen ethnic tensions. On balance, therefore, civic conceptions of citizenship offer more to leaders who seek to promote long-term political stability and harmonious ethnic relations.

CIVIL AND MINORITY RIGHTS POLICIES

Government policies on broad civil rights and specific minority rights are framed, first of all, by the attitude of the government in question to political rights and liberties in general. Authoritarian regimes—such as those in Burma, China, Indonesia, Malaysia, and Singapore—place limits on the rights of all citizens. Countries with democratic systems and comparatively strong constitutions—Australia, the Federated States of Micronesia, India, New Zealand, Papua New Guinea, and Vanuatu—are accustomed to defining and respecting the political rights of those who live therein.

Obviously, much also depends on the broad ethnic goals of the government in question. Governments that have unicultural visions of their

---

49. Until the 1970s, one also had to be Buddhist to be Thai. This criterion was dropped to strengthen the bonds between the country's Muslims and the Thai state.

countries and assimilationist agendas are mainly interested in limiting, not protecting, the activities of minorities. In cases such as these, the rights of minority groups are often trampled even when they are acknowledged in principle. For example, until the 1960s, Aboriginal Australians lacked the basic political rights enjoyed by citizens of the country. Moreover, special laws limited their rights of association and movement within the country, and, as noted above, the rights of Aborigines to keep their families intact were circumscribed until the 1970s. Burma's liberal 1947 constitution granted some ethnically defined states the right to secede from the union, but these provisions were later ignored in practice. All of China's post-1949 constitutions have contained special provisions to protect minority peoples and their cultures, but these provisions have been violated more than they have been observed. Sri Lanka's post-independence constitution contained a provision that prohibited the passage of any legislation that would be discriminatory with respect to any particular ethnic group; this provision was completely undercut in 1948 and 1949, when discriminatory citizenship laws were passed by the new parliament. Sinhalese eventually came to see majority rule as the essence of democracy, and the idea of minority rights was held in contempt. The Prevention of Terrorism Act of 1979 dramatically increased the authority of the central government to crack down on Tamil activists. Many Tamils were subsequently subjected to detention without trial.

In countries where multicultural visions and constitutional traditions hold sway, governments can and do make special efforts to protect and nurture minority communities.[50] Two main sets of initiatives are pursued. The first is aimed at what might be called the cultural rights of minority groups. It consists of laws and programs designed to preserve minority cultures, including linguistic and religious practices and other traditional ways. The Federated States of Micronesia, India, New Zealand, Papua New Guinea, and Vanuatu stand out as having made special efforts in this regard.[51] The second set of initiatives consists of laws and programs designed to protect the political rights of minorities and to ensure that minorities are properly represented in governmental bodies and the political life of the country. For example, five of the 120 seats in the New Zealand parliament are set aside for Maori (who captured a total of thirteen seats in the October 1996 election). In India, 119 of the 543 seats

---

50. For more discussion, see Jay A. Sigler, *Minority Rights: A Comparative Analysis* (Westport, Conn.: Greenwood Press, 1983), especially chaps. 6–7; Will Kymlicka, ed., *The Rights of Minority Cultures* (Oxford: Oxford University Press, 1995).

51. Language policies and policies on religion and religious groups will be discussed separately and in more detail later in this chapter.

in parliament are set aside for members of scheduled castes and tribes. Seats in state parliaments are also set aside.

Democratic leaders who are inclined to make good-faith efforts to protect minority groups should keep four guidelines in mind. First, constitutional and statutory protections are important, but they are not sufficient by themselves: they are not panaceas. The key to protecting minority groups is ending patterns of discrimination that threaten their viability. This, in turn, requires sustained political and educational efforts above and beyond the enactment of formal legal protections.

Second, governments should emphasize broad civil rights efforts aimed at the citizenry as a whole over minority rights provisions aimed only at specific groups. If the civil rights of all are robust and respected, then minority rights safeguards become superfluous. Alternatively, if the civil rights of all are trampled, then minority rights provisions are unlikely to offer much protection to minority groups. Broad civil rights efforts should be favored over special minority rights provisions, moreover, because they contribute to the depoliticization of ethnic issues. Special minority rights safeguards, on the other hand, are almost always contentious. If they intensify ethnic distinctions and generate ethnic backlashes, they can even be counterproductive.

Third, if special efforts are made on behalf of minority groups, political leaders should try to build broad-based coalitions in support of such efforts and thereby reduce the potential for ethnic backlashes. Finally, in this area as in all others, sustained efforts have to be made to implement policy initiatives. Implementation failures lead to disillusionment and disaffection, and compound ethnic problems in the long run.

POLICIES ON RELIGION AND RELIGIOUS GROUPS

Governments have to contend with two main sets of problems with respect to religion and religious groups: problems in state-group relations, and problems in inter-group relations.[52]

The easiest hurdle for governments to jump in the management of state-group relations is allowing groups and individuals to worship as they please. Most of the governments studied in this volume were willing to grant this most basic of religious freedoms to their citizens, with China being the most notable exception to this general rule.[53] A higher hurdle for governments to jump in the management of state-group relations—

---

52. This distinction comes from Kanti Bajpai; see his chapter on India in this volume.

53. In addition, Moros were persecuted for religious reasons by colonial and Philippine authorities.

one that many governments failed to clear—is resisting the temptation to establish an official religion. When governments single out one religion as the country's official religion, citizens who subscribe to other beliefs inevitably feel slighted and they often feel threatened. Governments in Malaysia, Pakistan, and Sri Lanka have nonetheless taken this step and elevated one system of beliefs above others. In Indonesia, five religions (Islam, Protestantism, Catholicism, Hinduism, and Buddhism) are officially recognized by the government. Under the Australian Citizenship Act of 1948, immigrants were required to swear allegiance to God, which some non-Christians found problematic. Alternatively, governments in India, the Federated States of Micronesia, New Zealand, Papua New Guinea, and Vanuatu have not taken the step of establishing official religions, which has eased at least one source of ethnic tension in these countries. Put another way, secularism has helped to depoliticize ethnicity in these countries.

Governments face two main obstacles in their efforts to manage inter-group relations, and each is formidable. The first is acting quickly and energetically to prevent and stop inter-group strife, such as disputes over religious sites, eruptions over religious processions, and communal violence in general. Many governments fail to address these problems effectively. In some cases, governments fail to act out of a sense of partisanship; politicians always find it hard to crack down on their supporters, even if their supporters are troublemakers. In other cases, government officials simply want to steer clear of highly charged and seemingly intractable problems. As a result, governments often dither and stall when it comes to inter-group religious disputes, hoping that complex problems will somehow resolve themselves. Even India, which has a commendable record in its handling of many religious issues, does not get high marks for its slow and ineffective responses to communal violence. The government of Pakistan gets even lower marks for its role in sponsoring religious extremists and contributing to a sharp escalation in sectarian violence.

The second problem with which governments have to contend in their efforts to manage inter-group relations is, if anything, even more challenging: developing norms of toleration between and among different religious groups. Governments in India have tried harder and accomplished more in this area than most of their counterparts in Asia and the Pacific: for five decades, most of India's leaders have preached the virtues of secularism and religious toleration. The persistence of communal violence in India shows, however, that even sustained governmental efforts cannot eliminate inter-group problems altogether.

LANGUAGE POLICIES

Language policies are extremely sensitive issues in countries where ethnicity is defined at least in part in linguistic terms. In ethnic settings such as these, language policies affect the prospects for group survival as well as the ability of group members to participate in governments, to be treated fairly by governmental agencies (courts, police, bureaucracies), to have access to governmental services, to take advantage of educational opportunities, and to pursue economic opportunities (including government employment and employment in the private sector). In addition, language is something to which many people attach great symbolic value. The challenge for governments in formulating language policies is striking a fair and sustainable balance between the need to promote national unity and the desires to preserve ethnic identities.

The track record of many governments in this area is good—even surprisingly good given the complexity of the challenges and the highly sensitive nature of the issue. The Indian government has handled this issue deftly, instituting a "three-language policy" that provides for Hindi, English, and non-Hindi languages to be used in official business and education. In addition, New Delhi reorganized states along linguistic lines, thereby giving linguistically defined ethnic groups more control over their own affairs. The government of Malaysia has also demonstrated flexibility on the language issue; although Malay has been promoted aggressively as the national language, English has been retained in a semi-official capacity to mollify the country's Chinese and Indian communities. The government of Papua New Guinea has showed great respect for the linguistic diversity of the country, in which some one thousand languages are spoken; Tokpisin, a form of pidgin and the country's *lingua franca*, has become the national language by default. The government of the Federated States of Micronesia has also demonstrated great tolerance on linguistic issues, although linguistic diversity is a more manageable problem in this case. In Vanuatu, which was governed as a colony by Great Britain and France at the same time, English, French, and Bislama are all official languages, and most newspapers and broadcast media are tri-lingual. English and French are the two principal languages of education, and most of Vanuatu's people are multilingual. Since the early 1970s, governments in New Zealand have made concerted efforts to nurture Maori language and culture. Governments in Indonesia and Thailand have had to contend with the formidable task of forging national identities in heterogenous societies, and they have consequently been aggressive in promoting the development of a national language (*bahasa Indonesia* and Thai, respectively). At the same time, they have been fairly tolerant of the continued use of minority languages outside of governmental settings.

Misguided language policies have contributed to ethnic polarization and violence in other countries. Pakistan's post-independence government made Urdu, which was spoken by Muhajirs and Punjabis in the western part of the country, the country's one and only official language, even though Bengalis, who lived in Pakistan's eastern wing, constituted a majority of the total population. Although this policy was said to be based on the need to forge a national identity, it also ensured the continued overrepresentation of Muhajirs and Punjabis in the civil bureaucracy and the military. In Sri Lanka, the passage of the Official Language Act in 1956 made Sinhala, the language of the numerically dominant Sinhalese population, the country's official language. This enraged Tamils, who saw the new policy as exclusionary and delegitimizing. At a practical level, it impinged on employment opportunities. The government's language policy was a major source of contention in subsequent decades. Although Tamil was also recognized as a national language in 1977, this conciliatory move came long after Sinhalese and Tamils had become polarized and the latter had become radicalized. Governments in Burma and China have engaged in linguistic imperialism for decades, arguing that *linguae francae* are needed to create and sustain national identities. Many ethnic minorities have become alienated as a result.

Governments that have developed tension-dampening rather than tension-inducing language policies—the Federated States of Micronesia, India, New Zealand, Papua New Guinea, and Vanuatu stand out—have generally done four things. First, they have been tolerant of and even respectful towards linguistic diversity. In particular, they been careful not to threaten the cultural survival of minorities through linguistic extermination. In many cases, they have allowed minority languages to be taught in schools. Second, in many of these countries, two or more languages have been designated as official languages. This keeps any one ethnic group from having a special status with respect to others, and, at a more practical level, it ensures that at least some minority languages can be used in governmental settings. This, in turn, makes it easier for members of minority groups to participate in governments, have access to governmental services, and secure employment either in the civil service or the private sector. Third, in federal or semi-federal settings such as the Federated States of Micronesia and India, minority languages have been designated official languages at state and local levels. This reassures the relevant groups about their cultural survival. Fourth, governments with good track records in the area of language policy have often sought to lower the salience of language as a political issue. In many cases, this has been done by promoting multilingualism in the population as a whole.

EDUCATION POLICIES

Education policies should be evaluated in terms of two criteria: the extent to which members of every ethnic group in society have equal access to educational opportunities, and the content of what is being taught in schools about the country's ethnic history and ethnic problems. The former usually receives more attention than the latter.

Only a few of the countries studied in this volume have good track records when it comes to providing equal access to educational opportunities. Indonesia and Thailand have done a better job than most, mainly because the governments in these countries have been determined to forge strong national identities; getting every child—members of ethnic minorities, in particular—into the classroom has been an important part of these nation-building efforts. In Thailand, for example, education has been compulsory since the first part of the twentieth century. Since the late 1960s, the government of Malaysia has been engaged in an aggressive campaign to improve educational opportunities for the country's Malay majority. This has involved a huge investment in schools (up to six percent of the gross domestic product) and easier acceptance standards for Malay applicants to universities. Although this effort has been successful in raising educational standards in the Malay community, it has generated much resentment in Chinese and Indian communities: English-language schools now give instruction in Malay; assistance to Chinese-language schools has been cut off; and Indian schools are very poor due to a lack of government funding. In India, a policy that reserves places in schools for members of scheduled castes and tribes seems to have accomplished little; elites within these communities have been the main beneficiaries of these policies, and discrimination against members of scheduled castes and tribes is still widespread.

In some places, education policies have failed even more starkly. In Sri Lanka, Tamil enrollment in universities was scaled back in the 1970s to make more slots available for Sinhalese students. This outraged the Tamil community, which saw higher education as one of the keys to social and economic advancement. Many Tamils became increasingly convinced that they would never be treated fairly by the Sinhalese, and they consequently began to see secession as their only alternative. The Sri Lankan government's restrictive educational policies pushed the country one very large step in the direction of civil war. In Australia and New Zealand, discrimination against indigenous peoples did not lead to violence, but decades of mistreatment on the educational front contributed to the many problems these communities experienced: low income levels, high unemployment levels, health and housing problems, and high levels of incarceration. Since the late 1960s and early 1970s, respectively, governments in Australia and New Zealand have turned over new leaves and made significant strides in their treatment of indigenous peoples, but much remains to be done in the educational arena and in other policy areas.

Four policy guidelines can be derived from the foregoing. First, if governments want to provide better educational opportunities for one ethnic group or another (or for the population as a whole), they must make long-term efforts comparable to what governments in Malaysia and Thailand, for example, have made. These efforts have to be sustained over decades, not just years. Second, governments have to make substantial investments in teachers, facilities, and financial aid programs for students who are burdened with talent but not wealth. Malaysia's campaign to raise Malay educational standards was successful because the government was willing and able to make a massive investment in this effort. Third, governments have to be exceedingly careful about instituting preferential admissions policies and quotas: such policies are always highly visible, and they invariably generate backlashes from those who do not receive special treatment. This, in turn, can lead to ethnic polarization. Policies that favor ethnic majorities, as in Malaysia and Sri Lanka, are particularly problematic because minorities may conclude that their survival is being threatened.[54] In Sri Lanka, this sentiment led to political radicalization and ultimately war. Fourth, since investment initiatives, preferential admissions policies, and quotas aimed at particular ethnic groups are bound to be contentious, leaders and governments should endeavor to build broad-based consensus for these affirmative action efforts. This will never be easy, but it will be one of the keys to riding out the political and social storms that follow.

The content of what is being taught in schools about the country's ethnic history and ethnic problems is also important. It is always difficult for leaders and governments to face up to the unpleasant aspects of their national histories, and it is particularly difficult for members of ethnic majorities to acknowledge past misbehavior. Groups tend to glorify and whitewash their own histories, and these sanitized versions of events

---

54. Ethnic majorities may oppose policies that favor minorities, but they are not likely to feel that their survival as groups is on the line.

usually find their way into textbooks and the classroom.[55] For example, it took until 1997 for a government-appointed board in Australia to acknowledge that the government's policy of forcibly taking Aboriginal children from their parents, a policy that was in effect from 1918 until the early 1970s, constituted a form of genocide.[56] Authoritarian rulers in Burma, China, and Indonesia have been energetic in their efforts to present past treatment of ethnic minorities in benign, self-serving ways.

Few countries handle this issue well. India has been more honest and more self-critical than most. Most of its governments have made serious efforts to inculcate toleration as a political and social norm. Since the early 1970s, governments in New Zealand have made an effort to acknowledge and atone for past mistreatment of Maori. Other governments should make similar efforts. If leaders and governments want to promote ethnic stability and justice in their countries, they have to acknowledge the high crimes that past governments and ethnic majorities have committed and make sure that unvarnished histories are taught in schools. This is one of the keys to true reconciliation. Leaders of ethnic minorities need to do the same. This is an issue that merits much more attention in scholarly, policymaking, and educational circles.

ECONOMIC POLICIES

Leaders and governments should be aware that general economic policies aimed at the country as a whole almost always have ethnic implications: changes in broad economic policies rarely if ever affect all groups in the same way. Decisions about instituting planned as opposed to market systems, for example, have implications for the amount of central control imposed on minority groups. In China, Mao Zedong's Great Leap Forward imposed economic collectivization and cultural assimilation on ethnic minorities. Deng Xiaoping's decentralization efforts in the 1970s and 1980s have weakened central control over minorities in borderlands, such as Tibet and Xinjiang. In addition, economic decentralization in China has worked more to the advantage of coastal areas than remote, interior areas; many of the latter are occupied by ethnic minorities. These groups consequently feel economically slighted at a time when they also have more room to take independent action. These developments could

---

55. See Snyder, "Nationalism and the Crisis of the Post-Soviet State"; Posen, "The Security Dilemma and Ethnic Conflict"; and Van Evera, "Hypotheses on Nationalism and War."

56. See Alan Thornhill, "Australia Rues Removal of Aboriginal Children," *Boston Globe*, May 21, 1997, p. A2.

mix in combustible ways. In New Zealand, the government's decision in the 1980s to privatize the economy and cut back on a range of social programs hit the Maori and Pacific Islander communities especially hard. Unemployment went up, especially in minority communities, just as safety net programs were scaled back. The New Zealand government, to its credit, made some efforts to soften this blow, but its initiatives did not fully insulate Maori and Pacific Islanders from the economic shock, the aftereffects of which were still being felt in the mid-1990s. Well-meaning governments will make concerted efforts to anticipate and minimize the disruptive effects of general economic policies on specific ethnic communities.

Agricultural and land reform policies are especially important because they usually have direct effects on ethnic geography and the well-being of specific ethnic groups. These effects are often intended. In Sri Lanka, for example, agricultural development projects in the north-central and eastern parts of the country were designed to promote Sinhalese settlement in Tamil parts of the island and thereby "recapture" these regions demographically. These projects were, of course, bitterly resented by Tamils, who had come to think of these regions as their own. The Indonesian government encouraged Javanese and Balinese to move from their densely populated islands to less populous parts of the country such as Irian Jaya, Kalimantan, Sulawesi, and Sumatra. The goal was to reduce population pressures on Java and Bali, and to develop agriculture elsewhere. Inevitably, this program generated ethnic tensions, because indigenous peoples hated having their lands taken by newcomers. In the Philippines during the Marcos era, land grabs and resettlement efforts in tribal and Moro areas were designed to enrich government officials, weaken Moro control in the south, and promote economic development (in that order). Fijian governments have been extremely attentive to land ownership issues, because they are adamant about retaining Fijian dominance of the country. Thoughtful leaders will make concerted efforts to anticipate the effects of agricultural and land reform policies on specific ethnic communities; well-meaning leaders will generally make efforts to minimize disruptive effects.

Finally, this volume sheds some light on affirmative action policies in the economic realm. One should distinguish, first of all, between programs designed to aid ethnic majorities and those targeted at minorities. In the countries studied in this volume, affirmative action efforts have often been made to improve the lot of ethnic majorities who, in many cases, were already in privileged economic positions. In Pakistan, for example, government policies generally discriminated in favor of the dominant Punjabis. In Burma, government initiatives have favored the

Burmese. In Sri Lanka, government policies worked to the benefit of Sinhalese, although these policies were rationalized as being necessary to make up for British policies that favored Tamils. In Malaysia, the government has worked since the late 1960s to improve the economic position of the country's majority Malay population, although this, too, is rationalized as being necessary to compensate for past inequities. In China, the central government has given Han Chinese economic incentives to resettle in Tibet and Xinjiang, where the new arrivals have come to play important, even dominant, roles in the local economies.

Efforts to help disadvantaged minority groups have been limited. India has a long-standing policy of reserving some government jobs for members of scheduled castes and tribes. In the 1970s, Pakistan established some quotas for minority employment in the government. In the Philippines, Ferdinand Marcos launched some development initiatives in Moro areas in the 1970s, but these were seen by Moros as attempts to strengthen ties between the south and the rest of the country, which would undercut Moro autonomy. Since the 1970s, governments in New Zealand have made some special efforts on behalf of the country's Maori population.

These programs have rarely brought about dramatic improvements in the economic prospects of the targeted groups, but they have almost always generated backlashes from other groups. Since affirmative action policies in the economic realm, like those in education, are bound to be contentious, leaders and governments should endeavor to build broad-based consensuses for such efforts. As noted above, this will never be easy, but it is one of the keys to seeing affirmative actions policies through to successful conclusions.

Policy Recommendations

I would like to conclude by putting forward two sets of broader policy recommendations: one for national leaders, in Asia and elsewhere, who would like to address ethnic problems and issues in their own countries in a constructive way; and one for international actors who are concerned about the promotion of ethnic stability and justice in other countries.

GUIDELINES FOR NATIONAL LEADERS

Returning to the broad themes and policy parameters discussed earlier, I would suggest that leaders who are interested in addressing ethnic problems constructively—that is, in a way that will promote both stability and harmony between and among ethnic groups—should endeavor to follow the five following guidelines.

First, leaders should think carefully about long-term policy goals.

More specifically, leaders should have visions of how ethnic relations in their countries should be structured, and these should be visions that can be supported by most if not all of the population. The problem, of course, is that different ethnic groups often have radically different ideas of how ethnic relations should be structured in their countries: numerically large, powerful groups naturally favor unicultural visions, while minorities are attracted to multicultural conceptions. The challenge for national leaders is to lead national discussions on these questions and to forge broad-based consensus. Countries that fail to come to a national understanding on this fundamental question are only postponing the inevitable and, in all probability, allowing existing ethnic problems to intensify.

Leaders should also keep in mind that the only thing worse that having no vision is having a bad vision—that is, an unrealistic vision that cannot be sustained over time. National leaders often favor unicultural visions because they are concerned about maintaining the political unity and territorial integrity of their countries. Unicultural visions also resonate well with large ethnic constituencies, and they provide rationales for strong central governments. However, unicultural agendas are not always realistic. Governments in Australia, New Zealand, the Philippines, and Sri Lanka have come to recognize that uniculturalism would not be sustainable in their countries, and they have consequently changed course. Governments in Burma, China, Indonesia, Malaysia, and Pakistan have had a great deal of trouble trying to impose unicultural visions on ethnic minorities. Maintaining political unity is a legitimate concern, but many secessionist problems are self-inflicted wounds brought about either by territorial expansion (China in Tibet, Indonesia in East Timor and Irian Jaya) or governmental mistreatment of the minorities in question (Burma, Pakistan, the Philippines, Sri Lanka). One could argue that unicultural visions and assimilationist agendas are prone to bringing about what they are ostensibly designed to prevent—secessionism. One could also argue that multicultural visions and accommodationist agendas do a better job of dampening ethnic tensions and secessionist tendencies than their unicultural and assimilationist counterparts. This is not to say that multicultural visions and agendas are trouble-free, only that they are more likely to lead to ethnic accommodation and, therefore, political stability. Many national leaders will find this highly counterintuitive. Many leaders will, in any event, continue to embrace unicultural visions and highly centralized political systems for self-serving political reasons.

Second, leaders should think strategically about the policy instruments they will employ to translate their ethnic visions into reality. In particular, leaders should be wary about relying on coercive policy instruments such as military force. Coercion has considerable appeal to leaders who have to contend with seemingly intractable ethnic problems: it holds out the promise of quick, permanent settlements to difficult policy problems. The problem is that military force usually fails to solve ethnic problems in the short term, while compounding them in the long term. As leaders in Burma, China, Indonesia, Sri Lanka, and elsewhere have discovered to their dismay, escalation is easy, de-escalation is hard, and the radicalization of ethnic groups is extremely difficult to reverse. It is hard to switch from coercive to persuasive approaches because it is hard to convince minorities, after they have been treated cruelly for years and even decades, that governments can be trusted partners.

This is not to say that coercion is always ineffective and inappropriate. For obvious reasons, coercive instruments are more likely to be effective if overwhelming force is used over long periods of time against small, weak minorities: British settlers successfully seized control of Australia, China has conquered Tibet, and Indonesian military forces have effective control over East Timor and Irian Jaya, for example. Significantly, in none of these cases has the government in question succeeded in assimilating minorities or winning over their hearts and minds. Coercion is more effective at conquering territory than at changing attitudes. It does not lead to ethnic accommodation; indeed, it makes accommodation more difficult. However, the use of force is appropriate under certain conditions: when secessionists refuse to compromise, and when secession would probably lead to the disintegration of the state in question; and when militant groups refuse to accept what disinterested observers would consider fair political compromises.[57] The problem, of course, is that leaders always believe that secessionist movements pose threats to national survival, and they always purport to believe that their peace offerings are fair. These perceptions and posturings, combined with a misguided faith in the efficacy of military force in ethnic settings, lead governments to engage in politically self-destructive behavior: excessive reliance on military force makes ethnic problems worse, political reconciliation harder, and political fragmentation more likely.

Third, leaders and governments should not neglect ethnic problems, hoping they will go away. Ethnic problems rarely go away on their own. Indeed, they almost always get worse if ignored. Leaders should try to take advantage of windows of opportunity when they come along—windows open and close; that is why they are called windows. In practical terms, this means that leaders should try to take action when things are going well: when ethnic groups are comparatively quiescent, when the

---

57. For more on the problems posed by militant groups, see Stephen John Stedman, "Spoiler Problems in Peace Processes," *International Security,* Vol. 22, No. 2 (Fall 1997).

economy is going well, and when the government's domestic political position is strong. This is when the odds of success are greatest. Taking action under these conditions will require a degree of initiative that many politicians lack, however. Most politicians will act only in response to a crisis—when ethnic groups are agitated, when economic problems are mounting, and when political difficulties are looming—and when the odds of taking effective action are poor.

Fourth, dramatic pronouncements and bold policy initiatives have to be followed by energetic implementation efforts. Declarations and proclamations are insufficient by themselves, and they can be counterproductive if talk is not translated into action. Partial or delayed implementation generates cynicism, which further aggravates ethnic problems. Sustained high-level attention and long-term resource commitments are the keys to addressing long-term problems, such as ethnic problems, effectively.

Finally, leaders need to recognize that, since ethnic conflict is inherent in multiethnic societies, ethnic problems cannot be eliminated—only managed.[58] There are no quick or permanent fixes to ethnic problems and conflicts. Leaders and governments should therefore prepare themselves for the long haul. There is no light at the end of the tunnel.

These recommendations—think carefully about long-term goals; think strategically about the use and misuse of policy instruments; address problems head on; make sure that talk is followed by action; and be prepared for the long haul—would be banal but for the fact that leaders and governments often do the opposite. Policy decisions are usually driven by the short-term political calculations and short-term planning horizons of alleged leaders. In countries where ethnic politics are intense, few politicians are able to rise above these political calculations and be true statesmen: Mahatma Gandhis and Nelson Mandelas are all too rare.

GUIDELINES FOR INTERNATIONAL ACTORS

In the spirit of even-handedness, let me also suggest five general guidelines for international actors—distant states, regional organizations, international organizations, and nongovernmental organizations—who might become engaged on these issues.

First, international actors need to recognize that their interests are often affected by ethnic conflicts in other countries, even far-off lands. Almost every ethnic conflict has regional dimensions—few are hermetically sealed—and ethnic conflicts often pose threats to regional security.

---

58. Esman, *Ethnic Politics*, p. 261.

Violent ethnic conflicts can trigger refugee flows, disrupt regional economic activities, and lead to military incursions in neighboring states. Neighboring states often meddle in the ethnic disputes of others to distract and weaken regional rivals. Inter-state wars can result. If regional security is an important international concern, then ethnic conflict should be as well. Ethnic conflicts are also important because they undermine regional and international organizations, such as the United Nations (whose stated purpose is the promotion of peace and security); international norms of behavior and international law (with respect to human rights, for example); and international order in general. These costs are difficult to measure, but they are real and they are paid by every actor in the international system. Policymakers in Washington and other international capitals should not be allowed to claim, as they often try to do, that ethnic problems in far-off lands are of no consequence to distant powers and the international community in general. These problems *are* consequential, and international actors should therefore be more engaged in efforts to prevent, manage, and resolve ethnic conflicts.

Second, ethnic problems are often horrible, but they are not always hopeless. Ethnic diversity does not always lead to violence, and ethnic violence is not always intractable. Australia, the Federated States of Micronesia, Malaysia, New Zealand, Singapore, Thailand, and Vanuatu, for example, have experienced little sustained violence in the last few decades of the twentieth century. India and Papua New Guinea have coped with extraordinary amounts of ethnic diversity surprisingly well. Australia and New Zealand have turned the corner in their treatment of indigenous peoples, and there are reasons for being hopeful about the resolution of the civil war between the government of the Philippines and the Moros. International actors, therefore, should not despair and walk away: ethnic problems are not necessarily intractable. International actors, moreover, should not be allowed to use the "ethnic conflicts are intractable" argument as an excuse for staying on the sidelines: it is analytically indefensible.

Third, in many cases international actors will be able to take constructive action with respect to ethnic problems. One of the main recommendations that flows from the foregoing analysis is that international actors should focus more attentively on governments and governmental policies as points of leverage in intra-state ethnic conflicts. Many of the factors that influence ethnic conflicts, such as demographic trends and modernization problems, are difficult to influence from a distance. Governments are discrete and identifiable actors, and governmental decisions, actions, and policies are discrete and identifiable events. National governments and their policies can therefore be targeted by international actors, and national governments are bodies over which international actors always have at least some influence.

Fourth, international actors should be careful to distinguish between situations where international involvement is welcome and situations where it is not. When international action is undertaken with the consent and cooperation of local parties, there is a great deal international actors can do to prevent, manage, and resolve ethnic conflicts. The international community should devote most of its efforts and resources to these kinds of cooperative undertakings. Effective international action is also possible when one or more of the parties on the ground opposes international involvement, but the costs of such action are higher and the probabilities of success are lower because international powers are engaged in coercion. This does not mean that coercive actions should never be undertaken: they are indeed warranted when the human and political costs of conflict are high and especially when moral outrages, such as genocide, are being committed. In cases such as these, there is still a lot the international community can do, provided that it has the strategic clarity, political will, and political consensus needed to coerce local parties into changing their behavior.[59] In short, coercive actions should be undertaken selectively, with great care, and with great determination.

Finally, international actors should develop a two-track strategy with respect to ethnic problems in specific countries.[60] One track should be a series of sustained, long-term efforts aimed at promoting political and economic development and civil rights, and overturning patterns of political, economic, and cultural discrimination. Developing blueprints for international action in these areas is beyond the scope of this book, but some steps—such as assisting democratic transitions and developing "mini-Marshall plans" for countries in need of special economic assistance—stand out.[61] These long-term efforts should be the international community's main focus. The international community's second track should be a series of more aggressive efforts focused on countries where ethnic problems are escalating and moving towards violence. This is not to say that preventing violence should be the international community's

---

59. See Chantal de Jonge Oudraat, *The United Nations and Internal Conflicts* (forthcoming).

60. This argument is developed in more detail in Brown, "Internal Conflict and International Action," pp. 606–614.

61. On "mini-Marshall plans," see de Jonge Oudraat, "The United Nations and Internal Conflict." For more discussion of long-term actions, see ibid., pp. 606–624.

only concern. Indeed, promoting political, economic, and social justice is the key to preventing ethnic violence in the long term.

Conclusions

In this book, we have shown how government policies can influence the course and trajectory of ethnic relations in multiethnic societies. In this concluding chapter, I have developed a framework for thinking about these issues, and put forward some analytical generalizations and policy recommendations. Obviously, much more research and analysis is needed in each of the policy areas discussed in these pages. One can easily imagine, for example, a large volume or even a series of volumes devoted exclusively to language policies, education policies, and policies on religion and religious groups, for example.

I believe that developing a clear understanding of how government policies influence ethnic groups, ethnic issues, and ethnic problems is important for both scholarly and practical reasons. If scholars are going to develop a grand unified theory of the dynamics of ethnic relations and the causes of ethnic conflicts, we will have to take government policies into account. These factors constitute an important, but often neglected, part of the broader analytic equation. Moreover, focusing on this part of the equation is useful because, of all the factors that influence ethnic relations and ethnic conflicts, government policies are among the most manipulable. Ethnic demography and geography, for example, usually change slowly. Broad economic developments and modernization processes are difficult to control with precision. Government policies are not infinitely flexible, but they are comparatively elastic. If one hopes that scholarly study of the dynamics of ethnic relations will ultimately lead to a theory of the causes of ethnic conflict and a strategy for conflict prevention, conflict management, and conflict resolution, then it makes sense to pay particular attention to government policies. This is an area where academic research could generate considerable leverage over important real-world problems.

Suggestions for Further Reading

Ethnic Relations and Ethnic Conflict: General Works

Anderson, Benedict. *Imagined Communities: Reflections on the Origins and Spread of Nationalism*. London: Verso, 1991.

Bell-Fialkoff, Andrew. "A Brief History of Ethnic Cleansing," *Foreign Affairs*, Vol. 72, No. 3 (Summer 1993), pp. 110–121.

Birch, Anthony H. *Nationalism and National Integration*. London: Unwin Hyman, 1989.

Brass, Paul, ed. *Ethnic Groups and the State*. London: Croom Helm, 1985.

Brass, Paul. *Ethnicity and Nationalism: Theory and Comparison*. Newbury Park, Calif.: Sage, 1991.

Brown, Michael E., ed. *Ethnic Conflict and International Security*. Princeton, N.J.: Princeton University Press, 1993.

Brown, Michael E., ed. *The International Dimensions of Internal Conflict*. Cambridge, Mass.: MIT Press, 1996.

Buchanan, Allen. *Secession: The Morality of Political Divorce from Fort Sumter to Lithuania and Quebec*. Boulder, Colo.: Westview Press, 1991.

Buchheit, Lee C. *Secession: The Legitimacy of Self-Determination*. New Haven, Conn.: Yale University Press, 1978.

Chaliand, Gerard, ed. *Minority Peoples in the Age of Nation-States*. London: Pluto, 1989.

Chazan, Naomi, ed. *Irredentism and International Politics*. Boulder, Colo.: Lynne Rienner, 1991.

Connor, Walker. *Ethnonationalism: The Quest for Understanding*. Princeton, N.J.: Princeton University Press, 1994.

De Silva, K.M., and Ronald J. May, eds. *Internationalization of Ethnic Conflict*. London: Pinter, 1991.

Enloe, Cynthia H. *Ethnic Conflict and Political Development*. Boston: Little, Brown, 1973.

Esman, Milton J., ed. *Ethnic Conflict in the Western World*. Ithaca, N.Y.: Cornell University Press, 1977.

Esman, Milton J. *Ethnic Politics*. Ithaca, N.Y.: Cornell University Press, 1994.

Etzioni, Amitai. "The Evils of Self-Determination," *Foreign Policy*, No. 89 (Winter 1992–93), pp. 21–35.

Gellner, Ernest. *Nations and Nationalism*. Ithaca, N.Y.: Cornell University Press, 1983.

Glazer, Nathan, and Daniel Moynihan, eds. *Ethnicity: Theory and Experience*. Cambridge, Mass.: Harvard University Press, 1975.

Gurr, Ted Robert. *Minorities at Risk: A Global View of Ethnopolitical Conflicts*. Washington, D.C.: U.S. Institute of Peace Press, 1993.

Gurr, Ted Robert. "Peoples Against States: Ethnopolitical Conflict and the Changing World System," *International Studies Quarterly*, Vol. 38, 1994, pp. 347–377.

Gurr, Ted Robert, and Barbara Harff. *Ethnic Conflict and World Politics*. Boulder, Colo.: Westview Press, 1994.

Halperin, Morton H. and David J. Scheffer with Patricia L. Small. *Self-Determination in the New World Order*. Washington, D.C.: Carnegie Endowment for International Peace, 1992.

Hannam, Hurst. *Autonomy, Sovereignty and Self Determination: The Accommodation of Conflicting Rights*. Philadelphia: University of Pennsylvania Press, 1990.

Heraclides, Alexis. "Secessionist Minorities and External Involvement," *International Organization*, Vol. 44, No. 3 (Summer 1990), pp. 341–378.

Heraclides, Alexis. *The Self-Determination of Minorities in International Politics*. London: Frank Cass, 1991.

Hobsbawm, Eric J. *Nations and Nationalism since 1980*. Cambridge, U.K: Cambridge University Press, 1990.

Horowitz, Donald L. *Ethnic Groups in Conflict*. Berkeley: University of California Press, 1985.

Juergensmeyer, Mark. *The New Cold War? Religious Nationalism Confronts the Secular State*. Berkeley: University of California Press, 1993.

Kellas, James G. *The Politics of Nationalism and Ethnicity*. London: Macmillan, 1991.

Lake, David A., and Donald Rothchild. "Containing Fear: The Origins and Management of Ethnic Conflict," *International Security*, Vol. 21, No. 2 (Fall 1996), pp. 41–75.

McNeill, William H. *Polyethnicity and National Unity in World History*. Toronto: University of Toronto Press, 1986.

Milne, Robert S. *Politics in Ethnically Bipolar Societies*. Vancouver: University of British Columbia Press, 1981.

Minahan, James. *Nations Without States: A Historical Dictionary of Contemporary National Movements*. Westport, Conn.: Greenwood Press, 1996.

Montville, Joseph V., ed. *Conflict and Peacekeeping in Multiethnic Societies*. Lexington, Mass.: Lexington Books, 1990.

Moynihan, Daniel Patrick. *Pandemonium: Ethnicity in International Politics*. Oxford: Oxford University Press, 1993.

Mulgan, Richard. "Should Indigenous Peoples Have Special Rights?" *Orbis*, Vol. 33, No. 3 (Summer 1989), pp. 375–388.

Newman, Saul. "Does Modernization Breed Ethnic Political Conflict?" *World Politics*, Vol. 43, No. 3 (April 1991), pp. 451–478.

Newman, Saul. *Ethnoregional Conflict in Democracies*. Westport, Conn.: Greenwood Press, 1996.

Philpott, Daniel. "In Defense of Self-Determination," *Ethics*, Vol. 105, No. 2 (January 1995), pp. 352–385.

Posen, Barry R. "The Security Dilemma and Ethnic Conflict," in Michael E. Brown, ed., *Ethnic Conflict and International Security.* Princeton, N.J.: Princeton University Press, 1993, pp. 103–124.

Premdas, Ralph, S.W.R. de A. Samarasinghe, and Alan Anderson, eds. *Secessionist Movements in Comparative Perspective.* London: Pinter, 1990.

Roosens, Eugene. *Creating Ethnicity: The Process of Ethnogenesis.* Newbury Park, Calif.: Sage, 1989.

Rothchild, Donald, and Alexander J. Groth. "Pathological Dimensions of Domestic and International Ethnicity," *Political Science Quarterly,* Vol. 110, No. 1 (Spring 1995), pp. 69–82.

Rothschild, Joseph. *Ethnopolitics: A Conceptual Framework.* New York: Columbia University Press, 1981.

Samarasinghe, S.W.R. de A., and Reed Coughlin, eds. *Economic Dimensions of Ethnic Conflict.* London: Pinter, 1991.

Schermerhorn, Richard A. *Comparative Ethnic Relations: A Framework for Theory and Research.* New York: Random House, 1970.

Sheffer, Gabriel, ed. *Modern Diasporas in International Politics.* London: Croom Helm, 1986.

Shehadi, Kamal S. *Ethnic Self-Determination and the Break-Up of the State.* Adelphi Paper No. 283. London: International Institute for Strategic Studies, 1993.

Smith, Anthony D. *The Ethnic Origins of Nations.* New York: Basil Blackwell, 1986.

Smith, Anthony D. *The Ethnic Revival in the Modern World.* New York: Cambridge University Press, 1981.

Smith, Anthony D. *National Identity.* London: Penguin, 1991.

Smith, Anthony D. *Nations and Nationalism in a Global Era.* Cambridge, U.K.: Polity Press, 1995.

Smith, Anthony D. *State and Nation in the Third World.* New York: St. Martin's, 1983.

Snyder, Jack. "Nationalism and the Crisis of the Post-Soviet State," in Michael E. Brown, ed., *Ethnic Conflict and International Security.* Princeton, N.J.: Princeton University Press, 1993, pp. 79–101.

Snyder, Jack, and Karen Ballentine. "Nationalism and the Marketplace of Ideas," *International Security,* Vol. 21, No. 2 (Fall 1996), pp. 5–40.

Snyder, Lewis L. *Global Mini-Nationalisms: Autonomy or Independence.* Westport, Conn.: Greenwood Press, 1982.

Stack, John F. *The Primordial Challenge: Ethnicity in the Contemporary World.* Westport, Conn.: Greenwood Press, 1986.

Suhrke, Astri, and Leila G. Noble, eds. *Ethnic Conflict in International Relations.* New York: Praeger, 1977.

Tilly, Charles, ed. *The Formation of National States in Western Europe.* Princeton, N.J.: Princeton University Press, 1975.

Van Evera, Stephen. "Hypotheses on Nationalism and War," *International Security,* Vol. 18, No. 4 (Spring 1994), pp. 5–39.

Watson, Michael, ed. *Contemporary Minority Nationalism.* London: Routledge, 1990.

Williams, Colin H. *National Separatism.* Cardiff, U.K.: University of Wales Press, 1982.

Young, Crawford. *The Politics of Cultural Pluralism*. Madison: University of Wisconsin Press, 1976.

Young, Elspeth. *Third World in the First: Development and Indigenous Peoples*. London: Routledge, 1995.

Politics and Ethnic Relations in Asia and the Pacific: General Works

Alagappa, Muthiah, ed. *Political Legitimacy in Southeast Asia: The Quest for Moral Authority*. Stanford, Calif.: Stanford University Press, 1995.

Barnes, Robert H., Andrew Gray, and Benedict Kingsbury, eds. *Indigenous Peoples of Asia*. Ann Arbor, Mich.: Association of Asian Studies, 1995.

Braibanti, Ralph. *Asian Bureaucratic Systems Emergent from the British Imperial Tradition*. Durham, N.C.: Duke University Press, 1966.

Brown, David. *The State and Ethnic Politics in Southeast Asia*. London: Routledge, 1994.

Campbell, I.C. *A History of the Pacific Islands*. Christchurch: University of Canterbury Press, 1992.

Chatterjee, Partha. *The Nation and its Fragments: Colonial and Postcolonial Histories*. Princeton, N.J.: Princeton University Press, 1993.

Diamond, Larry, Juan J. Linz, and Seymour Martin Lipset, eds. *Democracy in Developing Countries: Asia*. Vol. 3. Boulder, Colo.: Lynne Rienner, 1989.

Esposito, John L. *Islam in Asia: Religion, Politics, and Society*. Oxford: Oxford University Press, 1987.

Howe, Kerry R., Robert C. Kiste, and Brij V. Lal, eds. *Tides of History: the Pacific Islands in the Twentieth Century*. St. Leonards: Allen and Unwin, 1994.

Keyes, Charles F. *The Golden Peninsula: Culture and Adaptation in Mainland Southeast Asia*. Honolulu: University of Hawaii Press, 1995.

McCloud, Donald G. *Southeast Asia: Tradition and Modernity in the Contemporary World*. Boulder, Colo.: Westview Press, 1995.

Milne, Robert S. *Politics in Ethnically Bipolar States: Guyana, Malaysia, Fiji*. Vancouver: University of British Columbia Press, 1981.

Neher, Clark D., and Ross Marley. *Democracy and Development in Southeast Asia*. Boulder, Colo.: Westview Press, 1995.

Pye, Lucian W. *Asian Power and Politics: The Cultural Dimensions of Authority*. Cambridge, Mass.: Belknap Press, 1985.

Robie, David. *Blood on their Banner: Nationalist Struggles in the South Pacific*. New South Wales: Pluto Press, 1989.

Scarr, Deryck. *The History of the Pacific Islands: Kingdoms of the Reefs*. London: Macmillan, 1990.

Steinberg, David Joel, ed. *In Search of Southeast Asia: A Modern History*, rev. ed. Honolulu: University of Hawaii Press, 1987.

Tambiah, Stanley J. *Leveling Crowds: Ethnonationalist Conflicts and Collective Violence in South Asia*. Berkeley: University of California Press, 1996.

Trumbull, Robert. *Tin Roofs and Palm Trees: A Report on the New South Seas*. Seattle: University of Washington Press, 1977.

Von Der Mehden, Fred R. *South-East Asia, 1930–1970: The Legacy of Colonialism and Nationalism*. New York: W.W. Norton and Company, 1974.

Australia

Aboriginal and Torres Strait Islander Commission (ATSIC). *Recognition, Rights, and Reform: Report to Government on Native Title Social Justice Measures*. Canberra: ATSIC, 1995.

Bates, Daisy. *The Passing of the Aborigines: A Lifetime Spent Among the Natives of Australia*. London: John Murray, 1938.

Brennan, Frank. *One Land, One Nation*. Queensland: Queensland University Press, 1995.

Brennan, Frank. *Sharing the Country: The Case for an Agreement between Black and White Australians*. Victoria: Penguin, 1991, 1994.

Council of Australian Governments (COAG). *National Commitment to Improved Outcomes in the Delivery of Programs and Services for Aboriginal Peoples and Torres Strait Islanders*. Perth: COAG, 1992.

Dodson, Mick. *Aboriginal and Torres Strait Islander Social Justice Commissioner, 4th Report*. Canberra: Australian Government Publishing Service, 1996.

Finn, Paul. *Law and Government in Colonial Australia*. Melbourne: Oxford University Press, 1987.

Fletcher, Christine. *Aboriginal Politics: Intergovernmental Relations*. Melbourne: Melbourne University Press, 1992.

Fletcher, Christine. "The Australian Territories: Diversity in Governing," *Australian Journal of Political Science* (1992), pp. 159–176.

Fletcher, Christine. *Trapped in Civil Society: Aborigines and Federalism in Australia*. Discussion Paper No. 4. Darwin and Canberra: North Australia Research Unit, Australian National University, 1996.

House of Representatives Standing Committee on Aborginal Affairs. *Return to Country: The Aboriginal Homelands Movements in Australia*. Canberra: Australian Government Publishing Service, 1987.

Human Rights and Equal Opportunity Commission. *The Call for Recognition: A Report on the Situation of Australian South Sea Islanders, 15 December 1992*. Canberra: Australian Government Printing Service, 1992.

Long, T. "The Development of Government Aboriginal Policy: The Effect of Administrative Changes, 1829–1977," in R.M. and C.H. Berndt. *Aborigines of the West: Their Past and Their Present*. Perth: University of Western Australia, 1980.

Patience, Allan. "Immigration Policies," in B. Head and A. Patience, eds. *From Fraser to Hawke: Australian Public Policy in the 1980s*. Melbourne: Longman Cheshire, 1989.

Reynolds, H. *Aboriginal Sovereignty: Three Nations, One Australia*. Sydney: Allen and Unwin, 1996.

Sweeny, Brian and Associates. *A New Beginning: Community Attitudes Towards Aboriginal Reconciliation*. Study No. 9413. Canberra: Aboriginal Reconciliation Branch, Department of the Prime Minister and Cabinet, January 1996.

Turner, Patricia. *From Paternalism to Participation: The Role of the Commonwealth in the Administration of Aboriginal and Torres Strait Islander Affairs Policy*. Masters of Public Administration Thesis. Canberra: University of Canberra, 1994.

Burma

Chakravarti, Nalini R. *The Indian Minority in Burma: The Rise and Decline of an Immigrant Community.* London: Oxford University Press, 1971.

Ethnic Groups in Burma: Development, Democracy and Human Rights. London: Anti-Slavery International, 1994.

Falla, Jonathan. *True Love and Bartholomew: Rebels on the Burmese Border.* Cambridge, U.K.: Cambridge University Press, 1991.

Ghose, Rajeshwari, ed. "Ethnic Protest in Burma: Its Causes and Solutions," in *Protest Movements in South and Southeast Asia.* Hong Kong: Centre of Asian Studies, University of Hong Kong, 1987.

Lintner, Bertil. *Burma in Revolt: Opium and Insurgency Since 1948.* Boulder, Colo.: Westview Press, 1994.

Lintner, Bertil. "The Shans and the Shan State in Burma," *Contemporary Southeast Asia,* Vol. 5, No. 4 (1984), pp. 403–450.

Silverstein, Josef. *Burmese Politics: The Dilemma of National Unity.* New Brunswick, N.J.: Rutgers University Press, 1980.

Silverstein, Josef. "Federalism as a Solution to the Ethnic Problem in Burma," *Two Papers on Burma.* Discussion Paper No. 17. Canberra: Department of Political and Social Change, Research School of Pacific and Asian Affairs, Australian National University, 1996, pp. 15–23.

Silverstein, Josef. "National Unity in Burma: Is It Possible?" in Kusuma, Snitwongse, and Sukhumbhand Paribatra, eds. *Durable Stability in Southeast Asia.* Singapore: Institute of Asian Studies, 1987.

Smith, Martin J. *Burma: Insurgency and the Politics of Ethnicity.* London: Zed Books, 1991.

Smith, Martin. "A State of Strife: The Indigenous Peoples of Burma," in R.H. Barnes, Andrew Gray, and Benedict Kingsbury, eds. *Indigenous Peoples of Asia.* Ann Arbor, Mich.: Association for Asian Studies, Inc., 1995, pp. 221–245.

Steinberg, David. "Constitutional and Political Bases of Minority Insurrections in Burma," in Lim Joo-Jock and S. Vani, eds. *Armed Separatism in Southeast Asia.* Singapore: Institute of Southeast Asian Studies, 1984, pp. 49–80.

Taylor, Robert. "Perceptions of Ethnicity in the Politics of Burma," *Southeast Asian Journal of Social Science,* Vol. 10, No. 1 (1982), pp. 7–22.

Wiant, Jon A. "Insurgency in the Shan State," in Lim Joo-Jock and S. Vani, *Armed Separatism in Southeast Asia.* Singapore: Institute of Southeast Asian Studies, 1984, pp. 81–107.

Yawnghwe, Chao Tzang. *The Shan of Burma: Memoirs of a Shan Exile.* Singapore: Institute of Southeast Asian Studies, 1987.

China

Barnett, A. Doak. *China's Far West: Four Decades of Change.* Boulder, Colo.: Westview Press, 1993.

Barnett, Robin. *Cutting Off the Serpent's Head: Tightening Control in Tibet, 1994–95.* London: Tibet Information Network and New York: Human Rights Watch Asia, 1996.

Dreyer, June Teufel. *China's Forty Millions: Ethnic Minorities and National Integration in the People's Republic of China.* Cambridge, Mass.: Harvard University Press, 1976.

Dreyer, June Teufel. "The Islamic Community of China," *Central Asian Survey*, Vol. 1, No. 2/3 (November 1982), pp. 31–60.

Dreyer, June Teufel. "The PLA and Regionalism in Xinjiang," *Pacific Review*, Vol. 7, No. 1 (Winter 1994), pp. 41–55.

Dreyer, June Teufel. "Unrest in Tibet," *Current History* (September 1989), pp. 281–289.

Dreyer, June Teufel. "The Xinjiang Uighar Autonomous Region at Thirty: A Report Card," *Asian Survey*, Vol. 26, No. 7 (July 1986), pp. 721–744.

Gladney, Dru. *Muslim Chinese: Ethnic Nationalism in the People's Republic*. Cambridge, Mass.: Harvard Council on East Asian Studies, 1991.

Goldstein, Melvyn. *A History of Modern Tibet, 1913–1951: The Demise of the Lamaist State*. Berkeley: University of California Press, 1989.

Goldstein, Melvyn. *Nomads of Western Tibet*. Berkeley: University of California Press, 1990.

Heberer, Thomas. *China and Its National Minorities: Autonomy or Assimilation?* Armonk, N.Y.: M.E. Sharp, 1989.

Mackerras, Colin. *China's Minorities: Integration and Modernization in the 20th Century*. London: Oxford University Press, 1994.

Mackerras, Colin. *China's Minority Cultures: Identities and Integration Since 1912*. New York: St. Martin's, 1995.

Federated States of Micronesia

Gale, Roger W. *The Americanization of Micronesia: A Study of the Consolidation of U.S. Rule in the Pacific*. Washington, D.C.: American University Press, 1979.

Hughes, Daniel T. and Stanley K. Laughlin, Jr. "Key Elements in the Evolving Political Culture of the Federated States of Micronesia," in Jerry K. Loveland, ed. *Evolving Political Cultures in the Pacific Islands*. Laie, Hawaii: Institute for Polynesian Studies, 1982.

Kluge, Paul F. *The Edge of Paradise: America in Micronesia*. New York: Random House, 1991.

Petersen, Glenn. *Ethnicity and Interests at the 1990 Federated States of Micronesia Constitutional Convention*. Canberra: Research School of Pacific Studies, Australian National University, 1993.

Fiji

Lal, Brij V. *Broken Waves: A History of the Fiji Islands in the Twentieth Century*. Honolulu: University of Hawaii Press, 1992.

Lawson, Stephanie. *Ethnic Policies and the State in Fiji*. Canberra: Peace Research Centre, Australian National University, 1993.

Lawson, Stephanie. *Tradition Versus Democracy in the South Pacific: Fiji, Tonga and Western Samoa*. Cambridge, U.K.: Cambridge University Press, 1996.

Norton, Robert. *Race and Politics in Fiji*. 2nd ed. St. Lucia: University of Queensland Press, 1990.

Scarr, Deryck. *Fiji: The Politics of Illusion: The Military Coups in Fiji*. Kensington: University of New South Wales Press, 1988.

Sutherland, William. *Beyond the Politics of Race: An Alternative History of Fiji to 1992*. Canberra: Research School of Pacific Studies, Australian National University, 1992.

India

Baird, Robert D., ed. *Religion and Law in Independent India*. New Delhi: Manohar, 1993.

Das Gupta, Jyotindra. *Language Conflict and National Development: Group Politics and National Language Policy in India*. Bombay: Oxford University Press, 1970.

Datta, P.S. *Ethnic Peace Accords in India*. New Delhi: Vikas Publishing, 1995.

Derrett, Duncan M. *Religion, Law and the State in India*. London: Faber and Faber, 1968.

Engineer, Asghar Ali. *Babri Masjid-Ramjanambhoomi Controversy*. Delhi: Ajanta, 1990.

Galanter, Marc. *Competing Equalities: Law and the Backward Classes in India*. Delhi: Oxford University Press, 1984. Revised edition 1991.

Gupta, Shekhar. *India Redefines its Role*. Adelphi Paper No. 293. London: International Institute for Strategic Studies, 1995.

Hardgrave, Robert L., Jr., and Stanley A. Kochanek. *India: Government and Politics in a Developing Nation*, 5th ed. New York: Harcourt Brace Jovanovich, 1993.

Hazarika, Sanjoy. *Strangers in the Mist: Tales of War and Peace from India's Northeast*. New Delhi: Viking Penguin, 1994.

Jagmohan. *My Frozen Turbulence in Kashmir*, 3rd ed. New Delhi: Allied, 1993.

Jalal, Ayesha. *Democracy and Authoritarianism in South Asia*. New Delhi: Oxford University Press, 1995.

Kapur, Rajiv. *Sikh Separatism: The Politics of Faith*. London: Allen and Unwin, 1986.

Nayar, Kuldip and Khushwant Singh. *Tragedy of Punjab: Operation Bluestar and After*. New Delhi: Vision Books, 1984.

Pylee, M.V. *India's Constitution*. New Delhi: Asia Publishing House, 1967.

Rupesinghe, Kumar, and Khawar Mumtaz, eds. *Internal Conflicts in South Asia*. London: Sage, 1996.

Smith, Donald E. *India as a Secular State*. Princeton, N.J.: Princeton University Press, 1963.

Thomas, Raju G.C. *Perspectives on Kashmir: The Roots of Conflict in South Asia*. Boulder, Colo.: Westview Press, 1992.

Verghese, George. *India's Northeast*. New Delhi: Konarak Publishers, 1996.

Wallace, Paul, ed. *Region and Nation in India*. New Delhi: Oxford and IBH, 1985.

Weiner, Myron. *Sons of the Soil: Migration and Ethnic Conflict in India*. Princeton, N.J.: Princeton University Press, 1978.

Indonesia

Anderson, Benedict. *Language and Power: Exploring Political Cultures in Indonesia*. Ithaca, N.Y., Cornell University Press, 1990.

Bresnan, John. *Managing Indonesia: The Modern Political Economy*. New York: Columbia University Press, 1993.

Bourchier, David, and John Legge, eds. *Democracy in Indonesia: 1950s and 1990s*. Clayton, Victoria: Centre of Southeast Asia Studies, Monash University, 1994.

Crouch, Harold. *The Army and Politics in Indonesia*. Ithaca, N.Y.: Cornell University Press, 1978.

Eldridge, Philip. *Non-Government Organizations and Democratic Participation in Indonesia*. Oxford: Oxford University Press, 1995.

Grant, Bruce. *Indonesia*, 3rd ed. Melbourne: Melbourne University Press, 1996.

Hill, Hal. *The Indonesian Economy Since 1966: Southeast Asia's Emerging Giant*. Cambridge, U.K.: Cambridge University Press, 1996.

Hill, Hal. *Unity and Diversity: Regional Economic Development in Indonesia Since 1970*. Oxford: Oxford University Press, 1989.

Liddle, R. William. *Leadership and Culture in Indonesian Politics*. Sydney: Allen and Unwin, 1996.

MacIntyre, Andrew. *Business and Politics in Indonesia*. Sydney: Allen and Unwin, 1990.

Robinson, Richard. *Indonesia: The Rise of Capital*. Sydney: Allen and Unwin, 1986.

Schwarz, Adam. *A Nation in Waiting: Indonesia in the 1990s*. Sydney: Allen and Unwin, 1994.

Malaysia and Singapore

Andaya, Barbara Watson, and Leonard Y. Andaya. *A History of Malaysia*. Houndmills: Macmillan, 1982.

Crouch, Harold. *Government and Society in Malaysia*. Ithaca, N.Y.: Cornell University Press, 1996.

Gomez, Edmund Terence. *Political Business: Corporate Involvement of Malaysian Political Parties*. Townsville: James Cook University, 1994.

Hussin, Mutalib. *Islam and Ethnicity in Malay Politics*. Singapore: Oxford University Press, 1990.

Jesudason, James V. *Ethnicity and Economy: The State, Chinese Business, and Multinationals in Malaysia*. Singapore: Oxford University Press, 1989.

Mauzy, Diane K. *Barisan Nasional: Coalition Government in Malaysia*. Kuala Lumpur: Aliran, 1989.

Means, Gordon P. *Malaysian Politics: The Second Generation*. Singapore: Oxford University Press, 1991.

Milne, R.S., and Diane Mauzy. *Malaysia: Tradition, Modernity and Islam*. Boulder: Westview Press, 1985.

Muzaffar, Chandra. *Challenges and Choices in Malaysian Politics and Society*. Kuala Lumpur: Aliran, 1989.

Sundaram, Jomo Kwame. *Growth and Structural Change in the Malaysian Economy*. Houndmills: Macmillan, 1990.

New Zealand

Boston, Jonathan, John Martin, June Pallot, and Pat Walsh, eds. *Public Management: The New Zealand Model*. Auckland: Oxford University Press, 1996.

Boston, Jonathan, John Martin, June Pallot, and Pat Walsh, eds. *Reshaping the State*. Auckland: Oxford University Press, 1991.

Gold, Hyam. *New Zealand Politics in Perspective*. 3rd ed. Auckland: Longman Paul, 1992.

Gould, J.D. "Socio-Economic Differences between Maori Iwi," *Journal of the Polynesian Society*, Vol. 105, No. 2 (June 1996), pp. 165–183.

Greif, Stuart. *Immigration and National Identity in New Zealand*. Palmerston North: Dunmore Press, 1995.

Holland, Martin, and Jonathan Boston, eds. *The Fourth Labour Government: Policy and Politics in New Zealand*. 2nd ed. Auckland: Oxford University Press, 1990.

Kelsey, Jane. *The New Zealand Experiment: A World Model for Structural Adjustment?* Auckland: Auckland University Press/Bridget Williams Books, 1995.

Miller, Raymond, ed. *New Zealand Politics in Transition*. Auckland: Oxford University Press, 1997.

Mulgan, Richard G. *Politics in New Zealand*. 2nd ed. Auckland: Auckland University Press, 1997.

Rice, Geoffrey W. *The Oxford History of New Zealand*. 2nd ed. Auckland: Oxford University Press, 1992.

Sharp, Andrew. *Justice and the Maori: Maori Claims in New Zealand Political Argument in the 1980s*. 2nd ed. Auckland: Oxford University Press, 1997.

Sharp, Andrew, ed. *Leap Into the Dark: The Changing Role of the State in New Zealand since 1984*. Auckland: Auckland University Press, 1994.

Spoonley, Paul, ed. *Nga Patai: Racism and Ethnic Relations in Aotearoa/New Zealand*. Palmerston North: Dunmore Press, 1996.

Statistics New Zealand. *New Zealand Official Year Book*. Wellington: Department of Statistics, 1972–96.

Vasil, Raj, and Hon-Key Yoon. *New Zealanders of Asian Origin*. Wellington: Institute of Policy Studies, Victoria University of Wellington, 1996.

Wilson, Margaret, and Anna Yeatman, eds. *Justice and Identity: Antipodean Practices*. Wellington: Bridget Williams Books, 1995.

Pakistan

Alavi, Hamza. "Nationhood and the Nationalities in Pakistan," in Hastings Donnan and Prina Werbner, eds. *Economy and Culture in Pakistan: Migrants and Cities in a Muslim Society*. London: Macmillan, 1980.

Burki, Shahid Javed. *Pakistan under Bhutto, 1971–1977*. London: Macmillan, 1980.

Gankovsky, Y.V., and L. Gordon-Polonskaya. *A History of Pakistan (1947–1958)*. Lahore: People's Publishing House, 1971.

Gankovsky, Y.V., and V.N. Moskalenko. *The Three Constitutions of Pakistan*. Lahore: People's Publishing House, 1978.

Gardezi, Hasan, and Jamil Rashid, eds. *Pakistan: The Roots of Dictatorship: The Political Economy of a Praetorian State*. Delhi: Oxford University Press, 1986.

Hayes, Louis D. *Politics in Pakistan: The Struggle for Legitimacy*. Boulder, Colo.: Westview Press, 1984.

Jahan, Rounaq. *Pakistan: Failure in National Integration*. New York: Columbia University Press, 1972.

Kennedy, Charles H. "Policies of Ethnic Preference in Pakistan," *Asian Survey*, Vol. 24, No. 6 (June 1984), pp. 688–703.

Khan, Mohammed Asghar, ed. *Islam, Politics and the State: The Pakistan Experience.* London: Zed Books, 1985.

Noman, Omar. *The Political Economy of Pakistan 1947–1985.* New York: KPI, 1988.

Rashid, Abbas. "Pakistan: The Politics of 'Fundamentalism'," in Kumar Rupesinghe and Khawar Mumtaz, eds. *Internal Conflicts in South Asia.* London: Sage, 1996, pp. 55–80.

Rashid, Abbas, and Farida Shaheed. *Pakistan: Ethno-Politics and Contending Elites.* Geneva: United Nations Research Institute for Social Development, 1993.

Rizvi, Hasan-Askari. "The Military and Politics in Pakistan," in Charles H. Kennedy and David J. Loucher, eds. *Civil-Military Intervention in Asia and Africa.* Leiden: E.J. Brill, 1991.

Ziring, Lawrence. *Pakistan: The Enigma of Political Development.* Boulder, Colo.: Westview Press, 1980, pp. 795–812.

Ziring, Lawrence. "Public Policy Dilemmas and Pakistan's Nationality Problem: The Legacy of Zia," *Asian Survey,* Vol. 28, No. 8 (August 1988).

Papua New Guinea

Larmour, Peter. *Legitimacy, Sovereignty and Regime Change in the South Pacific: Comparisons Between the Fiji Coups and the Bougainville Rebellion.* Canberra: Research School of Pacific Studies, Australian National University, 1992.

Larmour, Peter. "The Politics of Race and Ethnicity: Theoretical Perspectives on Papua New Guinea," *Pacific Studies,* Vol. 15, No. 2 (1992).

Lawson, Stephanie. "Ethno-nationalist Dimensions of Internal Conflict: The Case of Bougainville Secessionism," in Kevin Clements, ed. *Peace and Security in the Asia Pacific Region: Post–Cold War Problems and Prospects.* Palmerston North: Dunmore Press, 1993.

May, Ronald J., ed. *Micronationalist Movements in Papua New Guinea.* Canberra: Australian National University, 1982.

May, Ronald J. and Matthew Spriggs, eds. *The Bougainville Crisis.* Bathurst, New South Wales: Crawford House Press, 1990.

Premdas, Ralph R. "Ethnicity and Nation-building: The Papua New Guinea Case," in Michael C. Howard, ed. *Ethnicity and Nation-building in the Pacific.* Tokyo: United Nations University, 1989.

The Philippines

Che Man, Wadir K. *Muslim Separatism: The Moros of Southern Philippines and the Malays of Southern Thailand.* Singapore: Oxford University Press, 1987.

Cordillera Studies Center (CSC). "Issues on Cordillera Autonomy: General Summary," CSC Working Paper 18. Baguio City: Cordillera Studies Center, University of the Philippines College, 1991.

Fry, Howard T. *A History of the Mountain Province.* Quezon City: New Day Publishers, 1983.

Gowing, Peter G. *Mandate in Moroland: The American Government of Muslim Filipinos 1899–1920.* Quezon City: Philippine Centre for Advanced Studies, University of the Philippines, 1977.

Gowing, Peter G. *Muslim Filippinos—Heritage and Horizon.* Quezon City: New Day Publishers, 1979.

Griffin, B. "National Policy on Minority Cultural Communities: The Philippine Case," *Asian Journal of Social Science,* Vol. 16, No. 2 (1988), pp. 5–16.

ICL Research Team. *A Report on Tribal Minorities in Mindanao.* Manila: Regal Publishing, 1983.

Lopez, Violeta B. *The Mangyans of Mindoro: An Ethnohistory.* Quezon City: University of the Philippines Press, 1976.

Lynch, O.J. "Tribal Land Law: A Mechanism for Upland Participatory Development," *Sandugo* (2nd Quarter, 1982), pp. 24–30 and (4th Quarter, 1982), pp. 14, 16, 18, 20.

Madale, Nagasura T. *Autonomy for Muslim Mindanao: The RCC Untold Story.* Manila: B-lal Publishers, 1989.

Majul, Cesar A. *The Contemporary Muslim Movement in the Philippines.* Berkeley, Calif.: Mizan Press, 1985.

May, Ronald J. "The Moro Movement in Southern Philippines," in Randal Stewart and Christine Jennett, eds. *Politics of the Future: The Role of Social Movements.* Melbourne: Macmillan Australia, 1989, pp. 321–339.

May, Ronald J. "Muslim and Tribal Filipinos," in Ronald J. May and Francisco Nemenzo, eds. *The Philippines after Marcos.* London: Croom Helm, 1985, pp. 110–129.

May, Ronald J. "The Wild West in the South: A Recent Political History of Mindanao," in Mark Turner, Ronald J. May, and Lulu R. Turner, eds. *Mindanao: Land of Unfulfilled Promise.* Quezon City: New Day Publishers, 1992, pp. 125–146.

Okamura, J.Y. "The Politics of Neglect: Philippine Ethnic Minority Policy," *Asian Journal of Social Science,* Vol. 17, No. 2 (1988), pp. 17–46.

Scott, William H. "The Creation of a Cultural Minority," in William Scott, ed. *Cracks in the Parchment Curtain.* Quezon City: New Day Publishers, 1985, pp. 28–41.

Scott, William H. *The Discovery of the Igorots: Spanish Contacts with the Pagans of Northern Luzon.* Quezon City: New Day Publishers, 1977.

Tan, A.S. *The Emergence of Philippine Chinese National and Political Consciousness.* Ph.D. Dissertation, University of California at Berkeley, 1969.

Wickberg, Edgar. *The Chinese in Philippine Life, 1850–1989.* New Haven, Conn.: Yale University Press, 1965.

Sri Lanka

Abeysekera, C., and N. Gunasinghe. *Facets of Ethnicity in Sri Lanka.* Colombo: Social Scientists Association, 1987.

Committee for Rational Development. *Sri Lanka, The Ethnic Conflict: Myths, Realities and Perspectives.* New Delhi: Navrang, 1984.

De Silva, K.M. *Managing Ethnic Tensions in Multi-Ethnic Societies: Sri Lanka 1880–1985.* New York: University Press of America, 1986.

Kodikara, Shelton U. *Indo-Sri Lanka Agreement of July 1987.* Colombo: University of Colombo, International Relations Program, 1989.

Manor, James. *Sri Lanka: In Change and Crisis.* London: Croom Helm, 1984.

Muni, S.D. *Pangs of Proximity: India and Sri Lanka's Ethnic Crisis.* Newbury Park, Calif.: Sage, 1993.

Phadnis, Urmila. *Religion and Politics in Sri Lanka*. New Delhi: South Asia Books, 1976.

Ponnambalam, S. *Sri Lanka: The National Question and the Tamil Liberation Struggle*. London: Zed Books, 1983.

Roberts, Michael, ed. *Collective Identities, Nationalisms, and Protest in Modern Sri Lanka*. Colombo: Marga Institute, 1979.

Schwarz, Walter. *The Tamils of Sri Lanka*. London: Minority Rights Group, 1988.

Shastri, Amita. "Sri Lanka's Provincial Council System: A Solution to the Ethnic Problem?" *Asian Survey*, Vol. 32, No. 8 (August 1992), pp. 401–421.

Spencer, Jonathan. *Sri Lanka: History and the Roots of Conflict*. New York: Routledge, 1990.

Tambiah, Stanley J. *Sri Lanka: Ethnic Fratricide and the Dismantling of Democracy*. Chicago: University of Chicago Press, 1986.

Wickramasinghe, Nira. *Ethnic Politics in Colonial Sri Lanka, 1927–1947*. New Delhi: Vikas Publishing House, 1995.

Wilson, A. Jeyaratnam. *The Break-up of Sri Lanka: The Sinhalese-Tamil Conflict*. London: C. Hurst, 1988.

Wriggins, William H. *Ceylon: Dilemmas of a New Nation*. Princeton, N.J.: Princeton University Press, 1960.

Thailand

Brown, David. *The State and Ethnic Politics in Southeast Asia*. London: Routledge, 1994.

Chaiwat, Satha-Anand. "Hijab and Moments of Legitimation: Islamic Resurgence in Thai Society," in Charles F. Keyes, Laurel Kendall, and Helen Hardacre, eds. *Asian Visions of Authority: Religion and the Modern States of East and Southeast Asia*. Honolulu: University of Hawaii Press, 1994, pp. 279–300.

Grabowsky, Volker, ed. *Regions and National Integration in Thailand, 1892–1992*. Wiesbaden: Otton Harrassowitz, 1995.

Kammerer, Cornelia A. "Territorial Imperatives: Akha Ethnic Identity and Thailand's National Integration," in R. Guideri, F. Pellizzi, and S.J. Tambiah, eds. *Ethnicities and Nations: Processes of Interethnic Relations in Latin America, Southeast Asia, and the Pacific*. Houston: Rothko Chapel, 1986, pp. 277–291.

Keyes, Charles F. *Isan: Regionalism in Northeastern Thailand*. Data Paper No. 65. Ithaca, N.Y.: Cornell University Southeast Asia Program, 1967.

Keyes, Charles F. *Thailand: Buddhist Kingdom as Modern Nation-State*. Boulder, Colo.: Westview Press, 1987.

Keyes, Charles F. "Who Are the Thai? Reflections on the Invention of Identities," in Lola Romanucci-Ross and George A. De Vos, eds. *Ethnic Identity: Creation Conflict and Accommodation*, 3rd ed. Walnut Creek, Calif.: Alta Mira Press, 1995, pp. 136–160.

McKinnon, John, and Bernard Vienne, eds. *Hill Tribes Today: Problems in Change*. Bangkok: White Lotus-Orstom, 1989.

McVey, Ruth. "Separatism and the Paradoxes of the Nation-State in Perspective," in Lim Joo-Jock and S. Vani, eds. *Armed Separatism in Southeast Asia*. Singapore: Institute of Southeast Asian Studies, 1984, pp. 3–29.

Rajah, Ananda. "Ethnicity, Nationalism, and the Nation-State: The Karen in Burma and Thailand," in Gehan Wijeyewardene, ed. *Ethnic Groups Across National Boundaries in*

Mainland Southeast Asia. Singapore: Institute of Southeast Asian Studies, 1990, pp. 102–133.

Skinner, G. William. *Chinese Society in Thailand.* Ithaca, N.Y.: Cornell University Press, 1957.

Smalley, William A. *Linguistic Diversity and National Unity: Language Ecology in Thailand.* Chicago: University of Chicago Press, 1994.

Thongchai, Winichakul. *Siam Mapped: A History of the Geo-Body of a Nation.* Honolulu: University of Hawaii Press, 1994.

Vanuatu

Aldrich, Robert. *France and the South Pacific since 1940.* London: Macmillan, 1993.

Lini, Walter. *Beyond Pandemonium: From the New Hebrides to Vanuatu.* Wellington: Asia Pacific Books, 1980.

Van Trease, Howard. *The Politics of Land in Vanuatu: From Colony to Independence.* Suva: Institute of Pacific Studies, University of the South Pacific, 1987.

Weisbrot, David. "Custom, Pluralism, and Realism in Vanuatu: Legal Development and the Role of Customary Law," *Pacific Studies,* Vol. 13, No. 1 (1989).

Contributors

Michael E. Brown is Associate Director of the International Security Program and Managing Editor of the journal *International Security* at the Center for Science and International Affairs, John F. Kennedy School of Government, Harvard University. He is the editor of *Ethnic Conflict and International Security* (Princeton University Press, 1993) and *The International Dimensions of Internal Conflict* (MIT Press, 1996), and co-editor of *East Asian Security* (MIT Press, 1996). He is writing a book on the causes of civil war.

Šumit Ganguly is Professor of Political Science at Hunter College of the City University of New York, where he teaches courses on South and Southeast Asian politics, and he is a member of the South Asian Institute at Columbia University. He is the author of *The Origins of War in South Asia* (Westview, 1994), and *The Crisis in Kashmir: Portents of War, Hopes of Peace* (Cambridge University Press and the Woodrow Wilson Center Press, 1997).

Samina Ahmed is a Research Fellow at the Institute of Regional Studies in Islamabad. She has written on Pakistan's relations with India and Central Asia, as well as on Pakistan's internal politics. Her most recent publication is "The Military and Ethnic Conflict in Sindh," in Charles H. Kennedy, ed., *Pakistan Briefing, 1995* (Westview, 1995).

Kanti Bajpai is Associate Professor at the School of International Studies, Jawaharlal Nehru University in New Delhi. His research and writings have dealt with regional security, ethnic conflict, and foreign policy issues in South Asia. He is the co-editor of *South Asia After the Cold War: International Perspectives* (Westview, 1993) and *Interpreting World Politics* (Sage, 1995).

June Teufel Dreyer is Professor of Political Science at the University of Miami. She has written on many aspects of China's domestic politics, and is the author of *China's Forty Millions: Minority Nationalities and National Integration in the People's Republic of China* (Harvard University Press, 1976).

Christine Fletcher is Director of the North Australian Research Unit, Australian National University, in Darwin. Previously, she was Senior Lecturer and Research Fellow at the National Centre for Development Studies, Australian National University, in Canberra. She is the author of *Aboriginal Politics: Intergovernmental Relations* (Melbourne University Press, 1992). Her recent publications include *Equity and Development Across Nations: Political and Fiscal Realities* (St. Martin's, 1996).

Charles Keyes is Professor of Anthropology and International Studies at the University of Washington and Director of the Northwest Regional Consortium for Southeast Asian Studies. He is the author of *The Golden Peninsula: Culture and Adaptation in Mainland Southeast Asia* (University of Hawaii Press, 1995) and *Thailand: Buddhist Kingdom as Modern Nation-State* (Westview, 1987), and editor of *Asian Visions of Authority: Religion and the Modern State in East and Southeast Asia* (University of Hawaii Press, 1994). He has conducted extensive research on the politics of cultural identity in Thailand and elsewhere in Southeast Asia.

Stephen Levine is a Reader in and Chairperson of the Department of Politics at Victoria University of Wellington, where he teaches courses on, *inter alia*, the politics of the South Pacific. He is Director of the New Zealand Political Change Project, and he is editor of *Political Science*, the journal of the New Zealand Political Studies Association.

R. William Liddle is Professor of Political Science at Ohio State University. He has written widely on Indonesian politics. He is the author of *Leadership and Culture in Indonesian Politics* (Allen and Unwin, 1996) and *Islam, Politics, and Modernization* (Sinar Harapan, 1997), and many scholarly articles and book chapters.

R.J. May is Senior Fellow in the Department of Political and Social Change at the Australian National University. He is the author, editor, or co-editor of over one dozen books on ethnic issues and Southeast Asia, including *Mindanao: Land of Unfulfilled Promise* (New Day Publishers, 1992) and *Managing Diversity? Governments and Ethnicity in Southeast Asia and the South Pacific* (forthcoming).

Andrew Sharp is Professor of Political Studies at the University of Auckland. He is the author of *Justice and the Maori: Maori Claims in New Zealand since the 1970s* (Oxford University Press, 2nd ed., 1997) and *The Political Ideas of the English Civil Wars, 1641–49* (Longmans, 1983). He is the editor of *Leap into the Dark: The Changing Role of the State in New Zealand since 1984* (Auckland University Press, 1994).

Amita Shastri is an Associate Professor in the Department of Political Science at San Francisco State University. Her research interests focus on the political economy of development, electoral politics, and ethnic politics in South Asia. Her work on the ethnic conflict in Sri Lanka has appeared in the *Journal of Asian Studies, Electoral Studies,* and *Asian Survey.*

Josef Silverstein is Professor of Political Science Emeritus at Rutgers University. He is the author of *Burma: Military Rule and the Politics of Stagnation* (Cornell University Press, 1977) and *Burmese Politics: The Dilemma of National Unity* (Rutgers University Press, 1980). He is also the editor of *Independent Burma at Forty Years: Six Assessments* (Cornell Southeast Asia Program, 1989).

Index

The Robert and Renée Belfer Center for Science and International Affairs

Graham T. Allison, Director
John F. Kennedy School of Government
Harvard University
79 JFK Street, Cambridge MA 02138
(617) 495-1400

The Belfer Center for Science and International Affairs (BCSIA) is the hub of research, teaching and training in international security affairs, environmental and resource issues, and science and technology policy at Harvard's John F. Kennedy School of Government. The Center's mission is to provide leadership in advancing policy-relevant knowledge about the most important challenges of international security and other critical issues where science, technology, and international affairs intersect.

BCSIA's leadership begins with the recognition of science and technology as driving forces transforming international affairs. The Center integrates insights of social scientists, natural scientists, technologists, and practitioners with experience in government, diplomacy, the military, and business to address these challenges. The Center pursues its mission in four complementary research programs:

- The International Security Program (ISP) addresses the most pressing threats to U.S. national interests and international security.

- The Environment and Natural Resources Program (ENRP) is the locus of Harvard's interdisciplinary research on resource and environmental problems and policy responses.

- The Science, Technology, and Public Policy (STPP) program analyzes ways in which science and technology policy influence international security, resources, environment, and development, and such cross-cutting issues as technological innovation and information infrastructure.

- The Strengthening Democratic Institutions (SDI) project catalyzes support for three great transformations in Russia, Ukraine, and the other republics of the former Soviet Union—to sustainable democracies, free market economies, and cooperative international relations.

The heart of the Center is its resident research community of more than one hundred scholars: Harvard faculty, analysts, practitioners, and each year a new, interdisciplinary group of research fellows. BCSIA sponsors frequent seminars, workshops, and conferences, many open to the public; maintains a substantial specialized library; and publishes a monograph series and discussion papers. The Center's International Security Program, directed by Steven E. Miller, publishes the CSIA Studies in International Security, and sponsors and edits the quarterly journal *International Security*.

The Center is supported by an endowment established with funds from Robert and Renée Belfer, the Ford Foundation, and Harvard University, by foundation grants, by individual gifts, and by occasional government contracts.